BARRON'S

HOW TO PREPARE FOR THE

CIVIL SERVICE EXAMINATION

FOR STENOGRAPHER, TYPIST, CLERK, AND OFFICE MACHINE OPERATOR

4TH EDITION

Jerry Bobrow, Ph.D.
Executive Director
Bobrow Test Preparation Services
Programs at major universities, colleges, and
law schools throughout California and Colorado
Lecturer, consultant, author of over eighteen
nationally known test preparation books

Peter Z. Orton, Ph.D.
Program Director, Global Curriculum Technology
IBM Management Development
Author and lecturer

William Covino, Ph.D.
Chairman, Department of English
Florida Atlantic University
Author and lecturer

D1611515

BARRON'S

Acknowledgments

I would like to thank the following people for their contributions to this work:

Dianne Young, M.S., professor of Typing and Office Skills, Santa Monica Community College

Pam Mason, M.A., instructor, Los Angeles Unified School District

Bob Stoneham, M.A., reading/writing specialist, California State University, Northridge

Joy Mondragon, Stacey Plaskoff, Dana Lind—for organization and proofreading

My special thanks for permission to use excerpts from existing works to:

Gregg Publishing Division, McGraw-Hill Book Company, Inc., Student's Transcript of *Gregg Short-hand Simplified for Colleges,* Volume Two, Second Edition, pages 12, 19, 26–27, 34, 81. Authors Louis A. Leslie, Charles E. Zoubek, and Russell J. Hosler. Copyright 1958, for transcription material beginning on page 271.

South-Western Publishing Company, *College Typewriting,* Tenth Edition, pages 310, 312, 313, 315, 345, 368, 370, 371. Authors Wanous, Duncan, Warner, Langford. Copyright 1980, for typing passages beginning on page 250.

And finally, my appreciation to my wife, Susan, and my children, Jennifer Lynn, 21, Adam Michael, 18, and Jonathan Matthew, 14, for their patience and moral support.

All inquiries should be addressed to:
Barron's Educational Series, Inc.
250 Wireless Boulevard
Hauppauge, New York 11788
http://www.barronseduc.com

Library of Congress Catalog Card No. 99-17933
International Standard Book No. 0-7641-0777-1

Library of Congress Cataloging-in-Publication Data

Bobrow, Jerry.
    How to prepare for the Civil Service examinations for stenographer,
typist, clerk, and office machine operator / by Jerry Bobrow, in
collaboration with Peter Z. Orton, William Covino. — 4th ed.
        p.   cm.
    ISBN 0-7641-0777-1
    1. Civil service—United States—Examinations.   2. Clerical ability
and aptitude tests.   I. Orton, Peter Z.   II. Covino, William   III. Title:
Civil Service examinations
JK717.C54B63   2000
651.3'741'076—dc21
                                                    99-17933
                                                    CIP

PRINTED IN THE UNITED STATES OF AMERICA
9 8 7 6 5 4 3 2

Contents

Will Studying Help Me?   v
Introduction   vi
   How to Get a Federal Government Job   vi
   Career Opportunities   vi
   The Tests   viii
   Additional Information About These Civil Service Positions and Tests   viii

PART ONE THE VERBAL ABILITIES TEST

Chapter 1   General Strategies/A Diagnostic Test with Answer
       Explanations/Analysis of Strengths and Weaknesses   3
Chapter 2   Understanding the Sections/Key Strategies/Practice,
       Practice, Practice   18
       Word Meaning   18
       Analogies   31
       Grammar   42
       Spelling   55
       Reading   62
Chapter 3   Four Model Tests with Answer Explanations   75

PART TWO THE CLERICAL ABILITIES TEST

Chapter 4   General Strategies/A Diagnostic Test with Answer
       Explanations/Analysis of Strengths and Weaknesses   121
Chapter 5   Understanding the Sections/Key Strategies/Practice,
       Practice, Practice   136
       Alike or Different   136
       Alphabetizing   149
       Arithmetic Computational Skills   170
       Number and Letter Scramble   184
Chapter 6   Four Model Tests with Answer Explanations   192

PART THREE THE TYPING TEST

Chapter 7   Introduction/A Diagnostic Test/Analysis   245
Chapter 8   Some Common Errors to Watch For/Practice,
       Practice, Practice   250

PART FOUR THE DICTATION TEST

Chapter 9   Introduction/A Diagnostic Test with Answers   259
Chapter 10 Practice, Practice, Practice   271

PART FIVE THE OFFICE MACHINE OPERATOR SPECIAL TESTS—SIMPLIFIED TYPING TEST/LETTER SERIES TEST

Chapter 11 Introduction to the Simplified Typing Test/
       A Diagnostic Test   293
Chapter 12 Practice, Practice, Practice   296
Chapter 13 Introduction to the Letter Series Test/A Diagnostic
       Test with Answer Explanations   304
Chapter 14 Practice, Practice, Practice   311

APPENDIX A

Samples of Questions for the
    Telephone Operator Test   324
      Accounting Clerk Test   325
      Computation Test   326
      Clerical Checking Test   328

APPENDIX B

Getting a Federal Government Job (flow chart)   330
Applying for a Federal Job (brochure)   331
OPM's Self-Service System for Employment
    Information (brochure)   331
1999 General Schedule—Hourly Basic Rates &
    Hourly Overtime   336
1999 General Schedule—Annual Rates by
    Grade and Step   337
Qualification Standards   337
Group Coverage Qualification Standards for
    Clerical and Administrative Support Positions   339
Clerical and Administrative Support Positions   343
Qualification Requirements   344
Clerical and Administrative Support Exam   346
Additional Testing Locations in Washington, D.C. area   347
Typing Proficiency Exam Locations in Washington, D.C. area   347
Special Pay Rates (Typing)   347
Official Sample Questions   348
Occupational Duty Sheet, Secretary   351
Secretary Positions   353
Declaration for Federal Employment
    (sample form)   354
Optional Application for Federal Employment
    (sample form)   356
Qualifications & Availability Form
    (sample grid form)   358
Answer Booklet (sample grid form)   363

Will Studying Help Me?

The most common questions involving exams are "Will studying help me?" and "If so, how should I study?"

Proper preparation *can* significantly improve your chances of doing your best on an exam. An exam gives you the opportunity to display your skills, knowledge, and ability to apply information. Your chances of doing your best and getting your best possible score will increase tremendously if you take the time to

1. become aware of the types of questions on the exam;
2. understand the techniques and strategies that will help you on these questions; and
3. practice applying your skills by using the techniques and strategies at home before the exam.

Once you learn what is on your exam, you can focus your study on specific types of material. You can review the basic skills that you need in order to do well on the exam.

But how you study is also important. Make sure that your study time is "quality" study time. This time should be uninterrupted blocks of one to two hours, but usually not more than that. Many study periods of one to two hours are usually much more effective than fewer, very long study periods. These study and practice times must be in a quiet, distraction-free setting that will make the study time more effective. This is important, as concentration is a key to good studying.

Make sure to have all the proper materials and supplies with you as you begin to study. It is easy to waste time and break concentration if you have to stop to find the proper materials.

An effective study plan will help you review in an organized manner. Take some time to set up a study schedule. Then stick to it. Once you've completed your study regimen, you should go in to take the test with a positive attitude because you've now prepared and are ready. Going in with this positive attitude will help you to apply what you know and will help you to do your best.

Will studying help you? If you study properly, it can give you the opportunity and the edge to do your best.

Why should you study? Because these exams are competitive and you want every advantage to do your best.

This book is designed to serve three purposes:

1. To provide information about the experience and training requirements for a variety of office occupations in the federal government, namely, stenographers, typists, clerks, and office machine operators.
2. To acquaint applicants with the step-by-step approach to getting a federal job and the tests required for these positions.
3. *To prepare applicants to do their best on the civil service exams.* This final purpose is the major emphasis of this book and includes
   —careful analysis of the test question types
   —important test-taking techniques
   —effective strategies for attacking each question type
   —basic skill review
   —extensive sample tests for practice and review

This introductory section (and Appendix B) will discuss How to Get a Federal Government Job, Career Opportunities, and Additional Information About These Civil Service Positions and Tests. The rest of the book focuses squarely on preparing for these important tests.

HOW TO GET A FEDERAL GOVERNMENT JOB

Step 1: Obtain an official announcement and application form from the federal government personnel office, whose local address and phone number are listed in your telephone directory. You can also get valuable information on the Internet at fjob.mail.opm.gov.

Step 2: Complete the application form, as instructed by the announcement. Send it, along with the required fee, to the Office of Personnel Management, whose address should be printed on the application and/or announcement.

Step 3: Become familiar with the test, its required basic skills, and effective test-taking strategies. This information is contained in this book, Barron's *How to Prepare for the Civil Service Examinations,* along with lots of practice tests to help you improve your basic skills as well as test-taking skills. Spend as much time as necessary for a thorough preparation.

Step 4: Meanwhile, you will receive by return mail an admission blank and instructions for taking a civil service test, if required. The instructions will list the location and time of the test, and the proper materials for you to bring to the exam (such as sharpened #2 pencils, a photo I.D., and more).

Step 5: Become familiar with the location of the test site so that . . .

Step 6: On the day of the exam, you arrive early and prepared to do your best.

Step 7: After your exam, the Office of Personnel Management evaluates your qualifications and places your application in its working files.

Step 8: The federal agency requests a list of names from the Office of Personnel Management of the best qualified candidates for its position openings.

Step 9: The Office of Personnel Management refers the best qualified candidates (hopefully *you!*).

Step 10: The federal agency interviews candidates and makes selections based upon candidate qualifications and interviews.

At this point, either you will be chosen to go to work or your name will be returned to the Office of Personnel Management for future referrals.

CAREER OPPORTUNITIES

CLERK-TYPIST AND CLERK-STENOGRAPHER

The positions filled from these examinations are paid under the General Schedule (see Appendix B), in which there are a number of grades that indicate the difficulty and responsibility of the work and the necessary qualifications requirements. Normal entrance levels* are GS-2 for Clerk-Typist positions and GS-3 for Clerk-Stenographer positions. This difference in grade reflects the greater difficulty of the stenographic work and the additional skill required.

Where there are concentrations of federal employees, the opportunities for well-qualified typists and stenographers are very favorable. The demand for GS-3 Clerk-Stenographers and GS-2 Clerk-Typists continues to be steady. There is also a need for persons with extra qualifications required for GS-4 Clerk-Stenographer and GS-3 Clerk-Typist.

There are about 61,100 Clerk-Typist and 8,100 Clerk-Stenographer full-time positions in the federal

---

*For current entrance salary rates, consult the latest examination announcement or the Salary Supplement if the announcement does not show salaries. These forms are available at Federal Job Information Centers.

government.* Vacancies are constantly occurring in these positions as employees are promoted to higher-grade positions, transfer to other jobs, or leave for personal reasons. Career development and promotion programs make Clerk-Stenographer and Clerk-Typist positions a good training ground and an avenue of promotion to higher-grade positions of these types and to secretarial positions, of which there are about 91,500. There are also opportunities for promotion to other kinds of positions, such as Administrative Assistant and related occupations.

CLERK

The title "Clerk" covers many specialized fields. While some positions at the GS-2 and GS-3 levels call for specialized experience or training, most of the specialized work is at the GS-4 and higher levels. In the federal service, clerks have many opportunities to advance to higher-level clerical, supervisory, and administrative positions. Descriptions of some of the major groups of jobs follow.

In *accounting, payroll,* and *fiscal* work, there are about 49,000 clerical and clerical-administrative positions, exclusive of those in professional accounting. Accounts Maintenance Clerks perform accounting clerical work that requires ability to learn and to apply specific instructions, rules, regulations, and procedures, but does not require technical knowledge of bookkeeping or accounting. Other clerks in this area work in the general accounting field; some of these positions provide experience in almost the full range of accounting duties and, when supplemented by appropriate education, help prepare employees for professional accounting careers. Related large occupational groups include Military Pay Clerks and Leave and Payroll Clerks.

A very important group comprises about 5,500 Voucher Examiners. These jobs begin at the GS-3 level, but most are at higher levels because of the responsible and difficult nature of the work.

A distinct job is Cash Processing Clerk. These clerks handle and watch for irregularities in cash items; they also learn and apply requirements for accepting documents that are the basis for the transactions of commercial, federal, and other financial institutions in processing cash items.

A very large group of clerical positions is in the *general clerical* and *administrative* field. This includes over 23,700 Mail and File Clerks, a much smaller group of Correspondence Clerks, and several thousand other clerical jobs of types too numerous to list here. Grades range from GS-1 through GS-6.

In the *personnel* field, clerks have an opportunity to advance to a variety of administrative and technical positions in support of professional personnel work.

The movement of people and material makes up a large part of the business of the federal government. In particular, the movement of military personnel and supplies and the movement of agricultural and other shipments offer additional opportunities for clerks. These clerical positions are in grades GS-2 through GS-5. Many of the positions provide opportunities for promotion to freight or passenger rate work or other higher-level assignments.

The huge problems of supply for the Department of Defense, Veterans Administration, and other agencies call for close to 39,400 clerks in *general supply, stock control,* and *storekeeping.* Most of these positions are in the two agencies just mentioned, but there are sizable numbers in the Treasury Department and in the General Services Administration, the agency in charge of procurement, supply, and maintenance of property for the federal government.

Finally, the extensive statistical programs of the federal government utilize about 2,300 skilled Statistical Assistants. Their work includes the collection and analysis of data from census and other surveys, crop prediction reports, work measurement studies, and many other functions. While the entry level into these jobs is usually at GS-3, many opportunities for advancement exist, and specialized training courses in statistics and in data processing are available to employees.

OFFICE MACHINE OPERATOR

Approximately 11,900 Data Transcribers operate numeric and alphabetic machines, using skills similar to those required in typewriting. There is a considerably smaller number of Electric Accounting Machine Operators, who operate a variety of tabulating equipment. In these groups most employees are at the GS-2, GS-3, and GS-4 levels.

These jobs provide an opportunity to work with and learn various data processing systems. With additional specialized training or experience, employees are able to prepare for careers in computer system operations, programming, and planning.

There are several thousand other Office Machine Operators, whose duties include the operation of one or more types of office imprinting (including embossing), duplicating, or reproducing machines, or the operation of miscellaneous office machines or equipment. Most of these positions are at the GS-2 level.

---

*The federal government also hires many part-time and temporary workers.

Bookkeeping Machine Operator and Calculating Machine Operator positions require special skills and training. Most of the positions in this group are GS-2 and GS-3.

THE TESTS

The tests required for the positions just described include

1. dictation
2. typing
3. verbal abilities
4. clerical skills

There are also some special tests for certain Office Machine Operator positions, including a simplified typing test for Teletypists and other operators of machines with alphabetic keyboards, and a test of abstract reasoning for Electric Accounting Machine Operators (Tabulating Machine Operators) and Cryptographic Equipment Operators.

With the diagnostic and model tests included in this book, candidates can determine if they have sufficient ability to meet the standards of the federal government, or if they need to build their skills and, if so, to what degree. These tests can also help candidates in identifying their shortcomings while there is time to focus their training accordingly. Applicants can thus diagnose areas needing improvement and then practice to strengthen their weak areas.

ADDITIONAL INFORMATION ABOUT THESE CIVIL SERVICE POSITIONS AND TESTS

The following paragraphs summarize current information concerning office positions, including stenographer and typist positions. (For the sake of brevity, in this book positions are often referred to as stenographer and typist positions rather than by the official titles of Clerk-Stenographer and Clerk-Typist.)

SALARIES AND OTHER BENEFITS

Appointments to stenographer positions are usually made at GS-3 and GS-4.* For the latter grade, 1 year of appropriate experience or education above the high school level is required. Appointments to typist, dictating machine transcriber, clerk, and office machine operator positions are usually made at GS-2 and GS-3. Appointments are also made at GS-4 to specialized clerk positions. Always consult your local announcement for current salary rates.

Group life insurance is available at a cost to the employee of 27½ cents biweekly per thousand dollars of insurance; the government pays the rest of the cost. The amount of insurance is $10,000 or the amount of the employee's salary (rounded to the next higher $1,000) plus $2,000, whichever is larger.

Group health insurance, partly paid for by the government as an employer, is also available. This voluntary program offers an employee a chance to join a group health benefits plan, with better rates and better protection than could be secured by an individual.

Paydays occur every 2 weeks. Deductions for federal income tax, as well as for retirement purposes, are withheld from the paycheck. Periodic increases of $250 to $425 a year, depending upon grade level, are provided for competent employees under salary schedules in effect in January 1993. Increases are at yearly intervals for the first 3 years of service in the grade, then at 2-year intervals for the next 6 years of service, and then at 3-year intervals until the maximum salary for the grade is reached. However, a promotion to higher levels, from an entry-level grade, would raise an employee's salary by an amount equal to at least two periodic increases. Thus, a grade-level promotion from GS-2 would give at least $950 a year more in salary.

Vacation benefits range from 13 working days a year to 20 days a year for employees with 3 to 15 years of service, and 26 days a year for those with more than 15 years of service.

All employees, regardless of length of service, earn 13 days of sick leave with pay each year. There is no restriction on the accumulation of unused sick leave.

TEST AND EXPERIENCE REQUIREMENTS

Tables 1 and 2 indicate the tests that are to be taken and the education and experience requirement for the positions.

Final numerical rating in the examination as a whole is based on the written tests of verbal and clerical abilities. Typing and dictation tests are qualifying only and are not added into the final rating. Higher scores are generally required for the higher grades.

*At the present time, a test is required for Clerk-Stenographer at the GS-4 level and for Secretary. For more information on the Secretary position, see "Occupational Duty Sheet, Secretary" in Appendix B.

Table 1
Clerk, Typist, and Stenographer

	Tests				Education/Experience**
	Verbal	*Clerical*	*Typing**	*Stenography**	
Clerk GS-2	Yes	Yes	No	No	High school graduate or 6 months
Typist GS-2	Yes	Yes	Yes	No	of appropriate experience.
Stenographer GS-3	Yes	Yes	Yes	Yes	
Clerk GS-3	Yes	Yes	No	No	1 year of appropriate experience
Typist GS-3	Yes	Yes	Yes	No	or 1 academic year of post-high
Stenographer GS-4	Yes	Yes	Yes	Yes	school education

*An acceptable proficiency certificate can be substituted for these tests—see section "Proficiency Certificates."

**The appropriate experience for clerk is progressively responsible clerical or office work. Appropriate experience for typist and stenographer is either (1) experience that included, as a significant part of the work, application of the required skill (i.e., typing, dictating machine transcribing, or stenography) or (2) any type of clerical work that demonstrates the ability to perform the duties of the position to be filled, provided that the applicant demonstrates an adequate degree of proficiency in the required skill(s).

Table 2
Office Machine Operator

	Tests	*Education/Experience**
GS-2	Verbal and clerical tests for all applicants. For additional tests for certain positions, see section "The Office Machine Operator Special Tests," page 245.	a) 6 months specialized experience, or b) specialized course of instruction in operation of appropriate machine and 3 months of experience, or c) successful completion of a federally financed course of instruction (e.g., Work Incentive Program, Job Corps, Comprehensive Employment Training Act Program, etc.) of appropriate content, intensity, and duration, or d) high school graduation. Education must have included training in operation of appropriate machine, unless a performance test is available for the particular occupation.
GS-3		a) 1 year of office-type experience of which at least 6 months is specialized, or b) 1 academic year of post-high school education, which included training in the operation of appropriate machine, unless a performance test is available for the particular occupation.

*Different requirements may be in effect in some localities. If so, these different requirements will be stated in the examination announcements for those localities.

PROFICIENCY CERTIFICATES

Arrangements have been made with many schools and other authorized training organizations to accept from the applicants a teacher's certificate of proficiency in typing and shorthand. Submission of such a certificate will excuse the applicant from taking the typing and/or shorthand tests. The certificate must be on the official form furnished by the Office of Personnel Management (OPM). On this form, a teacher may certify that the student has demonstrated proficiency in typing and/or shorthand on unfamiliar and continuous material at a standard at least high enough to meet the OPM's requirements. Certificates are valid for only a limited period and are usually issued only to those persons who are still in school. Applicants with satisfactory certificates will still have to take the verbal and clerical abilities tests. If you have any questions concerning the use of proficiency certificates, contact the area office of the U.S. Office of Personnel Management servicing your area.

PHYSICALLY HANDICAPPED APPLICANTS

Although applicants for federal employment must be able to perform the duties of a position, this does not prevent physically handicapped persons from being hired. Physically handicapped persons are encouraged to apply for positions in the federal government. Each area office of the Office of Personnel Management has a Selective Placement Specialist who is responsible for assuring that all handicapped applicants are able to take advantage of the available employment opportunities for which they apply. Federal agencies also have coordinators for selective placement to assist in job placements. In addition to regular competitive placements, severely handicapped persons may be able to secure excepted appointments in some positions.

Most clerical, typing, stenographer, and office machine operator jobs require good distance vision in one eye and the ability to read, without strain, material the size of typewritten characters. Glasses may be used. However, blind typists can fill many positions, such as dictating machine transcribers. Blind applicants should state on their application cards that they are blind, since special arrangements must be made for their examination.

Ability to hear the conversational voice is required for most positions; however, some positions are suitable for deaf applicants.

Be sure to tell the examiner ahead of time if you need special assistance in taking a civil service test. Often you can be accommodated by having more time to complete non-speeded portions of tests. Also, parts of tests may be waived for you.

If you have a disability and are interested in a civil service job with the federal government, another avenue for assistance is the federal Selective Placement Coordinator of the federal agency where you would like to work. Every agency and location has a personnel official who serves as a Selective Placement Coordinator. This person can place you directly in a position without the use of ability and aptitude tests. The appointment is a noncompetitive, excepted service appointment. If you perform the job successfully for two years, you can be converted noncompetitively to the competitive service. You will be treated the same as competitive service hires in terms of health benefits, life insurance, and retirement eligibility. Also, you will have the same leave benefits. In the case of an invisible disability, other employees will never know that you were hired under an excepted appointment. In any case, you will be treated with the same respect given anyone else. The main disadvantage to an excepted service appointment is that you are in a separate reduction-in-force category from competitive service appointments. (However, reductions in force are fairly rare.) There are no formal documentation requirements to enter these programs and a statement from a professional in a health field may be sufficient documentation. States also have special appointing authorities for hiring people with disabilities; these should be explored.

Your rehabilitation counselor can work with you in making contacts with the federal Selective Placement Coordinator or with the comparable state official. Also, if you are a veteran of the military services, the Department of Labor's Employment Services have excellent specialized services available to you; you need to mention that you are a veteran and ask for help as a veteran.

EQUIPMENT NEEDED FOR TESTS

In some localities, competitors taking the typing test must furnish a typewriter and a typing table for use in the examination. Applicants who wish to use an electric typewriter should ask the examining office, in advance of the examination date, whether there is an electric outlet in the examining room.

Stenographer applicants may use any system of taking and transcribing dictation provided it does not interfere with the dictation or with other competitors. Any system of manually written shorthand notes or any noiseless shorthand writing machine may be used provided the notes are given to the examiner after they have been transcribed. Blind persons may be required to furnish a transcribing machine for use in the examining room.

HOW AND WHERE TO APPLY

Civil Service examinations for typists and stenographers are usually announced together and given at the same time. Examinations for Clerk and for various types of Office Machine Operator, such as Data Transcriber, may be announced separately. However, some or all of these examinations may be combined in a single Office Assistant Examination. There may also be some training positions in these occupations. Check with your local U.S. Office of Personnel Management for details on positions, locations, and grade levels for which the examination is being held, and specific instructions on how to apply. Applicants are usually provided with samples of the tests to be given in the examination.

Full information about applying for these and other federal jobs is provided by Federal Job Information Centers throughout the country. These offices are usually listed in local telephone directories under "U.S. Government." If there are none listed in your directory, dial 800-555-1212 to obtain the toll-free number for your state.

INTERNET JOB SEARCH

The Internet is one of the best sources for jobs, both locally and nationally. It can be both time-consuming and fun. Working with a friend, you can do some very fascinating searches. However, you can work alone and have fun doing it as well. The following sources are current as of mid-March 1998.

America's Job Bank. http://www.dol.gov Select America's Job Bank. This is the Employment Service Internet line. It contains jobs for every state and local area. Also, it lists private placement firms that you can use. Most of these private placement firms charge the employer for a placement, not the applicant; you need to verify this with each one you contact.

OPM Federal Government Jobs. http://www.opm.gov Enter the file labeled USA Jobs. This is excellent and is updated on a 24-hour basis. Every job opening for every agency in the federal civil service is listed. Since many jobs are only open for 14 days, it is necessary to check listings on at least a weekly basis. You can apply for many federal jobs on-line by answering the various questions listed and typing in your background information.

Riley Guide. http://www.jobtrak.com/ This is an excellent source and provides great links to other information and the ability to apply for jobs on-line. Also, check out http://dbm.com/jobguide. This is a related guide developed by Margaret Riley Dikel, who is the leading Internet career developer.

Local Newspapers. Many newspapers list all job openings on the Internet. The employer is charged for both the written newspaper advertisement and the Internet advertisement. For example, The *Washington Post* provides job advertisements on the Internet. The *Post*'s site is: http://www.washingtonpost.com. You can use such a site and go to other sites through links provided. You will find all of the jobs listed in *The Washington Post*. Also, you will find help in writing resumes and cover letters as well as other assistance.

Career Path. http://www.careerpath.com This web site is one of the most used job search sites. It is very user-friendly. You can conduct a job search. You can put your resume on-line.

Online Career Center. http://www.occ.com You can search for jobs and company profiles here. Also, you can put your resume on-line.

Other Government Internet Systems. To go into all of the federal government's Internet systems, I suggest using the White House links as an entry source: http://whitehouse.gov

Yahoo and Other Browsers. If you are looking into areas to live or information about companies, or information about jobs, use a web browser. After you go into the web page, you will be asked for key words for your search. Yahoo is widely used and provides links for other browsers: http://www.yahoo.com.

Internet Availability. You can use the Internet at public libraries in most cities. Usually, you would be given 30 to 40 minutes of terminal time each time you request it. The librarian will show you how to do a search, if you are unfamiliar with the Internet. Also, many cities have large job-search collections in some libraries. Ask the reference librarian where these collections are held. There are extensive job search manuals and books to help in a job search for specific occupations and occupations in general. Also, there are many reference books that can be used for job searches.

Wherever you go, you will find the Internet easy to use. You will find instructions on how to enter into a file. Then when you are into a file, the different options will be shown as highlighted words, underlined words, or buttons. These can be pressed by the pointer and you will go into the section you want to search. The Internet is extensively cross-referenced with links to other sites so that you can go from one site to another in your job search. Also, if you are using library facilities in your job search, you may want to explore with the librarian how to set up an E-mail account through various free E-mail systems that will not interfere with the library's account, so that you can hear back from employers. (Do not be concerned if you cannot set up such an account; the prospective employer will call or write to you, if you do not have such an account.)

TEMPORARY APPOINTMENTS

If you are offered a temporary position, you should consider taking it. This is particularly true if it is for one year or longer. Temporary positions of one year or longer usually offer most of the same benefits as permanent positions offer. Also, temporary positions often are converted to permanent positions. The process for this conversion may require you to re-compete. However, if you retain a copy of your notice of rating, normally you will not need to retake a civil service examination.

COMPLETION OF ANSWER SHEET

Most test answer sheets are machine scored. Therefore, it is very important that they be filled out properly. Most tests allow only one answer for each question; if there is more than one answer, the scoring machine is programmed to score the answer as incorrect. Therefore, an applicant must be careful to erase an answer completely if he or she changes it.

Great care must be taken to insure that an applicant's name and Social Security account number is recorded properly.

VETERANS' PREFERENCE PROVISIONS

There are provisions for giving preference to veterans. For more information regarding these preferences contact the agencies or web sites listed below. The following "Notice to Veterans," dated 1998, discusses changes to these provisions.

NOTICE TO VETERANS

Subject—Changes to the Veterans' Preference Provisions contained in the Defense Authorization Act of November 18, 1997.

Two important changes have recently been enacted. The following changes have extended veterans' preference to persons who:

—served on active duty, regardless of where or how long, in the **Gulf War** from August 2, 1990, through January 2, 1992, and

—served in a campaign or expedition for which a campaign medal has been authorized, including El Salvador, Grenada, Haiti, Lebanon, Panama, Somalia, Southwest Asia, and Bosnia.

For more detailed information, request the *Federal Employment Info Line #3, Veterans Preference* through USA*Jobs*, the federal employment information system. By computer at www.usajobs.opm.gov, or fjob.opm.gov, or ftp.fjob.opm.gov; by phone at 202-606-2700, TDD 912-744-2299, or dial 912-757-3100; or visit the Self-Service Employment Information Center located at 1900 E Street, Room 1416, NW, Washington, D.C.

01/26/98

PART ONE

The Verbal Abilities Test

CHAPTER 1

General Strategies
A Diagnostic Test
with Answer Explanations
Analysis of Strengths and Weaknesses

THE VERBAL ABILITIES TEST

The Verbal Abilities Test includes questions that measure such language skills as knowledge of the meaning and relationship of words, ability to spell common words, and skill in recognizing sentences that are grammatically correct in contrast to others that are not acceptable. The test also includes questions that measure the ability to read and understand written material. There are 85 questions on the test, *with a time limit of 35 minutes.* *

Word meaning	25 questions
Analogy	20 questions
Grammar	10 questions
Spelling	20 questions
Reading	10 questions

The question types are "scrambled" throughout the test; that is, you will have 5 word meaning, then 4 analogy, then 2 grammar, then 4 spelling, then 2 reading questions. This series will repeat four times for a total of 85 questions. Each question has equal value toward your final score. Your score on the Verbal Abilities Test is the number of questions you answer correctly. There is no penalty for an incorrect answer.

PROCEDURE

You will have 3 minutes to study the directions and sample questions on the front of your test booklet and to mark the answers to these sample questions in the space provided. You will then be told when to begin the actual test, for which you will have 35 minutes.

GENERAL STRATEGIES

Since there is a limited amount of time (35 minutes) to answer 85 questions, some very important considerations regarding speed, marking, eliminating choices, and guessing come into play. We recommend you become familiar with the following strategies:

Marking in the Test Booklet

Many test takers don't take full advantage of opportunities to mark key words and cross out wrong choices *in the test booklet*. Remember that writing in your test booklet (as explained later) can significantly help you stay focused, as well as help you isolate the correct answer choices. It will also enable you to successfully use the following strategy.

The One-Check, Two-Check System

Many people score lower than they should on the Verbal Abilities Test simply because they do not get to many of the easier problems. They puzzle over difficult questions and use up the time that could be spent answering easy ones. In fact, the difficult questions are worth exactly the same as the easy ones, so it makes sense not to do the hard problems until you have answered all the easy ones.

To maximize your correct answers by focusing on the easier problems, use the following system:

1. Attempt the first question. If it is answerable quickly and easily, work the problem, circle the answer in the question booklet, and then

---

*The U.S. Office of Personnel Management currently plans to drop the analogies portion of this test at a future date. When this is done, the number of questions in the other sections will be increased to retain an 85-question test.

mark that answer on the answer sheet. The mark on the answer sheet should be a complete mark, not merely a dot, because you may not be given time at the end of the test to darken marks.

2. If a question seems impossible, place two checks (✔✔) on or next to the question number in the question booklet and mark the answer you guess on the answer sheet. (*There is no penalty for a wrong guess.*) The mark on the answer sheet should be a complete mark, not merely a dot, because you may not be given time at the end of the test to darken marks.

3. If you're in the midst of a question that seems to be taking too much time, or if you immediately spot that a question is answerable but time-consuming (that is, it will require a minute or more to answer), place one check (✔) next to the question number, mark an answer you guess on the answer sheet, and continue with the next question.

    NOTE THAT NO QUESTIONS ARE LEFT BLANK. AN ANSWER CHOICE IS *ALWAYS* FILLED IN BEFORE LEAVING THAT QUESTION, SINCE THERE IS NO PENALTY FOR GUESSING.

4. When all the problems in a section have been attempted in this manner, there may still be time left. If so, return to the single-check (✔) questions, working as many as possible, changing each guessed answer to a worked-out answer, if necessary.

5. If time remains after all the single-check (✔) questions are completed, you can choose between
    a. attempting those "impossible" double-check (✔✔) questions (sometimes a question later on in the test may trigger your memory to allow once-impossible questions to be solved);

    or

    b. spending time checking and reworking the easier questions to eliminate any careless errors.

6. You should try to use *all* the allotted time as effectively as possible.

Use this system as you work through the Verbal Ability diagnostic and model tests in this book; such practice will allow you to make "one-check, two-check" judgments quickly when you actually take your exam. As our extensive research has shown, use of this system results in less wasted time.

The Elimination Strategy

Faced with four or five answer choices, you will work more efficiently and effectively if you immediately *eliminate* unreasonable or obviously wrong choices. In many cases, several of the choices will immediately appear to be incorrect, and these should be crossed out *on your test booklet* immediately. Then, if a guess is necessary among the remaining choices, you will not reconsider these obvious wrong choices, but will choose from the remaining choices.

Consider the following reading question:

> According to the theory of aerodynamics, the bumblebee is unable to fly. This is because the size, weight, and shape of his body in relationship to his total wingspan make flying impossible. The bumblebee, being ignorant of this "scientific truth," flies anyway.

The paragraph best supports the statement that bumblebees
A) cannot fly in strong winds
B) are ignorant of other things but can't do all of them
C) do not actually fly but glide instead
D) may contradict the theory of aerodynamics

Test takers who do not immediately eliminate the unreasonable choices here, and instead try to analyze every choice, will find themselves becoming confused and anxious as they try to decide how even unreasonable choices might be correct. Their thinking might go something like this:

> "Hmmmm, I've never seen a bumblebee in a strong wind. I'm not sure what (B) means. I wonder if bumblebees do glide;
> I've never looked at them *that* closely. Hmmmm, (D) could be right, but what about the other three? I had better look at them again in case I missed something."

On and on they go, sometimes rereading choices three or four times. In a test of this nature—only 35 minutes allotted for 85 questions—they cannot afford to spend so much time on one question!

Using the elimination strategy, a confident test taker proceeds as follows:

"A)?   Ridiculous and irrelevant. Cross it out.
 B)?   I don't understand this. Put a question mark after it.
 C)?   That sounds ridiculous. Cross it out.
 D)?   That's possible. In fact, that's a much better choice than (B), which I'm not sure I even understand. The answer I'll mark is (D)."

This test taker, aware that most answer choices can be easily eliminated, does so without complicating the process by considering unreasonable possibilities.

To summarize this strategy:

—Look for incorrect answer choices. Cross them out in the test booklet.
—Put question marks after choices that chould be possible.
—Never reconsider choices you have eliminated.

Eliminating incorrect choices will lead you to correct choices more quickly and will increase your chances when you make a guess.

Guessing

As previously mentioned, there is no penalty for an incorrect answer, even if it is a guess. So *never* leave a blank on the Verbal Abilities Test. (This rule does not apply to the other tests, however.)

Whenever you are faced with a difficult, seemingly impossible, or time-consuming question, never leave it until you have *at least registered a guess on the answer sheet*.

Changing Answers and Stray Marks

If you find it necessary to change an answer on your answer sheet, make sure to erase the incorrect answer *completely*. Any partial marks in the answer spaces may be picked up by the scoring machine as a "second answer choice marked" on one question, and that question will be marked incorrect. Therefore take great care to erase completely and not to make stray marks on your answer sheet.

A DIAGNOSTIC TEST WITH ANSWER EXPLANATIONS

The purpose of this diagnostic test is to familiarize you with the Verbal Abilities Test. It is designed to introduce you to the testing areas and to assist you in evaluating your strengths and weaknesses. This will help you focus your review. Chapter 2 will give you a more complete range of problem types and specific strategies for each section. After correcting the diagnostic test and assessing your strengths and weaknesses, you should start your area reviews and practice in the next chapter.

The diagnostic test should be taken under strict test conditions.

First take 3 minutes to review the sample questions given here before starting the exam. (NOTE: Sample questions are usually distributed with the announcement and if so may not be given in the official examination.) Now tear out your answer sheet from this book, turn to the next page, and begin the exam.

REVIEWING THE KEY STRATEGIES

Remember to:

1. Answer easy questions first.

2. Skip "impossible" questions, marking them with the double check (✔✔).

3. Skip "time-consuming" questions, marking them with the single check (✔), coming back to these later, if possible.

4. Answer every question. Fill in a guess, if necessary.

5. Use *all* the allotted time.

ANSWER SHEET

SIGNATURE: _____
(Please Sign)

EXAMINATION TITLE: _____

PLACE OF EXAMINATION: _____

City _____

State _____

TODAY'S DATE: _____

SAMPLE Ⓐ ● Ⓒ Ⓓ Ⓔ

DIRECTIONS FOR MARKING ANSWER SHEET

Use only a **No. 2 (or softer) lead pencil.** Darken completely the circle corresponding to your answer. You **must** keep your mark within the circle. Stray marks may be counted as errors. Erase **completely** all marks except your answer.

SAMPLE NAME GRID

LAST NAME

1. In the boxes below, **PRINT** your name. Print only as many letters as will fit within the areas for the last name, first initial (F.I.), and middle initial (M.I.) Below each box, darken the circle containing the same letter. SEE SAMPLE NAME GRID

LAST NAME

2. In the boxes below, enter your 9-digit Social Security Number. Below each box, darken the circle in each column corresponding to the number you have entered.

SOCIAL SECURITY NUMBER

3. OCCUPATIONAL GROUP NUMBER

SECTION 1

PART

TEST SERIES

TEST NUMBER

Make no marks or entries in the columns to the right until you receive instructions from the administrator.

1 Ⓐ Ⓑ Ⓒ Ⓓ Ⓔ
2 Ⓐ Ⓑ Ⓒ Ⓓ Ⓔ
3 Ⓐ Ⓑ Ⓒ Ⓓ Ⓔ
4 Ⓐ Ⓑ Ⓒ Ⓓ Ⓔ
5 Ⓐ Ⓑ Ⓒ Ⓓ Ⓔ
6 Ⓐ Ⓑ Ⓒ Ⓓ Ⓔ
7 Ⓐ Ⓑ Ⓒ Ⓓ Ⓔ
8 Ⓐ Ⓑ Ⓒ Ⓓ Ⓔ
9 Ⓐ Ⓑ Ⓒ Ⓓ Ⓔ
10 Ⓐ Ⓑ Ⓒ Ⓓ Ⓔ

11 Ⓐ Ⓑ Ⓒ Ⓓ Ⓔ
12 Ⓐ Ⓑ Ⓒ Ⓓ Ⓔ
13 Ⓐ Ⓑ Ⓒ Ⓓ Ⓔ
14 Ⓐ Ⓑ Ⓒ Ⓓ Ⓔ
15 Ⓐ Ⓑ Ⓒ Ⓓ Ⓔ
16 Ⓐ Ⓑ Ⓒ Ⓓ Ⓔ
17 Ⓐ Ⓑ Ⓒ Ⓓ Ⓔ
18 Ⓐ Ⓑ Ⓒ Ⓓ Ⓔ
19 Ⓐ Ⓑ Ⓒ Ⓓ Ⓔ
20 Ⓐ Ⓑ Ⓒ Ⓓ Ⓔ

21 Ⓐ Ⓑ Ⓒ Ⓓ Ⓔ
22 Ⓐ Ⓑ Ⓒ Ⓓ Ⓔ
23 Ⓐ Ⓑ Ⓒ Ⓓ Ⓔ
24 Ⓐ Ⓑ Ⓒ Ⓓ Ⓔ
25 Ⓐ Ⓑ Ⓒ Ⓓ Ⓔ
26 Ⓐ Ⓑ Ⓒ Ⓓ Ⓔ
27 Ⓐ Ⓑ Ⓒ Ⓓ Ⓔ
28 Ⓐ Ⓑ Ⓒ Ⓓ Ⓔ
29 Ⓐ Ⓑ Ⓒ Ⓓ Ⓔ
30 Ⓐ Ⓑ Ⓒ Ⓓ Ⓔ

31 Ⓐ Ⓑ Ⓒ Ⓓ Ⓔ
32 Ⓐ Ⓑ Ⓒ Ⓓ Ⓔ
33 Ⓐ Ⓑ Ⓒ Ⓓ Ⓔ
34 Ⓐ Ⓑ Ⓒ Ⓓ Ⓔ
35 Ⓐ Ⓑ Ⓒ Ⓓ Ⓔ
36 Ⓐ Ⓑ Ⓒ Ⓓ Ⓔ
37 Ⓐ Ⓑ Ⓒ Ⓓ Ⓔ
38 Ⓐ Ⓑ Ⓒ Ⓓ Ⓔ
39 Ⓐ Ⓑ Ⓒ Ⓓ Ⓔ
40 Ⓐ Ⓑ Ⓒ Ⓓ Ⓔ

51 Ⓐ Ⓑ Ⓒ Ⓓ Ⓔ
52 Ⓐ Ⓑ Ⓒ Ⓓ Ⓔ
53 Ⓐ Ⓑ Ⓒ Ⓓ Ⓔ
54 Ⓐ Ⓑ Ⓒ Ⓓ Ⓔ
55 Ⓐ Ⓑ Ⓒ Ⓓ Ⓔ
56 Ⓐ Ⓑ Ⓒ Ⓓ Ⓔ
57 Ⓐ Ⓑ Ⓒ Ⓓ Ⓔ
58 Ⓐ Ⓑ Ⓒ Ⓓ Ⓔ
59 Ⓐ Ⓑ Ⓒ Ⓓ Ⓔ
60 Ⓐ Ⓑ Ⓒ Ⓓ Ⓔ

41 Ⓐ Ⓑ Ⓒ Ⓓ Ⓔ
42 Ⓐ Ⓑ Ⓒ Ⓓ Ⓔ
43 Ⓐ Ⓑ Ⓒ Ⓓ Ⓔ
44 Ⓐ Ⓑ Ⓒ Ⓓ Ⓔ
45 Ⓐ Ⓑ Ⓒ Ⓓ Ⓔ
46 Ⓐ Ⓑ Ⓒ Ⓓ Ⓔ
47 Ⓐ Ⓑ Ⓒ Ⓓ Ⓔ
48 Ⓐ Ⓑ Ⓒ Ⓓ Ⓔ
49 Ⓐ Ⓑ Ⓒ Ⓓ Ⓔ
50 Ⓐ Ⓑ Ⓒ Ⓓ Ⓔ

61 Ⓐ Ⓑ Ⓒ Ⓓ Ⓔ
62 Ⓐ Ⓑ Ⓒ Ⓓ Ⓔ
63 Ⓐ Ⓑ Ⓒ Ⓓ Ⓔ
64 Ⓐ Ⓑ Ⓒ Ⓓ Ⓔ
65 Ⓐ Ⓑ Ⓒ Ⓓ Ⓔ
66 Ⓐ Ⓑ Ⓒ Ⓓ Ⓔ
67 Ⓐ Ⓑ Ⓒ Ⓓ Ⓔ
68 Ⓐ Ⓑ Ⓒ Ⓓ Ⓔ
69 Ⓐ Ⓑ Ⓒ Ⓓ Ⓔ
70 Ⓐ Ⓑ Ⓒ Ⓓ Ⓔ

71 Ⓐ Ⓑ Ⓒ Ⓓ Ⓔ
72 Ⓐ Ⓑ Ⓒ Ⓓ Ⓔ
73 Ⓐ Ⓑ Ⓒ Ⓓ Ⓔ
74 Ⓐ Ⓑ Ⓒ Ⓓ Ⓔ
75 Ⓐ Ⓑ Ⓒ Ⓓ Ⓔ
76 Ⓐ Ⓑ Ⓒ Ⓓ Ⓔ
77 Ⓐ Ⓑ Ⓒ Ⓓ Ⓔ
78 Ⓐ Ⓑ Ⓒ Ⓓ Ⓔ
79 Ⓐ Ⓑ Ⓒ Ⓓ Ⓔ
80 Ⓐ Ⓑ Ⓒ Ⓓ Ⓔ

91 Ⓐ Ⓑ Ⓒ Ⓓ Ⓔ
92 Ⓐ Ⓑ Ⓒ Ⓓ Ⓔ
93 Ⓐ Ⓑ Ⓒ Ⓓ Ⓔ
94 Ⓐ Ⓑ Ⓒ Ⓓ Ⓔ
95 Ⓐ Ⓑ Ⓒ Ⓓ Ⓔ
96 Ⓐ Ⓑ Ⓒ Ⓓ Ⓔ
97 Ⓐ Ⓑ Ⓒ Ⓓ Ⓔ
98 Ⓐ Ⓑ Ⓒ Ⓓ Ⓔ
99 Ⓐ Ⓑ Ⓒ Ⓓ Ⓔ
100 Ⓐ Ⓑ Ⓒ Ⓓ Ⓔ

81 Ⓐ Ⓑ Ⓒ Ⓓ Ⓔ
82 Ⓐ Ⓑ Ⓒ Ⓓ Ⓔ
83 Ⓐ Ⓑ Ⓒ Ⓓ Ⓔ
84 Ⓐ Ⓑ Ⓒ Ⓓ Ⓔ
85 Ⓐ Ⓑ Ⓒ Ⓓ Ⓔ
86 Ⓐ Ⓑ Ⓒ Ⓓ Ⓔ
87 Ⓐ Ⓑ Ⓒ Ⓓ Ⓔ
88 Ⓐ Ⓑ Ⓒ Ⓓ Ⓔ
89 Ⓐ Ⓑ Ⓒ Ⓓ Ⓔ
90 Ⓐ Ⓑ Ⓒ Ⓓ Ⓔ

111 Ⓐ Ⓑ Ⓒ Ⓓ Ⓔ
112 Ⓐ Ⓑ Ⓒ Ⓓ Ⓔ
113 Ⓐ Ⓑ Ⓒ Ⓓ Ⓔ
114 Ⓐ Ⓑ Ⓒ Ⓓ Ⓔ
115 Ⓐ Ⓑ Ⓒ Ⓓ Ⓔ
116 Ⓐ Ⓑ Ⓒ Ⓓ Ⓔ
117 Ⓐ Ⓑ Ⓒ Ⓓ Ⓔ
118 Ⓐ Ⓑ Ⓒ Ⓓ Ⓔ
119 Ⓐ Ⓑ Ⓒ Ⓓ Ⓔ
120 Ⓐ Ⓑ Ⓒ Ⓓ Ⓔ

101 Ⓐ Ⓑ Ⓒ Ⓓ Ⓔ
102 Ⓐ Ⓑ Ⓒ Ⓓ Ⓔ
103 Ⓐ Ⓑ Ⓒ Ⓓ Ⓔ
104 Ⓐ Ⓑ Ⓒ Ⓓ Ⓔ
105 Ⓐ Ⓑ Ⓒ Ⓓ Ⓔ
106 Ⓐ Ⓑ Ⓒ Ⓓ Ⓔ
107 Ⓐ Ⓑ Ⓒ Ⓓ Ⓔ
108 Ⓐ Ⓑ Ⓒ Ⓓ Ⓔ
109 Ⓐ Ⓑ Ⓒ Ⓓ Ⓔ
110 Ⓐ Ⓑ Ⓒ Ⓓ Ⓔ

121 Ⓐ Ⓑ Ⓒ Ⓓ Ⓔ
122 Ⓐ Ⓑ Ⓒ Ⓓ Ⓔ
123 Ⓐ Ⓑ Ⓒ Ⓓ Ⓔ
124 Ⓐ Ⓑ Ⓒ Ⓓ Ⓔ
125 Ⓐ Ⓑ Ⓒ Ⓓ Ⓔ
126 Ⓐ Ⓑ Ⓒ Ⓓ Ⓔ
127 Ⓐ Ⓑ Ⓒ Ⓓ Ⓔ
128 Ⓐ Ⓑ Ⓒ Ⓓ Ⓔ
129 Ⓐ Ⓑ Ⓒ Ⓓ Ⓔ
130 Ⓐ Ⓑ Ⓒ Ⓓ Ⓔ

VERBAL ABILITIES DIAGNOSTIC TEST

Time allotted—35 minutes

Directions and Sample Questions

Study the sample questions carefully. Each question has four suggested answers. Decide which one is the best answer. Find the question number on the Sample Answer Sheet. Show your answer to the question by darkening completely the space corresponding to the letter that is the same as the letter of your answer. Keep your mark within the space. If you have to erase a mark, be sure to erase it completely. Mark only one answer for each question. Do NOT mark space E for any question.

Sample Questions

I. *Previous* means most nearly
   A) abandoned   C) timely
   B) former   D) younger

II. Just as the procedure of a collection department must be clear cut and definite, the steps being taken with the sureness of a skilled chess player, so the various paragraphs of a collection letter must show clear organization, giving evidence of a mind that, from the beginning, has had a specific end in view.

The paragraph best supports the statement that a collection letter should always
   A) show a spirit of sportsmanship
   B) be divided into several paragraphs
   C) be brief, but courteous
   D) be carefully planned

Decide which sentence is preferable with respect to grammar and usage suitable for a formal letter or report.

III. A) They do not ordinarily present these kind of reports in detail like this.
   B) A report of this kind is not hardly ever given in such detail as this one.
   C) This report is more detailed than what such reports ordinarily are.
   D) A report of this kind is not ordinarily presented in as much detail as this one is.

Find the correct spelling of the word and darken the proper answer space. If no suggested spelling is correct, darken space D.

IV. A) athalete   C) athlete
   B) athelete   D) none of these

V. SPEEDOMETER is related to POINTER as WATCH is related to
   A) case   C) dial
   B) hands   D) numerals

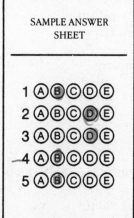

SAMPLE ANSWER SHEET

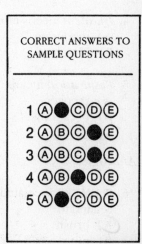

CORRECT ANSWERS TO SAMPLE QUESTIONS

Answer Explanations for Sample Questions

I. **(B)** *Previous* means came before, or *former*.
II. **(D)** "A specific end in view" indicates a careful plan in mind.
III. **(D)** In (A), "these kind" is incorrect; it should be "this kind." In (B), "not hardly ever" is incorrect; it should be "hardly ever." In (C), "than what such reports" is incorrect; the "what" should be deleted.
IV. **(C)** The correct spelling is *athlete*.
V. **(B)** The second word is the "indicator" on the first word.

THE TEST

Read each question carefully. Select the best answer and darken the proper space on the answer sheet.

Word Meaning

1. *Flexible* means most nearly
   A) breakable   C) pliable
   B) flammable   D) weak

2. *Option* means most nearly
   A) use   C) value
   B) choice   D) blame

3. To *verify* means most nearly to
   A) examine   C) confirm
   B) explain   D) guarantee

4. *Indolent* means most nearly
   A) moderate   C) selfish
   B) hopeless   D) lazy

5. *Respiration* means most nearly
   A) recovery   C) pulsation
   B) breathing   D) sweating

Analogies

6. PLUMBER is related to WRENCH as PAINTER is related to
   A) brush   C) shop
   B) pipe   D) hammer

7. LETTER is related to MESSAGE as PACKAGE is related to
   A) sender   C) insurance
   B) merchandise   D) business

8. FOOD is related to HUNGER as SLEEP is related to
   A) night   C) weariness
   B) dream   D) rest

9. KEY is related to TYPEWRITER as DIAL is related to
   A) sun   C) circle
   B) number   D) telephone

Grammar

10. A) I think that they will promote whoever has the best record.

B) The firm would have liked to have promoted all employees with good records.

C) Such of them that have the best records have excellent prospects of promotion.

D) I feel sure they will give the promotion to whomever has the best record.

11. A) The receptionist must answer courteously the questions of all them callers.

B) The receptionist must answer courteously the questions what are asked by the callers.

C) There would have been no trouble if the receptionist had have always answered courteously.

D) The receptionist should answer courteously the questions of all callers.

Spelling

12. A) collapsible   C) collapseble
    B) collapseable   D) none of these

13. A) ambigeuous   C) ambiguous
    B) ambigeous   D) none of these

14. A) predesessor   C) predecesser
    B) predecesar   D) none of these

15. A) sanctioned   C) sanctionned
    B) sancktioned   D) none of these

Reading

16. The secretarial profession is a very old one and has increased in importance with the passage of time. In modern times, the vast expansion of business and industry has greatly increased the need and opportunities for secretaries, and for the first time in history their number has become large.

    The paragraph best supports the statement that the secretarial profession
    A) is older than business and industry
    B) did not exist in ancient times
    C) has greatly increased in size
    D) demands higher training than it did formerly

17. Civilization started to move ahead more rapidly when people freed themselves of the shackles that restricted their search for the truth.

The paragraph best supports the statement that the progress of civilization

A) came as a result of people's dislike for obstacles

B) did not begin until restrictions on learning were removed

C) has been aided by people's efforts to find the truth

D) is based on continually increasing efforts

18. *Vigilant* means most nearly
A) sensible   C) suspicious
B) watchful   D) restless

19. *Incidental* means most nearly
A) independent C) infrequent
B) needless   D) casual

20. *Conciliatory* means most nearly
A) pacific   C) obligatory
B) contentious D) offensive

21. *Altercation* means most nearly
A) defeat   C) controversy
B) concurrence D) vexation

22. *Irresolute* means most nearly
A) wavering   C) impudent
B) insubordinate D) unobservant

23. DARKNESS is related to SUNLIGHT as STILLNESS is related to
A) quiet   C) sound
B) moonlight   D) dark

24. DESIGNED is related to INTENTION as ACCIDENTAL is related to
A) purpose   C) damage
B) caution   D) chance

25. ERROR is related to PRACTICE as SOUND is related to
A) deafness   C) muffler
B) noise   D) horn

26. RESEARCH is related to FINDINGS as TRAINING is related to
A) skill   C) supervision
B) tests   D) teaching

27. A) If properly addressed, the letter will reach my mother and I.

B) The letter had been addressed to myself and my mother.

C) I believe the letter was addressed to either my mother or I.

D) My mother's name, as well as mine, was on the letter.

28. A) The supervisors reprimanded the typists, whom she believed had made careless errors.

B) The typists would have corrected the errors had they of known that the supervisor would see the report

C) The errors in the typed reports were so numerous that they could hardly be overlooked.

D) Many errors were found in the reports which they typed and could not disregard them.

29. A) minieture   C) mineature
B) minneature   D) none of these

30. A) extemporaneous C) extemperaneous
B) extempuraneus   D) none of these

31. A) problemmatical C) problematicle
B) problematical   D) none of these

32. A) descendant   C) desendant
B) decendant   D) none of these

33. The likelihood of America's exhausting her natural resources seems to be growing less. All kinds of waste are being reworked and new uses are constantly being found for almost everything. We are getting more use out of our goods and are making many new byproducts out of what was formerly thrown away.

The paragraph best supports the statement that we seem to be in less danger of exhausting our resources because

A) economy is found to lie in the use of substitutes

B) more service is obtained from a given amount of material

C) we are allowing time for nature to restore them

D) supply and demand are better controlled

34. Telegrams should be clear, concise, and brief. Omit all unnecessary words. The parts of speech most often used in telegrams are nouns, verbs, adjectives, and adverbs. If possible, do without pronouns, prepositions, articles, and

copulative verbs. Use simple sentences rather than complex or compound ones.

The paragraph best supports the statement that in writing telegrams one should always use
A) common and simple words
B) only nouns, verbs, adjectives, and adverbs
C) incomplete sentences
D) only the words essential to the meaning

35. To *counteract* means most nearly to
A) undermine   C) preserve
B) censure   D) neutralize

36. *Deferred* means most nearly
A) reversed   C) considered
B) delayed   D) forbidden

37. *Feasible* means most nearly
A) capable   C) practicable
B) justifiable   D) beneficial

38. To *encounter* means most nearly to
A) meet   C) overcome
B) recall   D) retreat

39. *Innate* means most nearly
A) eternal   C) native
B) well-developed D) prospective

40. STUDENT is related to TEACHER as DISCIPLE is related to
A) follower   C) principal
B) master   D) pupil

41. LECTURE is related to AUDITORIUM as EXPERIMENT is related to
A) scientist   C) laboratory
B) chemistry   D) discovery

42. BODY is related to FOOD as ENGINE is related to
A) wheels   C) motion
B) fuel   D) smoke

43. SCHOOL is related to EDUCATION as THEATER is related to
A) management   C) recreation
B) stage   D) preparation

44. A) Most all these statements have been supported by persons who are reliable and can be depended upon.
B) The persons which have guaranteed these statements are reliable.

C) Reliable persons guarantee the facts with regards to the truth of these statements
D) These statements can be depended on, for their truth has been guaranteed by reliable persons.

45. A) The success of the book pleased both the publisher and authors.
B) Both the publisher and they was pleased with the success of the book.
C) Neither they or their publisher was disappointed with the success of the book.
D) Their publisher was as pleased as they with the success of the book.

46. A) extercate   C) extricate
B) extracate   D) none of these

47. A) hereditory   C) hereditairy
B) hereditary   D) none of these

48. A) auspiceous   C) auspicious
B) auspiseous   D) none of these

49. A) sequance   C) sequense
B) sequence   D) none of these

50. The prevention of accidents makes it necessary not only that safety devices be used to guard exposed machinery but also that mechanics be instructed in safety rules which they must follow for their own protection, and that the lighting in the plant be adequate.

The paragraph best supports the statement that industrial accidents
A) may be due to ignorance
B) are always avoidable
C) usually result from inadequate machinery
D) cannot be entirely overcome

51. The English language is peculiarly rich in synonyms, and there is scarcely a language spoken that has not some representative in English speech. The spirit of the Anglo-Saxon race has subjugated these various elements to one idiom, making not a patchwork, but a composite language.

The paragraph best supports the statement that the English language
A) has few idiomatic expressions
B) is difficult to translate
C) is used universally
D) has absorbed words from other languages

52. To *acquiesce* means most nearly to
   A) assent   C) complete
   B) acquire   D) participate

53. *Unanimity* means most nearly
   A) emphasis   C) harmony
   B) namelessness   D) impartiality

54. *Precedent* means most nearly
   A) example   C) law
   B) theory   D) conformity

55. *Versatile* means most nearly
   A) broad-minded   C) up-to-date
   B) well-known   D) many-sided

56. *Authentic* means most nearly
   A) detailed   C) valuable
   B) reliable   D) practical

57. BIOGRAPHY is related to FACT as NOVEL is related to
   A) fiction   C) narration
   B) literature   D) book

58. COPY is related to CARBON PAPER as MOTION PICTURE is related to
   A) theater   C) duplicate
   B) film   D) television

59. EFFICIENCY is related to REWARD as CARELESSNESS is related to
   A) improvement   C) reprimand
   B) disobedience   D) repetition

60. ABUNDANT is related to CHEAP as SCARCE is related to
   A) ample   C) inexpensive
   B) costly   D) unobtainable

61. A) Brown's & Company employees have recently received increases in salary.
   B) Brown & Company recently increased the salaries of all its employees.
   C) Recently Brown & Company has increased their employees' salaries.
   D) Brown & Company have recently increased the salaries of all its employees.

62. A) In reviewing the typists' work reports, the job analyst found records of unusual typing speeds.
   B) It says in the job analyst's report that some employees type with great speed.
   C) The job analyst found that, in reviewing the typists' work reports, that some unusual typing speeds had been made.
   D) In the reports of typists' speeds, the job analyst found some records that are kind of unusual.

63. A) oblitorate   C) obbliterate
   B) oblitterat   D) none of these

64. A) diagnoesis   C) diagnosis
   B) diagnossis   D) none of these

65. A) contenance   C) countinance
   B) countenance   D) none of these

66. A) conceivably   C) conceiveably
   B) concieveably   D) none of these

67. Through advertising, manufacturers exercise a high degree of control over consumers' desires. However, the manufacturer assumes enormous risks in attempting to predict what consumers will want and in producing goods in quantity and distributing them in advance of final selection by the consumers.

The paragraph best supports the statement that manufacturers
   A) can eliminate the risk of overproduction by advertising
   B) distribute goods directly to the consumers
   C) must depend upon the final consumers for the success of their undertakings
   D) can predict with great accuracy the success of any product they put on the market

68. In the relations of humans to nature, the procuring of food and shelter is fundamental. With the migration of humans to various climates, ever new adjustments to the food supply and to the climate became necessary.

The paragraph best supports the statement that the means by which humans supply their material needs are
   A) accidental
   B) varied
   C) limited
   D) inadequate

69. *Strident* means most nearly
   A) swaggering   C) angry
   B) domineering   D) harsh

70. To *confine* means most nearly to
   A) hide   C) eliminate
   B) restrict   D) punish

71. To *accentuate* means most nearly to
   A) modify   C) sustain
   B) hasten   D) intensify

72. *Banal* means most nearly
   A) commonplace   C) tranquil
   B) forceful   D) indifferent

73. *Incorrigible* means most nearly
   A) intolerable   C) irreformable
   B) retarded   D) brazen

74. POLICE OFFICER is related to ORDER as DOCTOR is related to
   A) physician   C) sickness
   B) hospital   D) health

75. ARTIST is related to EASEL as WEAVER is related to
   A) loom   C) threads
   B) cloth   D) spinner

76. CROWD is related to PERSONS as FLEET is related to
   A) expedition   C) navy
   B) officers   D) ships

77. CALENDAR is related to DATE as MAP is related to
   A) geography   C) mileage
   B) trip   D) vacation

78. A) Since the report lacked the needed information, it was of no use to them.
   B) This report was useless to them because there were no needed information in it.
   C) Since the report did not contain the needed information, it was not real useful to them.
   D) Being that the report lacked the needed information, they could not use it.

79. A) The company had hardly declared the dividend till the notices were prepared for mailing.
   B) They had no sooner declared the dividend when they sent the notices to the stockholders.
   C) No sooner had the dividend been declared than the notices were prepared for mailing.
   D) Scarcely had the dividend been declared than the notices were sent out.

80. A) compitition   C) competetion
    B) competition   D) none of these

81. A) occassion   C) ocassion
    B) occasion   D) none of these

82. A) knowlege   C) knowledge
    B) knolledge   D) none of these

83. A) deliborate   C) delibrate
    B) deliberate   D) none of these

84. What constitutes skill in any line of work is not always easy to determine; economy of time must be carefully distinguished from economy of energy, as the quickest method may require the greatest expenditure of muscular effort, and may not be essential or at all desirable.

The paragraph best supports the statement that
   A) the most efficiently executed task is not always the one done in the shortest time
   B) energy and time cannot both be conserved in performing a single task
   C) a task is well done when it is performed in the shortest time
   D) skill in performing a task should not be acquired at the expense of time

85. It is difficult to distinguish between bookkeeping and accounting. In attempts to do so, bookkeeping is called the art, and accounting the science, of recording business transactions. Bookkeeping gives the history of the business in a systematic manner; and accounting classifies, analyzes, and interprets the facts thus recorded.

The paragraph best supports the statement that
   A) accounting is less systematic than bookkeeping
   B) accounting and bookkeeping are closely related
   C) bookkeeping and accounting cannot be distinguished from one another
   D) bookkeeping has been superseded by accounting

ANSWER KEY

Word Meaning

1. C	18. B	35. D	52. A	69. D
2. B	19. D	36. B	53. C	70. B
3. C	20. A	37. C	54. A	71. D
4. D	21. C	38. A	55. D	72. A
5. B	22. A	39. C	56. B	73. C

Analogies

6. A	23. C	40. B	57. A	74. D
7. B	24. D	41. C	58. B	75. A
8. C	25. C	42. B	59. C	76. D
9. D	26. A	43. C	60. B	77. C

Grammar

10. A	27. D	44. D	61. B	78. A
11. D	28. C	45. D	62. A	79. C

Spelling

12. A	29. D	46. C	63. D	80. B
13. C	30. A	47. B	64. C	81. B
14. D	31. B	48. C	65. B	82. C
15. A	32. A	49. B	66. A	83. B

Reading

16. C	33. B	50. A	67. C	84. A
17. C	34. D	51. D	68. B	85. B

ANALYSIS CHART

Now that you've corrected your exam, use the following chart to analyze your results and spot your strengths and weaknesses. This analysis should help you focus your study and review efforts.

Section	Total Number of Questions	Number Correct	Number Incorrect	Number Unanswered*
Word Meaning	25			
Analogies	20			
Grammar	10			
Spelling	20			
Reading Comprehension	10			
TOTAL	85			

*Since there is no penalty for incorrect answers on the Verbal Abilities Test, you should have left no question unanswered. Even if you didn't have time to answer a question, at least you should have filled in the answer space with a guess.

ANSWER EXPLANATIONS

1. (C) *Flexible* means bendable, or *pliable*. *Flex* means bend.
2. (B) *Option* means selection or alternative, or *choice*.
3. (C) *To verify* means to prove, or to *confirm*.
4. (D) *Indolent* means not inclined to work, or *lazy*.
5. (B) *Respiration* means inhaling and exhaling, or *breathing*.
6. (A) The second word is a tool of the first word.
7. (B) The second word is sent or delivered in the first word.
8. (C) The first word eliminates the second word.
9. (D) The first word is the operative mechanism on the second word.
10. (A) In (B), the verb tenses should be "would like to have promoted." "Such of them" in (C) is incorrect. (D) should read: "whoever has the best record."
11. (D) In (A), "all them callers" is incorrect; it should be "all callers." In (B), "what are asked" is incorrect; it should be "asked." In (C), "had have" should be "had."
12. (A) collapsible
13. (C) ambiguous
14. (D) Correct spelling: predecessor.
15. (A) sanctioned
16. (C) "Their number has become large" indicates that the number of secretaries has greatly increased in size.
17. (C) "When people freed themselves of the shackles that restricted their search for the truth," civilization moved ahead. This indicates that civilization's progress was aided by people's efforts to find the truth.
18. (B) *Vigilant* means on guard, or *watchful*. Note the root word, *vigil*.
19. (D) *Incidental* means of minor event or circumstance, or *casual*.
20. (A) *Conciliatory* means to bring together or make peaceful. *Pacific* is the best synonym. Note the root word, *pacify*.
21. (C) *Altercation* is a quarrel, or *controversy*.
22. (A) *Resolute* means firm; *irresolute* means *wavering*.
23. (C) The first word is the absence of the second word.
24. (D) *Designed* means *by intention*. *Accidental* means *by chance*. The first word occurs through the action of the second word.

25. (C) The second word eliminates or lessens the first word.

26. (A) The second word is the intended result of the first word.

27. (D) In (A), (B), and (C), the phrase should be "my mother and me."

28. (C) In (A), "Whom" should be "who." In (B), "of known" is incorrect; it should be simply "known." In (D), "they" is vague, and "and could not disregard them" is awkward.

29. (D) Correct spelling: miniature

30. (A) extemporaneous

31. (B) problematical

32. (A) descendant

33. (B) "Getting more use out of our goods" indicates that more service is obtained from a given amount of material.

34. (D) "Concise" and "brief" indicate that, in telegrams, one should use only words essential to the meaning.

35. (D) To *counteract* means to check the effects of an action, or to *neutralize*. Note the prefix, *counter*, meaning against, and the root word, *act*.

36. (B) *Deferred* means put off, or *delayed*.

37. (C) *Feasible* means possible, able to be done, or *practicable*.

38. (A) To *encounter* means to come in contact with, or to *meet*.

39. (C) *Innate* means inborn, or *native*.

40. (B) The first word learns from the second word.

41. (C) The first word takes place in the second word.

42. (B) The first word consumes the second word for energy.

43. (C) The first word is a place for the purpose of the second word.

44. (D) In (A), "reliable and can be depended upon" is repetitious. In (B), "which" should be "who." In (C), "the facts with regards to the truth" is repetitious and awkward.

45. (D) In (A), "both" indicates two people, whereas "publisher and authors" must mean a minimum of three people. In (B), "was" should be "were," among other errors. (C) should be "Neither they *nor* . . ."

46. (C) extricate

47. (B) hereditary

48. (C) auspicious

49. (B) sequence

50. (A) The necessity that "mechanics be instructed in safety rules" indicates that accidents may be due to ignorance.

51. (D) "There is scarcely a language spoken that has not some representative in English speech" indicates that the English language has absorbed words from other languages.

52. (A) To *acquiesce* means to give in, or to *assent*.

53. (C) *Unanimity* means total agreement, or *harmony*. Notice the root, *unanimous*.

54. (A) *Precedent* means a standard, or *example*.

55. (D) *Versatile* means multiskilled, or *many-sided*.

56. (B) *Authentic* means worthy of trust or reliance, or *reliable*.

57. (A) The first word is a book using the second word.

58. (B) The first word is made by means of the second word.

59. (C) The first word results in the second word.

60. (B) The second word is the price of the first word.

61. (B) In (A), the *'s* should be on *Company*, not *Brown*. In (C), "has" and "their" must agree; the correct form is "its employees." In (D), "have" should be "has" to agree with "its."

62. (A) The error in (B) is the vague use of "it." The error in (C) is awkward sentence structure, not as direct or clear as it could be. The error in (D) is the informal phrase "kind of" unusual.

63. (D) Correct spelling: obliterate

64. (C) diagnosis

65. (B) countenance

66. (A) conceivably

67. (C) That "the manufacturer assumes enormous risks in attempting to predict what consumers will want" indicates that manufacturers must depend upon the final consumers for the success of their undertakings.

68. (B) "*New adjustments* to the food supply and to the climate" indicates that the means by which humans supply their material needs are varied.

69. (D) *Strident* means grating, or *harsh*.

70. (B) To *confine* means to keep within bounds, or to *restrict*.

71. (D) To *accentuate* means to increase, or to *intensify*.

72. (A) *Banal* means worn-out and predictable, or *commonplace*.

73. (C) *Incorrigible* means uncorrectable, or *irreformable*.

74. (D) The first word is the person who restores the second word.

75. **(A)** The second word is a tool of the first word.
76. **(D)** The first word is a collection or group of the second word.
77. **(C)** The second word is a unit comprising the first word.
78. **(A)** The main error in (B) is "were"; it should be "was." The main error in (C) is "real useful"; it should be "really useful," or simply "useful." The main error in (D) is a nonstandard phrase, "being that"; it should be "because."
79. **(C)** Each of the incorrect choices here is unclear about the relationship between declaring the dividend and sending the notices.

80. **(B)** competition
81. **(B)** occasion
82. **(C)** knowledge
83. **(B)** deliberate
84. **(A)** That "economy of time must be carefully distinguished from economy of energy" indicates that the most efficiently executed task is not always the one done in the shortest time.
85. **(B)** "It is difficult to distinguish between bookkeeping and accounting," as they are closely related.

CHAPTER 2

Understanding the Sections
Key Strategies
Practice, Practice, Practice

WORD MEANING

This question type tests your vocabulary. You are given words and must decide which choice means the same or most nearly the same as the given word. For example:

To *terminate* means most nearly
A) schedule C) finish
B) begin D) disallow

Since to *terminate* means to *cease* or to *put an end to*, the best choice is (C) *finish*.

HELPFUL TECHNIQUES AND STRATEGIES

1. Choose the most nearly correct word from among the choices given. Sometimes the best choice may not be perfect or convey exactly the same meaning you would use yourself, but if it is the *best* of the choices, it is the correct answer.
2. Work as quickly as you can. Scan the possible answers and decide immediately on the correct one. Take time out to study each individual choice only if the words are unfamiliar or especially difficult for you.
3. Although the words used should not be technical or obscure, they may be long and/or dif-

ficult. Break these words up into prefixes, suffixes, and roots to help in understanding the meaning. Item 6 contains a list of prefixes, suffixes, and roots.

4. If possible, use the given word in a short, clear sentence. This may help give you a context to work from and increase your understanding of the word's meaning. Then substitute the choices into your sentence to see if the sentence retains the same meaning.
5. Many words carry a strong connotation. If, for example, a word sounds "positive" or "good," then choose a word that has a positive connotation. If a word sounds "negative" or "bad," then your choice should reflect this negative connotation. Sometimes you may not know the exact meaning of a certain word, but it will just sound "positive" or "negative" to you. Trust your instincts and select the answer choice that reflects this connotation. Example:

Noxious means most nearly
A) clean C) famous
B) luminous D) poisonous

Since *noxious* has a strong negative connotation, you can eliminate all choices except (D) *poisonous*, which also is negative, and is the correct answer.

6. Review the list that follows.

SOME COMMON PREFIXES, SUFFIXES, AND ROOTS

Prefix	Meaning	Examples
ad-	to; at; near	*adhere* stick to
anti-	in opposition; against	*antislavery* against slavery
auto-	self; by self; of one's self	*automatic* self-acting
bene-	good; well	*benevolence* disposed to do good
bi-	two; twice; double	*bisect* cut into two equal parts
circum-	around; all around	*circumnavigate* sail around (the globe)
co-		*cooperate* perform together
com-; con-	with; together; altogether	*combine* merge with *connect* join together
contra-	against; contrary	*contradict* assert the contrary of
de-	down; from; away	*descend* travel down
dia-	through; between; across	*diagonal* across a figure
dis-	not; apart	*disapprove* not approve
ex-	out of; out; from	*expel* drive out
extra-	beyond; without	*extraordinary* beyond the ordinary
fer-	wild; untamed	*ferocity* wildness
fore-	beforehand; in front	*foresee* see beforehand
geo-	earth	*geography* the study of the earth and its inhabitants
hemi-	half	*hemisphere* one-half a sphere or globe
hyper-	too much; beyond; over	*hypersensitive* oversensitive
hypo-	beneath; too little	*hypodermic* beneath the skin
inter-	between; among	*interfere* enter between or among others
intro-	within; in; into	*introduce* bring or lead in
mal-, male-	bad; ill; badly	*malfunction* function badly
mis-	wrongly; badly	*misinformed* badly informed
mon-, mono-	single; having only one	*monomania* obsessed by one idea
non-	not	*nonprofessional* not belonging to a profession
omni-	all; everywhere	*omnipotent* all-powerful
per-	through; throughout; thoroughly	*perforate* pierce through
poly-	many	*polygamy* having many husbands or wives at one time
post-	after; behind	*postnatal* after birth
pre-	before; prior to	*preview* see beforehand
pro-	before; forth; forward	*produce* bring forth
re-	back; again	*recall* call back
sal-	health	*salutory* healthful
semi-	half	*semicircle* half circle
sub-	under; beneath; inferior	*subordinate* inferior in rank
super-	above; greater; more than	*superhuman* greater than human
trans-	across; through; beyond	*transport* carry across
un-	not	*uncommon* not common

Suffix	Meaning	Examples
-able	able to; capable of being	*lovable* capable of being loved
-acity	character; quality	*veracity* the quality of truth
-ence, -ance	a state of being	*abundance* the state of being abundant
-ful	full of	*grateful* full of gratitude
-fy	to make	*beautify* to make beautiful
-ion, -sion, -tion	the act or condition of	*reaction* the act of reacting
-ism	belief in; practice of; condition of	*activism* the practice of being actively involved
-less	free from; without	*penniless* without mercy
-logy	doctrine or science; the study of	*geology* the study of the earth
-ness	state of being	*emptiness* state of being empty
-some	abounding in; full of	*troublesome* full of trouble
-wise	in the manner of; in the direction of	*lengthwise* in the direction of length

Root	Meaning	Examples
acr	sharp; bitter	*acrimonious* bitter
ag, act	to do; to act	*agent* doer *retroactive* having a reverse action
agog	leader	*demagogue* false leader
agri, agrari	fields	*agrarian* farmer; one who works on fields
ali	another	*alias* another name
alt	high	*altitude* height
anim	mind; soul	*unanimous* of one mind
ann	year	*annuity* yearly payment *biennial* every two years
arch	ruler, government	*anarchy* no government
aqua	water	*aquatic* living in water
aud	to hear	*audible* can be heard
belli	war	*belligerent* carrying on war or aggression
ben, bene	good; well	*benefactor* one who does good
biblio	book	*bibliography* list of books
bio	life	*biography* story of a person's life
breve	short	*brevity* briefness; shortness
cap	head; to take	*captain* chief; headwaiter *capture* seize; to take captive
cede, cess	to go; to yield	*precede* to go before *concession* the act of yielding
chron, chrono	time	*chronicle* a register of events arranged in order of time *chronology* the time order of events

Root	Meaning	Examples
cid, cis	to kill; to cut	*homicide* killing of a person by another *incision* a cut
civi	citizen	*civil* relating to citizens
clos, clud	to close; to shut	*enclose* to close in *exclude* to shut out
dic, dict	to say; to speak	*diction* speech
domin	to rule	*dominate* to rule or have power over
duc	to lead	*induce* to lead or bring on
ego	I; self	*egocentric* self-centered
gam	marriage	*bigamy* marriage to two people at once
gen, gener	class; race; kind	*general* applying to a whole class or race
geo	earth	*geochemistry* the chemical study of the earth
greg	flock; herd; group	*gregarious* grouping together
jac, jact, ject	to throw	*projectile* something thrown forward
labor, laborat	to work	*laboratory* workplace
liber	book; free	*library* collection of books *liberty* freedom
man, mani, manu	hand	*manufacture* create; make by hand
mar	sea	*submarine* under the sea
mit, miss	to send	*transmit* send across *dismiss* to send away
mov, mot, mob	to move	*remove* to move away *emotion* "moving" feelings *mobile* movable
nav	ship	*navigate* sail a ship
pac	peace	*pacific* peaceful
port, portat	carry	*portable* able to be carried
put, putat	to calculate; to cut	*compute* to calculate *amputate* to cut off
quer, quisit	to ask	*query* to ask a question *inquisitive* questioning
quies	quiet	*acquiesce* to agree quietly, without protest
radi	ray	*irradiate* to shine light on
rap, rapt	to seize	*rapine* the act of seizing others' property by force *rapture* the state of being seized or carried away by emotion
rid, ris	to laugh	*deride* to laugh at scornfully *risible* capable of laughing
rog, rogate	to ask	*interrogate* to ask questions of
rupt	break	*rupture* a break
sag	wisdom	*sage* a wise person *sagacity* wisdom
sat, satis	enough	*satiate* to provide with enough or more than enough *satisfy* to meet the need of
schis, schiz	to cut; to split	*schism* a split or division *schizophrenia* a mental disorder characterized by separation of the thoughts and emotions

Root	Meaning	Examples
sci	to know	*science* knowledge
scop	to watch; to view	*telescope* an instrument for viewing things from a distance
scrib, script	to write	*prescribe* to write a medical prescription *transcript* a written copy
sec, sect	to cut	*section* to cut into parts *bisect* to cut in two
sed, sess, sid	to sit	*sedentary* doing much sitting *session* a meeting *preside* to sit in position of authority
sent, sens	to feel; to perceive	*resent* to feel annoyance *sensible* perceiving through the senses
sequ, secu, secut	to follow	*sequel* that which follows *consecutive* one following another
solv, solut	to loosen; to solve	*absolve* to free (loosen) from guilt *solution* act of solving a problem
soph	wise; wisdom	*sophisticate* a wordly-wise person
spec, spect, spic	to watch; to look; to appear	*spectator* observer *inspect* to look over *perspicacious* having sharp judgment
spir, spirit	to breathe	*expire* to exhale; to die *spirit* life
sta, stat	to stand	*stable* steady *stationary* fixed; unmoving
stru, struct	to build	*construe* to explain or deduce the meaning *structure* a building
suas, suad	to urge; to advise	*persuasive* having the power to cause something to change *dissuade* to advise someone against something
sum, sumpt	to take	*assume* to take on *resumption* taking up again
tact, tang	to touch	*tactile* perceptible through touch *intangible* unable to be touched
tempor	time	*contemporary* at the same time
ten, tent, tain	to hold	*tenure* holding of office *retentive* capable of holding *retain* to hold onto
tend, tens	to stretch	*extend* to stretch out or draw out *tense* to stretch tight
terr	land; earth	*terrestrial* pertaining to the earth
the, theo	god	*atheist* one who believes there is no God *theocracy* rule by God or by persons claiming to represent Him
thermo	heat	*thermal* relating to heat
tract	to draw	*attract* to draw
trud, trus	to thrust; to push	*protrude* to stick out *intrusive* pushing into or upon something
tum, tumid	to swell	*tumor* a swelling *tumify* to cause to swell
un, uni	one	*unanimous* of one opinion *uniform* of one form

Root	Meaning	Examples
urb	city	*suburban* outside the city
ut, util	to use; useful	*utility* the quality of being useful
vac	empty	*vacuum* empty space
ven, vent	to come	*intervene* come between *advent* an arrival
ver	true	*verify* to prove to be true
verb	words	*verbalize* using words *verbatim* word for word
verd	green	*verdant* green
vert, vers	to turn	*avert* to turn away
vi, via	way	*deviate* to turn from the prescribed way *via* by way of
vid, vis	to see	*evident* easily seen *invisible* unable to be seen
vinc, vict	to conquer; to win	*invincible* unconquerable *victorious* winning
vit, viv	to live	*vital* alive *vivacious* lively
voc, voke, vocat	to call	*revocable* capable of being called back *invoke* to call on *vocation* a calling
void	empty	*devoid* empty of (feeling)
volv, volut	to roll or turn around	*evolve* to develop by stages; to unfold *revolution* movement around
vol	to fly	*volatile* vaporizing quickly

PRACTICE SET 1

Select the best answer to each question and write the letter of your choice in the space provided.

1. To *amend* means most nearly to _____
   A) pass
   B) correct
   C) legislate
   D) finish

2. *Respite* means most nearly _____
   A) rest
   B) dine
   C) despite
   D) few

3. *Mammoth* means most nearly _____
   A) mammal
   B) extinct
   C) gigantic
   D) dead

4. *Iota* means most nearly _____
   A) tiny bit
   B) group
   C) speedster
   D) friend

5. *Latitude* means most nearly _____
   A) freedom
   B) style
   C) emotion
   D) worth

6. *Jargon* means most nearly _____
   A) puzzle
   B) lizard
   C) language
   D) container

7. *Knoll* means most nearly _____
   A) bell
   B) instrument
   C) hill
   D) harmony

8. *Liaison* means most nearly _____
   A) go-between
   B) foreigner
   C) rifle
   D) gallop

9. *Proximity* means most nearly _____
   A) closeness
   B) cleanliness
   C) prurient
   D) fitness

10. To *saturate* means most nearly to _____
    A) enjoy
    B) soak
    C) construct
    D) disturb

11. *Stamina* means most nearly _____
    A) strength
    B) root
    C) dye
    D) limb

12. To *tantalize* means most nearly to _____
    A) please
    B) seize
    C) tease
    D) freeze

13. *Toxic* means most nearly _____
    A) waste
    B) smelly
    C) poisonous
    D) growing

14. *Lesion* means most nearly _____
    A) league
    B) injury
    C) army
    D) ridicule

15. *Clandestine* means most nearly _____
    A) friendly
    B) remorseful
    C) secret
    D) pensive

16. *Combustible* means most nearly _____
    A) eatable
    B) breakable
    C) burnable
    D) thinkable

17. To *condone* means most nearly to _____
    A) condemn
    B) require
    C) forgive
    D) praise

18. *Frailty* means most nearly _____
    A) weakness
    B) frenzy
    C) real estate
    D) purpose

19. *Mandatory* means most nearly _____
    A) required
    B) able
    C) masculine
    D) separate

20. *Medley* means most nearly _____
    A) half-note
    B) interruption
    C) mixture
    D) snoop

21. *Lustrous* means most nearly _____
    A) lawsuit
    B) shining
    C) willowy
    D) fortunate

22. *Benevolent* means most nearly _____
    A) warlike
    B) generous
    C) angry
    D) rebellious

23. *Emaciated* means most nearly _____
    A) content
    B) strong
    C) wasted
    D) lofty

24. *Glossy* means most nearly _____
    A) free
    B) shiny
    C) stealthy
    D) refurbished

25. To *maim* means most nearly to _____
    A) defoliate
    B) beg
    C) issue
    D) injure

ANSWERS FOR PRACTICE SET 1

1. **(B)** correct
2. **(A)** rest
3. **(C)** gigantic
4. **(A)** tiny bit
5. **(A)** freedom
6. **(C)** language
7. **(C)** hill
8. **(A)** go-between
9. **(A)** closeness
10. **(B)** soak

11. **(A)** strength
12. **(C)** tease
13. **(C)** poisonous
14. **(B)** injury
15. **(C)** secret
16. **(C)** burnable
17. **(C)** forgive
18. **(A)** weakness

19. **(A)** required
20. **(C)** mixture
21. **(B)** shining
22. **(B)** generous
23. **(C)** wasted
24. **(B)** shiny
25. **(D)** injure

PRACTICE SET 2

Select the best answer to each question and write the letter of your choice in the space provided.

1. *Plagiarism* means most nearly ____
   A) theft
   B) anarchism
   C) illness
   D) evilness

2. To *reiterate* means most nearly to ____
   A) compound
   B) repeat
   C) affect
   D) retreat

3. *Monotonous* means most nearly ____
   A) large
   B) growing
   C) uninteresting
   D) jagged

4. *Futile* means most nearly ____
   A) engine
   B) missile
   C) useless
   D) decorative

5. *Pensive* means most nearly ____
   A) wealthy
   B) tense
   C) thoughtful
   D) idle

6. *Utilitarian* means most nearly ____
   A) useful
   B) despondent
   C) rich
   D) indolent

7. *Trepidation* means most nearly ____
   A) tearfulness
   B) anxiety
   C) hard work
   D) cleverness

8. *Labyrinth* means most nearly ____
   A) infantile
   B) hardship
   C) maze
   D) welcome

9. *Defection* means most nearly ____
   A) sickness
   B) problem
   C) bad temper
   D) desertion

10. *Cumbersome* means most nearly ____
    A) clumsy
    B) remarkable
    C) vegetation
    D) encompass

11. *Intimidation* means most nearly ____
    A) memory
    B) secret
    C) fear
    D) expectation

12. *Dais* means most nearly ____
    A) platform
    B) waste
    C) prejudice
    D) dress

13. *Candid* means most nearly ____
    A) hidden
    B) peeping
    C) frank
    D) funny

14. *Ambiguous* means most nearly ____
    A) long
    B) uncertain
    C) reliable
    D) aloof

15. *Chassis* means most nearly ____
    A) engine
    B) classic
    C) framework
    D) reliable

16. *Carmine* means most nearly ____
    A) model
    B) red
    C) sweet
    D) speedy

17. *Complacent* means most nearly ____
    A) self-satisfied
    B) ordered
    C) quiet
    D) natural

18. *Audible* means most nearly ____
    A) profitable
    B) knowledgeable
    C) hearable
    D) greedy

19. *Affluent* means most nearly ____
    A) proud
    B) keen
    C) wealthy
    D) understanding

20. To *loathe* means most nearly to ____
    A) bake
    B) detest
    C) clean
    D) limp

21. *Levity* means most nearly ____
    A) air
    B) measurement
    C) gaiety
    D) judgment

22. *Lethal* means most nearly ____
    A) ancient
    B) gas
    C) deadly
    D) formal

23. To *ferret* means most nearly to ____
    A) search out
    B) cut
    C) wander
    D) whip

24. *Genial* means most nearly ____
    A) scientific
    B) wizardly
    C) kindly
    D) superficial

25. *Vacuum* means most nearly _____
    A) utensil   C) blower
    B) cleaning   D) empty

ANSWERS FOR PRACTICE SET 2

1.	(A) theft	14.	(B) uncertain
2.	(B) repeat	15.	(C) framework
3.	(C) uninteresting	16.	(B) red
4.	(C) useless	17.	(A) self-satisfied
5.	(C) thoughtful	18.	(C) hearable
6.	(A) useful	19.	(C) wealthy
7.	(B) anxiety	20.	(B) detest
8.	(C) maze	21.	(C) gaiety
9.	(D) desertion	22.	(C) deadly
10.	(A) clumsy	23.	(A) search out
11.	(C) fear	24.	(C) kindly
12.	(A) platform	25.	(D) empty
13.	(C) frank		

PRACTICE SET 3

Select the best answer to each question and write the letter of your choice in the space provided.

1. *Oaf* means most nearly _____
    A) tree   C) stupid person
    B) rest   D) model

2. *Mobile* means most nearly _____
    A) fixed   C) movable
    B) gasoline   D) car

3. *Migratory* means most nearly _____
    A) protected   C) unhappy
    B) wandering   D) fickle

4. *Gusty* means most nearly _____
    A) enjoyable   C) windy
    B) throaty   D) happy

5. *Hapless* means most nearly _____
    A) unfortunate   C) disappointed
    B) sad   D) reliant

6. *Arcade* means most nearly _____
    A) passageway   C) games
    B) shipwreck   D) curvature

7. *Fraudulent* means most nearly _____
    A) perfect   C) deceitful
    B) friction   D) dangerous

8. To *goad* means most nearly to _____
    A) urge   C) bark
    B) punish   D) gather

9. *Homogenous* means most nearly _____
    A) pasteurized   C) similar
    B) blended   D) healthy

10. *Hubbub* means most nearly _____
    A) uproar   C) comedy
    B) friend   D) sidekick

11. *Omnipotent* means most nearly _____
    A) odorous   C) all-powerful
    B) obsolete   D) homesick

12. *Placid* means most nearly _____
    A) peaceful   C) perfunctory
    B) straight   D) foremost

13. *Tirade* means most nearly _____
    A) carnival   C) scolding
    B) fuselage   D) parade

14. *Stagnant* means most nearly _____
    A) smelling   C) playful
    B) motionless   D) ancient

15. *Succinct* means most nearly _____
    A) brief   C) loving
    B) achieving   D) tarnished

16. *Disgruntled* means most nearly _____
    A) belittled   C) discontent
    B) prudent   D) injured

17. To *amputate* means most nearly to _____
    A) hospitalize   C) prune
    B) dissolve   D) electrocute

18. *Apothecary* means most nearly _____
    A) talisman   C) curse
    B) druggist   D) opening

19. *Intermittent* means most nearly _____
    A) periodic   C) winterized
    B) settled   D) joking

20. To *aspire* means most nearly to _____
    A) sweat   C) seek
    B) hurry   D) allow

21. *Tenacious* means most nearly _____
    A) sportsmanlike C) steadfast
    B) boring   D) angry

22. *Haphazard* means most nearly _____
    A) deliberate   C) unfortunate
    B) accidental   D) hairy

23. *Infamous* means most nearly _____
    A) notorious   C) expensive
    B) heroic   D) unknown

24. *Inept* means most nearly _____
   A) worrisome   C) incompetent
   B) relentless   D) lazy

25. *Increment* means most nearly _____
   A) increase   C) infirmity
   B) prohibition   D) insufficient

ANSWERS FOR PRACTICE SET 3

1. (C) stupid person   14. (B) motionless
2. (C) movable   15. (A) brief
3. (B) wandering   16. (C) discontent
4. (C) windy   17. (C) prune
5. (A) unfortunate   18. (B) druggist
6. (A) passageway   19. (A) periodic
7. (C) deceitful   20. (C) seek
8. (A) urge   21. (C) steadfast
9. (C) similar   22. (B) accidental
10. (A) uproar   23. (A) notorious
11. (C) all-powerful   24. (C) incompetent
12. (A) peaceful   25. (A) increase
13. (C) scolding

PRACTICE SET 4

Select the best answer to each question and write
the letter of your choice in the space provided.

1. *Murkiness* means most nearly _____
   A) mud   C) gloom
   B) cheer   D) accident

2. *Perimeter* means most nearly _____
   A) area   C) boundary
   B) machine   D) yardstick

3. *Haughty* means most nearly _____
   A) dour   C) flabby
   B) proud   D) quick

4. *Forte* means most nearly _____
   A) strength   C) score
   B) battalion   D) barracks

5. To *engross* means most nearly to _____
   A) outnumber   C) absorb
   B) revile   D) dislike

6. To *deduce* means most nearly to _____
   A) reason   C) remain
   B) subtract   D) forbid

7. *Contorted* means most nearly _____
   A) aborted   C) twisted
   B) playful   D) harbored

8. To *cauterize* means most nearly to _____
   A) mix   C) burn
   B) count   D) dissuade

9. *Berserk* means most nearly _____
   A) frenzied   C) friend
   B) ornate   D) sheltered

10. To *rectify* means most nearly to _____
   A) make right   C) destruct
   B) turn away   D) build

11. *Pugnacious* means most nearly _____
   A) small   C) quarrelsome
   B) queasy   D) foreboding

12. *Mediocre* means most nearly _____
   A) brownish   C) ordinary
   B) healthful   D) small-minded

13. To *hone* means most nearly to _____
   A) sharpen   C) return
   B) possess   D) rank

14. To *reminisce* means most nearly to _____
   A) publish   C) answer
   B) remember   D) lessen

15. *Frivolous* means most nearly _____
   A) obstinate   C) trivial
   B) patient   D) ornate

16. To *flaunt* means most nearly to _____
   A) bury   C) praise
   B) allow   D) display

17. *Precarious* means most nearly _____
   A) not reckless   C) risky
   B) prepared   D) formidable

18. *Mishap* means most nearly _____
   A) sadness   C) strange looking
   B) accident   D) beggar

19. *Fiasco* means most nearly _____
   A) celebration   C) failure
   B) pottery   D) artwork

20. *Crony* means most nearly _____
   A) companion   C) retiree
   B) money   D) polish

21. *Scrutiny* means most nearly _____
   A) deceit   C) inspection
   B) wicked   D) fear

22. *Robust* means most nearly _____
   A) automaton   C) healthy
   B) decaying   D) stealing

23. To *relinquish* means most nearly to _____
    A) tie up   C) give up
    B) sum up   D) pick up

24. *Gnarled* means most nearly _____
    A) eaten   C) twisted
    B) fused   D) flabby

25. To *debilitate* means most nearly to _____
    A) ease   C) weaken
    B) pay back   D) show off

ANSWERS FOR PRACTICE SET 4

1. (C) gloom   14. (B) remember
2. (C) boundary   15. (C) trivial
3. (B) proud   16. (D) display
4. (A) strength   17. (C) risky
5. (C) absorb   18. (B) accident
6. (A) reason   19. (C) failure
7. (C) twisted   20. (A) companion
8. (C) burn   21. (C) inspection
9. (A) frenzied   22. (C) healthy
10. (A) make right   23. (C) give up
11. (C) quarrelsome   24. (C) twisted
12. (C) ordinary   25. (C) weaken
13. (A) sharpen

PRACTICE SET 5

Select the best answer to each question and write the letter of your choice in the space provided.

1. *Benediction* means most nearly _____
   A) argument   C) blessing
   B) retirement   D) treason

2. To *acquiesce* means most nearly to _____
   A) yield   C) understand
   B) familiarize   D) resolve

3. To *abhor* means most nearly to _____
   A) yell   C) dissolve
   B) force   D) detest

4. *Unwitting* means most nearly _____
   A) unconscious   C) droll
   B) ill-humored   D) stupid

5. To *recant* means most nearly to _____
   A) take back   C) allow
   B) deceive   D) forbid

6. *Morbid* means most nearly _____
   A) gruesome   C) allowable
   B) stiff   D) enthusiastic

7. *Occult* means most nearly _____
   A) mysterious   C) cold
   B) silent   D) oily

8. *Preposterous* means most nearly _____
   A) commonplace   C) profound
   B) skilled   D) absurd

9. To *resuscitate* means most nearly to _____
   A) revive   C) remind
   B) reneg   D) reproach

10. *Subtle* means most nearly _____
    A) soft   C) not obvious
    B) dirty   D) careless

11. *Uncanny* means most nearly _____
    A) pure   C) moldy
    B) strange   D) open

12. *Vigilant* means most nearly _____
    A) angry   C) forceful
    B) watchful   D) unknowledgeable

13. *Environs* means most nearly _____
    A) vicinity   C) chains
    B) forest   D) prison

14. *Entrepreneur* means most nearly _____
    A) roughneck   C) foreigner
    B) businessman   D) deceiver

15. To *poach* means most nearly to _____
    A) trespass   C) instruct
    B) model   D) hang

16. *Revelry* means most nearly _____
    A) merrymaking   C) anger
    B) reminder   D) overthrow

17. *Shoddy* means most nearly _____
    A) doubting   C) cheap
    B) intermittent D) ghostly

18. *Virile* means most nearly _____
    A) sick   C) manly
    B) deadly   D) watchful

19. *Mutinous* means most nearly _____
    A) silent   C) ponderous
    B) rebellious   D) changeable

20. *Profound* means most nearly _____
    A) discovered   C) very deep
    B) receptive   D) absurd

21. To *fabricate* means most nearly to _____
    A) enhance   C) lie
    B) free   D) urge

22. To *falter* means most nearly to _____
    A) blame   C) stumble
    B) draw out   D) decree

23. *Coy* means most nearly _____
    A) bashful   C) cowardly
    B) brief   D) aware

24. *Bland* means most nearly _____
    A) musical   C) mild
    B) friendly   D) happy

25. *Calligraphy* means most nearly _____
    A) measurement C) penmanship
    B) profession   D) communication

ANSWERS FOR PRACTICE SET 5

1.	(C) blessing	14.	(B)	businessman
2.	(A) yield	15.	(A)	trespass
3.	(D) detest	16.	(A)	merrymaking
4.	(A) unconscious	17.	(C)	cheap
5.	(A) take back	18.	(C)	manly
6.	(A) gruesome	19.	(B)	rebellious
7.	(A) mysterious	20.	(C)	very deep
8.	(D) absurd	21.	(C)	lie
9.	(A) revive	22.	(C)	stumble
10.	(C) not obvious	23.	(A)	bashful
11.	(B) strange	24.	(C)	mild
12.	(B) watchful	25.	(C)	penmanship
13.	(A) vicinity			

PRACTICE SET 6

Select the best answer to each question and write the letter of your choice in the space provided.

1. To *haggle* means most nearly to _____
    A) show off   C) bargain
    B) rob   D) raid

2. *Boisterous* means most nearly _____
    A) masculine   C) sentimental
    B) rowdy   D) trite

3. *Molten* means most nearly _____
    A) melted   C) lost
    B) furry   D) evil

4. *Mentor* means most nearly _____
    A) teacher   C) temperature
    B) salesperson D) adage

5. To *avow* means most nearly to _____
    A) marry   C) acknowledge
    B) adapt   D) help

6. *Mercenary* means most nearly _____
    A) greedy   C) murderous
    B) quick   D) reliable

7. To *reimburse* means most nearly to _____
    A) profit   C) pay back
    B) require   D) foretell

8. *Paltry* means most nearly _____
    A) chicken   C) insignificant
    B) friendship   D) white

9. *Mandatory* means most nearly _____
    A) masculine   C) required
    B) foolish   D) perceptive

10. To *petrify* means most nearly to _____
    A) harden   C) frighten
    B) kiss   D) embezzle

11. *Interim* means most nearly _____
    A) upset   C) meantime
    B) boundary   D) subject

12. To *desist* means most nearly to _____
    A) punish   C) stop
    B) forgive   D) allow

13. *Component* means most nearly _____
    A) part   C) circle
    B) conduct   D) conspiracy

14. *Avocation* means most nearly _____
    A) job   C) hobby
    B) trip   D) decoration

15. *Apathetic* means most nearly _____
    A) important   C) calm
    B) horrified   D) indifferent

16. *Compliant* means most nearly _____
    A) submissive   C) argument
    B) unhappy   D) restrictive

17. *Soothsayer* means most nearly _____
    A) dentist   C) predictor
    B) sleepwalker D) debater

18. *Sinister* means most nearly _____
    A) winding   C) evil
    B) smiling   D) truthful

19. *Redundant* means most nearly _____
    A) bouncing   C) self-reliant
    B) repetitious D) hardy

20. To *mimic* means most nearly to _____
    A) pander   C) imitate
    B) mumble   D) threaten

21. *Impeccable* means most nearly _____
   A) faultless   C) encouraging
   B) hairy   D) religious

22. *Idiosyncrasy* means most nearly _____
   A) peculiarity   C) rhythm
   B) weirdness   D) reliability

23. *Furtive* means most nearly _____
   A) sneaky   C) powerful
   B) sterile   D) limited

24. To *gorge* means most nearly to _____
   A) blast   C) cut short
   B) stuff   D) corrupt

25. *Dank* means most nearly _____
   A) dark   C) damp
   B) dim   D) dear

ANSWERS FOR PRACTICE SET 6

1.	(C) bargain	14.	(C) hobby
2.	(B) rowdy	15.	(D) indifferent
3.	(A) melted	16.	(A) submissive
4.	(A) teacher	17.	(C) predictor
5.	(C) acknowledge	18.	(C) evil
6.	(A) greedy	19.	(B) repetitious
7.	(C) pay back	20.	(C) imitate
8.	(C) insignificant	21.	(A) faultless
9.	(C) required	22.	(A) peculiarity
10.	(A) harden	23.	(A) sneaky
11.	(C) meantime	24.	(B) stuff
12.	(C) stop	25.	(C) damp
13.	(A) part		

REVIEWING THE KEY STRATEGIES

Remember to:

1. Look for the best, or closest, meaning.

2. Work as quickly as possible.

3. Use prefixes, suffixes, and roots.

4. Try the word in a clear sentence.

5. Look for positive or negative connotations.

ANALOGIES

This question type tests your vocabulary and your ability to understand relationships. Each question gives you one pair of related words, and one word from a second pair. You are given four choices for completing the second pair, so that it expresses a relationship similar to the first.

For example:

HEN is related to CHICK as HORSE is related to
A) bull   C) colt
B) milk   D) kitten

Notice the first pair, "HEN is related to CHICK." In this pair, the second word is a "young version" of the first word. Now look at the first word of the second pair: HORSE is related to . . . To complete this pair you must express the same relationship as in the first pair, so that the second word is a "young version" of the first word. The answer choice (second word) that best expresses that relationship is COLT. A COLT (second word) is a young version of a HORSE (first word). (C) is the correct answer.

HELPFUL TECHNIQUES AND STRATEGIES

1. Always try to determine the relationship expressed in the first pair of words. Is the relationship "cause to effect" or "part to whole," or what? Then look at the first word of the next pair.

2. It may help to read this question type by thinking to yourself, "A is related to B *in the same way* as C is related to (D)." The (D) word is the one you are looking for in your answer choices.

3. Remember that *order* must be the same in both pairs. For example,

STREAM is related to RIVER as LAKE is related to
A) pond   C) fish
B) ocean   D) water

Notice the relationship in the first pair: SMALL is to LARGE. Therefore the second pair should say that LAKE (small) is related to OCEAN (large). If you made the mistake of reversing the order in the second pair, you would have chosen (A) POND, which is incorrect.

4. The parts of speech in each pair should be consistent. Look at the question below:

SKYSCRAPER is related to TALL as FREIGHT TRAIN is related to
A) track   C) quickly
B) engine   D) long

Notice that the first word in each pair is a noun (person, place, or thing) and the second word in the first pair, TALL, is an adjective. Therefore the second word in the second pair must also be an adjective. Notice that answer choice (D), LONG, is an adjective, whereas the other choices are not: SKYSCRAPER (noun) is related to TALL (adjective) as FREIGHT TRAIN (noun) is related to LONG (adjective).

5. Remember that the second pair of words does not have to concern the same "subject" as the first. Look at the following question:

PUPPY is related to DOG as SAPLING is related to
A) house   C) leaf
B) tree   D) syrup

Notice that the "subject" of the first pair is animals and the "subject" of the second pair is plants. However, it is the *relationship* between words that is important. The relationship in the first pair is "younger" to "older." With this relationship in mind, you should conclude that SAPLING (younger) is related to TREE (older).

6. Look at all the choices before deciding on an answer, but don't spend too much time on any one question.

7. Usually you will be able to eliminate one or two choices immediately. Those that remain may all seem like good answers, but remember that you are looking for the *best* answer, one that best expresses the same relationship.

8. Analogies can be classified into specific categories. You will find it helpful to be able to recognize some of these categories and the common relationships immediately. Do not try to memorize these categories or to classify the analogies you are given on the exam. Instead, reason out the relationships shown in the first pair of analogies and then carefully choose a second pair that has a corresponding relationship.

    Following are some BASIC TYPES of analogies:

    a. CLASSIFICATIONS—sorts, kinds, general to specific, specific to general, thing to quality or characteristic, opposites, degree, etc.

A broad category is compared to a narrower category:

RODENT : SQUIRREL :: fish : flounder
(broad category) *(narrower category)* *(broad category)* *(narrower category)*

A person is compared to a characteristic:

SPRINTER : FAST :: jockey : small
(person) *(characteristic)* *(person)* *(characteristic)*

The general is compared to the specific:

SPORT : HOCKEY :: machine : typewriter
(general) *(specific)* *(general)* *(specific)*

A word is compared to a synonym of itself:

ENORMOUS : HUGE :: quick : speedy
(word) *(synonym)* *(word)* *(synonym)*

A word is compared to an antonym of itself:

SERVANT : MASTER :: sad : happy
(word) *(antonym)* *(word)* *(antonym)*

A word is compared to a definition of itself:

REGULATE : CONTROL :: segregate : separate
(word) *(definition)* *(word)* *(definition)*

A male is compared to a female:

ROOSTER : CHICKEN :: buck : doe
(male) *(female)* *(male)* *(female)*

A family relationship is compared to a similar family relationship:

AUNT : NIECE :: uncle : nephew
(family relationship) *(family relationship)*

A virtue is compared to a failing:

RESPONSIBILITY : CARELESSNESS :: honesty : dishonesty
(virtue) *(failing)* *(virtue)* *(failing)*

An element is compared to an extreme of itself:

DRY SPELL : DROUGHT :: water : flood
(element) *(extreme)* *(element)* *(extreme)*

A lesser degree is compared to a greater degree:

HAPPY : ECSTATIC :: hot : scorching
(lesser degree) *(greater degree)* *(lesser degree)* *(greater degree)*

The plural is compared to the singular:

CHILDREN : CHILD :: they : he
(plural) *(singular)* *(plural)* *(singular)*

b. STRUCTURALS—part to whole, whole to part, part to part, etc.

A part is compared to a whole:

FINGER : HAND :: room : house
(part) *(whole)* *(part)* *(whole)*

A whole is compared to a part:

DECK : CARD :: novel : chapter
(whole) *(part)* *(whole)* *(part)*

c. COMPONENTS—elements of a compound, ingredients of a recipe, etc.

An ingredient is compared to its finished result:

FLOUR : CAKE :: sulphur : gunpowder
(ingredient) *(finished product)* *(ingredient)* *(finished product)*

HYDROGEN : WATER :: sodium : salt
(element) *(compound)* *(element)* *(compound)*

d. OPERATIONALS—time sequence, operations, stages, phases, beginning to ending, before to after, etc.

One element of time is compared to another element of time:

DAWN : DUSK :: sunrise : sunset
(time element) *(time element)* *(time element)* *(time element)*

A time sequence relationship is expressed:

PROLOGUE : EPILOGUE :: birth : death
(beginning) *(ending)* *(beginning)* *(ending)*

A complete operation is compared to a stage:

FOOTBALL GAME : QUARTER :: baseball game : inning
(operation) *(stage)* *(operation)* *(stage)*

NOTE: Many analogies will overlap into more than one of the above basic types and will have to be analyzed by their purpose, use, cause-effect relationship, etc.

PRACTICE SET 1

Select the best answer to each question and write the letter of your choice in the space provded.

1. APPOINTMENT is related to CANCEL as BUILDING is related to _____
   A) construct   C) demolish
   B) conference   D) design

2. SPORT is related to SPECTATOR as TELEVISION is related to _____
   A) vision   C) viewer
   B) tube   D) channel

3. PURITY is related to WHITE as ANGER is related to _____
   A) yellow   C) mad
   B) red   D) mean

4. WALL is related to PAINTING as FLOOR is related to _____
   A) sweeping   C) house
   B) dirty   D) ironing

5. PLUMBER is related to WRENCH as LION-TAMER is related to _____
   A) lion   C) cage
   B) whip   D) fear

6. AUTOMOBILE is related to IGNITION as LAMP is related to _____
   A) bulb   C) switch
   B) wheel   D) steering wheel

7. IMPORTANT is related to INSIGNIFICANT as INTENDED is related to _____
   A) purpose   C) meaningless
   B) required   D) accidental

8. CUISINE is related to KITCHEN as EXPERIMENT is related to _____
   A) living room   C) stadium
   B) airport   D) laboratory

9. ORE is related to MINE as SAP is related to _____
   A) syrup   C) branch
   B) fluid   D) tree

10. WINDOW is related to AWNING as EYES is related to _____
    A) glasses   C) visor
    B) feet   D) hand

11. SALVAGE is related to TREASURE as RESCUE is related to _____
    A) ambulance   C) squad
    B) victim   D) hospital

12. ALLIES is related to ADVERSARIES as FRIENDS is related to _____
    A) foes   C) arbitrators
    B) helpers   D) peacemakers

13. LAGOON is related to BAY as BROOK is related to _____
    A) puddle   C) ocean
    B) river   D) aqueduct

14. TASK is related to FATIGUE as FASTING is related to _____
    A) food   C) weakness
    B) strength   D) slowness

15. DRAPE is related to WINDOW as COSTUME is related to _____
    A) seamstress   C) character
    B) Halloween   D) mask

16. DAWN is related to DAY as PREFACE is related to _____
    A) epilogue   C) book
    B) index   D) chapter

17. TRIAL is related to COURTROOM as BALLGAME is related to _____
    A) clubhouse   C) stadium
    B) league   D) uniform

18. MARRIAGE is related to BACHELOR as EXPERIENCE is related to _____
    A) fun   C) wizard
    B) novice   D) husband

19. HEART is related to HUMAN as ENGINE is related to _____
    A) carburetor   C) automobile
    B) gasoline   D) mechanic

20. BURGLAR is related to ALARM as TRESPASSER is related to _____
    A) bark   C) air raid
    B) steal   D) property

ANSWER EXPLANATIONS FOR PRACTICE SET 1

1. (C) The first word is eliminated by the second word.
2. (C) The first word is watched by the second word.
3. (B) The second word is the color symbolizing the first word.
4. (A) The second word is done to the first word.
5. (B) The second word is a tool of the first word.

6. **(C)** The second word turns on the first word.
7. **(D)** The first word is the opposite of the second word.
8. **(D)** The first word is produced in the second word.
9. **(D)** The first word is produced in the second word.
10. **(C)** The second word shades the first word.
11. **(B)** The first word saves the second word.
12. **(A)** The first word is the opposite of the second word.
13. **(B)** The first word is similar to but smaller than the second word.
14. **(C)** The first word causes the second word.
15. **(C)** The first word covers the second word.
16. **(C)** The first word begins the second word.
17. **(C)** The first word takes place in the second word.
18. **(B)** The first word ends the second word.
19. **(C)** The first word is the vital center of the second word.
20. **(A)** The first word is frightened away by the second word.

PRACTICE SET 2

Select the best answer to each question and write the letter of your choice in the space provided.

1. SOLO is related to ENSEMBLE as INDIVIDUAL is related to ___
   A) committee   C) instrument
   B) performance   D) partner

2. MELANCHOLY is related to CHEERFUL as TRAGEDY is related to ___
   A) death   C) play
   B) drama   D) comedy

3. BIGOT is related to TOLERANCE as MISER is related to ___
   A) generosity   C) hoard
   B) money   D) spendthrift

4. CLAW is related to LION as TALON is related to ___
   A) snake   C) hand
   B) hawk   D) finger

5. BUSINESS is related to BANKRUPT as TEAM is related to ___
   A) fall behind   C) teamwork
   B) forfeit   D) play

6. COFFEE is related to BEAN as TEA is related to ___
   A) bag   C) instant
   B) leaf   D) iced

7. HERD is related to CATTLE as FLOCK is related to ___
   A) lions   C) mice
   B) sheep   D) gather

8. ICE is related to GLACIER as SAND is related to ___
   A) beach   C) sandstorm
   B) heat   D) water

9. CAPTAIN is related to SHIP as PUBLISHER is related to ___
   A) newspaper   C) film
   B) mint   D) airplane

10. CATASTROPHE is related to EARTHQUAKE as BIRD is related to ___
    A) robin   C) accident
    B) flight   D) nest

11. EXTINCT is related to DINOSAUR as IMAGINARY is related to ___
    A) whale   C) unicorn
    B) fantasy   D) real

12. ASTRONOMY is related to STARS as GEOLOGY is related to ___
    A) geography   C) rocks
    B) maps   D) artifacts

13. REVOLUTION is related to TYRANNY as COURAGE is related to ___
    A) fear   C) government
    B) anger   D) heroism

14. SACRIFICE is related to MARTYR as RULE is related to ___
    A) lawyer   C) despot
    B) carpenter   D) measure

15. DAY is related to SOLAR as EVENING is related to ___
    A) night   C) dawn
    B) dark   D) lunar

16. GARAGE is related to VEHICLES as VAULT is related to ___
    A) burglar   C) valuables
    B) safe   D) combination

17. LIMP is related to INJURY as LAUGH is related to ___
    A) cry   C) joke
    B) pain   D) smile

18. WATER is related to EVAPORATE as ICE is related to _____
    A) freeze   C) cold
    B) melt   D) solid

19. MEAT is related to PROTEIN as POTATOES is related to _____
    A) fat   C) calories
    B) starch   D) butter

20. DISEMBARK is related to SHIP as DISMOUNT is related to _____
    A) train   C) horse
    B) rider   D) mountain

ANSWER EXPLANATIONS FOR PRACTICE SET 2

1. **(A)** The second word is the plural of the first word.
2. **(D)** The first word is the opposite of the second word.
3. **(A)** The first word lacks the second word.
4. **(B)** The second word grasps with the first word.
5. **(B)** The second word is the failure of the first word.
6. **(B)** The first word comes originally from the second word.
7. **(B)** The first word is a collection of the second word.
8. **(A)** The second word is composed of the first word.
9. **(A)** The first word is in charge of the second word.
10. **(A)** The second word is a specific example of the first word.
11. **(C)** The first word is a description of the second word.
12. **(C)** The first word is the study of the second word.
13. **(A)** The first word overcomes the second word.
14. **(C)** The first word is an action of the second word.
15. **(D)** The second word is the illumination of the first word.
16. **(C)** The first word stores the second word.
17. **(C)** The second word causes the first word.
18. **(B)** The first word changes by means of the second word.
19. **(B)** The first word provides the second word.
20. **(C)** The first word is the action of getting off the second word.

PRACTICE SET 3

Select the best answer to each question and write the letter of your choice in the space provided.

1. DUNCE is related to SCHOLAR as TRAITOR is related to _____
   A) spy   C) rogue
   B) teaser   D) hero

2. SCARCITY is related to PLENTY as FOOLISHNESS is related to _____
   A) wisdom   C) interests
   B) jokes   D) jesters

3. IMAGE is related to MIRAGE as FACT is related to _____
   A) fantasy   C) thought
   B) oasis   D) reality

4. BOOK is related to INDEX as APARTMENT BUILDING is related to _____
   A) doorbells   C) bedroom
   B) directory   D) driveway

5. IGLOO is related to ESKIMO as NEST is related to _____
   A) Indian   C) family
   B) bird   D) flock

6. NUN is related to HABIT as SOLDIER is related to _____
   A) rifle   C) uniform
   B) battalion   D) infantry

7. VIAL is related to BARREL as PAMPHLET is related to _____
   A) volume   C) leaflet
   B) box   D) discount

8. WAITER is related to TIP as ACTOR is related to _____
   A) applause   C) actress
   B) drama   D) stage

9. BLADE is related to SKATE as WHEEL is related to _____
   A) kick   C) bicycle
   B) foot   D) spoke

10. RAIN is related to DROP as SNOW is related to _____
    A) flake   C) ice
    B) icicle   D) hail

11. BALDNESS is related to HAIR as SILENCE is related to _____
    A) quiet   C) laughter
    B) noise   D) sunshine

12. CIRCLE is related to ARC as LINE is related to _____
A) parallel
B) segment
C) curve
D) perpendicular

13. DOG is related to WOLF as CAT is related to _____
A) kitty
B) tiger
C) bear
D) feline

14. FEATHERS is related to BIRD as SCALES is related to _____
A) weigh
B) notes
C) fish
D) animal

15. PACKAGE is related to RIBBON as CAKE is related to _____
A) chocolate
B) wedding
C) icing
D) sugar

16. FACE is related to EYES as HOUSE is related to _____
A) windows
B) doors
C) roof
D) ears

17. PUNCH is related to DUCK as QUESTION is related to _____
A) answer
B) understand
C) evade
D) teach

18. TREE is related to SAPLING as COW is related to _____
A) bull
B) milk
C) calf
D) barn

19. SOCCER is related to BALL as HOCKEY is related to _____
A) stick
B) ice
C) goal
D) puck

20. DROWSY is related to NAP as HUNGRY is related to _____
A) snack
B) starve
C) siesta
D) drink

ANSWER EXPLANATIONS FOR PRACTICE SET 3

1. (D) The first word is the opposite of the second word.
2. (A) The first word is the opposite of the second word.
3. (A) The second word is an imaginary first word.
4. (B) The second word is a contents listing of the first word.
5. (B) The second word builds and lives out of the first word.
6. (C) The first word wears the second word.
7. (A) The second word is a much larger first word.
8. (A) The second word is given in appreciation to the first word.
9. (C) The first word is a part of the second word.
10. (A) The first word falls in the form of the second word.
11. (B) The first word lacks the second word.
12. (B) The second word is a part of the first word.
13. (B) The first word is a domesticated animal in the same family as the second word.
14. (C) The first word is the body covering of the second word.
15. (C) The second word is what goes around the first word.
16. (A) The second word is the "viewing openings" of the first word.
17. (C) The second word avoids the first word.
18. (C) The second word is an immature first word.
19. (D) The second word is the object of control when playing the first word.
20. (A) The second word satisfies the biological condition of the first word.

PRACTICE SET 4

Select the best answer to each question and write the letter of your choice in the space provided.

1. LIFEGUARD is related to RESCUE as PROFESSOR is related to _____
A) instruct
B) college
C) school
D) student

2. JOKE is related to LAUGHTER as THREAT is related to _____
A) fear
B) discovery
C) happiness
D) brawny

3. DEPOSIT is related to WITHDRAWAL as POSITIVE is related to _____
A) neutral
B) negative
C) position
D) bankrupt

4. TREMOR is related to EARTHQUAKE as WIND is related to _____
A) hurricane
B) lightning
C) clock
D) thunder

5. JAR is related to JAM as SHOES is related to _____
A) sandals
B) laces
C) feet
D) soles

6. RADIO is related to TRANSISTOR as SAIL-BOAT is related to _____
   A) mast
   B) rudder
   C) engine
   D) wind

7. TOES is related to FOOT as HANDS is related to _____
   A) fingers
   B) clock
   C) glove
   D) house

8. PREDICTION is related to MYSTIC as PROGNOSIS is related to _____
   A) diagnosis
   B) prescription
   C) doctor
   D) patient

9. MEAT is related to MILK as FORK is related to _____
   A) knife
   B) straw
   C) dish
   D) cow

10. REHEARSE is related to IMPROVEMENT as PRACTICE is related to _____
    A) perfection
    B) study
    C) failure
    D) audition

11. HOUSE is related to ROOF as BOX is related to _____
    A) wall
    B) face
    C) side
    D) lid

12. TEETHING is related to PAIN as TICKLING is related to _____
    A) tenderness
    B) laughter
    C) friendship
    D) soothing

13. THROTTLE is related to GASOLINE as FAUCET is related to _____
    A) hose
    B) garden
    C) water
    D) car

14. WRING is related to WASHCLOTH as SQUEEZE is related to _____
    A) mop
    B) sponge
    C) pail
    D) pillow

15. STAMP is related to POSTAGE as PREMIUM is related to _____
    A) insurance
    B) accident
    C) coupon
    D) exceptional

16. WEIGHT is related to SCALE as LENGTH is related to _____
    A) speedometer
    B) tape measure
    C) clock
    D) width

17. SCULPTOR is related to MARBLE as NOVELIST is related to _____
    A) books
    B) paper
    C) literature
    D) characters

18. MODEST is related to HUMBLE as CAUTIOUS is related to _____
    A) accident
    B) careful
    C) reliable
    D) braggart

19. SAFARI is related to GAME as POSSE is related to _____
    A) animal
    B) human
    C) fugitive
    D) western

20. LULLABY is related to BABY as TAPS is related to _____
    A) trumpet
    B) soldier
    C) bedtime
    D) sleep

ANSWER EXPLANATIONS FOR PRACTICE SET 4

1. **(A)** The second word is the job task of the first word.
2. **(A)** The second word is the result of the first word.
3. **(B)** The first word is the opposite of the second word.
4. **(A)** The second word is larger in size than the first word.
5. **(C)** The first word contains the second word.
6. **(D)** The second word powers the first word.
7. **(B)** The first word is on or a part of the second word.
8. **(C)** The first word is a statement made by the second word.
9. **(B)** The first word relates to solid food; the second word to liquid food.
10. **(A)** The second word is the goal of the first word.
11. **(D)** The second word is atop the first word.
12. **(B)** The second word is a result of the first word.
13. **(C)** The first word regulates the flow of the second word.
14. **(B)** The first word empties the liquid from the second word.
15. **(A)** The first word pays for the second word.
16. **(B)** The second word measures the first word.
17. **(B)** The second word is the raw material used by the first word.
18. **(B)** The first word is a synonym for the second word.
19. **(C)** The second word is the object of capture of the first word.
20. **(B)** The first word precedes the sleeping of the second word.

PRACTICE SET 5

Select the best answer to each question and write the letter of your choice in the space provided.

1. NURSE is related to DOCTOR as SECRETARY is related to _____
   A) man
   B) office
   C) typewriter
   D) executive

2. ENCOURAGE is related to RIDICULE as SMILE is related to _____
   A) scowl
   B) happy
   C) rely
   D) wink

3. AMNESIA is related to MEMORIES as SILENCE is related to _____
   A) operation
   B) hearing
   C) melodies
   D) quiet

4. APPRENTICE is related to MASTER as STUDENT is related to _____
   A) scholar
   B) academic
   C) teacher
   D) studies

5. SIGNATURE is related to FORGERY as ORIGINAL is related to _____
   A) facsimile
   B) verbatim
   C) reasonable
   D) criminal

6. ACCIDENT is related to RECKLESSNESS as HUMILIATION is related to _____
   A) resoluteness
   B) tactlessness
   C) cleanliness
   D) determination

7. NAVIGATOR is related to SEXTANT as WOODSMAN is related to _____
   A) novel
   B) work
   C) axe
   D) timber

8. BOOK is related to CHAPTER as SYMPHONY is related to _____
   A) musician
   B) conductor
   C) movement
   D) instrument

9. ONION is related to TEARS as TIREDNESS is related to _____
   A) body
   B) bed
   C) yawn
   D) exercise

10. GALLOP is related to HORSE as SLITHER is related to _____
    A) snail
    B) rat
    C) spider
    D) snake

11. IRON is related to RUST as TOOTH is related to _____
    A) incisor
    B) toothpaste
    C) decay
    D) clean

12. TROPICAL is related to RAIN as ARCTIC is related to _____
    A) ice
    B) snow
    C) igloo
    D) water

13. ENGINE is related to FUEL as BODY is related to _____
    A) organs
    B) limb
    C) food
    D) breath

14. SCARCE is related to EXPENSIVE as PLENTIFUL is related to _____
    A) invaluable
    B) cheap
    C) rotten
    D) valuable

15. ENORMOUS is related to MINUTE as REWARD is related to _____
    A) reprimand
    B) value
    C) restitution
    D) hour

16. RECKLESS is related to CAREFUL as FACT is related to _____
    A) novel
    B) new
    C) fiction
    D) antique

17. GINGER is related to ROOT as CHOCOLATE is related to _____
    A) bar
    B) candy
    C) bean
    D) milk

18. BULLSEYE is related to TARGET as NOSE is related to _____
    A) eyes
    B) ears
    C) face
    D) body

19. BUTTER is related to MARGARINE as SUGAR is related to _____
    A) sweet
    B) salt
    C) saccharin
    D) oleomargarine

20. BIRD is related to WORM as CAT is related to _____
    A) dog
    B) mouse
    C) pet
    D) animal

ANSWER EXPLANATIONS FOR PRACTICE SET 5

1. **(D)** The first word assists the second word.
2. **(A)** The first word is the opposite of the second word.
3. **(C)** The first word is the absence of the second word.
4. **(C)** The first word learns from the second word.
5. **(A)** The second word is a copy of the first word.
6. **(B)** The first word results from the second word.

7. **(C)** The second word is a tool of the first word.
8. **(C)** The second word is a part of the first word.
9. **(C)** The first word causes the second word.
10. **(D)** The first word is how the second word moves.
11. **(C)** The second word is the corrosion of the first word.
12. **(B)** The second word is the precipitation occurring in the region of the first word.
13. **(C)** The second word powers the first word.
14. **(B)** The second word is the cost of the first word.
15. **(A)** The first word is the opposite of the second word.
16. **(C)** The first word is the opposite of the second word.
17. **(C)** The second word is the origin of the first word.
18. **(C)** The first word is the center of the second word.
19. **(C)** The second word is a substitute for the first word.
20. **(B)** The second word is the prey of the first word.

PRACTICE SET 6

Select the best answer to each question and write the letter of your choice in the space provided.

1. COACH is related to TEAM as CONDUCTOR is related to _____
   A) electricity   C) instruments
   B) orchestra   D) music

2. EWE is related to RAM as CHICKEN is related to _____
   A) hen   C) rooster
   B) chick   D) fowl

3. SWORD is related to KNIGHT as RIFLE is related to _____
   A) gun   C) pistol
   B) soldier   D) weapon

4. PAPER is related to INK as BLACKBOARD is related to _____
   A) writing   C) schoolroom
   B) lesson   D) chalk

5. COOL is related to FRIGID as WARM is related to _____
   A) torrid   C) crisp
   B) lukewarm   D) balmy

6. NEWS is related to HEARSAY as FACT is related to _____
   A) ideas   C) science
   B) newspaper   D) fiction

7. CROCUS is related to SPRING as THUNDERCLOUD is related to _____
   A) sky   C) winter
   B) storm   D) dark

8. OBESE is related to SLENDER as BABBLING is related to _____
   A) brook   C) talkative
   B) quiet   D) slim

9. LEMON is related to CITRUS as CHICKEN is related to _____
   A) rooster   C) fowl
   B) hen   D) barnyard

10. INFANTS is related to NURSERY as MINNOWS is related to _____
    A) hospital   C) babies
    B) hatchery   D) fish

11. WATER is related to JUG as LETTER is related to _____
    A) alphabet   C) stamp
    B) envelope   D) literate

12. HICK is related to SOPHISTICATION as BOOR is related to _____
    A) tactfulness   C) interesting
    B) money   D) rudeness

13. THUG is related to GUN as BULL is related to _____
    A) steer   C) matador
    B) horns   D) sports

14. SCHOLAR is related to ENCYCLOPEDIA as MECHANIC is related to _____
    A) dictionary   C) manual
    B) tools   D) transistor

15. OVERALLS is related to TRACTOR as TUXEDO is related to _____
    A) farming   C) cummerbund
    B) limousine   D) sportscar

16. FAME is related to DISGRACE as HERO is related to _____
    A) criminal   C) fortune
    B) friendship   D) popularity

17. PIANO is related to TUNED as HAIR is related to _____
    A) grown   C) blonde
    B) trimmed   D) shaggy

18. PODIUM is related to SPEAKER as STAGE is related to _____
   A) coach
   B) actor
   C) cowboy
   D) soldier

19. ANGLER is related to TROUT as WOLF is related to _____
   A) cub
   B) hunter
   C) lair
   D) rabbit

20. CRINGE is related to COWARD as DECEIVE is related to _____
   A) spy
   B) soldier
   C) actor
   D) hero

ANSWER EXPLANATIONS FOR PRACTICE SET 6

1. **(B)** The first word prepares and leads the second word.
2. **(C)** The first word is the female of the species; the second word is the male.
3. **(B)** The first word is the weapon used by the second word.
4. **(D)** The second word is the substance used to write on the first word.
5. **(A)** The second word is a greater degree of the first word.
6. **(D)** The first word is nearer the truth; the second word lacks truth.
7. **(B)** The first word is a sign of the second word.
8. **(B)** The first word is the opposite of the second word.
9. **(C)** The first word is a specific variety of the second word.
10. **(B)** The first word is where the second word lives immediately after birth.
11. **(B)** The second word contains the first word.
12. **(A)** The first word is lacking the second word.
13. **(B)** The second word is the weapon used by the first word.
14. **(C)** The second word is the reference book of the first word.
15. **(B)**. The first word is the attire worn by the person using the second word.
16. **(A)** The first word is the opposite of the second word.
17. **(B)** The second word puts the first word "in order."
18. **(B)** The first word is where the second word performs.
19. **(D)** The second word is the prey of the first word.
20. **(A)** The first word is the action of the second word.

PRACTICE SET 7

Select the best answer to each question and write the letter of your choice in the space provided.

1. SCALPEL is related to KNIFE as NURSE is related to _____
   A) doctor
   B) assistant
   C) hospital
   D) operation

2. BEGGAR is related to POOR as FOX is related to _____
   A) skunk
   B) slow
   C) large
   D) sly

3. FELONY is related to MISDEMEANOR as KILL is related to _____
   A) maim
   B) bury
   C) murder
   D) guilty

4. RETRACT is related to STATEMENT as VOID is related to _____
   A) escape
   B) avoidance
   C) contract
   D) empty

5. STOOPED is related to POSTURE as SLURRED is related to _____
   A) diction
   B) stance
   C) music
   D) action

6. MOVIES is related to PROJECTOR as RECORDS is related to _____
   A) speakers
   B) tape recorder
   C) phonograph
   D) radio

7. CHEMIST is related to LABORATORY as ARTIST is related to _____
   A) canvas
   B) museum
   C) easel
   D) studio

8. AGILE is related to NIMBLE as FAST is related to _____
   A) swift
   B) slow
   C) perpetual
   D) racy

9. DELICACY is related to GOURMET as INSECT is related to _____
   A) bee
   B) pollen
   C) frog
   D) hive

10. BOOK is related to CHAPTER as SONG is related to _____
   A) stanza
   B) sing
   C) music
   D) instrument

11. AMBIGUOUS is related to CLARITY as TEMPORARY is related to _____
   A) transient
   B) permanence
   C) clear
   D) fragile

12. SAW is related to CUT as YARDSTICK is related to _____
    A) foot   C) measure
    B) inch   D) tool

13. PROBLEM is related to SOLUTION as POISON is related to _____
    A) hemlock   C) arsenic
    B) nitrate   D) antidote

14. SUGGEST is related to REQUIRED as REQUEST is related to _____
    A) ask   C) suspect
    B) demand   D) allow

15. AUTOMOBILE is related to HIGHWAY as LOCOMOTIVE is related to _____
    A) station   C) track
    B) train   D) engine

16. DISTANCE is related to MILE as LIQUID is related to _____
    A) milk   C) water
    B) quart   D) meter

17. TAILOR is related to NEEDLE as MECHANIC is related to _____
    A) engineer   C) toolchest
    B) screwdriver   D) brush

18. PORCINE is related to PIG as BOVINE is related to _____
    A) boy   C) sheep
    B) cow   D) iodine

19. BREAD is related to BUTTER as POTATOES is related to _____
    A) gravy   C) margarine
    B) steak   D) lamb

20. GNASH is related to TEETH as LISTEN is related to _____
    A) hear   C) resolve
    B) ears   D) dissuade

ANSWERS AND EXPLANATIONS FOR PRACTICE SET 7

1. (B) The first word is the medical term for the second word.
2. (D) The second word is a characteristic of the first word.
3. (A) The first word is a more serious degree of the second word.
4. (C) The first word nullifies the second word.
5. (A) The first word is an impairment of the second word.
6. (C) The second word plays the first word.
7. (D) The second word is where the first word works.
8. (A) The first word is a synonym for the second word.
9. (C) The first word is eaten by the second word.
10. (A) The second word is a part of the first word.
11. (B) The first word is the opposite of the second word.
12. (C) The first word is the tool to do the second word.
13. (D) The second word overcomes the first word.
14. (B) The second word is an imperative ("must") of the first word.
15. (C) The first word travels on the second word.
16. (B) The second word is a measure of the first word.
17. (B) The second word is a tool of the first word.
18. (B) The first word means "pertaining to" the second word.
19. (A) The second is usually put on the first word.
20. (B) The first word is the action of the second word.

REVIEWING THE KEY STRATEGIES

Remember to:

1. Determine the relationship in the first pair.
2. Use "in the same way" to set up relationships.
3. Keep the order similar.
4. Keep parts of speech consistent.
5. Disregard subject matter; only relationship is important.
6. Look at all the choices before selecting one.
7. Eliminate wrong choices immediately.
8. Use categories to recognize relationships.

GRAMMAR

This question type tests your ability to recognize language that is unsuitable for a formal letter or written report. Knowledge of the rules and conventions of Standard Written English is necessary.

Each question consists of four different sentences. Three of them contain errors; one does not. Consider the following example:

A) Those who can remember well after a period of practice has an advantage over others.
B) Through regular practice, it is possible to develop a good memory, which can be very useful.
C) A good memory is not enjoyed by many people which do not practice at it.
D) Practice is required, being that memory is so difficult to get ahold of.

The correct answer is (B); it demonstrates grammar and usage suitable for a formal letter or report. An explanation of the errors in each of the other choices is included in the following discussion of helpful techniques and strategies.

HELPFUL TECHNIQUES AND STRATEGIES

1. Read all four sentences before considering which one is best. Don't jump to conclusions.
2. Sentences that are incorrect will often contain one of the following types of errors:
   a. INCORRECT VERBS—Pay special attention to the verbs in each sentence. One type of verb error occurs in choice (A) of the preceding example: "*Those* who can remember well after a period of practice *has* an advantage over others." In this case, the subject is "those," which is plural, and therefore the verb should also be plural, "have" instead of "has." In this case, the danger lies in presuming that "practice" is the subject of the sentence and concluding that because "practice has" is correct, the sentence is correct. When examining the verb in any sentence, be careful to identify correctly the subject (the "doer" of the action). Here is another sentence in which the subject does not agree with the verb:

   INCORRECT: A *crate* of office supplies have been stored in the closet, until some other space is found.

   CORRECT: A *crate* of office supplies has been stored in the closet, until some other space is found.

Besides checking for subject-verb agreement, make sure that the verb tense is correct. Consider the following example:

By the end of the year, every employee *will had been given* a 10 percent raise.

In this case, "had" is incorrect; the correct verb is "have."

   b. MISUSE OF PRONOUNS—Pay special attention to pronouns: he, she, him, her, we, us, you, who, whom, which, that. Choice (C) of the example contains a pronoun error: "A good memory is not enjoyed by many people *which* do not practice at it." The pronoun "which" does not refer correctly to "people"; the correct pronoun here is "who." The following sentences also illustrate pronoun errors.

   INCORRECT: When *one* has given dedicated service to the company for so many years, *you* expect a gift upon retirement.

   CORRECT: When *one* has given dedicated service to the company for so many years, *one* expects a gift upon retirement.

It would also be correct, in this case, to write "he expects" or "she expects." "He" and "she" agree with "one."

   INCORRECT: The man *whom* delivered the new copier to the office also installed it.

   CORRECT: The man *who* delivered the new copier to the office also installed it.

The pronoun "whom" refers to those who *receive action*, and the pronoun "who" refers to those who do an action. In this case, the man is doing an action, delivering the copier, so "who" is correct.
Another example of this:

INCORRECT: I will give the bonus to whomever fixes the machine.

In this sentence, *whomever* is incorrect. Although it appears that "whomever" is the object of the preposition "to" and therefore should be correct, it is not the object of "to." The entire phrase, "whomever fixes the machine," is the object of "to," and within that phrase, "whomever" is doing the action: "*whomever* fixes the machine." Therefore, "whomever," as the doer, is incorrect. It should be changed to "whoever."

CORRECT: I will give the bonus to whoever fixes the machine.

c. INCORRECT USAGE—A number of expressions commonly used in conversation are incorrect in Standard Written English. Choice (D) in the original example contains two such expressions: "Practice is required, *being that* memory is so difficult to *get ahold of*." Here is one way to rewrite this sentence correctly: "Because the improvement of memory is so difficult, practice is required." The following are some expressions that represent incorrect usage:

all the farther	hisself	ought to of
being as how	in regards	theirselves
being that	that	use to,
had to of	irregardless	suppose to
	no such a	

d. VAGUE OR UNCLEAR MEANING—The meaning of a sentence may be vague or unclear because (1) certain words in the sentence are not used clearly or (2) the structure of the sentence makes the meaning illogical or unclear. Consider the following set of four choices:

A) While proofreading the letter, a mistake was detected in the third line.
B) While proofreading a letter, one should be able to do this perfectly.
C) Through careful proofreading, a number of mistakes can appear in a letter.
D) Those who carefully proofread letters detect errors easily.

The correct choice is (D); the meaning of each of the other choices is unclear. In choice (B), the meaning of "this" is uncertain; "this" may or may not refer to proofreading. In choice (A), the structure of the sentence makes it seem as if "a mistake" is doing the proofreading! Choice (C) makes the inaccurate and illogical statement that mistakes "appear" through proofreading; it is more logical and accurate to say that mistakes are *detected* through proofreading.

e. REPETITION—A sentence is incorrect when it is unnecessarily wordy or repetitious. Consider the following examples:

The memorandum was sent to those who received it, the manager and me.
Everyone was asked to arrive for work early in the morning, at 6 A.M.

Here are less repetitious and wordy versions of the same sentences:

The memorandum was received by the manager and me.
Everyone was asked to arrive for work at 6 A.M.

A few more examples of common errors:

A) The quantity of child care centers have increased during the last decade, along with the increase in working parents.
B) For the work of parents, more child care centers have appeared during the last decade.
C) With more during the last decade, working parents appreciate child care centers.
D) During the last decade, the appearance of more working parents has coincided with the appearance of more child care centers.

Choice (D) is correct. In (A), the verb "have" should be replaced with "has," in order to agree with the subject, "quantity." In (B), "for the work of parents" is an unclear phrase. In (C), the meaning of "more" is unclear.

A) The sales force ought to of achieved much higher sales last week, but were not able to do so.
B) The sales force, who is usually very successful, did a very poor job last week.
C) Selling much less than usual, the weeks ahead might be more productive for the company sales force.

D) Putting a week of poor results behind them, the sales force hoped that the weeks ahead would be more productive.

Choice (D) is correct. In (A), "ought to of" is incorrect usage. In (B), the pronoun "who" is incorrect; "which" is the correct pronoun for referring to "the sales force." The structure of choice (C) makes it seem as if "the weeks ahead," rather than the sales force, are "selling much less than usual."

A) The lobby of the Brinker Building use to of been much less crowded than it is now.

B) If the lobby of the Brinker Building would have had been enlarged years ago, it would not be so crowded today.

C) The lobby of the Brinker Building is much more crowded now than it used to be.

D) When one enters the lobby of the Brinker Building, you immediately enter a crowd.

Choice (C) is correct. In (A), "use to of been" is incorrect usage. In (B), "would have had been" is an incorrect verb tense; "had been" is correct. In (D), the pronoun "you" is incorrect; "you" should be replaced with "one," "he," or "she," and "enter" should be changed to "enters."

PRACTICE SET 1

Decide which sentence is preferable with respect to grammar and usage suitable for a formal letter or report. Write the letter of your choice in the space provided.

1. A) The prohibition against laying down ____ on the furniture is posted in several places throughout the company lounge.
   B) During lunch and breaks, although laying one down in the company-lounge may be inviting, it is prohibited.
   C) Lying down on furniture in the company lounge is not allowed.
   D) With reference to the furnishings in the lounge, lying down or laying on it cannot be permitted.

2. A) Having the drinking of wine frequently in Italy and France contrasts ____ with the regular drinking of water in the United States.
   B) With water the frequent drink in the United States, wine is for Italy and France also a frequent drink.
   C) Drinking wine such as we in the United States drink water are the people of which are in Italy and France.
   D) Many people in Italy and France drink wine as frequently as we in the United States drink water.

3. A) Modern business psychologists, ____ with information on creativity and stress more than long ago, have contributed to improved morale and productivity.
   B) With valuable information on creativity and stress, modern business psychologists have contributed to improved morale and productivity.
   C) Improved morale and productivity has been of modern business psychology, with information on creativity and stress.
   D) Creativity and stress have improved morale and productivity, with information from modern business psychologists.

4. A) A longer lunch period will be provided, after it was reported that hastily eating lunch caused an upset stomach.
   B) Eating lunch too quickly, an upset stomach resulted in lengthening the lunch period.
   C) Returning from lunch feeling upset, a longer lunch period was instituted for everyone.
   D) Convinced that eating a hasty lunch is not healthy for anyone, we are instituting a longer lunch period.

5. A) People often read a book merely to ____ pass the time, to prove their intelligence, avoiding the real world, and many other ridiculous reasons.
   B) There are many good reasons for reading, and some ridiculous ones as well.
   C) Merely passing the time, to prove their intelligence, and to avoid the real world, many people read a book.
   D) Reading for ridiculous reasons are merely to pass the time, to prove their intelligence, and to avoid the real world, among others.

6. A) Manikins, each dressed in an expensive outfit, makes the store window attractive to passersby.
   B) There are two manikins, dressed in expensive clothes, in the store window.
   C) As shoppers pass the store window, expensively dressed manikins pass their view.
   D) As for clothes that are attractive and expensive, manikins are on display in the store window.

7. A) Empty since it appeared, a number ____ of you have requested a suggestion box for the office.
   B) The suggestion box that a number of you requested has remained empty since it appeared.
   C) The request for a suggestion box, to which was responded with one, has not as yet resulted with a suggestion.

D) Suggestions for the suggestion box have not appeared as yet, and it is still empty even though a number of you have requested it.

8. A) Having mislain the calendar, the appointments calendar was unable to verify where they should be and when.
   B) Scheduling was impossible because the appointments secretary had mislain the appointments calendar.
   C) The calendar listing everyone's appointments could not be found, with the result being that no one knew where to be and when.
   D) The appointments secretary mislaid his calendar, so no one knew whether any appointments had been scheduled.

9. A) Associates who we have not contacted for months should be informed of all recent decisions.
   B) Inform associates whom we have not contacted for months of all recent decisions.
   C) Of all associates that we have not contacted for months, inform them of recent decisions.
   D) Not contacting associates for months, we are informing them of all recent decisions.

10. A) When one has all ready publicized a decision, it is difficult to revoke it.
    B) With an already publicized decision, revoking it is difficult.
    C) With the revoking of a decision already publicized, revoking it is difficult.
    D) It is difficult to revoke a decision that has already been publicized.

ANSWER EXPLANATIONS FOR PRACTICE SET 1

1. (C) The most prominent error in each of the other choices is the incorrect use of "laying" for "lying."
2. (D) "Having" should be omitted in (A). (B) is both vague and repetitious (for example, "frequent drink"). "Such as we" is one incorrect phrase in (C).
3. (B) The sentence structure in each of the other choices is incoherent, and the meaning of several phrases is unclear.

4. (D) Choice (B) seems to say that an upset stomach is eating lunch, and (C) that the lunch period returns from lunch. The verb tenses in (A) are inconsistent.
5. (B) (A) and (C) have parallelism errors. (D) should begin, "Ridiculous reasons for reading . . ."
6. (B) In (A), the verb "makes" does not agree with the subject "manikins." (C) contains the illogical phrase "manikins pass." In (D), the connection between the first half of the sentence and the second half is unclear.
7. (B) The phrase "empty since it appeared" in (A) is misplaced. (C) contains awkward and wordy phrases, for instance, "to which was responded." (D) is wordy and repetitious.
8. (D) "Mislain" is incorrect in both (A) and (B). In (C), "with the result being that" is wordy and awkward.
9. (B) In (A), "who" is incorrect. In (C), the sentence structure is wordy and awkward, and "that" is used incorrectly. In (D), the verb tense of "not contacting" is incorrect.
10. (D) In (A), "all ready" is incorrect; "already" would be correct. Although (B) and (C) do use "already" correctly, both sentences are vague and wordy. The most clear, direct, and correct expression is (D).

PRACTICE SET 2

Decide which sentence is preferable with respect to grammar and usage suitable for a formal letter or report. Write the letter of your choice in the space provided.

1. A) Everyone differs greatly in the way they listen to and benefit from information.
   B) Listening closely to important information, in order to benefit from it, vary from person to person.
   C) Listening carefully is an important skill, especially when vital information is involved.
   D) Skillful listening is important, while everyone does theirs differently.

2. A) Neither wealth nor power are the desires of those majoring in business, according to a recent poll.
   B) Business majors polled recently denied that either wealth or power are their desire.
   C) Business majors desire neither wealth nor power as such in a recent poll.
   D) Wealth and power were not the stated goals of business majors polled recently.

3. A) Both the inventor and the manufacturer _____ received credit for the success of the product.
   B) The inventor was as responsible for the success of the product, with the manufacturer.
   C) High sales figures for the new product delighted not only their inventor, but also the manufacturer.
   D) The inventor and the manufacturer was given publicity for the popularity of their new product.

4. A) Government institutions have become _____ more powerful, but they have also lost the respect of many citizens.
   B) A rapidly decreasing respect for government institutions and that such institutions are becoming more powerful is a cause of concern.
   C) The status of government institutions, that has changed recently, can result in less respect.
   D) As for the status of government institutions, theirs is not as strong as it was formerly.

5. A) Dealing directly with the question are _____ minor errors in typing to be allowed.
   B) Some people question whether minor errors in typing should be allowed.
   C) The allowance of imperfectly typed manuscripts are not to be permitted.
   D) Although typing errors are difficult to avoid, it cannot be permitted.

6. A) Many will agree with the new retirement _____ policy, and many will disagree with it, taking the other side of the issue.
   B) Some changes in the retirement policy provokes both positive and negative responses.
   C) Those who drafted the new retirement policy welcome both positive and negative responses from all concerned.
   D) Retirement is an issue to get both pro and con viewpoints.

7. A) The City Council, consisting of twelve _____ members, were scheduled to meet for several hours.
   B) With all twelve members of the City Council scheduled to meet, several hours were scheduled.
   C) A City Council meeting may be scheduled soon, if all of the council members are available at a convenient time.
   D) Finding several hours for a meeting of the City Council members were not at all easy.

8. A) To type a letter accurately, spelling must _____ be part of what is watched.
   B) Accurate typing and correct spelling are both absolutely necessary.
   C) With accuracy, both for typing and for spelling, a letter will be acceptable.
   D) Typing, spelling, and accuracy are those which any letter must demonstrate.

9. A) Adam is a successful student who never _____ thinks of anything but grades.
   B) Adam is a successful student whom never thinks of anything but grades.
   C) Adam is a successful student for who grades are all that is important.
   D) Adam, for who grades are most important, is a successful student.

10. A) The people who neglect important tasks _____ until the last minute are usually unable to do a careful job.
    B) Those type of people which neglect important tasks usually rush to complete them.
    C) Types of people which neglect important tasks until the last minute do so in a rush.
    D) With the neglect of important tasks by those who prefer to rush, the last minute is popular.

ANSWER EXPLANATIONS FOR PRACTICE SET 2

1. **(C)** In (A), the pronoun "they" and the verbs "listen" and "benefit" should agree with the singular "everyone." One error in (B) is the incorrect use of "vary"; the verb should be "varies." In (D), "theirs" is a plural pronoun, but "everyone" is singular.

2. **(D)** In both (A) and (B), the verb "are" should be changed to "is." In (C), "as such" is awkward.

3. **(A)** In (B), either the "as" or the "with" is incorrect. In (C), "their" should be replaced with "its." In (D), the verb "was given" should be replaced with "were given," in order to agree with the plural subject.

4. **(A)** The sentence structure of (B) is awkward, and "is" is incorrect. (C) is unclear, and (D) is wordy.

5. **(B)** Choice (A) is not a complete sentence. In (C), "are" should be changed to "is" in order to agree with "allowance." In (D), "it" is an incorrect pronoun; "they" would be correct, to agree with "errors."

6. **(C)** Choice (A) is repetitious. In (B), "provokes" should be changed to "provoke," to agree with "changes." In (D), "to get" is an awkward phrase.

7. **(C)** In (A), the verb "were" does not agree with the subject, "City Council." In (B), the repetition of "scheduled" is awkward. In (D), the verb "were" should be changed to "was."

8. **(B)** Choice (A) seems to say that the "spelling" is doing the "typing"! In (C), both instances of "for" may be changed to "in." In (D), "those which" is an incomplete, unclear phrase.
9. **(A)** In the incorrect choices, "whom" and "for who" are used incorrectly.
10. **(A)** In (B), "those type" and "which" are incorrect. In (C), "which" is incorrect ("who" and "whom" are used to refer to people). In (D), "the last minute is popular" has no clear relation to the first part of the sentence.

PRACTICE SET 3

Decide which sentence is preferable with respect to grammar and usage suitable for a formal letter or report. Write the letter of your choice in the space provided.

1. A) The Back & Hammer Corporation has designed a new building that is round in shape and large in size. _____
   B) The new Back & Hammer building will be round and very large, according to the architect's design.
   C) With the new building's design submitted by the architect, Back & Hammer can look forward to a new size and shape.
   D) While conventional buildings are somewhat smaller and more square, the new Back & Hammer building's roundness and size is a reason it is different.

2. A) Whichever of the two companies submits the lowest bid will receive the contract. _____
   B) The contract will be awarded to whoever bids lowest.
   C) Bidding lower than the competitors, the contract will go to whomever does so.
   D) The contract bids are being reviewed by myself, who will select the lowest.

3. A) Those in the company who had worked all the hardest to handle the Christmas rush, were rewarded with large bonuses. _____
   B) Those who worked hardest to handle the Christmas rush will receive large bonuses.
   C) A well-deserved bonus was paid by the company to the hardest-working employees among them, during the Christmas rush
   D) Working hardly during the very busy Christmas season brought bonuses to a number of workers.

4. A) Whoever answers the phone must do so courteously. _____
   B) Courtesy is important, both away from it and on the phone.
   C) Without courtesy on the telephone, any secretary is lacking with a vital skill.
   D) A courteous phone voice, for whomever answers the phone, has great importance.

5. A) Although hundreds of people complained when they changed the taste of their soft drink, sales remained steady. _____
   B) Sales did not decrease after the company "improved" the taste of its soft drinks, but hundreds of people complained.
   C) The complaints of hundreds of people in the fact of a new taste for the cola had no effect on sales.
   D) Selling cola was no more difficult after changing their taste than before it.

6. A) After establishing its home office in Los Angeles, the small company failed to compete successfully with larger firms in the area. _____
   B) Although they intended to offer competition to larger firms in the Los Angeles area, the new company was not successful.
   C) Among successful competition among successful firms in the Los Angeles area, a smaller company is unlikely to be successful.
   D) Achieving success in the competitive Los Angeles area, the new company was not able to do so.

7. A) Child safety groups are demanding legislation forbidding the use of glass containers in public places. _____
   B) Fearing for the safety of children who might be injured by them, child safety groups are forbidding the public use of glass containers.
   C) Because broken glass containers may injure a child, they are demanding legislation prohibiting their public use.
   D) Children, because they may break, should not have access to glass containers.

8. A) One new employee was accused of complaining too much, but denied that he had done so. _____
   B) One new employee was overheard complaining about his job, but he claimed that he said no such a thing.

C) Accused of complaining too much, a new employee denied himself.

D) Complaining excessively, the job was obviously unpleasant for the new employee.

9. A) Everyone on the staff, as well as Jerry and _____ I, supports the new proposal.

B) Everyone on the staff, as well as Jerry and me, supports the new proposal.

C) The support of the new proposal by Jerry as well as me goes along with the support of the staff.

D) Me and Jerry and everyone on the staff support the new proposal.

10. A) Choosing every word carefully, a writer _____ can communicate even complex ideas with clarity and precision.

B) Choosing every word carefully, even complex ideas can be written with clarity and precision.

C) Writing complex ideas with clarity and precision, choosing every word carefully.

D) As for clarity and precision, it is the task of choosing every word carefully.

ANSWER EXPLANATIONS FOR PRACTICE SET 3

1. **(B)** In (A), "in shape" and "in size" are repetitious. In (C) there is no clear reference to a building, so "a new size and shape" is vague. In (D), the subjects "roundness and size" require a plural verb and "reasons."

2. **(B)** In (A) "lowest" should be "lower" (C) seems to say that the contract itself is doing the bidding, and "whomever" is not the correct form. In (D), "me" should be used, instead of "myself."

3. **(B)** In (A), "all the hardest" is incorrect. In (C), the meaning of "them" is not clear. In (D), "working hardly" is incorrect.

4. **(A)** Choices (B) and (D) both contain pronoun errors: in (B), "it" is vague, and in (D), "whomever" is incorrect. In (C), "lacking with" should be replaced with "lacking in."

5. **(B)** In (A), the meaning of "they" and "their" is not clear. In (C), "in the fact of" is an incorrect phrase. In (D), the meaning of "it" is not clear, and "their" should be "its."

6. **(A)** In (B), "they" is used incorrectly to refer to "company." In (C), "Among successful competition among" is repetitious. Choice (D) seems to contradict itself.

7. **(A)** In each of the other choices, the use of pronouns "they" and "them" is unclear.

8. **(A)** In (B), "no such thing" is incorrect. In (C), "denied himself" is not the appropriate phrase.

Choice (D), with its unclear sentence structure, seems to say that the "job" was "complaining excessively."

9. **(A)** In both (B) and (D), "me" is incorrect; "I" is the correct pronoun in both cases. (C) is an unnecessarily wordy expression.

10. **(A)** In (B), the "complex ideas" seem to be doing the "choosing." Choice (C) is not a complete sentence. In (D), "it" is a vague term.

PRACTICE SET 4

Decide which sentence is preferable with respect to grammar and usage suitable for a formal letter or report. Write the letter of your choice in the space provided.

1. A) If the report would have been completed _____ on schedule, everyone would have been able to take the weekend off.

B) Everyone will be required to work this weekend if the report is not completed on time.

C) With the possibility of completing the report in order to avoid working all weekend, everyone would have tried staying on schedule.

D) A report not completed by this weekend, the weekend off will not be available.

2. A) Both men and women, whomever are interested in administrative experience, are invited to apply for a summer internship program.

B) We are pleased to announce a summer internship program that offers substantial administrative experience.

C) Those whom are after administrative experience should apply for the summer internship program.

D) With administrative experience, the summer internship program invites applications from both men and women.

3. A) The special talents of every team member are rarely acknowledged by the coach.

B) Each member of the team is theirself a unique talent, even though the coach rarely gives anyone credit.

C) Without any credit of the coach, the unique talent of each team member goes unnoticed.

D) Talented and unique, the team goes without the acknowledgment of them by the coach.

4. A) In the opinion of the general public, it _____ believes that major corporations are not ethical.
   B) The general public questions the ethics of major corporations, in their opinion.
   C) With a belief regarding major corporations that their ethics are questionable, the general public voices its opinion.
   D) The general public believes that the practices of most major corporations are not ethical.

5. A) Most popular in relation to the flexible _____ interest rate is the fixed rate, even though it is often higher.
   B) With flexible versus fixed rates, the more popular one is the higher of the two.
   C) Flexible interest rates are less popular than fixed rates, even though fixed rates are usually higher.
   D) Less popularity has made flexible interest rates less appealing than the higher fixed rates.

6. A) Because Stupple & Whipple Industries _____ has discontinued the production of microcomputers, they are giving full attention to other possible products.
   B) Having decided to investigate other possibilities, Stupple & Whipple Industries is no longer producing microcomputers.
   C) Microcomputer production is not for Stupple & Whipple Industries any longer, after whose decision to explore other possibilities.
   D) Without microcomputers in production, other possibilities than the computer is the interest of Stupple & Whipple Industries.

7. A) As far as political forces were concerned, _____ industrial growth as well as business grows stronger before 1950.
   B) During the first half of this century, business and industry were becoming dominant political forces in the United States.
   C) As the growth of the United States progressed during the first half of the century, both business and industry was in the forefront.
   D) With the early years of this century came a dominant industry, as a political force, along with business.

8. A) The memorandum was addressed to the _____ office manager, the division supervisor, and me.

B) Those receiving the communication included myself, along with the division manager, and in addition, the office manager.
C) A memo—routed to the office manager via the division supervisor and me—was received.
D) After receiving a memo addressed also to the office manager and me, the division supervisor did also.

9. A) The president of the Rotary Club won re- _____ election being that his past achievements were so many.
   B) Being that his past achievements were so many, the president of the Rotary Club won reelection.
   C) The president of the Rotary Club won re-election because of his many past achievements.
   D) With his many past achievements in mind, reelection of the Rotary Club president was because of them.

10. A) In the court's judgment, the cause of the _____ accident was negligence rather than speeding.
    B) The cause of the accident was negligence rather than speeding in the court's judgment.
    C) The cause of the accident was negligence instead of speeding in the court's judgment.
    D) Negligence rather than speeding was the cause of the accident in the court judgment.

ANSWER EXPLANATIONS FOR PRACTICE SET 4

1. (B) In (A), "report would have been" should be "report had been." In both (C) and (D), the sentence structure is obviously confusing.
2. (B) "Whomever" and whom" are incorrect pronouns in (A) and (C). The sentence structure of (D) suggests that the "summer program" has "administrative experience."
3. (A) In (B), the pronoun "theirself" is incorrect, and in (D), the pronoun "them" is incorrect. In (C), "of the coach" should be "from the coach."
4. (D) In (A), "it believes" is repetitious. "Their" is incorrect in (B). In (C) "with a belief regarding . . . that" is awkward usage.
5. (C) In (A), "in relation to" is awkward. In (B), the meaning of the sentence is unclear. In (D), "less popularity" is an awkward phrase.

6. **(B)** In (A) and (C) there are pronoun errors: "they" is incorrect in (A), and "whose" contributes to poor sentence structure in (C). In (D), "is" should be "are" ("possibilities are").

7. **(B)** Both (A) and (C) contain incorrect verbs: "grows" in (A), and "was" in (C). The relationship between "business" and "industry" is not precisely stated in (D).

8. **(A)** Each of the other is wordy or awkward.

9. **(C)** In both (A) and (B), "being that" is an incorrect phrase; "because" is correct. Choice (D) is awkward and unclear.

10. **(A)** In (B), "speeding in the court's judgment" seems to say that the speeding took place in the court; this same confusing phrase occurs in (C). In (D), the comma is missing before the final phrase; "court" should be "court's."

PRACTICE SET 5

Decide which sentence is preferable with respect to grammar and usage suitable for a formal letter or report. Write the letter of your choice in the space provided.

1. A) A meeting was called for we project su- _____ pervisors and our assistants.
   B) It was important to all concerned that a meeting having been called for both supervisors and assistants be scheduled.
   C) Project supervisors and their assistants were called to a meeting.
   D) Meeting regularly, on the part of both supervisors and assistants, were important to all concerned.

2. A) Not likely to repeat what he had said a _____ moment ago, the teacher was not sure if whether the class understood him or not.
   B) Making an important point more than once, the class was not sure of the teacher's meaning until he had repeated it.
   C) Uncertain about whether the class had understood him, the teacher repeated what he had said a moment ago.
   D) After a few moments past, and the class still did not express any understanding, the teacher had repeated himself.

3. A) Several friends have decided to jog on a _____ weekend basis, which can gradually be increased as their heart and lungs grow stronger.

   B) Several friends have decided to jog together every Saturday, and perhaps more often as their hearts and lungs grow stronger.
   C) To jog more often as their heart and lungs grow stronger, several friends have decided to jog every Saturday.
   D) With every Saturday, several friends have begun jogging as their hearts and lungs grow stronger.

4. A) Finding the most efficient method for _____ completing a routine task can make it more pleasant.
   B) Routine assignments can be very unpleasant without which effort to find a method that is efficient.
   C) The founding of a method, although it does not change the requirement to do a routine task, can be more pleasant.
   D) Routine though they may be, a task can be much better if one is given an efficient method for completing it.

5. A) Friends for years, they suddenly began _____ arguing frequently and loudly.
   B) Arguments can upset years of friendship, as a frequent and loud one seemed to prove in a recent case.
   C) With years behind a friendship of frequent and loud arguments, those involved are often not capable of continuing the relationship.
   D) How violent an argument must be before a friendship is affected, and those involved in it must change their relationship.

6. A) As for other appliances, those installed _____ newly have energy efficiency ratings surpassed the older ones.
   B) Each of the appliances installed in the new offices is energy-efficient.
   C) New appliances, even though more expensive, compare favorably over those that required more energy in the past.
   D) Although new, the energy used by each new appliance in each new office could not be described as efficient.

7. A) All of his sentences are well constructed, _____ and it contributes to the clarity of his writing.
   B) His well-constructed sentences contribute to the clarity of his writing.
   C) Clear sentences, well-constructed, are contributory to clarity of writing.

D) All of his sentences are well-constructed, that being the contribution to the clarity of his writing.

8. A) Both days being the same birthday for _____ both Jean and Joan, we baked only one cake.
   B) On the same day as Joan, whose birthday falls along with Jean's, more than one cake for both of them was not necessary.
   C) We baked a cake for Jean, whose birthday fell on the same day as Joan's.
   D) With the other's birthday on the same day as Jean, namely Joan, we had already baked a cake for only one.

9. A) Reading the newspaper carefully, I no- _____ ticed that an old English sheepdog was advertised in the column labeled "Pets for Sale."
   B) Reading the newspaper carefully, an old English sheepdog that I noticed was advertised in the column labeled, "Pets for Sale."
   C) By reading the newspaper carefully, an old English sheepdog was advertised in the column labeled "Pets for Sale."
   D) In the column labeled "Pets for Sale," reading carefully, I noticed an old English sheepdog.

10. A) Everyone should be commended for _____ performing admirable well during a recent evaluation of the department.
    B) Everyone should be commended for performing admirably well during a recent evaluation of the department.
    C) With an admirably well performance, everyone in the department should be commended.
    D) An admirable good performance deserves commending everyone in the department.

ANSWER EXPLANATIONS FOR PRACTICE SET 5

1. **(C)** In (A), "for we" is incorrect; "for us" would be correct. In (B) the verb "having been called" is both unnecessary and incorrect. In (D), the verb "were" does not agree with the subject, "meeting"; "Meeting . . . *was* important" would be correct.
2. **(C)** In (A), "if whether" is incorrect; "if" alone would be sufficient. The sentence structure of (B) seems to say that the class, not the teacher, is "making a important point." In (D), both "past" and "had repeated" are incorrect.
3. **(B)** An error in (A) is "heart"; it should be "hearts." An obvious error in (C) is the repetition of "to jog." Choice (D) is unclear.
4. **(A)** In (B), "without which effort" is incorrect. One error in (C) is the incorrect use of "founding." In (D), "they" is used incorrectly to refer to "task."
5. **(A)** (B) is not as clear a statement as (A); the word "one" makes no sense with "frequent." In (C), "with years behind" is awkward. In (D), the sentence structure is not clear.
6. **(B)** In (A), "surpassed," "as for other appliances," and "installed newly" are used incorrectly. In (C), "compare favorably over" should be "compare favorably to". In (D), "new" seems to refer to "energy"; this is an illogical reference.
7. **(B)** "It" is an incorrect pronoun in (A); "they contribute" or just "contribute" would be correct. In (C), "contributory" is incorrect. In (D), "that being" is a vague phrase.
8. **(C)** The sentence structure of each of the other choices is obviously wordy, vague, and confusing.
9. **(A)** Both (B) and (C) seem to say that a sheepdog was reading the paper. In (D), "reading carefully" is placed in an awkward position in the sentence.
10. **(B)** In (A), "admirable" is incorrect. In (C), "admirably well performance" is incorrect. In (D), "admirable good" is incorrect. "Performing admirably well," in (B), is the correct expression.

PRACTICE SET 6

Decide which sentence is preferable with respect to grammar and usage suitable for a formal letter or report. Write the letter of your choice in the space provided.

1. A) A letterhead that is colorful but not hav- _____ ing adequate information is useless.
   B) Letterhead design is not nearly as important as the sufficiency of informing them who read it.
   C) If the information on the company letterhead is insufficient, they serve no purpose.
   D) Along with a colorful design, the company letterhead must include sufficient information.

2. A) Visitors are asked to park their cars away _____ from the main building during rush-hour traffic.
   B) Access to the main building during rush-hour traffic is prohibited on visitors.
   C) Parking space is available a long ways from the main building during rush-hour traffic.
   D) Finding a parking space near the main building for visitors is impossible during the rush hour.

3. A) After talking to the accountant, Mr. _____
Wright felt he should audit the report
prior to the noon conference.

B) Mr. Wright asked his accountant whether
auditing the report before his conference at noon was possible.

C) If he could audit the report before the
noon conference was what Mr. Wright
needed to know of his accountant.

D) Mr. Wright wondered if his accountant
would have time to audit the report prior
to the noon conference.

4. A) The final draft of a report should dem- _____
onstrate not only correct English, with
logical organization as well.

B) Correct English, as well as logical organization, are important in the final draft
of a report.

C) When drafting the final version of a report, writers must pay close attention to
both correct English and logical organization.

D) As for final matters, correctness and effective organization should be the focus
of any writer concerned with it.

5. A) Neither welfare benefits nor an im- _____
proved health plan was discussed by the
board members.

B) Neither welfare benefits or an improved
health plan was on the agenda at the
board meeting.

C) With more important matters to consider, the board members discussed not
welfare benefits or even an improved
health plan.

D) Without discussion of either welfare
benefits or an improved health plan at
the board meeting.

6. A) Those who require emergency medical _____
attention may do so without loss of pay.

B) When emergency medical attention is
necessary to interrupt the workday, no
loss of pay results.

C) Anyone who must leave work for emergency medical attention will not suffer
any loss of pay.

D) Loss of pay is not given to those who
need emergency medical attention during the workday.

7. A) "To Whom It May Concern" is one of _____
many popular grammatically correct
phrases.

B) Among grammatically popular and correct expressions, "To Whom It May Concern" is one of many.

C) When beginning correspondence with
"To Whom It May Concern," they can be
sure of a popular and grammatical
phrase.

D) A number of phrases are both popular
and grammatically correct; "To Whom It
May Concern" is one of which.

8. A) This year's expenditure for advertising _____
ought to of been much lower.

B) The firm must devote fewer of its budget
to advertising.

C) The advertising budget should be
reduced.

D) Reduction in the budget for advertising
would of been a good idea.

9. A) When only one security officer is on duty _____
in the building, there are those of which
take special precautions.

B) Those who work after hours should be
very cautious, being as how only one security officer is on duty.

C) Only one security officer patrols the
building after working hours, so everyone staying late should be very cautious.

D) All should take precautions over any
emergency after hours, rather than to depend on only one security officer.

10. A) An unused office, full of obsolete equip- _____
ment and discarded files, were made
ready for the newest member of the firm.

B) To find office space for someone new, an
unused area full of old files and useless
equipment is available.

C) New office space is scarce, except of an
area that had been used for storage.

D) A previously unused office will be reno-
vated for the use of the firm's newest
member.

ANSWER EXPLANATIONS FOR PRACTICE SET 6

1. (D) In (A), to be parallel, "not having" should
read "does not have." In (B), "sufficiency of informing them" is incorrect. In (C), "they serve"
should be replaced with "it serves."

2. (A) In (B), "prohibited on" is incorrect. In (C),
"ways" is incorrect. In (D), "for visitors" is awk-
wardly placed.

3. (D) In each of the other choices, the reference of
the pronoun "he" or "his" is not clear.

4. (C) In (A), the words following the comma are
incorrectly phrased; correct phrasing would be
"but also logical organization." In (B), "are"

should be replaced with "is," in order to agree with the singular subject, "correct English." In (D), "it" is a vague pronoun.

5. (A) Both (B) and (C) are incorrect because they do not use "neither/not . . . nor" correctly. (D) is not a complete sentence.

6. (C) In (A), "may do so" is an inappropriate phrase. In (B), "to interrupt the workday" is illogical. Choice (D) is also illogical, because "loss of pay" is not something that is "given."

7. (A) In (B), "grammatically popular" is an illogical phrase. In (C), "they" is unclear. In (D), "of which" is unnecessary.

8. (C) In (A), "ought to of" is incorrect. In (B), "fewer" should be replaced with "less." In (D), "would of been" is incorrect.

9. (C) In (A), "those of which" is an incorrect phrase. In (B), "being as how" is incorrect. In (D), one error is "precautions over," which should be replaced with "precautions for"; another is "rather than *to* depend"—"to" is incorrect.

10. (D) In (A), "were" should be replaced with "was," in order to agree with the subject, "office." (B) illustrates unclear sentence structure and seems to say that the "unused area" is "to find office space." In (C), "except of" should be replaced with "except for."

REVIEWING THE KEY STRATEGIES

Remember to:

1. Read all four sentences before selecting answer.

2. Look for common errors first:

   — incorrect verbs

   — misuse of pronouns

   — incorrect usage

   — unclear meaning

   — repetition

SPELLING

This question type tests your ability to recognize correct spelling. You are given three different spellings of a certain word and are required to choose the correct spelling, if it appears. If it does not appear, you are to choose answer D.

Helpful Techniques and Strategies

1. SEE the word. Very often, we do not recognize words that are misspelled because of the way they are pronounced. For instance, "accidentally" is pronounced "accident-ly" and may be misspelled for that reason.

    After looking at the three choices you are given, look away from the test page and attempt to *see* the word in your mind. Write the word mentally, letter by letter. Doing so may help you to avoid a misspelling based on pronunciation alone.

2. Before taking the test, study a list of commonly misspelled words, such as the following. The common trouble spots are underlined.

3. One way to prepare for this part of the test is to create your own sample questions, using the preceding list of commonly misspelled words. Keeping in mind some basic spelling rules and common spelling errors (some examples follow), devise possible misspellings of these words. This way you will become familiar not only with the correct spelling, but also with possible types of incorrect spellings that may appear on the test. Examples:

absolutely	absalutely	absolootly
foresee	forsee	foursea
vegetable	vegtable	vegetible

TABLE 3
SOME COMMONLY MISSPELLED WORDS

absence	bicycle	correspondence	equipped	independence	necessary	pursuing	sophomore
accept	bulletin	courageous	evidently	influential	neither	quarreling	specimen
accidentally	bureau	course	excitement	ingenious	nickel	really	speech
accommodate	cafeteria	courteous	existence	inoculate	niece	receipt	stomach
accordance	calendar	courtesy	expense	interesting	ninety	received	strength
achievement	campaign	criticism	extension	interfere	ninth	recognize	succeed
acknowledge	captain	crowd	familiar	jealous	noticeable	recommend	success
acquainted	careful	crucial	fascinating	jewelry	occasion	referee	sufficient
acquired	carriage	deceive	fatigue	judgment	occurred	referred	superintendent
across	ceiling	decided	forcibly	justice	often	refugee	surely
advice	cemetery	defendant	forehead	kindergarten	omitted	relieve	surprise
advisable	changeable	dependent	foreign	knowledge	owing	religious	suspense
advise	chaos	descent	foresee	laboratory	pamphlet	remittance	technical
affectionately	chief	desirable	forty	legible	parallel	repetition	terrible
aisle	climbed	despair	forward	lettuce	pastime	reservoir	therefore
allege	cloth	desperate	freight	library	permanent	resistance	thorough
all right	clothes	device	fugitive	lieutenant	personally	restaurant	tobacco
almost	college	disastrous	fundamental	lightning	personnel	rhyme	toward
already	colonel	discipline	further	losing	physically	rhythm	tragedy
altogether	column	disease	generally	lying	planning	ridiculous	transferred
amateur	committee	divided	government	maintenance	possesses	salary	twelfth
annual	common	doubt	grateful	magazine	possibility	sandwich	typical
anxious	comparative	duly	grievance	marriage	possible	scarcely	unusual
apparatus	competition	dying	guarantee	merchandise	preceding	schedule	useful
arctic	confident	effect	guard	miniature	prejudice	secretary	vegetable
article	congratulations	efficiency	handful	mischievous	privilege	seize	village
ascertain	conquer	eighth	harassed	misspelled	probably	sergeant	villain
assistance	conscience	eligible	height	mortgage	procedure	severely	weight
athletic	conscientious	embarrass	heroes	mournful	proceeded	shriek	weird
attacked	conscious	eminent	immediately	movable	prominent	siege	welfare
attendance	consequently	endeavor	incidentally	murmur	proved	sincerely	woman
beggar	convenience	environment	indefinitely	muscle	psychology	skiing	yield
benefited	coolly	equipment					

4. Be familiar with basic spelling rules. Study the following:

a. ADDING ENDINGS—When a word ends with "e," drop the "e" if the ending begins with a vowel (a, e, i, o, u), but do not drop the "e" if the ending begins with a consonant (b, c, d, f, g, h, etc.). Examples:

> age—aging (drop the "e" when adding "ing")
>
> manage—management (keep the "e" when adding "ment")

Change "y" to "i" when adding an ending, except when the ending is "ing." Examples:

> study—studies—studying

Keep the final "l" when you add "ly." Example:

> personal—personally

b. "I" BEFORE "E" EXCEPT AFTER "C." Examples:

> field   perceive
> relief   ceiling

When the sound of "ie" is not ē (ee), the usual spelling is "ei." Examples:

> neighbor
> weigh
> height

Exceptions to these rules: weird, leisure, friend, mischief

5. Be familiar with types of common spelling errors. We have already cautioned you to become familiar with words that are pronounced differently from the way they are spelled. Besides the confusion of pronunciation and spelling, another common error is *confusing words with the same sound but different spellings*. Study the following list:

TABLE 4
SOME COMMONLY CONFUSED WORDS

air; ere; heir	buy; by	grate; great
ate; eight	cent; scent; sent	groan; grown
blew; blue	coarse; course	hear; here
bough; bow	for; four	him; hymn
brake; break	forth; fourth	hole; whole

grate; great	right; write
groan; grown	road; rode
hear; here	sew; so; sow
him; hymn	scene; seen
hole; whole	stationary; stationery
hour; our	steal; steel
its; it's	straight; strait
knew; new	some; sum
know; no	son; sun
lead; led	sweet; suite
mail; male	their; there; they're
meat; meet	threw; through
pail; pale	to; too; two
pair; pare; pear	way; weigh
peace; piece	whose; who's
principal; principle	wood; would
read; red	

6. Keep a personal list of troublesome words. Jot down those words that give you particular spelling problems, and review them regularly.

Sample Questions

Find the correct spelling of the word and write the letter of your choice in the space provided. If no suggested spelling is correct, write choice D.

1. A) accomadate   C) accommodate   _____
   B) accomodate   D) none of these

2. A) calander   C) calendur   _____
   B) calendar   D) none of these

3. A) priviledge   C) privledge   _____
   B) privilege   D) none of these

4. A) recommend   C) recomend   _____
   B) reccommend   D) none of these

5. A) developement   C) devellopment   _____
   B) development   D) none of these

6. A) nickel   C) nickil   _____
   B) nickle   D) none of these

7. A) catagory   C) cattagory   _____
   B) category   D) none of these

Answers to Sample Questions

1. **C**	5. **B**
2. **B**	6. **A**
3. **B**	7. **B**
4. **A**	

PRACTICE SET 1

Find the correct spelling of the word and write the letter of your choice in the space provided. If no suggested spelling is correct, write choice D.

1. A) fourty   C) forety   _____
    B) forty   D) none of these

2. A) acheivement   C) acheivment   _____
    B) achievement   D) none of these

3. A) accross   C) acros   _____
    B) across   D) none of these

4. A) advertizement   C) advertisement   _____
    B) adverticement   D) none of these

5. A) salary   C) sallary   _____
    B) salery   D) none of these

6. A) permenent   C) purmenent   _____
    B) permanent   D) none of these

7. A) ajourn   C) adjourn   _____
    B) edjourn   D) none of these

8. A) artikle   C) articul   _____
    B) artical   D) none of these

9. A) scarcley   C) scarcly   _____
    B) scarcely   D) none of these

10. A) intresting   C) interesting   _____
    B) intrestting   D) none of these

11. A) magasine   C) magazine   _____
    B) maggazine   D) none of these

12. A) referance   C) reference   _____
    B) refrence   D) none of these

13. A) posible   C) posibel   _____
    B) possible   D) none of these

14. A) gentlemen   C) gentelmen   _____
    B) gentalmen   D) none of these

15. A) consequently   C) consecuentally   _____
    B) consequentally   D) none of these

16. A) captian   C) captein   _____
    B) captin   D) none of these

17. A) carrage   C) carriage   _____
    B) cariage   D) none of these

18. A) aquired   C) ackwiered   _____
    B) acuired   D) none of these

19. A) lutenant   C) liutenant   _____
    B) lieutenent   D) none of these

20. A) independance   C) independince   _____
    B) independence   D) none of these

ANSWERS FOR PRACTICE SET 1

1. (B) forty
2. (B) achievement
3. (B) across
4. (C) advertisement
5. (A) salary
6. (B) permanent
7. (C) adjourn
8. (D) Correct spelling: article
9. (B) scarcely
10. (C) interesting
11. (C) magazine
12. (C) reference
13. (B) possible
14. (A) gentlemen
15. (A) consequently
16. (D) Correct spelling: captain
17. (C) carriage
18. (D) Correct spelling: acquired
19. (D) Correct spelling: lieutenant
20. (B) independence

PRACTICE SET 2

Find the correct spelling of the word and write the letter of your choice in the space provided. If no suggested spelling is correct, write choice D.

1. A) stomach   C) stommack   _____
    B) stomack   D) none of these

2. A) jewlrey   C) jewelry   _____
    B) jewlry   D) none of these

3. A) superentendent   C) superentendant   _____
    B) superintendant   D) none of these

4. A) virticle   C) vertical   _____
    B) verticle   D) none of these

5. A) sofomore   C) sophmore   _____
    B) sophomore   D) none of these

6. A) sarjent   C) sargant   _____
    B) sargeant   D) none of these

7. A) vegtable C) vegetable _____
   B) vegtabel D) none of these

8. A) tobaco C) tabacco _____
   B) tobacco D) none of these

9. A) moregage C) morgage _____
   B) mortgage D) none of these

10. A) merchandice C) merchandise _____
   B) merchandize D) none of these

11. A) omited C) ommitted _____
   B) omitted D) none of these

12. A) memmorandem C) memmorandum _____
   B) memorandum D) none of these

13. A) minature C) minatoor _____
   B) miniature D) none of these

14. A) greatful C) graitful _____
   B) grateful D) none of these

15. A) fudjitive C) fugative _____
   B) fudgitive D) none of these

16. A) preperations C) preprarations _____
   B) preparations D) none of these

17. A) equiptment C) equipment _____
   B) eqwuiptment D) none of these

18. A) buereau C) bureau _____
   B) beaureau D) none of these

19. A) accordance C) acordance _____
   B) accordence D) none of these

20. A) assistence C) assistance _____
   B) assistince D) none of these

ANSWERS FOR PRACTICE SET 2

1. (A) stomach
2. (C) jewelry
3. (D) Correct spelling: superintendent
4. (C) vertical
5. (B) sophomore
6. (D) Correct spelling: sergeant
7. (C) vegetable
8. (B) tobacco
9. (B) mortgage
10. (C) merchandise
11. (B) omitted
12. (B) memorandum

13. (B) miniature
14. (B) grateful
15. (D) Correct spelling: fugitive
16. (B) preparations
17. (C) equipment
18. (C) bureau
19. (A) accordance
20. (C) assistance

PRACTICE SET 3

Find the correct spelling of the word and write the letter of your choice in the space provided. If no suggested spelling is correct, write choice D.

1. A) artic C) Artic _____
   B) arctic D) none of these

2. A) marrage C) marriage _____
   B) marraige D) none of these

3. A) chiminey C) chimeny _____
   B) chimney D) none of these

4. A) perfession C) profession _____
   B) profesion D) none of these

5. A) excape C) escape _____
   B) exkape D) none of these

6. A) surprize C) surprise _____
   B) serprise D) none of these

7. A) congradalations C) congratulations _____
   B) congradulations D) none of these

8. A) reconize C) recconise _____
   B) recognize D) none of these

9. A) tomorow C) tomorrow _____
   B) tommorrow D) none of these

10. A) atheltics C) athletics _____
   B) atheletics D) none of these

11. A) disasterous C) desasterous _____
   B) disastrous D) none of these

12. A) prespire C) perspire _____
   B) pirspire D) none of these

13. A) secratery C) secratary _____
   B) secretery D) none of these

14. A) umberella C) umberela _____
   B) umbrella D) none of these

15. A) lightining   C) litening   _____
    B) lightning   D) none of these

16. A) goverment   C) government   _____
    B) govrement   D) none of these

17. A) affectionitely   C) affectionately   _____
    B) affectionatly   D) none of these

18. A) requirment   C) requiremint   _____
    B) requirement   D) none of these

19. A) choclate   C) chocolit   _____
    B) chocolet   D) none of these

20. A) asociate   C) assoshiate   _____
    B) associate   D) none of these

ANSWERS FOR PRACTICE SET 3

1. (B) arctic
2. (C) marriage
3. (B) chimney
4. (C) profession
5. (C) escape
6. (C) surprise
7. (C) congratulations
8. (B) recognize
9. (C) tomorrow
10. (C) athletics
11. (B) disastrous
12. (C) perspire
13. (D) Correct spelling: secretary
14. (B) umbrella
15. (B) lightning
16. (C) government
17. (C) affectionately
18. (B) requirement
19. (D) Correct spelling: chocolate
20. (B) associate

PRACTICE SET 4

Find the correct spelling of the word and write the letter of your choice in the space provided. If no suggested spelling is correct, write choice D.

1. A) dependent   C) dependint   _____
    B) dependunt   D) none of these

2. A) equasion   C) equazion   _____
    B) equation   D) none of these

3. A) excitment   C) excitement   _____
    B) exsitement   D) none of these

4. A) presense   C) prescence   _____
    B) presence   D) none of these

5. A) envirement   C) environment   _____
    B) enviernment   D) none of these

6. A) campaine   C) campaign   _____
    B) campain   D) none of these

7. A) corespondence   C) corraspondence   _____
    B) corispondence   D) none of these

8. A) benefit   C) benafit   _____
    B) benifit   D) none of these

9. A) consequentally   C) consekwentally   _____
    B) consequently   D) none of these

10. A) attendence   C) attendance   _____
    B) atendance   D) none of these

11. A) promanent   C) promenint   _____
    B) promenent   D) none of these

12. A) height   C) heighth   _____
    B) hieght   D) none of these

13. A) dropt   C) dropped   _____
    B) droped   D) none of these

14. A) carefull   C) carful   _____
    B) careful   D) none of these

15. A) busness   C) business   _____
    B) bizness   D) none of these

16. A) suceed   C) succed   _____
    B) succede   D) none of these

17. A) english   C) English   _____
    B) Englesh   D) none of these

18. A) cooperation   C) cooparation   _____
    B) coaparation   D) none of these

19. A) vackume   C) vaccuum   _____
    B) vaccume   D) none of these

20. A) afourmentioned   C) aformentioned   _____
    B) aforementioned   D) none of these

ANSWERS FOR PRACTICE SET 4

1. (A) dependent
2. (B) equation
3. (C) excitement

4. **(B)** presence
5. **(C)** environment
6. **(C)** campaign
7. **(D)** Correct spelling: correspondence
8. **(A)** benefit
9. **(B)** consequently
10. **(C)** attendance
11. **(D)** Correct spelling: prominent
12. **(A)** height
13. **(C)** dropped
14. **(B)** careful
15. **(C)** business
16. **(D)** Correct spelling: succeed
17. **(C)** English
18. **(A)** cooperation
19. **(D)** Correct spelling: vacuum
20. **(B)** aforementioned

PRACTICE SET 5

Find the correct spelling of the word and write the letter of your choice in the space provided. If no suggested spelling is correct, write choice D.

1. A) relience   C) reliance   _____
   B) relyance   D) none of these

2. A) adition   C) addittion   _____
   B) addition   D) none of these

3. A) innoculate   C) inocculate   _____
   B) inoculate   D) none of these

4. A) probubly   C) probably   _____
   B) probly   D) none of these

5. A) Febuary   C) February   _____
   B) Febrary   D) none of these

6. A) testimonial   C) testemonial   _____
   B) testamonial   D) none of these

7. A) eficient   C) efficcient   _____
   B) effishient   D) none of these

8. A) necesary   C) necessary   _____
   B) nessesary   D) none of these

9. A) temprature   C) temperature   _____
   B) tempereture   D) none of these

10. A) corperation   C) corporation   _____
    B) corparation   D) none of these

11. A) comittment   C) commitment   _____
    B) committment   D) none of these

12. A) facetously   C) fascetiously   _____
    B) facitiously   D) none of these

13. A) barter   C) bartur   _____
    B) bartar   D) none of these

14. A) recquisite   C) recwisite   _____
    B) requisite   D) none of these

15. A) inteligent   C) intelligint   _____
    B) enteligent   D) none of these

16. A) transatory   C) transitory   _____
    B) transitorry   D) none of these

17. A) langauge   C) langwage   _____
    B) language   D) none of these

18. A) liberry   C) library   _____
    B) libary   D) none of these

19. A) resplendent   C) resplendint   _____
    B) resplendant   D) none of these

20. A) propelor   C) propeller   _____
    B) propellor   D) none of these

ANSWERS FOR PRACTICE SET 5

1. **(C)** reliance
2. **(B)** addition
3. **(B)** inoculate
4. **(C)** probably
5. **(C)** February
6. **(A)** testimonial
7. **(D)** Correct spelling: efficient
8. **(C)** necessary
9. **(C)** temperature
10. **(C)** corporation
11. **(C)** commitment
12. **(D)** Correct spelling: facetiously
13. **(A)** barter
14. **(B)** requisite
15. **(D)** Correct spelling: intelligent
16. **(C)** transitory
17. **(B)** language
18. **(C)** library
19. **(A)** resplendent
20. **(C)** propeller

PRACTICE SET 6

Find the correct spelling of the word and write the letter of your choice in the space provided. If no suggested spelling is correct, write choice D.

1. A) wield   C) weilde   _____
   B) weild   D) none of these

2. A) exhilarate   C) exhilerate   _____
   B) exilarate   D) none of these

3. A) misspell   C) misspel   _____
   B) mispell   D) none of these

4. A) grammer   C) grammar   _____
   B) gramar   D) none of these

5. A) existance   C) exsistence   _____
   B) existence   D) none of these

6. A) missile   C) misile   _____
   B) missle   D) none of these

7. A) procede   C) proseed   _____
   B) proceed   D) none of these

8. A) repitition   C) repittition   _____
   B) repetition   D) none of these

9. A) wierd   C) weerd   _____
   B) weird   D) none of these

10. A) embaras   C) embarrass   _____
    B) embarass   D) none of these

11. A) perogative   C) prerogotive   _____
    B) prerogative   D) none of these

12. A) their's   C) theyr's   _____
    B) theirs   D) none of these

13. A) guage   C) gaige   _____
    B) gauge   D) none of these

14. A) aggression   C) aggresion   _____
    B) agression   D) none of these

15. A) restarant   C) restaurant   _____
    B) restrant   D) none of these

16. A) marshul   C) marshalle   _____
    B) marshal   D) none of these

17. A) ristrain   C) restrain   _____
    B) restrane   D) none of these

18. A) cemetary   C) cemetery   _____
    B) cemitery   D) none of these

19. A) irresistible   C) irrisistable   _____
    B) irresistable   D) none of these

20. A) occassion   C) occasion   _____
    B) ocassion   D) none of these

ANSWERS FOR PRACTICE SET 6

1. (A) wield
2. (A) exhilarate
3. (A) misspell
4. (C) grammar
5. (B) existence
6. (A) missile
7. (B) proceed
8. (B) repetition
9. (B) weird
10. (C) embarrass
11. (B) prerogative
12. (B) theirs
13. (B) gauge
14. (A) aggression
15. (C) restaurant
16. (B) marshal
17. (C) restrain
18. (C) cemetery
19. (A) irresistible
20. (C) occasion

REVIEWING THE KEY STRATEGIES

Remember to:

1. "See" the word.

2. Review your list of commonly misspelled words.

3. Be familiar with basic spelling rules.

4. Be familiar with types of common errors.

5. Keep a personal list of troublesome words.

READING

This question type tests your ability to understand the essential meaning of brief paragraphs. No outside information or knowledge is required to answer each question.

Each paragraph is very brief, sometimes no more than one sentence. One question follows each paragraph, with four answer choices.

Helpful Techniques and Strategies for Reading Each Paragraph

1. Each paragraph usually contains only one main idea, often stated in the first sentence. Identify the main idea in the following sample paragraph:

   > As the legal profession becomes more specialized and complex, clerical assistance must become more specialized as well. One legal secretary might be an expert in bankruptcy law, another an expert in criminal justice.

   The first sentence, a general statement about increasing specialization in the legal profession, states the main idea. It is followed by a more specific statement, which gives additional information. You should practice recognizing this structure: *main idea + additional information.*

2. As you finish reading each paragraph, try to summarize the paragraph mentally, in a few words. For example, after reading the sample paragraph just given, you might summarize it by saying to yourself, "Legal secretaries specialize in different types of law."

3. Note whether the paragraph states a particular attitude toward the subject. Typically, the author will either *approve* or *disapprove* of the main point or remain *neutral*. In the sample passage just given, the author takes no position pro or con, but delivers the additional information in a matter-of-fact way. Consider the following sample passage:

   > In the majority of modern families, both husband and wife work full-time. However, many of these couples become more devoted to their jobs than to each other.

   Here, the main point receives criticism rather than support. The key to the author's attitude here is the contrast word "however"; when a *contrast word* follows the main point, it may indicate the author's disapproval of the main point.

4. If necessary, read the paragraph twice so that you understand it fully. These paragraphs are so brief that an *occasional* rereading will not seriously shorten your allotted time. However, never reread a paragraph until you have read it completely.

5. Don't dwell on unfamiliar words. Usually the context of a paragraph will help you to understand such words. Consider the following sample passage:

   > A regular diet of pizza and beer may have deleterious effects. These foods are loaded with fats and carbohydrates, and add more to one's waistline than to physical well-being.

   Although "deleterious" may be an unfamiliar word, the remainder of the paragraph makes it clear that the effects of pizza and beer are unhealthy, and suggests that "deleterious" has a meaning similar to "unhealthy."

Helpful Techniques and Strategies for Choosing an Answer

Consider once again a sample paragraph that we examined earlier, this time including a question:

> As the legal profession becomes more specialized and complex, clerical assistance must become more specialized as well. One legal secretary might be an expert in bankruptcy law, another an expert in criminal justice.

The paragraph best supports the statement that a legal secretary
A) may understand subjects other than law
B) may have special training in a particular branch of law
C) must be an expert in several types of law
D) is of no use to attorneys

1. When considering the answer choices, try first to eliminate incorrect answers. An incorrect answer often falls into one of three categories:

   a. *IRRELEVANT, OR NOT ADDRESSED*—Choice (A) is an irrelevant choice. Although particular types of law are mentioned, subjects other than law are not. Note that this statement may certainly be true for some legal secretaries, but receives no support *from the paragraph*.

   b. CONTRADICTORY—Choice (C) contradicts information in the passage. The paragraph discusses legal secretaries who specialize in *one* type of law, not several.

   c. UNREASONABLE—Choice (D) is an altogether unreasonable statement, according to the paragraph. The passage stresses the special expertise of legal secretaries thus making it unreasonable to conclude that they are useless.

2. In many cases, the correct answer choice will repeat the main point from the paragraph. In this case, the main point is that legal secretaries are becoming more specialized, and the correct answer emphasizes "special training." Notice also that the correct answer here refers as well to the second sentence, which contains additional information about particular branches of law.

   A few more samples:

A regular diet of pizza and beer may have deleterious effects. These foods are loaded with fats and carbohydrates, and add more to one's waistline than to physical well-being.

The paragraph best supports the statement that pizza and beer
A) should be consumed regularly if they are to have the proper effects
B) should definitely be eaten occasionally
C) can be harmful if they make up the main part of every meal
D) should be consumed separately rather than together

The correct answer is (C); it repeats the main point that pizza and beer, if eaten regularly, can have deleterious (harmful to health) effects. Choice (A) contradicts this point. Choice (B) contradicts the author's negative attitude toward pizza and beer. Choice (D) is irrelevant; the issue whether pizza and beer should be consumed separately or together is not addressed by the passage.

The belief that positive thinking is the key to success can lead to laziness. It encourages some people to engage in slipshod work, in the hope that an optimistic mental attitude will take the place of hard, careful, dedicated work.

The paragraph best supports the statement that laziness
A) is always the result of positive thinking
B) is practiced by successful people
C) is only permissible after one has completed a hard day's work
D) may result from a reliance on positive thinking

The correct choice is (D), which repeats the main point that "positive thinking . . . can lead to laziness." However, the paragraph does not say that laziness is *always* the result; therefore (A) is not the best answer. Choice (A) *overstates* the main point of the paragraph; the overstatement is evident in the use of the word "always." Choice (B) is unreasonable and is certainly contradicted by the paragraph. Choice (C) is irrelevant; the paragraph does not discuss *when* laziness is permissible.

PRACTICE SET 1

Select the best answer to each question and write the letter of your choice in the space provided.

1. Hundreds of new self-help books have been _____ published over the last decade. These books generally reflect a positive, optimistic approach to modern problems and challenges, informed by current research in psychology.

   The paragraph best supports the statement that the authors of self-help books

   A) are psychologists
   B) may be aware of current research in psychology
   C) are of greatest value to psychologists
   D) have only been published over the last ten years

2. The recent popularity of hot-air ballooning _____ is yet another instance of nostalgia for the past. Certainly these brightly colored floating globes of air are not modern inventions; rather, they recall the spectacle of county fairs and carnivals from the turn of the century.

   The paragraph best supports the statement that hot-air balloons

   A) could be seen at county fairs and carnivals of the past
   B) are more brightly colored today than they were at the turn of the century
   C) are most popular among those who lived at the turn of the century
   D) have been popular in every century

3. It has been said that a weed is a flower whose _____ virtue has not yet been discovered. As if to prove this point, a number of homeowners who are tired of constantly maintaining a pretty lawn and shrubbery have decided to let weeds run wild in their yards. The result, in some cases, has been quite an attractive array of lively shapes and colors.

   The paragraph best supports the statement that

   A) weeds are not flowers
   B) weeds make a pretty lawn even prettier
   C) weeds can be beautiful
   D) most homeowners prefer to let weeds run wild

4. Although every individual is thinking con- _____ stantly during the course of every day, no one is aware of his thoughts very often. Just walking a few steps entails a number of mental choices and activities that are performed more or less unconsciously. To become conscious of everything going on in the mind would be immobilizing.

   The paragraph best supports the statement that unconscious mental choices

   A) are performed by everyone every day
   B) are most dangerous when one is not thinking
   C) are immobilizing
   D) occur every few steps

5. Science fiction and fantasy have always ap- _____ pealed to the desire to escape from the boredom of conventional life and to experience the adventure and danger of a new environment. Thrilling to the excitement of "Star Wars" is a way of "getting away from it all."

   The paragraph best supports the statement that "Star Wars"

   A) is popular only with those who are bored with life
   B) provides excitement that conventional life does not
   C) is the best example of science fiction and fantasy
   D) is more thrilling than any other science fiction movie

6. Hitting a baseball is certainly one of the most _____ difficult feats in sports. Even the greatest hitters of all time have been able only to hit safely once for every three trips to the plate. In other words, even great hitters fail more often than they succeed.

   The paragraph best supports the statement that

   A) nothing succeeds like success
   B) it is unrealistic to expect to get a hit more than once in three tries
   C) great hitters must get used to being failures
   D) the difficulty of hitting a baseball causes many potential ballplayers to avoid the sport

7. The microwave oven has become a standard _____ appliance in many kitchens, mainly because it offers a fast way of cooking food, and therefore appeals to the growing number of households whose members maintain busy schedules, and have little time for the slow, conventional preparation of a meal.

   The paragraph best supports the statement that the microwave oven appeals to

A) everyone living in a busy household
B) those who need time to maintain a busy schedule in the kitchen
C) those who need more standard appliances in the kitchen
D) those who are not able to spend much time cooking

8. Clarity, correctness, and coherence are certainly elements of good writing, but interest is the most important element of all; writing that does not provoke and hold a reader's attention rarely succeeds as effective communication.

The paragraph best supports the statement that

A) clarity, correctness, and coherence are not important elements of good writing
B) good writers are always interesting people
C) it is possible for writing to be correct without being interesting
D) writing is the most effective means of communication

9. Because so many educators have concluded that interacting with students is more effective than dominating and commanding them, student-centered classrooms (typified by open discussion and sharing) have become more numerous than teacher-centered classrooms (typified by passive attention to lectures).

The paragraph best supports the statement that the number of student-centered classrooms

A) is larger than the number of teacher-centered classrooms
B) has been approved by educators
C) means that students are learning more than they ever have before
D) suggests that there are more students dominating teachers than there are teachers dominating students

10. Despite numerous medical studies that publicize health risks associated with caffeine, Americans continue to consume coffee in huge quantities. For most, the benefits of coffee apparently outweigh the dangers.

The paragraph best supports the statement that caffeine

A) is included in all brands of coffee
B) is a popular drink in America

C) receives unwarranted attention from the medical profession
D) is the victim of careless scientific research

ANSWER EXPLANATIONS FOR PRACTICE SET 1

1. **(B)** The paragraph states that self-help books are "generally . . . informed by current research in psychology." However, just because these books may contain research in psychology, they are not necessarily authored by psychologists, so (A) is not the best choice.
2. **(A)** The paragraph associates present-day hot-air balloons with those seen at county fairs and carnivals at the turn of the century.
3. **(C)** The passage states that a collection of weeds can be quite attractive.
4. **(A)** The paragraph states that every day "a number of mental choices" are performed "more or less unconsciously."
5. **(B)** The paragraph states that science fiction and fantasy (of which "Star Wars" is an example) provide "escape from the boredom of conventional life."
6. **(B)** Since even the greatest hitters hit safely only once in three tries, we may logically conclude that it is unrealistic to expect to do better than this.
7. **(D)** The paragraph says that the microwave oven appeals to those who have "little time" for the slow preparation of a meal.
8. **(C)** By emphasizing that interest is more important than correctness, the paragraph strongly implies that it is possible for writing to be correct without being interesting.
9. **(A)** Each of the other choices requires assumptions not supported by the paragraph. The paragraph does explicitly state that student-centered classrooms "have become more numerous" than teacher-centered classrooms.
10. **(B)** The paragraph explicitly states that "Americans . . . consume coffee in huge quantities."

PRACTICE SET 2

Select the best answer to each question and write the letter of your choice in the space provided.

1. Comedy is an art that is constantly changing. What was funny a few years ago seems merely silly now, mainly because the public tastes and public issues that are the substance of comedy have themselves changed. New events result in new blunders, and provide the material for new jokes.

The paragraph best supports the statement that

A) today's jokes are different than they were years ago
B) today's jokes refer only to current events
C) comedians are finding it difficult to write new material
D) comedy writers are constantly changing

2. Being new and different does not ensure the _____ success of a product. Advertisers must see to it that buyers who will use the product hear about it; they must place their advertising in the right spot. Little is gained by advertising denture adhesive during a Saturday morning cartoon show.

The paragraph best supports the statement that

A) Saturday morning cartoon shows do not contain advertisements
B) Saturday morning cartoon shows only advertise products that are not new and different
C) most buyers are shopping rather than watching television on Saturday mornings
D) those who use denture adhesive are not likely to be the viewers of Saturday morning cartoon shows

3. Some American auto factories are beginning _____ to resemble their Japanese counterparts. In many Japanese factories, the workers enjoy the same status and privileges as their bosses. Everyone works in harmony, and there is much less of the tension and anger that results when one group dominates another.

The paragraph best supports the statement that

A) everyone works in harmony in Japan
B) workers and bosses share the same status in some American factories
C) there is one main cause of tension and anger
D) Japanese factories have been influenced by the success of the American auto industry

4. Scientists persist in their efforts to improve _____ on nature. Making advances in genetic engineering, some researchers expect to invent new forms of life soon. One bacterium under development can consume and digest toxic wastes, and thus help clean up the environment.

The paragraph best supports the statement that

A) toxic wastes pose the most serious environmental problem, as far as scientists are concerned

B) it is the responsibility of scientists to improve on nature
C) a bacterium that can consume and digest toxic wastes would be a new form of life
D) inventing new forms of life takes persistence

5. The foliage and ground cover growing along _____ the nation's superhighways serve at least two functions. They help make traveling a more pleasant visual experience, and they help absorb the noise of thousands of automobile engines.

The paragraph best supports the statement that

A) foliage and ground cover are planted along superhighways for more than one reason
B) automobile engines become less noisy on superhighways
C) there are only two reasons for planting foliage and ground cover along superhighways
D) pleasant scenery results in safer driving

6. An emphasis on orderly behavior and disci- _____ pline in junior high school and high school prepares young adults to join the work force upon graduation, where they must adhere to rules and regulations. But a school experience that does not encourage free expression, individuality, and creativity may produce obedient workers who are not able to think for themselves.

The paragraph best supports the statement that junior high school and high school

A) are not educating young adults properly
B) do not employ teachers who can think for themselves
C) should encourage qualities other than orderly behavior and discipline
D) punish those who are creative

7. Comic strips can often provide a commentary _____ on everyday life, along with entertainment. The characters from "Peanuts," for instance, represent types of people that everyone encounters regularly: the bumbling nice guy; the brash, insensitive loudmouth; and the student for whom school is a bore.

The paragraph best supports the statement that the characters in "Peanuts"

A) do not represent particular individuals
B) handle real life better than real people
C) represent the three most common types of people one encounters in everyday life
D) appear in other comic strips as well

8. In the 1930s, the first modern health spas _____ were built, complete with efficient exercise equipment, swimming pools, and full-service locker rooms. But health spas did not become wildly popular until the 1980s; now one cannot travel very far in any big city without seeing one.

The paragraph best supports the statement that the popularity of health spas

A) is the result of improved exercise equipment
B) could not be measured in the 1930s
C) has increased since the 1930s
D) only exists in big cities

9. Poets who wish to compose a Japanese haiku _____ must follow a formula: There are three lines in all, a first line of five syllables, a second line of seven syllables, and a third line of five syllables. The restriction to precisely seventeen syllables makes the haiku form quite difficult to master.

The paragraph best supports the statement that writing a haiku

A) is difficult for someone who is not Japanese
B) may include more than three lines
C) extends beyond thirty-five syllables in special cases
D) is not an easy task, even though the form of the poem is simple

10. The length and structure of the workweek _____ have undergone a good deal of change in recent years. Workers who once labored eight hours each day, forty hours each week, Monday through Friday, are now allowed to determine their own schedules to some extent. Those who are able to complete assigned tasks efficiently and effectively during a shortened or irregular schedule, or those who can work better during different hours from the standard ones, are allowed an adjusted schedule by some companies.

The paragraph best supports the statement that some workers

A) are unable to work efficiently and effectively
B) may work on Saturday or Sunday
C) are employed by old-fashioned companies
D) work much more than forty hours each week

ANSWER EXPLANATIONS FOR PRACTICE SET 2

1.   (A) The paragraph repeatedly stresses that what is funny now is different from what was funny in the past.
2.   (D) The paragraph stresses that advertising must be placed in the "right spots" and concludes by implying that a cartoon show is not the right spot to appeal to "buyers who will use the product."
3.   (B) The passage states that some American factories are beginning to operate like those in Japan, relative to the relationship between workers and bosses.
4.   (C) The "bacterium under development" is mentioned as an example of "new forms of life."
5.   (A) The passage states that foliage and ground cover "serve at least two functions."
6.   (C) The passage calls for the encouragement of "free expression, individuality, and creativity."
7.   (A) The passage states that the comic strip's characters represent "types of people," thus strongly implying that they do not represent particular individuals.
8.   (C) The paragraph states that health spas became "wildly popular" in the 1980s.
9.   (D) The paragraph states explicitly that the haiku form is "quite difficult to master."
10.   (B) The paragraph stresses that some workers no longer work during the standard, Monday through Friday, workweek; this fact strongly implies that some workers may work on Saturday or Sunday. The paragraph does not suggest, however, that the workweek has become longer than forty hours, so (D) is not the best answer.

PRACTICE SET 3

Select the best answer to each question and write the letter of your choice in the space provided.

1. The relationship between architecture and _____ geometry becomes apparent once one surveys the newest buildings under construction in metropolitan areas. Each structure is a precise combination of triangles, rectangles, and trapezoids, arranged so that angles jut out in unusual places, in an array of lively designs.

The paragraph best supports the statement that new buildings

A) are more pleasant to look at than old ones
B) utilize a number of geometric shapes
C) were constructed to reflect a love of geometry
D) are designed to teach geometry to observers

2. Fast food is becoming more nutritious. Salad _____ bars are appearing at places that only served hamburgers once, offering diners the benefits of fresh vegetables. And the menus are expanding in other directions as well, offering chicken sandwiches on whole wheat buns, and low-fat yogurt desserts. With families cooking less often and eating out more often, the diet provided by fast-food chains has a great impact on the health of the nation; it would seem that the budget restaurants are taking seriously their responsibility to nourish us.

The paragraph best supports the statement that the improved nutrition of fast food is

A) affecting the health of many people
B) probably only a temporary trend
C) mainly based on the availability of more fresh vegetables
D) a response to widespread malnutrition

3. Few people understand poetry, and few prefer _____ to read it. Although English professors speak in glowing terms about the greatness of Pope's *Rape of the Lock* and Tennyson's *Ulysses*, it seems that only other professors share their enthusiasm. To appreciate the greatness of difficult poetry, readers must exercise great patience and concentration, and must tolerate the unusual, compressed language of rhythm and rhyme; with so many urgent issues demanding our attention at almost every hour of the day, choosing to figure out a poem seems an unlikely possibility.

The paragraph best supports the statement that poetry is popular

A) because so many people love the satisfaction that comes from understanding a great poem
B) because English professors have generated enthusiasm in so many of their students
C) with those who love rhymes
D) with a small, specialized group

4. Those who try to increase their vocabulary _____ by memorizing words and definitions are wasting time. Only by employing language in real situations do we make it familiar. Therefore, the most effective way to learn a new word is to use it, again and again.

The paragraph best supports the statement that people can increase their vocabulary by

A) memorizing more than just word lists and definitions

B) using only the words they need to use
C) creating situations that require unusual language
D) using new words whenever possible

5. Meteorology may qualify as a science, but _____ there is a great deal of guesswork involved as well. Even with tremendous knowledge about wind currents and weather patterns, and the most sophisticated equipment, forecasters' predictions are often wrong. The movement of a phenomenon as prominent as a hurricane cannot even be determined very far in advance. We remain the servants and victims of the weather, not its masters.

The paragraph best supports the statement that the science of weather prediction

A) is only accurate when the weather is fair
B) is useless when it comes to hurricanes
C) is not yet sophisticated enough to achieve accuracy consistently
D) does not qualify as a science

6. More children die each year from automobile accidents than from any other single _____ cause. This fact should be sufficient to force each of the 50 states to enact a mandatory seat belt law, but such laws have not yet swept the country. If we are to preserve our most precious natural resource, however, we must take steps that make buckling up imperative everywhere.

The paragraph best supports the statement that children are

A) our most precious natural resource
B) ignored in most states
C) not willing to wear seat belts
D) dying more frequently than ever

7. A baseball game can be described as a series _____ of solo performances: at any given moment, attention is focused on one player and one play. On the other hand, soccer involves all of the team most of the time: each player interacts with others constantly, so that no single individual seems responsible for success or failure. It is perhaps because spectators enjoy concentrating on individual personalities that baseball remains a much more popular spectator sport than soccer.

The paragraph best supports the statement that the popularity of baseball

A) will always be greater than the popularity of soccer
B) cannot be compared to the popularity of soccer
C) may be related to the preferences of spectators
D) will remain strong as long as individual players maintain their skills

8. Modern word processing equipment makes _____ the preparation of business correspondence easier and more efficient, perhaps. Typing errors disappear from the monitor at the touch of a button, and the final printout takes only seconds to produce. However, some typists have not yet become comfortable with staring at a text displayed on a screen; they are used to black letters on a white background, and cannot perceive textual errors as readily when faced with white letters on a dark background.

The paragraph best supports the statement that the typing errors that appear on a word processor screen

A) are more serious than those that appear on paper
B) are more difficult for some typists to recognize
C) disappear before they can be corrected
D) are more modern than errors produced on a typewriter

9. Student protesters are more polite than they _____ used to be. One need only recall the violent riots of the 1960s, led by ragged, long-haired political activists, to notice the difference that prevails today: while the demonstrators of yesteryear yelled obscenities at the police and openly flouted civic regulations, today's demonstrators cooperate almost meekly with law enforcement officials, maintaining a neat, orderly, peaceful display while they express political dissent.

The paragraph best supports the statement that

A) today's protesters are not as effective as the protesters of the 1960s
B) law enforcement officials encounter less hostility from protesters now than they did in the 1960s
C) today's protesters wear nice clothes and have short hair
D) civic regulations have changed since the 1960s, and are not so offensive to protesters anymore

10. Everyone who collects books is not an avid _____ reader. Some prefer to fill their homes with shelves of novels, travelogues, and self-help

guides for the purpose of display and decoration only. They enjoy the accessibility of knowledge and information, but rarely partake of the storehouse.

The paragraph best supports the statement that those who buy books

A) prefer only novels, travelogues, and self-help guides
B) decorate their homes with books alone
C) have added a storehouse onto their home
D) do not necessarily read them

ANSWER EXPLANATIONS FOR PRACTICE SET 3

1. **(B)** The passage states that new buildings display geometric shapes: triangles, rectangles, and trapezoids.
2. **(A)** The paragraph states that the availability of more nutritious fast food "has a great impact on the health of the nation."
3. **(D)** The paragraph states that poetry seems to be popular mainly with professors (2nd sentence); professors are a small, specialized group.
4. **(D)** All the other choices contradict the information in the passage; (D) repeats the point of the third sentence.
5. **(C)** Several times the passage makes the point that predicting the weather involves "a great deal of guesswork" and can be inaccurate.
6. **(A)** The value of children is stressed throughout the passage, and they are called "our most precious natural resource" in the final sentence.
7. **(C)** The final sentence of the paragraph proposes that what the spectators enjoy (individual personalities) may determine the greater popularity of baseball.
8. **(B)** The passage states that "some typists . . . cannot perceive textual errors as readily" on a word processor screen.
9. **(B)** The major change emphasized in the passage is the increased cooperation with law enforcement officials.
10. **(D)** The paragraph explicitly states that every collector of books "is not an avid reader."

PRACTICE SET 4

Select the best answer to each question and write the letter of your choice in the space provided.

1. The federal government is becoming more _____ vigilant when it comes to toxic waste. Probably as a result of widespread press coverage

of the Love Canal disaster a few years ago, politicians and bureaucrats are more sensitive to heightened public attention to mismanaged chemical dumps and the health hazards they pose. Heavy fines are being imposed upon those who have ignored regulations about safe waste disposal.

The paragraph best supports the statement that the Love Canal disaster

A) was the first disaster of its kind
B) led to a number of other, more serious disasters involving unsafe waste disposal
C) was the first disaster that attracted the attention of the federal government
D) involved the issue of toxic waste

2. Sociologists have noted that children today _____ are less "childish" than ever; when they are still very young, perhaps only six or seven years old, children are already mimicking adult fashions and leading relatively independent lives. Dressed in designer jeans, an elementary school child is likely to spend much of every day fending for herself, taking charge of her own life while waiting for her working parents to arrive home. Less dependent on adults for their day-to-day decisions, children "grow up" faster.

The paragraph best supports the statement that children today are

A) likely to wear only fashion jeans
B) likely to be more intelligent than children of six or seven years ago
C) not interested in the opinions of their parents
D) likely to have parents who are employed outside the home during the day

3. The new American revolution is an electronic one. Advances in sophisticated circuitry have yielded more gadgets than anyone could have imagined only a few years ago: calculators as small as a wristwatch and automobile dashboards full of digital readouts are two of the many products that have enhanced the quality of life. There is some fear, however, that we may become so dependent on solid-state circuits to do our thinking that we may forget how to do it ourselves.

The paragraph best supports the statement that although progress in electronic progress has improved the quality of life, it

A) may affect our ability to think independently

B) has merely provided gadgets
C) has made those who use electronic devices more afraid of them than ever
D) is not nearly as sophisticated as it will become in the next century

4. There are advantages and disadvantages to _____ clear, simple writing. Sentences that are easy to understand are processed more quickly and efficiently by readers; those who can express themselves in simple terms are rarely misunderstood. However, prose that is crystal clear often lacks both complexity and imagination. Whether one chooses a style that is simple and clear or complex and unusual often depends upon the tolerance of one's readers.

The paragraph best supports the statement that more tolerant readers will

A) be less willing to read simple and clear writing
B) be more willing to read complex and unusual writing
C) be confused easily
D) demand writing that is complex, unusual, and easy to misunderstand

5. Years ago, a nationwide poll concluded that _____ there are more televisions than there are bathtubs in American homes. No doubt that fact remains today, especially in light of the growing popularity of home computers. Now, in addition to owning televisions for entertainment, more and more families are purchasing TV monitors for use with a personal computer. We can guess safely that there are still many more people staring at a picture tube than singing in the shower.

The paragraph best supports the statement that

A) cleanliness is less important to Americans than it used to be
B) most homes do not require more than one bathtub
C) the general results of the nationwide poll taken years ago are still true
D) few people have televisions in the bathroom

6. Some have called Californians the nomads of _____ America. While those living in the Midwest, the South, and the East tend to reside in the same place for a number of years, Californians change addresses regularly. The constant mobility of California residents helps to keep the real estate industry in that state thriving.

The paragraph best supports the statement that real estate sales

A) are related to how frequently a population changes addresses
B) have always been better in California than in any other state
C) are more important to Californians than to the residents of other states
D) are virtually nonexistent outside California

7. Recently, cable television firms have faced _____ stiff competition from the home video industry. Given the choice of either renting movies for home viewing or subscribing to a cable service that offers recent films, consumers are choosing the rentals. Many say that local video stores offer a wider choice of movies than any cable station, and that renting movies allows viewers the freedom to watch them at any time, so they are not tied to the cable station schedule.

The paragraph best supports the statement that consumers

A) prefer to rent movies rather than buy them
B) value freedom of choice
C) would like to upgrade the quality of cable television firms
D) watch a greater number of movies than cable television firms have been able to provide

8. A recent experiment in psychology yielded _____ results that are difficult to interpret. Researchers found that whenever the light bulbs were changed in the workplace, production increased. Although the brightness in the room neither increased nor decreased, the workers worked better each time a custodial crew changed the bulbs. Perhaps just the sight of the light bulbs being changed led the workers to feel that conditions had improved, and to work better.

The paragraph best supports the statement that the results of the psychology experiment

A) will lead to a continual increase in production
B) had no effect on the work of the custodial crew
C) lead to no definite conclusions
D) will be used to improve working conditions in a number of companies

9. Some teachers prefer "creative" writers, and _____ some prefer "correct" writers. Rarely does one encounter a student who writes unconventional and exciting prose while also obey-ing all the rules and conventions of standard written English. It may be impossible for any writer to be both radical and obedient at the same time.

The paragraph best supports the statement that a writer who is both creative and correct

A) is rarely successful in school
B) is preferred by half of the teachers he encounters
C) tends to confuse being radical with being obedient
D) knows how to deviate from the rules of standard written English

10. Many aviators are also avid sailors, perhaps _____ because the principles of flying are so similar to the principles of sailing, so that participants in both sports enjoy the thrill of riding the wind.

The paragraph best supports the statement that

A) learning to sail qualifies one to fly an airplane
B) flying is most thrilling on windy days
C) many aviators are sailors, but no sailors are aviators
D) many aviators, when not flying, enjoy sailing

ANSWER EXPLANATIONS FOR PRACTICE SET 4

1. **(D)** The paragraph discusses government attention to toxic waste, and the Love Canal disaster is cited as a specific example.
2. **(D)** The individual who represents "children today" in the paragraph waits "for her working parents to arrive home"; the strong implication here is that the parents are employed outside the home.
3. **(A)** The final sentence of the paragraph contrasts the enhanced quality of life with the possibility that electronic devices may "do our thinking" for us.
4. **(B)** The paragraph associates a writer's chosen style with the tolerance of readers and implies that complex and unusual writing requires more tolerant readers because it is not understood as "quickly and efficiently" as simple and clear writing.
5. **(C)** The paragraph states that the "fact remains today" that there are more televisions than bathtubs in American homes.
6. **(A)** The passage associates the "mobility of California residents" with a thriving real estate industry, but does not support any of the other possible choices.
7. **(B)** The paragraph states that consumers prefer the freedom to choose both their movies and their viewing time.

8. **(C)** Although the paragraph reaches a conclusion that is "perhaps" true, it emphasizes that the results of the experiment "are difficult to interpret," and states no *definite* conclusions.

9. **(D)** The creative and correct writer knows the rules and also knows how to write "unconventional" prose, that is, prose that deviates from the rules.

10. **(D)** The paragraph explicitly states that "many aviators are also avid sailors."

PRACTICE SET 5

Select the best answer to each question and write the letter of your choice in the space provided.

1. Historians accept the fact that writing history _____ requires interpreting the past, not just cataloguing it. As a mere collection of facts, the history of the Civil War means nothing; only when the facts are analyzed and explained does this event become significant.

   The paragraph best supports the statement that a list of facts about the Civil War is

   A) what most historians are interested in
   B) mistaken for history by those who are not historians
   C) not so important as the analysis and explanation of those facts
   D) usually too dull for any historian

2. The automobile engine is an unappreciated _____ marvel. Consider its durability alone, as it endures tens of thousands of miles of wear and tear over years and years, and still starts up every morning.

   The paragraph best supports the statement that those who drive automobiles

   A) abuse their automobile engines
   B) do not usually consider the amazing durability of the engine
   C) run the engine longer than they should
   D) know almost nothing about how an automobile engine works

3. Babe Ruth still holds the official record for _____ the most home runs hit in one season. Roger Maris hit 61 home runs, to top Ruth's record of 60, but Maris batted in 162 games, compared to 154 games for Ruth.

   The paragraph best supports the statement that Roger Maris

   A) played in a number of unofficial baseball games, but hit home runs in none of them
   B) did not hit a home run again after the season in which he hit 61
   C) probably had more chances to hit home runs, during the season, than Babe Ruth did
   D) was a more powerful hitter than Babe Ruth, despite the existence of Ruth's record

4. Many gamblers seem unwilling to admit that _____ chance and luck largely determine who wins and loses. Many develop elaborate schemes and systems for winning at blackjack and roulette, but only very few leave the casino wealthier than when they entered.

   The paragraph best supports the statement that a system for winning at blackjack

   A) depends to a great extent upon chance and luck for its success
   B) should only be used by gamblers who consider themselves lucky
   C) can also be useful for winning at roulette and other casino games
   D) has been tried by many gamblers who have relied on chance and luck as well

5. Secretaries must be experts in human rela- _____ tions as well as office procedures. Much of their time every day is spent advising and counseling others about programs and policies, and repeatedly adjusting to the variety of persons and personalities that visits the office each day.

   The paragraph best supports the statement that the ability to interact effectively with a variety of different people

   A) should not be expected of a secretary, even though it is a valuable skill
   B) is only useful during the times that the office is very busy
   C) is a very important and necessary secretarial skill
   D) should only be demanded of secretaries who have had extensive training in human relations

6. Social observers have noted that "stress," _____ which is such a popular affliction in this decade, was virtually unheard-of in the recent past. Our grandparents accorded no special status to everyday tension, and they seem to have experienced less of such tension than we do now. If "stress" did not receive so much publicity these days, perhaps many of us would not feel compelled to suffer from it.

The paragraph best supports the statement that the widespread publicity of stress

A) is something that those of past generations would not have allowed
B) may actually influence the occurrence of stress
C) never compelled our grandparents to pay any attention to everyday tension
D) has gone unnoticed by many of us

7. A neat, orderly workplace encourages calmness and efficiency, just as a messy workplace provokes tension and wastefulness. In other words, the qualities of the workplace draw out related qualities in the workers.

The paragraph best supports the statement that the appearance of a workplace

A) is usually neat and orderly
B) is completely dependent on the abilities of the workers
C) can affect the behavior of the workers
D) must be maintained on a regular basis, just as personal qualities such as wastefulness must be maintained on a regular basis.

8. For inexperienced writers, often the most _____ difficult task is writing an introduction. Therefore, it is sometimes best to delay writing the introductory paragraph until after the body, or "middle" of the essay, is complete.

The paragraph best supports the statement that

A) experienced writers may not need to delay writing the introductory paragraph
B) experienced writers must always write the introductory paragraph before writing the body of the essay
C) without first reading the body of the essay, inexperienced writers cannot tell what they are supposed to write about
D) the introductory paragraph is always a disaster for inexperienced writers

9. As digital clocks replace traditional, radial _____ timepieces, the connection between time and the rotation of the earth is less evident. As the hands of a radial clock move in a circle, from hour to hour, they mimic the turning of the earth on its axis, during the course of each twenty-four-hour day.

The paragraph best supports the statement that the movement of a radial clock

A) reminds everyone of the rotation of the sun around the earth
B) is less accurate, but more natural, than the movement of a digital clock
C) only pretends to duplicate the rotation of the earth
D) is significantly different from the movement of a digital clock

10. The interior design of a restaurant can invite _____ customers to either dine leisurely, or eat and run. Dark, soft upholstery and soft lighting are conducive to a long, relaxed meal; on the other hand, stiff, thinly padded chairs and brightly illuminated dining areas seem to keep people from remaining for very long.

The paragraph best supports the statement that the length of time that one spends at a restaurant meal

A) is usually spent relaxing in a dark atmosphere
B) can vary with the quality of the food as well as the interior design of the restaurant
C) may be affected by the interior design of the restaurant
D) is never pleasant when the room is brightly lit and the chairs are thinly padded

ANSWER EXPLANATIONS FOR PRACTICE SET 5

1. (C) The paragraph stresses that analysis and explanation, rather than facts alone, are important to historians.
2. (B) The passage calls the automobile engine an "unappreciated marvel" and follows with a discussion of engine durability, thus implying that drivers do not usually consider the durability of the engine.
3. (C) The paragraph states that Maris hit 61 home runs in a season that was longer than the season during which Ruth set his record; therefore, we may conclude that Maris probably had more chances than Ruth to hit home runs.
4. (A) The paragraph states explicitly that "chance and luck largely determine who wins and loses."
5. (C) The importance of "adjusting to the variety of persons and personalities" is emphasized in the paragraph.
6. (B) The final sentence suggests a relationship between the publicity of stress and the occurrence of it.

7. **(C)** The paragraph compares the appearance of the workplace with the "qualities in the workers," pointing out that the workers are affected by the workplace.

8. **(A)** The paragraph suggests that inexperienced writers may need to delay writing the introductory paragraph, and thus implies that experienced writers may not need to delay writing the introductory paragraph.

9. **(D)** The passage contrasts digital clocks with radial timepieces, in the first sentence.

10. **(C)** It is the interior design of the restaurant that invites customers "to either dine leisurely, or eat and run."

REVIEWING THE KEY STRATEGIES

Remember to:

1. Eliminate incorrect answers first. They may be:
   — irrelevant
   — contradictory
   — unreasonable

2. Look for correct answer choices that repeat or re-emphasize main points of the passage.

CHAPTER 3

Four Verbal Abilities Model Tests
with Answer Explanations

This chapter contains four complete full-length model tests with answers and explanations. The purpose of this chapter is to help you master the techniques for working quickly under time pressure. After correcting each model test, assess your strengths and weaknesses and return to the specific review section for additional review.

The model tests should be taken under strict test conditions. This means:

—no scratch paper permitted

—any scratch work must be done on test booklet

—answers must be marked on answer sheet

—use #2 pencils with erasers

—follow time limits exactly. (Use an alarm clock.) Thirty-five minutes for each test. You may not proceed to test #2 until 35 minutes are up for test #1. Then you may not return to test #1.

—no interruptions allowed

—no aids permitted (such as dictionary, calculator, etc.)

NOTE: Sample questions are usually distributed with the announcement and if so may not be given in the official examinations.

Remember to tear out your answer sheet preceding each model test.

ANSWER SHEET

SIGNATURE: _____
(Please Sign)

EXAMINATION TITLE: _____

PLACE OF EXAMINATION: _____
City

_____
State

TODAY'S DATE: _____

SAMPLE Ⓐ ● Ⓒ Ⓓ Ⓔ

DIRECTIONS FOR MARKING ANSWER SHEET

Use only a **No. 2 (or softer) lead pencil**. Darken completely the circle corresponding to your answer. You **must** keep your mark within the circle. Stray marks may be counted as errors. Erase **completely** all marks except your answer.

1. In the boxes below, **PRINT** your name. Print only as many letters as will fit within the areas for the last name, first initial (F.I.), and middle initial (M.I.). Below each box, darken the circle containing the same letter. SEE SAMPLE NAME GRID

SAMPLE NAME GRID

LAST NAME — MCCABE   F.I. — C   M.I. — A

2. In the boxes below, enter your 9-digit Social Security Number. Below each box, darken the circle in each column corresponding to the number you have entered.

SOCIAL SECURITY NUMBER

3. OCCUPATIONAL GROUP NUMBER

LAST NAME   F.I.   M.I.

SECTION 1

PART

TEST SERIES

TEST NUMBER

Make no marks or entries in the columns to the right until you receive instructions from the administrator.

| 1 Ⓐ Ⓑ Ⓒ Ⓓ Ⓔ | 11 Ⓐ Ⓑ Ⓒ Ⓓ Ⓔ | 21 Ⓐ Ⓑ Ⓒ Ⓓ Ⓔ | 31 Ⓐ Ⓑ Ⓒ Ⓓ Ⓔ | 51 Ⓐ Ⓑ Ⓒ Ⓓ Ⓔ | 71 Ⓐ Ⓑ Ⓒ Ⓓ Ⓔ | 91 Ⓐ Ⓑ Ⓒ Ⓓ Ⓔ | 111 Ⓐ Ⓑ Ⓒ Ⓓ Ⓔ |

11 Ⓐ Ⓑ Ⓒ Ⓓ Ⓔ 31 Ⓐ Ⓑ Ⓒ Ⓓ Ⓔ 51 Ⓐ Ⓑ Ⓒ Ⓓ Ⓔ 71 Ⓐ Ⓑ Ⓒ Ⓓ Ⓔ 91 Ⓐ Ⓑ Ⓒ Ⓓ Ⓔ 111 Ⓐ Ⓑ Ⓒ Ⓓ Ⓔ
12 Ⓐ Ⓑ Ⓒ Ⓓ Ⓔ 32 Ⓐ Ⓑ Ⓒ Ⓓ Ⓔ 52 Ⓐ Ⓑ Ⓒ Ⓓ Ⓔ 72 Ⓐ Ⓑ Ⓒ Ⓓ Ⓔ 92 Ⓐ Ⓑ Ⓒ Ⓓ Ⓔ 112 Ⓐ Ⓑ Ⓒ Ⓓ Ⓔ
13 Ⓐ Ⓑ Ⓒ Ⓓ Ⓔ 33 Ⓐ Ⓑ Ⓒ Ⓓ Ⓔ 53 Ⓐ Ⓑ Ⓒ Ⓓ Ⓔ 73 Ⓐ Ⓑ Ⓒ Ⓓ Ⓔ 93 Ⓐ Ⓑ Ⓒ Ⓓ Ⓔ 113 Ⓐ Ⓑ Ⓒ Ⓓ Ⓔ
14 Ⓐ Ⓑ Ⓒ Ⓓ Ⓔ 34 Ⓐ Ⓑ Ⓒ Ⓓ Ⓔ 54 Ⓐ Ⓑ Ⓒ Ⓓ Ⓔ 74 Ⓐ Ⓑ Ⓒ Ⓓ Ⓔ 94 Ⓐ Ⓑ Ⓒ Ⓓ Ⓔ 114 Ⓐ Ⓑ Ⓒ Ⓓ Ⓔ
15 Ⓐ Ⓑ Ⓒ Ⓓ Ⓔ 35 Ⓐ Ⓑ Ⓒ Ⓓ Ⓔ 55 Ⓐ Ⓑ Ⓒ Ⓓ Ⓔ 75 Ⓐ Ⓑ Ⓒ Ⓓ Ⓔ 95 Ⓐ Ⓑ Ⓒ Ⓓ Ⓔ 115 Ⓐ Ⓑ Ⓒ Ⓓ Ⓔ
16 Ⓐ Ⓑ Ⓒ Ⓓ Ⓔ 36 Ⓐ Ⓑ Ⓒ Ⓓ Ⓔ 56 Ⓐ Ⓑ Ⓒ Ⓓ Ⓔ 76 Ⓐ Ⓑ Ⓒ Ⓓ Ⓔ 96 Ⓐ Ⓑ Ⓒ Ⓓ Ⓔ 116 Ⓐ Ⓑ Ⓒ Ⓓ Ⓔ
17 Ⓐ Ⓑ Ⓒ Ⓓ Ⓔ 37 Ⓐ Ⓑ Ⓒ Ⓓ Ⓔ 57 Ⓐ Ⓑ Ⓒ Ⓓ Ⓔ 77 Ⓐ Ⓑ Ⓒ Ⓓ Ⓔ 97 Ⓐ Ⓑ Ⓒ Ⓓ Ⓔ 117 Ⓐ Ⓑ Ⓒ Ⓓ Ⓔ
18 Ⓐ Ⓑ Ⓒ Ⓓ Ⓔ 38 Ⓐ Ⓑ Ⓒ Ⓓ Ⓔ 58 Ⓐ Ⓑ Ⓒ Ⓓ Ⓔ 78 Ⓐ Ⓑ Ⓒ Ⓓ Ⓔ 98 Ⓐ Ⓑ Ⓒ Ⓓ Ⓔ 118 Ⓐ Ⓑ Ⓒ Ⓓ Ⓔ
19 Ⓐ Ⓑ Ⓒ Ⓓ Ⓔ 39 Ⓐ Ⓑ Ⓒ Ⓓ Ⓔ 59 Ⓐ Ⓑ Ⓒ Ⓓ Ⓔ 79 Ⓐ Ⓑ Ⓒ Ⓓ Ⓔ 99 Ⓐ Ⓑ Ⓒ Ⓓ Ⓔ 119 Ⓐ Ⓑ Ⓒ Ⓓ Ⓔ
20 Ⓐ Ⓑ Ⓒ Ⓓ Ⓔ 40 Ⓐ Ⓑ Ⓒ Ⓓ Ⓔ 60 Ⓐ Ⓑ Ⓒ Ⓓ Ⓔ 80 Ⓐ Ⓑ Ⓒ Ⓓ Ⓔ 100 Ⓐ Ⓑ Ⓒ Ⓓ Ⓔ 120 Ⓐ Ⓑ Ⓒ Ⓓ Ⓔ
1 Ⓐ Ⓑ Ⓒ Ⓓ Ⓔ 21 Ⓐ Ⓑ Ⓒ Ⓓ Ⓔ 41 Ⓐ Ⓑ Ⓒ Ⓓ Ⓔ 61 Ⓐ Ⓑ Ⓒ Ⓓ Ⓔ 81 Ⓐ Ⓑ Ⓒ Ⓓ Ⓔ 101 Ⓐ Ⓑ Ⓒ Ⓓ Ⓔ 121 Ⓐ Ⓑ Ⓒ Ⓓ Ⓔ
2 Ⓐ Ⓑ Ⓒ Ⓓ Ⓔ 22 Ⓐ Ⓑ Ⓒ Ⓓ Ⓔ 42 Ⓐ Ⓑ Ⓒ Ⓓ Ⓔ 62 Ⓐ Ⓑ Ⓒ Ⓓ Ⓔ 82 Ⓐ Ⓑ Ⓒ Ⓓ Ⓔ 102 Ⓐ Ⓑ Ⓒ Ⓓ Ⓔ 122 Ⓐ Ⓑ Ⓒ Ⓓ Ⓔ
3 Ⓐ Ⓑ Ⓒ Ⓓ Ⓔ 23 Ⓐ Ⓑ Ⓒ Ⓓ Ⓔ 43 Ⓐ Ⓑ Ⓒ Ⓓ Ⓔ 63 Ⓐ Ⓑ Ⓒ Ⓓ Ⓔ 83 Ⓐ Ⓑ Ⓒ Ⓓ Ⓔ 103 Ⓐ Ⓑ Ⓒ Ⓓ Ⓔ 123 Ⓐ Ⓑ Ⓒ Ⓓ Ⓔ
4 Ⓐ Ⓑ Ⓒ Ⓓ Ⓔ 24 Ⓐ Ⓑ Ⓒ Ⓓ Ⓔ 44 Ⓐ Ⓑ Ⓒ Ⓓ Ⓔ 64 Ⓐ Ⓑ Ⓒ Ⓓ Ⓔ 84 Ⓐ Ⓑ Ⓒ Ⓓ Ⓔ 104 Ⓐ Ⓑ Ⓒ Ⓓ Ⓔ 124 Ⓐ Ⓑ Ⓒ Ⓓ Ⓔ
5 Ⓐ Ⓑ Ⓒ Ⓓ Ⓔ 25 Ⓐ Ⓑ Ⓒ Ⓓ Ⓔ 45 Ⓐ Ⓑ Ⓒ Ⓓ Ⓔ 65 Ⓐ Ⓑ Ⓒ Ⓓ Ⓔ 85 Ⓐ Ⓑ Ⓒ Ⓓ Ⓔ 105 Ⓐ Ⓑ Ⓒ Ⓓ Ⓔ 125 Ⓐ Ⓑ Ⓒ Ⓓ Ⓔ
6 Ⓐ Ⓑ Ⓒ Ⓓ Ⓔ 26 Ⓐ Ⓑ Ⓒ Ⓓ Ⓔ 46 Ⓐ Ⓑ Ⓒ Ⓓ Ⓔ 66 Ⓐ Ⓑ Ⓒ Ⓓ Ⓔ 86 Ⓐ Ⓑ Ⓒ Ⓓ Ⓔ 106 Ⓐ Ⓑ Ⓒ Ⓓ Ⓔ 126 Ⓐ Ⓑ Ⓒ Ⓓ Ⓔ
7 Ⓐ Ⓑ Ⓒ Ⓓ Ⓔ 27 Ⓐ Ⓑ Ⓒ Ⓓ Ⓔ 47 Ⓐ Ⓑ Ⓒ Ⓓ Ⓔ 67 Ⓐ Ⓑ Ⓒ Ⓓ Ⓔ 87 Ⓐ Ⓑ Ⓒ Ⓓ Ⓔ 107 Ⓐ Ⓑ Ⓒ Ⓓ Ⓔ 127 Ⓐ Ⓑ Ⓒ Ⓓ Ⓔ
8 Ⓐ Ⓑ Ⓒ Ⓓ Ⓔ 28 Ⓐ Ⓑ Ⓒ Ⓓ Ⓔ 48 Ⓐ Ⓑ Ⓒ Ⓓ Ⓔ 68 Ⓐ Ⓑ Ⓒ Ⓓ Ⓔ 88 Ⓐ Ⓑ Ⓒ Ⓓ Ⓔ 108 Ⓐ Ⓑ Ⓒ Ⓓ Ⓔ 128 Ⓐ Ⓑ Ⓒ Ⓓ Ⓔ
9 Ⓐ Ⓑ Ⓒ Ⓓ Ⓔ 29 Ⓐ Ⓑ Ⓒ Ⓓ Ⓔ 49 Ⓐ Ⓑ Ⓒ Ⓓ Ⓔ 69 Ⓐ Ⓑ Ⓒ Ⓓ Ⓔ 89 Ⓐ Ⓑ Ⓒ Ⓓ Ⓔ 109 Ⓐ Ⓑ Ⓒ Ⓓ Ⓔ 129 Ⓐ Ⓑ Ⓒ Ⓓ Ⓔ
10 Ⓐ Ⓑ Ⓒ Ⓓ Ⓔ 30 Ⓐ Ⓑ Ⓒ Ⓓ Ⓔ 50 Ⓐ Ⓑ Ⓒ Ⓓ Ⓔ 70 Ⓐ Ⓑ Ⓒ Ⓓ Ⓔ 90 Ⓐ Ⓑ Ⓒ Ⓓ Ⓔ 110 Ⓐ Ⓑ Ⓒ Ⓓ Ⓔ 130 Ⓐ Ⓑ Ⓒ Ⓓ Ⓔ

MODEL TEST 1

Time allotted—35 minutes

Directions

Each question has four suggested answers. Decide which one is the best answer. Find the question number on the Answer Sheet. Show your answer to the question by darkening completely the square corresponding to the letter of your answer. Keep your mark within the space. If you have to erase a mark, be sure to erase it completely. Mark only one answer for each question. Do NOT mark space E for any question.

Word Meaning

1. *Integrity* means most nearly
   A) wealth   C) honesty
   B) temper   D) understanding

2. *Frugal* means most nearly
   A) free   C) pretentious
   B) thrifty   D) profane

3. *Depravity* means most nearly
   A) corruption   C) greed
   B) slavery   D) boldness

4. *Awry* means most nearly
   A) distant   C) not straight
   B) bitter   D) ironic

5. *Unkempt* means most nearly
   A) neat   C) swollen
   B) untidy   D) closed

Analogies

6. ALUMNUS is related to ALUMNA as ROOSTER is related to
   A) hen   C) barnyard
   B) crow   D) chick

7. PRUNE is related to PLUM as RAISIN is related to
   A) kumquat   C) peach
   B) grape   D) cereal

8. RUNG is related to LADDER as STEP is related to
   A) march   C) stairway
   B) halt   D) prong

9. INTERSECTION is related to RED LIGHT as PROMONTORY is related to
   A) lighthouse   C) archipelago
   B) peninsula   D) island

Grammar

Decide which sentence is preferable with respect to grammar and usage suitable for a formal letter or report.

10. A) Each of the senior staff members regards his work serious enough to excel in every task, according to a recent evaluation.
    B) According to a recent evaluation, each senior staff member regards his work so seriously that he excels in every task.
    C) With a serious regard, according to a recent evaluation, each senior staff member excels in every task.
    D) The excelling in every task by each of the senior staff members is the result of taking work seriously according to a recent evaluation.

11. A) Although the floral arrangement smelled sweetly, several people complained about its gaudiness.
    B) Smelling sweetly, the floral arrangement still received complaints from those objecting to its gaudiness.
    C) The sweet-smelling floral arrangement had complaints of gaudiness.
    D) Although gaudy, the floral arrangement smelled sweet.

Spelling

Find the correct spelling to the word and darken the proper answer space. If no suggested spelling is correct, darken space D.

12. A) recieved   C) received
    B) receeved   D) none of these

13. A) posibility   C) possibility
    B) possibillity   D) none of these

14. A) musile   C) muscle
    B) musscle   D) none of these

15. A) kindergarten   C) kindergardin
    B) kindergarden   D) none of these

Reading

16. Any voice heard over the phone is associated with a face and personality, which are sometimes not at all appropriate to the actual person who is speaking. In other words, the telephone can be both an invaluable tool for communication and a source of mistaken impressions.

The paragraph best supports the statement that the way a person sounds over the phone
- A) will lead a listener to accurately imagine a face and personality
- B) will always fool a listener who is curious about what face and personality match the voice
- C) is often distorted by the mistaken impressions of the telephone
- D) may not always match the face and personality of the person

17. Teachers in several regions are being asked to take competency tests in order to demonstrate their educational preparation and literacy skills. Recently, some officials emphasized the need for a national test for teachers, and some teachers' groups responded angrily.

The paragraph best supports the statement that
- A) some teachers' groups do not believe that teachers can pass a competency test
- B) the competency tests already in use have received no angry responses
- C) the institution of a national competency test for teachers is a controversial issue
- D) the results of competency tests accurately reflect the educational preparation and literacy skills of teachers

18. *Unique* means most nearly
- A) singular
- B) sexless
- C) twisted
- D) clownish

19. *Proficient* means most nearly
- A) quick
- B) dubious
- C) skilled
- D) reliable

20. *Judicious* means most nearly
- A) trial
- B) wise
- C) debatable
- D) sweet

21. *Meticulous* means most nearly
- A) careful
- B) imitative
- C) asinine
- D) healthful

22. *Prognosis* means most nearly
- A) sickness
- B) difficulty
- C) forecast
- D) forked

23. SUNDIAL is related to CLOCK as ABACUS is related to
- A) stopwatch
- B) barometer
- C) calculator
- D) thermometer

24. TADPOLE is related to FROG as CATERPILLAR is related to
- A) worm
- B) fur
- C) butterfly
- D) forest

25. MAYOR is related to CITY as GOVERNOR is related to
- A) country
- B) nation
- C) village
- D) state

26. MARS is related to RED as SATURN is related to
- A) Jupiter
- B) rings
- C) planet
- D) moons

27. A) The most demanding professor on campus always requires term papers, insists on field studies, and reads all lab reports personally.
- B) The most demanding professor on campus always requires term papers, insists on field studies, and reading all lab reports personally.
- C) Personally reading all lab reports, insisting on field studies, and to require term papers make this professor the most demanding.
- D) With demanding term papers, insisting on field studies, and the reading of all lab reports, this professor is requiring.

28. A) The agency overseas sent several representatives, who present new ideas for marketing there after they arrived.
- B) The overseas representatives presented new ideas for marketing when they arrived here.
- C) The overseas representatives' arrival presented new ideas for marketing.
- D) Having had arrived here, the overseas representatives present new ideas.

29. A) hankerchef
- B) handkerchief
- C) hankerchefe
- D) none of these

30. A) proceedural
- B) procedural
- C) procederal
- D) none of these

31. A) pschology   C) psycholagy
    B) pschylogy   D) none of these

32. A) proffesor   C) professor
    B) profesor   D) none of these

33. Those who find themselves without the time to sit down and read a good book are listening to books instead. A number of literary classics have been recorded on audio cassettes and have become popular with busy professionals as well as with homemakers.

The paragraph best supports the statement that the time required to read books
A) may be used by some people for tasks other than reading
B) is better spent listening to books on audio cassettes
C) is less available today than it was earlier in this century
D) is probably spent on audio and video entertainment

34. The dozens of different languages spoken today may have a common root. A number of linguists and historians believe that the Indo-European language, spoken thousands of years ago, was the basis for many of the languages of more modern times. The precise nature of the Indo-European language is, however, very difficult to determine.

The paragraph best supports the statement that
A) Indo-European is no longer spoken anywhere in the world
B) there were dozens of different ancient languages that were all called Indo-European
C) linguists and historians are no longer interested in the precise nature of Indo-European
D) Indo-European is not the only language that was spoken

35. *Introverted* means most nearly
A) unarguable   C) strong
B) withdrawn   D) upset

36. *Heterogeneous* means most nearly
A) perverted   C) varied
B) healthy   D) recondite

37. *Feasible* means most nearly
A) practical   C) stealable
B) expensive   D) ridiculous

38. To *emulate* means most nearly to
A) imitate   C) require
B) disown   D) disparage

39. *Hirsute* means most nearly
A) historic   C) mounted
B) hairy   D) armored

40. PROFESSOR is related to CAMPUS as LIFEGUARD is related to
A) rescue   C) beach
B) save   D) summer

41. TELESCOPE is related to CLOSE as MICROSCOPE is related to
A) small   C) far
B) large   D) near

42. CHILD is related to BIB as ADULT is related to
A) wipe   C) napkin
B) neck   D) food

43. PEN is related to QUILL as PAPER is related to
A) pencil   C) ink
B) parchment   D) book

44. A) Waste can be eliminated, or at least reduced, if less pencils, pens, and paper clips are left lying around.
B) Waste can be eliminated, or at least reduced, if fewer pencils, pens, and paper clips are left lying around.
C) The fewer the pencils, pens, and paper clips, the more of waste is eliminated.
D) With pencils, pens, and paper clips less wasted, the more it can be eliminated or reduced.

45. A) When only six months old, the committee will review the success of the new management plan.
B) After the new management plan has been implemented for six months, the committee will have had it under review.
C) With six months behind them, the new management plan's success came under the review of the committee.
D) In six months the committee will review the effects of the new management plan.

46. A) heros   C) heroes
B) heeroes   D) none of these

47. A) imediately   C) immediately
     B) immedietly   D) none of these

48. A) influential   C) influensial
     B) influencial   D) none of these

49. A) eradicate   C) irradicate
     B) iradicate   D) none of these

50. Although reference books such as a dictionary, thesaurus, and grammar handbook are part of any writer's library, they are not usually consulted with regularity. Too much time looking into reference works leaves little time for the writing itself.

The paragraph best supports the statement that a writer's reference books
A) are best left untouched by any writer who wishes to be productive
B) may be books other than a dictionary, thesaurus, and grammar handbook
C) always require a great deal of time to consult
D) are indispensable for writers, but do not often improve the quality of any writer's work

51. When one is pressed to complete a writing task within a brief time limit, it is often useful to rely on a standard formula for organizing the writing. One very useful formula for writing the first paragraph of an essay is abbreviated TRI, topic-restriction-illustration. Using this formula, one first writes a very general sentence (topic), and then follows with a more focused statement (restriction) and a mention of the examples that will be discussed (illustration).

The paragraph best supports the statement that
A) writing within a brief time limit is very difficult for anyone who does not use a standard formula
B) the time available for writing may determine whether using a formula is necessary
C) those who rely on TRI for writing paragraphs will complete writing tasks more quickly than those who do not
D) there are no standard formulas for writing the paragraphs that follow the first one

52. *Pastoral* means most nearly
A) ancient   C) melodic
B) rural   D) starving

53. *Homage* means most nearly
A) honor   C) settle
B) estate   D) vision

54. *Aghast* means most nearly
A) fueled   C) horrified
B) exhaust   D) left over

55. *Innate* means most nearly
A) human   C) simplistic
B) overwrought   D) in-born

56. *Fetid* means most nearly
A) stinking   C) fallen
B) productive   D) satiated

57. APARTMENT is related to RENT as HOME is related to
A) paint   C) live
B) purchase   D) build

58. JOCKEY is related to SMALL as RACEHORSE is related to
A) big   C) fast
B) brown   D) old

59. PREFACE is related to BOOK as PREFIX is related to
A) novel   C) suffix
B) word   D) repair

60. RADIO is related to TELEVISION as AURAL is related to
A) oral   C) film
B) visual   D) station

61. A) Arriving at the office early, the sun was rising as the manager began work.
B) The sun rising and arriving at the office early, the manager began work.
C) The manager arrived at the office before sunrise and began work.
D) Managing a sunrise arrival at the office to begin work, the manager had been working.

62. A) Juries usually make correct decisions and perform their duties both correctly and effectively.
B) Juries usually make correct decisions.
C) Making correct decisions keep juries both correct and effective.
D) Juries usually make correct decisions and perform their duties both correct and effective.

63. A) garanteed   C) gauranteed
    B) guaranteed   D) none of these

64. A) fundimental   C) fundementel
    B) fundamental   D) none of these

65. A) murmer   C) mermer
    B) mermur   D) none of these

66. A) mornful   C) mournfull
    B) mournful   D) none of these

67. A skillful typist is much more than a transcriber of words. Given a rough draft filled with scribbles and awkward phrases, the typist must not only type the copy, but also decipher and make clear ideas that the original writer left vague.

The paragraph best supports the statement that
A) typists do not always receive rough drafts that are neat and clear
B) typists prefer to revise and correct the writer's rough draft
C) all typists have worked for writers who were imaginative but not able to produce a clear rough draft
D) most typists expect that a rough draft will be difficult to read

68. At most major universities, the availability of parking spaces is a substantial problem. There are always far fewer spaces than there are students, faculty, and staff who drive to school, and unless one arrives very early in the morning, the likelihood of securing a space is slim indeed.

The paragraph best supports the statement that many people who attend major universities
A) arrive early in the morning
B) do not park on campus
C) are not bothered by parking problems
D) prefer to walk to school

69. To *embellish* means most nearly to
A) signal   C) ornament
B) stomach   D) mortify

70. *Paraphernalia* means most nearly
A) spirits   C) fear
B) equipment   D) illegal

71. To *hinder* means most nearly to
A) restrain   C) sharpen
B) imply   D) pray

72. To *cull* means most nearly to
A) cut   C) select
B) desert   D) decay

73. *Chaste* means most nearly
A) pursuit   C) satisfaction
B) pure   D) punishment

74. PERSON is related to SURNAME as BOOK is related to
A) author   C) chapter
B) subject   D) title

75. ROOM is related to LAMP as SKY is related to
A) cloud   C) sun
B) night   D) day

76. CLOTHING is related to CLOSET as AMMUNITION is related to
A) armory   C) garage
B) general   D) storeroom

77. INDUSTRY is related to POLLUTION as TRAFFIC is related to
A) cars   C) highway
B) accidents   D) speed

78. A) Referring to known and proven facts is important in any effective argument.
B) To know and proving facts for an effective argument is important.
C) One should include persuasive facts in any argument.
D) One should put persuasive facts in their argument whenever possible.

79. A) Thirty-six hours, give or take a few minutes, are the length of time required for the special project.
B) Required for the special project are thirty-six hours, give or take a few minutes.
C) The special project will require approximately thirty-six hours.
D) With a requirement of thirty-six hours, more or less, the special project requires a precise length of time.

80. A) preperations   C) prepurations
B) prepirations   D) none of these

81. A) predjudice   C) prejudice
B) pregjudice   D) none of these

82. A) meaness   C) meenness
B) meanness   D) none of these

83. A) matteriel   C) material
     B) meterial   D) none of these

84. When individual personalities conflict, the best solution is honesty and compromise. Only by airing the problem and discussing mutually agreeable terms for solving it, can a group put conflict behind them and get on with useful work.

The paragraph best supports the statement that when a conflict arises between individuals,
   A) honesty on the part of either individual is unusual
   B) solving the problem is much more difficult than continuing to work together
   C) one of the individuals is not willing to be honest and compromise
   D) an individual who refuses to compromise is an obstacle to solving the problem

85. With advances in medical technology, and increased public interest in exercise and nutrition, the average life expectancy in America continues to increase, and consequently, the average age of the population continues to rise. America is getting older.

The paragraph best supports the statement that exercise and nutrition
   A) have offset the decay of American culture
   B) are less advanced than medical technology, but more interesting to the public
   C) have contributed to longer lives, and affected the average age of the population
   D) are most valuable before one passes the average age of the population

ANSWER KEY FOR MODEL TEST 1

Word Meaning

1. C	18. A	35. B	52. B	69. C
2. B	19. C	36. C	53. A	70. B
3. A	20. B	37. A	54. C	71. A
4. C	21. A	38. A	55. D	72. C
5. B	22. C	39. B	56. A	73. B

Analogies

6. A	23. C	40. C	57. B	74. D
7. B	24. C	41. B	58. C	75. C
8. C	25. D	42. C	59. B	76. A
9. A	26. B	43. B	60. B	77. B

Grammar

10. B	27. A	44. B	61. C	78. C
11. D	28. B	45. D	62. B	79. C

Spelling

12. C	29. B	46. C	63. B	80. D
13. C	30. B	47. C	64. B	81. C
14. C	31. D	48. A	65. D	82. B
15. A	32. C	49. A	66. B	83. C

Reading

16. D	33. A	50. B	67. A	84. D
17. C	34. A	51. B	68. B	85. C

ANALYSIS CHART FOR MODEL TEST 1

Now that you've corrected your exam, use the following chart to carefully analyze your results and spot your strengths and weaknesses. This analysis should help you focus your study and review efforts.

Section	Total Number of Questions	Number Correct	Number Incorrect	Number Unanswered*
Word Meaning	25			
Analogies	20			
Grammar	10			
Spelling	20			
Reading Comprehension	10			
TOTAL	85			

*Since there is no penalty for incorrect answers on the Verbal Abilities Test, you should have left no question unanswered. Even if you didn't have time to answer a question, at least you should have filled in the answer space with a guess.

ANSWER EXPLANATIONS FOR MODEL TEST 1

1. (C) honesty
2. (B) thrifty
3. (A) corruption
4. (C) not straight
5. (B) untidy
6. (A) The first word is the male version; the second word is the female version.
7. (B) The first word is the second word dried up.
8. (C) The first word is one of the parts of the second word.

9. **(A)** The second word is the signal located at the first word.
10. **(B)** In (A), "serious" should be "seriously." In (C), "with a serious regard" is unclear. Choice (D) is wordy.
11. **(D)** In both (A) and (B), "sweetly" should be "sweet." In (C), "had complaints of gaudiness" is an unclear phrase.
12. **(C)** received
13. **(C)** possibility
14. **(C)** muscle
15. **(A)** kindergarten
16. **(D)** The paragraph implies that listeners will not always *accurately* imagine the face and personality associated with a voice on the telephone, so (A) is not the best choice. (D) sums up the overall point of the paragraph.
17. **(C)** The paragraph states that "some officials" and "some teachers' groups" disagree about the need for a national competency test; such disagreement makes the issue controversial, rather than agreeable to all.
18. **(A)** singular
19. **(C)** skilled
20. **(B)** wise
21. **(A)** careful
22. **(C)** forecast
23. **(C)** The first word is an ancient version of the second word.
24. **(C)** The first word changes into the second word.
25. **(D)** The first word is the elected leader of the second word.
26. **(B)** The second word is a characteristic of the first word.
27. **(A)** Choices (B), (C), and (D) all exhibit faulty parallelism; for instance, in (C), "to require" should be "requiring."
28. **(B)** In both (A) and (D), the verbs are incorrect: "present" in both (A) and (D) should be "presented"; also, "having had" in (D) should be "having." In (C), the "arrival" rather than the "representatives" presented the new ideas.
29. **(B)** handkerchief
30. **(B)** procedural
31. **(D)** Correct spelling: psychology
32. **(C)** professor
33. **(A)** The paragraph stresses the popularity of books on cassettes and suggests that some people are listening to books rather than reading them, thus spending the time during which they might be reading in other ways.

34. **(A)** While (D) may be true, in general, it is not supported by information in the passage. Because the passage states that Indo-European is an ancient language that remains more or less unknown today, we may conclude that it is no longer spoken; otherwise, its nature would not be "difficult to determine."
35. **(B)** withdrawn
36. **(C)** varied
37. **(A)** practical
38. **(A)** imitate
39. **(B)** hairy
40. **(C)** The second word is where the first word works.
41. **(B)** The second word is the resulting action of the first word.
42. **(C)** The second word is used while the first word eats.
43. **(B)** The second word is an ancient version of the first word.
44. **(B)** In (A), "less" is used incorrectly; when describing items that are *countable,* "fewer" is correct. (C) is an illogical sentence, and "more of waste" is a vague expression. In (D), "less wasted" and "it" are unclear.
45. **(D)** In (A), the sentence seems to say that the committee is "only six months old." (B) contains a verb error: "will have had" is incorrect. (C) is awkward and not clear; "them" should be "it."
46. **(C)** heroes
47. **(C)** immediately
48. **(A)** influential
49. **(A)** eradicate
50. **(B)** Each of the other choices is an extreme conclusion that extends beyond the information in the paragraph. In the paragraph, the particular books mentioned are offered as examples of reference books in general and are not referred to as the *only* reference books useful or available to a writer.
51. **(B)** The paragraph mentions "time limit" as a factor related to using a formula for writing. Each of the other choices may be true in general, but none is supported by the paragraph.
52. **(B)** rural
53. **(A)** honor
54. **(C)** horrified
55. **(D)** in-born
56. **(A)** stinking
57. **(B)** The second word is the common way of obtaining the first word.

58. **(C)** The second word is a characteristic of the first word.
59. **(B)** The first word is the first part of the second word.
60. **(B)** The first word refers to hearing; the second word refers to sight.
61. **(C)** Choices (A) and (B) seem to say that the sun was arriving at the office early. Choice (D) is vague and wordy.
62. **(B)** Choices (A), (C) and (D) are unnecessarily repetitious. In (C), "keep" should be "keeps." In (D), "correct and effective" should be "correctly and effectively."
63. **(B)** guaranteed
64. **(B)** fundamental
65. **(D)** Correct spelling: murmur
66. **(B)** mournful
67. **(A)** The paragraph describes a rough draft that is neither neat nor clear as something that a typist may receive.
68. **(B)** The availability of "far fewer spaces" than drivers allows us to conclude that many people do not park on campus.
69. **(C)** ornament
70. **(B)** equipment
71. **(A)** restrain
72. **(C)** select
73. **(B)** pure
74. **(D)** The second word is the identifying name for the first word.

75. **(C)** The second word illuminates the first word.
76. **(A)** The first word is stored in the second word.
77. **(B)** The second word is a harmful result of the first word.
78. **(C)** In (A), "known and proven facts" is an unnecessarily wordy phrase. In (B), "proving" should be "to prove," and the verb should be plural ("are"). In (D), "their" is incorrect; "one's," "his," or "her" is correct in this case.
79. **(C)** In (A) and (B), the verb "are" should be singular, to agree with the single-unit subject. The sentence structure in (B) is also awkward. Choice (D) is repetitious and also illogical, because "thirty-six hours, more or less" is not a *precise* length of time."
80. **(D)** Correct spelling is preparations
81. **(C)** prejudice
82. **(B)** meanness
83. **(C)** material
84. **(D)** The paragraph connects compromise with the "best solution" and allows us to conclude that a solution is blocked by one who is unwilling to compromise.
85. **(C)** The passage explicitly states that exercise and nutrition have caused Americans to live longer.

ANSWER SHEET

SIGNATURE: _____
(Please Sign)

EXAMINATION TITLE: _____

PLACE OF EXAMINATION: _____

City _____

State _____

TODAY'S DATE: _____

SAMPLE Ⓐ ● Ⓒ Ⓓ Ⓔ

DIRECTIONS FOR MARKING ANSWER SHEET

Use only a **No. 2 (or softer) lead pencil.** Darken completely the circle corresponding to your answer. You **must** keep your mark within the circle. Stray marks may be counted as errors. Erase **completely** all marks except your answer.

1. In the boxes below, **PRINT** your name. Print only as many letters as will fit within the areas for the last name, first initial (F.I.), and middle initial (M.I.) Below each box, darken the circle containing the same letter. SEE SAMPLE NAME GRID

SAMPLE NAME GRID

LAST NAME

M.I.
F.I.

2. In the boxes below, enter your 9-digit Social Security Number. Below each box, darken the circle in each column corresponding to the number you have entered.

SOCIAL SECURITY NUMBER

3. OCCUPATIONAL GROUP NUMBER

LAST NAME

F.I.

M.I.

SECTION 1

PART

TEST SERIES

TEST NUMBER

| 1 Ⓐ Ⓑ Ⓒ Ⓓ Ⓔ | 11 Ⓐ Ⓑ Ⓒ Ⓓ Ⓔ | 31 Ⓐ Ⓑ Ⓒ Ⓓ Ⓔ | 51 Ⓐ Ⓑ Ⓒ Ⓓ Ⓔ | 71 Ⓐ Ⓑ Ⓒ Ⓓ Ⓔ | 91 Ⓐ Ⓑ Ⓒ Ⓓ Ⓔ | 111 Ⓐ Ⓑ Ⓒ Ⓓ Ⓔ |

11 Ⓐ Ⓑ Ⓒ Ⓓ Ⓔ 31 Ⓐ Ⓑ Ⓒ Ⓓ Ⓔ 51 Ⓐ Ⓑ Ⓒ Ⓓ Ⓔ 71 Ⓐ Ⓑ Ⓒ Ⓓ Ⓔ 91 Ⓐ Ⓑ Ⓒ Ⓓ Ⓔ 111 Ⓐ Ⓑ Ⓒ Ⓓ Ⓔ
12 Ⓐ Ⓑ Ⓒ Ⓓ Ⓔ 32 Ⓐ Ⓑ Ⓒ Ⓓ Ⓔ 52 Ⓐ Ⓑ Ⓒ Ⓓ Ⓔ 72 Ⓐ Ⓑ Ⓒ Ⓓ Ⓔ 92 Ⓐ Ⓑ Ⓒ Ⓓ Ⓔ 112 Ⓐ Ⓑ Ⓒ Ⓓ Ⓔ
13 Ⓐ Ⓑ Ⓒ Ⓓ Ⓔ 33 Ⓐ Ⓑ Ⓒ Ⓓ Ⓔ 53 Ⓐ Ⓑ Ⓒ Ⓓ Ⓔ 73 Ⓐ Ⓑ Ⓒ Ⓓ Ⓔ 93 Ⓐ Ⓑ Ⓒ Ⓓ Ⓔ 113 Ⓐ Ⓑ Ⓒ Ⓓ Ⓔ
14 Ⓐ Ⓑ Ⓒ Ⓓ Ⓔ 34 Ⓐ Ⓑ Ⓒ Ⓓ Ⓔ 54 Ⓐ Ⓑ Ⓒ Ⓓ Ⓔ 74 Ⓐ Ⓑ Ⓒ Ⓓ Ⓔ 94 Ⓐ Ⓑ Ⓒ Ⓓ Ⓔ 114 Ⓐ Ⓑ Ⓒ Ⓓ Ⓔ
15 Ⓐ Ⓑ Ⓒ Ⓓ Ⓔ 35 Ⓐ Ⓑ Ⓒ Ⓓ Ⓔ 55 Ⓐ Ⓑ Ⓒ Ⓓ Ⓔ 75 Ⓐ Ⓑ Ⓒ Ⓓ Ⓔ 95 Ⓐ Ⓑ Ⓒ Ⓓ Ⓔ 115 Ⓐ Ⓑ Ⓒ Ⓓ Ⓔ
16 Ⓐ Ⓑ Ⓒ Ⓓ Ⓔ 36 Ⓐ Ⓑ Ⓒ Ⓓ Ⓔ 56 Ⓐ Ⓑ Ⓒ Ⓓ Ⓔ 76 Ⓐ Ⓑ Ⓒ Ⓓ Ⓔ 96 Ⓐ Ⓑ Ⓒ Ⓓ Ⓔ 116 Ⓐ Ⓑ Ⓒ Ⓓ Ⓔ
17 Ⓐ Ⓑ Ⓒ Ⓓ Ⓔ 37 Ⓐ Ⓑ Ⓒ Ⓓ Ⓔ 57 Ⓐ Ⓑ Ⓒ Ⓓ Ⓔ 77 Ⓐ Ⓑ Ⓒ Ⓓ Ⓔ 97 Ⓐ Ⓑ Ⓒ Ⓓ Ⓔ 117 Ⓐ Ⓑ Ⓒ Ⓓ Ⓔ
18 Ⓐ Ⓑ Ⓒ Ⓓ Ⓔ 38 Ⓐ Ⓑ Ⓒ Ⓓ Ⓔ 58 Ⓐ Ⓑ Ⓒ Ⓓ Ⓔ 78 Ⓐ Ⓑ Ⓒ Ⓓ Ⓔ 98 Ⓐ Ⓑ Ⓒ Ⓓ Ⓔ 118 Ⓐ Ⓑ Ⓒ Ⓓ Ⓔ
19 Ⓐ Ⓑ Ⓒ Ⓓ Ⓔ 39 Ⓐ Ⓑ Ⓒ Ⓓ Ⓔ 59 Ⓐ Ⓑ Ⓒ Ⓓ Ⓔ 79 Ⓐ Ⓑ Ⓒ Ⓓ Ⓔ 99 Ⓐ Ⓑ Ⓒ Ⓓ Ⓔ 119 Ⓐ Ⓑ Ⓒ Ⓓ Ⓔ
20 Ⓐ Ⓑ Ⓒ Ⓓ Ⓔ 40 Ⓐ Ⓑ Ⓒ Ⓓ Ⓔ 60 Ⓐ Ⓑ Ⓒ Ⓓ Ⓔ 80 Ⓐ Ⓑ Ⓒ Ⓓ Ⓔ 100 Ⓐ Ⓑ Ⓒ Ⓓ Ⓔ 120 Ⓐ Ⓑ Ⓒ Ⓓ Ⓔ
1 Ⓐ Ⓑ Ⓒ Ⓓ Ⓔ 21 Ⓐ Ⓑ Ⓒ Ⓓ Ⓔ 41 Ⓐ Ⓑ Ⓒ Ⓓ Ⓔ 61 Ⓐ Ⓑ Ⓒ Ⓓ Ⓔ 81 Ⓐ Ⓑ Ⓒ Ⓓ Ⓔ 101 Ⓐ Ⓑ Ⓒ Ⓓ Ⓔ 121 Ⓐ Ⓑ Ⓒ Ⓓ Ⓔ
2 Ⓐ Ⓑ Ⓒ Ⓓ Ⓔ 22 Ⓐ Ⓑ Ⓒ Ⓓ Ⓔ 42 Ⓐ Ⓑ Ⓒ Ⓓ Ⓔ 62 Ⓐ Ⓑ Ⓒ Ⓓ Ⓔ 82 Ⓐ Ⓑ Ⓒ Ⓓ Ⓔ 102 Ⓐ Ⓑ Ⓒ Ⓓ Ⓔ 122 Ⓐ Ⓑ Ⓒ Ⓓ Ⓔ
3 Ⓐ Ⓑ Ⓒ Ⓓ Ⓔ 23 Ⓐ Ⓑ Ⓒ Ⓓ Ⓔ 43 Ⓐ Ⓑ Ⓒ Ⓓ Ⓔ 63 Ⓐ Ⓑ Ⓒ Ⓓ Ⓔ 83 Ⓐ Ⓑ Ⓒ Ⓓ Ⓔ 103 Ⓐ Ⓑ Ⓒ Ⓓ Ⓔ 123 Ⓐ Ⓑ Ⓒ Ⓓ Ⓔ
4 Ⓐ Ⓑ Ⓒ Ⓓ Ⓔ 24 Ⓐ Ⓑ Ⓒ Ⓓ Ⓔ 44 Ⓐ Ⓑ Ⓒ Ⓓ Ⓔ 64 Ⓐ Ⓑ Ⓒ Ⓓ Ⓔ 84 Ⓐ Ⓑ Ⓒ Ⓓ Ⓔ 104 Ⓐ Ⓑ Ⓒ Ⓓ Ⓔ 124 Ⓐ Ⓑ Ⓒ Ⓓ Ⓔ
5 Ⓐ Ⓑ Ⓒ Ⓓ Ⓔ 25 Ⓐ Ⓑ Ⓒ Ⓓ Ⓔ 45 Ⓐ Ⓑ Ⓒ Ⓓ Ⓔ 65 Ⓐ Ⓑ Ⓒ Ⓓ Ⓔ 85 Ⓐ Ⓑ Ⓒ Ⓓ Ⓔ 105 Ⓐ Ⓑ Ⓒ Ⓓ Ⓔ 125 Ⓐ Ⓑ Ⓒ Ⓓ Ⓔ
6 Ⓐ Ⓑ Ⓒ Ⓓ Ⓔ 26 Ⓐ Ⓑ Ⓒ Ⓓ Ⓔ 46 Ⓐ Ⓑ Ⓒ Ⓓ Ⓔ 66 Ⓐ Ⓑ Ⓒ Ⓓ Ⓔ 86 Ⓐ Ⓑ Ⓒ Ⓓ Ⓔ 106 Ⓐ Ⓑ Ⓒ Ⓓ Ⓔ 126 Ⓐ Ⓑ Ⓒ Ⓓ Ⓔ
7 Ⓐ Ⓑ Ⓒ Ⓓ Ⓔ 27 Ⓐ Ⓑ Ⓒ Ⓓ Ⓔ 47 Ⓐ Ⓑ Ⓒ Ⓓ Ⓔ 67 Ⓐ Ⓑ Ⓒ Ⓓ Ⓔ 87 Ⓐ Ⓑ Ⓒ Ⓓ Ⓔ 107 Ⓐ Ⓑ Ⓒ Ⓓ Ⓔ 127 Ⓐ Ⓑ Ⓒ Ⓓ Ⓔ
8 Ⓐ Ⓑ Ⓒ Ⓓ Ⓔ 28 Ⓐ Ⓑ Ⓒ Ⓓ Ⓔ 48 Ⓐ Ⓑ Ⓒ Ⓓ Ⓔ 68 Ⓐ Ⓑ Ⓒ Ⓓ Ⓔ 88 Ⓐ Ⓑ Ⓒ Ⓓ Ⓔ 108 Ⓐ Ⓑ Ⓒ Ⓓ Ⓔ 128 Ⓐ Ⓑ Ⓒ Ⓓ Ⓔ
9 Ⓐ Ⓑ Ⓒ Ⓓ Ⓔ 29 Ⓐ Ⓑ Ⓒ Ⓓ Ⓔ 49 Ⓐ Ⓑ Ⓒ Ⓓ Ⓔ 69 Ⓐ Ⓑ Ⓒ Ⓓ Ⓔ 89 Ⓐ Ⓑ Ⓒ Ⓓ Ⓔ 109 Ⓐ Ⓑ Ⓒ Ⓓ Ⓔ 129 Ⓐ Ⓑ Ⓒ Ⓓ Ⓔ
10 Ⓐ Ⓑ Ⓒ Ⓓ Ⓔ 30 Ⓐ Ⓑ Ⓒ Ⓓ Ⓔ 50 Ⓐ Ⓑ Ⓒ Ⓓ Ⓔ 70 Ⓐ Ⓑ Ⓒ Ⓓ Ⓔ 90 Ⓐ Ⓑ Ⓒ Ⓓ Ⓔ 110 Ⓐ Ⓑ Ⓒ Ⓓ Ⓔ 130 Ⓐ Ⓑ Ⓒ Ⓓ Ⓔ

MODEL TEST 2

Time allotted—35 minutes

Directions

Each question has four suggested answers. Decide which one is the best answer. Find the question number on the Answer Sheet. Show your answer to the question by darkening completely the square corresponding to the letter of your answer. Keep your mark within the space. If you have to erase a mark, be sure to erase it completely. Mark only one answer for each question. Do NOT mark space E for any question.

Word Meaning

1. *Criterion* means most nearly
   A) armor   C) soldier
   B) standard   D) fuel

2. *Slothful* means most nearly
   A) three-toed   C) lazy
   B) intermittent   D) ghostly

3. *Queasy* means most nearly
   A) nauseous   C) quiet
   B) enthusiastic   D) reliable

4. To *interject* means most nearly to
   A) upset   C) interrupt
   B) hint   D) fear

5. To *renounce* means most nearly to
   A) give up   C) enjoy
   B) remember   D) rectify

Analogies

6. TEETH is related to CHEW as NOSE is related to
   A) sweet   C) center
   B) smell   D) nostril

7. BAT is related to BASEBALL as DRUMSTICK is related to
   A) instrument   C) band leader
   B) triangle   D) drum

8. WOOD is related to GLASS as PAPER is related to
   A) cellophane   C) ripped
   B) page   D) book

9. STENOGRAPHER is related to WORDS as ACCOUNTANT is related to
   A) typist   C) numbers
   B) letters   D) terms

Grammar

10. A) Whomever reviews last month's financial statements must conclude that the company is in trouble.
    B) With a review of financial statements, one must conclude that it is all the better to see that the company is in trouble.
    C) A review of last month's financial statements suggests that the company is in trouble.
    D) The review of last month's financial statements should be referred to whomever will review it thoroughly.

11. A) The hazy ideas and concepts presented in the presentation were vague and indefinite.
    B) The presenter presented hazy ideas and concepts in a vague and indefinite way.
    C) Hazy ideas and concepts were presented only vaguely, and without definitions.
    D) The ideas presented were vague.

Spelling

12. A) rediculous   C) ridiculus
    B) ridiculious   D) none of these

13. A) pronunciation   C) pronunction
    B) pronounciation   D) none of these

14. A) desireable   C) desirable
    B) disireable   D) none of these

15. A) judgment   C) jugdment
    B) judgemint   D) none of these

Reading

16. Most college graduates do not pursue a career relevant to their college major. Part of the reason for this is a fast-changing job market, which creates new jobs and job categories, and eliminates old jobs and job categories, at such a rapid pace that college training in a particular area may become obsolete very quickly.

The paragraph best supports the statement that a student entering college today
- A) will encounter a much-changed job market when she graduates
- B) will be unable to find a job when she graduates
- C) will need to create a new job for herself, taking account of the old jobs that have been eliminated
- D) should not pursue a major that is not relevant to the future job market

17. The past is the mirror of the present. By studying history we encounter the same general problems that cultures and societies face today, and we learn possible solutions to those problems. We may also learn that some problems can never be absolutely solved.

The paragraph best supports the statement that history
- A) always provides the necessary solutions to modern social problems
- B) makes the solution of modern problems even more difficult
- C) is a source of solutions that may be used to address problems in modern times
- D) does not necessarily repeat itself

18. *Orifice* means most nearly
- A) building
- B) protrusion
- C) opening
- D) allowance

19. *Morose* means most nearly
- A) gloomy
- B) sprawling
- C) dissolved
- D) large

20. To *impede* means most nearly to
- A) instruct
- B) construct
- C) obstruct
- D) assume

21. *Fickle* means most nearly
- A) pretty
- B) sour
- C) changeable
- D) redolent

22. To *enthrall* means most nearly to
- A) tease
- B) test
- C) captivate
- D) require

23. COTTON is related to SOFT as WOOL is related to
- A) sheep
- B) warm
- C) expensive
- D) light

24. SMOKE is related to CHIMNEY as LIQUID is related to
- A) funnel
- B) ocean
- C) glass
- D) water

25. ATHLETE is related to ROOKIE as MOVIE is related to
- A) screening
- B) premiere
- C) award
- D) cancelation

26. PENDULUM is related to SWING as GYROSCOPE is related to
- A) stop
- B) measure
- C) spin
- D) boat

27.
- A) Because she demanded immediate improvement, the manager warned her that dismissal was a possibility.
- B) Demanding immediate improvement, the manager threatened her with dismissal.
- C) The manager threatened her with immediate improvement in mind.
- D) Because she demanded immediate improvement, she warned her that dismissal was a possibility.

28.
- A) Regulations must be enforced all the farther if they are to be effective.
- B) The farther enforcement of regulations will guarantee their effectiveness.
- C) Going farther with the enforcement of regulations guarantees farther effectiveness.
- D) Stronger enforcement will make the regulations more effective.

29.
- A) separate
- B) seperate
- C) seprate
- D) none of these

30.
- A) publically
- B) publicly
- C) publickally
- D) none of these

31.
- A) accomadate
- B) accomodate
- C) accommodate
- D) none of these

32.
- A) calander
- B) calendar
- C) calender
- D) none of these

33. Perhaps it is true, as the old saying goes, that knowledge is power. But sometimes knowledge brings pain rather than power: the more we learn and the more we read, the more we realize that the world is filled with violence and corruption. This knowledge may leave us feeling more powerless than powerful.

The paragraph best supports the statement that knowledge

A) may be possible only after violence and corruption are eliminated forever
B) is mainly the result of reading about violence and corruption
C) may not lead to power
D) really exists only in old sayings, and is rarely available from any other source

34. Office procedures are not inflexible. Although each employee has been assigned specific tasks to be performed at specific times, all must be sensitive to the needs and problems of others and help out whenever necessary. In order to be ready to help, everyone is advised to become familiar with the jobs and responsibilities of others, to become as skilled as possible in as many different tasks as possible.

The paragraph best supports the statement that
A) assisting coworkers is important and desirable
B) most employees are not willing to help one another
C) some employees are more skilled than others
D) learning many different tasks is difficult

35. *Dubious* means most nearly
   A) doubtful   C) long
   B) retired   D) dumb

36. *Ungainly* means most nearly
   A) bankrupt   C) not permanent
   B) swollen   D) awkward

37. To *lampoon* means most nearly to
   A) spear   C) ridicule
   B) harvest   D) light

38. To *fritter* means most nearly to
   A) waste   C) allow
   B) cook   D) seal

39. To *coerce* means most nearly to
   A) rely   C) force
   B) think over   D) agree

40. CHOREOGRAPHER is related to BALLET as INVENTOR is related to
   A) laboratory   C) electricity
   B) machine   D) imagination

41. BASEMENT is related to ATTIC as VALLEY is related to
   A) plateau   C) mountaintop
   B) crevasse   D) pasture

42. BOOK is related to LIBRARY as WHEAT is related to
   A) granary   C) food
   B) bread   D) milk

43. BUST is related to SCULPTOR as PLAY is related to
   A) playground   C) dramatist
   B) worker   D) entertainer

44. A) Merlo's Gift Shop and Nat's Novelty Store sells gifts created by local artists.
    B) Gifts created to local artists are sold in both Merlo's Gift Shop and Nat's Novelty Store.
    C) Merlo's and Nat's, selling gifts created by local artists.
    D) Merlo's Gift Shop and Nat's Novelty Store sell gifts created by local artists.

45. A) The office manager hired the most experienced of the two candidates who applied for a clerical position.
    B) Deciding experientially on who was better prepared clerically, the office manager decided to choose between two candidates.
    C) Primarily interested in the candidate with more experience, the office manager hired her for the new clerical position.
    D) With a clerical position in mind requiring experience, the decision was for the office manager.

46. A) curtale   C) certail
    B) curtail   D) none of these

47. A) bribery   C) bribary
    B) bribury   D) none of these

48. A) tommorow   C) tommorrow
    B) tomorrow   D) none of these

49. A) maneuver   C) manuver
    B) manuever   D) none of these

50. With expert clerical assistance, a business executive is free to concentrate on important issues and decisions, and can rely on the staff to give expert attention to correspondence, bookkeeping, and appointments. Without expert

clerical assistance, an executive must compromise her talents and her time. Clearly, it is the clerical staff that allows any executive to be an executive; a talented staff guarantees that business will thrive.

The paragraph best supports the statement that expert attention to correspondence, bookkeeping, and appointments
A) utilizes the talents and time of some business executives
B) leaves the staff free to concentrate on other issues
C) are tasks that all executives should master
D) are best accomplished by a talented staff

51. In most cases, prefer active verbs to passive verbs. A sentence such as "The salaries were raised by the board of directors," should be revised to read, "The board of directors raised the salaries." In this case, and in so many others, the active construction results in a more economical statement, one that is understood more quickly and clearly. Of course, passive constructions cannot and should not be discarded altogether.

The paragraph best supports the statement that passive constructions
A) will be thought incorrect by most readers
B) are useful at times
C) can be understood more clearly than active constructions
D) must always be revised

52. *Frigid* means most nearly
A) white   C) cold
B) smart   D) thick

53. *Bloated* means most nearly
A) shipwrecked C) swollen
B) hollow   D) embalmed

54. To *relish* means most nearly to
A) anger   C) protest
B) enjoy   D) upset

55. *Ailing* means most nearly
A) affected   C) ill
B) disordered   D) worn

56. *Cognizant* means most nearly
A) aware   C) hardy
B) wheeling   D) terminal

57. FLOWER is related to GARDEN as TREE is related to
A) stump   C) weeds
B) orchard   D) branches

58. SHEEP is related to WOOL as GOOSE is related to
A) gander   C) down
B) flock   D) beak

59. BLEEDING is related to TOURNIQUET as TRAFFIC is related to
A) green light C) automobile
B) red light   D) detour

60. FOOD is related to FASTING as EXERCISE is related to
A) conditioning C) resting
B) warming up   D) stretching

61. A) In order to cut expenses, the supervisor must decide whether to reduce the workload, lay off several employees, or forbid private use of the duplicating machine.
B) Reducing the workload, laying off several employees, or to forbid private use of the duplicating machine were several options open to the supervisor cutting employees.
C) Reduced workload, or employees, or no private duplication crossed the mind of the supervisor cutting expenses.
D) The supervisor thought about several ways to cut expenses: workload, employee reduction, or in the area of duplication.

62. A) Having been promoted suddenly, the board of directors extended their congratulations to the new vice-president.
B) The board of directors congratulated the new vice-president on his sudden promotion.
C) To the new vice-president, with promotion so sudden, the board of directors congratulated him.
D) The board of directors will have had congratulated the new vice-president after his sudden promotion.

63. A) histeria   C) hystaria
B) hysteria   D) none of these

64. A) misconseption C) misconception
B) misconcepsion D) none of these

65. A) disburce   C) disburse
     B) disberse   D) none of these

66. A) revinue   C) revenew
     B) revenue   D) none of these

67. County clerks, who issue marriage licenses and retain records of confidential marriages, have reported numerous abuses of the confidential marriage law. In San Diego, for instance, the Immigration and Naturalization Service has found that illegal aliens take advantage of the law's privacy to wed citizens they may never have met, in order to gain legal residency status.

The paragraph best supports the statement that the confidential marriage law
A) can be abused by illegal aliens who want to become legal residents
B) is often abused by the county clerks who issue marriage licenses
C) is used by illegal aliens to marry citizens outside the United States
D) privately issues licenses and records of marriage

68. By investing $10 million in the shuttle salvage operation, underwriters for the Palapa and Westar now have a chance to recover some of the $100 million they paid to the Indonesian government and to Western Union after the satellite launch fizzled last February.

The paragraph best supports the statement that the salvage operation
A) was a failure last February
B) will earn $100 million from the Indonesian government
C) may help reduce the losses incurred by the underwriters
D) will recover $100 million paid by Western Union

69. *Compunction* means most nearly
A) remorse   C) grammar
B) timely   D) gall

70. *Mundane* means most nearly
A) commonplace   C) religious
B) awkward   D) formidable

71. *Verbatim* means most nearly
A) babbling   C) word-for-word
B) argument   D) enticing

72. *Unequivocal* means most nearly
A) clear   C) mute
B) advantageous   D) mistaken

73. *Clemency* means most nearly
A) redundancy   C) leniency
B) illumination   D) tendency

74. HAIR is related to HEAD as NAIL is related to
A) hammer   C) arm
B) finger   D) cut

75. FENCE is related to YARD as BRACELET is related to
A) wrist   C) neck
B) ring   D) belt

76. SOLDIER is related to BARRACKS as ESKIMO is related to
A) Iceland   C) snow
B) arctic   D) igloo

77. SOCKET is related to PLUG as HOLE is related to
A) peg   C) shovel
B) pencil   D) axe

78. A) Promising a bright future, and to celebrate a wonderful past, the Hardy Company awarded each of its employees a bonus.
B) To promise a bright future and a wonderful past, the Hardy Company awarded each of its employees a bonus.
C) The future bright and the past wonderful, the bonus awarded to each of the Hardy Company employees.
D) The Hardy Company awarded each of its employees a bonus, promising them a bright future and thanking them for a wonderful past.

79. A) The lunch he ordered tasted better than the coworkers.
B) The lunch he ordered tasted better than the others' lunches.
C) The lunch he ordered tasted better than the coworkers lunching.
D) Lunching with the coworkers, the one he ordered tasted best.

80. A) modren   C) modern
B) modurn   D) none of these

81. A) aparatis   C) apparatus
B) aparatus   D) none of these

82. A) sumation   C) summation
    B) summashun   D) none of these

83. A) forein   C) foriegn
    B) foreign   D) none of these

84. With the growing popularity of radio talk shows, it becomes possible to spend most of the day listening to interesting conversations on a variety of significant topics, even while working at a solitary job. Listening to music all day may not be nearly as rewarding or informative.

The paragraph best supports the statement that listening to music
A) has become a popular alternative to listening to talk shows
B) is never as interesting as participating in a conversation
C) may be less preferable than listing to radio talk shows
D) makes it impossible to listen to radio talk shows

85. Those who have difficulty reading are usually those who have not read much. The habit of reading is probably instilled during childhood; those children with parents who like to read also tend to acquire a fondness for books. Adults who have never learned to like reading are likely to avoid it.

The paragraph best supports the statement that those who have avoided reading during childhood
A) will probably not find reading easier as they get older
B) will transmit a hateful attitude toward books and reading to their children
C) were probably kept from reading by their parents
D) did so only because interesting reading material was not made available by their parents

ANSWER KEY FOR MODEL TEST 2

Word Meaning

1. B	18. C	35. A	52. C	69. A
2. C	19. A	36. D	53. C	70. A
3. A	20. C	37. C	54. B	71. C
4. C	21. C	38. A	55. C	72. A
5. A	22. C	39. C	56. A	73. C

Analogies

6. B	23. B	40. B	57. B	74. B
7. D	24. A	41. C	58. C	75. A
8. A	25. B	42. A	59. B	76. D
9. C	26. C	43. C	60. C	77. A

Grammar

10. C	27. B	44. D	61. A	78. D
11. D	28. D	45. C	62. B	79. B

Spelling

12. D	29. A	46. B	63. B	80. C
13. A	30. B	47. A	64. C	81. C
14. C	31. C	48. B	65. C	82. C
15. A	32. B	49. A	66. B	83. B

Reading

16. A	33. C	50. D	67. A	84. C
17. C	34. A	51. B	68. C	85. A

ANALYSIS CHART FOR MODEL TEST 2

Now that you've corrected your exam, use the following chart to carefully analyze your results and spot your strengths and weaknesses. This analysis should help you focus your study and review efforts.

Section	Total Number of Questions	Number Correct	Number Incorrect	Number Unanswered*
Word Meaning	25			
Analogies	20			
Grammar	10			
Spelling	20			
Reading Comprehension	10			
TOTAL	85			

*Since there is no penalty for incorrect answers on the Verbal Abilities Test, you should have left no question unanswered. Even if you didn't have time to answer a question, at least you should have filled in the answer space with a guess.

ANSWER EXPLANATIONS FOR MODEL TEST 2

1. **(B)** standard
2. **(C)** lazy
3. **(A)** nauseous
4. **(C)** interrupt
5. **(A)** give up

6. **(B)** The second word is the action of the first word.
7. **(D)** The first word hits the second word.
8. **(A)** The second word has clear, "see-through" qualities, differentiating it from the first word.
9. **(C)** The first word works professionally with the second word.
10. **(C)** In (A), "whomever" is incorrect; "who-ever" would be correct. In (B), "all the bet-ter" is an incorrect expression. In (D), "whomever" should be "whoever."
11. **(D)** Each of the other choices is repetitious; for instance, "vague" repeats unnecessarily the meaning of "hazy."
12. **(D)** Correct spelling: ridiculous
13. **(A)** pronunciation
14. **(C)** desirable
15. **(A)** judgment
16. **(A)** The passage stresses the "fast-changing job market."
17. **(C)** The passage stresses the similarity be-tween the "general problems" of the past and those of the present, but does not suggest that the study of history will answer all questions or solve all problems.
18. **(C)** opening
19. **(A)** gloomy
20. **(C)** obstruct
21. **(C)** changeable
22. **(C)** captivate
23. **(B)** The second word is a quality of the first word.
24. **(A)** The first word travels through the sec-ond word.
25. **(B)** The second word is the initial introduc-tion of the first word.
26. **(C)** The second word is the movement of the first word.
27. **(B)** In both (A) and (D), the reference of "her" and of "she" is vague. In (C), the mean-ing of "in mind" is not clear.
28. **(D)** "All the farther" and "farther" are incor-rect in each of the other choices; "further" would be a better choice in all three cases.
29. **(A)** separate
30. **(B)** publicly
31. **(C)** accommodate
32. **(B)** calendar
33. **(C)** The passage states that having knowl-edge may leave the holder of such knowledge feeling "more powerless than powerful."
34. **(A)** None of the other choices is supported by information in the paragraph. (A) repeats the overall point of the paragraph.

35. **(A)** doubtful
36. **(D)** awkward
37. **(C)** ridicule
38. **(A)** waste
39. **(C)** force
40. **(B)** The first word creates the second word.
41. **(C)** The first word is at the bottom; the sec-ond word is at the top.
42. **(A)** The first word is stored in the second word.
43. **(C)** The second word creates the first word.
44. **(D)** In (A), the subject of the sentence is plu-ral, so the verb should be plural, "sell" in-stead of "sells." In (B), "to" should be "by." (C) is not a complete sentence.
45. **(C)** In (A), the correct phrase for comparing two people is "more experienced" rather than "most experienced." In (B), "experien-tially" improperly refers to the office man-ager. (D) is vague and illogical, saying that the decision had a mind and that the clerical po-sition was given to the office manager!
46. **(B)** curtail
47. **(A)** bribery
48. **(B)** tomorrow
49. **(A)** maneuver
50. **(D)** This choice restates the overall point of the paragraph.
51. **(B)** The final sentence states that "passive constructions . . . should not be discarded al-together" and thus implies that passive con-structions are useful at times.
52. **(C)** cold
53. **(C)** swollen
54. **(B)** enjoy
55. **(C)** ill
56. **(A)** aware
57. **(B)** The first word grows in the second word.
58. **(C)** The second word covers the first word.
59. **(B)** The second word stops the flow of the first word.
60. **(C)** The second word is the opposite of the first word.
61. **(A)** In (B), "to forbid" should be "forbid-ding" (so that it is parallel with "reducing" and "laying"). Both (C) and (D) are incom-plete and unclear.
62. **(B)** In both (A) and (C), the sentence struc-ture is awkward and unclear. Also in (A), the board of directors seems to have been pro-moted. In (D), "will have had congratulated" is an incorrect verb; "congratulated" alone would be sufficient here.
63. **(B)** hysteria
64. **(C)** misconception

65. **(C)** disburse
66. **(B)** revenue
67. **(A)** The passage states that illegal aliens take advantage of the law "in order to gain legal residency status."
68. **(C)** The paragraph states that the underwriters "now have a chance to recover" some of the money they lost because of the failed launch.
69. **(A)** remorse
70. **(A)** commonplace
71. **(C)** word-for-word
72. **(A)** clear
73. **(C)** leniency
74. **(B)** The first word grows out of the second word.
75. **(A)** The second word encircles the first word.
76. **(D)** The second word is the structure in which the first word lives.
77. **(A)** The second word fits into the first word.

78. **(D)** In (A), "to celebrate" should be "celebrating," parallel to "promising." Choice (B) is illogical: one cannot *promise* a "wonderful past." (C) is not a complete sentence.
79. **(B)** Choices (A) and (C) compare the taste of lunch with the taste of coworkers. In (D), "one" appears to refer to "coworkers."
80. **(C)** modern
81. **(C)** apparatus
82. **(C)** summation
83. **(B)** foreign
84. **(C)** The paragraph states that listening to music "may not be nearly as rewarding or informative" as listening to radio talk shows.
85. **(A)** The paragraph reveals that children who have not read much will probably become adults who avoid reading and have difficulty reading. Each of the other choices makes assumptions about parents that are not expressed or implied in the paragraph.

ANSWER SHEET

SIGNATURE: _____
(Please Sign)

EXAMINATION TITLE: _____

PLACE OF EXAMINATION: _____

City _____ State _____

TODAY'S DATE: _____

SAMPLE Ⓐ ● Ⓒ Ⓓ Ⓔ

DIRECTIONS FOR MARKING ANSWER SHEET

Use only a **No. 2 (or softer) lead pencil**. Darken completely the circle corresponding to your answer. You **must** keep your mark within the circle. Stray marks may be counted as errors. Erase **completely** all marks except your answer.

SAMPLE NAME GRID

M.I. | A
F.I. | C
LAST NAME | M C C A B E

1. In the boxes below, **PRINT** your name. Print only as many letters as will fit within the areas for the last name, first initial (F.I.), and middle initial (M.I.). Below each box, darken the circle containing the same letter. SEE SAMPLE NAME GRID

LAST NAME

F.I.

M.I.

2. In the boxes below, enter your 9-digit Social Security Number. Below each box, darken the circle in each column corresponding to the number you have entered.

SOCIAL SECURITY NUMBER

3. OCCUPATIONAL GROUP NUMBER

SECTION 1

PART

TEST SERIES

TEST NUMBER

Make no marks or entries in the columns to the right until you receive instructions from the administrator.

1 Ⓐ Ⓑ Ⓒ Ⓓ Ⓔ
2 Ⓐ Ⓑ Ⓒ Ⓓ Ⓔ
3 Ⓐ Ⓑ Ⓒ Ⓓ Ⓔ
4 Ⓐ Ⓑ Ⓒ Ⓓ Ⓔ
5 Ⓐ Ⓑ Ⓒ Ⓓ Ⓔ
6 Ⓐ Ⓑ Ⓒ Ⓓ Ⓔ
7 Ⓐ Ⓑ Ⓒ Ⓓ Ⓔ
8 Ⓐ Ⓑ Ⓒ Ⓓ Ⓔ
9 Ⓐ Ⓑ Ⓒ Ⓓ Ⓔ
10 Ⓐ Ⓑ Ⓒ Ⓓ Ⓔ
11 Ⓐ Ⓑ Ⓒ Ⓓ Ⓔ
12 Ⓐ Ⓑ Ⓒ Ⓓ Ⓔ
13 Ⓐ Ⓑ Ⓒ Ⓓ Ⓔ
14 Ⓐ Ⓑ Ⓒ Ⓓ Ⓔ
15 Ⓐ Ⓑ Ⓒ Ⓓ Ⓔ
16 Ⓐ Ⓑ Ⓒ Ⓓ Ⓔ
17 Ⓐ Ⓑ Ⓒ Ⓓ Ⓔ
18 Ⓐ Ⓑ Ⓒ Ⓓ Ⓔ
19 Ⓐ Ⓑ Ⓒ Ⓓ Ⓔ
20 Ⓐ Ⓑ Ⓒ Ⓓ Ⓔ
21 Ⓐ Ⓑ Ⓒ Ⓓ Ⓔ
22 Ⓐ Ⓑ Ⓒ Ⓓ Ⓔ
23 Ⓐ Ⓑ Ⓒ Ⓓ Ⓔ
24 Ⓐ Ⓑ Ⓒ Ⓓ Ⓔ
25 Ⓐ Ⓑ Ⓒ Ⓓ Ⓔ
26 Ⓐ Ⓑ Ⓒ Ⓓ Ⓔ
27 Ⓐ Ⓑ Ⓒ Ⓓ Ⓔ
28 Ⓐ Ⓑ Ⓒ Ⓓ Ⓔ
29 Ⓐ Ⓑ Ⓒ Ⓓ Ⓔ
30 Ⓐ Ⓑ Ⓒ Ⓓ Ⓔ
31 Ⓐ Ⓑ Ⓒ Ⓓ Ⓔ
32 Ⓐ Ⓑ Ⓒ Ⓓ Ⓔ
33 Ⓐ Ⓑ Ⓒ Ⓓ Ⓔ
34 Ⓐ Ⓑ Ⓒ Ⓓ Ⓔ
35 Ⓐ Ⓑ Ⓒ Ⓓ Ⓔ
36 Ⓐ Ⓑ Ⓒ Ⓓ Ⓔ
37 Ⓐ Ⓑ Ⓒ Ⓓ Ⓔ
38 Ⓐ Ⓑ Ⓒ Ⓓ Ⓔ
39 Ⓐ Ⓑ Ⓒ Ⓓ Ⓔ
40 Ⓐ Ⓑ Ⓒ Ⓓ Ⓔ
41 Ⓐ Ⓑ Ⓒ Ⓓ Ⓔ
42 Ⓐ Ⓑ Ⓒ Ⓓ Ⓔ
43 Ⓐ Ⓑ Ⓒ Ⓓ Ⓔ
44 Ⓐ Ⓑ Ⓒ Ⓓ Ⓔ
45 Ⓐ Ⓑ Ⓒ Ⓓ Ⓔ
46 Ⓐ Ⓑ Ⓒ Ⓓ Ⓔ
47 Ⓐ Ⓑ Ⓒ Ⓓ Ⓔ
48 Ⓐ Ⓑ Ⓒ Ⓓ Ⓔ
49 Ⓐ Ⓑ Ⓒ Ⓓ Ⓔ
50 Ⓐ Ⓑ Ⓒ Ⓓ Ⓔ
51 Ⓐ Ⓑ Ⓒ Ⓓ Ⓔ
52 Ⓐ Ⓑ Ⓒ Ⓓ Ⓔ
53 Ⓐ Ⓑ Ⓒ Ⓓ Ⓔ
54 Ⓐ Ⓑ Ⓒ Ⓓ Ⓔ
55 Ⓐ Ⓑ Ⓒ Ⓓ Ⓔ
56 Ⓐ Ⓑ Ⓒ Ⓓ Ⓔ
57 Ⓐ Ⓑ Ⓒ Ⓓ Ⓔ
58 Ⓐ Ⓑ Ⓒ Ⓓ Ⓔ
59 Ⓐ Ⓑ Ⓒ Ⓓ Ⓔ
60 Ⓐ Ⓑ Ⓒ Ⓓ Ⓔ
61 Ⓐ Ⓑ Ⓒ Ⓓ Ⓔ
62 Ⓐ Ⓑ Ⓒ Ⓓ Ⓔ
63 Ⓐ Ⓑ Ⓒ Ⓓ Ⓔ
64 Ⓐ Ⓑ Ⓒ Ⓓ Ⓔ
65 Ⓐ Ⓑ Ⓒ Ⓓ Ⓔ
66 Ⓐ Ⓑ Ⓒ Ⓓ Ⓔ
67 Ⓐ Ⓑ Ⓒ Ⓓ Ⓔ
68 Ⓐ Ⓑ Ⓒ Ⓓ Ⓔ
69 Ⓐ Ⓑ Ⓒ Ⓓ Ⓔ
70 Ⓐ Ⓑ Ⓒ Ⓓ Ⓔ
71 Ⓐ Ⓑ Ⓒ Ⓓ Ⓔ
72 Ⓐ Ⓑ Ⓒ Ⓓ Ⓔ
73 Ⓐ Ⓑ Ⓒ Ⓓ Ⓔ
74 Ⓐ Ⓑ Ⓒ Ⓓ Ⓔ
75 Ⓐ Ⓑ Ⓒ Ⓓ Ⓔ
76 Ⓐ Ⓑ Ⓒ Ⓓ Ⓔ
77 Ⓐ Ⓑ Ⓒ Ⓓ Ⓔ
78 Ⓐ Ⓑ Ⓒ Ⓓ Ⓔ
79 Ⓐ Ⓑ Ⓒ Ⓓ Ⓔ
80 Ⓐ Ⓑ Ⓒ Ⓓ Ⓔ
81 Ⓐ Ⓑ Ⓒ Ⓓ Ⓔ
82 Ⓐ Ⓑ Ⓒ Ⓓ Ⓔ
83 Ⓐ Ⓑ Ⓒ Ⓓ Ⓔ
84 Ⓐ Ⓑ Ⓒ Ⓓ Ⓔ
85 Ⓐ Ⓑ Ⓒ Ⓓ Ⓔ
86 Ⓐ Ⓑ Ⓒ Ⓓ Ⓔ
87 Ⓐ Ⓑ Ⓒ Ⓓ Ⓔ
88 Ⓐ Ⓑ Ⓒ Ⓓ Ⓔ
89 Ⓐ Ⓑ Ⓒ Ⓓ Ⓔ
90 Ⓐ Ⓑ Ⓒ Ⓓ Ⓔ
91 Ⓐ Ⓑ Ⓒ Ⓓ Ⓔ
92 Ⓐ Ⓑ Ⓒ Ⓓ Ⓔ
93 Ⓐ Ⓑ Ⓒ Ⓓ Ⓔ
94 Ⓐ Ⓑ Ⓒ Ⓓ Ⓔ
95 Ⓐ Ⓑ Ⓒ Ⓓ Ⓔ
96 Ⓐ Ⓑ Ⓒ Ⓓ Ⓔ
97 Ⓐ Ⓑ Ⓒ Ⓓ Ⓔ
98 Ⓐ Ⓑ Ⓒ Ⓓ Ⓔ
99 Ⓐ Ⓑ Ⓒ Ⓓ Ⓔ
100 Ⓐ Ⓑ Ⓒ Ⓓ Ⓔ
101 Ⓐ Ⓑ Ⓒ Ⓓ Ⓔ
102 Ⓐ Ⓑ Ⓒ Ⓓ Ⓔ
103 Ⓐ Ⓑ Ⓒ Ⓓ Ⓔ
104 Ⓐ Ⓑ Ⓒ Ⓓ Ⓔ
105 Ⓐ Ⓑ Ⓒ Ⓓ Ⓔ
106 Ⓐ Ⓑ Ⓒ Ⓓ Ⓔ
107 Ⓐ Ⓑ Ⓒ Ⓓ Ⓔ
108 Ⓐ Ⓑ Ⓒ Ⓓ Ⓔ
109 Ⓐ Ⓑ Ⓒ Ⓓ Ⓔ
110 Ⓐ Ⓑ Ⓒ Ⓓ Ⓔ
111 Ⓐ Ⓑ Ⓒ Ⓓ Ⓔ
112 Ⓐ Ⓑ Ⓒ Ⓓ Ⓔ
113 Ⓐ Ⓑ Ⓒ Ⓓ Ⓔ
114 Ⓐ Ⓑ Ⓒ Ⓓ Ⓔ
115 Ⓐ Ⓑ Ⓒ Ⓓ Ⓔ
116 Ⓐ Ⓑ Ⓒ Ⓓ Ⓔ
117 Ⓐ Ⓑ Ⓒ Ⓓ Ⓔ
118 Ⓐ Ⓑ Ⓒ Ⓓ Ⓔ
119 Ⓐ Ⓑ Ⓒ Ⓓ Ⓔ
120 Ⓐ Ⓑ Ⓒ Ⓓ Ⓔ
121 Ⓐ Ⓑ Ⓒ Ⓓ Ⓔ
122 Ⓐ Ⓑ Ⓒ Ⓓ Ⓔ
123 Ⓐ Ⓑ Ⓒ Ⓓ Ⓔ
124 Ⓐ Ⓑ Ⓒ Ⓓ Ⓔ
125 Ⓐ Ⓑ Ⓒ Ⓓ Ⓔ
126 Ⓐ Ⓑ Ⓒ Ⓓ Ⓔ
127 Ⓐ Ⓑ Ⓒ Ⓓ Ⓔ
128 Ⓐ Ⓑ Ⓒ Ⓓ Ⓔ
129 Ⓐ Ⓑ Ⓒ Ⓓ Ⓔ
130 Ⓐ Ⓑ Ⓒ Ⓓ Ⓔ

MODEL TEST 3

Time allotted—35 minutes

Directions

Each question has four suggested answers. Decide which one is the best answer. Find the question number on the Answer Sheet. Show your answer to the question by darkening completely the space corresponding to the letter of your answer. Keep your mark within the space. If you have to erase a mark, be sure to erase it completely. Mark only one answer for each question. Do NOT mark space E for any question.

Word Meaning

1. *Harried* means most nearly
   - A) rapid
   - B) disturbed
   - C) rushed
   - D) distant

2. To *scald* means most nearly to
   - A) climb
   - B) censure
   - C) raise
   - D) burn

3. To *decipher* means most nearly to
   - A) translate
   - B) number
   - C) funnel
   - D) determine

4. *Rationale* means most nearly
   - A) motive
   - B) emotion
   - C) reality
   - D) amount

5. *Antidote* means most nearly
   - A) joke
   - B) hospital
   - C) cure
   - D) story

Analogies

6. BANK is related to MONEY as ARMORY is related to
   - A) iron
   - B) coins
   - C) ammunition
   - D) soldiers

7. ADOLESCENCE is related to YOUNGSTER as MATURITY is related to
   - A) adult
   - B) child
   - C) teenager
   - D) corpse

8. CRIME is related to WITNESS as EVENT is related to
   - A) police
   - B) judge
   - C) spectator
   - D) stadium

9. BOTTLE is related to CORK as POT is related to
   - A) pan
   - B) handle
   - C) stove
   - D) lid

Grammar

Decide which sentence is preferable with respect to grammar and usage suitable for a formal letter or report.

10. A) All of them decided it would not be as good for the girls to stay home rather than go to the party.
    B) The girls all decided it would be best to stay at home rather to go to the party.
    C) All the girls decided it would be better to stay home than to go to the party.
    D) To stay home instead of going to the party was decided to be the best according to all the girls.

11. A) When a person reads the instructions, they should remember to follow directions as complete as possible.
    B) When reading the instructions, a person should follow directions as completely as possible.
    C) Following directions as completely as possible, a person reading the instructions.
    D) Remember when reading instructions and following directions as completely as possible.

Spelling

Find the correct spelling of the word and darken the proper answer space. If no suggested spelling is correct, darken space D.

12. A) juvenil
    B) juvanile
    C) juvinil
    D) none of these

13. A) drapht
    B) draft
    C) draph
    D) none of these

14. A) defence
    B) defense
    C) defensce
    D) none of these

15. A) territorrial
    B) teritorial
    C) territorial
    D) none of these

Reading

16. Noting that drug abuse has increased markedly since the 1960s, we must ask why. Put simply, people use drugs because the complexity and difficulty of modern life is simply overwhelming, and the temptation to escape from it all with cocaine is often impossible to resist.

The paragraph best supports the statement that cocaine

A) are difficult to recognize in one's own writing

B) are only apparent to professional editors who are not writers

C) are not usually a problem for an editor reading her own writing

D) must be pointed out before they are recognized

17. The ability to recognize grammar and usage errors in the writing of others is not the same as the ability to see such errors in one's own writing. Often a writer is not aware of his own errors until they are pointed out by a good editor.

The paragraph best supports the statement that errors in grammar and usage

A) are difficult to recognize in one's own writing

B) are only apparent to professional editors who are not writers

C) are not usually a problem for an editor reading her own writing

D) must be pointed out before they are recognized

18. *Hindrance* means most nearly
A) secret   C) aid
B) obstacle   D) medication

19. To *pacify* means most nearly to
A) cross   C) placate
B) attempt   D) conceal

20. *Maxim* means most nearly
A) amount   C) giant
B) proverb   D) poison

21. *Cavity* means most nearly
A) quill   C) sting
B) decay   D) hole

22. *Torrid* means most nearly
A) slow   C) fearful
B) hot   D) determined

23. PRESCRIPTION is related to PHARMACIST as BLUEPRINT is related to
A) builder   C) landlord
B) architect   D) tenant

24. GUILT is related to INNOCENCE as VICE is related to
A) crime   C) sin
B) punishment   D) virtue

25. ZOO is related to ANIMAL as GALLERY is related to
A) patrons   C) art
B) guards   D) building

26. CLOCK is related to HOUR as CALENDAR is related to
A) minute   C) month
B) hour   D) June

27. A) Be sure to double check your ticket location to make certain you are in the proper seat.
B) To make sure you are in the proper seat, double checking your ticket location is to be done.
C) Making certain you are in the proper seat, your ticket is to be double checked.
D) To double check your ticket location and to be certain you are in the proper seat.

28. A) Whatever he does or doesn't do, it's for sure that he really truly enjoys his work.
B) Depending on what he does or doesn't do, he sure likes his work.
C) Not mattering what he does or doesn't do, he enjoys his work.
D) Whatever he does or doesn't do, he at least enjoys his work.

29. A) tolerence   C) tolerance
B) tollerance   D) none of these

30. A) tommorrow   C) tomorrow
B) tommorow   D) none of these

31. A) lightening   C) litening
B) lightning   D) none of these

32. A) likeable   C) likible
B) likable   D) none of these

33. Since 1890, the federal government and the states have passed a number of laws against corrupt political practices. But today many feel that political corruption is a regular occurrence, and deeply mistrust their public leaders.

The paragraph best supports the statement that many citizens

A) are not in favor of laws against corrupt political practices
B) changed their attitude toward political corruption after 1890
C) think that their political leaders are probably corrupt
D) are even more corrupt than their political leaders

34. People who easily adapt themselves to different social situations, who mingle easily with many different personalities, might be compared to the chameleon, that lizard who changes color to match the environment.

The paragraph best supports the statement that

A) it is possible to compare people with animals
B) adaptable people tend to resemble reptiles
C) the chameleon is a very social animal
D) the ability to change color is not limited to the chameleon

35. *Garish* means most nearly
A) gaudy   C) worthless
B) decorative   D) abundant

36. *Regal* means most nearly
A) normal   C) young
B) immense   D) kingly

37. *Occult* means most nearly
A) youthful   C) swift
B) mysterious   D) fraudulent

38. *Parody* means most nearly
A) spoof   C) flock
B) equality   D) trap

39. To *beckon* means most nearly
A) desire   C) delight
B) reverse   D) summon

40. SAILBOAT is related to WIND as BICYCLE is related to
A) feet   C) road
B) wheels   D) chain

41. BLUNDER is related to MISCUE as PRECISION is related to
A) error   C) slang
B) accuracy   D) illusion

42. HORSE is related to STABLE as TENANT is related to
A) city   C) apartment
B) landlord   D) lease

43. RECIPE is related to INGREDIENTS as CAST is related to
A) play   C) arm
B) stage   D) characters

44. A) Typical of their species, the parrot will thrive where they can find enough fruits and nuts.
B) Like their species, parrots will thrive wherever it can find enough fruits and nuts.
C) Finding enough fruits and nuts will enable parrots to thrive like their species.
D) Typical of their species, parrots will thrive wherever they can find enough fruits and nuts.

45. A) Bernhouse obviously treasured the memory of his father's happiness as much as he did the memory of his own childhood.
B) The memory of his father's happiness was obviously treasured by Bernhouse as much as he did his father's treasured happiness.
C) Obviously treasuring his father's happiness as much as the memory of Bernhouse's own childhood.
D) Bernhouse treasured obviously the memory of his father's happiness as much as his own childhood memory.

46. A) allright   C) allrite
B) alright   D) none of these

47. A) hazardous   C) hazzardice
B) hazzardous   D) none of these

48. A) congradulatons C) congratalations
B) congradalations D) none of these

49. A) mannakin   C) mannequin
B) mannaquin   D) none of these

50. Some scientists have proposed that, over two hundred million years ago, one giant land mass—rather than various continents and islands—covered one-third of the earth.

The paragraph best supports the statement that the different continents that exist now

A) were all larger in the past
B) may not have always existed as such
C) have been challenged by scientists
D) now occupy two-thirds of the earth

51. Antifreeze lowers the melting point of any liquid to which it is added, so that the liquid will not freeze in cold weather. It is commonly used to maintain the cooling system in automobile radiators. Of course, the weather may become so cold that even antifreeze is not effective, but such a severe climatic condition rarely occurs in well-traveled places.

The paragraph best supports the statement that antifreeze is

A) usually effective only in automobile radiators
B) usually effective wherever automobile travel is common
C) usually effective even in the coldest climates on earth
D) not nearly as effective as it could be

52. *Frivolous* means most nearly
A) lighthearted   C) close
B) likable   D) equivalent

53. *Macabre* means most nearly
A) parrot   C) biblical
B) grotesque   D) paper

54. To *exert* means most nearly to
A) consume   C) forgive
B) acquit   D) exercise

55. To *infiltrate* means most nearly to
A) limit   C) disbelieve
B) intrude   D) deduce

56. *Callous* means most nearly
A) rough   C) sore
B) insensitive   D) conventional

57. HELIUM is related to BALLOON as WATER is related to
A) shore   C) aquarium
B) rain   D) fish

58. STONE is related to CHERRY as ATOM is related to
A) nucleus   C) molecule
B) electron   D) bomb

59. LAMB is related to SHEEP as CUB is related to
A) calf   C) bear
B) colt   D) den

60. DRY is related to PARCHED as WET is related to
A) soaked   C) dank
B) damp   D) rain

61. A) Music and films with a strong Latin theme has helped to unite the community.
B) Music, as well as films with a strong Latin theme, have been mostly helpful for the uniting of the community.
C) Music and films with a strong Latin theme have helped to unite the community.
D) Uniting the community, music and films with a strong Latin theme have been helpful.

62. A) Sitting in what he called his home away from home, Arnold thought concerning about his future.
B) Sitting in what he called his home away from home, concerning his future Arnold thought.
C) Having sat in what he is calling his home away from home, Arnold thinks about his future.
D) Sitting in what he called his home away from home, Arnold thought about the future.

63. A) musichan   C) musisian
B) musician   D) none of these

64. A) practicle   C) practical
B) practicul   D) none of these

65. A) servent   C) servant
B) servint   D) none of these

66. A) sincerly   C) sincerely
B) sinserely   D) none of these

67. In the twelfth century, people used the abacus (a simple device made of beads strung on wire) to perform complex calculations. Today we use electronic calculators, and the abacus has become obsolete. One thousand years from now, who knows?

The paragraph best supports the statement that

A) the abacus is useless for performing calculations today
B) in the distant future, the electronic calculator of today may seem obsolete
C) devices used for calculating undergo a vast improvement every 1,000 years
D) modern calculations are more complex than ancient calculations

68. It has been estimated that only one out of 500 drunken drivers on the highway is flagged down by the police. The odds against being arrested make it tempting for drinkers to give themselves the benefit of the doubt when they are considering whether they should get behind the wheel.

The paragraph best supports the statement that drinkers are

A) usually not driving when they are detained by the police
B) likely to drive even though they are drunk
C) quite frequently stopped by the police while on the highway
D) never stopped by the police while driving on the highway

69. To *elucidate* means most nearly to
A) explain   C) tighten
B) lose   D) forget

70. *Tawny* means most nearly
A) quiet   C) brown
B) soft   D) rowdy

71. *Despot* means most nearly
A) tyrant   C) inkwell
B) oasis   D) morsel

72. To *tarry* means most nearly to
A) hurry   C) blacken
B) linger   D) soil

73. *Lank* means most nearly
A) piece   C) amount
B) slender   D) common

74. CATERPILLAR is related to BUTTERFLY as TADPOLE is related to
A) lilypad   C) egg
B) pond   D) frog

75. PATRON is related to SUPPORT as ADMIRER is related to
A) compliment   C) contribution
B) money   D) desire

76. HOUSE is related to BASEMENT as CASTLE is related to
A) moat   C) dungeon
B) tower   D) parapet

77. MOTH is related to FLAME as IRON is related to
A) solder   C) filing
B) magnet   D) brass

78. A) Many at the time believed that the alliance with the allies is a trick to confuse their enemy.
B) Many at the time believes that the alliance with the allies was a trick to confuse their enemies.
C) Many at the time believed that their alliance with the allies confused the enemy as a trick.
D) Many at the time believed that their alliance with the allies was a trick to confuse their enemies.

79. A) Going a long way towards improvement of efficiency, they are no doubt useless, computers without humans.
B) Though they have gone a long way towards improvement of efficiency, computers are no doubt useless, having no humans.
C) Though they've made major improvements in efficiency, computers are useless without humans.
D) Being without humans, in spite of their improvements in efficiency, computers have gone a long way.

80. A) deceive   C) decieve
B) deceeve   D) none of these

81. A) vilence   C) violense
B) violence   D) none of these

82. A) misry   C) missery
    B) misary   D) none of these

83. A) heighth   C) hieght
    B) height   D) none of these

84. One of the most important works of the Middle Ages was *The Principles of Letter Writing,* authored by an anonymous Italian educator. It became the basis for formal communication, and many of the principles it advocates have become part of clerical education today.

The paragraph best supports the statement that clerical workers today

    A) should be more familiar with relevant books from the Middle Ages
    B) study some principles of communication that were available in the Middle Ages
    C) are not familiar with *The Principles of Letter Writing*
    D) study some principles that contradict those proposed in the Middle Ages

85. Although the acceptable format for writing reports varies from profession to profession, certain rules are invariable. For example, all writers must avoid faulty parallelism and misplaced modifiers; such grammatical errors are incorrect in any context.

The paragraph best supports the statement that different professions

    A) tend to disapprove of grammatical errors in written reports
    B) are only concerned with errors involving parallelism and modifiers
    C) consult grammatical rules before the preparation of any written report
    D) follow the same basic format for written reports, although there are variations

ANSWER KEY FOR MODEL TEST 3

Word Meaning

1. B	18. B	35. A	52. A	69. A
2. D	19. C	36. D	53. B	70. C
3. A	20. B	37. B	54. D	71. A
4. A	21. D	38. A	55. B	72. B
5. C	22. B	39. D	56. B	73. B

Analogies

6. C	23. A	40. A	57. C	74. D
7. A	24. D	41. B	58. A	75. A
8. C	25. C	42. C	59. C	76. C
9. D	26. C	43. D	60. A	77. B

Grammar

10. C	27. A	44. D	61. C	78. D
11. B	28. D	45. A	62. D	79. C

Spelling

12. D	29. C	46. D	63. B	80. A
13. B	30. C	47. A	64. C	81. B
14. B	31. B	48. D	65. C	82. D
15. C	32. B	49. C	66. C	83. B

Reading

16. D	33. C	50. B	67. B	84. B
17. A	34. A	51. B	68. B	85. A

ANALYSIS CHART FOR MODEL TEST 3

Now that you've corrected your exam, use the following chart to carefully analyze your results and spot your strengths and weaknesses. This analysis should help you focus your study and review efforts.

Section	Total Number of Questions	Number Correct	Number Incorrect	Number Unanswered*
Word Meaning	25			
Analogies	20			
Grammar	10			
Spelling	20			
Reading Comprehension	10			
TOTAL	85			

*Since there is no penalty for incorrect answers on the Verbal Abilities Test, you should have left no question unanswered. Even if you didn't have time to answer a question, at least you should have filled in the answer space with a guess.

ANSWER EXPLANATIONS FOR MODEL TEST 3

1. **(B)** disturbed
2. **(D)** burn
3. **(A)** translate
4. **(A)** motive
5. **(C)** cure

6. **(C)** The second word is stored in the first word.
7. **(A)** The first word is a condition of the second word.
8. **(C)** The second word observes the first word.
9. **(D)** The first word is closed up by the second word.
10. **(C)** In (A), "not be as good...rather than" is incorrect. In (B), "best" is incorrect when comparing two options. It should be "better." In (D), "according to" is awkward, and the sentence is better stated in the active, rather than passive.
11. **(B)** In (A), "they" incorrectly refers to "a person." (C) and (D) are sentence fragments.
12. **(D)** Correct spelling: juvenile
13. **(B)** draft
14. **(B)** defense
15. **(C)** territorial
16. **(D)** Cocaine is mentioned as a specific example of the general increase in drug abuse.
17. **(A)** The paragraph's second sentence strongly supports this choice.
18. **(B)** obstacle
19. **(C)** placate
20. **(B)** proverb
21. **(D)** hole
22. **(B)** hot
23. **(A)** The first word is given to the second word.
24. **(D)** The first word is the opposite of the second word.
25. **(C)** The first word displays the second word.
26. **(C)** The first word measures the second word.
27. **(A)** In (B), the sentence would be vastly improved if the phrases were in reverse order. In (C), "Making certain" should be "To make certain." (D) is a sentence fragment.
28. **(D)** In (A), "for sure" and "really truly" are unacceptable idioms, as is "Not mattering" in (C). In (B), "sure" should be "certainly."
29. **(C)** tolerance
30. **(C)** tomorrow
31. **(B)** lightning
32. **(B)** likable
33. **(C)** The passage states that "many...deeply mistrust their public leaders."
34. **(A)** The paragraph is itself a comparison between people and animals, thus supporting the statement that people and animals can be compared.
35. **(A)** gaudy
36. **(D)** kingly
37. **(B)** mysterious
38. **(A)** spoof
39. **(D)** summon
40. **(A)** The second word powers the first word.

41. **(B)** The first word is a synonym for the second word.
42. **(C)** The first word lives in the second word.
43. **(D)** The first word is composed of the second word.
44. **(D)** In (A), "the parrot" (singular) does not agree with "their" and "they." Similarly in (B), "parrots" does not agree with "it." In (C), "to thrive like their species" is vague.
45. **(A)** In (B), "as much as he did" is vague. (C) is a sentence fragment. In (D), "treasured obviously" is incorrect sentence structure.
46. **(D)** Correct spelling: all right
47. **(A)** hazardous
48. **(D)** Correct spelling: congratulations
49. **(C)** mannequin
50. **(B)** The paragraph discusses the possibility that the various continents of today were once contained in "one giant land mass."
51. **(B)** The final sentence implies that antifreeze is effective in "well-traveled places," that is, places where automobile travel is common.
52. **(A)** lighthearted
53. **(B)** grotesque
54. **(D)** exercise
55. **(B)** intrude
56. **(B)** insensitive
57. **(C)** The second word is filled with the first word.
58. **(A)** The second word is the center of the first word.
59. **(C)** The first word is a young second word.
60. **(A)** The second word is the extreme of the first word.
61. **(C)** In (A), "Music and films" (plural) require a plural verb, "have helped" instead of "has helped." In (B), the opposite is required: "Music...*has* helped," a singular subject takes a singular verb. Notice in (B) that "films" are not part of the subject. In (D), "have been helpful" is vague.
62. **(D)** In (A), "concerning about" is incorrect usage. (B) uses awkward structure. In (C), verb tenses are inconsistent.
63. **(B)** musician
64. **(C)** practical
65. **(C)** servant
66. **(C)** sincerely
67. **(B)** The paragraph concludes by questioning what sort of calculation device will exist in 1,000 years, strongly implying that the electronic calculator, like the abacus, will become obsolete.

68. **(B)** The paragraph states that drunken drivers are tempted to "give themselves the benefit of the doubt" when deciding whether to drive; in other words, drunken drivers are tempted to drive in spite of their condition.
69. **(A)** explain
70. **(C)** brown
71. **(A)** tyrant
72. **(B)** linger
73. **(B)** slender
74. **(D)** The first word transforms into the second word.
75. **(A)** The first word gives the second word.
76. **(C)** The second word is in the bottom of the first word.
77. **(B)** The first word is attracted to the second word.

78. **(D)** In (A), "is" should be "was." In (B), "believes" should be "believed." In (C), "confused the enemy as a trick" is awkward structure.
79. **(C)** In (A), "they" is vague, and the structure is awkward. In (B), "having no humans" is a vague phrase, as is "being without humans" in (D).
80. **(A)** deceive
81. **(B)** violence
82. **(D)** correct spelling: misery
83. **(B)** height
84. **(B)** The paragraph states that principles from the Middle Ages "have become part of clerical education today."
85. **(A)** The paragraph stresses the incorrectness of grammatical errors in all professions, saying that certain rules are "invariable."

ANSWER SHEET

SIGNATURE: _____
(Please Sign)

EXAMINATION TITLE: _____

PLACE OF EXAMINATION: _____
City _____ State

TODAY'S DATE: _____

SAMPLE Ⓐ ● Ⓒ Ⓓ Ⓔ

DIRECTIONS FOR MARKING ANSWER SHEET

Use only a **No. 2 (or softer) lead pencil.** Darken completely the circle corresponding to your answer. You **must** keep your mark within the circle. Stray marks may be counted as errors. Erase **completely** all marks except your answer.

SAMPLE NAME GRID

1. In the boxes below, **PRINT** your name. Print only as many letters as will fit within the areas for the last name, first initial (F.I.), and middle initial (M.I.) Below each box, darken the circle containing the same letter. SEE SAMPLE NAME GRID

LAST NAME   F.I.   M.I.

2. In the boxes below, enter your 9-digit Social Security Number. Below each box, darken the circle in each column corresponding to the number you have entered.

SOCIAL SECURITY NUMBER

3. OCCUPATIONAL GROUP NUMBER

SECTION 1

Make no marks or entries in the columns to the right until you receive instructions from the administrator.

PART

TEST SERIES

TEST NUMBER

| 1 Ⓐ Ⓑ Ⓒ Ⓓ Ⓔ | 21 Ⓐ Ⓑ Ⓒ Ⓓ Ⓔ | 41 Ⓐ Ⓑ Ⓒ Ⓓ Ⓔ | 61 Ⓐ Ⓑ Ⓒ Ⓓ Ⓔ | 81 Ⓐ Ⓑ Ⓒ Ⓓ Ⓔ | 101 Ⓐ Ⓑ Ⓒ Ⓓ Ⓔ | 121 Ⓐ Ⓑ Ⓒ Ⓓ Ⓔ |

11 Ⓐ Ⓑ Ⓒ Ⓓ Ⓔ   31 Ⓐ Ⓑ Ⓒ Ⓓ Ⓔ   51 Ⓐ Ⓑ Ⓒ Ⓓ Ⓔ   71 Ⓐ Ⓑ Ⓒ Ⓓ Ⓔ   91 Ⓐ Ⓑ Ⓒ Ⓓ Ⓔ   111 Ⓐ Ⓑ Ⓒ Ⓓ Ⓔ
12 Ⓐ Ⓑ Ⓒ Ⓓ Ⓔ   32 Ⓐ Ⓑ Ⓒ Ⓓ Ⓔ   52 Ⓐ Ⓑ Ⓒ Ⓓ Ⓔ   72 Ⓐ Ⓑ Ⓒ Ⓓ Ⓔ   92 Ⓐ Ⓑ Ⓒ Ⓓ Ⓔ   112 Ⓐ Ⓑ Ⓒ Ⓓ Ⓔ
13 Ⓐ Ⓑ Ⓒ Ⓓ Ⓔ   33 Ⓐ Ⓑ Ⓒ Ⓓ Ⓔ   53 Ⓐ Ⓑ Ⓒ Ⓓ Ⓔ   73 Ⓐ Ⓑ Ⓒ Ⓓ Ⓔ   93 Ⓐ Ⓑ Ⓒ Ⓓ Ⓔ   113 Ⓐ Ⓑ Ⓒ Ⓓ Ⓔ
14 Ⓐ Ⓑ Ⓒ Ⓓ Ⓔ   34 Ⓐ Ⓑ Ⓒ Ⓓ Ⓔ   54 Ⓐ Ⓑ Ⓒ Ⓓ Ⓔ   74 Ⓐ Ⓑ Ⓒ Ⓓ Ⓔ   94 Ⓐ Ⓑ Ⓒ Ⓓ Ⓔ   114 Ⓐ Ⓑ Ⓒ Ⓓ Ⓔ
15 Ⓐ Ⓑ Ⓒ Ⓓ Ⓔ   35 Ⓐ Ⓑ Ⓒ Ⓓ Ⓔ   55 Ⓐ Ⓑ Ⓒ Ⓓ Ⓔ   75 Ⓐ Ⓑ Ⓒ Ⓓ Ⓔ   95 Ⓐ Ⓑ Ⓒ Ⓓ Ⓔ   115 Ⓐ Ⓑ Ⓒ Ⓓ Ⓔ
16 Ⓐ Ⓑ Ⓒ Ⓓ Ⓔ   36 Ⓐ Ⓑ Ⓒ Ⓓ Ⓔ   56 Ⓐ Ⓑ Ⓒ Ⓓ Ⓔ   76 Ⓐ Ⓑ Ⓒ Ⓓ Ⓔ   96 Ⓐ Ⓑ Ⓒ Ⓓ Ⓔ   116 Ⓐ Ⓑ Ⓒ Ⓓ Ⓔ
17 Ⓐ Ⓑ Ⓒ Ⓓ Ⓔ   37 Ⓐ Ⓑ Ⓒ Ⓓ Ⓔ   57 Ⓐ Ⓑ Ⓒ Ⓓ Ⓔ   77 Ⓐ Ⓑ Ⓒ Ⓓ Ⓔ   97 Ⓐ Ⓑ Ⓒ Ⓓ Ⓔ   117 Ⓐ Ⓑ Ⓒ Ⓓ Ⓔ
18 Ⓐ Ⓑ Ⓒ Ⓓ Ⓔ   38 Ⓐ Ⓑ Ⓒ Ⓓ Ⓔ   58 Ⓐ Ⓑ Ⓒ Ⓓ Ⓔ   78 Ⓐ Ⓑ Ⓒ Ⓓ Ⓔ   98 Ⓐ Ⓑ Ⓒ Ⓓ Ⓔ   118 Ⓐ Ⓑ Ⓒ Ⓓ Ⓔ
19 Ⓐ Ⓑ Ⓒ Ⓓ Ⓔ   39 Ⓐ Ⓑ Ⓒ Ⓓ Ⓔ   59 Ⓐ Ⓑ Ⓒ Ⓓ Ⓔ   79 Ⓐ Ⓑ Ⓒ Ⓓ Ⓔ   99 Ⓐ Ⓑ Ⓒ Ⓓ Ⓔ   119 Ⓐ Ⓑ Ⓒ Ⓓ Ⓔ
20 Ⓐ Ⓑ Ⓒ Ⓓ Ⓔ   40 Ⓐ Ⓑ Ⓒ Ⓓ Ⓔ   60 Ⓐ Ⓑ Ⓒ Ⓓ Ⓔ   80 Ⓐ Ⓑ Ⓒ Ⓓ Ⓔ   100 Ⓐ Ⓑ Ⓒ Ⓓ Ⓔ   120 Ⓐ Ⓑ Ⓒ Ⓓ Ⓔ
1 Ⓐ Ⓑ Ⓒ Ⓓ Ⓔ   21 Ⓐ Ⓑ Ⓒ Ⓓ Ⓔ   41 Ⓐ Ⓑ Ⓒ Ⓓ Ⓔ   61 Ⓐ Ⓑ Ⓒ Ⓓ Ⓔ   81 Ⓐ Ⓑ Ⓒ Ⓓ Ⓔ   101 Ⓐ Ⓑ Ⓒ Ⓓ Ⓔ   121 Ⓐ Ⓑ Ⓒ Ⓓ Ⓔ
2 Ⓐ Ⓑ Ⓒ Ⓓ Ⓔ   22 Ⓐ Ⓑ Ⓒ Ⓓ Ⓔ   42 Ⓐ Ⓑ Ⓒ Ⓓ Ⓔ   62 Ⓐ Ⓑ Ⓒ Ⓓ Ⓔ   82 Ⓐ Ⓑ Ⓒ Ⓓ Ⓔ   102 Ⓐ Ⓑ Ⓒ Ⓓ Ⓔ   122 Ⓐ Ⓑ Ⓒ Ⓓ Ⓔ
3 Ⓐ Ⓑ Ⓒ Ⓓ Ⓔ   23 Ⓐ Ⓑ Ⓒ Ⓓ Ⓔ   43 Ⓐ Ⓑ Ⓒ Ⓓ Ⓔ   63 Ⓐ Ⓑ Ⓒ Ⓓ Ⓔ   83 Ⓐ Ⓑ Ⓒ Ⓓ Ⓔ   103 Ⓐ Ⓑ Ⓒ Ⓓ Ⓔ   123 Ⓐ Ⓑ Ⓒ Ⓓ Ⓔ
4 Ⓐ Ⓑ Ⓒ Ⓓ Ⓔ   24 Ⓐ Ⓑ Ⓒ Ⓓ Ⓔ   44 Ⓐ Ⓑ Ⓒ Ⓓ Ⓔ   64 Ⓐ Ⓑ Ⓒ Ⓓ Ⓔ   84 Ⓐ Ⓑ Ⓒ Ⓓ Ⓔ   104 Ⓐ Ⓑ Ⓒ Ⓓ Ⓔ   124 Ⓐ Ⓑ Ⓒ Ⓓ Ⓔ
5 Ⓐ Ⓑ Ⓒ Ⓓ Ⓔ   25 Ⓐ Ⓑ Ⓒ Ⓓ Ⓔ   45 Ⓐ Ⓑ Ⓒ Ⓓ Ⓔ   65 Ⓐ Ⓑ Ⓒ Ⓓ Ⓔ   85 Ⓐ Ⓑ Ⓒ Ⓓ Ⓔ   105 Ⓐ Ⓑ Ⓒ Ⓓ Ⓔ   125 Ⓐ Ⓑ Ⓒ Ⓓ Ⓔ
6 Ⓐ Ⓑ Ⓒ Ⓓ Ⓔ   26 Ⓐ Ⓑ Ⓒ Ⓓ Ⓔ   46 Ⓐ Ⓑ Ⓒ Ⓓ Ⓔ   66 Ⓐ Ⓑ Ⓒ Ⓓ Ⓔ   86 Ⓐ Ⓑ Ⓒ Ⓓ Ⓔ   106 Ⓐ Ⓑ Ⓒ Ⓓ Ⓔ   126 Ⓐ Ⓑ Ⓒ Ⓓ Ⓔ
7 Ⓐ Ⓑ Ⓒ Ⓓ Ⓔ   27 Ⓐ Ⓑ Ⓒ Ⓓ Ⓔ   47 Ⓐ Ⓑ Ⓒ Ⓓ Ⓔ   67 Ⓐ Ⓑ Ⓒ Ⓓ Ⓔ   87 Ⓐ Ⓑ Ⓒ Ⓓ Ⓔ   107 Ⓐ Ⓑ Ⓒ Ⓓ Ⓔ   127 Ⓐ Ⓑ Ⓒ Ⓓ Ⓔ
8 Ⓐ Ⓑ Ⓒ Ⓓ Ⓔ   28 Ⓐ Ⓑ Ⓒ Ⓓ Ⓔ   48 Ⓐ Ⓑ Ⓒ Ⓓ Ⓔ   68 Ⓐ Ⓑ Ⓒ Ⓓ Ⓔ   88 Ⓐ Ⓑ Ⓒ Ⓓ Ⓔ   108 Ⓐ Ⓑ Ⓒ Ⓓ Ⓔ   128 Ⓐ Ⓑ Ⓒ Ⓓ Ⓔ
9 Ⓐ Ⓑ Ⓒ Ⓓ Ⓔ   29 Ⓐ Ⓑ Ⓒ Ⓓ Ⓔ   49 Ⓐ Ⓑ Ⓒ Ⓓ Ⓔ   69 Ⓐ Ⓑ Ⓒ Ⓓ Ⓔ   89 Ⓐ Ⓑ Ⓒ Ⓓ Ⓔ   109 Ⓐ Ⓑ Ⓒ Ⓓ Ⓔ   129 Ⓐ Ⓑ Ⓒ Ⓓ Ⓔ
10 Ⓐ Ⓑ Ⓒ Ⓓ Ⓔ   30 Ⓐ Ⓑ Ⓒ Ⓓ Ⓔ   50 Ⓐ Ⓑ Ⓒ Ⓓ Ⓔ   70 Ⓐ Ⓑ Ⓒ Ⓓ Ⓔ   90 Ⓐ Ⓑ Ⓒ Ⓓ Ⓔ   110 Ⓐ Ⓑ Ⓒ Ⓓ Ⓔ   130 Ⓐ Ⓑ Ⓒ Ⓓ Ⓔ

MODEL TEST 4

Time allotted — 35 minutes

Directions

Each question has four suggested answers. Decide which one is the best answer. Find the question number on the Answer Sheet. Show your answer to the question by darkening completely the square corresponding to the letter of your answer. Keep your mark within the space. If you have to erase a mark, be sure to erase it completely. Mark only one answer for each question. Do NOT mark space E for any question.

Word Meaning

1. To *plead* means most nearly to
   A) direct   C) fold
   B) beg   D) inquire

2. *Auditor* means most nearly
   A) consultant   C) official
   B) applicant   D) listener

3. *Verbal* means most nearly
   A) wordy   C) oral
   B) active   D) written

4. To *scale* means most nearly
   A) weigh   C) dispute
   B) climb   D) descend

5. *Turbulent* means most nearly
   A) loud   C) sleep-inducing
   B) climb   D) accidental

Analogies

6. VEHICLE is related to TRUCK as REPTILE is related to
   A) animal   C) frog
   B) alligator   D) protozoan

7. DENTIST is related to TEETH as PSYCHIATRIST is related to
   A) heart   C) feet
   B) mind   D) thought

8. LEAF is related to SPINACH as ROOT is related to
   A) tomato   C) lettuce
   B) squash   D) carrot

9. IMPIOUS is related to BLASPHEMY as SLOTHFUL is related to
   A) greed   C) expense
   B) indolence   D) jungle

Grammar

Decide which sentence is preferable with respect to grammar and usage suitable for a formal letter or report.

10. A) The salad contains broccoli that has been cooked briefly, crabmeat, and it has two kinds of lettuce.
    B) The salad contains broccoli that is cooked briefly as well as crabmeat and contains two kinds of lettuce.
    C) The salad contains two kinds of lettuce, crabmeat, and also has briefly cooked broccoli.
    D) The salad contains broccoli that has been cooked briefly, crabmeat, and two kinds of lettuce.

11. A) Unlike most modern novelists, the novels of the Victorian age appeared first in magazines in serial form, sometimes for as long as one year.
    B) Appearing first in magazines in serial form, the novels of the Victorian age were sometimes as long as one year unlike most modern ones.
    C) Appearing first in magazines in serial form, sometimes over the length of a year, most Victorian novels were unlike modern novels.
    D) Unlike most modern novels, those of the Victorian age appeared first in magazines in serial form, sometimes for as long as a year.

Spelling

Find the correct spelling of the word and darken the proper answer space. If no suggested spelling is correct, darken space D.

12. A) address   C) addresse
    B) adress   D) none of these

13. A) embarassing   C) embarasing
    B) embarrassing   D) none of these

14. A) nucular   C) nuclear
    B) nuculear   D) none of these

15. A) niether   C) neether
    B) neither   D) none of these

Reading

16. Being the financial center of the United States has advantages and disadvantages. New York is also the fraud capital of the country, with more than a thousand criminal fraud convictions this year. Gullible investors lost more than five billion dollars.

    The paragraph best supports the statement that
    A) gains and losses on financial investments in New York are equal
    B) New York is the financial center of the United States
    C) convictions for criminal fraud are lowest where financial activity is lowest
    D) losses in financial fraud are seldom the fault of gullible investors

17. The tobacco industry has filed a law suit charging that the EPA report on second-hand smoke should be declared null and void because it overlooked evidence showing second-hand smoke is not dangerous. The report, the tobacco industry claims, has caused a sharp rise in the number of no smoking ordinances and a sharp decline in cigarette sales.

    The paragraph best supports the statement that
    A) the tobacco industry is genuinely concerned with scientific truth
    B) governments should pass no smoking ordinances to protect the health of the public
    C) the tobacco industry is concerned about the effect of the EPA report on tobacco sales
    D) the tobacco industry is likely to win its lawsuit

18. *Controversy* means most nearly
    A) indifference   C) refutation
    B) dispute   D) repetition

19. *To cite* means most nearly to
    A) quote   C) expect
    B) visualize   D) align

20. *Embargo* means most nearly
    A) customer   C) departure
    B) shipment   D) restriction

21. To *forsake* means most nearly to
    A) cherish   C) abandon
    B) disapprove   D) endear

22. *Expansive* means most nearly
    A) costly   C) unusual
    B) demonstrative   D) reticent

23. PLAY is related to ACT as NOVEL is related to
    A) prose   C) chapter
    B) reader   D) index

24. BULL is related to COW as DRAKE is related to
    A) duck   C) gosling
    B) bird   D) gander

25. SCISSORS is related to CLOTH as LAWNMOWER is related to
    A) garden   C) blades
    B) tool   D) grass

26. OVER is related to UNDER as INTO is related to
    A) next to   C) out of
    B) beside   D) between

27. A) Depressed by urban sprawl and the noise of the traffic, a one-acre garden of produce and flowers has cheered up ten patients at the Westway hospital.
    B) Depressed by urban sprawl and the noise of the traffic, ten patients at the Westway hospital have been cheered up by a one-acre garden of produce and flowers.
    C) Ten patients at the Westway hospital who have been cheered up by a one-acre garden of produce and flowers though once depressed by urban sprawl and the noise of the traffic.
    D) Urban sprawl and the noise of traffic depress ten patients at the Westway hospital, cheered up by a one-acre garden of produce and flowers.

28. A) The federal commission had decided to close the Boston Naval Shipyard, and this seemed the end of their jobs to hundreds of workers.
    B) The decision to close the Boston Naval Shipyard was reached by a federal commission, and this decision seems to be the end of their job for hundreds of workers.
    C) The federal commission's decision to close the Boston Naval Shipyard seemed to end the jobs of hundreds of workers.
    D) The federal commission decided to close the Boston Naval Shipyard, which seemingly ended the jobs of hundreds of workers.

29. A) commitee   C) committee
    B) comittee   D) none of these

30. A) desperite   C) despairate
    B) desparate   D) none of these

31. A) shutterred   C) shuttered
    B) shutered   D) none of these

32. A) forreign   C) forriegn
    B) foriegn   D) none of these

33. Just under 300,000 people have been murdered in the United States by guns in the last 25 years. Each year, an increasing percentage of these deaths involve children. Laws that punish adults who leave weapons where children can reach them cannot bring back a dead child. And these laws certainly do not prevent adults from buying the guns that kill the children.

    The paragraph best supports the statement that
    A) guns don't kill people, people do
    B) any laws controlling the sales or handling of a gun will fail to reduce the number of gun-related deaths
    C) more children are killed by guns in the United States every year
    D) we have not yet found a way to prevent the deaths by gunshot of a large number of American children

34. Throughout the nation, utility companies are looking for ways to reduce the consumption of energy instead of building new power plants. Since 20 percent of an average household's electricity is used to run refrigerators, any improvement in their energy efficiency would reduce the demand for electric power. A new, more efficient refrigerator developed by Whirlpool Corporation is expected to use just half as much electricity as older refrigerators, but should not cost buyers more than similar models cost now.

    The paragraph best supports the statement that
    A) consumers who use the new refrigerator can expect a drop of about 50 percent in their electric bills
    B) consumers who use the new refrigerator can expect a drop of about 10 percent in their electric bills
    C) the reduction of energy consumption is counterbalanced by an increase in the use of environmentally unsafe materials such as freon
    D) other companies will market energy efficient refrigerators at a lower price if the Whirlpool model is successful

35. To *appreciate* means most nearly to
    A) inquire   C) reduce
    B) increase   D) please

36. *Beret* means most nearly
    A) hairpin   C) cap
    B) wine glass   D) mushroom

37. *Futile* means most nearly
    A) useless   C) oracular
    B) plebeian   D) cheerful

38. *Commotion* means most nearly
    A) movement   C) accompaniment
    B) velocity   D) uproar

39. To *impose* means most nearly to
    A) guess   C) add
    B) levy   D) remove

40. WAITER is related to RESTAURANT as SURGEON is related to
    A) scalpel   C) operation
    B) medicine   D) hospital

41. GENEROUS is related to STINGY as GLUTTONOUS is related to
    A) fasting   C) pompous
    B) eating   D) overweight

42. CROWN is related to KING as BADGE is related to
    A) mayor   C) police officer
    B) handcuffs   D) jail

43. WARM is related to HOT as COOL is related to
    A) scorching   C) temperate
    B) chilly   D) icy

44. A) If you think carefully about your future, one must see the importance of education.
    B) If you think about your future carefully, you must see the importance of education.

C) If one thinks about your future carefully, one must see the importance of education.

D) You must see the importance of education, if one thinks about one's future carefully.

45. A) The final results at the end of the game were a total and complete surprise.

B) The final results of the game were a total and complete surprise.

C) The results of the game were a complete surprise.

D) The results at the end were totally and completely surprising.

46. A) repitition C) repetetion
    B) repetition D) none of these

47. A) manegeable C) managable
    B) manageable D) none of these

48. A) organically C) organicaly
    B) organicly   D) none of these

49. A) explane C) exsplain
    B) explain D) none of these

50. Federal law now requires all television sets to be equipped with built-in capacity to display captions. Captions enable the nation's 24 million hearing-impaired people to read subtitles on the screen. It will now be possible to watch television in a silent room, in case someone is sleeping. It will be easier for the illiterate to learn to read or for non-English speakers to learn English. The rise in the cost of television sets is expected to be no more than ten dollars, while separate decoders to access captions now cost much more.

The paragraph best supports the statement that

A) television sets with caption-display capabilities will be useful for both the hearing and the hearing-impaired public

B) technological advances usually are accompanied by a rise in cost for consumers

C) in the past, deaf people would not hear what was being said on television programs

D) captioned television programs will make the use of earphones obsolete

51. If the United States presses too hard on an issue, we are accused of forcing our views upon our allies. But if we consult with them and refuse to act without their agreement, we are accused of lack of leadership. It is difficult to find a way to be neither too hard nor too soft.

The paragraph best supports the statement that

A) the United States should give up trying to win the favor of its allies

B) the opinion of its allies plays a part in the policies of the United States

C) the United States should pay more attention to the concerns of its allies

D) the United States lacks leadership in world affairs

52. *Extinct* means most nearly
    A) noisome   C) ended
    B) darkened D) obscure

53. *Auction* means most nearly
    A) sale   C) request
    B) business D) implement

54. To *nurture* means most nearly to
    A) harm   C) grow accustomed
    B) educate D) foster

55. *Bleak* means most nearly
    A) liquid   C) white
    B) desolate D) optimistic

56. To *reap* means most nearly to
    A) plant C) winnow
    B) till   D) gather

57. RUG is related to WOOL as SAUCEPAN is related to
    A) soup   C) wood
    B) aluminum D) heat

58. COMPOSER is related to SONG as POET is related to
    A) meter   C) art
    B) writer D) ode

59. DOCTOR is related to PATIENT as LAWYER is related to
    A) lawsuit C) juror
    B) client   D) court

60. NEEDLE is related to THREAD as HAMMER is related to
    A) nail C) carpenter
    B) saw   D) wood

61. A) After he had mowed the lawn, the gardener put the lawnmower in the garage, and scatters the clippings on the garden.
    B) After he mows the lawn, the gardener put the lawnmower in the garage, and scattered the clippings in the garden.
    C) After he had mowed the lawn, the gardener put the lawnmower in the garage, and scattered the clippings on the garden.
    D) After mowing the lawn, the lawnmower was put into the garage and the clippings were scattered on the garden by the gardener.

62. A) Millions of farm workers who plant, tend, harvest, and package our food without any health insurance.
    B) Millions of farm workers who plant our food, tend it, harvest our food, and package it without any health insurance.
    C) Millions of farm workers, planting, tending, harvesting, and packaging our food without any health insurance.
    D) There are millions of farm workers who plant, tend, harvest, and package our food without any health insurance.

63. A) extrordinary   C) extraordinery
    B) extrardinary   D) none of these

64. A) appropriate   C) appropriette
    B) apropriate   D) none of these

65. A) assessories   C) accessories
    B) assesories   D) none of these

66. A) similar   C) similer
    B) similiar   D) none of these

67. In Indianapolis, sewer billing, microfilming, public golf courses, and building inspections are all handled by private firms. Public services, in competition with private operations, have become more efficient. But other communities that have turned public services over to private companies report higher costs while workers receive lower wages or fewer benefits. Privatization is not always the best choice a city can make.

The paragraph best supports the statement that
A) by privatizing such services as building inspections and microfilming, large cities can save money

B) in cities where privatization has been used, workers receive fewer benefits than in cities that retain control over the public services
C) a city should study the possible effects carefully before handing public services over to private industry
D) cities with both privatized and public services are more efficient than those having only one or the other.

68. As long as something is based on a true story, Americans are eager to buy it. Fiction is no longer necessary when so many facts are available. Television no longer shows mystery stories. It shows true stories of husbands who kill their wives or children who murder their parents. Is it any wonder that fiction sales fall lower every year?

The paragraph best supports the statement that novelists
A) are no longer interested in writing mystery stories
B) face a declining number of readers
C) can earn more money by writing for television than by writing novels
D) are more likely to write crime stories based upon real life than on imagined crimes

69. *Imprudent* means most nearly
    A) simple   C) rash
    B) introverted   D) stingy

70. *Tariff* means most nearly
    A) custom   C) law
    B) tax   D) decoration

71. *Wrenching* means most nearly
    A) spiteful   C) repairing
    B) convex   D) distorting

72. *Incentive* means most nearly
    A) stimulus   C) length
    B) precaution   D) vigilance

73. *Composure* means most nearly
    A) opus   C) prayer
    B) equanimity   D) restlessness

74. LION is related to PRIDE as WOLF is related to
    A) anger   C) pack
    B) fairy tale   D) forest

75. WHALE is related to OCEAN as MONKEY is related to
    A) liana
    B) mountain
    C) jungle
    D) land

76. EAGER is related to INDIFFERENT as FRESH is related to
    A) withdrawn
    B) modern
    C) recent
    D) rancid

77. AUTOMOBILE is related to GASOLINE as FLASH-LIGHT is related to
    A) battery
    B) bulb
    C) vision
    D) combustion

78. A) The senate, because the president, the chief justice, and the mayor were late, were unable to perform any business.
    B) Because the president, the chief justice, and the mayor were late, the senate was unable to perform any business.
    C) Being as the president, chief justice, and mayor were late, the senate was not able to perform any business.
    D) Because the president, chief justice, and mayor were late, the senate were unable to perform any business.

79. A) There is one thing that most kids would rather do with food than eat it: play with it.
    B) Most kids would rather play with food than eat food.
    C) For most kids, they would rather play with it than eat their foods.
    D) Food, most kids believe, is for playing with rather than for eating it.

80. A) counsil
    B) council
    C) councill
    D) none of these

81. A) visibally
    B) visiblly
    C) visibly
    D) none of these

82. A) parallel
    B) paralell
    C) parallell
    D) none of these

83. A) greef
    B) grief
    C) greif
    D) none of these

84. Everyone agrees that military bases that have been closed should be put to other uses; but as long as they are not cleaned up, no one can go near them safely. Half of the closed bases are dangerously polluted, either with hazardous chemicals or explosives. The federal government's willingness to sell these lands at somewhat reduced prices to the states is of no use unless the toxic wastes are cleaned up prior to the sale.

The paragraph best supports the statement that those states that purchase army bases from the federal government
    A) will be unable to use them for nonmilitary purposes
    B) should ascertain that the lands are pollution free before completing any transaction
    C) should use the land for the construction of prisons unwanted in other areas of the state
    D) can expect, in the long run, a modest improvement in the rate of unemployment

85. In South Africa, both the ruling government party and the African National Congress have been consistently willing to consider new ideas, to change positions, and to compromise. They are opponents, but both see the need to change South Africa. It is the extreme left and the extreme right that are incapable of seeing any point of view other than their own. Both are racist, violent, and determined that the flexible parties of the center will not succeed.

The paragraph best supports the statement that
    A) the ruling government party and the African National Congress are no longer the most important forces in South Africa
    B) the African National Congress is more willing to compromise than the ruling government party
    C) the extremists of both political persuasions present a real threat to the possible solution of political differences
    D) the most plausible solution to problems of South Africa is the separation of country into two independent nations

ANSWER KEY FOR MODEL TEST 4

Word Meaning

1. **B**	18. **B**	35. **B**	52. **C**	69. **C**
2. **D**	19. **A**	36. **C**	53. **A**	70. **B**
3. **C**	20. **D**	37. **A**	54. **D**	71. **D**
4. **B**	21. **C**	38. **D**	55. **B**	72. **A**
5. **B**	22. **B**	39. **B**	56. **D**	73. **B**

Analogies

6. **B**	23. **C**	40. **D**	57. **B**	74. **C**
7. **B**	24. **A**	41. **A**	58. **D**	75. **C**
8. **D**	25. **D**	42. **C**	59. **B**	76. **D**
9. **B**	26. **C**	43. **D**	60. **A**	77. **A**

Grammar

10. **D**	27. **B**	44. **B**	61. **C**	78. **B**
11. **D**	28. **C**	45. **C**	62 **D**	79. **A**

Spelling

12. **A**	29. **C**	46. **B**	63. **D**	80. **B**
13. **B**	30. **D**	47. **B**	64. **A**	81. **C**
14. **C**	31. **C**	48. **A**	65. **C**	82. **A**
15. **B**	32. **D**	49. **B**	66. **A**	83. **B**

Reading

16. **B**	33. **D**	50. **A**	67. **C**	84. **B**
17. **C**	34. **B**	51. **B**	68. **B**	85. **C**

ANALYSIS CHART FOR MODEL TEST 4

Now that you've corrected your exam use the following chart to carefully analyze your results and spot your strengths and weaknesses. This analysis should help you focus your study and review efforts.

Section	Total Number of Questions	Number Correct	Number Incorrect	Number Unanswered*
Word Meaning	25			
Analogies	20			
Grammar	10			
Spelling	20			
Reading Comprehension	10			
TOTAL	85			

*Since there is no penalty for incorrect answers on the Verbal Abilities Test, you should have left no question unanswered. Even if you didn't have time to answer a question, at least you should have filled in the answer space with a guess.

ANSWER EXPLANATIONS FOR MODEL TEST 4

1. **(B)** To *plead* is to *beg,* as in to plead for help.
2. **(D)** One meaning of the word *auditor* is listener. Words like audio, audience, and audition are derived from the Latin verb *audire,* to hear.
3. **(C)** *Verbal* is *oral.* Verbose is wordy.
4. **(B)** To *scale* means to *climb,* as in to scale the walls of a fort.
5. **(B)** *Turbulent* means *agitated,* noisy, violent.
6. **(B)** A broad category is followed by an example or member of that category.
7. **(B)** The second word is the part of the body with which the first word deals.
8. **(D)** The first word is the edible part of the second word.
9. **(B)** The second word is the likely action of a person the first adjective describes.
10. **(D)** (A), (B), and (C) have second verbs where one is sufficient.
11. **(D)** In (A), the opening phrase dangles. In (B), the verb "were" should be something like "extended" or "lasted." In (C), "novels" is repeated.
12. **(A)** address
13. **(B)** embarrassing
14. **(C)** nuclear
15. **(B)** neither
16. **(B)** The first sentence speaks of the "financial center" and the second of New York as *also* the fraud capital. None of the other answers is supported by the text of the paragraph.
17. **(C)** Though (A), (B), and (D) may be true, there is nothing to support them in the paragraph. That the tobacco industry has filed suit is a good indication of its concern with the effect of the report on sales.
18. **(B)** A *controversy* is a *dispute,* an argument, or disagreement.
19. **(A)** To *cite* is to *quote,* to refer to.
20. **(D)** An *embargo* is a *restriction,* especially a trade prohibition.
21. **(C)** To *forsake* is to *abandon,* to desert.
22. **(B)** *Expansive* is *demonstrative,* open, generous.
23. **(C)** The second word is a division or part of the first.
24. **(A)** The first word is a male, the second, a female.
25. **(D)** The first word is a tool that is used to cut the second word.
26. **(C)** The two prepositions are opposites.
27. **(B)** Choice (B) corrects the dangling modifier that begins (A). Choice (C) is a sentence fragment, lacking a main verb, and (D) places the final modifying clause so that it's unclear if it modifies "hospital" or "patients."

28. **(C)** Choice (C) is the most economical version and has no errors. (A) and (D) have a vague pronoun ("this") ("which"); (B) has an awkward repetition ("decision").

29. **(C)** committee

30. **(D)** Correct spelling: desperate

31. **(C)** shuttered

32. **(D)** Correct spelling: foreign

33. **(D)** The passage is concerned with the failure to prevent the death by gunshot of so many American children. The problem with (C) is that the passage speaks of an increasing percentage of children killed but not a larger number each year. It is possible the total would decline, while the percentage increased.

34. **(B)** Since the refrigerator consumes 20 percent of the average household electricity and the new refrigerators use only half as much energy, the electric bill should decrease by about 10 percent.

35. **(B)** To *appreciate* means to *increase*, as a stock appreciates in value. This is, of course, only one of the several meanings of this verb.

36. **(C)** A *beret* is a *cap*, especially worn in France.

37. **(A)** *Futile* means *useless*.

38. **(D)** A *commotion* is an *uproar*, a noisy disturbance.

39. **(B)** To *impose* is to *levy*, as in to impose a tax.

40. **(D)** The second word is workplace of the first.

41. **(A)** The two adjectives are opposites. A glutton is one who overeats.

42. **(C)** The first is worn by the second as a symbol of office.

43. **(D)** The second adjective is an extreme of the first.

44. **(B)** Only (B) uses only one pronoun (you, your) consistently. Each of the other three versions shifts from "one" to "you" or "you" to "one."

45. **(C)** Choice (C) is the most economical version. "Final" and "at the end," as well as "total and complete," are redundant.

46. **(B)** repetition

47. **(B)** manageable

48. **(A)** organically

49. **(B)** explain

50. **(A)** The paragraph points out the benefits of captions to both the hearing and the hearing-impaired audience. The other choices may be true but they are not nearly so well supported by this paragraph.

51. **(B)** Of the four answers, only choice (B) can be supported by the information in this paragraph. The paragraph implies that the United States wishes to find an answer because its allies do influence policy.

52. **(C)** *Extinct* means *ended*, extinguished, no longer alive.

53. **(A)** An *auction* is a kind of *sale*.

54. **(D)** To *nurture* is to *foster*, to nourish or maintain.

55. **(B)** The adjective *bleak* means *desolate*.

56. **(D)** To *reap* is to *gather*, to harvest.

57. **(B)** The second word is the material of which the first is made.

58. **(D)** The second word is a kind of work written by the first.

59. **(B)** The second word is the person who relies on the services of the first.

60. **(A)** The second word is moved by the first word to perform its function.

61. **(C)** The errors here are in the verb tenses. The correct version uses the past perfect "had mowed" in the clause with "after," and the past tense in the rest of the sentence.

62. **(D)** Only choice (D) is a complete sentence. The three other versions are sentence fragments, missing a main verb.

63. **(D)** Correct spelling: extraordinary

64. **(A)** appropriate

65. **(C)** accessories

66. **(A)** similar

67. **(C)** Since the paragraph presents both the possible advantages and disadvantages of privatization, it supports only choice (C). Choice (B) overstates and distorts a detail from the paragraph.

68. **(B)** Choices (A), (C), and (D) are not supported by the paragraph, but if fiction sales are falling, the novelist probably faces a declining number of readers.

69. **(C)** An *imprudent* person is *rash*, lacking in prudence.

70. **(B)** A *tariff* is a *tax*.

71. **(D)** *Wrenching* is *distorting* or twisting.

72. **(A)** An *incentive* is a *stimulus* or goad.

73. **(B)** *Composure* is *equanimity* or an even-tempered quality.

74. **(C)** The second term describes a group of the first word.

75. **(C)** The second word is the habitat of the first word.

76. **(D)** The two words are opposites.

77. **(A)** The first word is powered by the second.

78. **(B)** Choice (B) has the correct singular verb with "senate" and keeps the subjects and verbs close together. (A) and (D) have agreement errors, and (C) has an idiom error in "Being as."

79. **(A)** The first choice is correct; it avoids the repetition or awkward prepositions and pronouns of the other three.

80. **(B)** council

81. **(C)** visibly

82. **(A)** parallel

83. **(B)** grief

84. **(B)** The passage warns against pollution on army bases. Choice (A) overstates, while choices (C) and (D) may or may not be true but they are not relevant to this passage.

85. **(C)** The passage does prefer the African National Congress to the extremes, but not above the ruling party (B). Neither (A) nor (D) can be supported by this paragraph. The point of the paragraph is summed up by choice (C).

PART TWO

The Clerical Abilities Test

CHAPTER 4

General Strategies
A Diagnostic Test
with Answer Explanations
Analysis of Strengths and Weaknesses

THE CLERICAL ABILITIES TEST

The Clerical Abilities Test is a test of speed and accuracy on four clerical tasks. There are 120 questions with a *time limit of 15 minutes*. The categories are as follows:

Name and number checking	30 questions
Alphabetical order	30 questions
Arithmetic	30 questions
Letters and numbers	30 questions

The question types are "scrambled" throughout the test; that is, there are 5 questions of each type, repeated until they total 120 questions. Each question has equal value toward your final score. Your score on the Clerical Abilities Test, unlike that on the Verbal Abilities Test, is penalized for incorrect answers. (See the section on "Guessing" that follows.)

PROCEDURE

You will have 10 minutes to study the directions and sample questions on the front of your test booklet and to mark the answers to these sample questions in the space provided. (However, since time is at a premium on this test, it is important that you become familiar with the test question types *long before you take the actual exam.*) You will be told when to begin the actual test, for which you will have only 15 minutes.

GENERAL STRATEGIES

Since there is a limited amount of time (15 minutes) for 120 questions, some essential considerations come into play. We recommend that you reread the general strategies explained in the Verbal Abilities Test section of this book (pages 3–

5). There is one very *important* difference in the strategies for the Clerical Abilities Test, however, in regard to guessing.

Guessing

The score for this test, unlike the Verbal Abilities Test, is determined by the number of right answers *minus one-fourth* the number of wrong answers. Blank answers are given neither plus nor minus credit. Therefore every filled-in but incorrect answer lowers your test score very slightly. For example, if on this test you answer

90 questions correctly,
20 questions incorrectly, and leave
10 questions unanswered,

you will get 90 credits for your correct answers, minus 5 points for your incorrect answers ($\frac{1}{4} \times$ 20), for a total of 85 points. Notice that your final score is 5 points lower because of the 20 wrong answers.

Because of this adjustment, it is not wise to guess blindly on the Clerical Abilities Test, as a wrong choice can decrease your total score. (A "blind" guess is answering a question where you have no insight into the problem and no way of eliminating any choices.)

But if you are able to eliminate even one of the answer choices as incorrect, then you will have increased the odds of guessing correctly and, in the long run, you should get more points in your favor than taken away.

Of course, if you can eliminate *two* choices as incorrect, your chances of guessing correctly are even greater.

So, to summarize, don't guess blindly on this test, but do guess when you can eliminate one or more answer choices as incorrect.

Remember, if you skip a question, be careful to place your next answer mark in the proper space on your answer sheet, *not* in the space you just skipped!

Speed

The Clerical Abilities Test is primarily a test of *speed* in carrying out relatively simple clerical tasks. While accuracy on these tasks is important and will be taken into account in the scoring, experience has shown that many persons are so concerned about accuracy that they do the test more slowly than they should. Speed as well as accuracy is important to achieve a good score. Therefore, do not spend undue time on any particular question.

HOW TO DETERMINE THE TOTAL TEST SCORE

The score on the Verbal Abilities Test is the number of right answers. The score on the Clerical Abilities Test is the number of right answers minus ¼ the number of wrong answers (R − ¼W).

The scores on both tests will be added to determine total score. The passing point on the total test will vary according to the grade and kind of position to be filled. In general, a score of approximately 60 percent of the 85 questions on the Verbal Abilities Test is considered good performance. Therefore, a score of 50 or better on the Verbal Abilities Test and a score of 100 on the Verbal and Clerical Abilities Tests combined are considered good scores. These scores will probably qualify a prospective applicant, providing all other test and experience requirements for a particular position are met. Similarly, a score of less than 50 percent of the questions on the Verbal Abilities Test is considered poor. Less than 40 on the Verbal Abilities Test and less than 80 on the Verbal and Clerical Abilities Tests combined indicate relatively poor performance.

A review of how you answered the test questions in the Model Tests will provide useful information to see whether more work is needed in spelling, grammar, etc., whether greater speed or accuracy is needed in the Clerical Abilities Test, and whether the nature of the tasks in the two tests has been clearly understood.

A Diagnostic Test with Answer Explanations

The purpose of this diagnostic test is to familiarize you with the Clerical Abilities Test. It is designed to introduce you to the testing areas and assist you in evaluating your strengths and weaknesses. This will help you focus your review. Chapter 5 will give you a more complete range of problem types and specific strategies for each section. After correcting the diagnostic exam and assessing your strengths and weaknesses, you should start your area reviews and practice in the next chapter.

The diagnostic test should be taken under strict test conditions.

NOTE: Sample questions are usually distributed with the announcement and if so may not be given in the official examination.

First take 10 minutes to review the sample questions given here before starting this exam. Now tear out your answer sheet from this book, turn to the next page, and begin the exam.

ANSWER SHEET

SIGNATURE: _____
(Please Sign)

EXAMINATION TITLE: _____

PLACE OF EXAMINATION: _____
City

_____
State

TODAY'S DATE: _____

SAMPLE Ⓐ ● Ⓒ Ⓓ Ⓔ

DIRECTIONS FOR MARKING ANSWER SHEET

Use only a **No. 2 (or softer) lead pencil.** Darken completely the circle corresponding to your answer. You **must** keep your mark within the circle. Stray marks may be counted as errors. Erase **completely** all marks except your answer.

SAMPLE NAME GRID

LAST NAME

M C C A B E

F.I. C

M.I. A

1. In the boxes below, **PRINT** your name. Print only as many letters as will fit within the areas for the last name, first initial (F.I.), and middle initial (M.I.) Below each box, darken the circle containing the same letter. SEE SAMPLE NAME GRID

2. In the boxes below, enter your 9-digit Social Security Number. Below each box, darken the circle in each column corresponding to the number you have entered.

SOCIAL SECURITY NUMBER

3.

OCCUPATIONAL GROUP NUMBER

LAST NAME
F.I.
M.I.

SECTION 1

PART

TEST SERIES

TEST NUMBER

Make no marks or entries in the columns to the right until you receive instructions from the administrator.

1 Ⓐ Ⓑ Ⓒ Ⓓ Ⓔ
2 Ⓐ Ⓑ Ⓒ Ⓓ Ⓔ
3 Ⓐ Ⓑ Ⓒ Ⓓ Ⓔ
4 Ⓐ Ⓑ Ⓒ Ⓓ Ⓔ
5 Ⓐ Ⓑ Ⓒ Ⓓ Ⓔ
6 Ⓐ Ⓑ Ⓒ Ⓓ Ⓔ
7 Ⓐ Ⓑ Ⓒ Ⓓ Ⓔ
8 Ⓐ Ⓑ Ⓒ Ⓓ Ⓔ
9 Ⓐ Ⓑ Ⓒ Ⓓ Ⓔ
10 Ⓐ Ⓑ Ⓒ Ⓓ Ⓔ
11 Ⓐ Ⓑ Ⓒ Ⓓ Ⓔ
12 Ⓐ Ⓑ Ⓒ Ⓓ Ⓔ
13 Ⓐ Ⓑ Ⓒ Ⓓ Ⓔ
14 Ⓐ Ⓑ Ⓒ Ⓓ Ⓔ
15 Ⓐ Ⓑ Ⓒ Ⓓ Ⓔ
16 Ⓐ Ⓑ Ⓒ Ⓓ Ⓔ
17 Ⓐ Ⓑ Ⓒ Ⓓ Ⓔ
18 Ⓐ Ⓑ Ⓒ Ⓓ Ⓔ
19 Ⓐ Ⓑ Ⓒ Ⓓ Ⓔ
20 Ⓐ Ⓑ Ⓒ Ⓓ Ⓔ
21 Ⓐ Ⓑ Ⓒ Ⓓ Ⓔ
22 Ⓐ Ⓑ Ⓒ Ⓓ Ⓔ
23 Ⓐ Ⓑ Ⓒ Ⓓ Ⓔ
24 Ⓐ Ⓑ Ⓒ Ⓓ Ⓔ
25 Ⓐ Ⓑ Ⓒ Ⓓ Ⓔ
26 Ⓐ Ⓑ Ⓒ Ⓓ Ⓔ
27 Ⓐ Ⓑ Ⓒ Ⓓ Ⓔ
28 Ⓐ Ⓑ Ⓒ Ⓓ Ⓔ
29 Ⓐ Ⓑ Ⓒ Ⓓ Ⓔ
30 Ⓐ Ⓑ Ⓒ Ⓓ Ⓔ
31 Ⓐ Ⓑ Ⓒ Ⓓ Ⓔ
32 Ⓐ Ⓑ Ⓒ Ⓓ Ⓔ
33 Ⓐ Ⓑ Ⓒ Ⓓ Ⓔ
34 Ⓐ Ⓑ Ⓒ Ⓓ Ⓔ
35 Ⓐ Ⓑ Ⓒ Ⓓ Ⓔ
36 Ⓐ Ⓑ Ⓒ Ⓓ Ⓔ
37 Ⓐ Ⓑ Ⓒ Ⓓ Ⓔ
38 Ⓐ Ⓑ Ⓒ Ⓓ Ⓔ
39 Ⓐ Ⓑ Ⓒ Ⓓ Ⓔ
40 Ⓐ Ⓑ Ⓒ Ⓓ Ⓔ
41 Ⓐ Ⓑ Ⓒ Ⓓ Ⓔ
42 Ⓐ Ⓑ Ⓒ Ⓓ Ⓔ
43 Ⓐ Ⓑ Ⓒ Ⓓ Ⓔ
44 Ⓐ Ⓑ Ⓒ Ⓓ Ⓔ
45 Ⓐ Ⓑ Ⓒ Ⓓ Ⓔ
46 Ⓐ Ⓑ Ⓒ Ⓓ Ⓔ
47 Ⓐ Ⓑ Ⓒ Ⓓ Ⓔ
48 Ⓐ Ⓑ Ⓒ Ⓓ Ⓔ
49 Ⓐ Ⓑ Ⓒ Ⓓ Ⓔ
50 Ⓐ Ⓑ Ⓒ Ⓓ Ⓔ
51 Ⓐ Ⓑ Ⓒ Ⓓ Ⓔ
52 Ⓐ Ⓑ Ⓒ Ⓓ Ⓔ
53 Ⓐ Ⓑ Ⓒ Ⓓ Ⓔ
54 Ⓐ Ⓑ Ⓒ Ⓓ Ⓔ
55 Ⓐ Ⓑ Ⓒ Ⓓ Ⓔ
56 Ⓐ Ⓑ Ⓒ Ⓓ Ⓔ
57 Ⓐ Ⓑ Ⓒ Ⓓ Ⓔ
58 Ⓐ Ⓑ Ⓒ Ⓓ Ⓔ
59 Ⓐ Ⓑ Ⓒ Ⓓ Ⓔ
60 Ⓐ Ⓑ Ⓒ Ⓓ Ⓔ
61 Ⓐ Ⓑ Ⓒ Ⓓ Ⓔ
62 Ⓐ Ⓑ Ⓒ Ⓓ Ⓔ
63 Ⓐ Ⓑ Ⓒ Ⓓ Ⓔ
64 Ⓐ Ⓑ Ⓒ Ⓓ Ⓔ
65 Ⓐ Ⓑ Ⓒ Ⓓ Ⓔ
66 Ⓐ Ⓑ Ⓒ Ⓓ Ⓔ
67 Ⓐ Ⓑ Ⓒ Ⓓ Ⓔ
68 Ⓐ Ⓑ Ⓒ Ⓓ Ⓔ
69 Ⓐ Ⓑ Ⓒ Ⓓ Ⓔ
70 Ⓐ Ⓑ Ⓒ Ⓓ Ⓔ
71 Ⓐ Ⓑ Ⓒ Ⓓ Ⓔ
72 Ⓐ Ⓑ Ⓒ Ⓓ Ⓔ
73 Ⓐ Ⓑ Ⓒ Ⓓ Ⓔ
74 Ⓐ Ⓑ Ⓒ Ⓓ Ⓔ
75 Ⓐ Ⓑ Ⓒ Ⓓ Ⓔ
76 Ⓐ Ⓑ Ⓒ Ⓓ Ⓔ
77 Ⓐ Ⓑ Ⓒ Ⓓ Ⓔ
78 Ⓐ Ⓑ Ⓒ Ⓓ Ⓔ
79 Ⓐ Ⓑ Ⓒ Ⓓ Ⓔ
80 Ⓐ Ⓑ Ⓒ Ⓓ Ⓔ
81 Ⓐ Ⓑ Ⓒ Ⓓ Ⓔ
82 Ⓐ Ⓑ Ⓒ Ⓓ Ⓔ
83 Ⓐ Ⓑ Ⓒ Ⓓ Ⓔ
84 Ⓐ Ⓑ Ⓒ Ⓓ Ⓔ
85 Ⓐ Ⓑ Ⓒ Ⓓ Ⓔ
86 Ⓐ Ⓑ Ⓒ Ⓓ Ⓔ
87 Ⓐ Ⓑ Ⓒ Ⓓ Ⓔ
88 Ⓐ Ⓑ Ⓒ Ⓓ Ⓔ
89 Ⓐ Ⓑ Ⓒ Ⓓ Ⓔ
90 Ⓐ Ⓑ Ⓒ Ⓓ Ⓔ
91 Ⓐ Ⓑ Ⓒ Ⓓ Ⓔ
92 Ⓐ Ⓑ Ⓒ Ⓓ Ⓔ
93 Ⓐ Ⓑ Ⓒ Ⓓ Ⓔ
94 Ⓐ Ⓑ Ⓒ Ⓓ Ⓔ
95 Ⓐ Ⓑ Ⓒ Ⓓ Ⓔ
96 Ⓐ Ⓑ Ⓒ Ⓓ Ⓔ
97 Ⓐ Ⓑ Ⓒ Ⓓ Ⓔ
98 Ⓐ Ⓑ Ⓒ Ⓓ Ⓔ
99 Ⓐ Ⓑ Ⓒ Ⓓ Ⓔ
100 Ⓐ Ⓑ Ⓒ Ⓓ Ⓔ
101 Ⓐ Ⓑ Ⓒ Ⓓ Ⓔ
102 Ⓐ Ⓑ Ⓒ Ⓓ Ⓔ
103 Ⓐ Ⓑ Ⓒ Ⓓ Ⓔ
104 Ⓐ Ⓑ Ⓒ Ⓓ Ⓔ
105 Ⓐ Ⓑ Ⓒ Ⓓ Ⓔ
106 Ⓐ Ⓑ Ⓒ Ⓓ Ⓔ
107 Ⓐ Ⓑ Ⓒ Ⓓ Ⓔ
108 Ⓐ Ⓑ Ⓒ Ⓓ Ⓔ
109 Ⓐ Ⓑ Ⓒ Ⓓ Ⓔ
110 Ⓐ Ⓑ Ⓒ Ⓓ Ⓔ
111 Ⓐ Ⓑ Ⓒ Ⓓ Ⓔ
112 Ⓐ Ⓑ Ⓒ Ⓓ Ⓔ
113 Ⓐ Ⓑ Ⓒ Ⓓ Ⓔ
114 Ⓐ Ⓑ Ⓒ Ⓓ Ⓔ
115 Ⓐ Ⓑ Ⓒ Ⓓ Ⓔ
116 Ⓐ Ⓑ Ⓒ Ⓓ Ⓔ
117 Ⓐ Ⓑ Ⓒ Ⓓ Ⓔ
118 Ⓐ Ⓑ Ⓒ Ⓓ Ⓔ
119 Ⓐ Ⓑ Ⓒ Ⓓ Ⓔ
120 Ⓐ Ⓑ Ⓒ Ⓓ Ⓔ
121 Ⓐ Ⓑ Ⓒ Ⓓ Ⓔ
122 Ⓐ Ⓑ Ⓒ Ⓓ Ⓔ
123 Ⓐ Ⓑ Ⓒ Ⓓ Ⓔ
124 Ⓐ Ⓑ Ⓒ Ⓓ Ⓔ
125 Ⓐ Ⓑ Ⓒ Ⓓ Ⓔ
126 Ⓐ Ⓑ Ⓒ Ⓓ Ⓔ
127 Ⓐ Ⓑ Ⓒ Ⓓ Ⓔ
128 Ⓐ Ⓑ Ⓒ Ⓓ Ⓔ
129 Ⓐ Ⓑ Ⓒ Ⓓ Ⓔ
130 Ⓐ Ⓑ Ⓒ Ⓓ Ⓔ

CLERICAL ABILITIES DIAGNOSTIC TEST

Time allotted—15 minutes

Directions

This test contains four kinds of questions. There are some of each kind on each page in the booklet. The time limit for the test will be announced by the examiner.

Study the sample questions carefully. Each question has five suggested answers. Decide which one is the best answer. Find the question number on the Sample Answer Sheet. Show your answer to the question by darkening completely the space corresponding to the letter that is the same as the letter of your answer. Keep your mark within the space. If you have to erase a mark, be sure to erase it completely. Mark only one answer for each question.

Sample Questions

In each line across the page there are three names or numbers that are much alike. Compare the three names or numbers and decide which ones are exactly alike. On the Sample Answer Sheet at the right, mark the answer—

A if ALL THREE names or numbers are exactly ALIKE
B if only the FIRST and SECOND names or numbers are exactly ALIKE
C if only the FIRST and THIRD names or numbers are exactly ALIKE
D if only the SECOND and THIRD names or numbers are exactly ALIKE
E if ALL THREE names or numbers are DIFFERENT

I. Davis Hazen	David Hozen	David Hazen
II. Lois Appel	Lois Appel	Lois Apfel
III. June Allan	Jane Allan	Jane Allan
IV. 10235	10235	10235
V. 32614	32164	32614

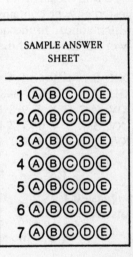

SAMPLE ANSWER SHEET

1 Ⓐ Ⓑ Ⓒ Ⓓ Ⓔ
2 Ⓐ Ⓑ Ⓒ Ⓓ Ⓔ
3 Ⓐ Ⓑ Ⓒ Ⓓ Ⓔ
4 Ⓐ Ⓑ Ⓒ Ⓓ Ⓔ
5 Ⓐ Ⓑ Ⓒ Ⓓ Ⓔ
6 Ⓐ Ⓑ Ⓒ Ⓓ Ⓔ
7 Ⓐ Ⓑ Ⓒ Ⓓ Ⓔ

It will be to your advantage to learn what A, B, C, D, and E stand for. If you finish the sample questions before you are told to turn to the test, study them.

In the next group of sample questions, there is a name in a box at the left, and four other names in alphabetical order at the right. Find the correct space for the boxed name so that it will be in alphabetical order with the others, and mark the letter of that space as your answer.

VI. | Jones, Jane |

A) →
   Goodyear, G. L.
B) →
   Haddon, Harry
C) →
   Jackson, Mary
D) →
   Jenkins, William
E) →

VII. | Kessler, Neilson |

A) →
   Kessel, Carl
B) →
   Kessinger, D. J.
C) →
   Kessler, Karl
D) →
   Kessner, Lewis
E) →

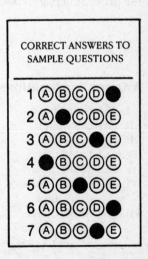

CORRECT ANSWERS TO SAMPLE QUESTIONS

1 Ⓐ Ⓑ Ⓒ Ⓓ ●
2 Ⓐ ● Ⓒ Ⓓ Ⓔ
3 Ⓐ Ⓑ Ⓒ ● Ⓔ
4 ● Ⓑ Ⓒ Ⓓ Ⓔ
5 Ⓐ Ⓑ ● Ⓓ Ⓔ
6 Ⓐ Ⓑ Ⓒ Ⓓ ●
7 Ⓐ Ⓑ Ⓒ ● Ⓔ

In the following questions, do whatever the question says, and find your answer among the list of suggested answers for that question. Mark the Sample Answer Sheet A, B, C or D, for the answer you obtained; or if your answer is not among these, mark E for that question.

VIII. Add:

22
+ 33

Answers
A) 44 B) 45
C) 54 D) 55
E) none of these

X. Multiply:

25
× 5

Answers
A) 100 B) 115
C) 125 D) 135
E) none of these

IX. Subtract:

24
− 3

A) 20 B) 21
C) 27 D) 29
E) none of these

XI. Divide:

6)126

A) 20 B) 22
C) 24 D) 26
E) none of these

There is one set of suggested answers for the next group of sample questions. Do not try to memorize these answers, because there will be a different set on each page in the test.

To find the answer to a question, find which suggested answer contains numbers and letters all of which appear in the question. If no suggested answer fits, mark E for that question.

XII. 8 N K 9 G T 4 6
XIII. T 9 7 Z 6 L 3 K
XIV. Z 7 G K 3 9 8 N
XV. 3 K 9 4 6 G Z L
XVI. Z N 7 3 8 K T 9

Suggested Answers
A = 7, 9, G, K
B = 8, 9, T, Z
C = 6, 7, K, Z
D = 6, 8, G, T
E = none of these

SAMPLE ANSWER SHEET	CORRECT ANSWERS TO SAMPLE QUESTIONS
1 Ⓐ Ⓑ Ⓒ Ⓓ Ⓔ	1 Ⓐ Ⓑ Ⓒ ● Ⓔ
2 Ⓐ Ⓑ Ⓒ Ⓓ Ⓔ	2 Ⓐ ● Ⓒ Ⓓ Ⓔ
3 Ⓐ Ⓑ Ⓒ Ⓓ Ⓔ	3 Ⓐ Ⓑ ● Ⓓ Ⓔ
4 Ⓐ Ⓑ Ⓒ Ⓓ Ⓔ	4 Ⓐ Ⓑ Ⓒ Ⓓ ●
5 Ⓐ Ⓑ Ⓒ Ⓓ Ⓔ	5 Ⓐ Ⓑ Ⓒ ● Ⓔ
6 Ⓐ Ⓑ Ⓒ Ⓓ Ⓔ	6 Ⓐ Ⓑ ● Ⓓ Ⓔ
7 Ⓐ Ⓑ Ⓒ Ⓓ Ⓔ	7 ● Ⓑ Ⓒ Ⓓ Ⓔ
8 Ⓐ Ⓑ Ⓒ Ⓓ Ⓔ	8 Ⓐ Ⓑ Ⓒ Ⓓ ●
9 Ⓐ Ⓑ Ⓒ Ⓓ Ⓔ	9 Ⓐ ● Ⓒ Ⓓ Ⓔ

After you have marked your answers to all the questions on the Sample Answer Sheets on this page and on the preceding page, check them with the answers in the boxes marked Correct Answers to Sample Questions.

Answer Explanations for Sample Questions

I. (E) Davi<u>s</u> Hazen	David Ho<u>z</u>en	David Hazen
II. (B) Lois A<u>p</u>pel	Lois Appel	Lois Ap<u>f</u>el
III. (D) <u>J</u>une Allan	Jane Allan	Jane All<u>a</u>n
IV. (A) 10235	10235	10235
V. (C) 32614	32<u>16</u>4	32614
VI. (E) Jenkins, William		
Jones, Jane		
VII. (D) Kessler, Karl		
Kessler, Neilson		
Kessner, Lewis		

VIII. (D) 55
IX. (B) 21
X. (C) 125
XI. (E) 21
XII. (D) 8 N K 9 <u>G T</u> 4 <u>6</u>
XIII. (C) T 9 <u>7</u> Z <u>6</u> L 3 <u>K</u>
XIV. (A) Z <u>7</u> <u>G</u> <u>K</u> 3 <u>9</u> 8 N
XV. (E) 3 <u>K</u> <u>9</u> <u>4</u> <u>6</u> <u>G</u> <u>Z</u> <u>L</u>
XVI. (B) <u>Z</u> N 7 3 <u>8</u> K <u>T</u> <u>9</u>

THE TEST

In questions 1 through 5, compare the three names or numbers, and mark the answer—
A if ALL THREE names or numbers are exactly ALIKE
B if only the FIRST and SECOND names or numbers are exactly ALIKE
C if only the FIRST and THIRD names or numbers are exactly ALIKE
D if only the SECOND and THIRD names or numbers are exactly ALIKE
E if ALL THREE names or numbers are DIFFERENT

1. 5261383	5261383	5261338
2. 8125690	8126690	8125609
3. W. E. Johnston	W. E. Johnson	W. E. Johnson
4. Vergil L. Muller	Vergil L. Muller	Vergil L. Muller
5. Atherton R. Warde	Asheton R. Warde	Atherton P. Warde

In questions 6 through 10, find the correct place for the name in the box.

6. | Hackett, Gerald |

A) →
   Habert, James
B) →
   Hachett, J. J.
C) →
   Hachetts, K. Larson
D) →
   Hachettson, Leroy
E) →

7. | Margenroth, Alvin |

A) →
   Margeroth, Albert
B) →
   Margestein, Dan
C) →
   Margestein, David
D) →
   Margue, Edgar
E) →

8. | Bobbitt, Olivier E. |

A) →
   Bobbitt, D. Olivier
B) →
   Bobbitt, Olive B.
C) →
   Bobbitt, Olivia H.
D) →
   Bobbitt, R. Olivia
E) →

9. | Mosely, Werner |

A) →
   Mosely, Albert J.
B) →
   Mosley, Alvin
C) →
   Mosley, S. M.
D) →
   Mozley, Vinson N.
E) →

10. | Youmuns, Frank L. |

A) →
   Youmons, Frank G.
B) →
   Youmons, Frank H.
C) →
   Youmons, Frank K.
D) →
   Youmons, Frank M.
E) →

GO ON TO THE NEXT COLUMN.

Answers

11. Add:
    43
    + 32

    A) 55   B) 65
    C) 66   D) 75
    E) none of these

12. Subtract:
    83
    − 4

    A) 73   B) 79
    C) 80   D) 89
    E) none of these

13. Multiply:
    41
    × 7

    A) 281   B) 287
    C) 291   D) 297
    E) none of these

14. Divide:
    6)306

    A) 44   B) 51
    C) 52   D) 60
    E) none of these

15. Add:
    37
    + 15

    A) 42   B) 52
    C) 53   D) 62
    E) none of these

For each question below, find which one of the suggested answers appears in that question.

16. 6 2 5 K 4 P T G

17. L 4 7 2 T 6 V K

18. 3 5 4 L 9 V T G

19. G 4 K 7 L 3 5 Z

20. 4 K 2 9 N 5 T G

Suggested Answers
A = 4, 5, K, T
B = 4, 7, G, K
C = 2, 5, G, L
D = 2, 7, L, T
E = none of these

GO ON TO THE NEXT PAGE.

In questions 21 through 25, compare the three names or numbers, and mark the answer—

A if ALL THREE names or numbers are exactly ALIKE
B if only the FIRST and SECOND names or numbers are exactly ALIKE
C if only the FIRST and THIRD names or numbers are exactly ALIKE
D if only the SECOND and THIRD names or numbers are exactly ALIKE
E if ALL THREE names or numbers are DIFFERENT

21. 2395890	2395890	2395890
22. 1926341	1926347	1926314
23. E. Owens McVey	E. Owen McVey	E. Owen McVay
24. Emily Neal Rouse	Emily Neal Rowse	Emily Neal Rowse
25. H. Merritt Audubon	H. Merriott Audubon	H. Merritt Audubon

In questions 26 through 30, find the correct place for the name in the box.

26. Watters, N. O.

A) →
Waters, Charles L.
B) →
Waterson, Nina P.
C) →
Watson, Nora J.
D) →
Wattwood, Paul A.
E) →

27. Johnston, Edward

A) →
Johnston, Edgar R.
B) →
Johnston, Edmond
C) →
Johnston, Edmund
D) →
Johnstone, Edmund A.
E) →

28. Rensch, Adeline

A) →
Ramsay, Amos
B) →
Remschel, Augusta
C) →
Renshaw, Austin
D) →
Rentzel, Becky
E) →

29. Schnyder, Maurice

A) →
Schneider, Martin
B) →
Schneider, Mertens
C) →
Schnyder, Newman
D) →
Schreibner, Norman
E) →

30. Freedenburg, C. Erma

A) →
Freedenberg, Emerson
B) →
Freedenberg, Erma
C) →
Freedenberg, Erma E.
D) →
Freedinberg, Erma F.
E) →

Answers

31. Subtract:
    68
    − 47

A) 10   B) 11
C) 20   D) 22
E) none of these

32. Multiply:
    50
    × 8

A) 400   B) 408
C) 450   D) 458
E) none of these

33. Divide:
    9)180

A) 20   B) 29
C) 30   D) 39
E) none of these

34. Add:
    78
    + 63

A) 131   B) 140
C) 141   D) 151
E) none of these

35. Subtract:
    89
    − 70

A) 9   B) 18
C) 19   D) 29
E) none of these

For each question below, find which one of the suggested answers appears in that question.

36. 9 G Z 3 L 4 6 N

37. L 5 N K 4 3 9 V

38. 8 2 V P 9 L Z 5

39. V P 9 Z 5 L 8 7

40. 5 T 8 N 2 9 V L

Suggested Answers

A = 4, 9, L, V
B = 4, 5, N, Z
C = 5, 8, L, Z
D = 8, 9, N, V
E = none of these

GO ON TO THE NEXT COLUMN. ————

GO ON TO THE NEXT PAGE.

In questions 41 through 45, compare the three names or numbers, and mark the answer—
A if ALL THREE names or numbers are exactly ALIKE
B if only the FIRST and SECOND names or numbers are exactly ALIKE
C if only the FIRST and THIRD names or numbers are exactly ALIKE
D if only the SECOND and THIRD names or numbers are exactly ALIKE
E if ALL THREE names or numbers are DIFFERENT

41. 6219354	6219354	6219354
42. 2312793	2312793	2312793
43. 1065407	1065407	1065047
44. Francis Ransdell	Frances Ramsdell	Francis Ramsdell
45. Cornelius Detwiler	Cornelius Detwiler	Cornelius Detwiler

In questions 46 through 50, find the correct place for the name in the box.

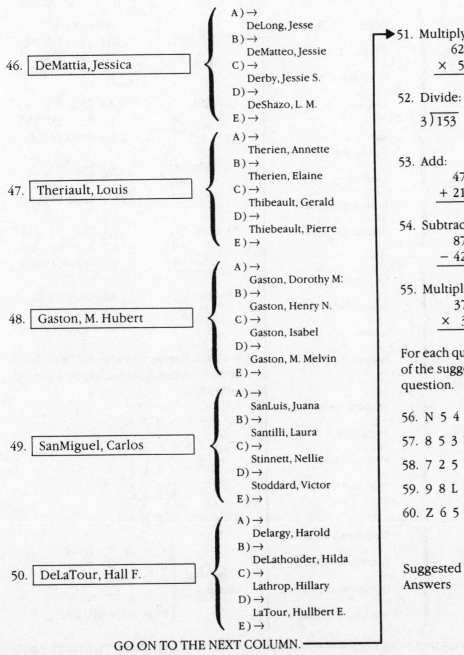

46. DeMattia, Jessica
A) →
DeLong, Jesse
B) →
DeMatteo, Jessie
C) →
Derby, Jessie S.
D) →
DeShazo, L. M.
E) →

47. Theriault, Louis
A) →
Therien, Annette
B) →
Therien, Elaine
C) →
Thibeault, Gerald
D) →
Thiebeault, Pierre
E) →

48. Gaston, M. Hubert
A) →
Gaston, Dorothy M.
B) →
Gaston, Henry N.
C) →
Gaston, Isabel
D) →
Gaston, M. Melvin
E) →

49. SanMiguel, Carlos
A) →
SanLuis, Juana
B) →
Santilli, Laura
C) →
Stinnett, Nellie
D) →
Stoddard, Victor
E) →

50. DeLaTour, Hall F.
A) →
Delargy, Harold
B) →
DeLathouder, Hilda
C) →
Lathrop, Hillary
D) →
LaTour, Hullbert E.
E) →

GO ON TO THE NEXT COLUMN.

Answers

51. Multiply:
62
× 5
A) 300 B) 310
C) 315 D) 360
E) none of these

52. Divide:
3⟌153
A) 41 B) 43
C) 51 D) 53
E) none of these

53. Add:
47
+ 21
A) 58 B) 59
C) 67 D) 68
E) none of these

54. Subtract:
87
− 42
A) 34 B) 35
C) 44 D) 45
E) none of these

55. Multiply:
37
× 3
A) 91 B) 101
C) 104 D) 114
E) none of these

For each question below, find which one of the suggested answers appears in that question.

56. N 5 4 7 T K 3 Z

57. 8 5 3 V L 2 Z N

58. 7 2 5 N 9 K L V

59. 9 8 L 2 5 Z K V

60. Z 6 5 V 9 3 9 N

Suggested Answers
A = 3, 8, K, N
B = 5, 8, N, V
C = 3, 9, V, Z
D = 5, 9, K, Z
E = none of these

GO ON TO THE NEXT PAGE.

In questions 61 through 65, compare the three names or numbers, and mark the answer—
A if ALL THREE names or numbers are exactly ALIKE
B if only the FIRST and SECOND names or numbers are exactly ALIKE
C if only the FIRST and THIRD names or numbers are exactly ALIKE
D if only the SECOND and THIRD names or numbers are exactly ALIKE
E if ALL THREE names or numbers are DIFFERENT

61. 6452054	6452654	6452054
62. 8501268	8501268	8501286
63. Ella Burk Newham	Ella Burk Newnham	Elena Burk Newnham
64. Jno. K. Ravencroft	Jno. H. Ravencroft	Jno. H. Ravencoft
65. Martin Wills Pullen	Martin Wills Pulen	Martin Wills Pullen

In questions 66 through 70, find the correct place for the name in the box.

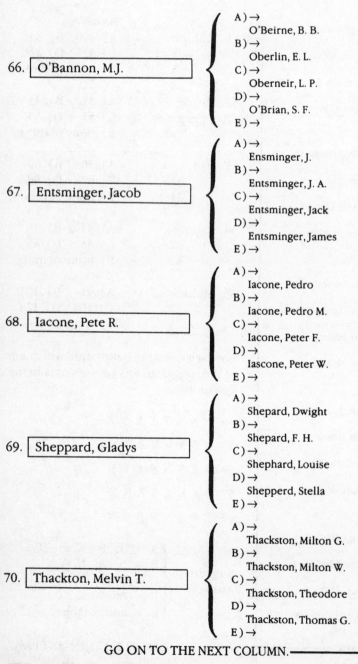

66. O'Bannon, M.J.
  A) →
  O'Beirne, B. B.
  B) →
  Oberlin, E. L.
  C) →
  Oberneir, L. P.
  D) →
  O'Brian, S. F.
  E) →

67. Entsminger, Jacob
  A) →
  Ensminger, J.
  B) →
  Entsminger, J. A.
  C) →
  Entsminger, Jack
  D) →
  Entsminger, James
  E) →

68. Iacone, Pete R.
  A) →
  Iacone, Pedro
  B) →
  Iacone, Pedro M.
  C) →
  Iacone, Peter F.
  D) →
  Iascone, Peter W.
  E) →

69. Sheppard, Gladys
  A) →
  Shepard, Dwight
  B) →
  Shepard, F. H.
  C) →
  Shephard, Louise
  D) →
  Shepperd, Stella
  E) →

70. Thackton, Melvin T.
  A) →
  Thackston, Milton G.
  B) →
  Thackston, Milton W.
  C) →
  Thackston, Theodore
  D) →
  Thackston, Thomas G.
  E) →

Answers

71. Divide:

7)357

A) 51 B) 52
C) 53 D) 54
E) none of these

72. Add:
58
+ 27

A) 75 B) 84
C) 85 D) 95
E) none of these

73. Subtract:
86
− 57

A) 18 B) 29
C) 38 D) 39
E) none of these

74. Multiply:
68
× 4

A) 242 B) 264
C) 272 D) 274
E) none of these

75. Divide:

9)639

A) 71 B) 73
C) 81 D) 83
E) none of these

For each question below, find which one of the suggested answers appears in that question.

76. 6 Z T N 8 7 4 V

77. V 7 8 6 N 5 P L

78. N 7 P V 8 4 2 L

79. 7 8 G 4 3 V L T

80. 4 8 G 2 T N 6 L

Suggested Answers
A = 2, 7, L, N
B = 2, 8, T, V
C = 6, 8, L, T
D = 6, 7, N, V
E = none of these

GO ON TO THE NEXT COLUMN.

GO ON TO THE NEXT PAGE.

In questions 81 through 85, compare the three names or numbers, and mark the answer—
A if ALL THREE names or numbers are exactly ALIKE
B if only the FIRST and SECOND names or numbers are exactly ALIKE
C if only the FIRST and THIRD names or numbers are exactly ALIKE
D if only the SECOND and THIRD names or numbers are exactly ALIKE
E if ALL THREE names or numbers are DIFFERENT

81. 3457988   3457986   3457986
82. 4695682   4695862   4695682
83. Stricklund Kanedy   Stricklund Kanedy   Stricklund Kanedy
84. Joy Harlor Witner   Joy Harloe Witner   Joy Harloe Witner
85. R. M. O. Uberroth   R. M. O. Uberroth   R. N. O. Uberroth

In questions 86 through 90, find the correct place for the name in the box.

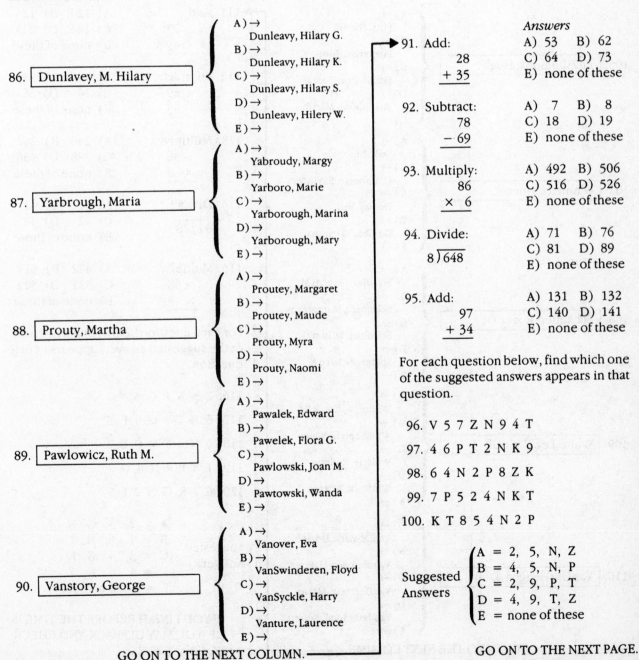

86. Dunlavey, M. Hilary
- A) →
  Dunleavy, Hilary G.
- B) →
  Dunleavy, Hilary K.
- C) →
  Dunleavy, Hilary S.
- D) →
  Dunleavy, Hilery W.
- E) →

87. Yarbrough, Maria
- A) →
  Yabroudy, Margy
- B) →
  Yarboro, Marie
- C) →
  Yarborough, Marina
- D) →
  Yarborough, Mary
- E) →

88. Prouty, Martha
- A) →
  Proutey, Margaret
- B) →
  Proutey, Maude
- C) →
  Prouty, Myra
- D) →
  Prouty, Naomi
- E) →

89. Pawlowicz, Ruth M.
- A) →
  Pawalek, Edward
- B) →
  Pawelek, Flora G.
- C) →
  Pawlowski, Joan M.
- D) →
  Pawtowski, Wanda
- E) →

90. Vanstory, George
- A) →
  Vanover, Eva
- B) →
  VanSwinderen, Floyd
- C) →
  VanSyckle, Harry
- D) →
  Vanture, Laurence
- E) →

GO ON TO THE NEXT COLUMN.

Answers

91. Add:
    28
 + 35

A) 53   B) 62
C) 64   D) 73
E) none of these

92. Subtract:
    78
 − 69

A) 7   B) 8
C) 18   D) 19
E) none of these

93. Multiply:
    86
 × 6

A) 492   B) 506
C) 516   D) 526
E) none of these

94. Divide:
8) 648

A) 71   B) 76
C) 81   D) 89
E) none of these

95. Add:
    97
 + 34

A) 131   B) 132
C) 140   D) 141
E) none of these

For each question below, find which one of the suggested answers appears in that question.

96. V 5 7 Z N 9 4 T

97. 4 6 P T 2 N K 9

98. 6 4 N 2 P 8 Z K

99. 7 P 5 2 4 N K T

100. K T 8 5 4 N 2 P

Suggested Answers
- A = 2, 5, N, Z
- B = 4, 5, N, P
- C = 2, 9, P, T
- D = 4, 9, T, Z
- E = none of these

GO ON TO THE NEXT PAGE.

In questions 101 through 105, compare the three names or numbers, and mark the answer—

A if ALL THREE names or numbers are exactly ALIKE
B if only the FIRST and SECOND names or numbers are exactly ALIKE
C if only the FIRST and THIRD names or numbers are exactly ALIKE
D if only the SECOND and THIRD names or numbers are exactly ALIKE
E if ALL THREE names or numbers are DIFFERENT

101. 1592514	1592574	1592574
102. 2010202	2010202	2010220
103. 6177396	6177936	6177396
104. Drusilla S. Ridgeley	Drusilla S. Ridgeley	Drusilla S. Ridgeley
105. Andrei I. Toumantzev	Andrei I. Tourmantzev	Aňdrei I. Toumantzov

In questions 106 through 110, find the correct place for the name in the box.

106. Fitzsimmons, Hugh
- A) →
- Fitts, Harold
- B) →
- Fitzgerald, June
- C) →
- FitzGibbon, Junius
- D) →
- FitzSimons, Martin
- E) →

107. D'Amato, Vincent
- A) →
- Daly, Steven
- B) →
- D'Amboise, S. Vincent
- C) →
- Daniel, Vail
- D) →
- DeAlba, Valentina
- E) →

108. Schaeffer, Roger D.
- A) →
- Schaffert, Evelyn M.
- B) →
- Schaffner, Margaret M.
- C) →
- Schafhirt, Milton G.
- D) →
- Shafer, Richard E.
- E) →

109. White-Lewis, Cecil
- A) →
- Whitelaw, Cordelia
- B) →
- White-Leigh, Nancy
- C) →
- Whitely, Rodney
- D) →
- Whitlock, Warren
- E) →

110. VanDerHeggen, Don
- A) →
- VanDemark, Doris
- B) →
- Vandenberg, H. E.
- C) →
- VanDercook, Marie
- D) →
- vanderLinden, Robert
- E) →

GO ON TO THE NEXT COLUMN.

Answers

111. Add:
$$\begin{array}{r} 75 \\ + 49 \\ \hline \end{array}$$
A) 124 B) 125
C) 134 D) 225
E) none of these

112. Subtract:
$$\begin{array}{r} 69 \\ - 45 \\ \hline \end{array}$$
A) 14 B) 23
C) 24 D) 26
E) none of these

113. Multiply:
$$\begin{array}{r} 36 \\ \times 8 \\ \hline \end{array}$$
A) 246 B) 262
C) 288 D) 368
E) none of these

114. Divide:
$$8\overline{)328}$$
A) 31 B) 41
C) 42 D) 48
E) none of these

115. Multiply:
$$\begin{array}{r} 58 \\ \times 9 \\ \hline \end{array}$$
A) 472 B) 513
C) 521 D) 522
E) none of these

For each question below, find which one of the suggested answers appears in that question.

116. Z 3 N P G 5 4 2

117. 6 N 2 8 G 4 P T

118. 6 N 4 T V G 8 2

119. T 3 P 4 N 8 G 2

120. 6 7 K G N 2 L 5

Suggested Answers
A = 2, 3, G, N
B = 2, 6, N, T
C = 3, 4, G, K
D = 4, 6, K, T
E = none of these

IF YOU FINISH BEFORE THE TIME IS UP, YOU MAY GO BACK AND CHECK YOUR ANSWERS.

ANSWER KEY FOR DIAGNOSTIC TEST

Alike or Different

1. B	21. A	41. A	61. C	81. D	101. D
2. E	22. E	42. A	62. B	82. C	102. B
3. D	23. E	43. B	63. E	83. A	103. C
4. A	24. D	44. E	64. E	84. D	104. A
5. E	25. C	45. A	65. C	85. B	105. E

Alphabetizing

6. E	26. D	46. C	66. A	86. A	106. D
7. A	27. D	47. A	67. D	87. E	107. B
8. D	28. C	48. D	68. C	88. C	108. A
9. B	29. C	49. B	69. D	89. C	109. C
10. E	30. D	50. C	70. E	90. B	110. D

Arithmetic

11. D	31. E	51. B	71. A	91. E	111. A
12. B	32. A	52. C	72. C	92. E	112. C
13. B	33. A	53. D	73. B	93. C	113. C
14. B	34. C	54. D	74. C	94. C	114. B
15. B	35. C	55. E	75. A	95. A	115. D

Letters and Numbers

16. A	36. E	56. E	76. D	96. D	116. A
17. D	37. A	57. B	77. D	97. C	117. B
18. E	38. C	58. E	78. A	98. E	118. B
19. B	39. C	59. D	79. E	99. B	119. A
20. A	40. D	60. C	80. C	100. B	120. E

ANALYSIS CHART FOR DIAGNOSTIC TEST

Now that you've corrected your exam, use the following chart to carefully analyze your results and spot your strengths and weaknesses. This analysis should help you focus your study and review efforts.

Section	Total Number of Questions	Number Correct	Number Incorrect	Number Unanswered*
Alike or Different	30			
Alphabetizing	30			
Arithmetic	30			
Letters and Numbers	30			
TOTAL	120			

*Since there is a small penalty for incorrect answers on the Clerical Abilities Test, you should not guess blindly. Try to eliminate one or more of the choices before you take your educated guess.

ANSWER EXPLANATIONS FOR DIAGNOSTIC TEST

1. (B) 5261383   5261383   5261338
2. (E) 8125690   8126690   8125609
3. (D) W. E. Johnston   W: E. Johnson   W. E. Johnson
4. (A) Vergil L. Muller   Vergil L. Muller   Vergil L. Muller
5. (E) Atherton R. Warde   Asheton R. Warde   Atherton P. Warde
6. (E) Hachettson, Leroy
   Hackett, Gerald
7. (A) *Margenroth, Alvin*
   Margeroth, Albert
8. (D) Bobbitt, Olivia H.
   Bobbitt, Olivier E.
   Bobbitt, R. Olivia
9. (B) Mosely, Albert J.
   Mosely Werner
   Mosley, Alvin
10. (E) Youmons, Frank M.
    Youmuns, Frank L.
11. (D) 75
12. (B) 79
13. (B) 287
14. (B) 51
15. (B) 52
16. (A) 6 2 5 K 4 P T G
17. (D) L 4 7 2 T 6 V K
18. (E) 3 5 4 L 9 V T G
19. (B) G 4 K 7 L 3 5 Z
20. (A) 4 K 2 9 N 5 T G
21. (A) 2395890   2395890   2395890
22. (E) 1926341   1926347   1926314
23. (E) E. Owens McVey   E. Owen McVey   E. Owen McVay
24. (D) Emily Neal Rouse   Emily Neal Rowse   Emily Neal Rowse
25. (C) H. Merritt Audubon   H. Merriott Audubon   H. Merritt Audubon
26. (D) Watson, Nora J.
    Watters, N. O.
    Wattwood, Paul A.
27. (D) Johnston, Edmund
    Jobnston, Edward
    Johnstone, Edmund A.
28. (C) Remschel, Augusta
    Renscb, Adeline
    Renshaw, Austin

29. (C) Schneider, Mertens
    Schnyder, Maurice
    Schnyder, Newman
30. (D) Freedenberg, Erma E.
    Freedenburg, C. Erma
    Freedinberg, Erma F.
31. (E) 21
32. (A) 400
33. (A) 20
34. (C) 141
35. (C) 19
36. (E) 9 G Z 3 L 4 6 N
37. (A) L 5 N K 4 3 9 V
38. (C) 8 2 V P 9 L Z 5
39. (C) V P 9 Z 5 L 8 7
40. (D) 5 T 8 N 2 9 V L
41. (A) 6219354   6219354   6219354
42. (A) 2312793   2312793   2312793
43. (B) 1065407   1065407   1065047
44. (E) Francis Ransdell   Francis Ramsdell   Francis Ramsdell
45. (A) Cornelius Detwiler   Cornelius Detwiler   Cornelius Detwiler
46. (C) DeMatteo, Jessie
    DeMattia, Jessica
    Derby, Jessie S.
47. (A) *Theriault, Louis*
    Therien, Annette
48. (D) Gaston, Isabel
    Gaston, M. Hubert
    Gaston, M. Melvin
49. (B) SanLuis, Juana
    San Miguel, Carlos
    Santilli, Laura
50. (C) DeLathouder, Hilda
    DeLaTour, Hall F.
    Lathrop, Hillary
51. (B) 310
52. (C) 51
53. (D) 68
54. (D) 45
55. (E) 111
56. (E) N 5 4 7 T K 3 Z
57. (B) 8 5 3 V L 2 Z N
58. (E) 7 2 5 N 9 K l V
59. (D) 9 8 L 2 5 Z K V

60. (C) Z 6 5 V 9 3 P N
61. (C) 6452054
62. (B) 8501268
63. (E) Ella Burk Newham
64. (E) Jno. K. Ravencroft
65. (C) Martin Wills Pullen
66. (A) O'Bannon, M. J.
    O'Beirne, B. B.
67. (D) Entsminger, Jack
    Entsminger, Jacob
    Entsminger, James
68. (C) Iacone, Pedro M.
    Iacone, Pete R.
    Iacone, Peter F.
69. (D) Shephard, Louise
    Sheppard, Gladys
    Shepperd, Stella
70. (E) Thackston, Thomas G.
    Thackton, Melvin T.
71. (A) 51
72. (C) 85
73. (B) 29
74. (C) 272
75. (A) 71
76. (D) 6 Z T N 8 7 4 V
77. (D) V 7 8 6 N 5 P L
78. (A) N 7 P V 8 4 2 L
79. (E) 7 8 G 4 3 V L T
80. (C) 4 8 G 2 T N 6 L
81. (D) 3457988
82. (C) 4695682
83. (A) Stricklund, Kanedy
84. (D) Joy Harlor Witner
85. (B) R. M. O. Uberroth
86. (A) Dunlavey, M. Hilary
    Dunleavy, Hilary G.
87. (E) Yarborough, Mary
    Yarbrough, Maria
88. (C) Prouty, Maude
    Prouty, Martha
    Prouty, Myra
89. (C) Pawelek, Flora G.
    Pawlowicz, Ruth M.
    Pawlowski, Joan M.

Comparison columns (items 61–65):

6452054	6452054
8501268	8501268
Ella Burk Newham	Elena Burk Newham
Jno. H. Ravencroft	Jno. H. Ravencroft
Martin Wills Pulen	Martin Wills Pullen

Comparison columns (items 81–85):

3457986	3457986
4695862	4695682
Stricklund, Kanedy	Stricklund, Kanedy
Joy Harloe Witner	Joy Harloe Witner
R. M. O. Uberroth	R. N. O. Uberroth

90. (B) Vanover, Eva
    Vanstory, George
    VanSwinderen, Floyd
91. (E) 63
92. (E) 9
93. (C) 516
94. (C) 81
95. (A) 131
96. (D) V 5 7 Z N 9 4 T
97. (C) 4 6 P T 2 N K 9
98. (E) 6 4 N 2 P 8 Z K
99. (B) 7 P 5 2 4 N K T
100. (B) K T 8 5 4 N 2 P
101. (D) 1592514
102. (B) 2010202
103. (C) 6177396
104. (A) Drusilla S. Ridgeley
105. (E) Andrei I. Toumantzev
106. (D) FitzGibbon, Junius
    Fitzsimmons, Hugh
    FitzSimons, Martin
107. (B) Daly, Steven
    D'Amato, Vincent
    D'Amboise, S. Vincent
108. (A) Schaeffer, Roger D.
    Schaffert, Evelyn M.
109. (C) White-Leigh, Nancy
    White-Lewis, Cecil
    Whitely, Podney
110. (D) VanDercook, Marie
    VanDerHeggen, Don
    vanderLinden, Robert
111. (A) 124
112. (C) 24
113. (C) 288
114. (B) 41
115. (D) 522
116. (A) Z 3 N P G 5 4 2
117. (B) 6 N 2 8 G 4 P T
118. (B) 6 N 4 T V G 8 2
119. (A) T 3 P 4 N 8 G 2
120. (E) 6 7 K G N 2 L 5

Comparison columns (items 101–105):

1592574	1592574
2010202	2010220
6177936	6177396
Drusilla S. Ridgeley	Drusilla S. Ridgeley
Andrei I. Toumantzov	Andrei I. Toumantzov

CHAPTER 5

Understanding the Sections
Key Strategies
Practice, Practice, Practice

ALIKE OR DIFFERENT

This question type tests your observation skills. You are given three names or three sets of numbers and are asked to determine if

ALL THREE are alike (answer A)
only the FIRST and SECOND are alike (answer B)
only the FIRST and THIRD are alike (answer C)
only the SECOND and THIRD are alike (answer D)
NONE of them are alike (answer E)

For example:

Harmon A. Killebrew   Harmon A. Killebrew   Harmonn A. Killebrew

Notice that the third name has a double "n", making it different from the first two names. Therefore since only the FIRST and SECOND are alike, the answer is B.

Or another example:

3546798   3547698   3546798

Notice here that the first and third are alike, but the second set of numbers is different—the 6 and 7 are reversed. Therefore the answer is C.

HELPFUL TECHNIQUES AND STRATEGIES

1. Before you take your actual test, be sure to understand and *memorize* what each answer choice indicates. You should not have to keep looking back and forth from the problems to the directions for every question.
2. Practice the many questions in this book, finding a particular technique that works best for you. Here are some suggestions:
    For the Numbers
    a. Since there are seven numbers in each set, you may read the set as if it's a telephone number. If you are used to working with

phone numbers, saying to yourself ("subvocalizing") a telephone "exchange" (the first three numbers) followed by four digits may be a helpful method.
For example:

2698621   2698612   2698612

Thus, you might subvocalize "269-8621" for the first set. Then, since the beginning of the next set, "269-," sounds the same, you continue with the last four digits—"8612." These sound different from the four digits in the first set. Therefore, you know sets 1 and 2 are different, because of the last four digits. Now try the third set: "269-" (the "exchange" sounds the same) "8612." Which last four digits does the third set duplicate? Quickly checking, you find the last four digits of set 2 are also "8612." The answer is (D).

b. This telephone technique has variations. You may wish to compare the first three digits (the "exchange") in each set separately; then compare the last four digits in each set—a divide and conquer strategy.
c. Or you may wish to try "Odd Man Out"—checking the first two sets to determine if they're similar. If they are, you then go to the third to see whether you have an (A) answer (all ALIKE) or a (B) answer (only the first two ALIKE). If the first two are different, then proceed to the third to see if the third matches the first set (answer C), or the second set (answer D), or neither set (answer E).
d. Whichever technique you develop, watch out for "reversals."
For example:

4695862   4695682   4695862

Notice that sets 1 and 3 are alike, but that 8 and 6 are reversed in set 2. Such reversals are often easily missed.

For the Names

a. Saying the names *carefully* in your mind may be helpful, but sometimes names spelled differently can sound alike.

b. You may wish to "divide and conquer": first comparing first names, then initials, then last names.

c. Watch out for the following:
Double letters. Often a letter will be single in one name but doubled in another.

Bob Uberroth   Bob Uberroth   Bob Uberoth

The third name has a single "r."
Silent letters

Emiley Smyth   Emiley Smyth   Emily Smith

Notice how all three first names will sound the same despite the last name not having the second "e."

Reversals. Especially look out for reversals of vowels, easy to miss. For example:

Annette Tharien   Annette Tharien   Annette Tharein

Notice the "i" and "e" reversed in the third name.

Different common spellings. Be aware of names (like Francis/Frances) that have more than one correct spelling. For example:

Francis Ramsdell   Frances Ramsdell   Frances Ramsdell

Only the second and the third names are alike, because "Francis" is spelled with an "i" in the first name.

Reverse letters. Some letters are the mirror image of other letters, and these can sometimes be confusing, especially if you are working at top speed. For example, "p" is the mirror image of "q." The letter "b" is the reverse of the letter "d." Some people have special difficulties with these kinds of letters. Try these:

Larry P. Dobkin   Larry P. Dobkin   Larry P. Dodkin

Notice the "d" in the last name; the others contain a "b."

Look-alike letters. And, finally, keep on your toes when you see certain letters that can be easily misread as other letters. For instance, an "m" may often be misread as an "n," and vice versa. An "s" may be misread as a "z," and a "q" as a "g." As you practice, you'll begin to spot these, and you should try to remember them. For example:

Ernest Ramsdell   Ernest Ransdell   Ernest Ramsdell

Notice that "Ramsdell" is spelled with an "n," rather than an "m," in the second case. Or:

Alfredo C. Lopes   Alfredo C. Lopez   Alfredo C. Lopez

Notice the "s" in the first name; the others end in "z."

PRACTICE SET 1

Compare the three names or numbers, and mark the answer—
  A if ALL THREE names or numbers are exactly ALIKE
  B if only the FIRST and SECOND names or numbers are exactly ALIKE
  C if only the FIRST and THIRD names or numbers are exactly ALIKE
  D if only the SECOND and THIRD names or numbers are exactly ALIKE
  E if ALL THREE names or numbers are DIFFERENT

1. 9854688	9854688	9854668	_____
2. 1003873	1003873	1003873	_____
3. 4837261	4837621	4837621	_____
4. Oswald Dunleavey	Oswald Dunleavey	Oswals Dunleavy	_____
5. Joseph Willierdite	Joseph Willierdite	Joseph Willierdite	_____
6. 6978459	6974859	6974589	_____
7. 3823145	3832145	3823145	_____
8. Stacey Baum Pleskoff	Stacy Baum Plesckoff	Stacey Baum Pleskof	_____
9. C. J. Farleighbacker	C. J. Farleighbacker	C. J. Farleighbacher	_____
10. Arnold M. Goulian	Arnold M. Goulain	Arnold M. Goulian	_____
11. 8093472	8093472	8093472	_____
12. 4768523	4765823	4765833	_____
13. 9487297	9482797	9482797	_____
14. Dona Leszyzski	Dona Leszyczski	Donna Leszyzski	_____
15. Joy Mondragon	Joy Mondragon	Joy Mondr'agan	_____
16. 7465938	7465398	7465938	_____
17. 1489235	1489325	1489325	_____
18. William E. Jerzsinski	William E. Jerszinski	William E. Jerzsinski	_____
19. Ernest VanSwickerton	Ernest VanSwikirten	Ernest VanSwickerten	_____
20. Fredda Wilmarettez	Fredda Wilmarettez	Freda Wilmarettez	_____
21. 5839287	5832987	5832987	_____
22. 9372638	9732368	9732368	_____
23. Lazaro F. Cosgrove	Lasaro F. Cosgrove	Lazaro F. Casgrove	_____
24. Lucila Fontanez	Lucila Fonanes	Lunita Fontanez	_____

25. Armand Cisalissi	Armand Cisilissi	Armand Cisalissi	_____
26. 4873983	4873983	4783983	_____
27. 9578246	9578246	9578246	_____
28. 5797358	5797358	5797538	_____
29. Robin I. Gastongauy	Robin I. Gastonguay	Robin I. Gastanquay	_____
30. Alfred Geisthardt	Alfred Geisthartd	Alfred Geisthardt	_____

ANSWER EXPLANATIONS FOR PRACTICE SET 1

1. (B) 9854688	9854688	9854668
2. (A) 1003873	1003873	1003873
3. (D) 4837261	4837621	4837621
4. (B) Oswald Dunleavey	Oswald Dunleavey	Oswals Dunleavy
5. (A) Joseph Willierdite	Joseph Willierdite	Joseph Willierdite
6. (E) 6978459	6974859	6974589
7. (C) 3823145	3832145	3823145
8. (E) Stacey Baum Pleskoff	Stacy Baum Plesckoff	Stacey Baum Pleskof
9. (B) C. J. Farleighbacker	C. J. Farleighbacker	C. J. Farleighbacher
10. (C) Arnold M. Goulian	Arnold M. Goulain	Arnold M. Goulian
11. (A) 8093472	8093472	8093472
12. (E) 4768523	4765823	4765833
13. (D) 9487297	9482797	9482797
14. (E) Dona Leszyzski	Dona Leszyczski	Donna Leszyzski
15. (B) Joy Mondragon	Joy Mondragon	Joy Mondragan
16. (C) 7465938	7465398	7465938
17. (D) 1489235	1489325	1489325
18. (C) William E. Jerzsinski	William E. Jerszinski	William E. Jerzsinski
19. (E) Ernest VanSwickerton	Ernest VanSwikirten	Ernest VanSwickerten
20. (B) Fredda Wilmarettez	Fredda Wilmarettez	Freda Wilmarettez
21. (D) 5839287	5832987	5832987
22. (D) 9372638	9732368	9732368
23. (E) Lazaro F. Cosgrove	Lasaro F. Cosgrove	Lazaro F. Casgrove
24. (E) Lucila Fontanez	Lucila Fonanes	Lunita Fontanez
25. (C) Armand Cisalissi	Armand Cisilissi	Armand Cisalissi
26. (B) 4873983	4873983	4783983
27. (A) 9578246	9578246	9578246
28. (B) 5797358	5797358	5797538
29. (E) Robin I. Gastongauy	Robin I. Gastonguay	Robin I. Gastanguay
30. (C) Alfred Geisthardt	Alfred Geisthartd	Alfred Geisthardt

PRACTICE SET 2

Compare the three names or numbers, and mark the answer—
   A if ALL THREE names or numbers are exactly ALIKE
   B if only the FIRST and SECOND names or numbers are exactly ALIKE
   C if only the FIRST and THIRD names or numbers are exactly ALIKE
   D if only the SECOND and THIRD names or numbers are exactly ALIKE
   E if ALL THREE names or numbers are DIFFERENT

1. 9358745	9358745	9357845	_____
2. 8574690	8547690	8547690	_____

3. Raymond H. Didsbury	Raymond H. Diddsbury	Raymond H. Didsburry	_____
4. Stephen M. Tranz	Stephen M. Tranz	Stephen M. Tramz	_____
5. Kevin C. Kretchmer	Kevin C. Kretchmer	Kevin C. Kretchmer	_____
6. 7534689	7354689	7534689	_____
7. 4736258	4736258	4736258	_____
8. 9273415	9274315	9274315	_____
9. Douglas S. Borghi	Douglass S. Borghi	Douglass S. Borghi	_____
10. Vartan Bergquist	Vartan Berquist	Vartan Berquist	_____
11. 7493876	4793876	4739876	_____
12. 9073484	9073484	9074384	_____
13. Shehani D. Housel	Shahani D. Housel	Shehani D. Housel	_____
14. Mansoor Hornblithe	Mansoor Hornblithe	Mansoor Hornblithe	_____
15. George Komashko	George Komashko	George Kamashko	_____
16. 7287394	7287934	7827934	_____
17. 4736297	4736297	4736297	_____
18. 5398247	5389247	5389247	_____
19. Steven P. Fuschia	Stephen P. Fuschia	Stephen P. Fuschia	_____
20. Farrah Berstmilier	Farrah Berstmilier	Farrah Berstmileir	_____
21. 3827394	3827394	3827934	_____
22. 4839271	4289271	4839271	_____
23. Powers S. Boothe	Powers S. Booth	Power S. Boothe	_____
24. Evyln Schaeffert	Evyln Shaeffert	Evyln Schaeffert	_____
25. Armantine Rogioso	Armatine Rogioso	Armatine Rogioso	_____
26. 9864837	9864387	9864837	_____
27. 8725137	8725137	8725137	_____
28. 6468931	6469831	6468931	_____
29. Rogers Hornsbrath	Rogers Hornsbrath	Rogers Hornsbrathe	_____
30. Mikael Maggliocco	Mikeal Maggliocco	Mikael Magglioco	_____

ANSWER EXPLANATIONS FOR PRACTICE SET 2

1. **(B)** 9358745	9358745	9357845
2. **(D)** 85<u>74</u>690	8547690	854<u>7</u>690
3. **(E)** Raymond H. Didsbury	Raymond H. Did<u>d</u>sbury	Raymond H. Didsbur<u>r</u>y
4. **(B)** Stephen M. Tranz	Stephen M. Tranz	Stephen M. Tram<u>z</u>
5. **(A)** Kevin C. Kretchmer	Kevin C. Kretchmer	Kevin C. Kretchmer
6. **(C)** 7<u>5</u>34689	7<u>3</u>54689	7534689
7. **(A)** 4736258	4736258	4736258
8. **(D)** 927<u>3</u>415	9274315	9274315
9. **(D)** Doug<u>l</u>as S. Borghi	Douglass S. Borghi	Douglass S. Borghi
10. **(D)** Vartan Ber<u>g</u>quist	Vartan Berquist	Vartan Berquist
11. **(E)** <u>7</u>493876	4793876	473<u>9</u>876
12. **(B)** 9073484	9073484	90<u>7</u>4384
13. **(C)** Shehani D. Housel	Sha<u>h</u>ani D. Housel	Shehani D. Housel
14. **(A)** Mansoor Hornblithe	Mansoor Hornblithe	Mansoor Hornblithe
15. **(B)** George Komashko	George Komashko	George K<u>a</u>mashko
16. **(E)** 7287<u>3</u>94	7287934	7827934
17. **(A)** 4736297	4736297	4736297
18. **(D)** 53<u>9</u>8247	5389247	5389247
19. **(D)** Ste<u>v</u>en P. Fuschia	Stephen P. Fuschia	Stephen P. Fuschia
20. **(B)** Farrah Berstmilier	Farrah Berstmilier	Farrah Berstmile<u>i</u>r
21. **(B)** 3827394	3827394	38279<u>3</u>4
22. **(C)** 4839271	4<u>2</u>89271	4839271
23. **(E)** Powers S. Booth<u>e</u>	Powers S. Booth	Power S. Booth<u>e</u>
24. **(C)** Evyln <u>S</u>chaeffert	Evyln <u>S</u>haeffert	Evyln Schaeffert
25. **(D)** Arma<u>n</u>tine Rogioso	Armatine Rogioso	Armatine Rogioso
26. **(C)** 9864<u>8</u>37	9864<u>3</u>87	9864837
27. **(A)** 8725137	8725137	8725137
28. **(C)** 64<u>68</u>931	64<u>69</u>831	6468931
29. **(B)** Rogers Hornsbrath	Rogers Hornsbrath	Rogers Hornsbrath<u>e</u>
30. **(E)** Mikael Maggliocco	Mik<u>ea</u>l Maggliocco	Mikael Magglio<u>co</u>

PRACTICE SET 3

Compare the three names or numbers, and mark the answer—
  A if ALL THREE names or numbers are exactly ALIKE
  B if only the FIRST and SECOND names or numbers are exactly ALIKE
  C if only the FIRST and THIRD names or numbers are exactly ALIKE
  D if only the SECOND and THIRD names or numbers are exactly ALIKE
  E if ALL THREE names or numbers are DIFFERENT

1. 5839478	5839478	5839478	_____
2. 9382739	9382789	9382789	_____
3. Alxis Kordumdrong	Alxis Kordumdrong	Alxis Kordomdrung	_____
4. Blossom Koneczka	Blossom Koneszka	Blossom Konezska	_____
5. Bethina Ploesser	Bethina Pleosser	Bettina Ploesser	_____
6. 3746893	3746983	3746983	_____
7. 4278345	4278345	4278345	_____
8. 2875291	2785291	2785291	_____

9. Krokor Pechakjian	Krokor Pechakjian	Krokor Pecharjian	_____
10. Lynette Preistley	Lynnette Preistley	Lynnette Priestley	_____
11. 3826387	3862837	3826837	_____
12. 4739826	4739836	4739826	_____
13. 3982635	3983625	3982635	_____
14. Rafael Morrison	Rafael Morrison	Rafael Morrisson	_____
15. Randise Rappoport	Randice Rappoport	Randice Rapopport	_____
16. 3675214	3675214	3675214	_____
17. 8672391	8673291	8672391	_____
18. Quenten C. Fischbeim	Quentin C. Fischbeim	Quentin C. Fischbiem	_____
19. Jenifer Robesgiase	Jenifer Robesgiase	Jennifer Robesgiase	_____
20. Florel Petersen	Florel Peterson	Florel Peterson	_____
21. 4872364	4873264	4873264	_____
22. 7483092	7480392	7480932	_____
23. 7348234	7348234	7348234	_____
24. G. Raymund Pafalcko	G. Ramund Pafalcko	G. Raymund Pafalcko	_____
25. M. L. K. Carrutthers	M. L. K. Carruthers	M. L. K. Carruthers	_____
26. 3678362	3687362	3687362	_____
27. 9376982	9736982	9736982	_____
28. 3892761	3892761	3892761	_____
29. Rogeiio Gonzalez	Rogeiio Gonzales	Rogeiio Gonzales	_____
30. Ferdinan Bulliekeir	Ferdinan Bulleikeir	Ferdinan Bulliekier	_____

ANSWER EXPLANATIONS FOR PRACTICE SET 3

1. (A) 5839478	5839478	5839478
2. (D) 9382739	9382789	9382789
3. (B) Alxis Kordumdrong	Alxis Kordumdrong	Alxis Kordomdrung
4. (E) Blossom Koneczka	Blossom Koneszka	Blossom Konezska
5. (E) Bethina Ploesser	Bethina Pleosser	Bettina Ploesser
6. (D) 3746893	3746983	3746983
7. (A) 4278345	4278345	4278345
8. (D) 2875291	2785291	2785291
9. (B) Krokor Pechakjian	Krokor Pechakjian	Krokor Pecharjian

10. (E) Lynette Preistley   Lynnette Preistley   Lynnette Priestley
11. (E) 3826387   3862837   3826837
12. (C) 4739826   4739836   4739826
13. (C) 3982635   3983625   3982635
14. (B) Rafael Morrison   Rafael Morrison   Rafael Morrisson
15. (E) Randise Rappoport   Randice Rappoport   Randice Rapopport
16. (A) 3675214   3675214   3675214
17. (C) 8672391   8673291   8672391
18. (E) Quenten C. Fischbeim   Quentin C. Fischbeim   Quentin C. Fischbiem
19. (B) Jenifer Robesgiase   Jenifer Robesgiase   Jennifer Robesgiase
20. (D) Florel Petersen   Florel Peterson   Florel Peterson
21. (D) 4872364   4873264   4873264
22. (E) 7483092   7480392   7480932
23. (A) 7348234   7348234   7348234
24. (C) G. Raymund Pafalcko   G. Ramund Pafalcko   G. Raymund Pafalcko
25. (D) M. L. K. Carrutthers   M. L. K. Carruthers   M. L. K. Carruthers
26. (D) 3678362   3687362   3687362
27. (D) 9376982   9736982   9736982
28. (A) 3892761   3892761   3892761
29. (D) Rogeiio Gonzalez   Rogeiio Gonzales   Rogeiio Gonzales
30. (E) Ferdinan Bulliekeir   Ferdinan Bulleikeir   Ferdinan Bulliekier

PRACTICE SET 4

Compare the three names or numbers, and mark the answer—
  A if ALL THREE names or numbers are exactly ALIKE
  B if only the FIRST and SECOND names or numbers are exactly ALIKE
  C if only the FIRST and THIRD names or numbers are exactly ALIKE
  D if only the SECOND and THIRD names or numbers are exactly ALIKE
  E if ALL THREE names or numbers are DIFFERENT

1. 5732837   5372837   5372837   _____

2. 4802736   4802736   4802376   _____

3. Michel St. Johns   Michel St. John   Mishel St. Johns   _____

4. Terrence Vanespreaux   Terrence Vanesprauex   Terrence Vanespreaux   _____

5. U. Yoshima Chaingo   U. Yoshina Chaingo   U. Yoshina Chiango   _____

6. 4869482   4869482   4869482   _____

7. 8394276   8392476   8392746   _____

8. 4829487   4829487   4892487   _____

9. Dana Cammer Lynd   Dana Cammer Lynde   Dana Cammer Lynde   _____

10. Epimena Sainzt   Epimena Saintz   Epimena Sainzt   _____

11. Louis Sagakuchi   Louis Sagsgughi   Louis Sagakuchi   _____

12. Festron Armandoff   Festron Armadoff   Festron Armadoff   _____

13. Hermine Pakhanians   Hermine Pakanians   Hermine Pakhanian   _____

14. 3846398	3846389	3846398	_____
15. 7493183	7493183	7493183	_____
16. 4839273	4832973	4839273	_____
17. 4698264	4698264	4698624	_____
18. Nicholas Palladino	Nickolas Palladino	Nicholas Palladino	_____
19. Jaime Prestridge	Jaime Pestridge	Jaime Pestredge	_____
20. Alonzo Forsythe	Alonzo Forsythe	Alonzo Forthythe	_____
21. 4832472	4832472	4832472	_____
22. 3659624	2695624	2695624	_____
23. 3825983	8325938	9325983	_____
24. Marietta Rogolizzo	Marieta Rogolizzo	Marieta Rogolizzo	_____
25. Jacob Rietdokog	Jacob Rietdokog	Jakob Rietdokog	_____
26. 5784963	5784693	5784963	_____
27. 3124785	3124785	3124875	_____
28. Edwardo Pimpernott	Edwardo Pimpernott	Eduardo Pimpernott	_____
29. Frencesca Moisely	Francesca Moisely	Francesca Moisely	_____
30. Olivier R. Dudlees	Oliver R. Dudlees	Oliver R. Dudless	_____

ANSWER EXPLANATIONS FOR PRACTICE SET 4

1. (D) 57**3**2837   5372837   5372837
2. (B) 4802736   4802736   4802**3**76
3. (E) Michel St. Johns   Michel St. John   Mishel St. Johns
4. (C) Terrence Vanespreaux   Terrence Vanesprauex   Terrence Vanespreaux
5. (E) U. Yoshima Chaingo   U. Yoshina Chaingo   U. Yoshina Chiango
6. (A) 4869482   4869482   4869482
7. (E) 8394276   8392476   8392746
8. (B) 4829487   4829487   4892487
9. (D) Dana Cammer Lynd   Dana Cammer Lynde   Dana Cammer Lynde
10. (C) Epimena Sainzt   Epimena Saintz   Epimena Sainzt
11. (C) Louis Sagakuchi   Louis Sagsgughi   Louis Sagakuchi
12. (D) Festron Armandoff   Festron Armadoff   Festron Armadoff
13. (E) Hermine Pakhanians   Hermine Pakanians   Hermine Pakhanian
14. (C) 3846398   3846389   3846398
15. (A) 7493183   7493183   7493183
16. (C) 4839273   4832973   4839273
17. (B) 4698264   4698264   4698624
18. (C) Nicholas Palladino   Nickolas Palladino   Nicholas Palladino
19. (E) Jaime Prestridge   Jaime Pestridge   Jaime Pestredge
20. (B) Alonzo Forsythe   Alonzo Forsythe   Alonzo Forthythe

21. (A) 4832472	4832472	4832472	
22. (D) 3659624	2695624	2695624	
23. (E) 3825983	8325938	9325983	
24. (D) Marietta Rogolizzo	Marieta Rogolizzo	Marieta Rogolizzo	
25. (B) Jacob Rietdokog	Jacob Rietdokog	Jakob Rietdokog	
26. (C) 5784963	5784693	5784963	
27. (B) 3124785	3124785	3124875	
28. (B) Edwardo Pimpernott	Edwardo Pimpernott	Eduardo Pimpernott	
29. (D) Frencesca Moisely	Francesca Moisely	Francesca Moisely	
30. (E) Olivier R. Dudlees	Oliver R. Dudlees	Oliver R. Dudless	

PRACTICE SET 5

Compare the three names or numbers, and mark the answer—
   A if ALL THREE names or numbers are exactly ALIKE
   B if only the FIRST and SECOND names or numbers are exactly ALIKE
   C if only the FIRST and THIRD names or numbers are exactly ALIKE
   D if only the SECOND and THIRD names or numbers are exactly ALIKE
   E if ALL THREE names or numbers are DIFFERENT

1. 9374653	9374653	9374653	_____
2. 4763981	4769381	4769831	_____
3. 5847291	5847291	5842791	_____
4. Atherton Jacquesman	Atherton Jaquesman	Atherton Jacqueman	_____
5. Willis Undertopper	Willis Undertopper	Willes Undertopper	_____
6. 6493759	6439759	6439759	_____
7. 3928404	3298404	3928404	_____
8. Langer F. Feltmann	Langer F. Feltman	Langar F. Feltman	_____
9. Oskar Fischman	Oskar Fischman	Oskar Ficshman	_____
10. Norris Feuchtwangar	Norris Feuchtwanger	Norris Fuechtwanger	_____
11. 4736948	4376948	4376948	_____
12. 4257389	4257389	4257389	_____
13. 8294735	2894735	8294735	_____
14. Arthur Fidelibus	Arthur Fidelibus	Arther Fidelibus	_____
15. Gerald M. Dudkins	Gerald M. Dudkins	Gerard M. Dudkins	_____
16. 4879326	4873926	4879326	_____
17. 6948732	6948732	6948732	_____
18. Haruko Kamakura	Hurako Kamakura	Hurako Kamakura	_____

19. Simmons Werthingten	Simmons Werthington	Simmins Werthington	_____
20. DeRonda Nocerino	DeRonda Nocerino	DaRonda Nocerino	_____
21. Marc Nochiela	Marc Nocheila	Marc Nochiela	_____
22. Cleveland Noburski	Cleveland Nobruski	Cleveland Nobruski	_____
23. 2839747	2839747	2839747	_____
24. 9372875	9732875	9732875	_____
25. 3729854	3729584	3798254	_____
26. 4839734	4839734	4837934	_____
27. 3526791	3526971	3526891	_____
28. 3749825	3749825	2949825	_____
29. Mallery J. Pearre	Mallory J. Peare	Mallory J. Pearre	_____
30. Stacey Rudashmann	Stacy Rudashmann	Stacey Rudashmann	_____

ANSWER EXPLANATIONS FOR PRACTICE SET 5

1. (A) 9374653	9374653	9374653
2. (E) 4763981	4769381	4769831
3. (B) 5847291	5847291	5842791
4. (E) Atherton Jacquesman	Atherton Jaquesman	Atherton Jacqueman
5. (B) Willis Undertopper	Willis Undertopper	Willes Undertopper
6. (D) 6493759	6439759	6439759
7. (C) 3928404	3298404	3928404
8. (E) Langer F. Feltmann	Langer F. Feltman	Langar F. Feltman
9. (B) Oskar Fischman	Oskar Fischman	Oskar Ficshman
10. (E) Norris Feuchtwangar	Norris Feuchtwanger	Norris Fuechtwanger
11. (D) 4736948	4376948	4376948
12. (A) 4257389	4257389	4257389
13. (C) 8294735	2894735	8294735
14. (B) Arthur Fidelibus	Arthur Fidelibus	Arther Fidelibus
15. (B) Gerald M. Dudkins	Gerald M. Dudkins	Gerard M. Dudkins
16. (C) 4879326	4873926	4879326
17. (A) 6948732	6948732	6948732
18. (D) Haruko Kamakura	Hurako Kamakura	Hurako Kamakura
19. (E) Simmons Werthingten	Simmons Werthington	Simmins Werthington
20. (B) DeRonda Nocerino	DeRonda Nocerino	DaRonda Nocerino
21. (C) Marc Nochiela	Marc Nocheila	Marc Nochiela
22. (D) Cleveland Noburski	Cleveland Nobruski	Cleveland Nobruski
23. (A) 2839747	2839747	2839747
24. (D) 9372875	9732875	9732875
25. (E) 3729854	3729584	3798254
26. (B) 4839734	4839734	4837934
27. (E) 3526791	3526971	3526891
28. (B) 3749825	3749825	2949825
29. (E) Mallery J. Pearre	Mallory J. Peare	Mallory J. Pearre
30. (C) Stacey Rudashmann	Stacy Rudashmann	Stacey Rudashmann

PRACTICE SET 6

Compare the three names or numbers, and mark the answer—
- A if ALL THREE names or numbers are exactly ALIKE
- B if only the FIRST and SECOND names or numbers are exactly ALIKE
- C if only the FIRST and THIRD names or numbers are exactly ALIKE
- D if only the SECOND and THIRD names or numbers are exactly ALIKE
- E if ALL THREE names or numbers are DIFFERENT

1. Abebaye Tearleney	Abebaya Tearleney	Abebaya Tearleney	_____
2. Mimi P. Teisan	Mimi P. Tiesman	Mimi P. Tiesman	_____
3. Forest Peuterman	Forrest Peuterman	Forrest Peuterman	_____
4. 6483947	6483947	6438947	_____
5. 3926598	3925698	3925968	_____
6. 4378947	4378947	4378947	_____
7. 4628479	4624879	4628479	_____
8. Claude Versailes	Claude Versailles	Claude Versailles	_____
9. Phillip Waddillove	Phillip Waddillove	Philip Waddillove	_____
10. Pinkerten Chesneiy	Pinkerton Chesneiy	Pinkerton Chesniey	_____
11. 4893263	4893262	4893623	_____
12. 4832764	4832764	4832746	_____
13. 6382749	6832749	6832749	_____
14. Hugh L. Wyannicki	Huge L. Wyannicki	Hugh L. Wyannicki	_____
15. Otto C. Wichert	Otto C. Wichert	Otto C. Wichirt	_____
16. Maurice E. Tyson	Maurice E. Tyson	Maurice E. Tyson	_____
17. Tzivskos Tittlemen	Tzivzkos Tittlemen	Tzvizkos Tittlemen	_____
18. Peter E. Villasenor	Peter E. Villiasenor	Peter E. Villiasenor	_____
19. 7362456	7364256	7342456	_____
20. 3829756	3829576	3829756	_____
21. 4839876	4839876	4839876	_____
22. 7328631	7328361	7328631	_____
23. 3907356	3907356	3907365	_____
24. Illay Vischmid	Illay Vischmed	Illay Vischmed	_____

25. Benjamin Weinenger	Benjamen Weinenger	Benjamin Weininger	____
26. 4983675	4983675	4983675	____
27. 8109354	8109534	8109354	____
28. Marion Wyanicki	Marian Wyanicki	Marian Wyanicki	____
29. Whitney Williston	Whitney Willisten	Whitney Wiliston	____
30. Garry Wohmgemuth	Garry Wohmgemuth	Garry Wohmgemuth	____

ANSWER EXPLANATIONS FOR PRACTICE SET 6

1. (D) Abebaye Tearleney — Abebaya Tearleney — Abebaya Tearleney
2. (D) Mimi P. Teisan — Mimi P. Tiesman — Mimi P. Tiesman
3. (D) Forest Peuterman — Forrest Peuterman — Forrest Peuterman
4. (B) 6483947 — 6483947 — 6438947
5. (E) 3926598 — 3925698 — 3925968
6. (A) 4378947 — 4378947 — 4378947
7. (C) 4628479 — 4624879 — 4628479
8. (D) Claude Versailes — Claude Versailles — Claude Versailles
9. (B) Phillip Waddillove — Phillip Waddillove — Philip Waddillove
10. (E) Pinkerten Chesneiy — Pinkerton Chesneiy — Pinkerton Chesniey
11. (E) 4893263 — 4893262 — 4893623
12. (B) 4832764 — 4832764 — 4832746
13. (D) 6382749 — 6832749 — 6832749
14. (C) Hugh L. Wyannicki — Huge L. Wyannicki — Hugh L. Wyannicki
15. (B) Otto C. Wichert — Otto C. Wichert — Otto C. Wichirt
16. (A) Maurice E. Tyson — Maurice E. Tyson — Maurice E. Tyson
17. (E) Tzivskos Tittlemen — Tzivzkos Tittlemen — Tzvizkos Tittlemen
18. (D) Peter E. Villasenor — Peter E. Villiasenor — Peter E. Villiasenor
19. (E) 7362456 — 7364256 — 7342456
20. (C) 3829756 — 3829576 — 3829756
21. (A) 4839876 — 4839876 — 4839876
22. (C) 7328631 — 7328361 — 7328631
23. (B) 3907356 — 3907356 — 3907365
24. (D) Illay Vischmid — Illay Vischmed — Illay Vischmed
25. (E) Benjamin Weinenger — Benjamen Weinenger — Benjamin Weininger
26. (A) 4983675 — 4983675 — 4983675
27. (C) 8109354 — 8109534 — 8109354
28. (D) Marion Wyanicki — Marian Wyanicki — Marian Wyanicki
29. (E) Whitney Williston — Whitney Willisten — Whitney Wiliston
30. (A) Garry Wohmgemuth — Garry Wohmgemuth — Garry Wohmgemuth

REVIEWING THE KEY STRATEGIES

Remember to:

1. Understand and memorize the directions before your test.

2. Find the technique that works best for you, and practice it.

3. Watch out for those "troublesome" numbers and letters.

ALPHABETIZING

The rules for placing names in proper alphabetical order are simple and straightforward. They require you to follow several steps:

Different Last Names
1. First, alphabetize by the first letter of the last name:
   Brown, James
   Harris, Arthur
   Thomas, Peter
2. If two or more last names begin with the same letter, then look to the second letter in the last name:
   Brown, James
   Sanders, Fred
   Smith, Gloria
   Notice that both "S" names come after *Brown* and that *Sanders* comes before *Smith* because of their second letters ("a" and "m").
3. If the first *and* second letters of the last name are alike, then look to the third letter:
   Peterson, Roberta
   Pezzari, Thomas
   Ulmer, Janice
4. If the first three letters of the last name are similar, look to the fourth letter, and so on:
   Bronson, Eloise
   Brown, Ferdinand
   Browvort, Michael
   Notice in the last example that *Bron* comes before *Brow,* but *Brown* comes before *Browv.*
5. If the letters are identical in two names, but one name is longer, the shorter name, which "runs out of letters," goes first. For example,
   Prout, Marie
   Proute, Harry
   Notice that *Prout* comes before *Proute.*
6. Don't let lowercase letters, apostrophes, or hyphens in last names confuse you. Continue to follow rules 1 to 5. For example:
   Daly, Ernest
   D'Ambrose, Evelyn
   Above, *Dal* comes before *DAm*. Or:
   VanDercook, Stephen
   vanLitton, Morris
   Vans-Harrold, Martha
   Notice the order: VanD, vanL, Vans.

Identical Last Names
What happens if the last names are exactly the same? Then look at the first name or first initial and follow these rules:

7. Alphabetize, using the first letter of the first name:
   Smith, Albert
   Smith, George
   Smith, Harold
8. If the first name begins with the same letter, look to the second letter:
   Jones, Richard
   Jones, Roberta
   Jones, Ruben
9. If a first name is merely an initial, that initial will precede any first name beginning with that same letter. For example:
   White, N.
   White, Norbert
10. Even if there is a middle name after the first initial, or two initials, a first initial will always precede a full first name:
    Chan, G. Ling
    Chan, George
    Another example:
    Forrest, R. Peter
    Forrest, Rae
11. Of course, if the first initial comes after the first letter of the full first name, it must follow the usual alphabetical rules. For example:
    Johnson, Albert
    Johnson, C. David
    Johnson, Charles
    Johnson, F. K.
    Johnson, Louise
12. And, of course, given only first initials, follow the usual rules:
    Abbott, C.
    Abbott, C. A.
    Abbott, E.
    Abbott, F.
    Abbott, H.
    Note that Abbott, C. A. comes after Abbott, C.
13. Finally, if the first names are exactly the same, or the first initials are the same, then look to the middle initial or the middle name, and follow the standard rules. For example:
    Brown, John
    Brown, John A.
    Brown, John Albert
    Brown, John H.
    Brown, John Herbert
    Brown, John Thomas
    Brown, John Z.
    Notice that here the alphabetizing begins with the middle name or initial: *Brown, John* is first because there is no middle name or initial; then *A.*, then *Albert*, then *H.*, then *Herbert,* then *Thomas*, then *Z.*

PRACTICE SET 1

Find the correct place for the name in the box, and mark the letter of that space as your answer.

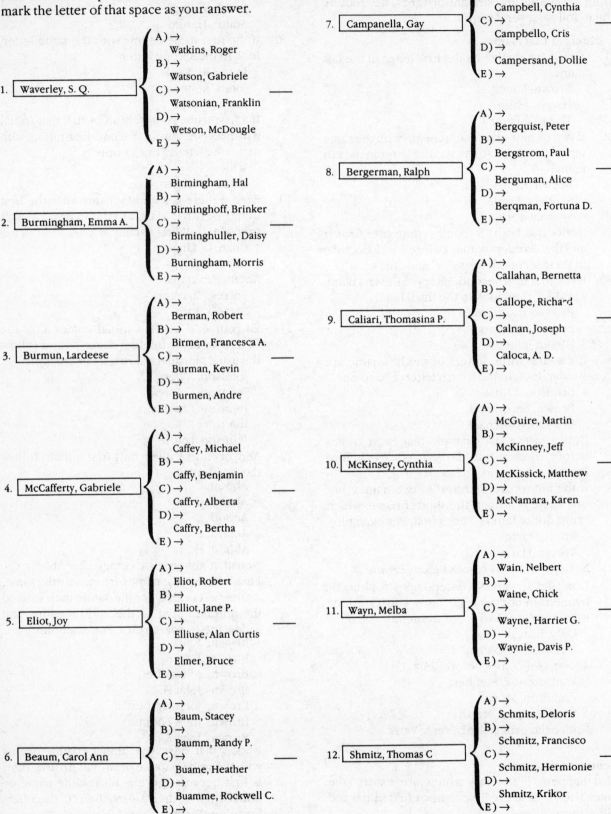

1. Waverley, S. Q.
   A) →
   Watkins, Roger
   B) →
   Watson, Gabriele
   C) → ___
   Watsonian, Franklin
   D) →
   Wetson, McDougle
   E) →

2. Burmingham, Emma A.
   A) →
   Birmingham, Hal
   B) →
   Birminghoff, Brinker
   C) → ___
   Birminghuller, Daisy
   D) →
   Burningham, Morris
   E) →

3. Burmun, Lardeese
   A) →
   Berman, Robert
   B) →
   Birmen, Francesca A.
   C) → ___
   Burman, Kevin
   D) →
   Burmen, Andre
   E) →

4. McCafferty, Gabriele
   A) →
   Caffey, Michael
   B) →
   Caffy, Benjamin
   C) → ___
   Caffry, Alberta
   D) →
   Caffry, Bertha
   E) →

5. Eliot, Joy
   A) →
   Eliot, Robert
   B) →
   Elliot, Jane P.
   C) → ___
   Elliuse, Alan Curtis
   D) →
   Elmer, Bruce
   E) →

6. Beaum, Carol Ann
   A) →
   Baum, Stacey
   B) →
   Baumm, Randy P.
   C) → ___
   Buame, Heather
   D) →
   Buamme, Rockwell C.
   E) →

7. Campanella, Gay
   A) →
   Cambell, Colin M.
   B) →
   Campbell, Cynthia
   C) → ___
   Campbello, Cris
   D) →
   Campersand, Dollie
   E) →

8. Bergerman, Ralph
   A) →
   Bergquist, Peter
   B) →
   Bergstrom, Paul
   C) → ___
   Berguman, Alice
   D) →
   Berqman, Fortuna D.
   E) →

9. Caliari, Thomasina P.
   A) →
   Callahan, Bernetta
   B) →
   Callope, Richard
   C) → ___
   Calnan, Joseph
   D) →
   Caloca, A. D.
   E) →

10. McKinsey, Cynthia
    A) →
    McGuire, Martin
    B) →
    McKinney, Jeff
    C) → ___
    McKissick, Matthew
    D) →
    McNamara, Karen
    E) →

11. Wayn, Melba
    A) →
    Wain, Nelbert
    B) →
    Waine, Chick
    C) → ___
    Wayne, Harriet G.
    D) →
    Waynie, Davis P.
    E) →

12. Shmitz, Thomas C
    A) →
    Schmits, Deloris
    B) →
    Schmitz, Francisco
    C) → ___
    Schmitz, Hermionie
    D) →
    Shmitz, Krikor
    E) →

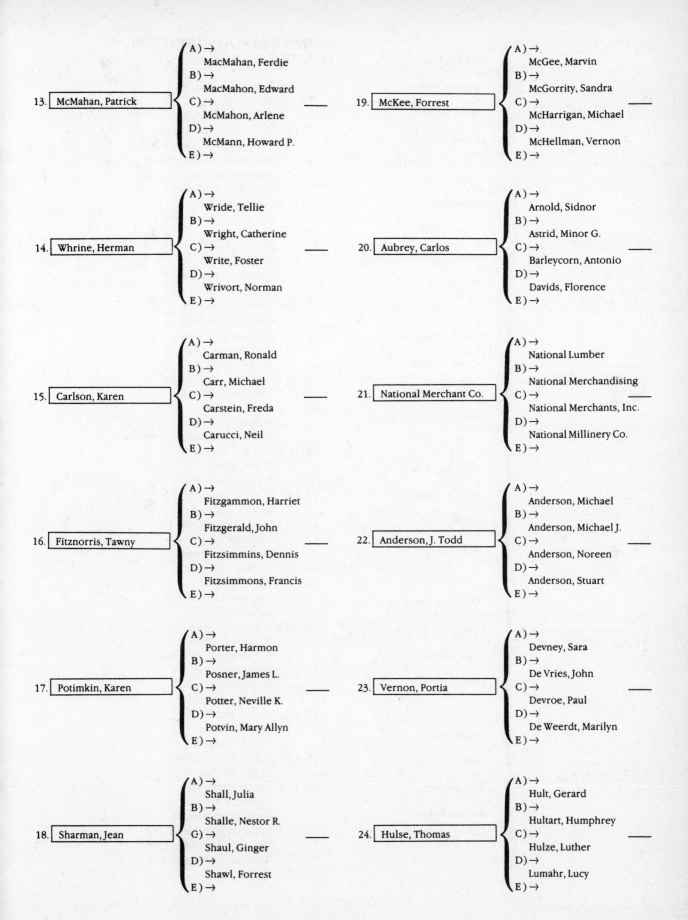

13. McMahan, Patrick
- A) →
- MacMahan, Ferdie
- B) →
- MacMahon, Edward
- C) → ___
- McMahon, Arlene
- D) →
- McMann, Howard P.
- E) →

14. Whrine, Herman
- A) →
- Wride, Tellie
- B) →
- Wright, Catherine
- C) → ___
- Write, Foster
- D) →
- Wrivort, Norman
- E) →

15. Carlson, Karen
- A) →
- Carman, Ronald
- B) →
- Carr, Michael
- C) → ___
- Carstein, Freda
- D) →
- Carucci, Neil
- E) →

16. Fitznorris, Tawny
- A) →
- Fitzgammon, Harriet
- B) →
- Fitzgerald, John
- C) → ___
- Fitzsimmins, Dennis
- D) →
- Fitzsimmons, Francis
- E) →

17. Potimkin, Karen
- A) →
- Porter, Harmon
- B) →
- Posner, James L.
- C) → ___
- Potter, Neville K.
- D) →
- Potvin, Mary Allyn
- E) →

18. Sharman, Jean
- A) →
- Shall, Julia
- B) →
- Shalle, Nestor R.
- G) → ___
- Shaul, Ginger
- D) →
- Shawl, Forrest
- E) →

19. McKee, Forrest
- A) →
- McGee, Marvin
- B) →
- McGorrity, Sandra
- C) → ___
- McHarrigan, Michael
- D) →
- McHellman, Vernon
- E) →

20. Aubrey, Carlos
- A) →
- Arnold, Sidnor
- B) →
- Astrid, Minor G.
- C) → ___
- Barleycorn, Antonio
- D) →
- Davids, Florence
- E) →

21. National Merchant Co.
- A) →
- National Lumber
- B) →
- National Merchandising
- C) → ___
- National Merchants, Inc.
- D) →
- National Millinery Co.
- E) →

22. Anderson, J. Todd
- A) →
- Anderson, Michael
- B) →
- Anderson, Michael J.
- C) → ___
- Anderson, Noreen
- D) →
- Anderson, Stuart
- E) →

23. Vernon, Portia
- A) →
- Devney, Sara
- B) →
- De Vries, John
- C) → ___
- Devroe, Paul
- D) →
- De Weerdt, Marilyn
- E) →

24. Hulse, Thomas
- A) →
- Hult, Gerard
- B) →
- Hultart, Humphrey
- C) → ___
- Hulze, Luther
- D) →
- Lumahr, Lucy
- E) →

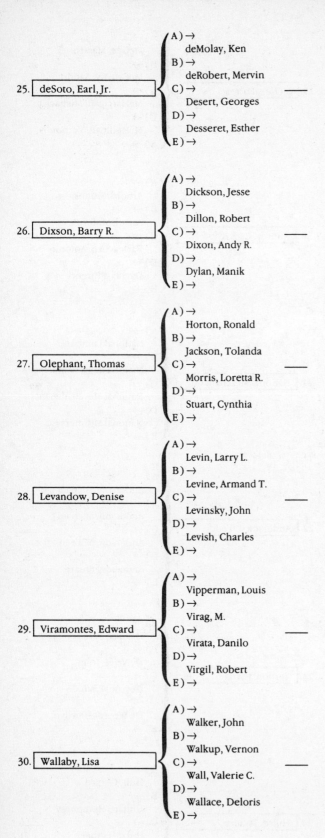

25. deSoto, Earl, Jr.
   - A) →
   - deMolay, Ken
   - B) →
   - deRobert, Mervin
   - C) → ___
   - Desert, Georges
   - D) →
   - Desseret, Esther
   - E) →

26. Dixson, Barry R.
   - A) →
   - Dickson, Jesse
   - B) →
   - Dillon, Robert
   - C) → ___
   - Dixon, Andy R.
   - D) →
   - Dylan, Manik
   - E) →

27. Olephant, Thomas
   - A) →
   - Horton, Ronald
   - B) →
   - Jackson, Tolanda
   - C) → ___
   - Morris, Loretta R.
   - D) →
   - Stuart, Cynthia
   - E) →

28. Levandow, Denise
   - A) →
   - Levin, Larry L.
   - B) →
   - Levine, Armand T.
   - C) → ___
   - Levinsky, John
   - D) →
   - Levish, Charles
   - E) →

29. Viramontes, Edward
   - A) →
   - Vipperman, Louis
   - B) →
   - Virag, M.
   - C) → ___
   - Virata, Danilo
   - D) →
   - Virgil, Robert
   - E) →

30. Wallaby, Lisa
   - A) →
   - Walker, John
   - B) →
   - Walkup, Vernon
   - C) → ___
   - Wall, Valerie C.
   - D) →
   - Wallace, Deloris
   - E) →

ANSWER EXPLANATIONS FOR PRACTICE SET 1

1. **(D)** Watsonian, Franklin
   Waverley, S. Q.
   Wetson, McDougle
2. **(D)** Birminghuller, Daisy
   Burmingham, Emma A.
   Burningham, Morris
3. **(E)** Burmen, Andre
   Burmun, Lardeese
4. **(E)** Caffry, Bertha
   McCafferty, Gabriele
5. **(A)** *Eliot, Joy*
   Eliot, Robert
6. **(C)** Baumm, Randy P.
   Beaum, Carol Ann
   Buame, Heather
7. **(B)** Cambell, Colin M.
   Campanella, Gay
   Campbell, Cynthia
8. **(A)** *Bergerman, Ralph*
   Bergquist, Peter
9. **(A)** *Caliari, Thomasina P.*
   Callahan, Bernetta
10. **(C)** McKinney, Jeff
    McKinsey, Cynthia
    McKissick, Matthew
11. **(C)** Waine, Chick
    Wayn, Melba
    Wayne, Harriet G.
12. **(E)** Shmitz, Krikor
    Shmitz, Thomas C.
13. **(C)** MacMahon, Edward
    McMahan, Patrick
    McMahon, Arlene
14. **(A)** *Whrine, Herman*
    Wride, Tellie
15. **(A)** *Carlson, Karen*
    Carman, Ronald
16. **(C)** Fitzgerald, John
    Fitznorris, Tawny
    Fitzsimmins, Dennis
17. **(C)** Posner, James L.
    Potimkin, Karen
    Potter, Neville K.
18. **(C)** Shalle, Nestor R.
    Sharman, Jean
    Shaul, Ginger
19. **(E)** McHellman, Vernon
    McKee, Forrest
20. **(C)** Astrid, Minor G.
    Aubrey, Carlos
    Barleycorn, Antonio
21. **(C)** National Merchandising
    National Merchant Co.
    National Merchants, Inc.

22. **(A)** *Anderson, J. Todd*
    Anderson, Michael
23. **(E)** De Weerdt, Marilyn
    Vernon, Portia
24. **(A)** *Hulse, Thomas*
    Hult, Gerard
25. **(D)** Desert, Georges
    deSoto, Earl, Jr.
    Desseret, Esther
26. **(D)** Dixon, Andy R.
    Dixson, Barry R.
    Dylan, Manik
27. **(D)** Morris, Loretta R.
    Olephant, Thomas
    Stuart, Cynthia
28. **(A)** *Levandow, Denise*
    Levin, Larry L.
29. **(C)** Virag, M.
    Viramontes, Edward
    Virata, Danilo
30. **(D)** Wall, Valerie C.
    Wallaby, Lisa
    Wallace, Deloris

PRACTICE SET 2

Find the correct place for the name in the box, and mark the letter of that space as your answer.

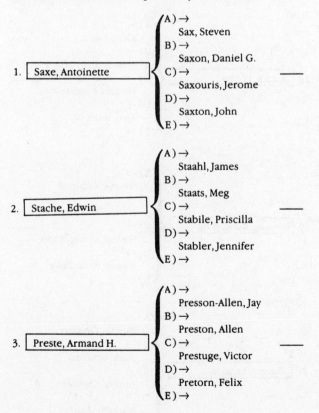

1. Saxe, Antoinette

A) →
  Sax, Steven
B) →
  Saxon, Daniel G.
C) →
  Saxouris, Jerome
D) →
  Saxton, John
E) →

2. Stache, Edwin

A) →
  Staahl, James
B) →
  Staats, Meg
C) →
  Stabile, Priscilla
D) →
  Stabler, Jennifer
E) →

3. Preste, Armand H.

A) →
  Presson-Allen, Jay
B) →
  Preston, Allen
C) →
  Prestuge, Victor
D) →
  Pretorn, Felix
E) →

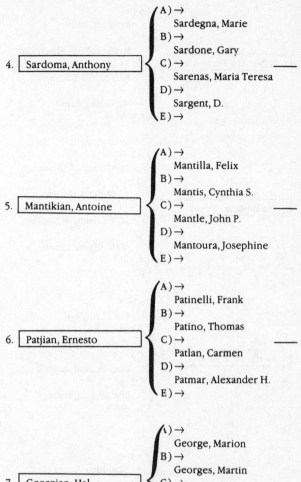

4. Sardoma, Anthony

A) →
  Sardegna, Marie
B) →
  Sardone, Gary
C) →
  Sarenas, Maria Teresa
D) →
  Sargent, D.
E) →

5. Mantikian, Antoine

A) →
  Mantilla, Felix
B) →
  Mantis, Cynthia S.
C) →
  Mantle, John P.
D) →
  Mantoura, Josephine
E) →

6. Patjian, Ernesto

A) →
  Patinelli, Frank
B) →
  Patino, Thomas
C) →
  Patlan, Carmen
D) →
  Patmar, Alexander H.
E) →

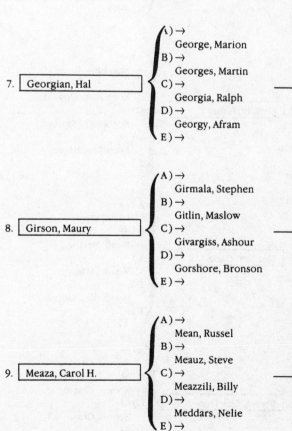

7. Georgian, Hal

A) →
  George, Marion
B) →
  Georges, Martin
C) →
  Georgia, Ralph
D) →
  Georgy, Afram
E) →

8. Girson, Maury

A) →
  Girmala, Stephen
B) →
  Gitlin, Maslow
C) →
  Givargiss, Ashour
D) →
  Gorshore, Bronson
E) →

9. Meaza, Carol H.

A) →
  Mean, Russel
B) →
  Meauz, Steve
C) →
  Meazzili, Billy
D) →
  Meddars, Nelie
E) →

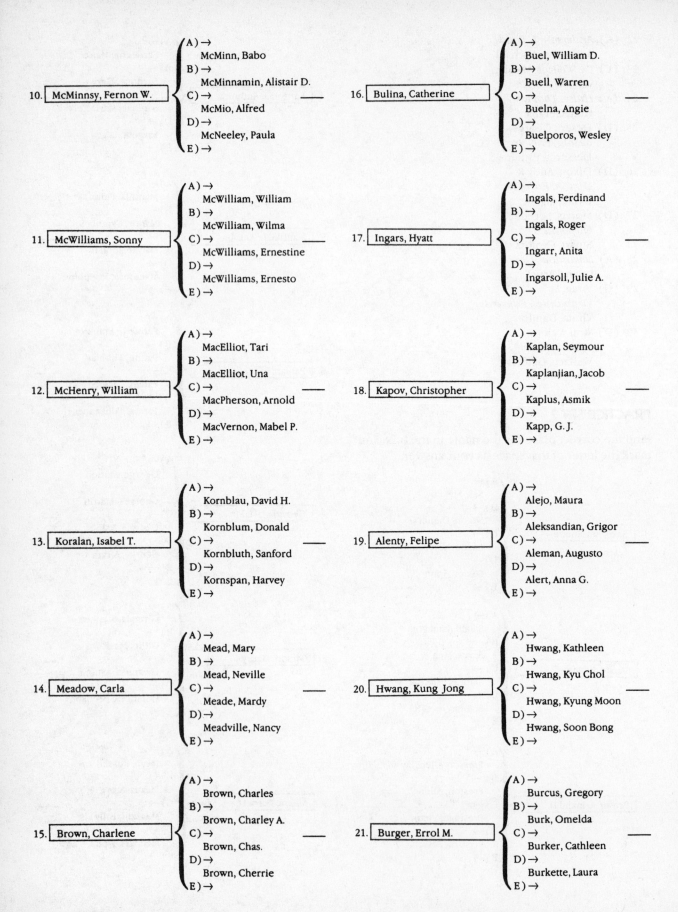

10. McMinnsy, Fernon W.
A) →
McMinn, Babo
B) →
McMinnamin, Alistair D.
C) → ____
McMio, Alfred
D) →
McNeeley, Paula
E) →

11. McWilliams, Sonny
A) →
McWilliam, William
B) →
McWilliam, Wilma
C) → ____
McWilliams, Ernestine
D) →
McWilliams, Ernesto
E) →

12. McHenry, William
A) →
MacElliot, Tari
B) →
MacElliot, Una
C) → ____
MacPherson, Arnold
D) →
MacVernon, Mabel P.
E) →

13. Koralan, Isabel T.
A) →
Kornblau, David H.
B) →
Kornblum, Donald
C) → ____
Kornbluth, Sanford
D) →
Kornspan, Harvey
E) →

14. Meadow, Carla
A) →
Mead, Mary
B) →
Mead, Neville
C) → ____
Meade, Mardy
D) →
Meadville, Nancy
E) →

15. Brown, Charlene
A) →
Brown, Charles
B) →
Brown, Charley A.
C) → ____
Brown, Chas.
D) →
Brown, Cherrie
E) →

16. Bulina, Catherine
A) →
Buel, William D.
B) →
Buell, Warren
C) → ____
Buelna, Angie
D) →
Buelporos, Wesley
E) →

17. Ingars, Hyatt
A) →
Ingals, Ferdinand
B) →
Ingals, Roger
C) → ____
Ingarr, Anita
D) →
Ingarsoll, Julie A.
E) →

18. Kapov, Christopher
A) →
Kaplan, Seymour
B) →
Kaplanjian, Jacob
C) → ____
Kaplus, Asmik
D) →
Kapp, G. J.
E) →

19. Alenty, Felipe
A) →
Alejo, Maura
B) →
Aleksandian, Grigor
C) → ____
Aleman, Augusto
D) →
Alert, Anna G.
E) →

20. Hwang, Kung Jong
A) →
Hwang, Kathleen
B) →
Hwang, Kyu Chol
C) → ____
Hwang, Kyung Moon
D) →
Hwang, Soon Bong
E) →

21. Burger, Errol M.
A) →
Burcus, Gregory
B) →
Burk, Omelda
C) → ____
Burker, Cathleen
D) →
Burkette, Laura
E) →

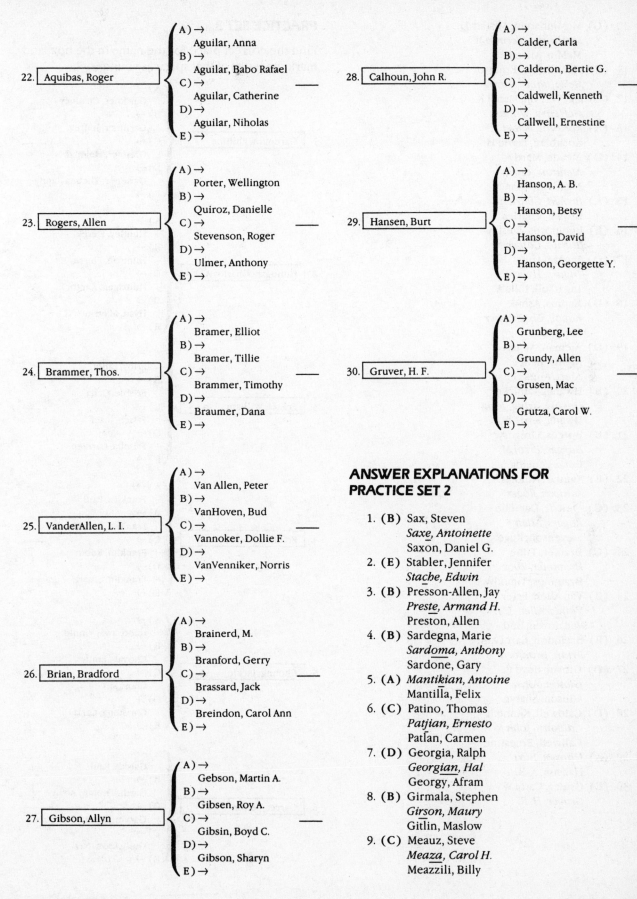

22. Aquibas, Roger
A) →
Aguilar, Anna
B) →
Aguilar, Babo Rafael
C) → _____
Aguilar, Catherine
D) →
Aguilar, Niholas
E) →

23. Rogers, Allen
A) →
Porter, Wellington
B) →
Quiroz, Danielle
C) → _____
Stevenson, Roger
D) →
Ulmer, Anthony
E) →

24. Brammer, Thos.
A) →
Bramer, Elliot
B) →
Bramer, Tillie
C) → _____
Brammer, Timothy
D) →
Braumer, Dana
E) →

25. VanderAllen, L. I.
A) →
Van Allen, Peter
B) →
VanHoven, Bud
C) → _____
Vannoker, Dollie F.
D) →
VanVenniker, Norris
E) →

26. Brian, Bradford
A) →
Brainerd, M.
B) →
Branford, Gerry
C) → _____
Brassard, Jack
D) →
Breindon, Carol Ann
E) →

27. Gibson, Allyn
A) →
Gebson, Martin A.
B) →
Gibsen, Roy A.
C) → _____
Gibsin, Boyd C.
D) →
Gibson, Sharyn
E) →

28. Calhoun, John R.
A) →
Calder, Carla
B) →
Calderon, Bertie G.
C) → _____
Caldwell, Kenneth
D) →
Callwell, Ernestine
E) →

29. Hansen, Burt
A) →
Hanson, A. B.
B) →
Hanson, Betsy
C) → _____
Hanson, David
D) →
Hanson, Georgette Y.
E) →

30. Gruver, H. F.
A) →
Grunberg, Lee
B) →
Grundy, Allen
C) → _____
Grusen, Mac
D) →
Grutza, Carol W.
E) →

ANSWER EXPLANATIONS FOR PRACTICE SET 2

1. **(B)** Sax, Steven
   Saxe, Antoinette
   Saxon, Daniel G.

2. **(E)** Stabler, Jennifer
   Stache, Edwin

3. **(B)** Presson-Allen, Jay
   Preste, Armand H.
   Preston, Allen

4. **(B)** Sardegna, Marie
   Sardoma, Anthony
   Sardone, Gary

5. **(A)** *Mantikian, Antoine*
   Mantilla, Felix

6. **(C)** Patino, Thomas
   Patjian, Ernesto
   Patlan, Carmen

7. **(D)** Georgia, Ralph
   Georgian, Hal
   Georgy, Afram

8. **(B)** Girmala, Stephen
   Girson, Maury
   Gitlin, Maslow

9. **(C)** Meauz, Steve
   Meaza, Carol H.
   Meazzili, Billy

10. (C) McMinnamin, Alistair D.
McMinnsy, Fernon W.
McMio, Alfred

11. (E) McWilliams, Ernesto
McWilliams, Sonny

12. (E) MacVernon, Mabel R.
McHenry, William

13. (A) *Koralan, Isabel T.*
Kornblau, David H.

14. (D) Meade, Mardy
Meadow, Carla
Meadville, Nancy

15. (A) *Brown, Charlene*
Brown, Charles

16. (E) Buelporos, Wesley
Bulina, Catherine

17. (D) Ingarr, Anita
Ingars, Hyatt
Ingarsoll, Julie A.

18. (D) Kaplus, Asmik
Kapov, Christopher
Kapp, G. J.

19. (D) Aleman, Augusto
Alenty, Relipe
Alert, Anna G.

20. (B) Hwang, Kathleen
Hwang, Kung, Jong
Hwang, Kyu Chol

21. (B) Burcus, Gregory
Burger, Errol M.
Burk, Omelda

22. (E) Aguilar, Niholas
Aquibas, Roger

23. (C) Quiroz, Danielle
Rogers, Allen
Stevenson, Roger

24. (C) Bramer, Tillie
Brammer, Thos.
Brammer, Timothy

25. (B) Van Allen, Peter
VanderAllen, L. I.
VanHoven, Bud

26. (E) Breindon, Carol Ann
Brian, Bradford

27. (D) Gibsin, Boyd C.
Gibson, Allyn
Gibson, Sharyn

28. (D) Caldwell, Kenneth
Calhoun, John R.
Callwell, Ernestine

29. (A) *Hansen, Burt*
Hanson, A. B.

30. (E) Grutza, Carol W.
Gruver, H. F.

PRACTICE SET 3

Find the correct place for the name in the box, and mark the letter of that space as your answer.

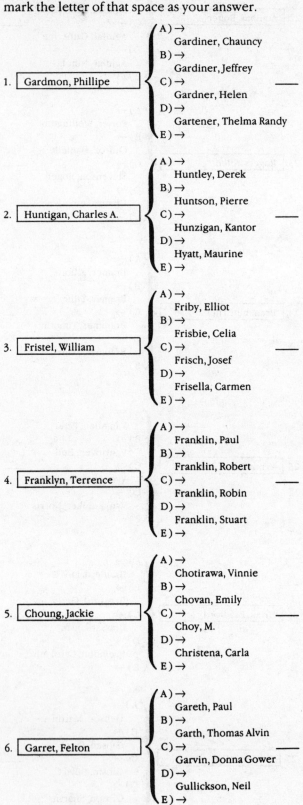

1. Gardmon, Phillipe
A) →
Gardiner, Chauncy
B) →
Gardiner, Jeffrey
C) → ____
Gardner, Helen
D) →
Gartener, Thelma Randy
E) →

2. Huntigan, Charles A.
A) →
Huntley, Derek
B) →
Huntson, Pierre
C) → ____
Hunzigan, Kantor
D) →
Hyatt, Maurine
E) →

3. Fristel, William
A) →
Friby, Elliot
B) →
Frisbie, Celia
C) → ____
Frisch, Josef
D) →
Frisella, Carmen
E) →

4. Franklyn, Terrence
A) →
Franklin, Paul
B) →
Franklin, Robert
C) → ____
Franklin, Robin
D) →
Franklin, Stuart
E) →

5. Choung, Jackie
A) →
Chotirawa, Vinnie
B) →
Chovan, Emily
C) → ____
Choy, M.
D) →
Christena, Carla
E) →

6. Garret, Felton
A) →
Gareth, Paul
B) →
Garth, Thomas Alvin
C) → ____
Garvin, Donna Gower
D) →
Gullickson, Neil
E) →

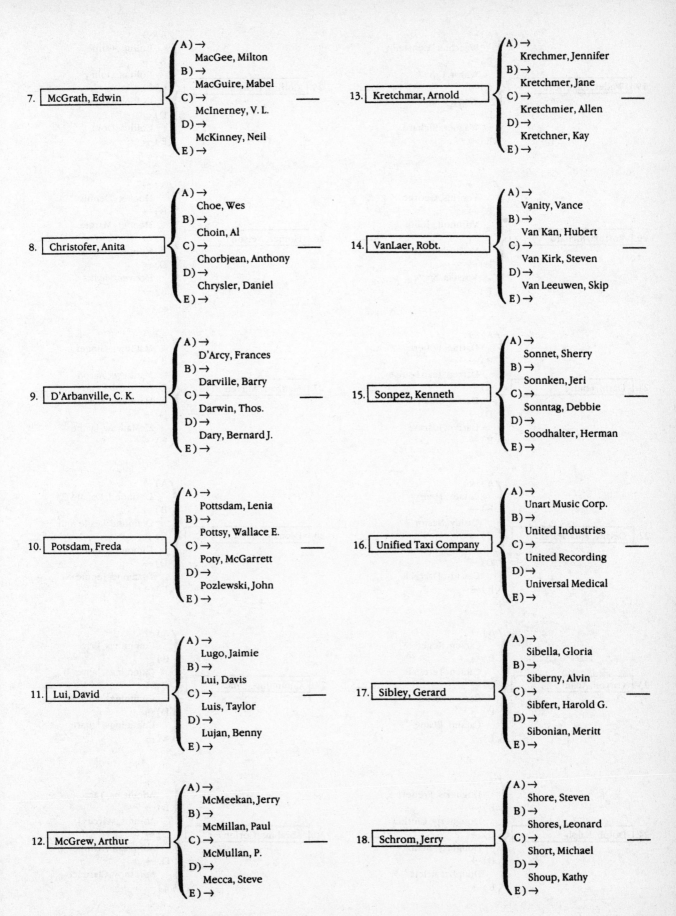

7. McGrath, Edwin
A) →
  MacGee, Milton
B) →
  MacGuire, Mabel
C) →   ___
  McInerney, V. L.
D) →
  McKinney, Neil
E) →

8. Christofer, Anita
A) →
  Choe, Wes
B) →
  Choin, Al
C) →   ___
  Chorbjean, Anthony
D) →
  Chrysler, Daniel
E) →

9. D'Arbanville, C. K.
A) →
  D'Arcy, Frances
B) →
  Darville, Barry
C) →   ___
  Darwin, Thos.
D) →
  Dary, Bernard J.
E) →

10. Potsdam, Freda
A) →
  Pottsdam, Lenia
B) →
  Pottsy, Wallace E.
C) →   ___
  Poty, McGarrett
D) →
  Pozlewski, John
E) →

11. Lui, David
A) →
  Lugo, Jaimie
B) →
  Lui, Davis
C) →   ___
  Luis, Taylor
D) →
  Lujan, Benny
E) →

12. McGrew, Arthur
A) →
  McMeekan, Jerry
B) →
  McMillan, Paul
C) →   ___
  McMullan, P.
D) →
  Mecca, Steve
E) →

13. Kretchmar, Arnold
A) →
  Krechmer, Jennifer
B) →
  Kretchmer, Jane
C) →   ___
  Kretchmier, Allen
D) →
  Kretchner, Kay
E) →

14. VanLaer, Robt.
A) →
  Vanity, Vance
B) →
  Van Kan, Hubert
C) →   ___
  Van Kirk, Steven
D) →
  Van Leeuwen, Skip
E) →

15. Sonpez, Kenneth
A) →
  Sonnet, Sherry
B) →
  Sonnken, Jeri
C) →   ___
  Sonntag, Debbie
D) →
  Soodhalter, Herman
E) →

16. Unified Taxi Company
A) →
  Unart Music Corp.
B) →
  United Industries
C) →   ___
  United Recording
D) →
  Universal Medical
E) →

17. Sibley, Gerard
A) →
  Sibella, Gloria
B) →
  Siberny, Alvin
C) →   ___
  Sibfert, Harold G.
D) →
  Sibonian, Meritt
E) →

18. Schrom, Jerry
A) →
  Shore, Steven
B) →
  Shores, Leonard
C) →   ___
  Short, Michael
D) →
  Shoup, Kathy
E) →

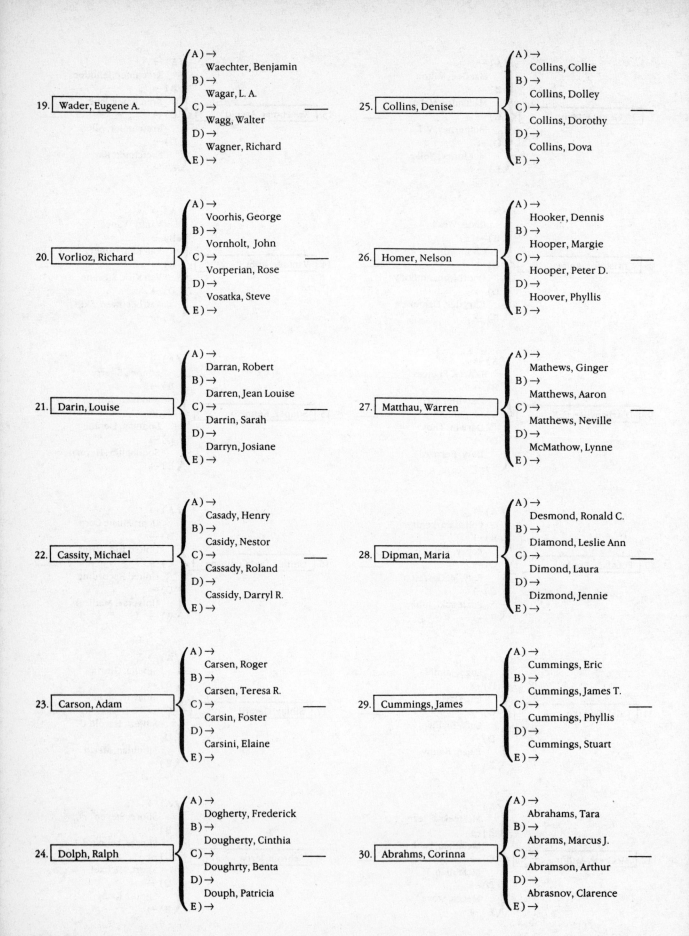

19. Wader, Eugene A.
- A) →
  Waechter, Benjamin
- B) →
  Wagar, L. A.
- C) →
  Wagg, Walter
- D) →
  Wagner, Richard
- E) →

———

20. Vorlioz, Richard
- A) →
  Voorhis, George
- B) →
  Vornholt, John
- C) →
  Vorperian, Rose
- D) →
  Vosatka, Steve
- E) →

———

21. Darin, Louise
- A) →
  Darran, Robert
- B) →
  Darren, Jean Louise
- C) →
  Darrin, Sarah
- D) →
  Darryn, Josiane
- E) →

———

22. Cassity, Michael
- A) →
  Casady, Henry
- B) →
  Casidy, Nestor
- C) →
  Cassady, Roland
- D) →
  Cassidy, Darryl R.
- E) →

———

23. Carson, Adam
- A) →
  Carsen, Roger
- B) →
  Carsen, Teresa R.
- C) →
  Carsin, Foster
- D) →
  Carsini, Elaine
- E) →

———

24. Dolph, Ralph
- A) →
  Dogherty, Frederick
- B) →
  Dougherty, Cinthia
- C) →
  Doughrty, Benta
- D) →
  Douph, Patricia
- E) →

———

25. Collins, Denise
- A) →
  Collins, Collie
- B) →
  Collins, Dolley
- C) →
  Collins, Dorothy
- D) →
  Collins, Dova
- E) →

———

26. Homer, Nelson
- A) →
  Hooker, Dennis
- B) →
  Hooper, Margie
- C) →
  Hooper, Peter D.
- D) →
  Hoover, Phyllis
- E) →

———

27. Matthau, Warren
- A) →
  Mathews, Ginger
- B) →
  Matthews, Aaron
- C) →
  Matthews, Neville
- D) →
  McMathow, Lynne
- E) →

———

28. Dipman, Maria
- A) →
  Desmond, Ronald C.
- B) →
  Diamond, Leslie Ann
- C) →
  Dimond, Laura
- D) →
  Dizmond, Jennie
- E) →

———

29. Cummings, James
- A) →
  Cummings, Eric
- B) →
  Cummings, James T.
- C) →
  Cummings, Phyllis
- D) →
  Cummings, Stuart
- E) →

———

30. Abrahms, Corinna
- A) →
  Abrahams, Tara
- B) →
  Abrams, Marcus J.
- C) →
  Abramson, Arthur
- D) →
  Abrasnov, Clarence
- E) →

———

ANSWER EXPLANATIONS FOR PRACTICE SET 3

1. (C) Gardiner, Jeffrey
   Gardmon, Phillipe
   Gardner, Helen
2. (A) *Huntigan, Charles A.*
   Huntley, Derek
3. (E) Frisella, Carmen
   Fristel, William
4. (E) Franklin, Stuart
   Franklyn, Terrence
5. (B) Chotirawa, Vinnie
   Choung, Jackie
   Chovan, Emily
6. (B) Gareth, Paul
   Garret, Felton
   Garth, Thomas Alvin
7. (C) MacGuire, Mabel
   McGrath, Edwin
   McInerney, V. L.
8. (D) Chorbjean, Anthony
   Christofer, Anita
   Chrysler, Daniel
9. (A) *D'Arbanville, C. K.*
   D'Arcy, Frances
10. (A) *Potsdam, Freda*
    Pottsdam, Lenia
11. (B) Lugo, Jaimie
    Lui, David
    Lui, Davis
12. (A) *McGrew, Arthur*
    McMeekan, Jerry
13. (B) Krechmer, Jennifer
    Kretchmar, Arnold
    Kretchmer, Jane
14. (D) Van Kirk, Steven
    VanLaer, Robt.
    Van Leeuwen, Skip
15. (D) Sonntag, Debbie
    Sonpez, Kenneth
    Soodhalter, Herman
16. (B) Unart Music Corp.
    Unified Taxi Company
    United Industries
17. (D) Sibfert, Harold G.
    Sibley, Gerard
    Sibonian, Meritt
18. (A) *Schrom, Jerry*
    Shore, Steven
19. (A) *Wader, Eugene A.*
    Waechter, Benjamin
20. (B) Voorhis, George
    Vorlioz, Richard
    Vornholt, John
21. (A) *Darin, Louise*
    Darran, Robert
22. (E) Cassidy, Darryl R.
    Cassity, Michael
23. (E) Carsini, Elaine
    Carson, Adam
24. (B) Dogherty, Frederick
    Dolph, Ralph
    Dougherty, Cinthia
25. (B) Collins, Collie
    Collins, Denise
    Collins, Dolley
26. (A) *Homer, Nelson*
    Hooker, Dennis
27. (B) Mathews, Ginger
    Matthau, Warren
    Matthews, Aaron
28. (D) Dimond, Laura
    Dipman, Maria
    Dizmond, Jennie
29. (B) Cummings, Eric.
    Cummings, James
    Cummings, James T.
30. (B) Abrahams, Tara
    Abrahms, Corinna
    Abrams, Marcus J.

PRACTICE SET 4

Find the correct place for the name in the box, and mark the letter of that space as your answer.

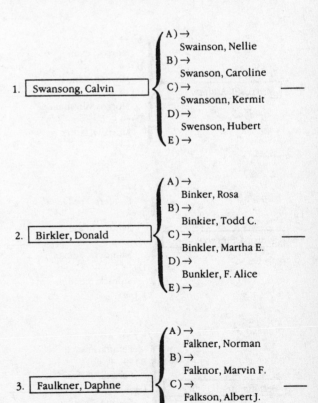

1. Swansong, Calvin
   A) →
   Swainson, Nellie
   B) →
   Swanson, Caroline
   C) →
   Swansonn, Kermit
   D) →
   Swenson, Hubert
   E) →

2. Birkler, Donald
   A) →
   Binker, Rosa
   B) →
   Binkier, Todd C.
   C) →
   Binkler, Martha E.
   D) →
   Bunkler, F. Alice
   E) →

3. Faulkner, Daphne
   A) →
   Falkner, Norman
   B) →
   Falknor, Marvin F.
   C) →
   Falkson, Albert J.
   D) →
   Faulkner, Erica
   E) →

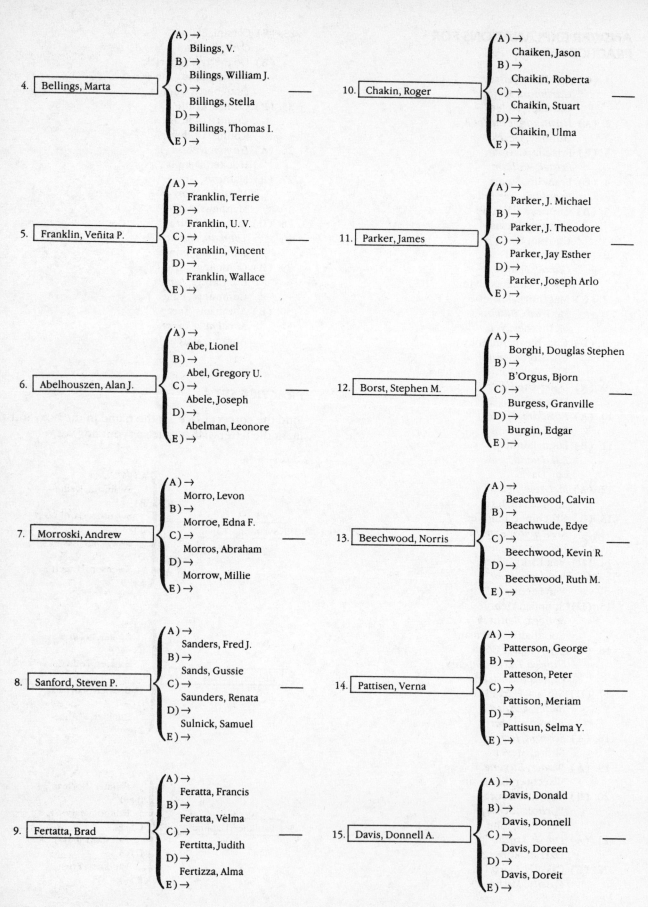

4. Bellings, Marta
- A) →
- Bilings, V.
- B) →
- Bilings, William J.
- C) →
- Billings, Stella
- D) →
- Billings, Thomas I.
- E) →

5. Franklin, Veñita P.
- A) →
- Franklin, Terrie
- B) →
- Franklin, U. V.
- C) →
- Franklin, Vincent
- D) →
- Franklin, Wallace
- E) →

6. Abelhouszen, Alan J.
- A) →
- Abe, Lionel
- B) →
- Abel, Gregory U.
- C) →
- Abele, Joseph
- D) →
- Abelman, Leonore
- E) →

7. Morroski, Andrew
- A) →
- Morro, Levon
- B) →
- Morroe, Edna F.
- C) →
- Morros, Abraham
- D) →
- Morrow, Millie
- E) →

8. Sanford, Steven P.
- A) →
- Sanders, Fred J.
- B) →
- Sands, Gussie
- C) →
- Saunders, Renata
- D) →
- Sulnick, Samuel
- E) →

9. Fertatta, Brad
- A) →
- Feratta, Francis
- B) →
- Feratta, Velma
- C) →
- Fertitta, Judith
- D) →
- Fertizza, Alma
- E) →

10. Chakin, Roger
- A) →
- Chaiken, Jason
- B) →
- Chaikin, Roberta
- C) →
- Chaikin, Stuart
- D) →
- Chaikin, Ulma
- E) →

11. Parker, James
- A) →
- Parker, J. Michael
- B) →
- Parker, J. Theodore
- C) →
- Parker, Jay Esther
- D) →
- Parker, Joseph Arlo
- E) →

12. Borst, Stephen M.
- A) →
- Borghi, Douglas Stephen
- B) →
- B'Orgus, Bjorn
- C) →
- Burgess, Granville
- D) →
- Burgin, Edgar
- E) →

13. Beechwood, Norris
- A) →
- Beachwood, Calvin
- B) →
- Beachwude, Edye
- C) →
- Beechwood, Kevin R.
- D) →
- Beechwood, Ruth M.
- E) →

14. Pattisen, Verna
- A) →
- Patterson, George
- B) →
- Patteson, Peter
- C) →
- Pattison, Meriam
- D) →
- Pattisun, Selma Y.
- E) →

15. Davis, Donnell A.
- A) →
- Davis, Donald
- B) →
- Davis, Donnell
- C) →
- Davis, Doreen
- D) →
- Davis, Doreit
- E) →

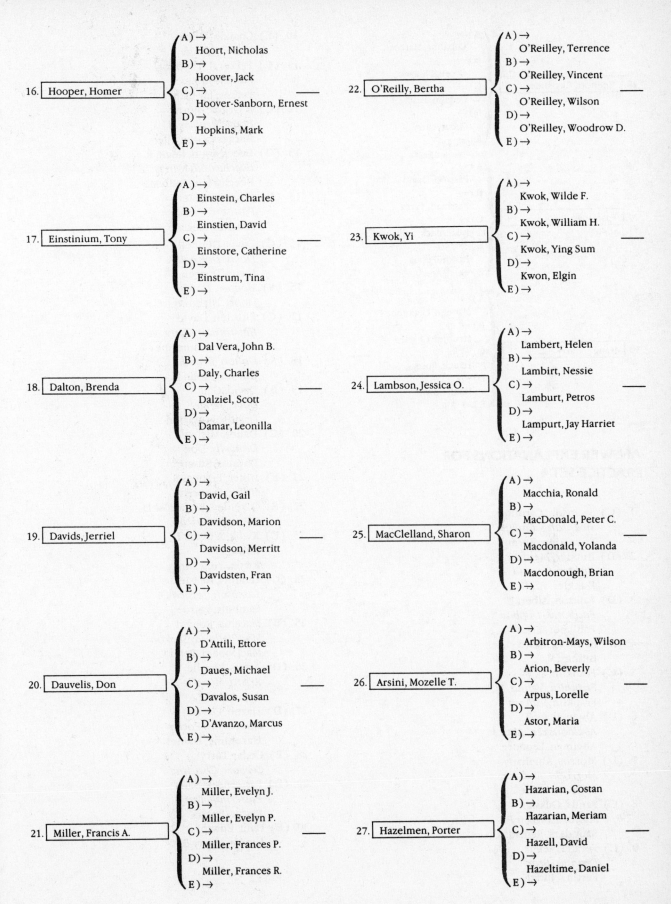

16. Hooper, Homer
A) →
Hoort, Nicholas
B) →
Hoover, Jack
C) → ___
Hoover-Sanborn, Ernest
D) →
Hopkins, Mark
E) →

17. Einstinium, Tony
A) →
Einstein, Charles
B) →
Einstien, David
C) → ___
Einstore, Catherine
D) →
Einstrum, Tina
E) →

18. Dalton, Brenda
A) →
Dal Vera, John B.
B) →
Daly, Charles
C) → ___
Dalziel, Scott
D) →
Damar, Leonilla
E) →

19. Davids, Jerriel
A) →
David, Gail
B) →
Davidson, Marion
C) → ___
Davidson, Merritt
D) →
Davidsten, Fran
E) →

20. Dauvelis, Don
A) →
D'Attili, Ettore
B) →
Daues, Michael
C) → ___
Davalos, Susan
D) →
D'Avanzo, Marcus
E) →

21. Miller, Francis A.
A) →
Miller, Evelyn J.
B) →
Miller, Evelyn P.
C) → ___
Miller, Frances P.
D) →
Miller, Frances R.
E) →

22. O'Reilly, Bertha
A) →
O'Reilley, Terrence
B) →
O'Reilley, Vincent
C) → ___
O'Reilley, Wilson
D) →
O'Reilley, Woodrow D.
E) →

23. Kwok, Yi
A) →
Kwok, Wilde F.
B) →
Kwok, William H.
C) → ___
Kwok, Ying Sum
D) →
Kwon, Elgin
E) →

24. Lambson, Jessica O.
A) →
Lambert, Helen
B) →
Lambirt, Nessie
C) → ___
Lamburt, Petros
D) →
Lampurt, Jay Harriet
E) →

25. MacClelland, Sharon
A) →
Macchia, Ronald
B) →
MacDonald, Peter C.
C) → ___
Macdonald, Yolanda
D) →
Macdonough, Brian
E) →

26. Arsini, Mozelle T.
A) →
Arbitron-Mays, Wilson
B) →
Arion, Beverly
C) → ___
Arpus, Lorelle
D) →
Astor, Maria
E) →

27. Hazelmen, Porter
A) →
Hazarian, Costan
B) →
Hazarian, Meriam
C) → ___
Hazell, David
D) →
Hazeltime, Daniel
E) →

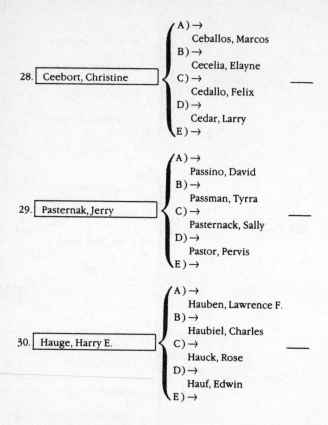

28. Ceebort, Christine
A) →
Ceballos, Marcos
B) →
Cecelia, Elayne
C) →
Cedallo, Felix
D) →
Cedar, Larry
E) →

29. Pasternak, Jerry
A) →
Passino, David
B) →
Passman, Tyrra
C) →
Pasternack, Sally
D) →
Pastor, Pervis
E) →

30. Hauge, Harry E.
A) →
Hauben, Lawrence F.
B) →
Haubiel, Charles
C) →
Hauck, Rose
D) →
Hauf, Edwin
E) →

ANSWER EXPLANATIONS FOR PRACTICE SET 4

1. (C) Swanson, Caroline
Swansong, Calvin
Swansonn, Kermit

2. (D) Binkler, Martha E.
Birkler, Donald
Bunkler, F. Alice

3. (D) Falkson, Albert J.
Faulkner, Daphne
Faulkner, Erica

4. (A) *Bellings, Marta*
Bilings, V.

5. (C) Franklin, U. V.
Franklin, Venita, P.
Franklin, Vincent

6. (D) Abele, Joseph
Abelhouszen, Alan J.
Abelman, Leonore

7. (D) Morros, Abraham
Morroski, Andrew
Morrow, Millie

8. (C) Sands, Gussie
Sanford, Steven P.
Saunders, Renata

9. (C) Feratta, Velma
Fertatta, Brad
Fertitta, Judith

10. (E) Chaikin, Ulma
Chakin, Roger

11. (C) Parker, J. Theodore
Parker, James
Parker, Jay Esther

12. (C) B'Orgus, Bjorn
Borst, Stephen M.
Burgess, Granville

13. (D) Beechwood, Kevin R.
Beechwood, Norris
Beechwood, Ruth M.

14. (C) Patteson, Peter
Pattisen, Verna
Pattison, Meriam

15. (C) Davis, Donnell
Davis, Donnell A.
Davis, Doreen

16. (A) *Hooper, Homer*
Hoort, Nicholas

17. (C) Einstien, David
Einstinium, Tony
Einstore, Catherine

18. (A) *Dalton, Brenda*
Dal Vera, John B.

19. (B) David, Gail
Davis, Jerriel
Davidson, Marion

20. (C) Daues, Michael
Dauvelis, Don
Davalos, Susan

21. (E) Miller, Frances R.
Miller, Francis A.

22. (E) O'Reilley, Woodrow D.
O'Reilly, Bertha

23. (C) Kwok, William H.
Kwok, Yi
Kwok, Ying Sum

24. (C) Lambirt, Nessie
Lambson, Jessica O.
Lamburt, Petros

25. (B) Macchia, Ronald
MacClelland, Sharon
MacDonald, Peter C.

26. (D) Arpus, Lorelle
Arsini, Mozelle T.
Astor, Maria

27. (D) Hazell, David
Hazelmen, Porter
Hazeltime, Daniel

28. (E) Cedar, Larry
Ceebort, Christine

29. (D) Pasternack, Sally
Pasternak, Jerry
Pastor, Pervis

30. (E) Hauf, Edwin
Hauge, Harry E.

PRACTICE SET 5

Find the correct place for the name in the box, and mark the letter of that space as your answer.

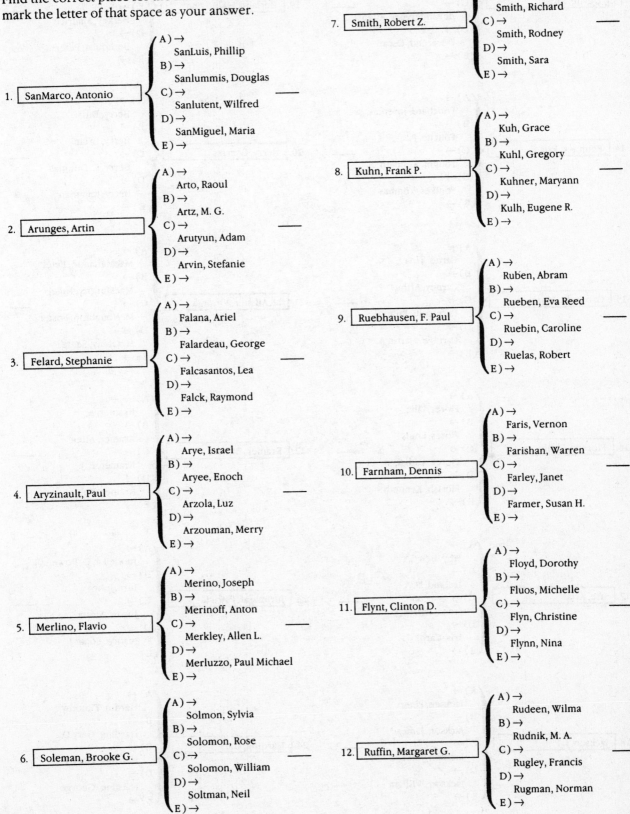

1. **SanMarco, Antonio**
   - A) →
     SanLuis, Phillip
   - B) →
     Sanlummis, Douglas
   - C) → ___
     Sanlutent, Wilfred
   - D) →
     SanMiguel, Maria
   - E) →

2. **Arunges, Artin**
   - A) →
     Arto, Raoul
   - B) →
     Artz, M. G.
   - C) → ___
     Arutyun, Adam
   - D) →
     Arvin, Stefanie
   - E) →

3. **Felard, Stephanie**
   - A) →
     Falana, Ariel
   - B) →
     Falardeau, George
   - C) → ___
     Falcasantos, Lea
   - D) →
     Falck, Raymond
   - E) →

4. **Aryzinault, Paul**
   - A) →
     Arye, Israel
   - B) →
     Aryee, Enoch
   - C) → ___
     Arzola, Luz
   - D) →
     Arzouman, Merry
   - E) →

5. **Merlino, Flavio**
   - A) →
     Merino, Joseph
   - B) →
     Merinoff, Anton
   - C) → ___
     Merkley, Allen L.
   - D) →
     Merluzzo, Paul Michael
   - E) →

6. **Soleman, Brooke G.**
   - A) →
     Solmon, Sylvia
   - B) →
     Solomon, Rose
   - C) → ___
     Solomon, William
   - D) →
     Soltman, Neil
   - E) →

7. **Smith, Robert Z.**
   - A) →
     Smith, R. Ruth
   - B) →
     Smith, Richard
   - C) → ___
     Smith, Rodney
   - D) →
     Smith, Sara
   - E) →

8. **Kuhn, Frank P.**
   - A) →
     Kuh, Grace
   - B) →
     Kuhl, Gregory
   - C) → ___
     Kuhner, Maryann
   - D) →
     Kulh, Eugene R.
   - E) →

9. **Ruebhausen, F. Paul**
   - A) →
     Ruben, Abram
   - B) →
     Rueben, Eva Reed
   - C) → ___
     Ruebin, Caroline
   - D) →
     Ruelas, Robert
   - E) →

10. **Farnham, Dennis**
    - A) →
      Faris, Vernon
    - B) →
      Farishan, Warren
    - C) → ___
      Farley, Janet
    - D) →
      Farmer, Susan H.
    - E) →

11. **Flynt, Clinton D.**
    - A) →
      Floyd, Dorothy
    - B) →
      Fluos, Michelle
    - C) → ___
      Flyn, Christine
    - D) →
      Flynn, Nina
    - E) →

12. **Ruffin, Margaret G.**
    - A) →
      Rudeen, Wilma
    - B) →
      Rudnik, M. A.
    - C) → ___
      Rugley, Francis
    - D) →
      Rugman, Norman
    - E) →

13. Devile, Albert
- A) →
- deStefano, Ann
- B) →
- deStepho, Pietro
- C) → ____
- deVanderveer, August
- D) →
- Deverend, Oscar
- E) →

14. Fouhner, Esta C.
- A) →
- Fouchard, Joseph
- B) →
- Fouche, P.
- C) → ____
- Fought, Kenneth
- D) →
- Foulkes, Thomas
- E) →

15. Carnieski, Morris
- A) →
- Carne, Tina
- B) →
- Carney, Arthur
- C) → ____
- Carnicelli, Ruben
- D) →
- Carnow, Martin A.
- E) →

16. Floretta, Philip
- A) →
- Flores, Lilia
- B) →
- Flores, Louis
- C) → ____
- Florez, Didi S.
- D) →
- Florish, Kenneth
- E) →

17. Irie, Kris
- A) →
- Irby, Ben C.
- B) →
- Ireland, N. A.
- C) → ____
- Irena, Perris
- D) →
- Iris, Carol
- E) →

18. Jackson, J. P.
- A) →
- Jacksen, Peter
- B) →
- Jackson, James
- C) → ____
- Jackson, John
- D) →
- Jackson, William
- E) →

19. Berland, Helen Ann
- A) →
- Berk, Lillian O.
- B) →
- Berker, S. R.
- C) → ____
- Berkey, Maurice
- D) →
- Berkquist, Peter
- E) →

20. Berry, Charles
- A) →
- Berry, Bill
- B) →
- Berry, Brian
- C) → ____
- Berry, C. Douglas
- D) →
- Berry, Jonathan
- E) →

21. McAllister, Virginia
- A) →
- MacMenamin, Peter
- B) →
- MacMullory, Nigel
- C) → ____
- McNoughton, Foster
- D) →
- McOleny, Santa
- E) →

22. Kramer, Edward
- A) →
- Kramer, A.
- B) →
- Kramer, Allen
- C) → ____
- Kramer, E. J.
- D) →
- Kramer, Rubin
- E) →

23. Jurimasat, Patricia
- A) →
- Juodeika, G. Rowena
- B) →
- Jura, John
- C) → ____
- Jurow, Stasia
- D) →
- Justice, Edgar J.
- E) →

24. Harding, Gary
- A) →
- Hardin, Timothy
- B) →
- Harding, Gary D.
- C) → ____
- Harding, Gary T.
- D) →
- Harding, George
- E) →

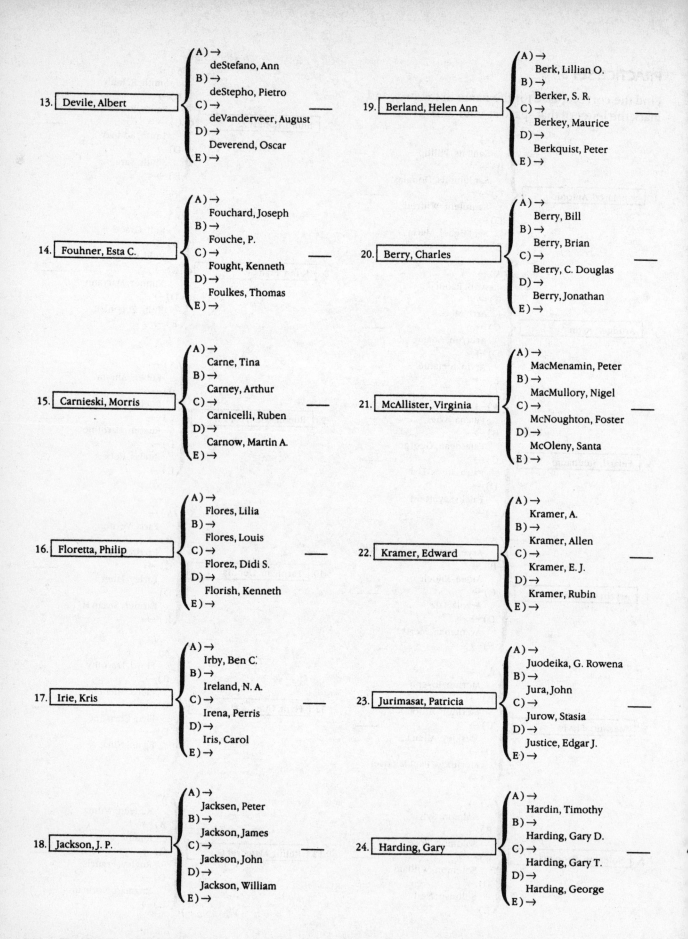

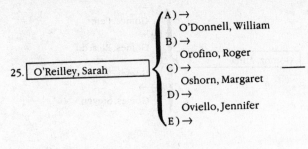

25. O'Reilley, Sarah
- A) →
  O'Donnell, William
- B) →
  Orofino, Roger
- C) →
  Oshorn, Margaret
- D) →
  Oviello, Jennifer
- E) →

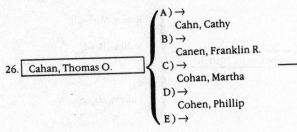

26. Cahan, Thomas O.
- A) →
  Cahn, Cathy
- B) →
  Canen, Franklin R.
- C) →
  Cohan, Martha
- D) →
  Cohen, Phillip
- E) →

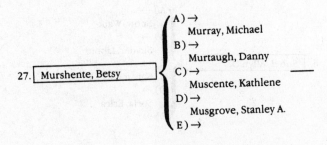

27. Murshente, Betsy
- A) →
  Murray, Michael
- B) →
  Murtaugh, Danny
- C) →
  Muscente, Kathlene
- D) →
  Musgrove, Stanley A.
- E) →

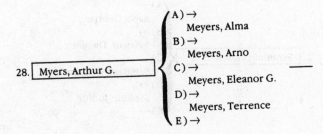

28. Myers, Arthur G.
- A) →
  Meyers, Alma
- B) →
  Meyers, Arno
- C) →
  Meyers, Eleanor G.
- D) →
  Meyers, Terrence
- E) →

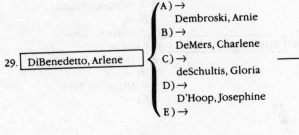

29. DiBenedetto, Arlene
- A) →
  Dembroski, Arnie
- B) →
  DeMers, Charlene
- C) →
  deSchultis, Gloria
- D) →
  D'Hoop, Josephine
- E) →

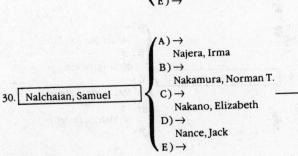

30. Nalchaian, Samuel
- A) →
  Najera, Irma
- B) →
  Nakamura, Norman T.
- C) →
  Nakano, Elizabeth
- D) →
  Nance, Jack
- E) →

ANSWER EXPLANATIONS FOR PRACTICE SET 5

1. **(D)** Sanlutent, Wilfred
   SanMarco, Antonio
   SanMiguel, Maria
2. **(C)** Artz, M. G.
   Arunges, Artin
   Arutyun, Adam
3. **(E)** Falck, Raymond
   Felard, Stephanie
4. **(C)** Aryee, Enoch
   Aryzinault, Paul
   Arzola, Luz
5. **(D)** Merkley, Allen L.
   Merlino, Flavio
   Merluzzo, Paul Michael
6. **(A)** *Soleman, Brooke G.*
   Solmon, Sylvia
7. **(C)** Smith, Richard
   Smith, Robert Z.
   Smith, Rodney
8. **(C)** Kuhl, Gregory
   Kuhn, Frank P.
   Kuhner, Maryann
9. **(C)** Rueben, Eva Reed
   Ruebhausen, F. Paul
   Ruebin, Caroline
10. **(E)** Farmer, Susan H.
    Farnham, Dennis
11. **(E)** Flynn, Nina
    Flynt, Clinton D.
12. **(C)** Rudnik, M. A.
    Ruffin, Margaret G.
    Rugley, Francis
13. **(E)** Deverend, Oscar
    Devile, Albert
14. **(D)** Fought, Kenneth
    Fouhner, Esta C.
    Foulkes, Thomas
15. **(D)** Carnicelli, Ruben
    Carnieski, Morris
    Carnow, Martin A.
16. **(C)** Flores, Louis
    Floretta, Philip
    Florez, Didi S.
17. **(D)** Irena, Perris
    Irie, Kris
    Iris, Carol
18. **(B)** Jacksen, Peter
    Jackson, J. P.
    Jackson, James
19. **(E)** Berkquist, Peter
    Berland, Helen Ann
20. **(D)** Berry, C. Douglas
    Berry, Charles
    Berry, Jonathan
21. **(C)** MacMullory, Nigel
    McAllister, Virginia
    McNoughton, Foster

22. **(D)** Kramer, E. J.
Kramer, Edward
Kramer, Rubin

23. **(C)** Jura, John
Jurimasat, Patricia
Jurow, Stasia

24. **(B)** Hardin, Timothy
Harding, Gary
Harding, Gary D.

25. **(B)** O'Donnell, William
O'Reilley, Sarah
Orofino, Roger

26. **(A)** _Caban, Thomas O._
Cahn, Cathy

27. **(B)** Murray, Michael
Murshente, Betsy
Murtaugh, Danny

28. **(E)** Meyers, Terrence
Myers, Arthur G.

29. **(E)** D'Hoop, Josephine
DiBenedetto, Arlene

30. **(D)** Nakano, Elizabeth
Nalchaian, Samuel
Nance, Jack

PRACTICE SET 6

Find the correct place for the name in the box, and mark the letter of that space as your answer.

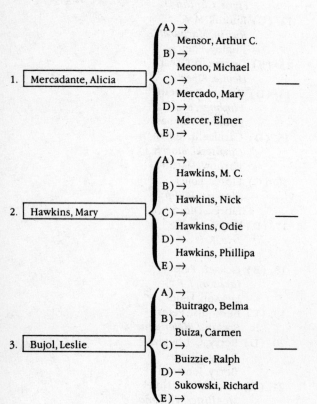

1. Mercadante, Alicia
(A) →
Mensor, Arthur C.
(B) →
Meono, Michael
(C) →
Mercado, Mary
(D) →
Mercer, Elmer
(E) →

2. Hawkins, Mary
(A) →
Hawkins, M. C.
(B) →
Hawkins, Nick
(C) →
Hawkins, Odie
(D) →
Hawkins, Phillipa
(E) →

3. Bujol, Leslie
(A) →
Buitrago, Belma
(B) →
Buiza, Carmen
(C) →
Buizzie, Ralph
(D) →
Sukowski, Richard
(E) →

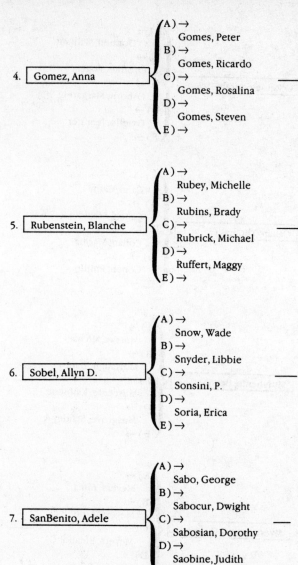

4. Gomez, Anna
(A) →
Gomes, Peter
(B) →
Gomes, Ricardo
(C) →
Gomes, Rosalina
(D) →
Gomes, Steven
(E) →

5. Rubenstein, Blanche
(A) →
Rubey, Michelle
(B) →
Rubins, Brady
(C) →
Rubrick, Michael
(D) →
Ruffert, Maggy
(E) →

6. Sobel, Allyn D.
(A) →
Snow, Wade
(B) →
Snyder, Libbie
(C) →
Sonsini, P.
(D) →
Soria, Erica
(E) →

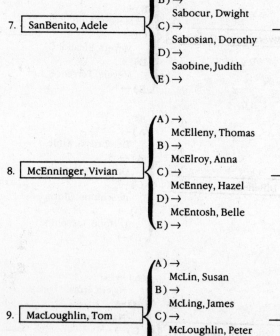

7. SanBenito, Adele
(A) →
Sabo, George
(B) →
Sabocur, Dwight
(C) →
Sabosian, Dorothy
(D) →
Saobine, Judith
(E) →

8. McEnninger, Vivian
(A) →
McElleny, Thomas
(B) →
McElroy, Anna
(C) →
McEnney, Hazel
(D) →
McEntosh, Belle
(E) →

9. MacLoughlin, Tom
(A) →
McLin, Susan
(B) →
McLing, James
(C) →
McLoughlin, Peter
(D) →
McMahan, Daisy
(E) →

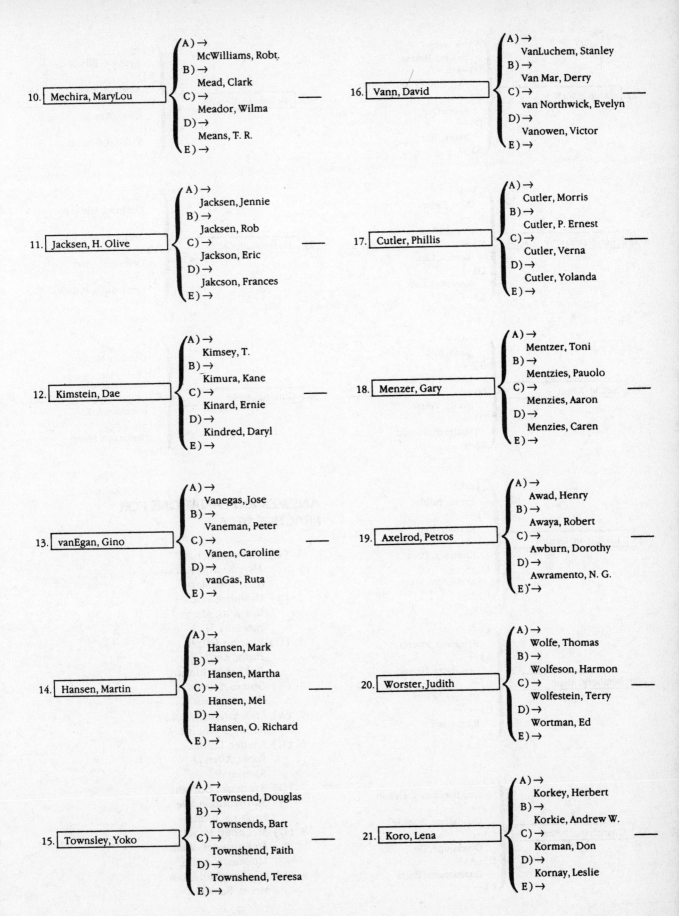

10. Mechira, MaryLou
A) →
McWilliams, Robt.
B) →
Mead, Clark
C) →
Meador, Wilma
D) →
Means, T. R.
E) →
____

16. Vann, David
A) →
VanLuchem, Stanley
B) →
Van Mar, Derry
C) →
van Northwick, Evelyn
D) →
Vanowen, Victor
E) →
____

11. Jacksen, H. Olive
A) →
Jacksen, Jennie
B) →
Jacksen, Rob
C) →
Jackson, Eric
D) →
Jakcson, Frances
E) →
____

17. Cutler, Phillis
A) →
Cutler, Morris
B) →
Cutler, P. Ernest
C) →
Cutler, Verna
D) →
Cutler, Yolanda
E) →
____

12. Kimstein, Dae
A) →
Kimsey, T.
B) →
Kimura, Kane
C) →
Kinard, Ernie
D) →
Kindred, Daryl
E) →
____

18. Menzer, Gary
A) →
Mentzer, Toni
B) →
Mentzies, Pauolo
C) →
Menzies, Aaron
D) →
Menzies, Caren
E) →
____

13. vanEgan, Gino
A) →
Vanegas, Jose
B) →
Vaneman, Peter
C) →
Vanen, Caroline
D) →
vanGas, Ruta
E) →
____

19. Axelrod, Petros
A) →
Awad, Henry
B) →
Awaya, Robert
C) →
Awburn, Dorothy
D) →
Awramento, N. G.
E) →
____

14. Hansen, Martin
A) →
Hansen, Mark
B) →
Hansen, Martha
C) →
Hansen, Mel
D) →
Hansen, O. Richard
E) →
____

20. Worster, Judith
A) →
Wolfe, Thomas
B) →
Wolfeson, Harmon
C) →
Wolfestein, Terry
D) →
Wortman, Ed
E) →
____

15. Townsley, Yoko
A) →
Townsend, Douglas
B) →
Townsends, Bart
C) →
Townshend, Faith
D) →
Townshend, Teresa
E) →
____

21. Koro, Lena
A) →
Korkey, Herbert
B) →
Korkie, Andrew W.
C) →
Korman, Don
D) →
Kornay, Leslie
E) →
____

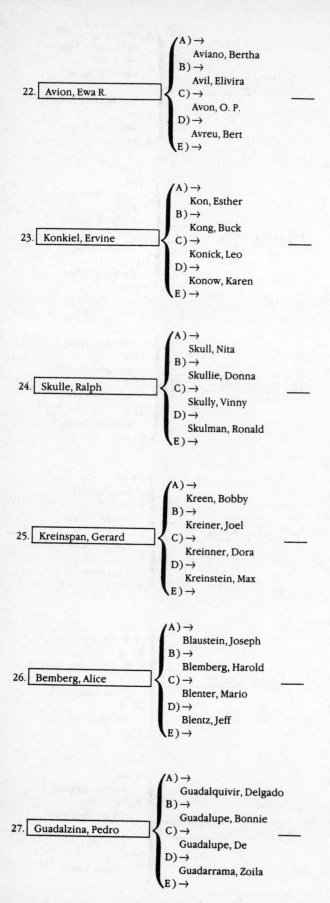

22. Avion, Ewa R.
- A) →
- Aviano, Bertha
- B) →
- Avil, Elivira
- C) →
- Avon, O. P.
- D) →
- Avreu, Bert
- E) →

23. Konkiel, Ervine
- A) →
- Kon, Esther
- B) →
- Kong, Buck
- C) →
- Konick, Leo
- D) →
- Konow, Karen
- E) →

24. Skulle, Ralph
- A) →
- Skull, Nita
- B) →
- Skullie, Donna
- C) →
- Skully, Vinny
- D) →
- Skulman, Ronald
- E) →

25. Kreinspan, Gerard
- A) →
- Kreen, Bobby
- B) →
- Kreiner, Joel
- C) →
- Kreinner, Dora
- D) →
- Kreinstein, Max
- E) →

26. Bemberg, Alice
- A) →
- Blaustein, Joseph
- B) →
- Blemberg, Harold
- C) →
- Blenter, Mario
- D) →
- Blentz, Jeff
- E) →

27. Guadalzina, Pedro
- A) →
- Guadalquivir, Delgado
- B) →
- Guadalupe, Bonnie
- C) →
- Guadalupe, De
- D) →
- Guadarrama, Zoila
- E) →

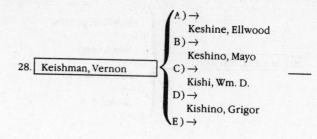

28. Keishman, Vernon
- A) →
- Keshine, Ellwood
- B) →
- Keshino, Mayo
- C) →
- Kishi, Wm. D.
- D) →
- Kishino, Grigor
- E) →

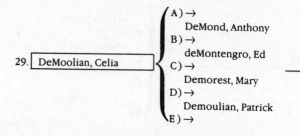

29. DeMoolian, Celia
- A) →
- DeMond, Anthony
- B) →
- deMontengro, Ed
- C) →
- Demorest, Mary
- D) →
- Demoulian, Patrick
- E) →

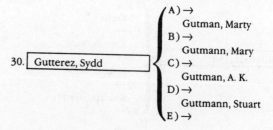

30. Gutterez, Sydd
- A) →
- Gutman, Marty
- B) →
- Gutmann, Mary
- C) →
- Guttman, A. K.
- D) →
- Guttmann, Stuart
- E) →

ANSWER EXPLANATIONS FOR PRACTICE SET 6

1. **(C)** Meono, Michael
Mercadante, Alicia
Mercado, Mary
2. **(B)** Hawkins, M. C.
Hawkins, Mary
Hawkins, Nick
3. **(D)** Buizzie, Ralph
Bujol, Leslie
Bukowski, Richard
4. **(E)** Gomes, Steven
Gomez, Anna
5. **(A)** *Rubenstein, Blanche*
Rubey, Michelle
6. **(C)** Snyder, Libbie
Sobel, Allyn D.
Sonsini, P.
7. **(D)** Sabosian, Dorothy
SanBenito, Adele
Saobine, Judith
8. **(D)** McEnney, Hazel
McEnninger, Vivian
McEntosh, Belle
9. **(A)** *MacLoughlin, Tom*
McLin, Susan

10. **(E)** Means, T. R.
Mechira, MaryLou
11. **(A)** *Jacksen, H. Olive*
Jacksen, Jennie
12. **(B)** Kimsey, T.
Kimstein, Dae
Kimura, Kane
13. **(A)** *vanEgan, Gino*
Vanegas, Jose
14. **(C)** Hansen, Martha
Hansen, Martin
Hansen, Mel
15. **(E)** Townshend, Teresa
Townsley, Yoko
16. **(C)** Van Mar, Derry
Vann, David
van Northwick, Evelyn
17. **(C)** Cutler, P. Ernest
Cutler, Phillis
Cutler, Verna
18. **(C)** Mentzies, Pauolo
Menzer, Gary
Menzies, Aaron
19. **(E)** Awramento, N. G.
Axelrod, Petros
20. **(D)** Wolfestein, Terry
Worster, Judith
Wortman, Ed

21. **(E)** Kornay, Leslie
Koro, Lena
22. **(C)** Avil, Elivira
Avion, Ewa R.
Avon, O. P.
23. **(D)** Konick, Leo
Konkiel, Ervine
Konow, Karen
24. **(B)** Skull, Nita
Skulle, Ralph
Skullie, Donna
25. **(D)** Kreinner, Dora
Kreinspan, Gerard
Kreinstein, Max
26. **(A)** *Bemberg, Alice*
Blaustein, Joseph
27. **(D)** Guadalupe, De
Guadalzina, Pedro
Guadarrama, Zoila
28. **(A)** *Keishman, Vernon*
Keshine, Ellwood
29. **(C)** deMontengro, Ed
DeMoolian, Celia
Demorest, Mary
30. **(C)** Gutmann, Mary
Gutterez, Sydd
Guttman, A. K.

REVIEWING THE KEY STRATEGIES

Remember to:

1. Learn the definite rules for alphabetizing.

2. Practice them.

ARITHMETIC COMPUTATIONAL SKILLS

These question types measure your ability to do simple computations, without the use of an adding machine or calculator. There are four types of questions: addition, subtraction, multiplication, and division.

ADDITION

Add:
$$\begin{array}{r} 19 \\ + 23 \end{array}$$

To answer this question type you must be familiar with basic addition facts (for example, 9 + 3 = 12). You should also know how to "carry." In the example just given, for the ones column 9 + 3 equals 12. The 2 is written in the total ones column, but the 1 (from the 12) is carried to the tens column, which now equals 1 + 1 + 2 = 4. The answer is 42.

$$\begin{array}{r} {}^{1}19 \\ + 23 \\ \hline 42 \end{array}$$

SUBTRACTION

Subtract:
$$\begin{array}{r} 92 \\ - 37 \end{array}$$

To answer this question type, you must be familiar with basic subtraction facts (for example, 12 − 7 = 5). You should also know how to "borrow." Notice in the example just given, in the one's column, you cannot compute 2 − 7. Therefore, you must borrow a 1 (which means 10) from the 9 (ninety), and add it to the 2, which now becomes 12:

$$\begin{array}{r} 8 \\ 9^{1}2 \\ - 37 \end{array}$$

When you borrow 1 (ten) from the 9 (tens), the 9 (ninety) now becomes 8 (eighty), and the 2 becomes 12. Now you can subtract in the ones column, 12 − 7 = 5, and in the tens column, 8 − 3 = 5. The answer is 55.

$$\begin{array}{r} 8 \\ 9^{1}2 \\ - 37 \\ \hline 55 \end{array}$$

A TIP: You may check your subtraction, by adding up from the total. In this example:

$$\begin{array}{r} 92 \\ - 37 \\ \hline 55 \end{array}$$

Does 55 + 37 = 92? It should, if 55 is the correct answer. If it does not, then you have made a calculation error.

MULTIPLICATION

Multiply:
$$\begin{array}{r} 46 \\ \times 3 \end{array}$$

To answer this question type, you must be familiar with basic multiplication skills (times tables). You should also know how to "carry." In the example just given, the 3 is first multiplied with the 6:

$$\begin{array}{r} {}^{1}46 \\ \times 3 \\ \hline 8 \end{array}$$

3 × 6 = 18. Notice that the 8 is placed in the ones column, but the 1 (ten) is carried to the tens column. Now the 4 is multiplied by the 3: 3 × 4 = 12. And the "1" (ten) carried over is added on to the 12: 12 + 1 = 13.

$$\begin{array}{r} {}^{1}46 \\ \times 3 \\ \hline 138 \end{array}$$

DIVISION

Divide: $6\overline{)258}$

To answer this question type, you must be familiar with basic division skills (for example, 15 divided by 3 = 5). You should also know how to do simple "long division." In the example just given, 6 does not go into 2, but it will go into 25 a total of 4 times. Write the 4 above the 5 in 25:

$$6\overline{)258}^{\,4}$$

Now multiply 4 × 6, and write the answer, 24, below the 25:

$$\begin{array}{r} 4 \\ 6\overline{)258} \\ 24 \end{array}$$

Now subtract:

$$
\begin{array}{r}
4 \\
6{\overline{\smash{\big)}\,258}} \\
\underline{24} \\
1
\end{array}
$$

Now "bring down" the next digit, 8:

$$
\begin{array}{r}
4 \\
6{\overline{\smash{\big)}\,258}} \\
\underline{24} \\
18
\end{array}
$$

Does 6 go into 18? Yes, 3 times. Therefore, write 3 on the line above the 8:

$$
\begin{array}{r}
43 \\
6{\overline{\smash{\big)}\,258}} \\
\underline{24} \\
18
\end{array}
$$

Now multiply, as before: $3 \times 6 = 18$. Write that below the 18 and subtract:

$$
\begin{array}{r}
43 \\
6{\overline{\smash{\big)}\,258}} \\
\underline{24} \\
18 \\
\underline{18} \\
0
\end{array}
$$

Since the difference is 0, there is no remainder. (The questions on your test will not have any remainder answer.) The final answer is 43.

A TIP: One quick way to check your answer is to multiply it by the divisor: in this case, 43×6. The result should be 258.

HELPFUL TECHNIQUES AND STRATEGIES

1. Review the basic addition and subtraction facts, as well as the multiplication (times tables) and division facts, long before taking your exam. If you are weak in any area, try to strengthen your skills in that area so that it will not slow you down when you are taking the test.
2. Practice the many arithmetic question types in this book to increase your speed, skill, and confidence.
3. Although the words "add," "subtract," "divide," or "multiply" are printed above each arithmetic question on the actual test, it is wise also to look at the "sign" in the question. For example:

    Subtract:

$$
\begin{array}{r}
85 \\
-\,32
\end{array}
$$

    The minus sign reinforces this as a subtraction problem. Under time and test pressure it can be easy to make a careless mistake and *add* when you should be *subtracting*. Looking at the sign will help reinforce the operation required.
4. All the problems have answer (E), "none of these." If the answer you arrive at is not listed in choices (A), (B), (C), or (D), then you are to choose answer (E).
5. As with the other question types on the test, if any particular question gives you trouble, then skip it; if you can eliminate one choice take a guess, or come back to it later if time permits.

PRACTICE SET 1

Make the following computations, and indicate which of the answer choices is the correct one.

Answers

1. Add:
   82
   + 41

   A) 121   B) 123
   C) 133   D) 141
   E) none of these
   _____

2. Subtract:
   90
   − 31

   A) 59   B) 61
   C) 63   D) 69
   E) none of these
   _____

3. Multiply:
   57
   × 2

   A) 104   B) 114
   C) 124   D) 134
   E) none of these
   _____

4. Divide:
   7)602

   A) 68   B) 76
   C) 86   D) 88
   E) none of these
   _____

5. Add:
   24
   + 16

   A) 30   B) 40
   C) 50   D) 60
   E) none of these
   _____

6. Subtract:
   86
   − 21

   A) 57   B) 65
   C) 67   D) 78
   E) none of these
   _____

7. Multiply:
   85
   × 5

   A) 405   B) 415
   C) 425   D) 435
   E) none of these
   _____

8. Divide:
   2)682

   A) 324   B) 340
   C) 341   D) 342
   E) none of these
   _____

9. Add:
   123
   + 348

   A) 461   B) 463
   C) 471   D) 473
   E) none of these
   _____

10. Subtract:
    88
    − 31

    A) 57   B) 59
    C) 67   D) 119
    E) none of these
    _____

11. Multiply:
    72
    × 3

    A) 213   B) 246
    C) 261   D) 266
    E) none of these
    _____

12. Divide:
    6)630

    A) 102   B) 105
    C) 150   D) 160
    E) none of these
    _____

Answers

13. Add:
    91
    + 45

    A) 126   B) 136
    C) 146   D) 156
    E) none of these
    _____

14. Subtract:
    72
    − 14

    A) 52   B) 58
    C) 62   D) 68
    E) none of these
    _____

15. Multiply:
    52
    × 8

    A) 406   B) 412
    C) 416   D) 418
    E) none of these
    _____

16. Divide:
    9)981

    A) 19   B) 101
    C) 109   D) 190
    E) none of these
    _____

17. Add:
    82
    + 14

    A) 76   B) 84
    C) 86   D) 92
    E) none of these
    _____

18. Subtract:
    89
    − 14

    A) 73   B) 75
    C) 85   D) 93
    E) none of these
    _____

19. Multiply:
    23
    × 7

    A) 141   B) 151
    C) 171   D) 181
    E) none of these
    _____

20. Divide:
    6)204

    A) 34   B) 36
    C) 44   D) 48
    E) none of these
    _____

21. Add:
    36
    + 57

    A) 81   B) 83
    C) 91   D) 93
    E) none of these
    _____

22. Subtract:
    162
    − 87

    A) 65   B) 75
    C) 77   D) 85
    E) none of these
    _____

23. Multiply:
    28
    × 5

    A) 140   B) 144
    C) 160   D) 164
    E) none of these
    _____

24. Divide:
    5)350

    A) 70   B) 71
    C) 75   D) 80
    E) none of these
    _____

25. Add:
    36
    + 52

    A) 84   B) 86
    C) 88   D) 98
    E) none of these
    _____

26. Subtract: *Answers*

26. Subtract:
82
− 17

A) 63 B) 65
C) 73 D) 75
E) none of these   ———

27. Multiply:
72
× 4

A) 282 B) 284
C) 288 D) 298
E) none of these   ———

28. Divide:
4)860

A) 205 B) 215
C) 225 D) 235
E) none of these   ———

29. Add:
29
+ 35

A) 64 B) 66
C) 68 D) 74
E) none of these   ———

30. Subtract:
134
− 21

A) 113 B) 118
C) 123 D) 128
E) none of these   ———

ANSWERS FOR PRACTICE SET 1

1. (B) 123
2. (A) 59
3. (B) 114
4. (C) 86
5. (B) 40
6. (B) 65
7. (C) 425
8. (C) 341
9. (C) 471
10. (A) 57
11. (E) Correct answer: 216.
12. (B) 105
13. (B) 136
14. (B) 58
15. (C) 416
16. (C) 109
17. (E) Correct answer: 96.
18. (B) 75
19. (E) Correct answer: 161.
20. (A) 34
21. (D) 93
22. (B) 75
23. (A) 140
24. (A) 70
25. (C) 88
26. (B) 65
27. (C) 288
28. (B) 215
29. (A) 64
30. (A) 113

PRACTICE SET 2

Make the following computations, and indicate which of the answer choices is the correct one.

Answers

1. Multiply:
30
× 4

A) 12 B) 102
C) 120 D) 140
E) none of these   ———

2. Divide:
9)810

A) 19 B) 91
C) 99 D) 100
E) none of these   ———

3. Add:
32
+ 84

A) 106 B) 108
C) 110 D) 118
E) none of these   ———

4. Subtract:
93
− 15

A) 77 B) 78
C) 88 D) 93
E) none of these   ———

5. Multiply:
82
× 5

A) 401 B) 410
C) 411 D) 420
E) none of these   ———

6. Divide:
7)497

A) 17 B) 70
C) 71 D) 77
E) none of these   ———

7. Add:
15
+ 82

A) 83 B) 87
C) 93 D) 98
E) none of these   ———

8. Subtract:
89
− 34

A) 54 B) 55
C) 65 D) 66
E) none of these   ———

9. Multiply:
54
× 4

A) 216 B) 226
C) 236 D) 264
E) none of these   ———

10. Divide:
3)219

A) 71 B) 72
C) 73 D) 75
E) none of these   ———

11. Add:
74
+ 18

A) 82 B) 84
C) 92 D) 94
E) none of these   ———

12. Subtract:
71
− 13

A) 58 B) 62
C) 63 D) 68
E) none of these   ———

13. Multiply:
38
× 5

Answers

A) 150 B) 154
C) 180 D) 190
E) none of these

_____

14. Divide:
9⟌720

A) 8 B) 18
C) 80 D) 81
E) none of these

_____

15. Add:
39
+ 52

A) 81 B) 87
C) 91 D) 97
E) none of these

_____

16. Subtract:
92
− 36

A) 46 B) 48
C) 56 D) 58
E) none of these

_____

17. Multiply:
23
× 6

A) 128 B) 135
C) 136 D) 148
E) none of these

_____

18. Divide:
7⟌357

A) 50 B) 51
C) 53 D) 57
E) none of these

_____

19. Add:
38
+ 45

A) 73 B) 78
C) 80 D) 83
E) none of these

_____

20. Subtract:
95
− 32

A) 60 B) 62
C) 67 D) 73
E) none of these

_____

21. Multiply:
15
× 7

A) 85 B) 95
C) 105 D) 115
E) none of these

_____

22. Divide:
6⟌366

A) 60 B) 61
C) 66 D) 71
E) none of these

_____

23. Add:
19
+ 57

A) 76 B) 79
C) 84 D) 86
E) none of these

_____

24. Subtract:
93
− 48

A) 35 B) 45
C) 55 D) 58
E) none of these

_____

25. Multiply:
19
× 7

A) 103 B) 113
C) 133 D) 153
E) none of these

_____

26. Divide:
8⟌648

Answers

A) 80 B) 81
C) 88 D) 91
E) none of these

_____

27. Add:
26
+ 39

A) 64 B) 65
C) 67 D) 75
E) none of these

_____

28. Subtract:
93
− 51

A) 38 B) 42
C) 48 D) 52
E) none of these

_____

29. Multiply:
84
× 3

A) 222 B) 322
C) 332 D) 342
E) none of these

_____

30. Divide:
5⟌325

A) 55 B) 61
C) 65 D) 68
E) none of these

_____

ANSWERS FOR PRACTICE SET 2

1. (C) 120
2. (E) Correct answer: 90.
3. (E) Correct answer: 116.
4. (B) 78
5. (B) 410
6. (C) 71
7. (E) Correct answer: 97.
8. (B) 55
9. (A) 216
10. (C) 73
11. (C) 92
12. (A) 58
13. (D) 190
14. (C) 80
15. (C) 91
16. (C) 56
17. (E) Correct answer: 138.
18. (B) 51
19. (D) 83
20. (E) Correct answer: 63.
21. (C) 105
22. (B) 61
23. (A) 76
24. (B) 45
25. (C) 133
26. (B) 81
27. (B) 65
28. (B) 42
29. (E) Correct answer: 252
30. (C) 65

PRACTICE SET 3

Make the following computations, and indicate which of the answer choices is the correct one.

Answers

1. Add:
   25
   + 36
   A) 51   B) 61
   C) 63   D) 71
   E) none of these   _____

2. Subtract:
   71
   − 35
   A) 34   B) 36
   C) 46   D) 56
   E) none of these   _____

3. Multiply:
   17
   × 4
   A) 28   B) 48
   C) 58   D) 68
   E) none of these   _____

4. Divide:
   7) 287
   A) 41   B) 47
   C) 51   D) 57
   E) none of these   _____

5. Add:
   44
   + 71
   A) 105   B) 113
   C) 115   D) 125
   E) none of these   _____

6. Multiply:
   23
   × 9
   A) 181   B) 191
   C) 201   D) 207
   E) none of these   _____

7. Subtract:
   53
   − 21
   A) 21   B) 23
   C) 32   D) 33
   E) none of these   _____

8. Divide:
   8) 168
   A) 12   B) 20
   C) 21   D) 22
   E) none of these   _____

9. Add:
   19
   + 56
   A) 65   B) 77
   C) 78   D) 85
   E) none of these   _____

10. Multiply:
    22
    × 3
    A) 60   B) 62
    C) 66   D) 69
    E) none of these   _____

11. Subtract:
    92
    − 13
    A) 71   B) 75
    C) 79   D) 81
    E) none of these   _____

12. Divide:
    8) 248
    A) 13   B) 23
    C) 30   D) 31
    E) none of these   _____

Answers

13. Add:
    49
    + 34
    A) 73   B) 81
    C) 85   D) 93
    E) none of these   _____

14. Multiply:
    13
    × 6
    A) 48   B) 68
    C) 78   D) 88
    E) none of these   _____

15. Subtract:
    89
    − 64
    A) 23   B) 27
    C) 35   D) 37
    E) none of these   _____

16. Divide:
    7) 357
    A) 41   B) 50
    C) 55   D) 61
    E) none of these   _____

17. Add:
    53
    + 25
    A) 77   B) 78
    C) 87   D) 88
    E) none of these   _____

18. Subtract:
    84
    − 17
    A) 67   B) 69
    C) 75   D) 77
    E) none of these   _____

19. Multiply:
    23
    × 3
    A) 66   B) 68
    C) 69   D) 96
    E) none of these   _____

20. Divide:
    4) 256
    A) 61   B) 62
    C) 64   D) 66
    E) none of these   _____

21. Add:
    17
    + 81
    A) 76   B) 88
    C) 97   D) 98
    E) none of these   _____

22. Subtract:
    84
    − 13
    A) 61   B) 69
    C) 71   D) 73
    E) none of these   _____

23. Multiply:
    24
    × 7
    A) 148   B) 158
    C) 168   D) 188
    E) none of these   _____

24. Divide:
    8) 648
    A) 81   B) 82
    C) 83   D) 84
    E) none of these   _____

25. Add:
    28
    + 54
    A) 72   B) 74
    C) 82   D) 84
    E) none of these   _____

26. Subtract:
93
− 31

A) 60 B) 61
C) 62 D) 63
E) none of these   _____

27. Multiply:
93
× 4

A) 362 B) 366
C) 372 D) 376
E) none of these   _____

28. Divide:
7)805

A) 113 B) 120
C) 125 D) 127
E) none of these   _____

29. Add:
83
+ 59

A) 132 B) 138
C) 142 D) 144
E) none of these   _____

30. Subtract:
169
− 23

A) 144 B) 146
C) 156 D) 158
E) none of these   _____

ANSWERS FOR PRACTICE SET 3

1. (B) 61
2. (B) 36
3. (D) 68
4. (A) 41
5. (C) 115
6. (D) 207
7. (C) 32
8. (C) 21
9. (E) Correct answer: 75.
10. (C) 66
11. (C) 79
12. (D) 31
13. (E) Correct answer: 83.
14. (C) 78
15. (E) Correct answer: 25.
16. (E) Correct answer: 51.
17. (B) 78
18. (A) 67
19. (C) 69
20. (C) 64
21. (D) 98
22. (C) 71
23. (C) 168
24. (A) 81
25. (C) 82
26. (C) 62
27. (C) 372
28. (E) Correct answer: 115.
29. (C) 142
30. (B) 146

PRACTICE SET 4

Make the following computations, and indicate which of the answer choices is the correct one.

Answers

1. Multiply:
82
× 7

A) 546 B) 564
C) 568 D) 574
E) none of these   _____

2. Divide:
5)850

A) 107 B) 130
C) 170 D) 190
E) none of these   _____

3. Add:
23
+ 81

A) 104 B) 106
C) 108 D) 114
E) none of these   _____

4. Subtract:
812
− 408

A) 402 B) 404
C) 408 D) 410
E) none of these   _____

5. Multiply:
92
× 3

A) 216 B) 236
C) 256 D) 276
E) none of these   _____

6. Divide:
8)648

A) 18 B) 80
C) 88 D) 89
E) none of these   _____

7. Add:
81
+ 18

A) 98 B) 99
C) 100 D) 109
E) none of these   _____

8. Subtract:
98
− 31

A) 37 B) 39
C) 67 D) 69
E) none of these   _____

9. Multiply:
72
× 4

A) 238 B) 288
C) 328 D) 368
E) none of these   _____

10. Divide:
7)497

A) 17 B) 70
C) 71 D) 701
E) none of these   _____

11. Add:
35
+ 81

A) 106 B) 111
C) 116 D) 119
E) none of these   _____

12. Subtract:
52
− 19

A) 31 B) 33
C) 41 D) 43
E) none of these   _____

13. Multiply:
    106
    × 5

A) 53   B) 503
C) 530 D) 630
E) none of these   _____

14. Divide:
    6)612

A) 21   B) 102
C) 111 D) 112
E) none of these   _____

15. Add:
    123
    + 304

A) 227 B) 337
C) 427 D) 437
E) none of these   _____

16. Subtract:
    82
    − 31

A) 31   B) 41
C) 51   D) 61
E) none of these   _____

17. Multiply:
    72
    × 8

A) 562 B) 566
C) 568 D) 574
E) none of these   _____

18. Divide:
    4)256

A) 44   B) 46
C) 64   D) 66
E) none of these   _____

19. Add:
    19
    + 82

A) 81   B) 83
C) 91   D) 101
E) none of these   _____

20. Subtract:
    101
    − 48

A) 43   B) 45
C) 55   D) 58
E) none of these   _____

21. Multiply:
    21
    × 8

A) 160 B) 168
C) 169 D) 186
E) none of these   _____

22. Divide:
    6)906

A) 115 B) 150
C) 151 D) 155
E) none of these   _____

23. Add:
    56
    + 81

A) 135 B) 137
C) 139 D) 147
E) none of these   _____

24. Subtract:
    92
    − 31

A) 61   B) 63
C) 67   D) 71
E) none of these   _____

25. Multiply:
    23
    × 5

A) 105 B) 115
C) 135 D) 155
E) none of these   _____

26. Divide:
    7)784

A) 112 B) 114
C) 118 D) 121
E) none of these   _____

27. Add:
    62
    + 35

A) 93   B) 97
C) 107 D) 111
E) none of these   _____

28. Subtract:
    148
    − 74

A) 64   B) 68
C) 72   D) 74
E) none of these   _____

29. Multiply:
    74
    × 3

A) 144 B) 212
C) 222 D) 224
E) none of these   _____

30. Divide:
    3)936

A) 302 B) 311
C) 313 D) 318
E) none of these   _____

ANSWERS FOR PRACTICE SET 4

1. (D) 574
2. (C) 170
3. (A) 104
4. (B) 404
5. (D) 276
6. (E) Correct answer: 81.
7. (B) 99
8. (C) 67
9. (B) 288
10. (C) 71
11. (C) 116
12. (B) 33
13. (C) 530
14. (B) 102
15. (C) 427
16. (C) 51
17. (E) Correct answer: 576.
18. (C) 64
19. (D) 101
20. (E) Correct answer: 53.
21. (B) 168
22. (C) 151
23. (B) 137
24. (A) 61
25. (B) 115
26. (A) 112
27. (B) 97
28. (D) 74
29. (C) 222
30. (E) Correct answer: 312.

PRACTICE SET 5

Make the following computations, and indicate which of the answer choices is the correct one.

Answers

1. Add:
   82
   + 21
   A) 102 B) 113
   C) 137 D) 143
   E) none of these

2. Subtract:
   96
   − 41
   A) 45 B) 47
   C) 55 D) 57
   E) none of these

3. Multiply:
   81
   × 3
   A) 241 B) 243
   C) 253 D) 283
   E) none of these

4. Divide:
   8)840
   A) 15 B) 51
   C) 105 D) 150
   E) none of these

5. Add:
   87
   + 83
   A) 160 B) 170
   C) 180 D) 190
   E) none of these

6. Subtract:
   182
   − 31
   A) 111 B) 141
   C) 143 D) 151
   E) none of these

7. Multiply:
   71
   × 5
   A) 350 B) 355
   C) 365 D) 375
   E) none of these

8. Divide:
   7)910
   A) 13 B) 103
   C) 130 D) 133
   E) none of these

9. Add:
   283
   + 46
   A) 229 B) 289
   C) 329 D) 349
   E) none of these

10. Subtract:
    261
    − 130
    A) 130 B) 131
    C) 138 D) 141
    E) none of these

11. Multiply:
    23
    × 8
    A) 164 B) 174
    C) 184 D) 194
    E) none of these

12. Divide:
    4)484
    A) 112 B) 120
    C) 121 D) 122
    E) none of these

Answers

13. Add:
    92
    + 18
    A) 100 B) 106
    C) 108 D) 110
    E) none of these

14. Subtract:
    82
    − 15
    A) 57 B) 59
    C) 67 D) 77
    E) none of these

15. Multiply:
    18
    × 3
    A) 34 B) 44
    C) 54 D) 64
    E) none of these

16. Divide:
    8)168
    A) 12 B) 22
    C) 24 D) 31
    E) none of these

17. Add:
    42
    + 57
    A) 92 B) 95
    C) 99 D) 109
    E) none of these

18. Subtract:
    130
    − 42
    A) 68 B) 78
    C) 88 D) 98
    E) none of these

19. Multiply:
    19
    × 7
    A) 123 B) 132
    C) 143 D) 153
    E) none of these

20. Divide:
    6)366
    A) 61 B) 66
    C) 71 D) 76
    E) none of these

21. Add:
    32
    + 81
    A) 131 B) 133
    C) 137 D) 141
    E) none of these

22. Subtract:
    122
    − 38
    A) 76 B) 84
    C) 86 D) 94
    E) none of these

23. Multiply:
    23
    × 4
    A) 82 B) 88
    C) 92 D) 104
    E) none of these

24. Divide:
    3)243
    A) 18 B) 38
    C) 80 D) 81
    E) none of these

25. Add:
    56
    + 32
    A) 84 B) 86
    C) 94 D) 98
    E) none of these

26. Subtract:
    84
    − 31

Answers
A) 47   B) 53
C) 55   D) 57
E) none of these   _____

27. Multiply:
    96
    × 4

A) 342   B) 344
C) 364   D) 384
E) none of these   _____

28. Divide:
    7) 392

A) 52   B) 53
C) 54   D) 55
E) none of these   _____

29. Add:
    472
    + 319

A) 781   B) 783
C) 791   D) 797
E) none of these   _____

30. Subtract:
    94
    − 25

A) 69   B) 71
C) 77   D) 79
E) none of these   _____

ANSWERS FOR PRACTICE SET 5

1. (E) Correct answer: 103.
2. (C) 55
3. (B) 243
4. (C) 105
5. (B) 170
6. (D) 151
7. (B) 355
8. (C) 130
9. (C) 329
10. (B) 131
11. (C) 184
12. (C) 121
13. (D) 110
14. (C) 67
15. (C) 54
16. (E) Correct answer: 21.
17. (C) 99
18. (C) 88
19. (E) Correct answer: 133.
20. (A) 61
21. (E) Correct answer: 113.
22. (B) 84
23. (C) 92
24. (D) 81
25. (E) Correct answer: 88.
26. (B) 53
27. (D) 384
28. (E) Correct answer: 56.
29. (C) 791
30. (A) 69

PRACTICE SET 6

Make the following computations, and indicate which of the answer choices is the correct one.

Answers

1. Multiply:
   32
   × 5

A) 150   B) 155
C) 160   D) 170
E) none of these   _____

2. Divide:
   8) 248

A) 13   B) 30
C) 31   D) 41
E) none of these   _____

3. Add:
   52
   + 49

A) 91   B) 97
C) 101   D) 103
E) none of these   _____

4. Subtract:
   44
   − 13

A) 19   B) 21
C) 31   D) 39
E) none of these   _____

5. Multiply:
   28
   × 6

A) 148   B) 168
C) 188   D) 208
E) none of these   _____

6. Divide:
   6) 384

A) 34   B) 44
C) 64   D) 74
E) none of these   _____

7. Add:
   123
   + 38

A) 141   B) 151
C) 161   D) 171
E) none of these   _____

8. Subtract:
   47
   − 19

A) 18   B) 26
C) 28   D) 36
E) none of these   _____

9. Multiply:
   31
   × 3

A) 39   B) 36
C) 91   D) 93
E) none of these   _____

10. Divide:
    2) 572

A) 266   B) 271
C) 281   D) 286
E) none of these   _____

11. Add:
    84
    + 32

A) 114   B) 118
C) 126   D) 132
E) none of these   _____

12. Subtract:
    92
    − 35

A) 57   B) 59
C) 63   D) 67
E) none of these   _____

13. Multiply:
81
× 4

Answers
A) 314 B) 324
C) 342 D) 432
E) none of these

_____

14. Divide:
3)372

A) 122 B) 126
C) 128 D) 132
E) none of these

_____

15. Add:
95
+ 28

A) 121 B) 123
C) 131 D) 133
E) none of these

_____

16. Subtract:
142
− 71

A) 61 B) 71
C) 73 D) 79
E) none of these

_____

17. Multiply:
56
× 7

A) 352 B) 372
C) 392 D) 402
E) none of these

_____

18. Divide:
4)108

A) 23 B) 27
C) 29 D) 32
E) none of these

_____

19. Add:
28
+ 91

A) 111 B) 119
C) 121 D) 127
E) none of these

_____

20. Subtract:
88
− 32

A) 54 B) 55
C) 56 D) 57
E) none of these

_____

21. Multiply:
17
× 7

A) 109 B) 119
C) 129 D) 131
E) none of these

_____

22. Divide:
9)918

A) 92 B) 98
C) 102 D) 120
E) none of these

_____

23. Add:
57
+ 93

A) 141 B) 144
C) 153 D) 157
E) none of these

_____

24. Subtract:
108
− 21

A) 77 B) 78
C) 87 D) 97
E) none of these

_____

25. Multiply:
28
× 8

A) 164 B) 194
C) 204 D) 224
E) none of these

_____

26. Divide:
8)624

Answers
A) 73 B) 78
C) 79 D) 83
E) none of these

_____

27. Add:
78
+ 45

A) 127 B) 132
C) 133 D) 143
E) none of these

_____

28. Subtract:
92
− 44

A) 46 B) 48
C) 52 D) 56
E) none of these

_____

29. Multiply:
18
× 4

A) 42 B) 52
C) 62 D) 72
E) none of these

_____

30. Divide:
7)539

A) 73 B) 77
C) 79 D) 83
E) none of these

_____

ANSWERS FOR PRACTICE SET 6

1. (C) 160
2. (C) 31
3. (C) 101
4. (C) 31
5. (B) 168
6. (C) 64
7. (C) 161
8. (C) 28
9. (D) 93
10. (D) 286
11. (E) Correct answer: 116.
12. (A) 57
13. (B) 324
14. (E) Correct answer: 124.
15. (B) 123
16. (B) 71
17. (C) 392
18. (B) 27
19. (B) 119
20. (C) 56
21. (B) 119
22. (C) 102
23. (E) Correct answer: 150.
24. (C) 87
25. (D) 224
26. (B) 78
27. (E) Correct answer: 123.
28. (B) 48
29. (D) 72
30. (B) 77

PRACTICE SET 7

Make the following computations, and indicate which of the answer choices is the correct one.

Answers

1. Add:
   29
   + 47
   A) 66   B) 67
   C) 76   D) 78
   E) none of these   _____

2. Subtract:
   108
   − 32
   A) 66   B) 76
   C) 78   D) 88
   E) none of these   _____

3. Multiply:
   19
   × 8
   A) 132   B) 138
   C) 152   D) 158
   E) none of these   _____

4. Divide:
   8)472
   A) 57   B) 58
   C) 59   D) 61
   E) none of these   _____

5. Add:
   147
   + 204
   A) 321   B) 331
   C) 341   D) 441
   E) none of these   _____

6. Subtract:
   75
   − 38
   A) 33   B) 37
   C) 39   D) 43
   E) none of these   _____

7. Multiply:
   210
   × 4
   A) 480   B) 640
   C) 840   D) 1040
   E) none of these   _____

8. Divide:
   9)369
   A) 38   B) 39
   C) 41   D) 49
   E) none of these   _____

9. Add:
   27
   + 98
   A) 123   B) 125
   C) 127   D) 129
   E) none of these   _____

10. Subtract:
    92
    − 18
    A) 76   B) 78
    C) 84   D) 86
    E) none of these   _____

11. Multiply:
    35
    × 9
    A) 275   B) 295
    C) 305   D) 315
    E) none of these   _____

12. Divide:
    4)3240
    A) 801   B) 810
    C) 811   D) 880
    E) none of these   _____

Answers

13. Add:
    483
    + 235
    A) 618   B) 638
    C) 718   D) 738
    E) none of these   _____

14. Subtract:
    92
    − 31
    A) 59   B) 61
    C) 69   D) 71
    E) none of these   _____

15. Multiply:
    19
    × 6
    A) 94   B) 96
    C) 104   D) 114
    E) none of these   _____

16. Divide:
    4)488
    A) 64   B) 82
    C) 108   D) 112
    E) none of these   _____

17. Add:
    203
    + 318
    A) 511   B) 515
    C) 521   D) 535
    E) none of these   _____

18. Subtract:
    106
    − 48
    A) 54   B) 56
    C) 58   D) 62
    E) none of these   _____

19. Multiply:
    27
    × 7
    A) 169   B) 183
    C) 191   D) 199
    E) none of these   _____

20. Divide:
    3)903
    A) 31   B) 301
    C) 311   D) 313
    E) none of these   _____

21. Add:
    39
    + 64
    A) 93   B) 95
    C) 103   D) 105
    E) none of these   _____

22. Subtract:
    98
    − 32
    A) 64   B) 66
    C) 68   D) 74
    E) none of these   _____

23. Multiply:
    32
    × 4
    A) 124   B) 128
    C) 132   D) 136
    E) none of these   _____

24. Divide:
    8)656
    A) 80   B) 81
    C) 82   D) 83
    E) none of these   _____

25. Add:
    94
    + 32
    A) 124   B) 126
    C) 136   D) 144
    E) none of these   _____

26. Subtract:
29
− 14

Answers
A) 5   B) 13
C) 18   D) 19
E) none of these   _____

27. Multiply:
13
× 8

A) 84   B) 94
C) 104   D) 114
E) none of these   _____

28. Divide:
7)385

A) 51   B) 53
C) 55   D) 61
E) none of these   _____

29. Add:
85
+ 66

A) 141   B) 143
C) 151   D) 153
E) none of these   _____

30. Subtract:
92
− 37

A) 53   B) 55
C) 65   D) 67
E) none of these   _____

ANSWERS FOR PRACTICE SET 7

1. (C) 76
2. (B) 76
3. (C) 152
4. (C) 59
5. (E) Correct answer: 351
6. (B) 37
7. (C) 840
8. (C) 41
9. (B) 125
10. (E) Correct answer: 74.
11. (D) 315
12. (B) 810
13. (C) 718
14. (B) 61
15. (D) 114
16. (E) Correct answer: 122.
17. (C) 521
18. (C) 58
19. (E) Correct answer: 189
20. (B) 301
21. (C) 103
22. (B) 66
23. (B) 128
24. (C) 82
25. (B) 126
26. (E) Correct answer: 15.
27. (C) 104
28. (C) 55
29. (C) 151
30. (B) 55

PRACTICE SET 8

Make the following computations, and indicate which of the answer choices is the correct one.

Answers

1. Multiply:
23
× 6

A) 122   B) 128
C) 138   D) 198
E) none of these   _____

2. Divide:
4)168

A) 41   B) 42
C) 43   D) 48
E) none of these   _____

3. Add:
46
+ 31

A) 74   B) 75
C) 87   D) 89
E) none of these   _____

4. Subtract:
98
− 41

A) 55   B) 57
C) 67   D) 73
E) none of these   _____

5. Multiply:
72
× 8

A) 562   B) 566
C) 568   D) 576
E) none of these   _____

6. Divide:
7)637

A) 90   B) 91
C) 92   D) 97
E) none of these   _____

7. Add:
23
+ 84

A) 107   B) 109
C) 117   D) 119
E) none of these   _____

8. Subtract:
96
− 31

A) 64   B) 65
C) 75   D) 86
E) none of these   _____

9. Multiply:
19
× 6

A) 54   B) 64
C) 104   D) 114
E) none of these   _____

10. Divide:
6)660

A) 11   B) 101
C) 112   D) 118
E) none of these   _____

11. Add:
28
+ 57

A) 55   B) 65
C) 75   D) 85
E) none of these   _____

12. Subtract:
92
− 86

A) 2   B) 4
C) 6   D) 16
E) none of these   _____

13. Multiply:
26
× 4

A) 84 B) 88
C) 94 D) 114
E) none of these

_____

Answers

14. Divide:
3)288

A) 92 B) 94
C) 96 D) 98
E) none of these

_____

15. Add:
93
+ 41

A) 123 B) 134
C) 143 D) 144
E) none of these

_____

16. Subtract:
75
− 18

A) 53 B) 57
C) 63 D) 67
E) none of these

_____

17. Multiply:
58
× 3

A) 154 B) 164
C) 174 D) 182
E) none of these

_____

18. Divide:
8)824

A) 13 B) 18
C) 103 D) 108
E) none of these

_____

19. Add:
28
+ 38

A) 64 B) 66
C) 68 D) 76
E) none of these

_____

20. Subtract:
81
− 17

A) 64 B) 68
C) 74 D) 78
E) none of these

_____

21. Multiply:
19
× 8

A) 72 B) 92
C) 132 D) 152
E) none of these

_____

22. Divide:
7)784

A) 111 B) 121
C) 122 D) 128
E) none of these

_____

23. Add:
93
+ 81

A) 172 B) 174
C) 176 D) 178
E) none of these

_____

24. Subtract:
82
− 14

A) 62 B) 66
C) 68 D) 72
E) none of these

_____

25. Multiply:
23
× 4

A) 82 B) 102
C) 112 D) 122
E) none of these

_____

Answers

26. Divide:
3)138

A) 42 B) 46
C) 64 D) 68
E) none of these

_____

27. Add:
83
+ 95

A) 172 B) 175
C) 178 D) 183
E) none of these

_____

28. Subtract:
134
− 62

A) 70 B) 72
C) 78 D) 82
E) none of these

_____

29. Multiply:
28
× 5

A) 140 B) 150
C) 170 D) 190
E) none of these

_____

30. Divide:
9)108

A) 12 B) 21
C) 28 D) 81
E) none of these

_____

ANSWERS FOR PRACTICE SET 8

1. **(C)** 138
2. **(B)** 42
3. **(E)** Correct answer: 77.
4. **(B)** 57
5. **(D)** 576
6. **(B)** 91
7. **(A)** 107
8. **(B)** 65
9. **(D)** 114
10. **(E)** Correct answer: 110.
11. **(D)** 85
12. **(C)** 6
13. **(E)** Correct answer: 104.
14. **(C)** 96
15. **(B)** 134
16. **(B)** 57
17. **(C)** 174
18. **(C)** 103
19. **(B)** 66
20. **(A)** 64
21. **(D)** 152
22. **(E)** Correct answer: 112.
23. **(B)** 174
24. **(C)** 68
25. **(E)** Correct answer: 92.
26. **(B)** 46
27. **(C)** 178
28. **(B)** 72
29. **(A)** 140
30. **(A)** 12

NUMBER AND LETTER SCRAMBLE

This question type tests your observation skills. You are given five sets of eight letters and numbers (four of each), followed by five suggested answers, (A), (B), (C), (D), and (E). Answer (E) is always "none of these." For example:

1. V 5 7 Z N 9 4 T

2. 4 6 P T 2 N K 9

3. 6 4 N 2 P 8 Z K

4. 7 P 5 2 4 N K T

5. K T 8 5 4 N 2 P

Suggested Answers
$$
\begin{cases}
A = 2, & 5, & N, & Z \\
B = 4, & 5, & N, & P \\
C = 2, & 9, & P, & T \\
D = 4, & 9, & T, & Z \\
E = \text{none of these}
\end{cases}
$$

For each numbered question, you must find which of the suggested answers contains letters and numbers *all,* of which appear in that question. For example, the answer to question 1 is (D), because all of the numbers and letters in answer (D) (4, 9, T, Z) appear in question 1.

SUGGESTED STRATEGY

Since the first problem is solved, let's go on to question 2. Place your finger so that it points to the numbers in question 2, and now look at the two numbers in (A): 2 and 5. Are they contained in question 2? The 2 is, but 5 is not, so go on to answer (B). The two numbers there are 4 and 5. The 4 is in question 2, but the 5 is not, so go on to answer (C). The two numbers there are 2 and 9, *both* of which are contained in question 2. So keep going in answer (C) to the letters: P and T. Are they contained in question 2? They are, so you can stop—the answer to question 2 is (C).

If either P or T were *not* contained in the question, you would then have gone on to answer (D). If the numbers and letters in (D) were not contained in question 2, you would then choose answer (E).

Now try practicing this technique to increase your skill and speed.

Reminders:

1. Only one suggested answer will be correct for each question.
2. A suggested answer, (A), (B), (C), (D), or (E), may be used more than once for different questions in each five-question set. For example, the answers to 1, 2, 3, 4 and 5 are (D), (C), (E), (B), and (B). Notice that the (B) answer appears twice in this set of five questions.

PRACTICE SET 1

For each of the following questions, find which one of the suggested answers appears in that question.

1. F 2 Q S W 4 3 9 _____

2. 5 Q 9 7 W 3 S Z _____

3. 5 Q 3 Z X W 7 9 _____

4. Z 2 S 3 Q 7 W 9 _____

5. 5 7 H W Q 9 J 4 _____

Suggested Answers
{
A = 9, 2, W, Q
B = 9, 5, Q, Z
C = 2, 3, W, H
D = 3, 5, H, Z
E = none of these
}

6. Q 4 3 6 Z H 2 F _____

7. 7 4 2 X J 9 F Q _____

8. 6 9 4 Q 8 H J X _____

9. 8 7 J 9 4 F H X _____

10. F 5 4 X 8 2 S Q _____

Suggested Answers
{
A = 2, 7, H, Q
B = 4, 7, Q, X
C = 2, 8, X, F
D = 4, 8, H, F
E = none of these
}

11. 5 9 4 H 3 S Z W _____

12. J 3 6 9 Z 5 X H _____

13. 2 4 3 J 8 X Z W _____

14. W 3 H 6 J 2 4 F _____

15. 3 H 9 8 Q 4 Z W _____

Suggested Answers
{
A = 3, 4, H, Z
B = 3, 6, W, H
C = 9, 4, W, J
D = 9, 6, J, Z
E = none of these
}

16. 8 W F 2 J 3 5 Q _____

17. J 4 Q H 3 2 8 X _____

18. 7 9 X S 8 J F 4 _____

19. X S 8 F 4 J 7 6 _____

20. 4 Z 7 Q 9 8 X J _____

Suggested Answers
{
A = 3, 8, J, X
B = 3, 4, Q, F
C = 4, 7, J, F
D = 7, 8, Q, X
E = none of these
}

21. 5 F Z Q 7 6 3 X _____

22. X 6 7 5 Q 4 S J _____

23. Q 6 S X 7 3 9 J _____

24. 6 7 W 3 2 X J Z _____

25. 3 7 W 9 Z Q 5 J _____

Suggested Answers
{
A = 9, 6, J, Q
B = 9, 7, Z, X
C = 5, 7, J, Z
D = 5, 6, Q, X
E = none of these
}

26. X 4 6 F Q 8 3 Z _____

27. 3 5 S Z 9 Q H 8 _____

28. 5 3 Q 9 S 7 F H _____

29. 6 S 4 9 3 Q H Z _____

30. H Z 7 4 3 Q 9 S _____

Suggested Answers
{
A = 9, 4, Q, F
B = 3, 4, Q, S
C = 9, 8, S, Z
D = 3, 8, Z, F
E = none of these
}

1. (A) F 2 Q S W 4 3 9
2. (B) 5 Q 9 7 W 3 S Z
3. (B) 5 Q 3 Z X W 7 9
4. (A) Z 2 S 3 Q 7 W 9
5. (E) 5 7 H W Q 9 J 4
6. (E) Q 4 3 6 Z H 2 F
7. (B) 7 4 2 X J 9 F Q
8. (E) 6 9 4 Q 8 H J X
9. (D) 8 7 J 9 4 F H X
10. (C) F 5 4 X 8 2 S Q
11. (A) 5 9 4 H 3 S Z W
12. (D) J 3 6 9 Z 5 X H
13. (E) 2 4 3 J 8 X Z W
14. (B) W 3 H 6 J 2 4 F
15. (A) 3 H 9 8 Q 4 Z W
16. (E) 8 W F 2 J 3 5 Q
17. (A) J 4 Q H 3 2 8 X
18. (C) 7 9 X S 8 J F 4
19. (C) X S 8 F 4 J 7 6
20. (D) 4 Z 7 Q 9 8 X J
21. (D) 5 F Z Q 7 6 3 X
22. (D) X 6 7 5 Q 4 S J
23. (A) Q 6 S X 7 3 9 J
24. (E) 6 7 W 3 2 X J Z
25. (C) 3 7 W 9 Z Q 5 J
26. (D) X 4 6 F Q 8 3 Z
27. (C) 3 5 S Z 9 Q H 8
28. (E) 5 3 Q 9 S 7 F H
29. (B) 6 S 4 9 3 Q H Z
30. (B) H Z 7 4 3 Q 9 S

PRACTICE SET 2

For each of the following questions, find which one of the suggested answers appears in that question.

1. Y 5 R U H 7 6 4 _____

2. 8 R 4 2 H 6 U Z _____

3. 8 R 6 Z I H 2 4 _____

4. Z 5 U 6 R 2 H 4 _____

5. 8 9 X H R 4 M 7 _____

Suggested Answers
$\begin{cases} A = 4, 5, H, R \\ B = 4, 8, R, Z \\ C = 5, 6, H, X \\ D = 6, 8, X, Z \\ E = \text{none of these} \end{cases}$

6. 8 4 7 X 6 U Z H _____

7. M 6 9 4 Z 8 I X _____

8. 5 7 6 M 3 I Z H _____

9. H 6 X 9 M 5 7 Y _____

10. 6 X 4 3 R 7 Z H _____

Suggested Answers
$\begin{cases} A = 6, 7, X, Z \\ B = 6, 9, H, X \\ C = 4, 7, H, M \\ D = 4, 9, M, Z \\ E = \text{none of these} \end{cases}$

11. 3 H Y 5 M 6 8 R _____

12. M 7 R X 6 5 3 I _____

13. 2 4 I U 3 M Y 7 _____

14. I U 3 Y 7 M 2 9 _____

15. 7 Z 2 R 4 3 I M _____

Suggested Answers
$\begin{cases} A = 6, 3, M, I \\ B = 6, 7, R, Y \\ C = 7, 2, M, Y \\ D = 2, 3, R, I \\ E = \text{none of these} \end{cases}$

16. 8 Y Z R 2 9 6 I _____

17. I 9 2 8 R 7 U M _____

18. R 9 U I 2 6 4 M _____

19. 9 2 H 6 5 I M Z _____

20. 6 2 H 4 Z R 8 M _____

Suggested Answers
$\begin{cases} A = 4, 9, M, R \\ B = 4, 2, Z, I \\ C = 8, 2, M, Z \\ D = 8, 9, R, I \\ E = \text{none of these} \end{cases}$

21. I 7 9 Y R 3 6 Z _____

22. 6 8 U Z 4 R X 3 _____

23. 8 6 R 4 U 2 Y X _____

24. 9 U 7 4 R X Z _____

25. X Z 2 7 6 R 4 U _____

Suggested Answers $\left\{\begin{array}{l} A = 4, \ 7, \ R, \ Y \\ B = 6, \ 7, \ R, \ U \\ C = 4, \ 3, \ U, \ Z \\ D = 6, \ 3, \ Z, \ Y \\ E = \text{none of these} \end{array}\right.$

26. R 7 6 9 Z X 5 Y ____

27. 2 7 5 I M 4 Y R ____

28. 9 4 7 R 3 X M I ____

29. 3 2 M 4 7 Y X I ____

30. Y 8 7 I 3 5 U R ____

Suggested Answers $\left\{\begin{array}{l} A = 5, \ 2, \ X, \ R \\ B = 7, \ 2, \ R, \ I \\ C = 5, \ 3, \ I, \ Y \\ D = 7, \ 3, \ X, \ Y \\ E = \text{none of these} \end{array}\right.$

ANSWER EXPLANATIONS FOR PRACTICE SET 2

1. (A) Y 5 R U H 7 6 4
2. (B) 8 R 4 2 H 6 U Z
3. (B) 8 R 6 Z I H 2 4
4. (A) Z 5 U 6 R 2 H 4
5. (E) 8 9 X H R 4 M 7
6. (A) 8 4 7 X 6 U Z H
7. (D) M 6 9 4 Z 8 I X
8. (E) 5 7 6 M 3 I Z H
9. (B) H 6 X 9 M 5 7 Y
10. (A) 6 X 4 3 R 7 Z H
11. (E) 3 H Y 5 M 6 8 I
12. (A) M 7 R X 6 5 3 I
13. (C) 2 4 I U 3 M Y 7
14. (C) I U 3 Y 7 M 2 9
15. (D) 7 Z 2 R 4 3 I M
16. (D) 8 Y Z R 2 9 6 I
17. (D) I 9 2 8 R 7 U M
18. (A) R 9 U I 2 6 4 M
19. (E) 9 2 H 6 5 I M Z
20. (C) 6 2 H 4 Z R 8 M
21. (D) I 7 9 Y R 3 6 Z
22. (C) 6 8 U Z 4 R X 3
23. (E) 8 6 R 4 U 2 Y X
24. (E) 9 U 7 4 R X Z
25. (B) X Z 2 7 6 R 4 U
26. (E) R 7 6 9 Z X 5 Y
27. (B) 2 7 5 I M 4 Y R
28. (E) 9 4 7 R 3 X M I
29. (D) 3 2 M 4 7 Y X I
30. (C) Y 8 7 I 3 5 U R

PRACTICE SET 3

For each of the following questions, find which one of the suggested answers appears in that question.

1. Q 9 8 3 X Z 7 M ____

2. 4 9 7 U W 6 M Q ____

3. 3 6 9 Q 5 Z W U ____

4. 5 4 W 6 9 M Z U ____

5. M 2 9 U 5 7 R Q ____

Suggested Answers $\left\{\begin{array}{l} A = 7, \ 4, \ Z, \ Q \\ B = 9, \ 4, \ Q, \ U \\ C = 7, \ 5, \ U, \ M \\ D = 9, \ 5, \ Z, \ M \\ E = \text{none of these} \end{array}\right.$

6. U 9 3 M Q 5 8 X ____

7. 8 2 R X 6 Q Z 5 ____

8. 2 8 Q 6 R 4 M Z ____

9. 3 R 9 6 8 Q Z X ____

10. Z X 4 9 8 Q 6 R ____

Suggested Answers $\left\{\begin{array}{l} A = 6, \ 9, \ Q, \ M \\ B = 8, \ 9, \ Q, \ R \\ C = 6, \ 5, \ R, \ X \\ D = 8, \ 5, \ X, \ M \\ E = \text{none of these} \end{array}\right.$

11. 2 M X Q 4 3 8 U ____

12. U 3 4 2 Q 9 R W ____

13. Q 3 R U 4 8 6 W ____

14. 3 4 F 8 7 U W X ____

15. 8 4 F 6 X Q 2 W ____

Suggested Answers $\left\{\begin{array}{l} A = 6, \ 3, \ W, \ Q \\ B = 6, \ 4, \ X, \ U \\ C = 2, \ 4, \ W, \ X \\ D = 2, \ 3, \ Q, \ U \\ E = \text{none of these} \end{array}\right.$

16. 5 F M 7 W 8 2 Q   ——

17. W 9 Q Z 8 7 5 U   ——

18. 4 6 U R 5 W M 9   ——

19. U R 5 M 9 W 4 3   ——

20. 9 X 4 Q 6 5 U W   ——

Suggested Answers
{
A = 8, 5, W, U
B = 8, 9, Q, M
C = 9, 4, W, M
D = 4, 5, Q, U
E = none of these
}

21. 2 6 9 Z 8 R X F   ——

22. W 8 3 6 X 2 U Z   ——

23. 7 9 8 W 5 U X F   ——

24. F 8 Z 3 W 7 9 M   ——

25. 8 Z 6 5 Q 9 X F   ——

Suggested Answers
{
A = 8, 9, Z, X
B = 8, 3, F, Z
C = 6, 9, F, W
D = 6, 3, W, X
E = none of these
}

26. M 7 Q R F 9 8 6   ——

27. 2 Q 6 4 F 8 R X   ——

28. 2 Q 8 X U F 4 6   ——

29. X 7 R 8 Q 4 F 6   ——

30. 2 3 Z F Q 6 W 9   ——

Suggested Answers
{
A = 6, 7, F, Q
B = 6, 2, Q, X
C = 7, 8, F, Z
D = 8, 2, Z, X
E = none of these
}

ANSWER EXPLANATIONS FOR PRACTICE SET 3

1. (E) Q 9 8 3 X Z 7 M
2. (B) $\underline{4}$ $\underline{9}$ 7 U W 6 M $\underline{Q}$
3. (E) $\overline{3}$ $\overline{6}$ 9 $\overline{Q}$ 5 Z W $\overline{U}$
4. (D) $\underline{5}$ $\underline{4}$ W 6 9 M Z U
5. (C) $\underline{M}$ 2 9 U $\underline{5}$ $\underline{7}$ R Q
6. (D) $\underline{U}$ 9 3 $\underline{M}$ Q $\underline{5}$ 8 X
7. (C) 8 2 $\underline{R}$ $\underline{X}$ 6 $\underline{Q}$ Z $\underline{5}$
8. (E) 2 8 $\overline{Q}$ $\overline{6}$ R 4 M Z
9. (B) 3 R $\underline{9}$ 6 $\underline{8}$ $\underline{Q}$ Z X
10. (B) Z X 4 $\underline{9}$ $\underline{8}$ $\underline{Q}$ $\overline{6}$ R
11. (D) $\underline{2}$ M X $\underline{Q}$ $\overline{4}$ $\underline{3}$ 8 $\underline{U}$
12. (D) $\underline{U}$ 3 4 $\underline{2}$ $\underline{Q}$ $\overline{9}$ R $\overline{W}$
13. (A) Q $\underline{3}$ R $\underline{U}$ 4 8 $\underline{6}$ $\underline{W}$
14. (E) 3 4 F 8 7 U $\overline{W}$ $\overline{X}$
15. (C) 8 $\underline{4}$ F 6 $\underline{X}$ Q 2 $\underline{W}$
16. (E) 5 F M 7 $\overline{W}$ 8 $\overline{2}$ Q
17. (A) $\underline{W}$ 9 Q Z $\underline{8}$ 7 $\underline{5}$ $\underline{U}$
18. (C) $\underline{4}$ 6 U R 5 $\underline{W}$ $\underline{M}$ $\underline{9}$
19. (C) $\underline{U}$ R 5 $\underline{M}$ $\underline{9}$ $\overline{W}$ 4 3
20. (D) 9 X $\underline{4}$ $\underline{Q}$ 6 $\underline{5}$ $\underline{U}$ W
21. (A) 2 6 $\underline{9}$ $\underline{Z}$ 8 R $\underline{X}$ F
22. (D) W 8 $\underline{3}$ $\underline{6}$ X 2 $\underline{U}$ Z
23. (E) $\overline{7}$ 9 8 $\overline{W}$ $\overline{5}$ U X F
24. (B) F $\underline{8}$ $\underline{Z}$ $\underline{3}$ W 7 9 M
25. (A) $\underline{8}$ $\underline{Z}$ 6 5 Q $\underline{9}$ $\underline{X}$ F
26. (A) $\overline{M}$ $\underline{7}$ Q R $\underline{F}$ $\underline{9}$ 8 $\underline{6}$
27. (B) 2 $\underline{Q}$ $\underline{6}$ 4 F 8 R $\underline{X}$
28. (B) $\underline{2}$ $\underline{Q}$ 8 X U F 4 $\overline{6}$
29. (A) $\underline{X}$ $\underline{7}$ R 8 $\underline{Q}$ 4 $\underline{F}$ $\overline{6}$
30. (E) 2 $\overline{3}$ Z F $\overline{Q}$ 6 $\overline{W}$ $\overline{9}$

PRACTICE SET 4

For each of the following questions, find which one of the suggested answers appears in that question.

1. 4 5 J Q M 8 H 3   ——

2. Y 9 R 2 M 6 Q 8   ——

3. 4 M 2 Y W Q 6 8   ——

4. 4 M 8 6 Q 2 R Y   ——

5. S 9 M R Q 3 2 8   ——

Suggested Answers
{
A = 8, 9, Q, M
B = 8, 4, M, Y
C = 9, 2, Q, J
D = 2, 4, J, Y
E = none of these
}

6. 2 J 8 7 M 3 Y Q   ——

7. Q 2 J 5 H 9 3 S   ——

8. 9 3 2 H 7 W Y Q   ——

9. H 2 5 8 Y 4 W J   ——

10. 4 8 3 J 2 R Y Q   ——

Suggested Answers
{
A = 2, 3, J, Y
B = 2, 5, Q, J
C = 8, 3, Q, H
D = 8, 5, H, Y
E = none of these
}

11. 3 Y 6 M 8 7 W H   ——

12. W R 7 S 3 H 6 5   ——

13. 6 8 W R 7 H S 3   ——

14. H 3 M J 2 9 7 W   ——

15. 7 Q S 9 H 2 4 M   ——

Suggested Answers
{
A = 2, 7, H, W
B = 2, 3, M, S
C = 3, 6, H, S
D = 6, 7, M, W
E = none of these
}

16. 2 6 Q 8 Y M 4 H   ——

17. 5 6 Q 2 9 W H Y   ——

18. M 5 R W 6 2 8 H   ——

19. W 5 6 4 M 3 R H   ——

20. 4 S Y M 6 5 2 W   ——

Suggested Answers
{
A = 8, 5, H, M
B = 8, 6, Y, W
C = 4, 6, H, Y
D = 4, 5, M, W
E = none of these
}

21. J Y 6 3 2 M 8 R   ——

22. 5 R 3 8 2 M J Y   ——

23. 4 2 M 8 R 6 S J   ——

24. 2 4 R Y 8 M J 7   ——

25. W 3 5 S M 7 2 Y   ——

Suggested Answers
{
A = 8, 3, M, S
B = 2, 3, M, R
C = 8, 7, R, Y
D = 2, 7, Y, S
E = none of these
}

26. S 4 3 W 7 9 R M   ——

27. 7 6 H 8 3 S J W   ——

28. 5 8 3 M 7 J H W   ——

29. 6 3 9 W H 8 S M   ——

30. M 3 2 5 Y J 9 S   ——

Suggested Answers
{
A = 9, 6, J, M
B = 3, 6, M, W
C = 9, 7, W, S
D = 3, 7, J, S
E = none of these
}

ANSWER EXPLANATIONS FOR PRACTICE SET 4

1. (E) 4 5 J Q M 8 H 3
2. (A) Y 9 R 2 M 6 Q 8
3. (B) 4 M 2 Y W Q 6 8
4. (B) 4 M 8 6 Q 2 R Y
5. (A) S 9 M R Q 3 2 8
6. (A) 2 J 8 7 M 3 Y Q
7. (B) Q 2 J 5 H 9 3 S
8. (E) 9 3 2 H 7 W Y Q
9. (D) H 2 5 8 Y 4 W J
10. (A) 4 8 3 J 2 R Y Q
11. (D) 3 Y 6 M 8 7 W H
12. (C) W R 7 S 3 H 6 5
13. (C) 6 8 W R 7 H S 3
14. (A) H 3 M J 2 9 7 W
15. (E) 7 Q S 9 H 2 4 M
16. (C) 2 6 Q 8 Y M 4 H
17. (E) 5 6 Q 2 9 W H Y
18. (A) M 5 R W 6 2 8 H
19. (D) W 5 6 4 M 3 R H
20. (D) 4 S Y M 6 5 2 W
21. (B) J Y 6 3 2 M 8 R
22. (B) 5 R 3 8 2 M J Y
23. (E) 4 2 M 8 R 6 S J
24. (C) 2 4 R Y 8 M J 7
25. (D) W 3 5 S M 7 2 Y
26. (C) S 4 3 W 7 9 R M
27. (D) 7 6 H 8 3 S J W
28. (E) 5 8 3 M 7 J H W
29. (B) 6 3 9 W H 8 S M
30. (E) M 3 2 5 Y J 9 S

PRACTICE SET 5

For each of the following questions, find which one of the suggested answers appears in that question.

1. T 3 2 G 6 8 L K _____

2. 6 5 P 7 2 T N G _____

3. 4 7 2 K 6 N P G _____

4. 5 2 8 G P 7 T K _____

5. K 2 9 4 Z N 8 T _____

Suggested Answers
$\begin{cases} A = 8, & 5, & N, & K \\ B = 2, & 5, & K, & G \\ C = 8, & 6, & G, & T \\ D = 2, & 6, & N, & T \\ E = \text{none of these} \end{cases}$

6. N Z 5 2 9 K 7 L _____

7. 4 L 2 7 9 K N Z _____

8. 3 9 K 7 L 5 T N _____

9. 9 3 L Z 7 K N 6 _____

10. G 2 4 T K 6 9 Z _____

Suggested Answers
$\begin{cases} A = 7, & 6, & Z, & T \\ B = 9, & 2, & K, & L \\ C = 7, & 6, & L, & Z \\ D = 9, & 6, & Z, & T \\ E = \text{none of these} \end{cases}$

11. 9 5 V 7 Z K 3 P _____

12. 4 5 V 9 8 G P Z _____

13. K 4 L G 5 9 7 P _____

14. G 4 5 3 K 2 L P _____

15. 3 T Z K 5 4 9 G _____

Suggested Answers
$\begin{cases} A = 7, & 4, & P, & K \\ B = 7, & 5, & Z, & G \\ C = 3, & 5, & P, & Z \\ D = 3, & 4, & K, & G \\ E = \text{none of these} \end{cases}$

16. 2 Z 5 K 7 6 G P _____

17. G L 6 T 2 P 5 4 _____

18. 5 7 G L 6 P T 2 _____

19. P 2 K N 9 8 6 G _____

20. 6 V T 8 P 9 3 K _____

Suggested Answers
$\begin{cases} A = 9, & 6, & P, & G \\ B = 9, & 2, & K, & T \\ C = 2, & 5, & P, & T \\ D = 5, & 6, & K, & G \\ E = \text{none of these} \end{cases}$

21. 9 N 7 6 K 2 Z V _____

22. V 9 N 4 P 8 2 T _____

23. 8 2 9 P 6 G Z V _____

24. P 9 3 7 Z 3 G N _____

25. 3 7 2 N 9 L Z V _____

Suggested Answers
$\begin{cases} A = 9, & 2, & N, & Z \\ B = 9, & 3, & V, & N \\ C = 7, & 2, & V, & P \\ D = 7, & 3, & P, & Z \\ E = \text{none of these} \end{cases}$

26. 3 4 N V K 7 P 2 _____

27. Z 8 L 9 K 5 V 7 _____

28. 3 K 9 Z G V 5 7 _____

29. 3 K 7 5 V 9 L Z _____

30. T 8 K L V 2 9 7 _____

Suggested Answers
$\begin{cases} A = 7, & 8, & V, & K \\ B = 7, & 3, & K, & Z \\ C = 8, & 9, & V, & N \\ D = 9, & 3, & N, & Z \\ E = \text{none of these} \end{cases}$

ANSWER EXPLANATIONS FOR PRACTICE SET 5

1. (C) T 3 2 <u>G</u> <u>6</u> <u>8</u> L K
2. (D) <u>6</u> 5 P <u>7</u> <u>2</u> <u>T</u> N G
3. (E) <u>4</u> 7 2 K <u>6</u> <u>N</u> P G
4. (B) <u>5</u> 2 8 <u>G</u> P 7 T <u>K</u>
5. (E) <u>K</u> 2 9 <u>4</u> Z N 8 <u>T</u>
6. (B) N Z 5 <u>2</u> <u>9</u> K 7 <u>L</u>
7. (B) 4 L <u>2</u> <u>7</u> <u>9</u> K N <u>Z</u>
8. (E) 3 <u>9</u> K 7 L 5 T N
9. (C) 9 3 L <u>Z</u> <u>7</u> K N <u>6</u>
10. (D) G 2 <u>4</u> T K 6 <u>9</u> <u>Z</u>
11. (C) 9 5 V <u>7</u> Z K <u>3</u> <u>P</u>
12. (E) 4 <u>5</u> V 9 8 G <u>P</u> <u>Z</u>
13. (A) <u>K</u> 4 L G 5 9 <u>7</u> P
14. (D) <u>G</u> <u>4</u> 5 <u>3</u> K 2 <u>L</u> P
15. (D) <u>3</u> T Z <u>K</u> 5 4 9 <u>G</u>
16. (D) 2 Z <u>5</u> <u>K</u> 7 6 G P
17. (C) G L <u>6</u> <u>T</u> 2 <u>P</u> <u>5</u> 4
18. (C) <u>5</u> 7 G <u>L</u> 6 <u>P</u> <u>T</u> 2
19. (A) <u>P</u> 2 K N <u>9</u> 8 <u>6</u> <u>G</u>
20. (E) <u>6</u> V T 8 P 9 <u>3</u> K
21. (A) <u>9</u> <u>N</u> 7 6 K <u>2</u> <u>Z</u> V
22. (E) <u>V</u> 9 N 4 P 8 <u>2</u> T
23. (E) 8 2 9 P 6 G Z V
24. (D) <u>P</u> 9 <u>3</u> 7 Z <u>3</u> G N
25. (A) <u>3</u> 7 2 <u>N</u> 9 L <u>Z</u> V
26. (E) 3 4 N V K 7 P 2
27. (A) Z 8 L 9 K 5 <u>V</u> <u>7</u>
28. (B) <u>3</u> <u>K</u> 9 Z G V <u>5</u> <u>7</u>
29. (B) <u>3</u> <u>K</u> <u>7</u> <u>5</u> V 9 L <u>Z</u>
30. (A) T <u>8</u> K L <u>V</u> 2 9 <u>7</u>

CHAPTER 6

Four Clerical Abilities Model Tests
with Answer Explanations

This chapter contains four complete full-length model tests with answers and explanations. The purpose of this chapter is to help you master the techniques for working quickly under time pressure. After correcting each model test, assess your strengths and weaknesses and return to the specific review section for additional review.

The model tests should be taken under strict test conditions. This means:

—no scratch paper permitted

—any scratch work must be done on test booklet

—answers must be marked on answer sheet

—use #2 pencils with erasers

—follow time limits exactly. (Use an alarm clock.) Fifteen minutes for each test. You may not proceed to test #2 until 15 minutes are up for test #1. Then you may not return to test #1.

—no interruptions allowed

—no aids permitted (such as dictionary, calculator, etc.)

NOTE: Sample questions are usually distributed with the announcement and if so may not be given in the official examinations.

Remember to tear out your answer sheet preceding each model test.

ANSWER SHEET

SIGNATURE: _____
(Please Sign)

EXAMINATION TITLE: _____

PLACE OF EXAMINATION: _____
City   State

TODAY'S DATE: _____

SAMPLE Ⓐ ● Ⓒ Ⓓ Ⓔ

DIRECTIONS FOR MARKING ANSWER SHEET

Use only a **No. 2 (or softer) lead pencil.** Darken completely the circle corresponding to your answer. You **must** keep your mark within the circle. Erase **completely** all marks except your answer. Stray marks may be counted as errors.

SAMPLE NAME GRID

LAST NAME — M C C A B E
F.I. — C
M.I. — A

1. In the boxes below, **PRINT** your name. Print only as many letters as will fit within the areas for the last name, first initial (F.I.), and middle initial (M.I.). Below each box, darken the circle containing the same letter. SEE SAMPLE NAME GRID

LAST NAME   F.I.   M.I.

2. In the boxes below, enter your 9-digit Social Security Number. Below each box, darken the circle in each column corresponding to the number you have entered.

SOCIAL SECURITY NUMBER

3. OCCUPATIONAL GROUP NUMBER

SECTION 1

Make no marks or entries in the columns to the right until you receive instructions from the administrator.

TEST NUMBER
TEST SERIES
PART

1 Ⓐ Ⓑ Ⓒ Ⓓ Ⓔ   11 Ⓐ Ⓑ Ⓒ Ⓓ Ⓔ   31 Ⓐ Ⓑ Ⓒ Ⓓ Ⓔ   51 Ⓐ Ⓑ Ⓒ Ⓓ Ⓔ   71 Ⓐ Ⓑ Ⓒ Ⓓ Ⓔ   91 Ⓐ Ⓑ Ⓒ Ⓓ Ⓔ   111 Ⓐ Ⓑ Ⓒ Ⓓ Ⓔ
2 Ⓐ Ⓑ Ⓒ Ⓓ Ⓔ   12 Ⓐ Ⓑ Ⓒ Ⓓ Ⓔ   32 Ⓐ Ⓑ Ⓒ Ⓓ Ⓔ   52 Ⓐ Ⓑ Ⓒ Ⓓ Ⓔ   72 Ⓐ Ⓑ Ⓒ Ⓓ Ⓔ   92 Ⓐ Ⓑ Ⓒ Ⓓ Ⓔ   112 Ⓐ Ⓑ Ⓒ Ⓓ Ⓔ
3 Ⓐ Ⓑ Ⓒ Ⓓ Ⓔ   13 Ⓐ Ⓑ Ⓒ Ⓓ Ⓔ   33 Ⓐ Ⓑ Ⓒ Ⓓ Ⓔ   53 Ⓐ Ⓑ Ⓒ Ⓓ Ⓔ   73 Ⓐ Ⓑ Ⓒ Ⓓ Ⓔ   93 Ⓐ Ⓑ Ⓒ Ⓓ Ⓔ   113 Ⓐ Ⓑ Ⓒ Ⓓ Ⓔ
4 Ⓐ Ⓑ Ⓒ Ⓓ Ⓔ   14 Ⓐ Ⓑ Ⓒ Ⓓ Ⓔ   34 Ⓐ Ⓑ Ⓒ Ⓓ Ⓔ   54 Ⓐ Ⓑ Ⓒ Ⓓ Ⓔ   74 Ⓐ Ⓑ Ⓒ Ⓓ Ⓔ   94 Ⓐ Ⓑ Ⓒ Ⓓ Ⓔ   114 Ⓐ Ⓑ Ⓒ Ⓓ Ⓔ
5 Ⓐ Ⓑ Ⓒ Ⓓ Ⓔ   15 Ⓐ Ⓑ Ⓒ Ⓓ Ⓔ   35 Ⓐ Ⓑ Ⓒ Ⓓ Ⓔ   55 Ⓐ Ⓑ Ⓒ Ⓓ Ⓔ   75 Ⓐ Ⓑ Ⓒ Ⓓ Ⓔ   95 Ⓐ Ⓑ Ⓒ Ⓓ Ⓔ   115 Ⓐ Ⓑ Ⓒ Ⓓ Ⓔ
6 Ⓐ Ⓑ Ⓒ Ⓓ Ⓔ   16 Ⓐ Ⓑ Ⓒ Ⓓ Ⓔ   36 Ⓐ Ⓑ Ⓒ Ⓓ Ⓔ   56 Ⓐ Ⓑ Ⓒ Ⓓ Ⓔ   76 Ⓐ Ⓑ Ⓒ Ⓓ Ⓔ   96 Ⓐ Ⓑ Ⓒ Ⓓ Ⓔ   116 Ⓐ Ⓑ Ⓒ Ⓓ Ⓔ
7 Ⓐ Ⓑ Ⓒ Ⓓ Ⓔ   17 Ⓐ Ⓑ Ⓒ Ⓓ Ⓔ   37 Ⓐ Ⓑ Ⓒ Ⓓ Ⓔ   57 Ⓐ Ⓑ Ⓒ Ⓓ Ⓔ   77 Ⓐ Ⓑ Ⓒ Ⓓ Ⓔ   97 Ⓐ Ⓑ Ⓒ Ⓓ Ⓔ   117 Ⓐ Ⓑ Ⓒ Ⓓ Ⓔ
8 Ⓐ Ⓑ Ⓒ Ⓓ Ⓔ   18 Ⓐ Ⓑ Ⓒ Ⓓ Ⓔ   38 Ⓐ Ⓑ Ⓒ Ⓓ Ⓔ   58 Ⓐ Ⓑ Ⓒ Ⓓ Ⓔ   78 Ⓐ Ⓑ Ⓒ Ⓓ Ⓔ   98 Ⓐ Ⓑ Ⓒ Ⓓ Ⓔ   118 Ⓐ Ⓑ Ⓒ Ⓓ Ⓔ
9 Ⓐ Ⓑ Ⓒ Ⓓ Ⓔ   19 Ⓐ Ⓑ Ⓒ Ⓓ Ⓔ   39 Ⓐ Ⓑ Ⓒ Ⓓ Ⓔ   59 Ⓐ Ⓑ Ⓒ Ⓓ Ⓔ   79 Ⓐ Ⓑ Ⓒ Ⓓ Ⓔ   99 Ⓐ Ⓑ Ⓒ Ⓓ Ⓔ   119 Ⓐ Ⓑ Ⓒ Ⓓ Ⓔ
10 Ⓐ Ⓑ Ⓒ Ⓓ Ⓔ   20 Ⓐ Ⓑ Ⓒ Ⓓ Ⓔ   40 Ⓐ Ⓑ Ⓒ Ⓓ Ⓔ   60 Ⓐ Ⓑ Ⓒ Ⓓ Ⓔ   80 Ⓐ Ⓑ Ⓒ Ⓓ Ⓔ   100 Ⓐ Ⓑ Ⓒ Ⓓ Ⓔ   120 Ⓐ Ⓑ Ⓒ Ⓓ Ⓔ
21 Ⓐ Ⓑ Ⓒ Ⓓ Ⓔ   41 Ⓐ Ⓑ Ⓒ Ⓓ Ⓔ   61 Ⓐ Ⓑ Ⓒ Ⓓ Ⓔ   81 Ⓐ Ⓑ Ⓒ Ⓓ Ⓔ   101 Ⓐ Ⓑ Ⓒ Ⓓ Ⓔ   121 Ⓐ Ⓑ Ⓒ Ⓓ Ⓔ
22 Ⓐ Ⓑ Ⓒ Ⓓ Ⓔ   42 Ⓐ Ⓑ Ⓒ Ⓓ Ⓔ   62 Ⓐ Ⓑ Ⓒ Ⓓ Ⓔ   82 Ⓐ Ⓑ Ⓒ Ⓓ Ⓔ   102 Ⓐ Ⓑ Ⓒ Ⓓ Ⓔ   122 Ⓐ Ⓑ Ⓒ Ⓓ Ⓔ
23 Ⓐ Ⓑ Ⓒ Ⓓ Ⓔ   43 Ⓐ Ⓑ Ⓒ Ⓓ Ⓔ   63 Ⓐ Ⓑ Ⓒ Ⓓ Ⓔ   83 Ⓐ Ⓑ Ⓒ Ⓓ Ⓔ   103 Ⓐ Ⓑ Ⓒ Ⓓ Ⓔ   123 Ⓐ Ⓑ Ⓒ Ⓓ Ⓔ
24 Ⓐ Ⓑ Ⓒ Ⓓ Ⓔ   44 Ⓐ Ⓑ Ⓒ Ⓓ Ⓔ   64 Ⓐ Ⓑ Ⓒ Ⓓ Ⓔ   84 Ⓐ Ⓑ Ⓒ Ⓓ Ⓔ   104 Ⓐ Ⓑ Ⓒ Ⓓ Ⓔ   124 Ⓐ Ⓑ Ⓒ Ⓓ Ⓔ
25 Ⓐ Ⓑ Ⓒ Ⓓ Ⓔ   45 Ⓐ Ⓑ Ⓒ Ⓓ Ⓔ   65 Ⓐ Ⓑ Ⓒ Ⓓ Ⓔ   85 Ⓐ Ⓑ Ⓒ Ⓓ Ⓔ   105 Ⓐ Ⓑ Ⓒ Ⓓ Ⓔ   125 Ⓐ Ⓑ Ⓒ Ⓓ Ⓔ
26 Ⓐ Ⓑ Ⓒ Ⓓ Ⓔ   46 Ⓐ Ⓑ Ⓒ Ⓓ Ⓔ   66 Ⓐ Ⓑ Ⓒ Ⓓ Ⓔ   86 Ⓐ Ⓑ Ⓒ Ⓓ Ⓔ   106 Ⓐ Ⓑ Ⓒ Ⓓ Ⓔ   126 Ⓐ Ⓑ Ⓒ Ⓓ Ⓔ
27 Ⓐ Ⓑ Ⓒ Ⓓ Ⓔ   47 Ⓐ Ⓑ Ⓒ Ⓓ Ⓔ   67 Ⓐ Ⓑ Ⓒ Ⓓ Ⓔ   87 Ⓐ Ⓑ Ⓒ Ⓓ Ⓔ   107 Ⓐ Ⓑ Ⓒ Ⓓ Ⓔ   127 Ⓐ Ⓑ Ⓒ Ⓓ Ⓔ
28 Ⓐ Ⓑ Ⓒ Ⓓ Ⓔ   48 Ⓐ Ⓑ Ⓒ Ⓓ Ⓔ   68 Ⓐ Ⓑ Ⓒ Ⓓ Ⓔ   88 Ⓐ Ⓑ Ⓒ Ⓓ Ⓔ   108 Ⓐ Ⓑ Ⓒ Ⓓ Ⓔ   128 Ⓐ Ⓑ Ⓒ Ⓓ Ⓔ
29 Ⓐ Ⓑ Ⓒ Ⓓ Ⓔ   49 Ⓐ Ⓑ Ⓒ Ⓓ Ⓔ   69 Ⓐ Ⓑ Ⓒ Ⓓ Ⓔ   89 Ⓐ Ⓑ Ⓒ Ⓓ Ⓔ   109 Ⓐ Ⓑ Ⓒ Ⓓ Ⓔ   129 Ⓐ Ⓑ Ⓒ Ⓓ Ⓔ
30 Ⓐ Ⓑ Ⓒ Ⓓ Ⓔ   50 Ⓐ Ⓑ Ⓒ Ⓓ Ⓔ   70 Ⓐ Ⓑ Ⓒ Ⓓ Ⓔ   90 Ⓐ Ⓑ Ⓒ Ⓓ Ⓔ   110 Ⓐ Ⓑ Ⓒ Ⓓ Ⓔ   130 Ⓐ Ⓑ Ⓒ Ⓓ Ⓔ

MODEL TEST 1

Time allotted—15 minutes

Directions

Each question has five suggested answers. Decide which one is the best answer. Find the question number on the Answer Sheet. Show your answer to the question by darkening completely the space corresponding to the letter that is the same as the letter of your answer. Keep your mark within the space. If you have to erase a mark, be sure to erase it completely. Mark only one answer for each question.

In questions 1 through 5, compare the three names or numbers, and mark the answer—
A if ALL THREE names or numbers are exactly ALIKE
B if only the FIRST and SECOND names or numbers are exactly ALIKE
C if only the FIRST and THIRD names or numbers are exactly ALIKE
D if only the SECOND and THIRD names or numbers are exactly ALIKE
E if ALL THREE names or numbers are DIFFERENT

1. 4826489	4824689	4826489
2. 3825431	3825431	3825431
3. 4763901	4769301	4769301
4. Worthington Pistle	Worthington Pistel	Worthington Pistle
5. Merriam Riwonla	Merriam Riwonia	Merriam Riwonia

In questions 6 through 10, find the correct place for the name in the box.

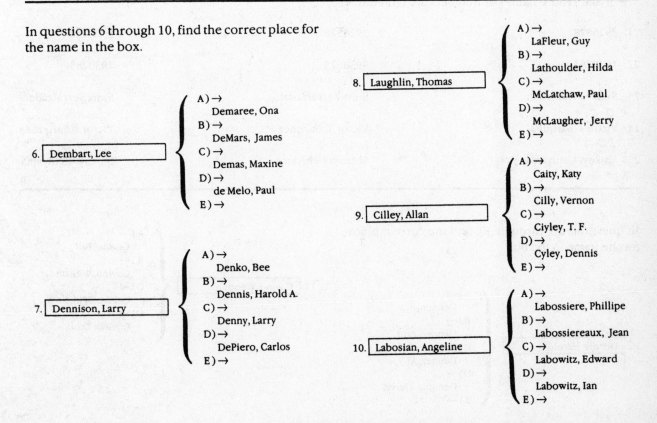

6. Dembart, Lee
   A) →
      Demaree, Ona
   B) →
      DeMars, James
   C) →
      Demas, Maxine
   D) →
      de Melo, Paul
   E) →

7. Dennison, Larry
   A) →
      Denko, Bee
   B) →
      Dennis, Harold A.
   C) →
      Denny, Larry
   D) →
      DePiero, Carlos
   E) →

8. Laughlin, Thomas
   A) →
      LaFleur, Guy
   B) →
      Lathoulder, Hilda
   C) →
      McLatchaw, Paul
   D) →
      McLaugher, Jerry
   E) →

9. Cilley, Allan
   A) →
      Caity, Katy
   B) →
      Cilly, Vernon
   C) →
      Ciyley, T. F.
   D) →
      Cyley, Dennis
   E) →

10. Labosian, Angeline
    A) →
       Labossiere, Phillipe
    B) →
       Labossiereaux, Jean
    C) →
       Labowitz, Edward
    D) →
       Labowitz, Ian
    E) →

11. Add:

   58
   + 17

Answers

A) 73   B) 75
C) 78   D) 85
E) none of these

12. Subtract:

   98
   − 51

A) 47   B) 50
C) 53   D) 57
E) none of these

13. Multiply:

   12
   × 7

A) 64   B) 74
C) 84   D) 94
E) none of these

14. Divide:

   3) 189

A) 60   B) 63
C) 65   D) 68
E) none of these

15. Add:

   23
   + 71

A) 84   B) 87
C) 92   D) 97
E) none of these

In questions 16 through 20, find which one of the suggested answers appears in that question.

16. 3 P U 4 M T 7 9

17. T 4 2 R 9 Y 6 U

18. R 2 M U 6 4 3 P

19. 6 U 4 7 9 M R Y

20. R P 2 6 3 U T 4

Suggested Answers

A = 2, 4, M, U
B = 3, 4, T, R
C = 9, 2, U, R
D = 9, 3, M, T
E = none of these

In questions 21 through 25, compare the three names or numbers, and mark the answer—

A if ALL THREE names or numbers are exactly ALIKE
B if only the FIRST and SECOND names or numbers are exactly ALIKE
C if only the FIRST and THIRD names or numbers are exactly ALIKE
D if only the SECOND and THIRD names or numbers are exactly ALIKE
E if ALL THREE names or numbers are DIFFERENT

21. 3926528   3926528   3925628

22. 1930283   1930823   1930283

23. Sima Serrafzadeh   Sima Serrafzadah   Sima Serrafzadeh

24. Victor I. Sarquez   Victor T. Sarquez   Victor I. Sarquez

25. Shizuyi Uchiyama   Shizuyi Uchiyama   Shizuyi Uchiyama

In questions 26, through 30, find the correct place for the name in the box.

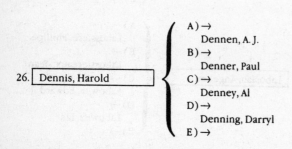

26. Dennis, Harold

A) →
   Dennen, A. J.
B) →
   Denner, Paul
C) →
   Denney, Al
D) →
   Denning, Darryl
E) →

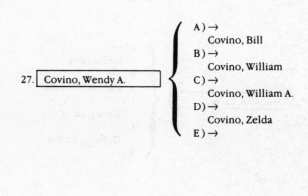

27. Covino, Wendy A.

A) →
   Covino, Bill
B) →
   Covino, William
C) →
   Covino, William A.
D) →
   Covino, Zelda
E) →

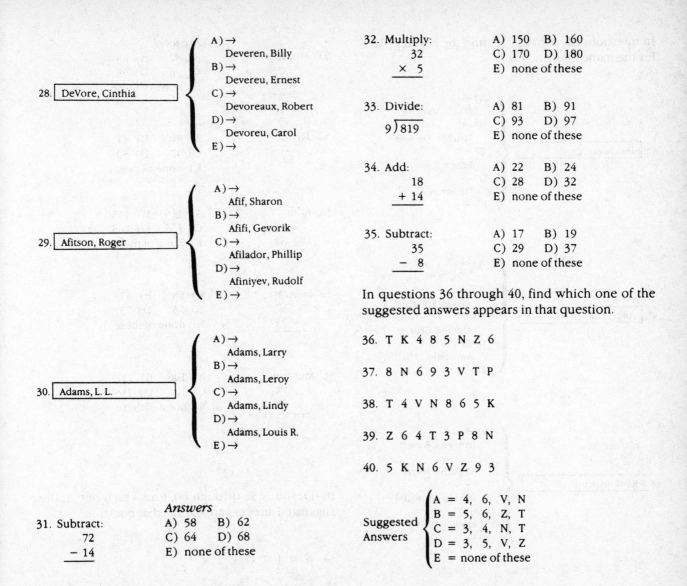

28. DeVore, Cinthia
- A) →
  Deveren, Billy
- B) →
  Devereu, Ernest
- C) →
  Devoreaux, Robert
- D) →
  Devoreu, Carol
- E) →

29. Afitson, Roger
- A) →
  Afif, Sharon
- B) →
  Afifi, Gevorik
- C) →
  Afilador, Phillip
- D) →
  Afiniyev, Rudolf
- E) →

30. Adams, L. L.
- A) →
  Adams, Larry
- B) →
  Adams, Leroy
- C) →
  Adams, Lindy
- D) →
  Adams, Louis R.
- E) →

31. Subtract:
$$\begin{array}{r} 72 \\ -\ 14 \\ \hline \end{array}$$

Answers
A) 58   B) 62
C) 64   D) 68
E) none of these

32. Multiply:
$$\begin{array}{r} 32 \\ \times\ 5 \\ \hline \end{array}$$
A) 150   B) 160
C) 170   D) 180
E) none of these

33. Divide:
$9\overline{)819}$
A) 81   B) 91
C) 93   D) 97
E) none of these

34. Add:
$$\begin{array}{r} 18 \\ +\ 14 \\ \hline \end{array}$$
A) 22   B) 24
C) 28   D) 32
E) none of these

35. Subtract:
$$\begin{array}{r} 35 \\ -\ 8 \\ \hline \end{array}$$
A) 17   B) 19
C) 29   D) 37
E) none of these

In questions 36 through 40, find which one of the suggested answers appears in that question.

36. T K 4 8 5 N Z 6

37. 8 N 6 9 3 V T P

38. T 4 V N 8 6 5 K

39. Z 6 4 T 3 P 8 N

40. 5 K N 6 V Z 9 3

Suggested Answers
- A = 4, 6, V, N
- B = 5, 6, Z, T
- C = 3, 4, N, T
- D = 3, 5, V, Z
- E = none of these

In questions 41 through 45, compare the three names or numbers, and mark the answer—
A if ALL THREE names or numbers are exactly ALIKE
B if only the FIRST and SECOND names or numbers are exactly ALIKE
C if only the FIRST and THIRD names or numbers are exactly ALIKE
D if only the SECOND and THIRD names or numbers are exactly ALIKE
E if ALL THREE names or numbers are DIFFERENT

41. 9038717   9037217   9037218

42. 2983014   2983014   2938014

43. 3826798   3826978   3826978

44. Leonard Wibbelsman   Leonard Wibblesman   Leonard Wibbelsmann

45. Heidi Claire Whotlock   Heidi Claire Whotlock   Hiedi Claire Whotlock

In questions 46, through 50, find the correct place for the name in the box.

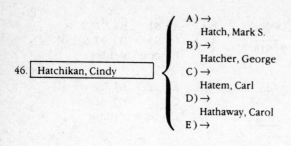

46. | Hatchikan, Cindy |
- A) →
  Hatch, Mark S.
- B) →
  Hatcher, George
- C) →
  Hatem, Carl
- D) →
  Hathaway, Carol
- E) →

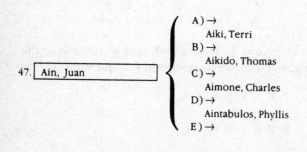

47. | Ain, Juan |
- A) →
  Aiki, Terri
- B) →
  Aikido, Thomas
- C) →
  Aimone, Charles
- D) →
  Aintabulos, Phyllis
- E) →

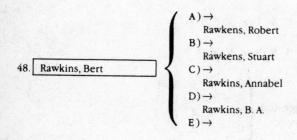

48. | Rawkins, Bert |
- A) →
  Rawkens, Robert
- B) →
  Rawkens, Stuart
- C) →
  Rawkins, Annabel
- D) →
  Rawkins, B. A.
- E) →

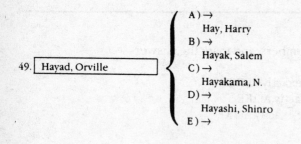

49. | Hayad, Orville |
- A) →
  Hay, Harry
- B) →
  Hayak, Salem
- C) →
  Hayakama, N.
- D) →
  Hayashi, Shinro
- E) →

50. | Odom, Rick |
- A) →
  O'Davorin, Kenneth
- B) →
  O'Day, Dennis
- C) →
  O'Dell, David
- D) →
  O'Donnell, Gene
- E) →

Answers

51. Multiply:

    23
  × 4

  A) 82   B) 88
  C) 96   D) 98
  E) none of these

52. Divide:

  2)82

  A) 40   B) 41
  C) 42   D) 50
  E) none of these

53. Add:

    93
  + 52

  A) 135   B) 145
  C) 155   D) 165
  E) none of these

54. Subtract:

    87
  − 24

  A) 65   B) 67
  C) 73   D) 75
  E) none of these

55. Multiply:

    17
  × 8

  A) 106   B) 116
  C) 126   D) 136
  E) none of these

In questions 56 through 60, find which one of the suggested answers appears in that question.

56. 6 M J 7 Q Y 2 4

57. Y 7 5 S 4 H 9 J

58. S 5 Q J 9 7 6 M

59. 9 J 7 2 4 Q S H

60. S M 5 9 6 J Y 7

Suggested Answers

- A = 5, 7, Q, J
- B = 6, 7, Y, S
- C = 4, 5, J, S
- D = 4, 6, Q, Y
- E = none of these

In questions 61 through 65, compare the three names or numbers, and mark the answer—
  A if ALL THREE names or numbers are exactly ALIKE
  B if only the FIRST and SECOND names or numbers are exactly ALIKE
  C if only the FIRST and THIRD names or numbers are exactly ALIKE
  D if only the SECOND and THIRD names or numbers are exactly ALIKE
  E if ALL THREE names or numbers are DIFFERENT

61. 8372918	8372981	8372981
62. 2837192	2837912	2837192
63. Sigemin Ziegler	Sigemin Zeigler	Sigemin Ziegler
64. Fern Frederics	Fern Fredricks	Fern Fredericks
65. J. Michael Zigovras	J. Michael Zigovras	J. Michael Zigorvas

---

In questions 66 through 70, find the correct place
for the name in the box.

66. Hawkins, Norbert
- A) →
  - Hawkins, Lee
- B) →
  - Hawkins, Lewis
- C) →
  - Hawkins, N. M.
- D) →
  - Hawkins, Wm. S.
- E) →

67. Gutierrez, Beth
- A) →
  - Gutana, Edmund
- B) →
  - Gutenberg, Bessie
- C) →
  - Gutentag, Chas.
- D) →
  - Guthrie, Bob
- E) →

68. Ole, Bente
- A) →
  - O'Lares, Enid
- B) →
  - O'Leary, Tim
- C) →
  - Oleas, Patrick
- D) →
  - Olender, Missy
- E) →

69. Pott, Gregory
- A) →
  - Potvin, Pam
- B) →
  - Potvist, Tilly
- C) →
  - Potwin, Allan
- D) →
  - Potwort, Freda
- E) →

70. Gunther, Edward
- A) →
  - Gunn, Elliot
- B) →
  - Gunnell, S. F.
- C) →
  - Gura, Franklin
- D) →
  - Guralt, Luke
- E) →

Answers

71. Divide:

7)357

  A) 45   B) 50
  C) 51   D) 53
  E) none of these

72. Add:
  29
  + 37

  A) 56   B) 65
  C) 66   D) 76
  E) none of these

73. Subtract:
  91
  − 19

  A) 72   B) 78
  C) 82   D) 83
  E) none of these

74. Multiply:
  24
  × 3

  A) 66   B) 68
  C) 72   D) 74
  E) none of these

75. Divide:

9)837

  A) 91   B) 92
  C) 93   D) 97
  E) none of these

In questions 76 through 80, find which one of the suggested answers appears in that question.

76. M Q 3 7 4 Z X 5

77. 7 Z 5 8 2 F M W

78. M 3 F Z 7 5 4 Q

79. X 5 3 M 2 W 7 Z

80. 4 Q Z 5 F X 8 2

Suggested Answers
A = 3, 5, F, Z
B = 4, 5, X, M
C = 2, 3, Z, M
D = 2, 4, F, X
E = none of these

In questions 81 through 85, compare the three names or numbers, and mark the answer—
A if ALL THREE names or numbers are exactly ALIKE
B if only the FIRST and SECOND names or numbers are exactly ALIKE
C if only the FIRST and THIRD names or numbers are exactly ALIKE
D if only the SECOND and THIRD names or numbers are exactly ALIKE
E if ALL THREE names or numbers are DIFFERENT

81. 4819287	4819287	3891287
82. 3782619	3782619	3782619
83. 2736510	2735610	2736510
84. Judith A. Streigel	Judith A. Streigel	Judith A. Striegel
85. Nicholas Strimling	Nicholas Strimler	Nichlas Strimling

In questions 86 through 90, find the correct place for the name in the box.

86. Groener, Tim
A) →
   Groobin, J.
B) →
   Groom, James
C) →
   Groot, Roger
D) →
   Gropman, Paula
E) →

87. Grzchbien, Solly
A) →
   Gruzzi, Maria
B) →
   Grzanka, Stanley
C) →
   Grzebien, Gary W.
D) →
   Grzibiewski, John
E) →

88. Cicci, Thomas
A) →
   Cinader, Alice
B) →
   Cinciarelli, John
C) →
   Cinco, Josepfina
D) →
   Cinecoe, Robt.
E) →

89. Haack, Martin
A) →
   Ha, Young Soon
B) →
   Haack, Ernest
C) →
   Haan, Patricia
D) →
   Haase, Sherie
E) →

90. Amore, Joseph
A) →
   Amo, Efrin
B) →
   Amor, Bartolo
C) →
   Amorde, Todd
D) →
   Amores, Mercedes
E) →

91. Add:

   92
   + 37

Answers
A) 139   B) 142
C) 149   D) 152
E) none of these

92. Subtract:

   132
   − 45

A) 77   B) 78
C) 97   D) 94
E) none of these

93. Multiply:

   19
   × 8

A) 152   B) 157
C) 158   D) 164
E) none of these

94. Divide:

   6)372

A) 16   B) 61
C) 62   D) 67
E) none of these

95. Add:

   18
   + 82

A) 90   B) 100
C) 110   D) 120
E) none of these

In questions 96 through 100, find which one of the suggested answers appears in that question.

96. 7 Q H 8 W Z 3 5

97. Z 8 6 F 5 J 2 H

98. F 6 W H 2 8 7 Q

99. 2 H 8 3 5 W F J

100. F Q 6 2 7 H Z 8

Suggested Answers
$\begin{cases} A = 6, 8, W, H \\ B = 7, 8, Z, F \\ C = 5, 6, H, F \\ D = 5, 7, W, Z \\ E = \text{none of these} \end{cases}$

In questions 101 through 105, compare the three names or numbers, and mark the answer—
A if ALL THREE names or numbers are exactly ALIKE
B if only the FIRST and SECOND names or numbers are exactly ALIKE
C if only the FIRST and THIRD names or numbers are exactly ALIKE
D if only the SECOND and THIRD names or numbers are exactly ALIKE
E if ALL THREE names or numbers are DIFFERENT

101. 3921038 · 3912038 · 3923038

102. 2710935 · 2701935 · 2701935

103. Neilson Saemaidahr · Neilson Saemaidhar · Neilson Saemaidahr

104. Stephanie R. Sharron · Stephanie R. Sharon · Stephanie R. Sharon

105. Jefferey Paige Sacks · Jefferey Paige Sachs · Jeffrey Paige Sachs

In questions 106 through 110, find the correct place for the name in the box.

106. Andeson, Louis

$\begin{cases} A) \rightarrow \\ \quad \text{Anderson, L. P.} \\ B) \rightarrow \\ \quad \text{Anderson, Peter} \\ C) \rightarrow \\ \quad \text{Andersonian, Frank} \\ D) \rightarrow \\ \quad \text{Andino, Vincent} \\ E) \rightarrow \end{cases}$

107. Rupolo, Victor

$\begin{cases} A) \rightarrow \\ \quad \text{Ruonala, Kenneth} \\ B) \rightarrow \\ \quad \text{Rupe, Arthur} \\ C) \rightarrow \\ \quad \text{Rupen, Osgood} \\ D) \rightarrow \\ \quad \text{Rupert, Corinne} \\ E) \rightarrow \end{cases}$

108. | American Filmathon

A) →
    American Business Supply
B) →
    American Cinema Editors
C) →
    American Film Institute
D) →
    American Foreign Services
E) →

109. | Ryan, J. Patrick

A) →
    Ryan, Ernest
B) →
    Ryan, John
C) →
    Ryan, Kerry
D) →
    Ryan, Larry
E) →

110. | Sabersky, Stephen

A) →
    Saber, Ron
B) →
    Sabrinsky, Judith
C) →
    Sabur, Zena
D) →
    Sabzinsky, Jonathan
E) →

Answers

111. Subtract:
   121
 − 84

A) 35 B) 37
C) 47 D) 49
E) none of these

112. Multiply:
  19
 × 4

A) 72 B) 74
C) 76 D) 78
E) none of these

113. Divide:
 9)810

A) 9 B) 19
C) 90 D) 91
E) none of these

114. Add:
  98
 + 37

A) 125 B) 135
C) 137 D) 139
E) none of these

115. Subtract:
  88
 − 31

A) 57 B) 63
C) 67 D) 77
E) none of these

In questions 116 through 120, find which one of the suggested answers appears in that question.

116. Y R 9 5 2 X Z 3

117. 5 X 3 6 8 H Y M

118. Y 9 H X 5 3 2 R

119. Z 3 9 Y 8 M 5 X

120. 2 R X 3 H Z 6 8

Suggested Answers

A = 9, 3, H, X
B = 2, 3, Z, Y
C = 8, 9, X, Y
D = 8, 2, H, Z
E = none of these

IF YOU FINISH BEFORE THE TIME IS UP, YOU MAY GO BACK AND CHECK YOUR ANSWERS.

ANSWER KEY FOR MODEL TEST 1

Alike or Different

1. C	21. B	41. E	61. D	81. B	101. E
2. A	22. C	42. B	62. C	82. A	102. D
3. D	23. C	43. D	63. C	83. C	103. C
4. C	24. C	44. E	64. E	84. B	104. D
5. D	25. A	45. B	65. B	85. E	105. E

Alphabetizing

6. D	26. E	46. C	66. D	86. A	106. D
7. C	27. B	47. D	67. E	87. C	107. E
8. C	28. C	48. E	68. B	88. A	108. D
9. B	29. E	49. B	69. A	89. C	109. B
10. A	30. A	50. D	70. C	90. D	110. B

Arithmetic

11. B	31. A	51. E	71. C	91. E	111. B
12. A	32. B	52. B	72. C	92. E	112. C
13. C	33. B	53. B	73. A	93. A	113. C
14. B	34. D	54. E	74. C	94. C	114. B
15. E	35. E	55. D	75. C	95. B	115. A

Letters and Numbers

16. D	36. B	56. D	76. B	96. D	116. B
17. C	37. E	57. C	77. E	97. C	117. E
18. A	38. A	58. A	78. A	98. A	118. A
19. E	39. C	59. E	79. C	99. E	119. C
20. B	40. D	60. B	80. D	100. B	120. D

ANALYSIS CHART FOR MODEL TEST 1

Now that you've corrected your exam, use the following chart to carefully analyze your results and spot your strengths and weaknesses. This analysis should help you focus your study and review efforts.

Section	Total Number of Questions	Number Correct	Number Incorrect	Number Unanswered*
Alike or Different	30			
Alphabetizing	30			
Arithmetic	30			
Letters and Numbers	30			
TOTAL	120			

*Since there is a small penalty for incorrect answers on the Clerical Abilities Test, you should not guess "blindly." Try to eliminate one or more of the choices before you take your educated guess.

ANSWER EXPLANATIONS FOR MODEL TEST 1

1. (C) 4826489   4824689   4826489
2. (A) 3825431   3825431   3825431
3. (D) 4763901   4769301   4769301
4. (C) Worthington Pistle   Worthington Pistel   Worthington Pistle
5. (D) Merriam Riwonia   Merriam Riwonia   Merriam Riwonia
6. (D) Demas, Maxine
   Dembart, Lee
   de Melo, Paul
7. (C) Dennis, Harold A.
   Dennison, Larry
   Denny, Larry
8. (C) Lathoulder, Hilda
   Laughlin, Thomas
   McLatchaw, Paul
9. (B) Caity, Katy
   Cilley, Allan
   Cilly, Vernon
10. (A) Labosian, Angeline
    Labossiere, Phillipe
11. (B) 75
12. (A) 47
13. (C) 84
14. (B) 63
15. (E) Correct answer: 94.
16. (D) 3 P U 4 M T 7 9
17. (C) T 4 2 R 9 Y 6 U
18. (A) R 2 M U 6 4 3 P
19. (E) 6 U 4 7 9 M R Y
20. (B) R P 2 6 3 U T 4
21. (B) 3926528   3925628
22. (C) 1930283   1930823
23. (C) Sima Serrafzadeh   Sima Serrafzadah   Sima Serrafzadeh
24. (C) Victor I. Sarquez   Victor T. Sarquez   Victor I. Sarquez
25. (A) Shizuyi Uchiyama   Shizuyi Uchiyama   Shizuyi Uchiyama
26. (E) Denning, Darryl
    Dennis, Harold
27. (B) Covino, Bill
    Covino, Wendy A.
    Covino, William
28. (C) Devereu, Ernest
    DeVore, Cinthia
    Devoreaux, Robert

29. (E) Afiniyév, Rudolf
    Afitson, Roger
30. (A) Adams, L. L.
    Adams, Larry
31. (A) 58
32. (B) 160
33. (B) 91
34. (D) 32
35. (E) Correct answer: 27.
36. (B) T K 4 8 5 N Z 6
37. (E) 8 N 6 9 3 V T P
38. (A) T 4 V N 8 6 5 K
39. (C) Z 6 4 T 3 P 8 N
40. (D) 5 K N 6 V Z 9 3
41. (E) 9038717   9037217   9037218
42. (B) 2983014   2983014   2983014
43. (D) 3826798   3826978   3826978
44. (E) Leonard Wibbelsman   Leonard Wibblesman   Leonard Wibbelsmann
45. (B) Heidi Claire Whotlock   Heidi Claire Whotlock   Hiedi Claire Whotlock
46. (C) Hatcher, George
    Hatchikan, Cindy
    Hatem, Carl
47. (D) Aimone, Charles
    Ain, Juan
    Aintabulos, Phyllis
48. (E) Rawkins, B. A.
    Rawkins, Bert
49. (B) Hay, Harry
    Hayad, Orville
    Hayak, Salem
50. (D) O'Dell, David
    Odom, Rick
    O'Donnell, Gene
51. (E) Correct answer: 92.
52. (B) 41
53. (B) 145
54. (E) Correct answer: 63.
55. (D) 136
56. (D) 6 M J 7 Q Y 2 4
57. (C) Y 7 5 S 4 H 9 J
58. (A) S 5 Q J 9 7 6 M
59. (E) 9 J 7 2 4 Q S H
60. (B) S M 5 9 6 J Y 7

61. (D) 8372918 / 8372981 / 8372981
62. (C) 2837192 / 2837912 / 2837192
63. (C) Sigemin Ziegler / Sigemin Zeigler / Sigemin Ziegler
64. (E) Fern Frederics / Fern Fredricks / Fern Fredericks
65. (B) J. Michael Zigovras / J. Michael Zigovras / J. Michael Zigorvas
66. (D) Hawkins, N. M. / *Hawkins, Norbert* / Hawkins, Wm. S.
67. (E) Guthrie, Bob / *Gutierrez, Beth*
68. (B) O'Lares, Enid / *Ole, Bente* / O'Leary, Tim
69. (A) *Pott, Gregory* / Potvin, Pam
70. (C) Gunnell, S. F. / *Gunther, Edward* / Gura, Franklin
71. (C) 51
72. (C) 66
73. (A) 72
74. (C) 72
75. (C) 93
76. (B) M Q 3 7 4 Z X 5
77. (E) 7 Z 5 8 2 F M W
78. (A) M 3 F Z 7 5 4 Q
79. (C) X 5 3 M 2 W 7 Z
80. (D) 4 Q Z 5 F X 8 2
81. (B) 4819287 / 4819287 / 4891287
82. (A) 3782619 / 3782619 / 3782619
83. (C) 2736510 / 2735610 / 2736510
84. (B) Judith A. Streigel / Judith A. Streigel / Judith A. Striegel
85. (E) Nicholas Strimling / Nicholas Strimler / Nichlas Strimling
86. (A) *Groener, Tim* / Groobin, J.
87. (C) Grzanka, Stanley / *Grzchbien, Solly* / Grzebien, Gary W.
88. (A) *Cicci, Thomas* / Cinader, Alice
89. (C) Haack, Ernest / *Haack, Martin* / Haan, Patricia

90. (D) Amorde, Todd / *Amore, Joseph* / Amores, Mercedes
91. (E) Correct answer: 129.
92. (E) Correct answer: 87.
93. (A) 152
94. (C) 62
95. (B) 100
96. (D) 7 Q H 8 W Z 3 5
97. (C) Z 8 6 F 5 J 2 H
98. (A) F 6 W H 2 8 7 Q
99. (E) 2 H 8 3 5 W F J
100. (B) F Q 6 2 7 H Z 8
101. (E) 3921038 / 3912038 / 3923038
102. (D) 2701935 / 2701935 / 2701935
103. (C) Neilson Saemaidahr / Neilson Saemaidhar / Neilson Saemaidahr
104. (D) Stephanie R. Sharron / Stephanie R. Sharon / Stephanie R. Sharon
105. (E) Jefferey Paige Sacks / Jefferey Paige Sachs / Jeffrey Paige Sachs
106. (D) Andersonian, Frank / *Andeson, Louis* / Andino, Vincent
107. (E) Rupert, Corinne / *Rupolo, Victor*
108. (D) American Film Institute / *American Filmatbon* / American Foreign Services
109. (B) Ryan, Ernest / *Ryan, J. Patrick* / Ryan, John
110. (B) Saber, Ron / *Sabersky, Stephen* / Sabrinsky, Judith
111. (B) 37
112. (C) 76
113. (C) 90
114. (B) 135
115. (A) 57
116. (B) Y R 9 5 2 X Z 3
117. (E) 5 X 3 6 8 H Y M
118. (A) Y 9 H X 5 3 2 R
119. (C) Z 3 9 Y 8 M 5 X
120. (D) 2 R X 3 H Z 6 8

ANSWER SHEET

SIGNATURE: _____
(Please Sign)

EXAMINATION TITLE: _____

PLACE OF EXAMINATION: _____

City _____ State _____

TODAY'S DATE: _____

SAMPLE Ⓐ ● Ⓒ Ⓓ Ⓔ

DIRECTIONS FOR MARKING ANSWER SHEET

Use only a **No. 2 (or softer) lead pencil.** Darken completely the circle corresponding to your answer. You **must** keep your mark within the circle. Stray marks may be counted as errors. Erase **completely** all marks except your answer.

SAMPLE NAME GRID

1. In the boxes below, **PRINT** your name. Print only as many letters as will fit within the areas for the last name, first initial (F.I.), and middle initial (M.I.) Below each box, darken the circle containing the same letter. SEE SAMPLE NAME GRID

2. In the boxes below, enter your 9-digit Social Security Number. Below each box, darken the circle in each column corresponding to the number you have entered.

SOCIAL SECURITY NUMBER

3. OCCUPATIONAL GROUP NUMBER

LAST NAME   F.I.   M.I.

SECTION 1

Make no marks or entries in the columns to the right until you receive instructions from the administrator.

TEST NUMBER ⓪①②③④⑤⑥⑦⑧⑨

TEST SERIES
ⓐⒷⒸⒹⒺⒻⒼⒽⒾ
⓪①②③④⑤⑥⑦⑧⑨
⓪①②③④⑤⑥⑦⑧⑨
⓪①②③④⑤⑥⑦⑧⑨

PART ⓪①②③④⑤⑥⑦⑧⑨

1 Ⓐ Ⓑ Ⓒ Ⓓ Ⓔ
2 Ⓐ Ⓑ Ⓒ Ⓓ Ⓔ
3 Ⓐ Ⓑ Ⓒ Ⓓ Ⓔ
4 Ⓐ Ⓑ Ⓒ Ⓓ Ⓔ
5 Ⓐ Ⓑ Ⓒ Ⓓ Ⓔ
6 Ⓐ Ⓑ Ⓒ Ⓓ Ⓔ
7 Ⓐ Ⓑ Ⓒ Ⓓ Ⓔ
8 Ⓐ Ⓑ Ⓒ Ⓓ Ⓔ
9 Ⓐ Ⓑ Ⓒ Ⓓ Ⓔ
10 Ⓐ Ⓑ Ⓒ Ⓓ Ⓔ
11 Ⓐ Ⓑ Ⓒ Ⓓ Ⓔ
12 Ⓐ Ⓑ Ⓒ Ⓓ Ⓔ
13 Ⓐ Ⓑ Ⓒ Ⓓ Ⓔ
14 Ⓐ Ⓑ Ⓒ Ⓓ Ⓔ
15 Ⓐ Ⓑ Ⓒ Ⓓ Ⓔ
16 Ⓐ Ⓑ Ⓒ Ⓓ Ⓔ
17 Ⓐ Ⓑ Ⓒ Ⓓ Ⓔ
18 Ⓐ Ⓑ Ⓒ Ⓓ Ⓔ
19 Ⓐ Ⓑ Ⓒ Ⓓ Ⓔ
20 Ⓐ Ⓑ Ⓒ Ⓓ Ⓔ
21 Ⓐ Ⓑ Ⓒ Ⓓ Ⓔ
22 Ⓐ Ⓑ Ⓒ Ⓓ Ⓔ
23 Ⓐ Ⓑ Ⓒ Ⓓ Ⓔ
24 Ⓐ Ⓑ Ⓒ Ⓓ Ⓔ
25 Ⓐ Ⓑ Ⓒ Ⓓ Ⓔ
26 Ⓐ Ⓑ Ⓒ Ⓓ Ⓔ
27 Ⓐ Ⓑ Ⓒ Ⓓ Ⓔ
28 Ⓐ Ⓑ Ⓒ Ⓓ Ⓔ
29 Ⓐ Ⓑ Ⓒ Ⓓ Ⓔ
30 Ⓐ Ⓑ Ⓒ Ⓓ Ⓔ
31 Ⓐ Ⓑ Ⓒ Ⓓ Ⓔ
32 Ⓐ Ⓑ Ⓒ Ⓓ Ⓔ
33 Ⓐ Ⓑ Ⓒ Ⓓ Ⓔ
34 Ⓐ Ⓑ Ⓒ Ⓓ Ⓔ
35 Ⓐ Ⓑ Ⓒ Ⓓ Ⓔ
36 Ⓐ Ⓑ Ⓒ Ⓓ Ⓔ
37 Ⓐ Ⓑ Ⓒ Ⓓ Ⓔ
38 Ⓐ Ⓑ Ⓒ Ⓓ Ⓔ
39 Ⓐ Ⓑ Ⓒ Ⓓ Ⓔ
40 Ⓐ Ⓑ Ⓒ Ⓓ Ⓔ
41 Ⓐ Ⓑ Ⓒ Ⓓ Ⓔ
42 Ⓐ Ⓑ Ⓒ Ⓓ Ⓔ
43 Ⓐ Ⓑ Ⓒ Ⓓ Ⓔ
44 Ⓐ Ⓑ Ⓒ Ⓓ Ⓔ
45 Ⓐ Ⓑ Ⓒ Ⓓ Ⓔ
46 Ⓐ Ⓑ Ⓒ Ⓓ Ⓔ
47 Ⓐ Ⓑ Ⓒ Ⓓ Ⓔ
48 Ⓐ Ⓑ Ⓒ Ⓓ Ⓔ
49 Ⓐ Ⓑ Ⓒ Ⓓ Ⓔ
50 Ⓐ Ⓑ Ⓒ Ⓓ Ⓔ
51 Ⓐ Ⓑ Ⓒ Ⓓ Ⓔ
52 Ⓐ Ⓑ Ⓒ Ⓓ Ⓔ
53 Ⓐ Ⓑ Ⓒ Ⓓ Ⓔ
54 Ⓐ Ⓑ Ⓒ Ⓓ Ⓔ
55 Ⓐ Ⓑ Ⓒ Ⓓ Ⓔ
56 Ⓐ Ⓑ Ⓒ Ⓓ Ⓔ
57 Ⓐ Ⓑ Ⓒ Ⓓ Ⓔ
58 Ⓐ Ⓑ Ⓒ Ⓓ Ⓔ
59 Ⓐ Ⓑ Ⓒ Ⓓ Ⓔ
60 Ⓐ Ⓑ Ⓒ Ⓓ Ⓔ
61 Ⓐ Ⓑ Ⓒ Ⓓ Ⓔ
62 Ⓐ Ⓑ Ⓒ Ⓓ Ⓔ
63 Ⓐ Ⓑ Ⓒ Ⓓ Ⓔ
64 Ⓐ Ⓑ Ⓒ Ⓓ Ⓔ
65 Ⓐ Ⓑ Ⓒ Ⓓ Ⓔ
66 Ⓐ Ⓑ Ⓒ Ⓓ Ⓔ
67 Ⓐ Ⓑ Ⓒ Ⓓ Ⓔ
68 Ⓐ Ⓑ Ⓒ Ⓓ Ⓔ
69 Ⓐ Ⓑ Ⓒ Ⓓ Ⓔ
70 Ⓐ Ⓑ Ⓒ Ⓓ Ⓔ
71 Ⓐ Ⓑ Ⓒ Ⓓ Ⓔ
72 Ⓐ Ⓑ Ⓒ Ⓓ Ⓔ
73 Ⓐ Ⓑ Ⓒ Ⓓ Ⓔ
74 Ⓐ Ⓑ Ⓒ Ⓓ Ⓔ
75 Ⓐ Ⓑ Ⓒ Ⓓ Ⓔ
76 Ⓐ Ⓑ Ⓒ Ⓓ Ⓔ
77 Ⓐ Ⓑ Ⓒ Ⓓ Ⓔ
78 Ⓐ Ⓑ Ⓒ Ⓓ Ⓔ
79 Ⓐ Ⓑ Ⓒ Ⓓ Ⓔ
80 Ⓐ Ⓑ Ⓒ Ⓓ Ⓔ
81 Ⓐ Ⓑ Ⓒ Ⓓ Ⓔ
82 Ⓐ Ⓑ Ⓒ Ⓓ Ⓔ
83 Ⓐ Ⓑ Ⓒ Ⓓ Ⓔ
84 Ⓐ Ⓑ Ⓒ Ⓓ Ⓔ
85 Ⓐ Ⓑ Ⓒ Ⓓ Ⓔ
86 Ⓐ Ⓑ Ⓒ Ⓓ Ⓔ
87 Ⓐ Ⓑ Ⓒ Ⓓ Ⓔ
88 Ⓐ Ⓑ Ⓒ Ⓓ Ⓔ
89 Ⓐ Ⓑ Ⓒ Ⓓ Ⓔ
90 Ⓐ Ⓑ Ⓒ Ⓓ Ⓔ
91 Ⓐ Ⓑ Ⓒ Ⓓ Ⓔ
92 Ⓐ Ⓑ Ⓒ Ⓓ Ⓔ
93 Ⓐ Ⓑ Ⓒ Ⓓ Ⓔ
94 Ⓐ Ⓑ Ⓒ Ⓓ Ⓔ
95 Ⓐ Ⓑ Ⓒ Ⓓ Ⓔ
96 Ⓐ Ⓑ Ⓒ Ⓓ Ⓔ
97 Ⓐ Ⓑ Ⓒ Ⓓ Ⓔ
98 Ⓐ Ⓑ Ⓒ Ⓓ Ⓔ
99 Ⓐ Ⓑ Ⓒ Ⓓ Ⓔ
100 Ⓐ Ⓑ Ⓒ Ⓓ Ⓔ
101 Ⓐ Ⓑ Ⓒ Ⓓ Ⓔ
102 Ⓐ Ⓑ Ⓒ Ⓓ Ⓔ
103 Ⓐ Ⓑ Ⓒ Ⓓ Ⓔ
104 Ⓐ Ⓑ Ⓒ Ⓓ Ⓔ
105 Ⓐ Ⓑ Ⓒ Ⓓ Ⓔ
106 Ⓐ Ⓑ Ⓒ Ⓓ Ⓔ
107 Ⓐ Ⓑ Ⓒ Ⓓ Ⓔ
108 Ⓐ Ⓑ Ⓒ Ⓓ Ⓔ
109 Ⓐ Ⓑ Ⓒ Ⓓ Ⓔ
110 Ⓐ Ⓑ Ⓒ Ⓓ Ⓔ
111 Ⓐ Ⓑ Ⓒ Ⓓ Ⓔ
112 Ⓐ Ⓑ Ⓒ Ⓓ Ⓔ
113 Ⓐ Ⓑ Ⓒ Ⓓ Ⓔ
114 Ⓐ Ⓑ Ⓒ Ⓓ Ⓔ
115 Ⓐ Ⓑ Ⓒ Ⓓ Ⓔ
116 Ⓐ Ⓑ Ⓒ Ⓓ Ⓔ
117 Ⓐ Ⓑ Ⓒ Ⓓ Ⓔ
118 Ⓐ Ⓑ Ⓒ Ⓓ Ⓔ
119 Ⓐ Ⓑ Ⓒ Ⓓ Ⓔ
120 Ⓐ Ⓑ Ⓒ Ⓓ Ⓔ
121 Ⓐ Ⓑ Ⓒ Ⓓ Ⓔ
122 Ⓐ Ⓑ Ⓒ Ⓓ Ⓔ
123 Ⓐ Ⓑ Ⓒ Ⓓ Ⓔ
124 Ⓐ Ⓑ Ⓒ Ⓓ Ⓔ
125 Ⓐ Ⓑ Ⓒ Ⓓ Ⓔ
126 Ⓐ Ⓑ Ⓒ Ⓓ Ⓔ
127 Ⓐ Ⓑ Ⓒ Ⓓ Ⓔ
128 Ⓐ Ⓑ Ⓒ Ⓓ Ⓔ
129 Ⓐ Ⓑ Ⓒ Ⓓ Ⓔ
130 Ⓐ Ⓑ Ⓒ Ⓓ Ⓔ

MODEL TEST 2

Time allotted—15 minutes

Directions

Each question has five suggested answers. Decide which one is the best answer. Find the question number on the Answer Sheet. Show your answer to the question by darkening completely the space corresponding to the letter of your answer. Keep your mark within the space. If you have to erase a mark, be sure to erase it completely. Mark only one answer for each question.

In questions 1 through 5, compare the three names or numbers, and mark the answer—
A if ALL THREE names or numbers are exactly ALIKE
B if only the FIRST and SECOND names or numbers are exactly ALIKE
C if only the FIRST and THIRD names or numbers are exactly ALIKE
D if only the SECOND and THIRD names or numbers are exactly ALIKE
E if ALL THREE names or numbers are DIFFERENT

1. 3870936	3879036	3870963
2. 3827092	3827902	3827902
3. 3701234	3702324	3701234
4. Arno Wojecieski	Arno Wojeceiski	Arno Wojecieski
5. Laurence Zwisen	Laurence Zwisen	Lawrence Zwisen

In questions 6 through 10, find the correct place for the name in the box.

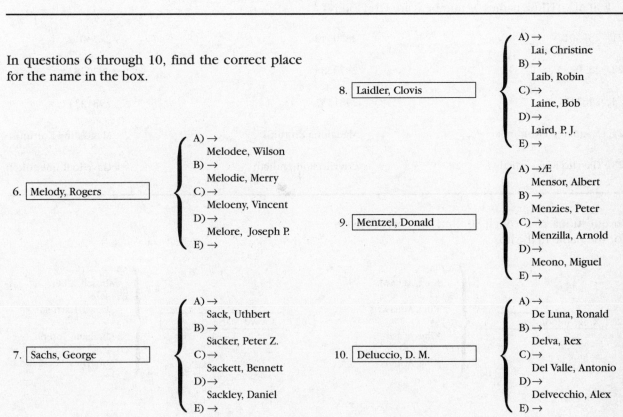

Answers

11. Multiply:
    18
    × 7

A) 122 B) 124
C) 132 D) 134
E) none of these

12. Divide:
    8) 696

A) 78 B) 83
C) 87 D) 89
E) none of these

13. Add:
    92
    + 35

A) 117 B) 127
C) 137 D) 139
E) none of these

14. Subtract:
    108
    − 42

A) 56 B) 64
C) 76 D) 78
E) none of these

15. Multiply:
    92
    × 5

A) 440 B) 450
C) 460 D) 550
E) none of these

In questions 16 through 20, find which one of the suggested answers appears in that question.

16. R 6 7 4 F M 8 Q

17. 3 6 8 X V 9 Q R

18. 4 9 6 R 2 M V X

19. 2 3 V 9 6 Q M X

20. Q 5 6 X 2 8 Z R

Suggested Answers
{
A = 8, 3, M, R
B = 6, 3, R, X
C = 8, 2, X, Q
D = 6, 2, M, Q
E = none of these
}

In questions 21 through 25, compare the three names or numbers, and mark the answer—
A if ALL THREE names or numbers are exactly ALIKE
B if only the FIRST and SECOND names or numbers are exactly ALIKE
C if only the FIRST and THIRD names or numbers are exactly ALIKE
D if only the SECOND and THIRD names or numbers are exactly ALIKE
E if ALL THREE names or numbers are DIFFERENT

21. 2873012   2870312   2873012

22. 2870283   2870283   2870283

23. 2983121   2981231   2981231

24. Magdalena Koltunik   Madalena Koltunik   Magdalina Koltunik

25. Gavrilo Romendicth   Gavrilo Romendicth   Gavrilo Romenditch

In questions 26 through 30, find the correct place for the name in the box.

26. | King, Anthony P. |
{
A) →
   King, Alma M.
B) →
   King, Anna Kris
C) →
   King, Arden
D) →
   King, Arthur
E) →
}

27. | Abovid, Maria |
{
A) →
   Abosch, Albert
B) →
   Abowd, Harriet
C) →
   Abraham, Joseph
D) →
   Abrahams, Roasamid
E) →
}

28. Addison, Tracey
- A) →
  - Addams, Dick
- B) →
  - Adderly, D. J.
- C) →
  - Addotta, Cosimo
- D) →
  - Adduman, Nikolas
- E) →

29. Mouton, N. G.
- A) →
  - Mouton, Betty
- B) →
  - Mouton, Carla
- C) →
  - Mouton, Lee
- D) →
  - Mouton, Nellie
- E) →

30. Moya, Antonio
- A) →
  - Moy, Richard
- B) →
  - Moy, Toon
- C) →
  - Moya, Adelaide
- D) →
  - Moya, Armando
- E) →

Answers

31. Divide:

5)195

A) 40 B) 41
C) 44 D) 49
E) none of these

32. Add:

35
+ 46

A) 71 B) 75
C) 79 D) 83
E) none of these

Answers

33. Subtract:

81
− 36

A) 35 B) 38
C) 45 D) 55
E) none of these

34. Multiply:

72
× 6

A) 422 B) 432
C) 442 D) 452
E) none of these

35. Divide:

3)921

A) 37 B) 39
C) 307 D) 370
E) none of these

In questions 36 through 40, find which one of the suggested answers appears in that question.

36. 5 9 6 M 7 Z F Y

37. V 7 4 9 F 5 X M

38. 8 6 7 V 2 X F Ẏ

39. Y 7 M 4 V 8 6 Q

40. 7 M 9 2 R 6 F Y

Suggested Answers
- A = 7, 6, M, F
- B = 7, 4, Y, M
- C = 9, 6, Y, V
- D = 9, 4, V, F
- E = none of these

In questions 41 through 45, compare the three names or numbers, and mark the answer—
A if ALL THREE names or numbers are exactly ALIKE
B if only the FIRST and SECOND names or numbers are exactly ALIKE
C if only the FIRST and THIRD names or numbers are exactly ALIKE
D if only the SECOND and THIRD names or numbers are exactly ALIKE
E if ALL THREE names or numbers are DIFFERENT

41. Ronald T. Kullaway	Ronald T. Kullaway	Ronald F. Kullaway
42. Ernest Teversen	Ernest Iversen	Ernest Ieversen
43. 4836194	4836914	4836194
44. 3129378	3123978	3129738
45. 2356421	2354621	2354621

In questions 46 through 50, find the correct place for the name in the box.

46. | Van Horn, Jay |

- A) →
  - Vanhimberger, Jos.
- B) →
  - VanHorne, Robt.
- C) →
  - Van Horssen, A. M.
- D) →
  - Van Hung, Nguyen
- E) →

47. | Jenkins, T. R. |

- A) →
  - Jenkins, Sylvia
- B) →
  - Jenkins, T. C.
- C) →
  - Jenkins, Thomas
- D) →
  - Jenkins, Thorman
- E) →

48. | Nay, Eleanor |

- A) →
  - Nawaz, M. B.
- B) →
  - Nawrocki, Lonny
- C) →
  - Nawrot, Edmund
- D) →
  - Nayar, Sami
- E) →

49. | Vetrono, Peter |

- A) →
  - Vetlugin, Rudolf
- B) →
  - Vetsikyan, Aaron
- C) →
  - Vette, E. C.
- D) →
  - Vetter, Wayne
- E) →

50. | Standards and Co. |

- A) →
  - Standard Fire Ass.
- B) →
  - Standard Testing
- C) →
  - Standards Improvement
- D) →
  - Standards Research
- E) →

Answers

51. Add:

$$27$$
$$+\ 38$$

A) 45 B) 55
C) 65 D) 75
E) none of these

52. Subtract:

$$95$$
$$-\ 37$$

A) 59 B) 58
C) 62 D) 68
E) none of these

53. Multiply:

$$35$$
$$\times\ 3$$

A) 95 B) 105
C) 115 D) 125
E) none of these

54. Divide:

$$6\overline{)102}$$

A) 12 B) 14
C) 16 D) 17
E) none of these

55. Add:

$$28$$
$$+\ 34$$

A) 62 B) 64
C) 66 D) 72
E) none of these

In questions 56 through 60, find which one of the suggested answers appears in that question.

56. X 6 4 Q R 2 7 F

57. 7 5 Z F 9 R M 2

58. 5 7 R 9 Z 3 Q M

59. 4 Z 6 9 7 R M F

60. M F 3 6 7 R 9 Z

Suggested Answers

A = 9, 6, R, Q
B = 7, 6, R, Z
C = 9, 2, Z, F
D = 7, 2, F, Q
E = none of these

In questions 61 through 65, compare the three names or numbers, and mark the answer—

A if ALL THREE names or numbers are exactly ALIKE
B if only the FIRST and SECOND names or numbers are exactly ALIKE
C if only the FIRST and THIRD names or numbers are exactly ALIKE
D if only the SECOND and THIRD names or numbers are exactly ALIKE
E If ALL THREE names or numbers are DIFFERENT

61. Lorraine Timbershun   Lorraine Timbershun   Loraine Timbershun

62. Michele R. Spencer   Michelle R. Spencer   Michele R. Spenser

63. Jake Lazarwitz	Jake Lazarwits	Jake Lazarwitz
64. 3826129	3826129	3826127
65. 4837910	4837910	4837910

In questions 66 through 70, find the correct place for the name in the box.

Answers

71. Subtract:
  38
  − 19

  A) 9   B) 11
  C) 19   D) 29
  E) none of these

66. | Andravillo, Frank |

A) →
  Andrade, Fred
B) →
  Andrades, Lee
C) →
  Andranik, Sami
D) →
  Andravin, Paul
E) →

72. Multiply:
  46
  × 4

  A) 164 B) 168
  C) 174 D) 178
  E) none of these

73. Divide:
  8) 648

  A) 80   B) 81
  C) 82   D) 88
  E) none of these

67. | Saary, Armand |

A) →
  Saarinen, Eric
B) →
  Saarinter, Lois
C) →
  Saasnow, Allyn
D) →
  Saavedra, Jake William
E) →

74. Add:
  15
  + 82

  A) 73   B) 93
  C) 87   D) 97
  E) none of these

75. Subtract:
  48
  − 31

  A) 11   B) 13
  C) 21   D) 27
  E) none of these

68. | Ryder, R. Thomas |

A) →
  Rider, Robert
B) →
  Ryder, Rob
C) →
  Ryder, Robert
D) →
  Ryder, Russell
E) →

In questions 76 through 80, find which one of the suggested answers appears in that question.

69. | Chan, Jinny |

A) →
  Chan, Cyrus A.
B) →
  Chan, James C.
C) →
  Chan, Jimmie R.
D) →
  Chan, Jin Ho
E) →

76. 5 Q F R 3 4 7 X

77. X 4 3 5 R 6 Z V

78. R 4 Z X 3 7 9 V

79. 4 3 Y 7 8 X V F

80. 7 3 Y 9 F R 5 V

70. | Chanler, Egan |

A) →
  Chandler, Katherine
B) →
  Chandler, Lilly
C) →
  Chanler, Doris
D) →
  Chanler, Ralph
E) →

Suggested Answers
A = 9, 4, V, R
B = 9, 3, F, X
C = 5, 3, V, F
D = 5, 4, R, X
E = none of these

In questions 81 through 85, compare the three names or numbers, and mark the answer—
   A if ALL THREE names or numbers are exactly ALIKE
   B if only the FIRST and SECOND names or numbers are exactly ALIKE
   C if only the FIRST and THIRD names or numbers are exactly ALIKE
   D if only the SECOND and THIRD names or numbers are exactly ALIKE
   E if ALL THREE names or numbers are DIFFERENT

81. 9810236   9810236   9870236

82. 3784615   3786415   3786415

83. 3892767   3892767   3892767

84. Kelley Millie Laykin   Kelley Millie Layken   Kelley Millie Layken

85. Alexander Mueller   Alexandra Mueller   Alexandra Meuller

---

In questions 86 through 90, find the correct place
for the name in the box.

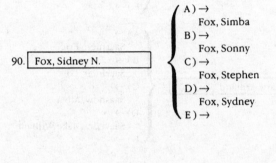

90. Fox, Sidney N.
   A) →
      Fox, Simba
   B) →
      Fox, Sonny
   C) →
      Fox, Stephen
   D) →
      Fox, Sydney
   E) →

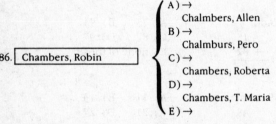

86. Chambers, Robin
   A) →
      Chalmbers, Allen
   B) →
      Chalmburs, Pero
   C) →
      Chambers, Roberta
   D) →
      Chambers, T. Maria
   E) →

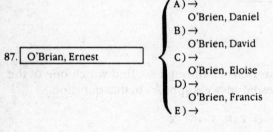

87. O'Brian, Ernest
   A) →
      O'Brien, Daniel
   B) →
      O'Brien, David
   C) →
      O'Brien, Eloise
   D) →
      O'Brien, Francis
   E) →

Answers

91. Multiply: A) 66   B) 69
       23   C) 89   D) 96
     × 3   E) none of these

92. Divide: A) 13   B) 17
                     C) 19   D) 27
    5) 135   E) none of these

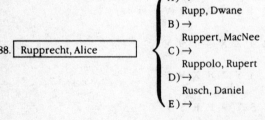

88. Rupprecht, Alice
   A) →
      Rupp, Dwane
   B) →
      Ruppert, MacNee
   C) →
      Ruppolo, Rupert
   D) →
      Rusch, Daniel
   E) →

93. Add: A) 129   B) 139
       48   C) 149   D) 157
     + 81   E) none of these

94. Subtract: A) 67   B) 77
       92   C) 79   D) 87
     − 15   E) none of these

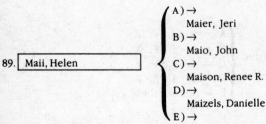

89. Maii, Helen
   A) →
      Maier, Jeri
   B) →
      Maio, John
   C) →
      Maison, Renee R.
   D) →
      Maizels, Danielle
   E) →

95. Multiply: A) 148   B) 164
       24   C) 168   D) 186
     × 7   E) none of these

In questions 96 through 100, find which one of the suggested answers appears in that question.

96. Q 8 R Z Y 6 7 9

97. 5 R 9 3 Y 7 Z F

98. 5 R 7 F X Y 3 9

99. F 8 Z 7 R 3 Y 9

100. 5 4 M Y R 9 V 6

Suggested Answers
$\begin{cases} A = 9, 8, Y, R \\ B = 9, 5, R, F \\ C = 8, 7, Y, M \\ D = 7, 5, M, F \\ E = \text{none of these} \end{cases}$

In questions 101 through 105, compare the three names or numbers, and mark the answer—
A if ALL THREE names or numbers are exactly ALIKE
B if only the FIRST and SECOND names or numbers are exactly ALIKE
C if only the FIRST and THIRD names or numbers are exactly ALIKE
D if only the SECOND and THIRD names or numbers are exactly ALIKE
E if ALL THREE names or numbers are DIFFERENT

101. 3829742	3829742	3829742
102. 3783465	3738465	3783465
103. L. M. Pisarkiewicz	L. M. Pisarkiewicz	M. L. Pisarkiewicz
104. Francis Pivrnec	Frances Pivrnec	Francis Pivnrec
105. Lloyd J. Pfitzer	Lloyd J. Pfitzer	Lloyd J. Pfitzer

In questions 106 through 110, find the correct place for the name in the box.

106. Krost, Barry
$\begin{cases} A) \to \\ \quad \text{Krose, Michael} \\ B) \to \\ \quad \text{Krosman, Tracy} \\ C) \to \\ \quad \text{Kross, Neil} \\ D) \to \\ \quad \text{Krotin, Felice Erica} \\ E) \to \end{cases}$

107. Kruger, Charlotte A.
$\begin{cases} A) \to \\ \quad \text{Koury, Allen} \\ B) \to \\ \quad \text{Kouster, Marty} \\ C) \to \\ \quad \text{Kroubman, Peter} \\ D) \to \\ \quad \text{Kruber, Tillie May} \\ E) \to \end{cases}$

108. Hurly, Van
$\begin{cases} A) \to \\ \quad \text{Hurley, James R.} \\ B) \to \\ \quad \text{Hurley, James S.} \\ C) \to \\ \quad \text{Hurley, Robin C.} \\ D) \to \\ \quad \text{James, Harold W.} \\ E) \to \end{cases}$

109. Ingersoll, Robert
$\begin{cases} A) \to \\ \quad \text{Inoue, Yoshiko} \\ B) \to \\ \quad \text{Instram, Tyrone} \\ C) \to \\ \quad \text{Inverness, George Allen} \\ D) \to \\ \quad \text{Ishimini, Leo P.} \\ E) \to \end{cases}$

110. | Sullivan, John L. |

A) →
    Sullivan, Jack
B) →
    Sullivan, Jim
C) →
    Sullivan, John
D) →
    Sullivan, Jon
E) →

Answers

111. Divide:

$7\overline{)217}$

A) 30   B) 31
C) 32   D) 37
E) none of these

112. Add:
    29
 + 51

A) 70   B) 78
C) 80   D) 90
E) none of these

113. Subtract:
    89
 − 18

A) 71   B) 73
C) 79   D) 81
E) none of these

114. Multiply:
    52
 × 9

A) 452   B) 458
C) 462   D) 466
E) none of these

115. Divide:

$6\overline{)384}$

A) 62   B) 64
C) 66   D) 68
E) none of these

In questions 116 through 120, find which one of the suggested answers appears in that question.

116. 2 Y Q 8 V 7 5 R

117. V 6 R M 7 8 2 X

118. 3 9 X Z 2 V Q 6

119. X Z 2 Q 6 V 3 4

120. 6 F 3 R 9 2 X V

Suggested Answers
A = 7, 2, V, X
B = 7, 6, R, Q
C = 6, 3, V, Q
D = 3, 2, R, X
E = none of these

IF YOU FINISH BEFORE THE TIME IS UP, YOU MAY GO BACK AND CHECK YOUR ANSWERS.

ANSWER KEY FOR MODEL TEST 2

Alike or Different

1. E	21. C	41. B	61. B	81. B	101. A
2. D	22. A	42. E	62. E	82. D	102. C
3. C	23. D	43. C	63. C	83. A	103. B
4. C	24. E	44. E	64. B	84. D	104. E
5. B	25. B	45. D	65. A	85. E	105. A

Alphabetizing

6. C	26. C	46. B	66. D	86. D	106. D
7. A	27. B	47. C	67. C	87. A	107. E
8. C	28. C	48. D	68. B	88. D	108. D
9. B	29. D	49. B	69. E	89. B	109. A
10. A	30. D	50. C	70. D	90. A	110. D

Arithmetic

11. E	31. E	51. C	71. C	91. B	111. B
12. C	32. E	52. B	72. E	92. D	112. C
13. B	33. C	53. B	73. B	93. A	113. A
14. E	34. B	54. D	74. D	94. 5	114. E
15. C	35. C	55. A	75. E	95. C	115. B

Letters and Numbers

16. E	36. A	56. D	76. D	96. A	116. E
17. B	37. D	57. C	77. D	97. B	117. A
18. E	38. E	58. E	78. A	98. B	118. C
19. D	39. B	59. B	79. E	99. A	119. C
20. C	40. A	60. B	80. C	100. E	120. D

ANALYSIS CHART FOR MODEL TEST 2

Now that you've corrected your exam, use the following chart to carefully analyze your results and spot your strengths and weaknesses. This analysis should help you focus your study and review efforts.

Section	Total Number of Questions	Number Correct	Number Incorrect	Number Unanswered*
Alike or Different	30			
Alphabetizing	30			
Arithmetic	30			
Letters and Numbers	30			
TOTAL	120			

*Since there is a small penalty for incorrect answers on the Clerical Abilities Test, you should not guess "blindly." Try to eliminate one or more of the choices before you take your educated guess.

ANSWER EXPLANATIONS FOR MODEL TEST 2

1. (E) 3870936   3879036   3870963
2. (D) 3827092   3827902   3827902
3. (C) 3701234   3702324   3701234
4. (C) Arno Wojecieski   Arno Wojeceiski   Arno Wojecieski
5. (B) Laurence Zwisen   Laurence Zwisen   Lawrence Zwisen
6. (C) Melodie, Merry
      Melody, Rogers
      Meloeny, Vincent
7. (A) *Sachs, George*
      Sack, Uthbert
8. (C) Laib, Robin
      Laidler, Clovis
      Laine, Bob
9. (B) Mensor, Albert
      Mentzel, Donald
      Menzies, Peter
10. (A) *Deluccio, D. M.*
       De Luna, Ronald
11. (E) Correct answer: 126.
12. (C) 87
13. (B) 127
14. (E) Correct answer: 66.
15. (C) 460
16. (E) R 6 7 4 F M 8 Q
17. (B) 3 6 8 X V 9 Q R
18. (E) 4 9 6 R 2 M V X
19. (D) 2 3 V 9 6 Q M X
20. (C) Q 5 6 X 2 8 Z R
21. (C) 2873012   2870312
22. (A) 2870283   2870283
23. (D) 2981231   2983121
24. (E) Magdalena Koltunik   Madalena Koltunik
25. (B) Gavrilo Romendicth   Gavrilo Romendicth
26. (C) King, Anna Kris
      King, Anthony P.
      King, Arden
27. (B) Abosch, Albert
      Abovid, Maria
      Abowd, Harriet
28. (C) Adderly, D.J.
      Addison, Tracey
      Addotta, Cosimo

29. (D) Mouton, Lee
      Mouton, N. G.
      Mouton, Nellie
30. (D) Moya, Adelaide
      Moya, Antonio
      Moya, Armando
31. (E) Correct answer: 39.
32. (E) Correct answer: 81.
33. (C) 45
34. (B) 432
35. (C) 307
36. (A) 5 9 6 M 7 Z F Y
37. (D) V 7 4 9 F 5 X M
38. (E) 8 6 7 V 2 X F Y
39. (B) Y 7 M 4 V 8 6 Q
40. (A) 7 M 9 2 R 6 F Y
41. (B) Ronald T. Kullaway   Ronald F. Kullaway
42. (E) Ernest Iversen   Ernest Iversen
43. (C) 4836914   4836194
44. (E) 3129378   3129738
45. (D) 2356421   2354621
46. (B) Vanhimberger, Jos.
      Van Horn, Jay
      VanHorne, Robt.
47. (C) Jenkins, T. C.
      Jenkins, T. R.
      Jenkins, Thomas
48. (D) Nawrot, Edmund
      Nay, Eleanor
      Nayar, Sami
49. (B) Vetlugin, Rudolf
      Vetrono, Peter
      Vetsikyan, Aaron
50. (C) Standard Testing
      Standards and Co.
      Standards Improvement
51. (C) 65
52. (B) 58
53. (B) 105
54. (D) 17
55. (A) 62
56. (D) X 6 4 Q R 2 7 F
57. (C) 7 5 Z F 9 R M 2
58. (E) 5 7 R 9 Z 3 Q M

59. (B) 4 Z 6 9 7 R M F
60. (B) M F 3 6 7 R 9 Z
61. (B) Lorraine Timbershun Lorraine Timbershun Lorraine Timbershun
62. (E) Michele R. Spencer Michelle R. Spencer Michele R. Spencer
63. (C) Jake Lazarwitz Jake Lazarwitz Jake Lazarwitz
64. (B) 3826129 3826129 3826127
65. (A) 4837910 4837910 4837910
66. (D) Andranik, Sami
        Andravillo, Frank
        Andravin, Paul
67. (C) Saarinter, Lois
        Saary, Armand
        Saasnow, Allyn
68. (B) Rider, Robert
        Ryder, R. Thomas
        Ryder, Rob
69. (E) Chan, Jin Ho
        Chan, Jimmy
70. (D) Chanler, Doris
        Chanler, Egan
        Chanler, Ralph
71. (C) 19
72. (E) Correct answer: 184.
73. (B) 81
74. (D) 97
75. (E) Correct answer: 17.
76. (D) 5 Q F R 3 4 7 X
77. (D) X 4 3 5 R 6 Z V
78. (A) R 4 Z X 3 7 9 V
79. (E) 4 3 Y 7 8 X V F
80. (C) 7 3 Y 9 F R 5 V
81. (B) 9810236 9810236
82. (D) 3786415 3786415
83. (A) 3892767 3892767
84. (D) Kelley Millie Laykin Kelley Millie Layken
85. (E) Alexander Mueller Alexandra Mueller
86. (D) Chambers, Roberta
        Chambers, Robin
        Chambers, T. Maria
87. (A) O'Brian, Ernest
        O'Brien, Daniel
88. (D) Ruppolo, Rupert
        Rupprecht, Alice
        Rusch, Daniel

89. (B) Maier, Jeri
        Maii, Helen
        Maio, John
90. (A) Fox, Sidney N.
        Fox, Simba
91. (B) 69
92. (D) 27
93. (A) 129
94. (B) 77
95. (C) 168
96. (A) Q 8 R Z Y 6 7 9
97. (B) 5 R 9 3 Y 7 Z F
98. (B) 5 R 7 F X Y 3 9
99. (A) F 8 Z 7 R 3 Y 9
100. (E) 5 4 M Y R 9 V 6
101. (A) 3829742 3829742 3829742
102. (C) 3783465 3783465 3783465
103. (B) L. M. Pisarkiewicz M. L. Pisarkiewicz
104. (E) Francis Pivrnec Francis Pivrnec
105. (A) Lloyd J. Pfitzer Lloyd J. Pfitzer
106. (D) Kross, Neil
        Krost, Barry
        Krotin, Felice Erica
107. (E) Kruber, Tillie May
        Kruger, Charlotte A.
108. (D) Hurley, Robin C.
        Hurly, Van
        James, Harold W.
109. (A) Ingersoll, Robert
        Inoue, Yoshiko
110. (D) Sullivan, John
        Sullivan, John L.
        Sullivan, Jon
111. (B) 31
112. (C) 80
113. (A) 71
114. (E) Correct answer: 468.
115. (B) 64
116. (E) 2 Y Q 8 V 7 5 R
117. (A) V 6 R M 7 8 2 X
118. (C) 3 9 X Z 2 V Q 6
119. (C) X Z 2 Q 6 V 3 4
120. (D) 6 F 3 R 9 2 X V

ANSWER SHEET

SIGNATURE: _____
(Please Sign)

EXAMINATION TITLE: _____

PLACE OF EXAMINATION: _____
City

_____
State

TODAY'S DATE: _____

SAMPLE Ⓐ ● Ⓒ Ⓓ Ⓔ

DIRECTIONS FOR MARKING ANSWER SHEET

Use only a **No. 2 (or softer) lead pencil**. Darken completely the circle corresponding to your answer. You **must** keep your mark within the circle. Stray marks may be counted as errors. Erase **completely** all marks except your answer.

SAMPLE NAME GRID

LAST NAME

M C C A B E

F.I. C

M.I. A

1. In the boxes below, **PRINT** your name. Print only as many letters as will fit within the areas for the last name, first initial (F.I.), and middle initial (M.I.) Below each box, darken the circle containing the same letter. SEE SAMPLE NAME GRID

LAST NAME

F.I.

M.I.

2. In the boxes below, enter your 9-digit Social Security Number. Below each box, darken the circle in each column corresponding to the number you have entered.

SOCIAL SECURITY NUMBER

3.
OCCUPATIONAL GROUP NUMBER

SECTION 1

Make no marks or entries in the columns to the right until you receive instructions from the administrator.

PART Ⓐ Ⓑ Ⓒ Ⓓ Ⓔ Ⓕ Ⓖ Ⓗ Ⓘ Ⓙ

TEST SERIES

TEST NUMBER

1 Ⓐ Ⓑ Ⓒ Ⓓ Ⓔ	11 Ⓐ Ⓑ Ⓒ Ⓓ Ⓔ	21 Ⓐ Ⓑ Ⓒ Ⓓ Ⓔ	31 Ⓐ Ⓑ Ⓒ Ⓓ Ⓔ	41 Ⓐ Ⓑ Ⓒ Ⓓ Ⓔ

11 Ⓐ Ⓑ Ⓒ Ⓓ Ⓔ 31 Ⓐ Ⓑ Ⓒ Ⓓ Ⓔ 51 Ⓐ Ⓑ Ⓒ Ⓓ Ⓔ 71 Ⓐ Ⓑ Ⓒ Ⓓ Ⓔ 91 Ⓐ Ⓑ Ⓒ Ⓓ Ⓔ 111 Ⓐ Ⓑ Ⓒ Ⓓ Ⓔ
12 Ⓐ Ⓑ Ⓒ Ⓓ Ⓔ 32 Ⓐ Ⓑ Ⓒ Ⓓ Ⓔ 52 Ⓐ Ⓑ Ⓒ Ⓓ Ⓔ 72 Ⓐ Ⓑ Ⓒ Ⓓ Ⓔ 92 Ⓐ Ⓑ Ⓒ Ⓓ Ⓔ 112 Ⓐ Ⓑ Ⓒ Ⓓ Ⓔ
13 Ⓐ Ⓑ Ⓒ Ⓓ Ⓔ 33 Ⓐ Ⓑ Ⓒ Ⓓ Ⓔ 53 Ⓐ Ⓑ Ⓒ Ⓓ Ⓔ 73 Ⓐ Ⓑ Ⓒ Ⓓ Ⓔ 93 Ⓐ Ⓑ Ⓒ Ⓓ Ⓔ 113 Ⓐ Ⓑ Ⓒ Ⓓ Ⓔ
14 Ⓐ Ⓑ Ⓒ Ⓓ Ⓔ 34 Ⓐ Ⓑ Ⓒ Ⓓ Ⓔ 54 Ⓐ Ⓑ Ⓒ Ⓓ Ⓔ 74 Ⓐ Ⓑ Ⓒ Ⓓ Ⓔ 94 Ⓐ Ⓑ Ⓒ Ⓓ Ⓔ 114 Ⓐ Ⓑ Ⓒ Ⓓ Ⓔ
15 Ⓐ Ⓑ Ⓒ Ⓓ Ⓔ 35 Ⓐ Ⓑ Ⓒ Ⓓ Ⓔ 55 Ⓐ Ⓑ Ⓒ Ⓓ Ⓔ 75 Ⓐ Ⓑ Ⓒ Ⓓ Ⓔ 95 Ⓐ Ⓑ Ⓒ Ⓓ Ⓔ 115 Ⓐ Ⓑ Ⓒ Ⓓ Ⓔ
16 Ⓐ Ⓑ Ⓒ Ⓓ Ⓔ 36 Ⓐ Ⓑ Ⓒ Ⓓ Ⓔ 56 Ⓐ Ⓑ Ⓒ Ⓓ Ⓔ 76 Ⓐ Ⓑ Ⓒ Ⓓ Ⓔ 96 Ⓐ Ⓑ Ⓒ Ⓓ Ⓔ 116 Ⓐ Ⓑ Ⓒ Ⓓ Ⓔ
17 Ⓐ Ⓑ Ⓒ Ⓓ Ⓔ 37 Ⓐ Ⓑ Ⓒ Ⓓ Ⓔ 57 Ⓐ Ⓑ Ⓒ Ⓓ Ⓔ 77 Ⓐ Ⓑ Ⓒ Ⓓ Ⓔ 97 Ⓐ Ⓑ Ⓒ Ⓓ Ⓔ 117 Ⓐ Ⓑ Ⓒ Ⓓ Ⓔ
18 Ⓐ Ⓑ Ⓒ Ⓓ Ⓔ 38 Ⓐ Ⓑ Ⓒ Ⓓ Ⓔ 58 Ⓐ Ⓑ Ⓒ Ⓓ Ⓔ 78 Ⓐ Ⓑ Ⓒ Ⓓ Ⓔ 98 Ⓐ Ⓑ Ⓒ Ⓓ Ⓔ 118 Ⓐ Ⓑ Ⓒ Ⓓ Ⓔ
19 Ⓐ Ⓑ Ⓒ Ⓓ Ⓔ 39 Ⓐ Ⓑ Ⓒ Ⓓ Ⓔ 59 Ⓐ Ⓑ Ⓒ Ⓓ Ⓔ 79 Ⓐ Ⓑ Ⓒ Ⓓ Ⓔ 99 Ⓐ Ⓑ Ⓒ Ⓓ Ⓔ 119 Ⓐ Ⓑ Ⓒ Ⓓ Ⓔ
20 Ⓐ Ⓑ Ⓒ Ⓓ Ⓔ 40 Ⓐ Ⓑ Ⓒ Ⓓ Ⓔ 60 Ⓐ Ⓑ Ⓒ Ⓓ Ⓔ 80 Ⓐ Ⓑ Ⓒ Ⓓ Ⓔ 100 Ⓐ Ⓑ Ⓒ Ⓓ Ⓔ 120 Ⓐ Ⓑ Ⓒ Ⓓ Ⓔ

1 Ⓐ Ⓑ Ⓒ Ⓓ Ⓔ 21 Ⓐ Ⓑ Ⓒ Ⓓ Ⓔ 41 Ⓐ Ⓑ Ⓒ Ⓓ Ⓔ 61 Ⓐ Ⓑ Ⓒ Ⓓ Ⓔ 81 Ⓐ Ⓑ Ⓒ Ⓓ Ⓔ 101 Ⓐ Ⓑ Ⓒ Ⓓ Ⓔ 121 Ⓐ Ⓑ Ⓒ Ⓓ Ⓔ
2 Ⓐ Ⓑ Ⓒ Ⓓ Ⓔ 22 Ⓐ Ⓑ Ⓒ Ⓓ Ⓔ 42 Ⓐ Ⓑ Ⓒ Ⓓ Ⓔ 62 Ⓐ Ⓑ Ⓒ Ⓓ Ⓔ 82 Ⓐ Ⓑ Ⓒ Ⓓ Ⓔ 102 Ⓐ Ⓑ Ⓒ Ⓓ Ⓔ 122 Ⓐ Ⓑ Ⓒ Ⓓ Ⓔ
3 Ⓐ Ⓑ Ⓒ Ⓓ Ⓔ 23 Ⓐ Ⓑ Ⓒ Ⓓ Ⓔ 43 Ⓐ Ⓑ Ⓒ Ⓓ Ⓔ 63 Ⓐ Ⓑ Ⓒ Ⓓ Ⓔ 83 Ⓐ Ⓑ Ⓒ Ⓓ Ⓔ 103 Ⓐ Ⓑ Ⓒ Ⓓ Ⓔ 123 Ⓐ Ⓑ Ⓒ Ⓓ Ⓔ
4 Ⓐ Ⓑ Ⓒ Ⓓ Ⓔ 24 Ⓐ Ⓑ Ⓒ Ⓓ Ⓔ 44 Ⓐ Ⓑ Ⓒ Ⓓ Ⓔ 64 Ⓐ Ⓑ Ⓒ Ⓓ Ⓔ 84 Ⓐ Ⓑ Ⓒ Ⓓ Ⓔ 104 Ⓐ Ⓑ Ⓒ Ⓓ Ⓔ 124 Ⓐ Ⓑ Ⓒ Ⓓ Ⓔ
5 Ⓐ Ⓑ Ⓒ Ⓓ Ⓔ 25 Ⓐ Ⓑ Ⓒ Ⓓ Ⓔ 45 Ⓐ Ⓑ Ⓒ Ⓓ Ⓔ 65 Ⓐ Ⓑ Ⓒ Ⓓ Ⓔ 85 Ⓐ Ⓑ Ⓒ Ⓓ Ⓔ 105 Ⓐ Ⓑ Ⓒ Ⓓ Ⓔ 125 Ⓐ Ⓑ Ⓒ Ⓓ Ⓔ
6 Ⓐ Ⓑ Ⓒ Ⓓ Ⓔ 26 Ⓐ Ⓑ Ⓒ Ⓓ Ⓔ 46 Ⓐ Ⓑ Ⓒ Ⓓ Ⓔ 66 Ⓐ Ⓑ Ⓒ Ⓓ Ⓔ 86 Ⓐ Ⓑ Ⓒ Ⓓ Ⓔ 106 Ⓐ Ⓑ Ⓒ Ⓓ Ⓔ 126 Ⓐ Ⓑ Ⓒ Ⓓ Ⓔ
7 Ⓐ Ⓑ Ⓒ Ⓓ Ⓔ 27 Ⓐ Ⓑ Ⓒ Ⓓ Ⓔ 47 Ⓐ Ⓑ Ⓒ Ⓓ Ⓔ 67 Ⓐ Ⓑ Ⓒ Ⓓ Ⓔ 87 Ⓐ Ⓑ Ⓒ Ⓓ Ⓔ 107 Ⓐ Ⓑ Ⓒ Ⓓ Ⓔ 127 Ⓐ Ⓑ Ⓒ Ⓓ Ⓔ
8 Ⓐ Ⓑ Ⓒ Ⓓ Ⓔ 28 Ⓐ Ⓑ Ⓒ Ⓓ Ⓔ 48 Ⓐ Ⓑ Ⓒ Ⓓ Ⓔ 68 Ⓐ Ⓑ Ⓒ Ⓓ Ⓔ 88 Ⓐ Ⓑ Ⓒ Ⓓ Ⓔ 108 Ⓐ Ⓑ Ⓒ Ⓓ Ⓔ 128 Ⓐ Ⓑ Ⓒ Ⓓ Ⓔ
9 Ⓐ Ⓑ Ⓒ Ⓓ Ⓔ 29 Ⓐ Ⓑ Ⓒ Ⓓ Ⓔ 49 Ⓐ Ⓑ Ⓒ Ⓓ Ⓔ 69 Ⓐ Ⓑ Ⓒ Ⓓ Ⓔ 89 Ⓐ Ⓑ Ⓒ Ⓓ Ⓔ 109 Ⓐ Ⓑ Ⓒ Ⓓ Ⓔ 129 Ⓐ Ⓑ Ⓒ Ⓓ Ⓔ
10 Ⓐ Ⓑ Ⓒ Ⓓ Ⓔ 30 Ⓐ Ⓑ Ⓒ Ⓓ Ⓔ 50 Ⓐ Ⓑ Ⓒ Ⓓ Ⓔ 70 Ⓐ Ⓑ Ⓒ Ⓓ Ⓔ 90 Ⓐ Ⓑ Ⓒ Ⓓ Ⓔ 110 Ⓐ Ⓑ Ⓒ Ⓓ Ⓔ 130 Ⓐ Ⓑ Ⓒ Ⓓ Ⓔ

MODEL TEST 3

Time allotted—15 minutes

Directions

Each question has five suggested answers. Decide which one is the best answer. Find the question number on the Answer Sheet. Show your answer to the question by darkening completely the space corresponding to the letter of your answer. Keep your mark within the space. If you have to erase a mark, be sure to erase it completely. Mark only one answer for each question.

In questions 1 through 5, compare the names or numbers, and mark the answer—
A if ALL THREE names or numbers are exactly ALIKE
B if only the FIRST and SECOND names or numbers are exactly ALIKE
C if only the FIRST and THIRD names or numbers are exactly ALIKE
D if only the SECOND and THIRD names or numbers are exactly ALIKE
E if ALL THREE names or numbers are DIFFERENT

1. Willie MacCovey	Willie McCovey	Willie MacCovey
2. Antony Frennsdorff	Anthony Frennsdorf	Anthony Frensdorff
3. Frederick Kurt	Fredrick Kurt	Frederic Kurt
4. Terrence Garrity	Terrence Garrity	Terence Garrity
5. 4930752	4930572	4930572

In questions 6 through 10, find the correct place for the name in the box.

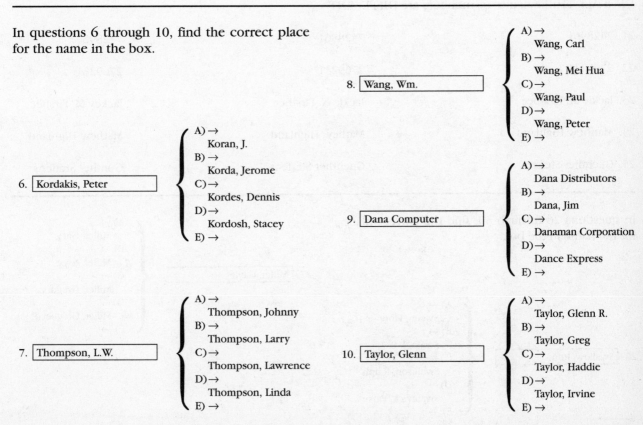

8. Wang, Wm.
   A) →
   Wang, Carl
   B) →
   Wang, Mei Hua
   C) →
   Wang, Paul
   D) →
   Wang, Peter
   E) →

6. Kordakis, Peter
   A) →
   Koran, J.
   B) →
   Korda, Jerome
   C) →
   Kordes, Dennis
   D) →
   Kordosh, Stacey
   E) →

9. Dana Computer
   A) →
   Dana Distributors
   B) →
   Dana, Jim
   C) →
   Danaman Corporation
   D) →
   Dance Express
   E) →

7. Thompson, L.W.
   A) →
   Thompson, Johnny
   B) →
   Thompson, Larry
   C) →
   Thompson, Lawrence
   D) →
   Thompson, Linda
   E) →

10. Taylor, Glenn
    A) →
    Taylor, Glenn R.
    B) →
    Taylor, Greg
    C) →
    Taylor, Haddie
    D) →
    Taylor, Irvine
    E) →

11. Multiply:
    32
    × 6

Answers
A) 182 B) 192
C) 196 D) 202
E) none of these

In questions 16 through 20, find which one of the suggested answers appears in that question.

16. 7 U 5 4 P 8 T M

12. Divide:

    7)217

A) 30 B) 31
C) 33 D) 37
E) none of these

17. M 7 U 2 Y 6 8 R

18. 6 8 7 Y 4 X T M

13. Add:
    58
    + 63

A) 101 B) 105
C) 111 D) 118
E) none of these

19. Y 7 2 5 T 9 X U

14. Subtract:
    93
    − 78

A) 15 B) 17
C) 23 D) 25
E) none of these

20. 9 5 8 U 7 Q T M

Suggested Answers
$\begin{cases} A = 7, & 8, & U, & T \\ B = 7, & 2, & M, & U \\ C = 5, & 8, & M, & Y \\ D = 5, & 2, & Y, & T \\ E = \text{none of these} \end{cases}$

15. Multiply:
    26
    × 4

A) 84 B) 94
C) 104 D) 114
E) none of these

In questions 21 through 25, compare the three names or numbers, and mark the answer—
  A if ALL THREE names or numbers are exactly ALIKE
  B if only the FIRST and SECOND names or numbers are exactly ALIKE
  C if only the FIRST and THIRD names or numbers are exactly ALIKE
  D if only the SECOND and THIRD names or numbers are exactly ALIKE
  E if ALL THREE names or numbers are DIFFERENT

21. 7428961   7428961   7428961

22. 2796231   2769231   2769231

23. Jackie M. Firstbee   Jackie N. Firstbee   Jackey M. Firsbee

24. Matthew Highland   Mathew Highland   Mathew Highland

25. Guenther Steffens   Guenther Steffens   Gunther Steffens

In questions 26 through 30, find the correct place for the name in the box.

27. | Miller, Gayle |
$\begin{cases} \text{A)} \rightarrow \\ \quad \text{Miller, Gary} \\ \text{B)} \rightarrow \\ \quad \text{Miller, Greg} \\ \text{C)} \rightarrow \\ \quad \text{Miller, Gregory} \\ \text{D)} \rightarrow \\ \quad \text{Miller, Gregory P.} \\ \text{E)} \rightarrow \end{cases}$

26. | Swallow, Ron |
$\begin{cases} \text{A)} \rightarrow \\ \quad \text{Swaim, Flora} \\ \text{B)} \rightarrow \\ \quad \text{Swain, J. E.} \\ \text{C)} \rightarrow \\ \quad \text{Swainson, Ralph} \\ \text{D)} \rightarrow \\ \quad \text{Swainvick, Patsy} \\ \text{E)} \rightarrow \end{cases}$

28. Sanders, Michael Jas.
A) →
Sanders, Michael
B) →
Sanders, Michael J.
C) →
Sanders, Nicholas
D) →
Sanders, Sandra
E) →

29. Baskin, Mark
A) →
Basket World
B) →
Baslow, Brigitte
C) →
Bassett, Robert
D) →
Bastean, Richard
E) →

30. Grella, Christa
A) →
Gaston, M.P.
B) →
Greenhaulgh, Vera
C) →
Greenleaf, Douglas
D) →
Greenlee, Kitty
E) →

Answers

31. Divide:

9)828

A) 19   B) 91
C) 92   D) 99
E) none of these

32. Add:
74
+ 29

A) 83   B) 93
C) 95   D) 103
E) none of these

33. Subtract:
82
− 56

A) 26   B) 28
C) 32   D) 36
E) none of these

34. Multiply:
71
× 5

A) 350   B) 365
C) 375   D) 385
E) none of these

35. Divide:

7)714

A) 12   B) 102
C) 120   D) 122
E) none of these

In questions 36 through 40, find which one of the suggested answers appears in that question.

36. 8 T 3 P 5 4 X Y

37. X Q 4 R 8 Y 3 2

38. 3 5 X Q 4 Y R 8

39. Y 8 P U 7 6 4 X

40. 4 M R 6 Y 7 9 P

Suggested Answers
A = 7, 4, Y, X
B = 7, 8, P, R
C = 8, 3   Y, R
D = 3, 4, P, X
E = none of these

In questions 41 through 45, compare the three names or numbers, and mark the answer—
A if ALL THREE names or numbers are exactly ALIKE
B if only the FIRST and SECOND names or numbers are exactly ALIKE
C if only the FIRST and THIRD names or numbers are exactly ALIKE
D if only the SECOND and THIRD names or numbers are exactly ALIKE
E if ALL THREE names or numbers are DIFFERENT

41. William Parkherst	William Parkhurst	William Parkhurst
42. Alan Wyzandowsky	Alan Wyzandosky	Allan Wyzandowsky
43. Bente Larsen	Bente Larsen	Bente Larson
44. John Lesczyznski	John Lesczyznski	John Lesczyznski
45. 7396932	7369632	7369632

In questions 46 through 50, find the correct place for the name in the box.

50. | Sam's Auto |

{
A) →
  Sampson, Steven
B) →
  Samsel, Ozzie
C) →
  Samuel, Tomas
D) →
  Sanchez, Joe
E) →
}

46. | Sandberg, Kate |

{
A) →
  Sandefur, Harold
B) →
  Sanders, Marvine
C) →
  Sandor, Dominick
D) →
  Sands, Janice
E) →
}

Answers

51. Add:
    97
  + 82

A) 155 B) 169
C) 179 D) 197
E) none of these

52. Subtract:
    81
  − 14

A) 57 B) 67
C) 75 D) 77
E) none of these

47. | Orloff, Bradford Lee |

{
A) →
  Orlean, Glenna
B) →
  Orlowski, Floyd
C) →
  Orme, Gaylord
D) →
  Orr, Fred
E) →
}

53. Multiply:
    39
  × 3

A) 97 B) 99
C) 107 D) 117
E) none of these

54. Divide:

  3)159

A) 35 B) 53
C) 59 D) 63
E) none of these

55. Add:
    39
  + 74

A) 103 B) 105
C) 113 D) 115
E) none of these

In questions 56 through 60, find which one of the suggested answers appears in that question.

48. | Otis, Graphics |

{
A) →
  Otis, G.
B) →
  Otis, Lance N.
C) →
  Otis, T.
D) →
  Otis, Wm. L.
E) →
}

56. R 9 8 X 4 6 Q P

57. 4 3 Y 5 8 R U X

58. 2 5 8 P 4 U Y X

59. 3 8 6 X Y 5 R P

49. | Green, M.L. |

{
A) →
  Green, Jean
B) →
  Green, Krisy
C) →
  Green, M.
D) →
  Greene, Patricia
E) →
}

60. P 8 7 2 T U 6 R

Suggested
Answers

{
A = 6, 3, U, P
B = 8, 3, P, X
C = 6, 4, X, R
D = 8, 4, U, R
E = none of these
}

In questions 61 through 65, compare the three names or numbers, and mark the answer—
    A if ALL THREE names or numbers are exactly ALIKE
    B if only the FIRST and SECOND names or numbers are exactly ALIKE
    C if only the FIRST and THIRD names or numbers are exactly ALIKE
    D if only the SECOND and THIRD names or numbers are exactly ALIKE
    E if ALL THREE names or numbers are DIFFERENT

61. 8646808   8648608   8646808

62. 4583201   4583021   4538021

63. 6854238   6845238   6854238

64. 9324685   9324685   9324685

65. Marion L. Woodside   Marion L. Woodside   Marion L. Woodside

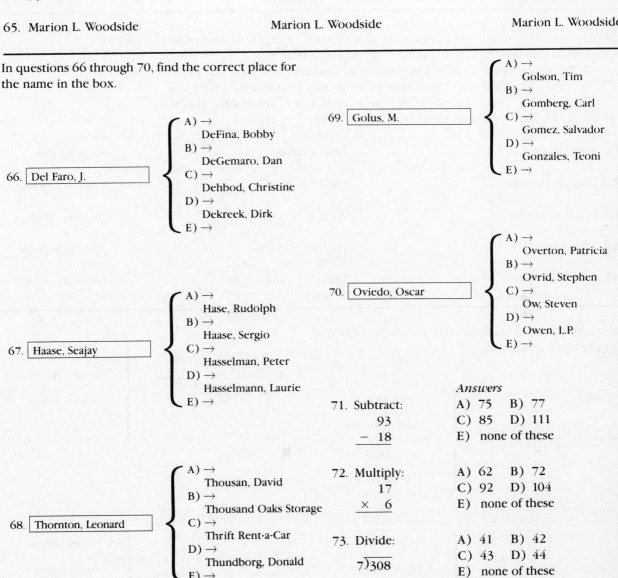

In questions 66 through 70, find the correct place for the name in the box.

66. Del Faro, J.
    A) →
        DeFina, Bobby
    B) →
        DeGemaro, Dan
    C) →
        Dehbod, Christine
    D) →
        Dekreek, Dirk
    E) →

67. Haase, Seajay
    A) →
        Hase, Rudolph
    B) →
        Haase, Sergio
    C) →
        Hasselman, Peter
    D) →
        Hasselmann, Laurie
    E) →

68. Thornton, Leonard
    A) →
        Thousan, David
    B) →
        Thousand Oaks Storage
    C) →
        Thrift Rent-a-Car
    D) →
        Thundborg, Donald
    E) →

69. Golus, M.
    A) →
        Golson, Tim
    B) →
        Gomberg, Carl
    C) →
        Gomez, Salvador
    D) →
        Gonzales, Teoni
    E) →

70. Oviedo, Oscar
    A) →
        Overton, Patricia
    B) →
        Ovrid, Stephen
    C) →
        Ow, Steven
    D) →
        Owen, L.P.
    E) →

Answers

71. Subtract: A) 75   B) 77
        93   C) 85   D) 111
      − 18   E) none of these

72. Multiply: A) 62   B) 72
        17   C) 92   D) 104
      × 6   E) none of these

73. Divide: A) 41   B) 42
                       C) 43   D) 44
    7)308   E) none of these

74. Add:
      29
    + 31

    A) 50   B) 60
    C) 70   D) 80
    E) none of these

75. Subtract:
      92
    − 37

    A) 55   B) 58
    C) 63   D) 63
    E) none of these

77. 2 3 M 7 6 X Y T

78. P 2 Q X 3 7 5 Y

79. X 2 3 9 P 8 Q Y

80. 9 R T P 3 2 7 X

In questions 76 through 80, find which one of the suggested answers appears in that question.

Suggested Answers
A = 5, 2, Y, P
B = 5, 3, T, X
C = 9, 3, Y, T
D = 9, 2, P, X
E = none of these

76. 7 3 M 5 T P 9 Y

In questions 81 through 85, compare the three names or numbers, and mark the answer—
    A if ALL THREE names or numbers are exactly ALIKE
    B if only the FIRST and SECOND names or numbers are exactly ALIKE
    C if only the FIRST and THIRD names or numbers are exactly ALIKE
    D if only the SECOND and THIRD names or numbers are exactly ALIKE
    E if ALL THREE names or numbers are DIFFERENT

81. Smiley Yarnell   Smiley Yarnel   Smily Yarnell

82. Lee P. Wangerrine   Lee P. Wangerrine   Lee P. Wangerine

83. Douglas Watkins   Douglas Watkins   Douglass Watkins

84. Tricia Connelley   Trishia Connelley   Trishia Connelly

85. Jeffrey Armantos   Jeffrey Armantos   Jeffrey Armontos

In questions 86 through 90, find the correct place for the name in the box.

86. Calloway, Larry
    A) →
    Callari, Peter
    B) →
    Callear, Clarence
    C) →
    Callis, Raymond
    D) →
    Callison, Jas. K.
    E) →

87. Pagan, Lester
    A) →
    Pagano, Rafael
    B) →
    Pagano, Samuel
    C) →
    Page, Denice
    D) →
    Pallazi, Shirley
    E) →

88. Snyder, Martin
    A) →
    Snider, Edwin
    B) →
    Snider, Marion
    C) →
    Snider, Robert
    D) →
    Snider, Wm. G.
    E) →

89. Smith, Jeffrey
    A) →
    Smith, Jefferey
    B) →
    Smith, Jeffrey A.
    C) →
    Smith, Jeffrey C.
    D) →
    Smith, Josephine
    E) →

90. Laitner, Phyllis

A) →
  Lakadner, Brian
B) →
  Lake, Donald
C) →
  Laker, Christene
D) →
  Lemon, Craig G.
E) →

Answers

91. Multiply: A) 268 B) 278
        72   C) 288 D) 308
      × 4   E) none of these

92. Divide: A) 47   B) 48
                 C) 49   D) 58
      8)376   E) none of these

93. Add: A) 78   B) 94
        91   C) 104 D) 114
      + 13   E) none of these

94. Subtract: A) 37   B) 47
        72   C) 57   D) 67
      − 15   E) none of these

95. Multiply: A) 355 B) 425
        51   C) 428 D) 435
      × 7   E) none of these

In questions 96 through 100, find which one of the suggested answers appears in that question.

96. U T 3 8 7 P 5 Q

97. 2 Q 8 5 7 P U T

98. 9 7 P 5 Q 3 R U

99. 7 9 Q T 5 P U 4

100. X 8 2 R P 4 7 T

Suggested Answers
A = 5, 8, P, R
B = 7, 8, P, Q
C = 5, 4, Q, T
D = 7, 4, T, R
E = none of these

In questions 101 through 105, compare the three names or numbers, and mark the answer—
A if ALL THREE names or numbers are exactly ALIKE
B if only the FIRST and SECOND names or numbers are exactly ALIKE
C if only the FIRST and THIRD names or numbers are exactly ALIKE
D if only the SECOND and THIRD names or numbers are exactly ALIKE
E if ALL THREE names or numbers are DIFFERENT

101. 5892542   5829542   5829542

102. 7483984   7483984   7483984

103. 3869457   3869457   3869547

104. 2749572   2794572   2749572

105. Maryjean Bremmeuth   Maryjean Bremmeuth   Maryjean Bremmueth

In questions 106 through 110, find the correct place for the name in the box.

106. La More, Leonard B.

A) →
  La Perche, Benny
B) →
  La Reina, Dora
C) →
  La Rossa, Michael
D) →
  Lacosta, Manuel
E) →

107. Townsend, Mary A.

A) →
  Townsend, Carole
B) →
  Townsend, Natalie
C) →
  Townsende, Claire
D) →
  Townsende, Tony
E) →

108. | Hunt, Randall G. |

- A) →
  Hunt, A. Raymond
- B) →
  Hunt, Rosalie
- C) →
  Hunt, Thomas
- D) →
  Hunt, Victoria
- E) →

109. | Bole, Stacey |

- A) →
  Bogush, Joann
- B) →
  Bolduc, Rick
- C) →
  Bolgna, Vincent
- D) →
  Bolin, Buford
- E) →

110. | Printmasters, Inc. |

- A) →
  Post Time Printing Co.
- B) →
  Print Able, Inc.
- C) →
  Quick Print
- D) →
  Randolph Printers, Inc.
- E) →

Answers

111. Divide:

6)384

A) 62 B) 64
C) 68 D) 72
E) none of these

112. Add:

29
+ 39

A) 58 B) 68
C) 78 D) 88
E) none of these

113. Subtract:

174
− 32

A) 140 B) 142
C) 144 D) 148
E) none of these

114. Multiply:

92
× 3

A) 267 B) 273
C) 276 D) 296
E) none of these

115. Divide:

7)707

A) 11 B) 110
C) 111 D) 112
E) none of these

In questions 116 through 120, find which one of the suggested answers appears in that question.

116. 9 2 U M P 5 Y 8

117. T 6 Q 7 P 3 M 5

118. 9 P 7 T X M 3 5

119. 9 P 5 3 M 7 Q T

120. R 6 P Q M 8 7 5

Suggested Answers
- A = 5, 6, M, P
- B = 5, 9, P, T
- C = 6, 7, M, U
- D = 7, 9, U, T
- E = none of these

IF YOU FINISH BEFORE THE TIME IS UP, YOU MAY GO BACK AND CHECK YOUR ANSWERS.

ANSWER KEY FOR MODEL TEST 3

Alike or Different

1. C	21. A	41. D	61. C	81. E	101. D
2. E	22. D	42. E	62. E	82. B	102. A
3. E	23. E	43. B	63. C	83. B	103. B
4. B	24. D	44. A	64. A	84. E	104. C
5. D	25. B	45. D	65. A	85. B	105. B

Alphabetizing

6. C	26. E	46. A	66. E	86. E	106. A
7. B	27. B	47. B	67. A	87. A	107. B
8. E	28. C	48. B	68. A	88. E	108. B
9. A	29. B	49. D	69. B	89. B	109. C
10. A	30. E	50. B	70. B	90. A	110. C

Arithmetic

11. B	31. C	51. C	71. A	91. C	111. B
12. B	32. D	52. B	72. E	92. A	112. B
13. E	33. A	53. D	73. D	93. C	113. B
14. A	34. E	54. B	74. B	94. C	114. C
15. C	35. B	55. C	75. A	95. E	115. E

Letters and Numbers

16. A	36. D	56. C	76. C	96. B	116. E
17. B	37. C	57. D	77. E	97. B	117. A
18. E	38. C	58. E	78. A	98. E	118. B
19. D	39. A	59. B	79. D	99. C	119. B
20. A	40. E	60. E	80. D	100. D	120. A

ANALYSIS CHART FOR MODEL TEST 3

Now that you've corrected your exam, use the following chart to carefully analyze your results and spot your strengths and weaknesses. This analysis should help you focus your study and review efforts.

Section	Total Number of Questions	Number Correct	Number Incorrect	Number Unanswered*
Alike or Different	30			
Alphabetizing	30			
Arithmetic	30			
Letters and Numbers	30			
TOTAL	120			

*Since there is a small penalty for incorrect answers on the Clerical Abilities Test, you should not guess "blindly." Try to eliminate one or more of the choices before you take your educated guess.

ANSWER EXPLANATIONS FOR MODEL TEST 3

1. (C) Willie MacCovey | Willie McCovey | Willie MacCovey
2. (E) Antony Frennsdorff | Anthony Frennsdorf | Anthony Frennsdorff
3. (E) Frederick Kurt | Fredrick Kurt | Frederic Kurt
4. (B) Terrence Garrity | Terrence Garrity | Terrence Garrity
5. (D) 4930752 | 4930572 | 4930572
6. (C) Korda, Jerome | *Kordakis, Peter* | Kordes, Dennis
7. (B) Thompson, Johnny | *Thompson, L.W.* | Thompson, Larry
8. (E) Wang, Peter | *Wang, Wm.*
9. (A) *Dana Computer* | Dana Distributors
10. (A) *Taylor, Glenn* | Taylor, Glenn R.
11. (B) 192
12. (B) 31
13. (E) Correct answer: 121.
14. (A) 15
15. (C) 104
16. (A) Z U 5 4 P 8 T M
17. (B) M Z U 2 Y 6 8 R
18. (E) 6 8 7 Y 4 X T M
19. (D) Y 7 2 5 T 9 X U
20. (A) 9 5 8 U Z Q T M
21. (A) 7428961 | 7428961
22. (D) 2796231 | 2769231
23. (E) Jackie M. Firstbee | Jackie N. Firstbee | Jackey M. Firsbee
24. (D) Matthew Highland | Mathew Highland | Mathew Highland
25. (B) Guenther Steffens | Guenther Steffens | Gunther Steffens
26. (E) Swainvick, Patsy | *Svatlou, Ron*
27. (B) Miller, Gary | *Miller, Gayle* | Miller, Greg
28. (C) Sanders, Michael J. | *Sanders, Michael Jas.* | Sanders, Nicholas

29. (B) Basket World | *Baskin, Mark* | Baslow, Brigitte
30. (E) Greenlee, Kitty | *Grella, Cbrista*
31. (C) 92
32. (D) 103
33. (A) 26
34. (E) Correct answer: 355.
35. (B) 102
36. (D) 8 T 3 P 5 4 X Y
37. (C) X Q 4 R 8 Y 3 2
38. (C) 3 5 X Q 4 Y R 8
39. (A) Y 8 P U 7 6 4 X
40. (E) 4 M R 6 Y 7 9 P
41. (D) William Parkherst | William Parkhurst | William Parkhurst
42. (E) Alan Wyzandosky | Alan Wyzandowsky | Allan Wyzandowsky
43. (B) Bente Larsen | Bente Larsen | Bente Larson
44. (A) John Lesczyznski | John Lesczyznski | John Lesczyznski
45. (D) 7396932 | 7396932 | 7369632
46. (A) *Sandberg, Kate* | Sandefur, Harold
47. (B) Orlean, Glenna | *Orloff, Bradford Lee* | Orlowski, Floyd
48. (B) Otis, G | *Otis, Graphics* | Otis, T
49. (D) Green, M. | *Green, M.L.* | Greene, Patricia
50. (B) Sampson, Steven | *Sam's Auto* | Samsel, Ozzie
51. (C) 179
52. (B) 67
53. (D) 117
54. (B) 53
55. (C) 113
56. (C) R 9 8 X 4 6 Q P
57. (D) 4 3 Y 5 8 R U X
58. (E) 2 5 8 P 4 U Y X
59. (B) 3 8 6 X Y 5 R P
60. (E) P 8 7 2 T U 6 R

61. (C) 8646808   8648608   8646808
62. (E) 4583201   4583021   4583021
63. (C) 6854238   6845238   6854238
64. (A) 9324685   9324685   9324685
65. (A) Marion L. Woodside   Marion L. Woodside   Marion L. Woodside
66. (E) Dekreek, Dirk
     Del Faro, J.
67. (A) Haase, Seajay
     Hase, Rudolph
68. (A) Thornton, Leonard
     Thousan, David
69. (B) Golson, Tim
     Golus, M.
     Gomberg, Carl
70. (B) Overton, Patricia
     Oviedo, Oscar
     Ovrid, Stephen
71. (A) 75
72. (E) Correct answer: 102.
73. (D) 44
74. (B) 60
75. (A) 55
76. (C) 7 3 M 5 T P 9 Y
77. (E) 2 3 M 7 6 X Y T
78. (A) P 2 Q X 3 7 5 Y
79. (D) X 2 3 9 P 8 Q Y
80. (D) 9 R T P 3 2 7 X
81. (E) Smiley Yarnell   Smiley Yarnel   Smily Yarnell
82. (B) Lee P. Wangerrine   Lee P. Wangerrine   Lee P. Wangerine
83. (B) Douglass Watkins   Douglas Watkins   Douglass Watkins
84. (E) Tricia Connelley   Trishia Connelley   Trishia Connelly
85. (B) Jeffrey Armantos   Jeffrey Armantos   Jeffrey Armontos
86. (E) Callison, Jas. K.
     Callouvay, Larry
87. (A) Pagan, Lester
     Pagano, Rafael
88. (E) Snider, Wm. G.
     Snyder, Martin
89. (B) Smith, Jefferey
     Smith, Jeffrey
     Smith, Jeffrey A.

90. (A) Laitner, Phyllis
     Lakadner, Brian
91. (C) 288
92. (A) 47
93. (C) 104
94. (C) 57
95. (E) Correct answer: 357.
96. (B) U T 3 8 7 P 5 Q
97. (B) 2 Q 8 5 7 P U T
98. (E) 9 7 P 5 Q 3 R U
99. (C) 7 9 Q T 5 P U 4
100. (D) X 8 2 R P 4 7 T
101. (D) 5892542   5829542
102. (A) 7483984   7483984
103. (B) 3869457   3869547
104. (C) 2749572   2749572
105. (B) Maryjean Bremmeuth Maryjean Bremmeuth Maryjean Bremmeuth
106. (A) La More, Leonard B.
     La Perche, Benny
107. (B) Townsend, Carole
     Townsend, Mary A.
     Townsend, Natalie
108. (B) Hunt, A. Raymond
     Hunt, Randall G.
     Hunt, Rosalie
109. (C) Bolduc, Rick
     Bole, Stacey
     Bolgna, Vincent
110. (C) Print Able, Inc.
     Printmasters, Inc.
     Quick Print
111. (B) 64
112. (B) 68
113. (B) 142
114. (C) 276
115. (E) Correct answer: 101.
116. (E) 9 2 U M P 5 Y 8
117. (A) T 6 Q 7 P 3 M 5
118. (B) 9 P 7 T X M 3 5
119. (B) 9 P 5 3 M 7 Q T
120. (A) R 6 P Q M 8 7 5

ANSWER SHEET

SIGNATURE: _____
(Please Sign)

EXAMINATION TITLE: _____

PLACE OF EXAMINATION: _____

TODAY'S DATE: _____

City _____   State _____

SAMPLE Ⓐ ● Ⓒ Ⓓ Ⓔ

DIRECTIONS FOR MARKING ANSWER SHEET

Use only a **No. 2 (or softer) lead pencil.** Darken completely the circle corresponding to your answer. You **must** keep your mark within the circle. Stray marks may be counted as errors. Erase **completely** all marks except your answer.

SAMPLE NAME GRID

LAST NAME

M C C A B E

M.I. — A

F.I. — C

1. In the boxes below, **PRINT** your name. Print only as many letters as will fit within the areas for the last name, first initial (F.I.), and middle initial (M.I.) Below each box, darken the circle containing the same letter. SEE SAMPLE NAME GRID

LAST NAME   F.I.   M.I.

2. In the boxes below, enter your 9-digit Social Security Number. Below each box, darken the circle in each column corresponding to the number you have entered.

SOCIAL SECURITY NUMBER

3.
OCCUPATIONAL
GROUP NUMBER

SECTION 1

PART

TEST SERIES

TEST NUMBER

Make no marks or entries in the columns to the right until you receive instructions from the administrator.

1 ABCDE	11 ABCDE	31 ABCDE	51 ABCDE	71 ABCDE	91 ABCDE	111 ABCDE
2 ABCDE	12 ABCDE	32 ABCDE	52 ABCDE	72 ABCDE	92 ABCDE	112 ABCDE
3 ABCDE	13 ABCDE	33 ABCDE	53 ABCDE	73 ABCDE	93 ABCDE	113 ABCDE
4 ABCDE	14 ABCDE	34 ABCDE	54 ABCDE	74 ABCDE	94 ABCDE	114 ABCDE
5 ABCDE	15 ABCDE	35 ABCDE	55 ABCDE	75 ABCDE	95 ABCDE	115 ABCDE
6 ABCDE	16 ABCDE	36 ABCDE	56 ABCDE	76 ABCDE	96 ABCDE	116 ABCDE
7 ABCDE	17 ABCDE	37 ABCDE	57 ABCDE	77 ABCDE	97 ABCDE	117 ABCDE
8 ABCDE	18 ABCDE	38 ABCDE	58 ABCDE	78 ABCDE	98 ABCDE	118 ABCDE
9 ABCDE	19 ABCDE	39 ABCDE	59 ABCDE	79 ABCDE	99 ABCDE	119 ABCDE
10 ABCDE	20 ABCDE	40 ABCDE	60 ABCDE	80 ABCDE	100 ABCDE	120 ABCDE
	21 ABCDE	41 ABCDE	61 ABCDE	81 ABCDE	101 ABCDE	121 ABCDE
	22 ABCDE	42 ABCDE	62 ABCDE	82 ABCDE	102 ABCDE	122 ABCDE
	23 ABCDE	43 ABCDE	63 ABCDE	83 ABCDE	103 ABCDE	123 ABCDE
	24 ABCDE	44 ABCDE	64 ABCDE	84 ABCDE	104 ABCDE	124 ABCDE
	25 ABCDE	45 ABCDE	65 ABCDE	85 ABCDE	105 ABCDE	125 ABCDE
	26 ABCDE	46 ABCDE	66 ABCDE	86 ABCDE	106 ABCDE	126 ABCDE
	27 ABCDE	47 ABCDE	67 ABCDE	87 ABCDE	107 ABCDE	127 ABCDE
	28 ABCDE	48 ABCDE	68 ABCDE	88 ABCDE	108 ABCDE	128 ABCDE
	29 ABCDE	49 ABCDE	69 ABCDE	89 ABCDE	109 ABCDE	129 ABCDE
	30 ABCDE	50 ABCDE	70 ABCDE	90 ABCDE	110 ABCDE	130 ABCDE

MODEL TEST 4

Time allotted—15 minutes

Directions

Each question has five suggested answers. Decide which one is the best answer. Find the question number on the Answer Sheet. Show your answer to the question by darkening completely the space corresponding to the letter of your answer. Keep your mark within the space. If you have to erase a mark, be sure to erase it completely. Mark only one answer for each question.

In questions 1 through 5, compare the three names or numbers, and mark the answer—
A if ALL THREE names or numbers are exactly ALIKE
B if only the FIRST and SECOND names or numbers are exactly ALIKE
C if only the FIRST and THIRD names or numbers are exactly ALIKE
D if only the SECOND and THIRD names or numbers are exactly ALIKE
E if ALL THREE names or numbers are DIFFERENT

1.	3827192	3827192	3827192
2.	4982521	4982521	4892521
3.	2819034	2891034	2189034
4.	Forrester Halmonds	Forester Halmonds	Forrester Hamlonds
5.	Suzanna Freemon	Suzanna Freeman	Suzanna Freemon

In questions 6 through 10, find the correct place for the name in the box.

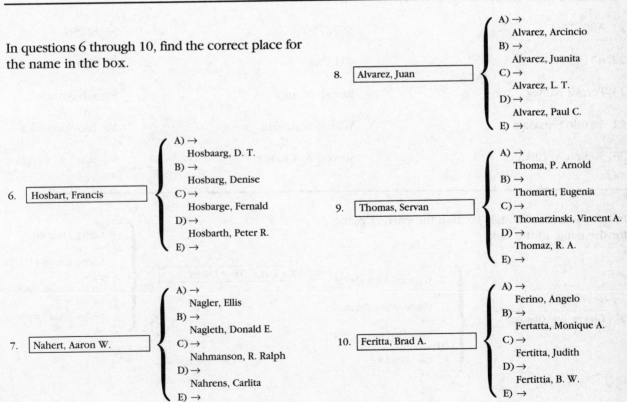

6. | Hosbart, Francis |
A) →
  Hosbaarg, D. T.
B) →
  Hosbarg, Denise
C) →
  Hosbarge, Fernald
D) →
  Hosbarth, Peter R.
E) →

7. | Nahert, Aaron W. |
A) →
  Nagler, Ellis
B) →
  Nagleth, Donald E.
C) →
  Nahmanson, R. Ralph
D) →
  Nahrens, Carlita
E) →

8. | Alvarez, Juan |
A) →
  Alvarez, Arcincio
B) →
  Alvarez, Juanita
C) →
  Alvarez, L. T.
D) →
  Alvarez, Paul C.
E) →

9. | Thomas, Servan |
A) →
  Thoma, P. Arnold
B) →
  Thomarti, Eugenia
C) →
  Thomarzinski, Vincent A.
D) →
  Thomaz, R. A.
E) →

10. | Feritta, Brad A. |
A) →
  Ferino, Angelo
B) →
  Fertatta, Monique A.
C) →
  Fertitta, Judith
D) →
  Fertittia, B. W.
E) →

11. Add:

    38
   + 17

Answers

A) 53 B) 55
C) 57 D) 63
E) none of these

12. Subtract:

    91
   − 19

A) 72 B) 74
C) 76 D) 78
E) none of these

13. Multiply:

    14
   × 9

A) 112 B) 116
C) 122 D) 126
E) none of these

14. Divide:

  4)184

A) 24 B) 28
C) 42 D) 44
E) none of these

15. Add:

    53
   + 17

A) 36 B) 60
C) 70 D) 80
E) none of these

In questions 16 through 20, find which one of the suggested answers appears in that question.

16. 9 D Q 2 U B 6 8

17. K 3 9 B A 7 X 2

18. H F 2 8 C 5 V 4

19. P Z 1 A R 3 8 W

20. Y S 6 D L 7 X V

Suggested Answers $\begin{cases} A = 6, 7, V, Y \\ B = 2, 9, A, X \\ C = 2, 6, B, Q \\ D = 2, 8, F, V \\ E = \text{none of these} \end{cases}$

In questions 21 through 25, compare the three names or numbers, and mark the answer—
  A if ALL THREE names or numbers are exactly ALIKE
  B if only the FIRST and SECOND names or numbers are exactly ALIKE
  C if only the FIRST and THIRD names or numbers are exactly ALIKE
  D if only the SECOND and THIRD names or numbers are exactly ALIKE
  E If ALL THREE names or numbers are DIFFERENT

21. 3892756	3892756	3892756
22. 4715309	4713509	4715309
23. Ferash Nunez	Faresh Nunez	Faresh Nunez
24. Yoshio Sunasata	Yoshio Sunasata	Yoshio Sunasaka
25. Steven A. Chafee	Steven A. Chafee	Stephen A. Chaffee

In questions 26 through 30, find the correct place for the name in the box.

26. Gimon, Eric Gustave

$\begin{cases} A) \rightarrow \\ \quad \text{Gilmore, John Owen} \\ B) \rightarrow \\ \quad \text{Gilmour, Joan Marie} \\ C) \rightarrow \\ \quad \text{Gim, Soyoun} \\ D) \rightarrow \\ \quad \text{Gin, Brian R.} \\ E) \rightarrow \end{cases}$

27. Sacks, David Oliver

$\begin{cases} A) \rightarrow \\ \quad \text{Sachs, Elizabeth} \\ B) \rightarrow \\ \quad \text{Sachs, Jennifer L.} \\ C) \rightarrow \\ \quad \text{Sachs, Steven Mark} \\ D) \rightarrow \\ \quad \text{Sachs, Todd Stephen} \\ E) \rightarrow \end{cases}$

28. De Koker, Rudi

- A) →
  De Merlier, Anne-Marie
- B) →
  Demko, Zachary P.
- C) →
  De Ney, Laura Leigh
- D) →
  Dennig, Paul August
- E) →

29. O'Shei, Cynthia

- A) →
  Osgood, Elisabeth
- B) →
  Osgood, Richard Magee III
- C) →
  O'Shaughnessy, Michael
- D) →
  Oshidari, Allyson
- E) →

30. Wong, Hijoung

- A) →
  Wolverton, M. John
- B) →
  Won, Dana Chung
- C) →
  Wong, Andrea
- D) →
  Wong, Christopher Jurn
- E) →

Answers

31. Subtract:
    92
    − 16

    A) 62   B) 66
    C) 72   D) 76
    E) none of these

32. Multiply:
    43
    × 6

    A) 238 B) 248
    C) 258 D) 268
    E) none of these

33. Divide

   6)372

    A) 56 B) 58
    C) 64 D) 66
    E) none of these

34. Add:
    19
    + 28

    A) 37 B) 39
    C) 45 D) 47
    E) none of these

35. Subtract:
    26
    − 17

    A) 7 B) 9
    C) 11 D) 19
    E) none of these

In questions 36 through 40, find which one of the suggested answers appears in that question.

36. P W 8 2 6 N Q 3

37. B S 9 T H 5 1 R

38. C F 7 T 3 J 8 Z

39. Z D 4 Y 7 W 2 S

40. Q Y 5 R W 4 9 K

Suggested Answers

- A = 3, 7, C, J
- B = 2, 3, N, P
- C = 4, 5, R, Y
- D = 2, 4, W, Y
- E = none of these

In questions 41 through 45, compare the three names or numbers, and mark the answer—

A if ALL THREE names or numbers are exactly ALIKE
B if only the FIRST and SECOND names or numbers are exactly ALIKE
C if only the FIRST and THIRD names or numbers are exactly ALIKE
D if only the SECOND and THIRD names or numbers are exactly ALIKE
E if ALL THREE names or numbers are DIFFERENT

41. 3728102	3278102	3728102
42. 2841739	2847139	2874139
43. Lauren Handleman	Lauren Handleman	Lauren Handelman
44. Ingrid Sappoldt	Ingrid Sappoldt	Ingrid Sappoldt
45. Porter Ermanovick	Porter Ermanovich	Porter Ermanovick

In questions 46 through 50, find the correct place for the name in the box.

46. Delagi, Bruce

A)→
  Dekker, George G.
B)→
  DeLaCruz, Margaret
C)→
  De La Grandville, Oliver
D)→
  Dellwo, Pablo
E)→

47. Kurtzman, Angela

A)→
  Kurz, Roland
B)→
  Kusa, Kyle A.
C)→
  Kutzscher, Brenda
D)→
  Kwong, Joanne W.
E)→

48. Camdipan, Lorie

A)→
  Camberos, Jose A.
B)→
  Cameros, Brian Leigh
C)→
  Campbell, Celest
D)→
  Campwala, David
E)→

49. Unehara, Barbara

A)→
  Unechi, Taro
B)→
  Uneda, Lance G.
C)→
  Uppal, Sanjay
D)→
  Urizar, Lorenzo Colin
E)→

50. Mrizek, Lori

A)→
  Moslet, Tambra
B)→
  Moss, Carol A.
C)→
  Moynihan, Robert
D)→
  Mueller, Gerhard
E)→

Answers

51. Multiply:
    34
    × 7

A) 218 B) 228
C) 238 D) 248
E) none of these

52. Divide:

    5)365

A) 65 B) 75
C) 85 D) 95
E) none of these

53. Add:
    56
    + 18

A) 64 B) 72
C) 74 D) 82
E) none of these

54. Subtract:
    62
    − 26

A) 44 B) 46
C) 48 D) 88
E) none of these

55. Multiply:
    32
    × 4

A) 128 B) 132
C) 138 D) 144
E) none of these

In questions 56 through 60, find which one of the suggested answers appears in that question.

56. 7 M K 3 W P 5 4

57. Y V 4 6 X 2 M 3

58. 8 T G 2 S D 7 A

59. 7 C S U 5 W T 4

60. Y F 5 R C 9 Q 2

Suggested Answers

A = 4, 5, C, T
B = 2, 3, M, V
C = 2, 5, C, Y
D = 3, 5, K, P
E = none of these

In questions 61 through 65, compare the three names or numbers, and mark the answer—
  A if ALL THREE names or numbers are exactly ALIKE
  B if only the FIRST and SECOND names or numbers are exactly ALIKE
  C if only the FIRST and THIRD names or numbers are exactly ALIKE
  D if only the SECOND and THIRD names or numbers are exactly ALIKE
  E if ALL THREE names or numbers are DIFFERENT

61. 4985639   4985369   4985369

62. 3692415   3692415   3692415

63. Jijentra Cheleen   Jijentra Cheleen   Jijentra Chileen

64. Patricia Mackinnon   Patricia MacKinnan   Patrick MacKinnan

65. Hongbin Issac   Hongbin Isaac   Hongbin Isaac

In questions 66 through 70, find the correct place for the name in the box.

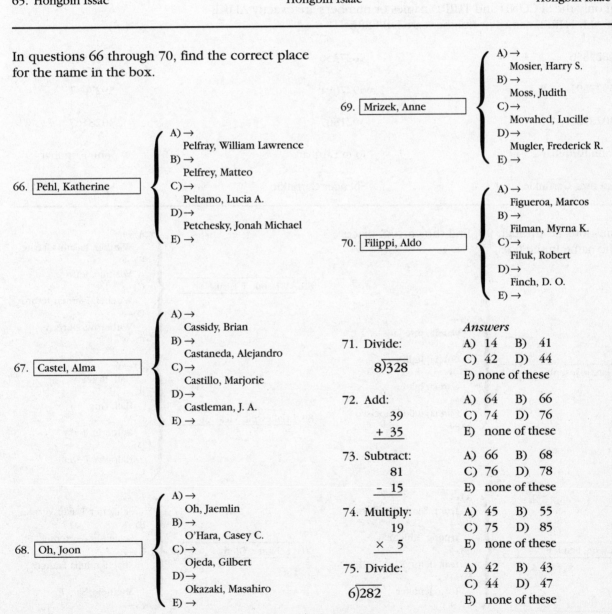

66. Pehl, Katherine
  A) →
    Pelfray, William Lawrence
  B) →
    Pelfrey, Matteo
  C) →
    Peltamo, Lucia A.
  D) →
    Petchesky, Jonah Michael
  E) →

67. Castel, Alma
  A) →
    Cassidy, Brian
  B) →
    Castaneda, Alejandro
  C) →
    Castillo, Marjorie
  D) →
    Castleman, J. A.
  E) →

68. Oh, Joon
  A) →
    Oh, Jaemlin
  B) →
    O'Hara, Casey C.
  C) →
    Ojeda, Gilbert
  D) →
    Okazaki, Masahiro
  E) →

69. Mrizek, Anne
  A) →
    Mosier, Harry S.
  B) →
    Moss, Judith
  C) →
    Movahed, Lucille
  D) →
    Mugler, Frederick R.
  E) →

70. Filippi, Aldo
  A) →
    Figueroa, Marcos
  B) →
    Filman, Myrna K.
  C) →
    Filuk, Robert
  D) →
    Finch, D. O.
  E) →

Answers

71. Divide:
    8)328
    A) 14   B) 41
    C) 42   D) 44
    E) none of these

72. Add:
      39
    + 35
    A) 64   B) 66
    C) 74   D) 76
    E) none of these

73. Subtract:
      81
    - 15
    A) 66   B) 68
    C) 76   D) 78
    E) none of these

74. Multiply:
      19
    × 5
    A) 45   B) 55
    C) 75   D) 85
    E) none of these

75. Divide:
    6)282
    A) 42   B) 43
    C) 44   D) 47
    E) none of these

In questions 76 through 80, find which one of the suggested answers appears in that question.

79. 4 T P 9 E C 6 U

80. R G 3 6 V T 4 X

76. N G 4 8 5 A W 7

77. 8 X 4 7 9 K Y C

78. F V 2 6 H P 4 A

Suggested
Answers
$\begin{cases} A = 2, & 4, & A, & H \\ B = 3, & 4, & V, & X \\ C = 7, & 8, & C, & Y, \\ D = 4, & 6, & C, & P \\ E = \text{none of these} \end{cases}$

In questions 81 through 85, compare the three names or numbers, and mark the answer—
A if ALL THREE names or numbers are exactly ALIKE
B if only the FIRST and SECOND names or numbers are exactly ALIKE
C if only the FIRST and THIRD names or numbers are exactly ALIKE
D if only the SECOND and THIRD names or numbers are exactly ALIKE
E if ALL THREE names or numbers are DIFFERENT

81. 9827356	9827356	9827536
82. 5927691	5927691	5927691
83. 3028167	3021867	3028167
84. John Farquhar	John Farqhar	John Farguhar
85. Spenser Garfinkle	Spencer Garfinkle	Spencer Garfinkle

In questions 86 through 90, find the correct place for the name in the box.

88. | Wissink, J. Ulrike |
$\begin{cases} A) \rightarrow \\ \quad \text{Winther, Rasmus Rayne} \\ B) \rightarrow \\ \quad \text{Wishnie, Jeffrey} \\ C) \rightarrow \\ \quad \text{Witchel, Emmett Jethro} \\ D) \rightarrow \\ \quad \text{Witherow, Doris A.} \\ E) \rightarrow \end{cases}$

86. | Garcia, Joseph |
$\begin{cases} A) \rightarrow \\ \quad \text{Garcia, Jose Luis} \\ B) \rightarrow \\ \quad \text{Garcia, Judith} \\ C) \rightarrow \\ \quad \text{Garcia, Julio} \\ D) \rightarrow \\ \quad \text{Garcia, Julio Francisco} \\ E) \rightarrow \end{cases}$

89. | Hallewell, Vicki |
$\begin{cases} A) \rightarrow \\ \quad \text{Hall, Bruce W.} \\ B) \rightarrow \\ \quad \text{Hall, Guy} \\ C) \rightarrow \\ \quad \text{Halperin, Jerry} \\ D) \rightarrow \\ \quad \text{Halpern, J. Dee} \\ E) \rightarrow \end{cases}$

87. | Tseng, Frank F. |
$\begin{cases} A) \rightarrow \\ \quad \text{Truitt, Sarah Taliaferro} \\ B) \rightarrow \\ \quad \text{Truong, Khiem Si} \\ C) \rightarrow \\ \quad \text{Tsai, Bi-Ru} \\ D) \rightarrow \\ \quad \text{Tsao, Jennifer} \\ E) \rightarrow \end{cases}$

90. | Schaffer, Glen |
$\begin{cases} A) \rightarrow \\ \quad \text{Schaeffer, David Vernon} \\ B) \rightarrow \\ \quad \text{Schaeffer, Portemus} \\ C) \rightarrow \\ \quad \text{Shaeffer, Julia Frances} \\ D) \rightarrow \\ \quad \text{Sheffield, Sara E.} \\ E) \rightarrow \end{cases}$

		Answers
91. Add:		A) 94 B) 102
	83	C) 104 D) 112
	+ 19	E) none of these

92. Subtract:		A) 9 B) 11
	48	C) 17 D) 19
	- 29	E) none of these

93. Multiply:		A) 88 B) 98
	27	C) 108 D) 118
	× 4	E) none of these

94. Divide:	A) 13 B) 103
	C) 113 D) 130
3)450	E) none of these

95. Add:		A) 36 B) 38
	26	C) 46 D) 48
	+ 18	E) none of these

In questions 96 through 100, find which one of the suggested answers appears in that question.

96. 8 G P 9 S T 3 6

97. F Y 7 2 R Q 4 3

98. 6 D A V 4 9 K F

99. P M 6 3 X F 9 W

100. E W 9 C V 4 U 8

Suggested Answers
A = 3, 9, F, M
B = 2, 3, Q, Y
C = 6, 9, F, V
D = 8, 9, C, U
E = none of these

In questions 101 through 105, compare the three names or numbers, and mark the answer—
  A if ALL THREE names or numbers are exactly ALIKE
  B if only the FIRST and SECOND names or numbers are exactly ALIKE
  C if only the FIRST and THIRD names or numbers are exactly ALIKE
  D if only the SECOND and THIRD names or numbers are exactly ALIKE
  E if ALL THREE names or numbers are DIFFERENT

101.	9423746	9423746	9423746
102.	3832615	3832165	3836215
103.	David M. Saraniti	David W. Saraniti	David M. Saraniti
104.	Larius Thornburg	Larius Thornburg	Larius Thornberg
105.	Hillary Beth Price	Hilary Beth Price	Hilary Beth Price

In questions 106 through 110, find the correct place for the name in the box.

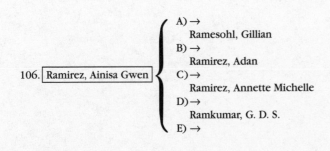

106. Ramirez, Ainisa Gwen
A) →
  Ramesohl, Gillian
B) →
  Ramirez, Adan
C) →
  Ramirez, Annette Michelle
D) →
  Ramkumar, G. D. S.
E) →

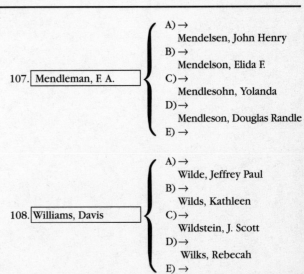

107. Mendleman, F. A.
A) →
  Mendelsen, John Henry
B) →
  Mendelson, Elida F.
C) →
  Mendlesohn, Yolanda
D) →
  Mendleson, Douglas Randle
E) →

108. Williams, Davis
A) →
  Wilde, Jeffrey Paul
B) →
  Wilds, Kathleen
C) →
  Wildstein, J. Scott
D) →
  Wilks, Rebecah
E) →

109. Fierstein, Katy

A) →
Fiore, Rozanne Linda
B) →
Fiorentino, Franklin
C) →
Firehammer, Antoine
D) →
Fish, Daniel Edmond
E) →

110. Shim, Brian

A) →
Shen, Raymond Tei-Lein
B) →
Shen, Ying
C) →
Shi, Carol Rachel
D) →
Shiau, Danny Ten-Yen
E) →

Answers

111. Subtract:
283
– 95

A) 88   B) 98
C) 108 D) 188
E) none of these

112. Multiply:
17
× 6

A) 72   B) 82
C) 92   D) 102
E) none of these

113. Divide:
3)288

A) 87   B) 91
C) 96   D) 99
E) none of these

114. Add:
87
+ 36

A) 111 B) 113
C) 121 D) 123
E) none of these

115. Subtract:
92
– 37

A) 35   B) 45
C) 55   D) 65
E) none of these

In questions 116 through 120, find which one of the suggested answers appears in that question.

116. R E 8 4 7 C V 6

117. 8 G K 4 R 2 3 X

118. 4 P Q 6 N Z W 8

119. D H 7 3 B 6 2 R

120. 6 T P 2 X M 4 G

Suggested Answers

A = 6, 8, W, Z
B = 6, 8, E, V
C = 4, 6, M, X
D = 4, 8, G, X
E = none of these

IF YOU FINISH BEFORE TIME IS UP, YOU MAY GO BACK AND CHECK YOUR ANSWERS.

ANSWER KEY FOR MODEL TEST 4

Alike or Different

1. A	21. A	41. C	61. D	81. B	101. A
2. B	22. C	42. E	62. A	82. A	102. E
3. E	23. D	43. B	63. B	83. C	103. C
4. E	24. B	44. A	64. E	84. E	104. B
5. C	25. B	45. C	65. D	85. D	105. D

Alphabetizing

6. D	26. D	46. C	66. A	86. B	106. C
7. C	27. E	47. A	67. C	87. E	107. C
8. B	28. A	48. B	68. B	88. C	108. E
9. D	29. D	49. C	69. D	89. C	109. A
10. B	30. E	50. D	70. B	90. C	110. E

Arithmetic

11. B	31. C	51. C	71. C	91. B	111. D
12. A	32. C	52. E	72. C	92. D	112. D
13. D	33. E	53. C	73. A	93. C	113. E
14. E	34. D	54. E	74. E	94. E	114. D
15. C	35. B	55. A	75. D	95. E	115. C

Letters and Numbers

16. C	36. B	56. D	76. E	96. E	116. B
17. B	37. E	57. B	77. C	97. B	117. D
18. D	38. A	58. E	78. A	98. C	118. A
19. E	39. D	59. A	79. D	99. A	119. E
20. A	40. C	60. C	80. B	100. D	120. C

ANALYSIS CHART FOR MODEL TEST 4

Now that you've corrected your exam, use the following chart to carefully analyze your results and spot your strengths and weaknesses. This analysis should help you focus your study and review efforts.

Section	Total Number of Questions	Number Correct	Number Incorrect	Number Unanswered*
Alike or Different	30			
Alphabetizing	30			
Arithmetic	30			
Letters and Numbers	30			
TOTAL	120			

*Since there is a small penalty for incorrect answers on the Clerical Abilities Test, you should not guess "blindly." Try to eliminate one or more of the choices before you take your educated guess.

ANSWER EXPLANATIONS FOR MODEL TEST 4

1. (A) 3827192   3827192   3827192
2. (B) 4982521   4982521   4892521
3. (E) 2819034   2891034   2189034
4. (E) Forrester Halmonds   Forrester Halmonds   Forrester Halmonds
5. (C) Suzanna Freemon   Suzanna Freeman   Suzanna Freemon

In questions 6 through 10, find the correct place for the name in the box.

6. (D) Hosbarge, Fernald   Hosbarth, Peter R.   Hosbart, Francis
7. (C) Nagleth, Donald E.   Nahmanson, R. Ralph   Nahert, Aaron W.
8. (B) Alvarez, Arcincio   Alvarez, Juanita   Alvarez, Juan
9. (D) Thomarzinski, Vincent A.   Thomaz, R. A.   Thomas, Servan
10. (B) Ferino, Angelo   Fertatta, Monique A.   Feritta, Brad
11. (B)
12. (A)
13. (D)
14. (E) Correct answer: 46
15. (C)
16. (C) 9 D Q 2 U B 6 8
17. (B) K 3 9 B A 7 X 2
18. (D) H E 2 8 C 5 Y 4
19. (E) P Z 1 A R 3 8 W
20. (A) Y S 6 D L Z X Y
21. (A) 3892756   3892756   3892756
22. (C) 4715309   4713509   4715309
23. (D) Ferash Nunez   Faresh Nunez   Faresh Nunez
24. (B) Yoshio Sunasata   Yoshio Sunasata   Yoshio Sunasaka
25. (B) Steven A. Chafee   Steven A. Chafee   Stephen A. Chaffee
26. (D) Gim, Soyoun   Gimon, Eric Gustave   Gin, Brian
27. (E) Sachs, Todd Stephen   Sacks, David Oliver
28. (A) De Koker, Rudi   De Merlier, Anne-Marie
29. (D) O'Shaughnessy, Michael   O'Shei, Cynthia   Oshidari, Allyson
30. (E) Wong, Christopher Jum   Wong, Hijourn
31. (C)
32. (C)
33. (E) Correct answer: 62
34. (D)
35. (B)

36. (B) P W 8 2 6 N Q 3
37. (E) B S 9 T H 5 1 R
38. (A) C F Z T 3 I 8 Z
39. (D) Z D 4 Y 7 W 2 s
40. (C) Q Y 5 R W 4 9 K
41. (C) 3728102   3278102   3728102
42. (E) 2847139   2847139   2874139
43. (B) Lauren Handleman   Lauren Handleman   Lauren Handelman
44. (A) Ingrid Sappoldt   Ingrid Sappoldt   Ingrid Sappoldt
45. (C) Porter Ermanovich   Porter Ermanovich   Porter Ermanovick
46. (C) DelaCruz, Margaret   De La Grandville, Oliver
47. (A) Kurtzman, Angela   Kurtzman, Angela   Kurz, Roland
48. (B) Camberos, Jose A.   Camdipan, Lorie   Cameros, Brian Leigh
49. (C) Uneda, Lance G.   Unehara, Barbara   Uppal, Sanjay
50. (D) Moynihan, Robert   Mrizek, Lori   Mueller, Gerhard
51. (B)
52. (E) Correct answer: 73
53. (C)
54. (E) Correct answer: 36
55. (A)
56. (D) 7 M K 3 W P 5 4
57. (B) Y V 4 6 X 2 M 3
58. (E) 8 T G 2 S D 7 A
59. (A) 7 C S U 5 W T 4
60. (C) Y F 5 R C 9 Q 2
61. (D) 4985639   4985369   4985369
62. (A) 3692415   3692415   3692415
63. (B) Jijentra Cheleen   Jijentra Cheleen   Jijentra Chileen
64. (E) Patricia MacKinnon   Patricia MacKinnan   Patrick MacKinnan
65. (D) Hongbin Issac   Hongbin Isaac   Hongbin Isaac
66. (A) Pehl, Katherine   Pelfray, William Lawrence
67. (C) Castaneda, Alejandro   Castel, Alma   Castillo, Marjorie
68. (B) Oh, Jaemlin   Oh, Joon   O'Hara, Casey C.
69. (D) Movahed, Lucille   Mrizek, Anne   Mugler, Frederick R.
70. (B) Figueroa, Marcos   Filippi, Aldo   Filman, Myrna K.
71. (C)
72. (C)
73. (A)
74. (E) Correct answer: 95
75. (D)

76. (E) N G 4 8 5 A W 7
77. (C) 8 X 4 Z 9 K Y C
78. (A) F V 2 6 H P 4 A
79. (D) 4 T P 9 E C 6 U
80. (B) R G 3 6 Y T 4 X
81. (B) 9827356 9827356 9827536
82. (A) 5927691 5927691 5927691
83. (C) 3028167 3021867 3028167
84. (E) John Farquhar — John Farquhar
85. (D) Spenser Garfinkle — Spencer Garfinkle
86. (B) Garcia, Jose Luis — Garcia, Joseph — Garcia, Judith
87. (E) Tsao, Jennifer — Tseng, Frank F.
88. (C) Wishnie, Jeffrey — Wissink, J. Ulrike — Witchel, Emmett Jethro
89. (C) Hall, Guy — Hallewell, Vicki — Halperin, Jerry
90. (C) Schaeffer, Portemus — Schaffer, Glen — Shaeffer, Julia Frances
91. (B)
92. (D)
93. (C)
94. (E) Correct answer: 150
95. (E) Correct answer: 44
96. (E) 8 G P 9 S T 3 6
97. (B) F Y 7 2 R Q 4 3
98. (C) 6 D A V 4 9 K E
99. (A) P M 6 3 X E 9 W
100. (D) E W 2 C V 4 U 8

101. (A) 9423746 — 9423746 — 9423746
102. (E) 3832615 — 3832165 — 3836215
103. (C) David M. Saraniti — David W. Saraniti — David M. Saraniti
104. (B) Larius Thornburg — Larius Thornburg — Larius Thornberg
105. (D) Hillary Beth Price — Hillary Beth Price — Hillary Beth Price
106. (C) Ramirez, Adan — Ramirez, Ainisa Gwen — Ramirez, Annette Michele
107. (C) Mendelson, Elida F. — Mendleman, F. A. — Mendlesohn, Yolanda
108. (E) Wilks, Rebecah — Williams, Davis
109. (A) Fierstein, Katy
110. (E) Shiau, Danny Ten-Yen — Shim, Brian
111. (D)
112. (D)
113. (E) Correct answer: 93
114. (D)
115. (C)
116. (B) R E 8 4 7 C Y 6
117. (D) 8 G K 4 R 2 3 X
118. (A) 4 P Q 6 N Z W 8
119. (E) D H 7 3 B 6 2 R
120. (C) 6 T P 2 X M 4 G

PART THREE

The Typing Test

CHAPTER 7

Introduction
A Diagnostic Test
Analysis

THE TYPING TEST—COPYING FROM PLAIN COPY

In this test, which is part of the Stenographer-Typist Examination, the applicant meets a single task, that of copying material exactly as it is presented. The candidate must demonstrate how rapidly he or she can do so and with what accuracy.

The typing test is used by agencies at the agencies' discretion. Agencies may use the tests developed by the Office of Personnel Management or a different test.

The Office of Personnel Management has recently included an automated version of the Typing Performance Test. This enables agencies to administer the Typing Performance Test using a computer keyboard instead of a typewriter. This version only tests typing skills, not word-processing skills.

HOW THE TEST IS GIVEN

In the usual typewriter examination procedure, each competitor is given a copy of the test and two sheets of typewriter paper. About 15 minutes is needed for the complete typing test.

Three minutes are allowed for reading the instructions on the face of the test and 3 minutes for the practice typing. The practice exercise consists of typing instructions as to spacing, capitalization, etc., and contains a warning that any erasures will be penalized. The practice typing helps make sure that the typewriter is functioning properly.

After the 3 minutes' practice typing, the competitors put fresh paper in their machines, and turn the test page over and read the test for 2 minutes. After the 2 minutes, they are instructed to start typing the test. Five minutes are allowed for the test proper.

HOW THE TEST IS RATED

The exercise must have been typed about once to meet the speed requirement of 40 words a minute. If this speed is not attained, the test is not scored for accuracy. As shown in Example A, which follows the Diagnostic Test, a test paper that contains 17 lines meets the minimum speed requirement. Applicants have been instructed to begin and end each line precisely as in the printed test copy. From Example A it can be quickly determined whether a typing test is to be rated for accuracy and, if so, the greatest number of errors permitted for the lines typed.

The next step is to compare the test paper with the printed test exercise and to mark and charge errors. The basic principles in charging typing errors are as follows:

Charge 1 for each—
  WORD or PUNCTUATION MARK incorrectly typed or in which there is an erasure. (An error in spacing which follows an incorrect word or punctuation mark is not further charged.)
  SERIES of consecutive words omitted, repeated, inserted, transposed, or erased. Charge for errors within such series, but the total charge cannot exceed the number of words.
  LINE or part of line typed over other material, typed with all capitals, or apparently typed with the fingers on the wrong keys.
  Change from the MARGIN where most lines begun by the applicant or from the PARAGRAPH INDENTION most frequently used by the applicant.

The typing score used in the official examination reflects both speed and accuracy, with accuracy weighted twice as heavily as speed. Other methods of rating typing often used in schools are based on gross words per minute or net words per minute (usually with not more than a fixed number of errors). Using Example B, teachers and applicants can calculate typing proficiency in terms of gross words per minute and errors, and can determine whether that proficiency meets the minimum standards of eligibility required in the regular Civil Service examination.

Example B, following the Diagnostic Test, gives the maximum number of errors permitted at various typing speeds. For example, at the minimum acceptable speed of 17 lines, or 40 gross words per minute, 3 errors are permitted for eligibility.

DIAGNOSTIC TEST

The purpose of this diagnostic test and analysis is to familiarize you with the Typing Test and to help you assess your typing skills.

Chapter 8 will give you eight full-length practice sets.

TYPING TEST—COPYING FROM PLAIN COPY

Directions

A practice exercise appears at the bottom of this page and the text exercise itself is on the next page.

First study these directions. Then, when the signal is given, begin to practice by typing the practice exercise below on the paper that has been given you. The examiner will tell you when to stop typing the practice exercise.

In both the practice and the test exercises, *space, paragraph, spell, punctuate, capitalize, and begin and end each line* precisely as shown in the exercise.

The examiner will tell you the exact time you will have to make repeated copies of the test exercise. Each time you complete the exercise, simply double space and begin again. If you fill up one side of the paper, turn it over and continue typing on the other side. Keep on typing until told to stop.

Keep in mind that you must meet minimum standards in both speed and accuracy and that, above these standards, accuracy is twice as important as speed. Make no erasures, insertions, or other corrections in this plain-copy test. Since errors are penalized whether or not they are erased or otherwise "corrected," it is best to keep on typing even though you detect an error.

Practice Exercise

```
        This practice exercise is similar in form and in diffi-
culty to the one that you will be required to typewrite for
the plain-copy test. You are to space, capitalize, punctu-
ate, spell, and begin and end each line precisely as in the
copy. Make no erasures, insertions, or other changes in
this test because errors will be penalized even if they are
erased or otherwise corrected. Practice typewriting this
material on scratch paper until the examiner tells you to stop,
remembering that for this examination it is more important
for you to typewrite accurately than to typewrite rapidly.
```

DO NOT TURN TO THE TEST UNTIL TOLD TO DO SO BY THE EXAMINER.

Test Exercise

        Because they have often learned to know types of archi-
tecture by decoration, casual observers sometimes fail to
realize that the significant part of a structure is not the
ornamentation but the body itself. Architecture, because
of its close contact with human lives, is peculiarly and
intimately governed by climate. For instance, a home built
for comfort in the cold and snow of the northern areas of
this country would be unbearably warm in a country with
weather such as that of Cuba. A Cuban house, with its open
court, would prove impossible to heat in a northern winter.

        Since the purpose of architecture is the construction of
shelters in which human beings may carry on their numerous
activities, the designer must consider not only climatic conditions but also the function of a building. Thus, although
the climate of a certain locality requires that an auditorium
and a hospital have several features in common, the purposes
for which they will be used demand some difference in structure. For centuries builders have first complied with these
two requirements and later added whatever ornamentation they
wished. Logically, we should see as mere additions, not as
basic parts, the details by which we identify architecture.

EACH TIME YOU REACH THIS POINT, DOUBLE SPACE AND BEGIN AGAIN.

Example A—Line Key for Typing Test

(LINE KEY FOR 5 MINUTE TYPING TEST SHOWING MAXIMUM NUMBER OF ERRORS PERMISSIBLE FOR VARIOUS TYPING SPEEDS, AT GRADES GS–2 TYPIST AND GS–3 STENOGRAPHER)

Speed.—In the following example, more than 16 lines must have been typed for any speed rating. This sample key is constructed on the premise that if the competitor made the first stroke in the final line (even if it was an error), he or she is given credit for that line in determining the gross words per minute.

Accuracy.—The gross words per minute typed, at any line, is the number *outside* the parentheses opposite that line. The numbers *in* the parentheses show the maximum number of errors permitted for that number of gross words per minute typed. The number of errors permitted increases with the speed. If the number of strokes per line were different, this table would have to be altered accordingly.

	Maximum Number of Errors Per Gross Words Per Minute Typed	
	1st typing of exercise	2d typing of exercise
Because they have often learned to know types of archi-	....	52(7)
tecture by decoration, casual observers sometimes fail to	....	54(7)
realize that the significant part of a structure is not the	....	56(8)
ornamentation but the body itself. Architecture, because	....	59(8)
of its close contact with human lives, is peculiarly and	....	61(9)
intimately governed by climate. For instance, a home built	....	64(9)
for comfort in the cold and snow of the northern areas of	....	66(10)
this country would be unbearably warm in a country with	....	68(10)
weather such as that of Cuba. A Cuban house, with its open	....	71(11)
court, would prove impossible to heat in a northern winter.	....	73(11)
Since the purpose of architecture is the construction of	....	76(12)
shelters in which human beings may carry on their numerous	....	78(12)
activities, the designer must consider not only climatic con-	....	80(12)[2]
ditions, but also the function of a building. Thus, although	....	....
the climate of a certain locality requires that an auditorium	....	....
and a hospital have several features in common, the purposes	....	....
for which they will be used demand some difference in struc-	40(3)[1]	....
ture. For centuries builders have first complied with these	42(4)	....
two requirements and later added whatever ornamentation they	44(5)	....
wished. Logically, we should see as mere additions, not as	47(6)	....
basic parts, the details by which we identify architecture.	49(6)	....

[1]The minimum rated speed is 40 gross words per minute for typing from printed copy.
[2]Any material typed after 80 gross words per minute (which is considered 100 in speed) is *not* rated for accuracy.
Note: The number of errors shown above must be proportionately increased for tests that are longer than 5 minutes.

Table 5

Example B—Errors Permitted at Various Typing Speeds

(MAXIMUM NUMBER OF ERRORS PERMITTED ON 5-MINUTE TESTS AT VARIOUS SPEEDS FOR TYPING SCORES REQUIRED FOR TYPIST AND STENOGRAPHER POSITIONS)

Speed	Maximum Number of Errors Permitted
Gross Words	*GS-2, GS-3, GS-4 Clerk-Typist*
Per Minute	*GS-3, GS-4, GS-5 Clerk-Stenographer*
Under 40	Ineligible
40	3
41–42	4
43–44	5
45–47	6
48–49	6
50–52	7
53–54	7
55–56	8
57–59	8
60–61	9
62–64	9
65–66	10
67–68	10
69–71	11
72–73	11
74–76	12
77–78	12
79–80	12

NOTE: THE NUMBER OF ERRORS SHOWN ABOVE MUST BE PROPORTIONATELY INCREASED FOR TESTS THAT ARE LONGER THAN 5 MINUTES.

CHAPTER 8

Some Common Errors to Watch For
Practice, Practice, Practice

(NOTE: Each practice set should be taken as a 5-minute timed writing. Gross words a minute are listed next to each line.)

Common Typing Errors to Watch For

As you practice, beware of the following most common typing errors:

1. *Striking one letter for another*. The most common examples of this are hitting "r" for "t," or "t" for "r"; hitting "i" for "o," or "o" for "i"; hitting "a" for "s," or "s" for "a"; hitting "i" for "e," or "e" for "i"; and hitting "m" for "n," or "n" for "m." As you look over your practice typing watch for these errors.

2. *Transposing letters*. Some common examples of typing letters in reverse order are: "re" instead of "er"; "op" instead of "po"; "ew" instead of "we"; "oi" instead of "io"; and "to" instead of "ot." If you find these in your work, practice hitting those letters in the correct order.

3. *Omitted letter errors*. Incorrect hand alignment, weakness in the smaller fingers, and reading too far ahead may cause omitted-letter errors. If you find letters missing in your words, you may wish to practice improving in this area.

PRACTICE SET 1

Type the following exercise, being careful to space, paragraph, spell, punctuate, capitalize, and begin and end each line precisely as shown. Each time you complete the exercise, double space and begin again. If you fill up one side of the paper, turn it over and continue typing on the other side. Keep typing until the time is up. Make no erasures, insertions, or other corrections.

	wpm: 5
Most people want to make sure their own welfare is being taken	3
care of properly. This need will embrace such items as job security,	6
fringe benefits, and final retirement. There are dozens of other items	8
that could be grouped under personal welfare; but, people can cope with	11
these other items if the basic three are covered. For most people, per-	14
sonal welfare means more than acquiring the mere basics of life—food,	17
clothing, and shelter; they want to be able to afford a few luxuries.	20
Job security, to some, is recognized as the single most critical	22
category of these items. If you do not possess good job security, you	25
may not have adequate fringe benefits and a good retirement program. If	28
you are like most people, you expect a job that is pleasant and finan-	31
cially rewarding as well; however, a good environment is ofttimes of more	34

importance than wages to some people. Your whole outlook on life can be   37
more positive when there is no significant concern about your job security.   40
The next category that is of big concern to most workers is fringe   42
benefits. Some of the most common fringe benefits that we now tend to   45
expect are health and major medical insurance, sick leave, retirement   48
paid for by the employer, and adequate vacation and holidays. Even   51
though wages are often the center of concern for most people, the single   54
largest item of controversy between workers and employers is the size of   57
the fringe benefits package that will be paid for by the firm.   59

Retirement should be a major item of concern to all individuals.   62
Today, more than ever, the need for well-planned and well-financed   64
retirement programs is essential. Most of us can expect to spend many   67
years in retirement; hence, we should begin planning for retirement the   70
day we begin our very first job. After we have arranged the financial   73
part of our retirement, we must be just as eager to organize the kinds   76
of activities in which we can participate when we finally quit working.   79

PRACTICE SET 2

Type the following exercise, being careful to space, paragraph, spell, punctuate, capitalize, and begin and end each line precisely as shown. Each time you complete the exercise, double space and begin again. If you fill up one side of the paper, turn it over and continue typing on the other side. Keep typing until the time is up. Make no erasures, insertions, or other corrections.

wpm: 5

On display at several of the offices in our city is a small sign   3
showing what is surely a very important message. The sign says quite   5
simply "Think." Busy workers and customers hastily look at the sign,   8
and it is interesting to conjecture that maybe the message says some-   11
thing a little bit different to every one who reads it. To some, for   14
example, it might portend that they should exercise greater caution in   17
their work; to others, it could offer encouragement to attack a pressing   19
problem that needs solving; while a third group might interpret it to be   22
a note of stimulation toward expanded creativity. That a five-letter   25
word printed on a sign should, like a tiny, mystical beacon, flash an   28
individualized message to those who read it, is itself thought provoking.   31

Every person can think. In the kingdom of animals, anthropologists   34
tell us, the power to reason is a distinctive characteristic of humans.   37
Although there appears to be little unanimity about why people can think,   40
it seems evident that we do our best job of it when faced with the pos-   42
sibility of making a mistake. At such times, we feel quite forced to   45
"act wisely," to "make a basic decision," to "use good judgment"—in   48
other words, to "think." The ability to think, therefore, is a valuable   51
prize to us; and, we will, ideally speaking, take advantage of any chance   54
to improve our capacity for it if in so doing we can develop our abil-   57
ity to avoid dangerous and expensive errors that could affect our family,   59
our friends, our city, our employer—and us.   61

PRACTICE SET 3

Type the following exercise, being careful to space, paragraph, spell, punctuate, capitalize, and begin and end each line precisely as shown. Each time you complete the exercise, double space and begin again. If you fill up one side of the paper, turn it over and continue typing on the other side. Keep typing until the time is up. Make no erasures, insertions, or other corrections.

	wpm: 5
You can safely consider that poor stroking habits are generally the	3
cause of failure to achieve high typing speeds and are the major reasons	5
for plateaus; but you can find material especially designed to help develop	8
quick, easy stroking. Use a part of the drill period each day to	11
work on these special drill exercises. You may not notice an immediate	14
change, but it will come if you work for it and if you analyze your	18
stroking habits very carefully. Among other specific ideas to keep before	21
you is the advice that all drills must be practiced with a definite goal in	24
mind. Unless you know what you are trying to attain, you can't hope to	26
achieve any particular degree of success. It is useless to pound away at	30
the keyboard day after day, hoping that practice will make your typing per-	32
fect. Your drills should be done with very specific objectives in mind. Ask	35
yourself about your objectives to determine if your exercises are right for	38
you.	38
A good course has long-term goals, or at least desired outcomes,	41
for all of its students. In order to reach these goals, each student	43
must decide upon the daily practice objectives that are appropriate to his	46
or her immediate requirements. There should be a specific objective for	49
a specific need. At times, a student will need to increase speed;	52
at other times, a student will require a reduction in speed in order to elim-	55
inate error. At still other times, the goal may be to improve a	58
vital technique: keystroking, spacing, shifting, and the like.	60

PRACTICE SET 4

Type the following exercise, being careful to space, paragraph, spell, punctuate, capitalize, and begin and end each line precisely as shown. Each time you complete the exercise, double space and begin again. If you fill up one side of the paper, turn it over and continue typing on the other side. Keep typing until the time is up. Make no erasures, insertions, or other corrections.

	wpm: 5
A business firm may use one of many letter formats that are in	3
use today; but, most companies are using one of the following styles:	6
block, modified block, and modified block with paragraphs indented.	8
Some companies have now decided to use a letter style that helps them	11
to avoid sex bias in their letter writing. That style is a simplified	14
letter style, which does not include a salutation, and, therefore,	17
does not show the bias against women that was found in the usual salu-	19

tations of the past. The block style and the simplified style are quite easy   23
to type because all parts of both styles begin at the left margin. The major   26
difference between the block style and the simplified style is that the   28
salutation and the complimentary close are included in the block style but   31
are excluded from the simplified format. In addition, the simplified letter   34
style always has a subject line; the block style may or may not include one.   37
According to one study, the block style is used in about a fourth of business   40
firms. The simplified style, however, enjoys only limited use.   43

    The modified block style differs from the block and the simplified   46
styles in that the date and the closing lines in the former begin at   49
the horizontal center of the paper rather than at the left margin.   51
The modified block style—which may use paragraph indention, but more   54
often does not—is the most generally used letter style. It results in   57
a well-balanced, attractive letter with only a limited amount of time   60
spent in operating the tab control to indent the date and closing lines.   63

PRACTICE SET 5

Type the following exercise, being careful to space, paragraph, spell, punctuate, capitalize, and begin and end each line precisely as shown. Each time you complete the exercise, double space and begin again. If you fill up one side of the paper, turn it over and continue typing on the other side. Keep typing until the time is up. Make no erasures, insertions, or other corrections.

wpm: 5

    A typist for an accounting firm is expected to be one who can type   3
a great quantity of numbers and symbols quickly and accurately. Some-   6
times the job is almost entirely quantitative, which means that the   8
typist must be alert to see that no errors are allowed to remain uncor-   11
rected. A wrong number or symbol can't be recognized like a misspelled   14
word, so a typist must make sure that the number or symbol has been   17
typed correctly. Accuracy is very important. The preparation of charts and   19
tables will just naturally become a considerable part of the work-load   21
arrangement when you become a typist in an accounting office. Since so   24
much accounting work is quantitative, it stands to reason that some parts   27
of longer reports can be presented best in graphic or tabulated form, such   30
as charts or tables. It is not unusual for a longer report to have, perhaps, as   33
many as a dozen displays in its appendix.   36

    A typist in an accounting office may not journalize but will type   39
many letters and memorandums. When a change in procedure is to be ef-   42
fected, a memo is typed and sent to all concerned. A typist will need   45
to know the exact number of copies to make before starting to type. This   48
ensures that all people affected will be sure to receive the notice of   51
change. Most internal communication queries between the accounting of-   53
fice and other locations within the business are done by memo.   56

PRACTICE SET 6

Type the following exercise, being careful to space, paragraph, spell, punctuate, capitalize, and begin and end each line precisely as shown. Each time you complete the exercise, double space and begin again. If you fill up one side of the paper, turn it over and continue typing on the other side. Keep typing until the time is up. Make no erasures, insertions, or other corrections.

wpm: 5

Telephone etiquette demands that a person should follow specific	3
rules when answering a telephone call. First, answer quickly; no one	5
likes a delay. If at all possible, the telephone should be picked up	8
on the first ring. Second, identify yourself properly; give your com-	11
pany's name, then your own name. Third, screen an incoming call; tell	14
why your boss cannot talk now, and then mention some other way in which	17
you may aid the caller. Fourth, give only essential information; you	20
must be very careful not to give any information that your employer may	22
not want you to provide. Fifth, get the necessary information from the	25
person; be polite, but try to determine who is calling and why he or	28
she is calling. And sixth, take messages accurately; have a pencil and	31
pad by your phone on which to jot down messages. If you will abide by	34
these simple rules, you will avoid many problems.	36
When placing a telephone call, be sure to follow the advice given	38
by the experts. First, be sure you have the correct number; a wrong	41
area code may cause a delay and embarrassment. Second, know the name of	44
the person you are calling; even a short hesitation may cause difficul-	47
ties with the person to whom you are speaking. Third, plan your con-	50
versation prior to making the call; respect the other person and don't	53
waste time. Fourth, give the person you are calling time to answer the	55
telephone; a rule of thumb is to allow the phone to ring a minimum of	58
ten times. Fifth, identify yourself properly and give the reason for	61
the call; avoid embarrassment and delays—the person you are calling	64
may not recognize your voice. And sixth, terminate your call promptly	67
and thank the individual you called for helping you.	69

PRACTICE SET 7

Type the following exercise, being careful to space, paragraph, spell, punctuate, capitalize, and begin and end each line precisely as shown. Each time you complete the exercise, double space and begin again. If you fill up one side of the paper, turn it over and continue typing on the other side. Keep typing until the time is up. Make no erasures, insertions, or other corrections.

wpm: 5

What factors determine if an employee will be a success? The three	3
basic factors of success on the job are: good technical skills, good	6
human relations skills, and a good work attitude. A person must be able	8
to exhibit the required technical skills in order to perform in an ade-	11
quate manner. Also, the need to get along with other people is equal	14
in importance to technical skills. And, even if a person builds good	17
technical skills and good human relations skills, a positive feeling	20
about the job is still essential in order to be a success. Cognizance	22
of these factors plays an important part in attaining success; if any	25
one of them is not realized, an employee may feel unsuccessful.	28
A person needs to prepare adequately in order to succeed on a job.	31
Preparation for a job must start long before the first day at work. A	33

part of this preparation is building a job entry-level skill. Also, an 36
employee must learn to develop a good, positive interpersonal relation- 39
ship with others. This ability to get along well with others is not an 42
instinct—much time and effort must be devoted to achieving good human 45
relations skills. Finally, an employee should look forward to work with plea- 48
sure; therefore, a positive attitude toward work must be developed 51
if the job is to be rewarding. Remember, anyone can learn to succeed as 54
an employee; all it takes is a real desire and work. 56

PRACTICE SET 8

Type the following exercise, being careful to space, paragraph, spell, punctuate, capitalize, and begin and end each line precisely as shown. Each time you complete the exercise, double space and begin again. If you fill up one side of the paper, turn it over and continue typing on the other side. Keep typing until the time is up. Make no erasures, insertions, or other corrections.

wpm: 5

The development and expanded use of the computer has not caused 3
the large number of jobs to be lost that so many people expected about 6
twenty-five years ago. In fact, the total number of people in the work force 8
has increased during the past twenty-five years, and the computer has 11
had the effect of creating many of the new jobs. While it is indeed 14
true that the development of the computer has made many of the routine, 17
less-skilled jobs unnecessary, it has also created many other highly 20
skilled jobs that call for employees who are trained for such fields 22
as data entry and computer operations, programming, and systems analy- 25
sis. In short, the occupations that call for specialized training, judgment, 28
and knowledge have increased in number; and thus, the computer has, in 31
fact, helped to create even more jobs and, in turn, to increase wages. 34

There are many people who insist that the computer has not had a 37
positive effect on the worker. They assert that many firms are more 39
concerned with net profit than they are with satisfied workers. In 42
many firms, the telephone calls, the invoices, the letters, and the 45
reports can all be done with the aid of a computer. Some firms are now 48
to the point where they can see how negative the impact of technology is 51
on their employees, and these firms are beginning job enrichment pro- 53
grams that will help their employees gain greater personal satisfaction 56
from their jobs. Perhaps the development of the computer may, in the end, 59
force firms to do what should have been done earlier—create pleas- 62
ant and satisfying jobs for all workers. 64

REVIEWING THE KEY STRATEGIES

Watch out for common errors:

— striking one letter for another

— transposing letters

— omitted letter errors

PART FOUR

The Dictation Test

CHAPTER 9

Introduction
A Diagnostic Test
with Answers

THE DICTATION TEST

The dictation test, which is a part of the Stenographer-Typist Examination, includes a practice dictation and a test exercise, each consisting of 240 words. The rate of dictation is 80 words a minute.

The dictation passages are nontechnical subject matter that might be given a stenographer in a government office. Sentence structure is not complicated and sentences are not extremely long or short. The words average 1.5 syllables in length.

As shown in Example C, Practice Dictation, each dictation passage is printed with spacing to show the point that the dictator should reach at the end of each 10 seconds in order to maintain an even dictation rate of 80 words a minute. This indication of timing is one device for assisting all examiners to conform to the intended dictation rate. All examiners are also sent instructions for dictating and a sample passage to be used in practicing dictating before the day of the test. By using these devices for securing uniform dictating and by providing alternate dictation passages that are as nearly equal as possible, the U. S. Office of Personnel Management can give each applicant a test that is neither harder nor easier than those given others competing for the same jobs.

The test differs from the conventional dictation test in the method of transcribing the notes. The applicant is not required to type a transcript of the notes, but follows a procedure that permits machine scoring of the test. When typewritten transcripts were still required, examiners rated the test by comparing every word of a competitor's paper with the material dictated and by charging errors. Fairness to those competing for employment required that comparable errors be penalized equally. Because of the variety of errors and combinations of errors that can be made in transcripts, the scoring of typewritten transcripts required considerable training and consumed much time—many months for large nationwide examinations. After years of experimentation, a transcript booklet procedure was devised that simplified and speeded the scoring procedure.

HOW THE TRANSCRIPT BOOKLET WORKS

The transcript booklet (see Example D, Diagnostic Test) gives the stenographer parts of the dictated passage, but leaves blank spaces where many of the words belong. With adequate shorthand notes, the stenographer can readily fit the correct words into the blank spaces, which are numbered 1 through 125. At the left of the printed partial transcript is a list of words, each word with a capital letter A, B, C, or D beside it. Knowing from the notes what word belongs in a blank space, the competitor looks for it among the words in the list. The letter beside the word or phrase in the list is the answer to be marked in the space on the transcript. In the list there are other words that a competitor with inadequate notes might guess belong in that space, but the capital letter beside these words would be an incorrect answer. *(Some persons find it helpful to write the word or the shorthand symbol in the blank space before looking for it in the word list. There is no objection to doing this.)*

Look, for example, at the Practice Dictation Transcript Sheet, Example D, question 10. The word dictated is "physical"; it is in the word list with a capital "D." In the transcript, blank number 10 should be answered "D."

None of the words in the list is marked "E," because the answer "E" is reserved for any question when the word dictated for that spot does not appear in the list. Every transcript booklet has spots for which the list does not include the correct words. This provision reduces the possibility that competitors may guess correct answers.

After the stenographer has written the letter of the missing word or phrase in each numbered blank of the transcript, he or she transfers the answers to the proper spaces on the answer sheet. Directions for marking the separate answer sheet are given on page 1 of Example E, Diagnostic Test.

HOW THE TEST IS ADMINISTERED

Each competitor is given a copy of the Practice Dictation Transcript Sheet (Example D), a copy of the Transcript Booklet (Example C), and an answer sheet. These are distributed at the times indicated below.

First, the Practice Dictation (see Example C) is dictated at the rate indicated by the 10-second divisions in which it is printed. This will be at the rate of 80 words a minute, for a total of 3 minutes. Then each competitor is given a copy of the Practice Dictation Transcript Sheet and allowed 7 minutes to study the instructions and to transcribe part of the practice dictation.

The test exercise (reverse side—here, page 238— of Example C) is also dictated at the rate of 80 words a minute, for 3 minutes. Then each competitor is given a Transcript Booklet and an answer sheet, and is told that he or she will have 3 minutes to read the directions on the face page, followed by 30 minutes to write the answers in the blank spaces, and then 10 minutes to transfer the answers to the answer sheet. These time limits have been found ample.

HOW THE ANSWER SHEET IS SCORED

In some rare instances where the typewritten transcript is still used, the passing standard on the total transcript is 24 or fewer errors for GS–3 Clerk-Stenographer and GS–4. Comparable standards on the parts of the dictation measured by the machine-scored method of transcription are 14 or fewer errors for GS–3 and GS–4 positions.

A stenographer who can take dictation at 80 words a minute with this degree of accuracy is considered fully qualified. Positions such as Reporting Stenographer and Shorthand Reporter require ability to take dictation at much higher speeds. The test for Reporting Stenographer is dictated at 120 words a minute. Two rates of dictation, 160 and 175 words a minute, are used for the Shorthand Reporter tests for different grade levels.

A DIAGNOSTIC TEST WITH ANSWERS

The purpose of this diagnostic exam is to familiarize you with the Dictation Test and to help you focus your practice.

Chapter 8 will give you five practice sets to help build strengths and reduce weaknesses.

ANSWER SHEET

SIGNATURE: _____
(Please Sign)

EXAMINATION TITLE: _____

PLACE OF EXAMINATION: _____
City   State

TODAY'S DATE: _____

SAMPLE Ⓐ ● Ⓒ Ⓓ Ⓔ

DIRECTIONS FOR MARKING ANSWER SHEET

Use only a **No. 2 (or softer) lead pencil.** Darken completely the circle corresponding to your answer. **You must keep** your mark within the circle. Stray marks may be counted as errors. Erase **completely** all marks except your answer.

SAMPLE NAME GRID

1. In the boxes below, **PRINT** your name. Print only as many letters as will fit within the areas for the last name, first initial (F.I.), and middle initial (M.I.) Below each box, darken the circle containing the same letter. SEE SAMPLE NAME GRID

2. In the boxes below, enter your 9-digit Social Security Number. Below each box, darken the circle in each column corresponding to the number you have entered.

SOCIAL SECURITY NUMBER

3. OCCUPATIONAL GROUP NUMBER

LAST NAME   F.I.   M.I.

SECTION 1

Make no marks or entries in the columns to the right until you receive instructions from the administrator.

PART

TEST SERIES

TEST NUMBER

1 Ⓐ Ⓑ Ⓒ Ⓓ Ⓔ	11 Ⓐ Ⓑ Ⓒ Ⓓ Ⓔ	31 Ⓐ Ⓑ Ⓒ Ⓓ Ⓔ	51 Ⓐ Ⓑ Ⓒ Ⓓ Ⓔ	71 Ⓐ Ⓑ Ⓒ Ⓓ Ⓔ	91 Ⓐ Ⓑ Ⓒ Ⓓ Ⓔ	111 Ⓐ Ⓑ Ⓒ Ⓓ Ⓔ
2 Ⓐ Ⓑ Ⓒ Ⓓ Ⓔ	12 Ⓐ Ⓑ Ⓒ Ⓓ Ⓔ	32 Ⓐ Ⓑ Ⓒ Ⓓ Ⓔ	52 Ⓐ Ⓑ Ⓒ Ⓓ Ⓔ	72 Ⓐ Ⓑ Ⓒ Ⓓ Ⓔ	92 Ⓐ Ⓑ Ⓒ Ⓓ Ⓔ	112 Ⓐ Ⓑ Ⓒ Ⓓ Ⓔ
3 Ⓐ Ⓑ Ⓒ Ⓓ Ⓔ	13 Ⓐ Ⓑ Ⓒ Ⓓ Ⓔ	33 Ⓐ Ⓑ Ⓒ Ⓓ Ⓔ	53 Ⓐ Ⓑ Ⓒ Ⓓ Ⓔ	73 Ⓐ Ⓑ Ⓒ Ⓓ Ⓔ	93 Ⓐ Ⓑ Ⓒ Ⓓ Ⓔ	113 Ⓐ Ⓑ Ⓒ Ⓓ Ⓔ
4 Ⓐ Ⓑ Ⓒ Ⓓ Ⓔ	14 Ⓐ Ⓑ Ⓒ Ⓓ Ⓔ	34 Ⓐ Ⓑ Ⓒ Ⓓ Ⓔ	54 Ⓐ Ⓑ Ⓒ Ⓓ Ⓔ	74 Ⓐ Ⓑ Ⓒ Ⓓ Ⓔ	94 Ⓐ Ⓑ Ⓒ Ⓓ Ⓔ	114 Ⓐ Ⓑ Ⓒ Ⓓ Ⓔ
5 Ⓐ Ⓑ Ⓒ Ⓓ Ⓔ	15 Ⓐ Ⓑ Ⓒ Ⓓ Ⓔ	35 Ⓐ Ⓑ Ⓒ Ⓓ Ⓔ	55 Ⓐ Ⓑ Ⓒ Ⓓ Ⓔ	75 Ⓐ Ⓑ Ⓒ Ⓓ Ⓔ	95 Ⓐ Ⓑ Ⓒ Ⓓ Ⓔ	115 Ⓐ Ⓑ Ⓒ Ⓓ Ⓔ
6 Ⓐ Ⓑ Ⓒ Ⓓ Ⓔ	16 Ⓐ Ⓑ Ⓒ Ⓓ Ⓔ	36 Ⓐ Ⓑ Ⓒ Ⓓ Ⓔ	56 Ⓐ Ⓑ Ⓒ Ⓓ Ⓔ	76 Ⓐ Ⓑ Ⓒ Ⓓ Ⓔ	96 Ⓐ Ⓑ Ⓒ Ⓓ Ⓔ	116 Ⓐ Ⓑ Ⓒ Ⓓ Ⓔ
7 Ⓐ Ⓑ Ⓒ Ⓓ Ⓔ	17 Ⓐ Ⓑ Ⓒ Ⓓ Ⓔ	37 Ⓐ Ⓑ Ⓒ Ⓓ Ⓔ	57 Ⓐ Ⓑ Ⓒ Ⓓ Ⓔ	77 Ⓐ Ⓑ Ⓒ Ⓓ Ⓔ	97 Ⓐ Ⓑ Ⓒ Ⓓ Ⓔ	117 Ⓐ Ⓑ Ⓒ Ⓓ Ⓔ
8 Ⓐ Ⓑ Ⓒ Ⓓ Ⓔ	18 Ⓐ Ⓑ Ⓒ Ⓓ Ⓔ	38 Ⓐ Ⓑ Ⓒ Ⓓ Ⓔ	58 Ⓐ Ⓑ Ⓒ Ⓓ Ⓔ	78 Ⓐ Ⓑ Ⓒ Ⓓ Ⓔ	98 Ⓐ Ⓑ Ⓒ Ⓓ Ⓔ	118 Ⓐ Ⓑ Ⓒ Ⓓ Ⓔ
9 Ⓐ Ⓑ Ⓒ Ⓓ Ⓔ	19 Ⓐ Ⓑ Ⓒ Ⓓ Ⓔ	39 Ⓐ Ⓑ Ⓒ Ⓓ Ⓔ	59 Ⓐ Ⓑ Ⓒ Ⓓ Ⓔ	79 Ⓐ Ⓑ Ⓒ Ⓓ Ⓔ	99 Ⓐ Ⓑ Ⓒ Ⓓ Ⓔ	119 Ⓐ Ⓑ Ⓒ Ⓓ Ⓔ
10 Ⓐ Ⓑ Ⓒ Ⓓ Ⓔ	20 Ⓐ Ⓑ Ⓒ Ⓓ Ⓔ	40 Ⓐ Ⓑ Ⓒ Ⓓ Ⓔ	60 Ⓐ Ⓑ Ⓒ Ⓓ Ⓔ	80 Ⓐ Ⓑ Ⓒ Ⓓ Ⓔ	100 Ⓐ Ⓑ Ⓒ Ⓓ Ⓔ	120 Ⓐ Ⓑ Ⓒ Ⓓ Ⓔ
	21 Ⓐ Ⓑ Ⓒ Ⓓ Ⓔ	41 Ⓐ Ⓑ Ⓒ Ⓓ Ⓔ	61 Ⓐ Ⓑ Ⓒ Ⓓ Ⓔ	81 Ⓐ Ⓑ Ⓒ Ⓓ Ⓔ	101 Ⓐ Ⓑ Ⓒ Ⓓ Ⓔ	121 Ⓐ Ⓑ Ⓒ Ⓓ Ⓔ
	22 Ⓐ Ⓑ Ⓒ Ⓓ Ⓔ	42 Ⓐ Ⓑ Ⓒ Ⓓ Ⓔ	62 Ⓐ Ⓑ Ⓒ Ⓓ Ⓔ	82 Ⓐ Ⓑ Ⓒ Ⓓ Ⓔ	102 Ⓐ Ⓑ Ⓒ Ⓓ Ⓔ	122 Ⓐ Ⓑ Ⓒ Ⓓ Ⓔ
	23 Ⓐ Ⓑ Ⓒ Ⓓ Ⓔ	43 Ⓐ Ⓑ Ⓒ Ⓓ Ⓔ	63 Ⓐ Ⓑ Ⓒ Ⓓ Ⓔ	83 Ⓐ Ⓑ Ⓒ Ⓓ Ⓔ	103 Ⓐ Ⓑ Ⓒ Ⓓ Ⓔ	123 Ⓐ Ⓑ Ⓒ Ⓓ Ⓔ
	24 Ⓐ Ⓑ Ⓒ Ⓓ Ⓔ	44 Ⓐ Ⓑ Ⓒ Ⓓ Ⓔ	64 Ⓐ Ⓑ Ⓒ Ⓓ Ⓔ	84 Ⓐ Ⓑ Ⓒ Ⓓ Ⓔ	104 Ⓐ Ⓑ Ⓒ Ⓓ Ⓔ	124 Ⓐ Ⓑ Ⓒ Ⓓ Ⓔ
	25 Ⓐ Ⓑ Ⓒ Ⓓ Ⓔ	45 Ⓐ Ⓑ Ⓒ Ⓓ Ⓔ	65 Ⓐ Ⓑ Ⓒ Ⓓ Ⓔ	85 Ⓐ Ⓑ Ⓒ Ⓓ Ⓔ	105 Ⓐ Ⓑ Ⓒ Ⓓ Ⓔ	125 Ⓐ Ⓑ Ⓒ Ⓓ Ⓔ
	26 Ⓐ Ⓑ Ⓒ Ⓓ Ⓔ	46 Ⓐ Ⓑ Ⓒ Ⓓ Ⓔ	66 Ⓐ Ⓑ Ⓒ Ⓓ Ⓔ	86 Ⓐ Ⓑ Ⓒ Ⓓ Ⓔ	106 Ⓐ Ⓑ Ⓒ Ⓓ Ⓔ	126 Ⓐ Ⓑ Ⓒ Ⓓ Ⓔ
	27 Ⓐ Ⓑ Ⓒ Ⓓ Ⓔ	47 Ⓐ Ⓑ Ⓒ Ⓓ Ⓔ	67 Ⓐ Ⓑ Ⓒ Ⓓ Ⓔ	87 Ⓐ Ⓑ Ⓒ Ⓓ Ⓔ	107 Ⓐ Ⓑ Ⓒ Ⓓ Ⓔ	127 Ⓐ Ⓑ Ⓒ Ⓓ Ⓔ
	28 Ⓐ Ⓑ Ⓒ Ⓓ Ⓔ	48 Ⓐ Ⓑ Ⓒ Ⓓ Ⓔ	68 Ⓐ Ⓑ Ⓒ Ⓓ Ⓔ	88 Ⓐ Ⓑ Ⓒ Ⓓ Ⓔ	108 Ⓐ Ⓑ Ⓒ Ⓓ Ⓔ	128 Ⓐ Ⓑ Ⓒ Ⓓ Ⓔ
	29 Ⓐ Ⓑ Ⓒ Ⓓ Ⓔ	49 Ⓐ Ⓑ Ⓒ Ⓓ Ⓔ	69 Ⓐ Ⓑ Ⓒ Ⓓ Ⓔ	89 Ⓐ Ⓑ Ⓒ Ⓓ Ⓔ	109 Ⓐ Ⓑ Ⓒ Ⓓ Ⓔ	129 Ⓐ Ⓑ Ⓒ Ⓓ Ⓔ
	30 Ⓐ Ⓑ Ⓒ Ⓓ Ⓔ	50 Ⓐ Ⓑ Ⓒ Ⓓ Ⓔ	70 Ⓐ Ⓑ Ⓒ Ⓓ Ⓔ	90 Ⓐ Ⓑ Ⓒ Ⓓ Ⓔ	110 Ⓐ Ⓑ Ⓒ Ⓓ Ⓔ	130 Ⓐ Ⓑ Ⓒ Ⓓ Ⓔ

Example C—Practice Dictation

INSTRUCTIONS TO THE EXAMINER: This Practice Dictation and one exercise will be dictated at the rate of 80 words a minute. Do not dictate the punctuation except for periods, but dictate with the expression that the punctuation indicates. Use a watch with a second hand to enable you to read the exercises at the proper speed.

Exactly on a minute, start dictating.

Finish reading each two lines at the number of seconds indicated below

I realize that this practice dictation is not a part of the examination	10
proper and is not to be scored. (Period) The work of preventing and correcting	20
physical defects in children is becoming more effective as a result of a change	30
in the attitude of many parents. (Period) In order to bring about this change,	40
mothers have been invited to visit the schools when their children are being examined	50
and to discuss the treatment necessary for the correction of defects. (Period)	1 min.
There is a distinct value in having a mother see that her child is not the	10
only one who needs attention. (Period) Otherwise a few parents might feel that they	20
were being criticized by having the defects of their children singled out for medical	30
treatment. (Period) The special classes that have been set up have shown the value of	40
the scientific knowledge that has been applied in the treatment of children. (Period)	50
In these classes the children have been taught to exercise by a trained teacher	2 min.
under medical supervision. (Period) The hours of the school day have been divided	10
between school work and physical activity that helps not only to correct their defects	20
but also to improve their general physical condition. (Period) This method of treatment	30
has been found to be very effective except for those who have severe medical	40
defects. (Period) Most parents now see how desirable it is to have these classes	50
that have been set up in the regular school system to meet special needs. (Period)	3 min.

After dictating the practice, pause for 15 seconds to permit competitors to complete their notes. Then continue in accordance with the directions for conducting the examination.

After the Practice Dictation Transcript has been completed, dictate the test from the next page.

THE TEST

Finish reading
each two lines
at the number
of seconds in-
dicated below

Exactly on a minute, start dictating.

The number enrolled in shorthand classes in the
high schools has shown a marked increase. (Period)　　10

Today this subject is one of the most
popular offered in the field of　　20

business education. (Period) When shorthand was
first taught, educators claimed that it was of　　30

value mainly in sharpening the powers
of observation and discrimination. (Period)　　40

However, with the growth of business and
the increased demand for office workers,　　50

educators have come to realize the
importance of stenography as a vocational　　1 min.

tool. (Period) With the differences
in the aims of instruction came changes in　　10

the grade placement of the subject. (Period)
The prevailing thought has always been that it　　20

should be offered in high school. (Period)
When the junior high school first came into　　30

being, shorthand was moved down to that level
with little change in the manner in which　　40

the subject was taught. (Period) It was soon
realized that shorthand had no place there　　50

because the training had lost its vocational
utility by the time the student could　　2 min.

graduate. (Period) Moreover, surveys
of those with education only through junior　　10

high school seldom found them at work as
stenographers. (Period) For this reason, shorthand　　20

was returned to the high school level and is
offered as near as possible to the time　　30

of graduation so that the skill will be
retained when the student takes a job. (Period)　　40

Because the age at which students enter
office jobs has advanced, there is now　　50

a tendency to upgrade business education
into the junior college. (Period)　　3 min.

After completing the dictation, pause for 15 seconds.
Give a Transcript to each competitor.

Example D—Practice Dictation Transcript Sheet

The TRANSCRIPT below is part of the material that was dictated to you for practice, except that many of the words have been left out. From your notes, you are to tell what the missing words are. Proceed as follows:

Compare your notes with the TRANSCRIPT and, when you come to a blank in the TRANSCRIPT, decide what word or words belong there. For example, you will find that the word "practice" belongs in blank number 1. Look at the WORD LIST to see whether you can find the same word there. Notice what letter (A, B, C, or D) is printed beside it, and write that letter in the blank. For example, the word "practice" is listed, followed by the letter "B." We have already written "B" in blank number 1 to show you how you are to record your choice. Now decide what belongs in each of the other blanks. (You may also write the word or words, or the shorthand for them, if you wish.) The same word may belong in more than one blank. If the exact answer is not listed, write "E" in the blank.

ALPHABETIC WORD LIST

about—B	paper—B
against—C	parents—B
attitude—A	part—C
	physical—D
being—D	portion—D
	practical—A
childhood—B	practice—B
children—A	preliminary—D
correcting—C	preventing—B
	procedure—A
doctors—B	proper—C
effective—D	reason for—A
efficient—A	result—B
examination—A	result of—C
examining—C	
	schools—C
for—B	
	to be—C
health—B	to prevent—A
mothers—C	
never—C	
not—D	

TRANSCRIPT

I realize that this **B** dictation is _____
                               1   2

a _____ of the _____ _____ and is _____ _____
  3   4   5   6   7

scored.

The work of _____ and _____ _____ defects in
               8   9   10

_____ is becoming more _____ as a _____ a change
11   12   13

in the _____ of many _____ . . . .
    14   15

Each numbered blank in the TRANSCRIPT is a question. You will be given a separate answer sheet like the sample here, to which you will transfer your answers. The answer sheet has a numbered row of circles for each question. The answer for blank number 1 is "B." We have already transferred this to number 1 in the Sample Answer Sheet, by darkening the circle marked "B."

Now transfer your answer for each of questions 2 through 15 to the answer sheet. That is, beside each number on the answer sheet find the letter that is the same as the letter you wrote in the blank with the same number in the TRANSCRIPT, and darken the circle marked with that letter.

After you have marked 15, continue with blank number 16 on the next page WITHOUT WAITING FOR A SIGNAL.

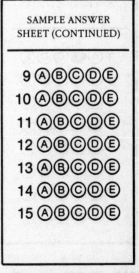

Example D—continued.

ALPHABETIC WORD LIST

all—A	know—A	to discover—A
at—C	knows—D	to discuss—D
		to endorse—C
bring—A	needed—B	to visit—B
collection—B	promote—B	treatments—A
correction—C		
	recognizing—D	understand—D
discuss—C		undertake—B
during—D	reducing—A	
		virtue—D
friend—A	satisfied—D	visit—A
	say—C	volume—B
indicated—C	see—B	
insisted—D	soon—C	young—C
is—B		
is not—A	their—D	

TRANSCRIPT (continued)

In order to ___ ___ this change, mothers
           16   17

have been invited ___ the schools when ___
              18   19

children are being examined and ___ the ___
                    20   21

necessary for the ___ of defects. There is a
              22

distinct ___ in having a mother ___ that her
        23   24

child ___ the only one who needs attention. . . .
    25

(The rest of the practice dictation is not transcribed here.)

SAMPLE ANSWER SHEET

16 Ⓐ Ⓑ Ⓒ Ⓓ Ⓔ
17 Ⓐ Ⓑ Ⓒ Ⓓ Ⓔ
18 Ⓐ Ⓑ Ⓒ Ⓓ Ⓔ
19 Ⓐ Ⓑ Ⓒ Ⓓ Ⓔ
20 Ⓐ Ⓑ Ⓒ Ⓓ Ⓔ
21 Ⓐ Ⓑ Ⓒ Ⓓ Ⓔ
22 Ⓐ Ⓑ Ⓒ Ⓓ Ⓔ
23 Ⓐ Ⓑ Ⓒ Ⓓ Ⓔ
24 Ⓐ Ⓑ Ⓒ Ⓓ Ⓔ
25 Ⓐ Ⓑ Ⓒ Ⓓ Ⓔ

Your notes should show that the word "bring" goes in blank 16, and "about" in blank 17. But "about" is *not in the list;* so "E" should be your answer for question 17.

The two words, "to visit—B," are needed for 18, and the one word "visit—A," would be an incorrect answer.

Compare your answers with the correct answers. If one of your answers does not agree with the correct answer, again compare your notes with the samples and make certain you understand the instructions. The correct answers for 16 through 25 are as follows: 16 A; 17 E; 18 B; 19 D; 20 D; 21 E; 22 C; 23 E; 24 B; and 25 A.

For the actual test you will use a separate answer sheet. As scoring will be done by an electronic scoring machine, it is important that you follow directions carefully. Use a medium No. 2 pencil. You must keep your mark for a question within the box. If you have to erase a mark, be sure to erase it completely. Mark only one answer for each question.

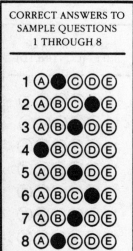

CORRECT ANSWERS TO SAMPLE QUESTIONS 1 THROUGH 8

1 Ⓐ ● Ⓒ Ⓓ Ⓔ
2 Ⓐ Ⓑ Ⓒ ● Ⓔ
3 Ⓐ Ⓑ ● Ⓓ Ⓔ
4 ● Ⓑ Ⓒ Ⓓ Ⓔ
5 Ⓐ Ⓑ ● Ⓓ Ⓔ
6 Ⓐ Ⓑ Ⓒ ● Ⓔ
7 Ⓐ Ⓑ ● Ⓓ Ⓔ
8 Ⓐ ● Ⓒ Ⓓ Ⓔ

For any stenographer who missed the practice dictation, part of it is given below:

"I realize that this practice dictation is not a part of the examination proper and is not to be scored.

"The work of preventing and correcting physical defects in children is becoming more effective as a result of a change in the attitude of many parents. In order to bring about this change, mothers have been invited to visit the schools when their children are being examined and to discuss the treatment necessary for the correction of defects. There is a distinct value in having a mother see that her child is not the only one who needs attention. . . ."

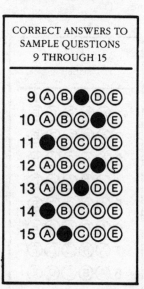

CORRECT ANSWERS TO SAMPLE QUESTIONS 9 THROUGH 15

9 Ⓐ Ⓑ ● Ⓓ Ⓔ
10 Ⓐ Ⓑ Ⓒ ● Ⓔ
11 ● Ⓑ Ⓒ Ⓓ Ⓔ
12 Ⓐ Ⓑ Ⓒ ● Ⓔ
13 Ⓐ Ⓑ ● Ⓓ Ⓔ
14 ● Ⓑ Ⓒ Ⓓ Ⓔ
15 Ⓐ ● Ⓒ Ⓓ Ⓔ

(Page 2 of Example D)

Example E—
Dictation Test Transcript Booklet

Directions for Completing the Transcript

A TRANSCRIPT of the dictation you have just taken is given on the following pages. As in the TRANSCRIPT for the practice dictation, there are numbered blank spaces for many of the words that were dictated. You are to compare your notes with the TRANSCRIPT and, when you come to a blank, decide what word or words belong there. For most of the blanks the words are included in the list beside the TRANSCRIPT; each is followed by a letter, A, B, C, or D. To show that you know which word or words belong in each blank space, you are to *write the letter in* the blank. You are to write E if the answer is NOT listed. (In addition you may write the word or words, or the shorthand for them, if you wish.) The same choice may belong in more than one blank.

After you have compared your notes with the TRANSCRIPT and have chosen the answer for each blank space, you will be given additional time to transfer your answers to a separate answer sheet.

Directions for Marking the Separate
Answer Sheet

On the answer sheet, each question number stands for the blank with the same number in the TRANSCRIPT. For each number, you are to darken the circle with the letter that is the same as the letter you wrote in the TRANSCRIPT. (The answers in this booklet will not be rated.) Be sure to use your pencil and record your answers on the separate answer sheet. You must keep your mark within the circle. If you have to erase a mark, be sure to erase it completely. Make only one mark for each question.

Work quickly so that you will be able to finish in the time allowed. First you should darken the circles on the answer sheet for the blanks you have lettered. You may continue to use your notes if you have not finished writing letters in the blanks in the TRANSCRIPT, or if you wish to make sure you have lettered them correctly.

DO NOT OPEN THIS BOOKLET UNTIL TOLD TO DO SO.

WORD LIST

Write E if the answer is NOT listed.

administration—C	increase—A	shorthand—D
along the—B	in the—D	shown—C
area—A		stenography—B
at first—A	known—D	study—C
		subject—A
claimed—C	line—C	
classes—B		taught—D
concluded—D	mainly—B	that—C
could be—D	marked—B	the—D
courses—C	mostly—D	these—B
		this—A
decrease—D	observation—B	thought—B
discriminating—C	observing—A	to be—A
discrimination—D	offered—C	training—D
	of value—C	
education—B	open—A	valuable—A
enrolled—D		vast—A
entering—A	popular—B	
	power—B	
field—D	powers—D	
first—D	practical—A	
given—B	shaping—A	
great—C	sharpen—B	

TRANSCRIPT

The number ___ in shorthand ___ ___ high
    1   2   3

schools has ___ a ___ ___. Today ___ ___
         4   5   6   7   8

is one of the most ___ ___ ___ ___ of
                   9   10   11   12

business ___. When ___ ___ ___ ___ ___
        13   14   15   16   17

educators ___ that it ___ ___ ___ in
        18   19   20   21   22

___ ___ of ___ and ___....
23   24   25   26

WORD LIST

Write E if the answer is NOT listed.

a change—D	has—C	schools—D
administration—C	had—B	shorthand—D
aims—A	have come—A	should be—A
always been—A	high school—B	significance—C
		stenography—B
begun—D	increased—D	study—C
businesses—A	increasing—C	subject—A
	institutions—D	
came—D	instruction—C	thinking—C
changes—B	it—B	this—A
come—C		thought—B
	offered—C	tool—B
defects—B	office—A	to realize—B
demand—B	official—C	to recognize—B
differences—D	often been—B	
	ought to be—B	valuable—A
education—B		vocational—C
educators—D	place—B	
	placement—D	when the—D
for—D	prevailing—B	with—A
		without—C
given—B	rule—D	workers—C
grade—C		
grading—B		

TRANSCRIPT (continued)

...However, ___ the growth of ___ and the
              27   28

___ ___ for ___ ___, ___ have ___
29   30   31   32   33   34

___ the ___ of ___ a ___ ___.
35   36   37   38   39   40

With the ___ in the ___ of ___ ___ ___
          41   42   43   44   45

in the ___ ___ of the ___. The ___
        46   47   48   49

___ ___ ___ that ___ ___ ___ in
50 51 52   53   54   55

___....
56

CONTINUE ON THE NEXT PAGE WITHOUT WAITING FOR A SIGNAL.

(Page 2 of Example C)

WORD LIST

Write *E* if the answer is NOT listed.

became—B	junior high—D	study—C
because—B		subject—A
	less—B	
came—D	lessened—C	taught—D
change—A	level—C	that—C
changed—C	little—A	the—D
could—C	lost—D	their—B
could be—D		there—B
	manner—B	this—A
date—D	method—C	time—B
	moved—C	training—D
first—D	moved down—B	
		usefulness—B
graduate—D	occupational—B	utility—C
graduated—B		
	recognized—A	vocational—C
had little—C		
had no—A	shorthand—D	which—A
here—D	since—C	
high—C	soon—C	
	stenography—B	
into being—A	student—A	
into business—C	students—C	

TRANSCRIPT (continued)

... When the _____ school _____ _____ _____ , _____
             57   58   59   60   61

was _____ to _____ _____ with _____ _____ in _____
      62   63   64   65   66   67

_____ _____ the _____ was _____ . It was _____ _____
 68   69   70   71   72   73

that _____ _____ place _____ _____ the _____ had
      74   75   76   77   78

_____ _____ _____ _____ by the _____ the _____
 79   80   81   82   83   84

_____ _____ ....
 85   86

WORD LIST

Write *E* if the answer is NOT listed.

advanced—A	job—B	showed—A
age—A	junior high—D	so—A
as far as—C		stenographers—C
at which—D	level—C	studies—B
at work—A		surveys—A
	may be—C	
be—B		takes—A
	near as—A	taught—D
date—D	nearly as—C	tendency—B
		that—C
education—B	offered—C	there—B
enter—D	often—B	this—A
	only—B	through—D
found—D		time—B
	possible—D	training—D
graduating—A		
graduation—C	rarely—D	undertake—A
	reason—B	until—A
has—C	reasons—D	upgrade—D
high school—B	retained—B	
		when—C
in—A	school—A	which—A
in order—D	secretaries—D	will—B
increased—D	secures—D	would—D
into—B	seldom—C	working—B

TRANSCRIPT (continued)

...Moreover, _____ of _____ with _____ _____ _____
                  87   88   89   90   91

_____ school _____ _____ them _____ as _____ . For
 92   93   94   95   96

_____ _____ , shorthand was _____ to the _____
 97   98   99   100

_____ and is _____ as _____ _____ to the _____ of
 101   102   103   104   105

_____ _____ _____ the skill _____ _____ _____
 106   107   108   109   110   111

_____ the student _____ a _____ . Because the _____
 112   113   114   115

_____ students _____ office _____ _____ _____ ,
 116   117   118   119   120

there is _____ a _____ to _____ _____ education
       121   122   123   124

_____ the junior college.
 125

(Page 3 of Example C)

ANSWER KEY

1.	D	26.	D	51.	C	76.	B	101.	C
2.	B	27.	A	52.	A	77.	B	102.	C
3.	D	28.	E	53.	B	78.	D	103.	A
4.	C	29.	D	54.	A	79.	D	104.	D
5.	B	30.	B	55.	C	80.	E	105.	B
6.	A	31.	A	56.	B	81.	C	106.	C
7.	A	32.	C	57.	D	82.	C	107.	A
8.	A	33.	D	58.	D	83.	B	108.	C
9.	B	34.	C	59.	D	84.	A	109.	B
10.	C	35.	B	60.	A	85.	C	110.	B
11.	D	36.	E	61.	D	86.	D	111.	B
12.	D	37.	E	62.	B	87.	A	112.	C
13.	B	38.	E	63.	C	88.	E	113.	A
14.	D	39.	C	64.	C	89.	B	114.	B
15.	E	40.	B	65.	A	90.	B	115.	A
16.	D	41.	D	66.	A	91.	D	116.	D
17.	D	42.	A	67.	D	92.	D	117.	D
18.	C	43.	C	68.	B	93.	C	118.	E
19.	E	44.	D	69.	E	94.	D	119.	C
20.	C	45.	B	70.	A	95.	A	120.	A
21.	B	46.	C	71.	D	96.	C	121.	E
22.	E	47.	D	72.	C	97.	A	122.	B
23.	D	48.	A	73.	E	98.	B	123.	D
24.	D	49.	B	74.	D	99.	E	124.	E
25.	B	50.	B	75.	A	100.	B	125.	B

CHAPTER 10

Practice, Practice, Practice

(NOTE: You will need another person to dictate each practice exercise. Allow 30 minutes to finish the transcript and mark your answers.)

PRACTICE SET 1

The Dictation

Finish reading each two lines at the number of seconds indicated below

To be able to express your ideas simply and clearly, it is necessary	10
that you have a good command of the language. (Period) The greater your vocabulary,	20
the more interesting and effective your conversation. (Period) Dr. Eliot, former	30
president of Harvard, said, "I recognize but one mental acquisition that	40
is an essential part of the education of a lady or a gentleman; namely,	50
an accurate and refined use of the mother tongue." (Period) Fortunately, this	1 min.
is an acquisition within the reach of everyone. (Period) Only two things	10
are necessary: a good dictionary and a desire to speak well. (Period)	20
Add to these the association with educated, intelligent people	30
and ready access to a public library, and there is no reason	40
in the world why you cannot acquire a rich and colorful	50
vocabulary. (Period) When you hear a new word or read it in	2 min.
a book, learn its meaning and pronunciation. (Period) Until you are	10
wholly familiar with the word and are able to use it in	20
your conversation, it is not a part of your vocabulary. (Period) It	30
is not enough to know how to pronounce a word and to have a general	40
idea of its meaning; you must know how to use it correctly in	50
your speech. (Period) Remember that there is always a right word for every purpose. (Period)	3 min.

Reprinted with permission from Gregg Shorthand Simplified for Colleges, *Leslie, Zoubeck, and Hosler, 1958, Gregg Publishing Division, McGraw-Hill Book Co., Inc.*

The Transcript

Compare your notes with the transcript. Then select the correct word for each blank space and write the letter of your choice in the space.

WORD LIST

Write *E* if the answer is NOT listed.

ability—B	goal—B	one—D
able—C	great—C	only—B
accurate—D	greater—B	our—D
acquire—D	greatest—D	
acquisition—B		part—A
acquisitive—C	Harvard—C	partial—C
actual—C		present—D
	ideal—B	president—A
capable—D	ideas—A	
clear—C	interest—B	realize—D
clearly—B	interesting—A	refined—D
command—C		remind—C
conservation—B	ladies—A	
conversation—B	lady—B	sensual—B
converse—C	language—A	simple—D
	length—B	
educate—C		to exist—C
effect—C	many—B	to express—B
effecting—B	mature—D	tongue—C
effective—D	medical—C	
essence—D	mental—A	use—A
essential--C	more—C	used—B
	mortal—D	
formal—C	most—A	woman—C
former—A		won—C
	natural—C	
gentleman—A	necessary—D	your—C
gentlemen—C	needed—C	

TRANSCRIPT

To be ___ ___ ___ ___ ___ and
  1   2   3   4   5

___, it is ___ that you have a ___
6   7   8

___ of the ___. The ___ your ___, the
9   10   11   12

___ ___ and ___ your ___.
13 14   15   16

Dr. Eliot, ___ ___ of ___, said, "I ___
           17 18   19   20

but ___ ___ ___ that is an ___
    21 22 23   24

___ of the ___ of a ___ or a ___;
25   26   27   28

namely, an ___ and ___ ___ of the
           29   30 31

___ ___."...
32 33

- -

WORD LIST

Write *E* if the answer is NOT listed.

acquaint—D	intellect—B	their—A
acquire—C	intelligent—A	there—D
acquired—B		these—A
acquisition—A	liberty—D	they're—B
association—B		this—B
assumption—D	necessary—D	those—B
	needed—A	to—B
can—B	no—A	to say—B
cannot—A	now—C	to speak—C
colored—D		too—D
colorful—B	people—C	two—A
	persons—B	
desire—A	public—B	vocality—C
dream—D		
	rare—B	well—B
educated—D	rationale—B	when—C
education—C.	reach—C	where—A
everybody—C	reading—A	why—D
everyone—B	realm—B	will—D
	reason—C	within—D
grand—B	republic—C	without—C
great—D	rich—C	

TRANSCRIPT (continued)

...Fortunately, ___ is an ___ ___ the ___ of
               34   35 36   37

___. Only ___ ___ are ___: a ___ ___
38   39 40   41   42 43

and a ___ ___ ___. Add to ___ the ___
      44 45 46   47   48

with ___, ___ and ___ ___ to a ___
     49   50   51 52   53   54

___, and ___ is ___ ___ in the ___ ___
55   56   57 58   59 60

you ___ ___ a ___ and ___ ___....
    61 62   63   64 65

272   The Dictation Test

WORD LIST

Write *E* if the answer is NOT listed.

a—C	is—B	the—A
able—A	it—A	these—B
air—D	its—C	this—C
also—D		to abuse—D
an—B	know—C	to lose—B
and—B		to use—C
as—A	lean—A	
	learn—D	vocabulary—B
book—B	learned—C	vocality—D
buck—D		
	meaning—B	which—B
conservation—C	means—C	whole—D
conversation—A	mental—D	wholly—B
converse—B	moaning—A	within—A
		word—B
familiar—D	new—D	world—D
family—C	now—B	
		you—B
hear—C	our—B	your—D
heard—D		
here—B	part—D	
holy—C	partial—B	
	pronounced—C	
in—C		
into—D	red—C	

TRANSCRIPT (continued)

... When _____ _____ a _____ _____ or _____ _____
66   67   68   69   70   71

_____ a _____, _____ _____ _____ and _____. Until
72   73   74   75   76   77

you _____ _____ _____ _____ _____ word _____
78   79   80   81   82   83

are _____ _____ it in _____ _____, it _____ _____
84   85   86   87   88   89

_____ _____ _____ your _____. ...
90   91   92   93

- -

WORD LIST

Write *E* if the answer is NOT listed.

all—C	into—B	there—A
alright—B	is—D	to abuse—A
an—A	it—C	to have—C
as—A	its—B	to hold—B
		to know—A
correct—B	meaning—C	to pronounce—B
correction—C	morning—B	to propose—D
correctly—D	most—D	to say—C
	must—B	to use—B
		to utilize—C
every—D	not—B	tonight—B
everyone—B	now—C	
		us—C
for—C	our—C	
four—A		warn—C
	propose—A	who—C
general—A		word—A
gentle—C		work—B
	speak—D	write—C
how—D	speech—A	
idea—D		
ideal—B	than—C	your—B
in—A	that—D	
inside—C	their—B	

TRANSCRIPT (continued)

... It _____ _____ _____ _____ _____ _____ a _____
94   95   96   97   98   99   100

_____ _____ a _____ _____ of _____ _____ ;
101   102   103   104   105   106

you _____ know _____ _____ it _____ _____ _____
107   108   109   110   111   112

_____ .
113

Remember _____ _____ is _____ a _____ word
114   115   116   117

_____ _____ _____ .
118   119   120

ANSWERS FOR PRACTICE SET 1

1. C	25. A	49. D	73. B	97. A
2. B	26. E	50. A	74. D	98. C
3. C	27. B	51. C	75. C	99. B
4. A	28. A	52. E	76. B	100. A
5. E	29. D	53. E	77. E	101. E
6. B	30. D	54. B	78. C	102. C
7. D	31. A	55. E	79. B	103. A
8. E	32. E	56. D	80. D	104. D
9. C	33. C	57. A	81. E	105. B
10. A	34. B	58. C	82. A	106. C
11. B	35. A	59. B	83. B	107. B
12. E	36. D	60. D	84. A	108. D
13. C	37. C	61. A	85. C	109. B
14. A	38. B	62. C	86. D	110. D
15. D	39. A	63. C	87. A	111. A
16. B	40. E	64. B	88. B	112. B
17. A	41. D	65. E	89. E	113. A
18. A	42. E	66. B	90. C	114. D
19. C	43. E	67. C	91. D	115. A
20. E	44. A	68. D	92. E	116. E
21. D	45. C	69. B	93. B	117. E
22. A	46. B	70. E	94. D	118. C
23. B	47. A	71. A	95. B	119. D
24. C	48. B	72. C	96. E	120. E

PRACTICE SET 2

The Dictation

Finish reading each two lines at the number of seconds indicated below

Each year you, with millions of other Americans, spend an agonizing	10
period of indecision considering the pros and cons of the various trips presented	20
in the travel folders you have accumulated. (Period) The fact that your	30
budget may be definitely limited does not detract from the enjoyment you	40
derive from reading of the far-off places so attractively described and	50
pictured in the literature of the various bus, railroad, steamship, and	1 min.
airlines. (Period) The annual search for something different to do during the	10
vacation period adds to the zest of the vacation itself. (Period) The extensive	20
airline services now available make it possible for one to consider trips that	30
previously were impossible because of time limitations. (Period) High among	40
the trips that might appeal to you is travel in Europe. (Period) You can relax	50
in the scenic splendor of the Old World and revel in its art masterpieces,	2 min.
its colorful native pageants, and its quaint customs and costumes. (Period)	10
Flying the Atlantic to Europe will save you precious days of that	20
all-too-short vacation period. (Period) You will have more time to spend	30
in visiting each country. (Period) It will be possible for you to become better	40
acquainted with the people and their everyday pursuits. (Period) You can	50
see some of the byways that the average tourist so frequently misses. (Period)	3 min.

Reprinted with permission from Gregg Shorthand Simplified for Colleges, Leslie, Zoubeck, and Hosler, 1958, Gregg Publishing Division, McGraw-Hill Book Co., Inc.

The Transcript

Compare your notes with the transcript. Then select the correct word for each blank space and write the letter of your choice in the space.

WORD LIST

Write *E* if the answer is NOT listed.

accumulated—A   enjoyable—D   present—C
accustomed—C   enjoyment—B   presented—D
airlines—C   pros—D
airplanes—D   faced—D   prose—A
airways—B   fact—C
Americas—D   fat—B   railroad—B
Americans—A   folders—B   railway—C
another—B   folds—D   reading—A
attraction—D   reads—B
attractively—C   indecision—A
                    indigestion—B   spend—D
budding—A   spent—B
budget—B   limitation—B   steamer—A
bus—A   literate—D   steamship—D
bussed—B   literature—B
                                    trail—C
cans—C   million—C   travel—A
cons—B   millions—D   traveled—B
considerate—C
                                    tricks—A
                     organizing—A
defined—C   other—C   varied—D
definitely—D   various—C
derailed—D   period—C   very—B
derived—C   picture—A
describe—C   pictured—D   year—B
detract—A   pitcher—C   your—C
distract—C   placed—B
disturbed—B   places—A

TRANSCRIPT

Each _____ you, with _____ of _____ _____, _____
      1   2   3   4   5

an _____ of _____ _____ the _____ and _____
  6   7   8   9   10   11

of the _____ _____ _____ in the _____ _____ you
       12   13   14   15   16

have _____. The _____ that your _____ may be _____
     17   18   19   20

_____ does not _____ from the _____ you _____
21   22   23   24

from _____ of the far-off _____ so _____ _____ and
    25   26   27   28

_____ in the _____ of the _____ _____, _____, _____,
29   30   31   32   33   34

and _____ ....
  35

WORD LIST

Write *E* if the answer is NOT listed.

aids—C   limitations—D   siege—B
airplane—B   limitless—A   someone—A
annual—B   limits—C
annul—C   time—B
are—B   made—A   to conclude—C
available—B   make—D   to conduct—A
availed—D   mate—C   to dew—D
                                      to do—B
because—A   new—D   to due—A
become—C   now—C   tricks—D
                                      trips—A
different—C   one—B
diverse—D   vacation—A
during—C   period—D   vocation—B
                   possible—A
expensive—A   predated—D   wear—A
extensive—D   previously—B   were—C
                   probable—C   won—D
improbable—B
its—C   search—A   zeal—B
itself—B   seek—D   zest—C
                   servants—D
just—D   services—A

TRANSCRIPT (continued)

... The _____ _____ for _____ _____ _____ _____ the
      36   37   38   39   40   41

_____ _____ _____ to the _____ of the vacation
42   43   44   45

_____ .
46

The _____ _____ _____ _____ _____ _____ _____ it _____
     47   48   49   50   51   52   53

for _____ _____ _____ that _____ _____ _____ _____
   54   55   56   57   58   59   60

of _____ _____ ....
  61   62

WORD LIST

Write _E_ if the answer is NOT listed.

able—A	masterworks—B	scene—C
aged—D	may—A	scenery—A
amid—D	might—D	scenic—B
among—B		splendid—C
appear—C	native—A	
arch—C	natural—B	than—B
art—A	nature—D	that—C
	night—B	travail—D
can—D		travel—C
can't—C	old—C	tricks—C
colored—A		trips—A
colorful—C	pageants—A	
costumes—B	pages—B	world—A
customs—D		
	quaint—C	you—B
England—B	queer—D	your—A
Europe—A	quick—A	
globe—B	rebel—C	
	relapse—B	
it's—A	relax—D	
its—D	revel—B	

TRANSCRIPT (continued)

... High _____ the _____ _____ _____ _____ to
          63   64   65   66   67

_____ is _____ in _____. You _____ _____ in the
68   69   70   71   72

_____ _____ of the _____ _____ and _____ in
73   74   75   76   77

_____ _____ _____, its _____ _____ _____, and its
78   79   80   81   82   83

_____ _____ and _____ . . . .
84   85   86

- -

WORD LIST

Write _E_ if the answer is NOT listed.

acquainted—A	misses—A	than—B
acquitted—D	misuse—C	their—C
Atlanta—B	more—C	there—B
Atlantic—B	most—D	to become—A
avarice—D	Mrs.—B	to begin—B
average—C	much—A	to share—B
		to spend—A
be—B	often—D	tourism—D
best—B	overage—B	tourist—A
better—C		twist—C
bylaws—A	passable—C	
byways—B	people—D	Utopia—A
	period—C	
can—B	person—C	vacation—A
could—D	possible—D	visited—B
country—A	possibility—A	visiting—C
county—B	precious—B	visitor—A
	precocious—D	vocation—C
day—B	pursues—B	
days—C	pursuits—C	will—D
daze—A		would—C
	safe—C	
every—C	save—A	
everyday—A	sea—A	
everyone—D	see—D	
	shall—A	
had—A	some—A	
have—B	sum—C	

TRANSCRIPT (continued)

... Flying the _____ to _____ will _____ you _____
         87   88   89   90

_____ of _____ all-too-short _____ _____. You _____
91   92   93   94   95

_____ _____ _____ _____ in _____ _____ _____. It
96   97   98   99   100 101 102

_____ _____ _____ for you _____ _____ _____
103   104 105   106 107 108

with the _____ and _____ _____ _____. You _____
        109   110 111 112   113

_____ _____ of the _____ that the _____ _____
114 115   116   117 118

so _____ _____.
  119   120

ANSWERS FOR PRACTICE SET 2

1. B	25. A	49. A	73. B	97. C
2. D	26. A	50. C	74. E	98. E
3. C	27. C	51. B	75. C	99. A
4. A	28. E	52. D	76. A	100. C
5. D	29. D	53. A	77. B	101. E
6. E	30. B	54. B	78. D	102. A
7. C	31. C	55. D	79. A	103. D
8. A	32. A	56. A	80. E	104. B
9. E	33. B	57. B	81. C	105. D
10. D	34. D	58. C	82. A	106. A
11. B	35. C	59. E	83. A	107. C
12. C	36. B	60. A	84. C	108. A
13. E	37. A	61. B	85. D	109. D
14. D	38. E	62. D	86. B	110. C
15. A	39. C	63. B	87. C	111. A
16. B	40. B	64. A	88. E	112. C
17. A	41. C	65. C	89. A	113. B
18. C	42. A	66. D	90. B	114. D
19. B	43. D	67. E	91. C	115. A
20. D	44. E	68. B	92. E	116. B
21. E	45. C	69. C	93. A	117. C
22. A	46. B	70. A	94. C	118. A
23. B	47. D	71. D	95. D	119. E
24. C	48. E	72. D	96. B	120. A

PRACTICE SET 3

The Dictation

Finish reading
each two lines
at the number
of seconds in-
dicated below

The boy was ten years old, and
he had a passion for machinery. (Period) He   10

tinkered with all the clocks in the old
white farmhouse until they kept time   20

properly. (Period) One Sunday morning after
church a neighbor took out his big gold   30

huntingcase watch. (Period) He said, "Henry,
can you fix my old turnip?" (Question mark) The   40

boy found that a jewel was loose in the
works. (Period) He put it back into place and   50

the watch ran. (Period) The neighbors around
Dearborn began to bring their ailing old   1 min.

timepieces. (Period) So young Henry Ford set up
shop on a shelf in his bedroom, working   10

nights after chores. (Period) In the winter
he kept warm with an oil lantern   20

between his feet. (Period) He ground a shingle
nail down into a tiny screwdriver and made   30

files from knitting needles. (Period) All
his life he tinkered with watches and   40

never had to use a jeweler's eyeglass. (Period)
He could almost see with his long, thin,   50

steel-spring fingers: the fingers of
the hands that put the nation on wheels. (Period)   2 min.

His passion for machinery became an
idea, and the power of that idea has   10

rolled on through the years. (Period) He
learned how to run, repair, and make every   20

kind of machine there was. (Period) Then
he began on the machine that wasn't—   30

a horseless carriage. (Period) In 1896,
seven years before the founding of the   40

Ford Motor Company, he trundled his
first little two-passenger machine out   50

into one of the alleys of Detroit and
ran it around the block. (Period)   3 min.

Reprinted with permission from Gregg Shorthand Simplified for Colleges, *Leslie,
Zoubeck, and Hosler, 1958, Gregg Publishing Division, McGraw-Hill Book Co., Inc.*

The Transcript

Compare your notes with the transcript. Then select the correct word for each blank space and write the letter of your choice in the space.

WORD LIST

Write E if the answer is NOT listed.

all—C	large—B	till—B
		time—A
big—B	machine—C	timed—B
bigger—D	machinery—B	tinker—A
boat—D	meaning—C	tinkered—D
boy—A	morning—A	took—D
		turned—A
can—D	neighbor—B	turnip—B
can't—C	neighbors—C	
charge—B		until—D
church—C	oil—D	
clock—A	our—D	watch—B
		water—A
farm—A	passion—A	while—B
farmhouse—C	position—C	white—A
fix—A	proper—D	
fixed—C	properly—C	years—C
fox—B	property—A	yours—A
gold—C	take—A	
good—D	taken—B	
	ten—D	
keep—C	then—C	
kept—B	tied—C	

TRANSCRIPT

The ____ was ____ ____ ____ , and he had a
   1   2   3   4

____ for ____ . He ____ with ____ the ____ in
 5   6   7   8   9

the ____ ____ ____ ____ they ____ ____
   10   11   12   13   14   15

____ .
16

One ____ ____ ____ ____ a ____
    17   18   19   20   21   22

____ his ____ ____ huntingcase ____ . He said,
 23   24   25   26

"Henry, ____ you ____ my ____ ____ ?" . . .
       27   28   29   30

WORD LIST

Write E if the answer is NOT listed.

abound—C	in—A	sat—A
ailed—B	into—B	self—D
ailing—C		sharp—A
around—A	jewel—B	shelf—C
	jeweler—D	ship—B
back—C		shop—D
backed—B	keep—D	sit—D
bedroom--B	lecture—B	
begin—A	loose—C	their—D
between—C	lose—D	there—C
bog—C		timepieces—A
book—D	neighborhood—D	timers—D
bottom—D	neighborhoods—A	to bring—B
brought—C	night—D	
	nights—C	under—C
chores—B	oil—A	
	old—D	warm—B
feel—C		warn—C
feet—D	pat—C	water—A
find—B	please—C	winner—C
foot—B	put—D	winter—D
found—D		work—B
	ran—D	worked—D
him—B	run—C	works—A
his—A		

TRANSCRIPT (continued)

. . . The ____ ____ that a ____ was ____ in the
       31   32   33   34

____ . He ____ it ____ ____ ____ and the ____
35   36   37   38   39   40

____ .
41

The ____ ____ Dearborn ____ ____ ____
     42   43   44   45   46

____ ____ ____ . So ____ Henry Ford ____
 47   48   49   50   51

____ ____ on a ____ in his ____ , ____ ____
52   53   54   55   56   57

after ____ . In the ____ he ____ ____ with an
     58   59   60   61

____ ____ ____ his ____ . . . .
62   63   64   65

WORD LIST

Write _E_ if the answer is NOT listed.

almost—B	knitted—C	puts—D
always—C	knitting—B	
	knotting—A	saw—C
can—D		see—D
could—C	life—C	seen—A
	live—B	single—C
down—B	long—B	
	lung—A	than—C
eyeball—B		then—D
eyeglass—A	made—A	thin—A
	maid—B	tinny—C
file—D	make—A	tiny—D
filed—A		
files—C	nail—D	us—B
fingered—A	nailed—B	used—A
fingers—B	nation—C	
	national—A	watched—D
grind—B	needled—A	watches—A
ground—A	needles—D	wheeled—B
	noodles—C	wheels—D
had—D	null—A	
hard—C		
	pat—B	
jewels—C	put—A	

TRANSCRIPT (continued)

...He ___ a ___ ___ ___ into a ___
66   67   68   69   70

___ and ___ ___ from ___ ___. All his
71   72   73   74   75

___ he tinkered with ___ and ___ ___ to
76   77   78   79

___ a ___ ___.
80   81   82

He ___ ___ ___ with his ___, ___, steel-
83   84   85   86   87

spring ___: the fingers of the ___ that ___
88   89   90

the ___ on ___ ....
91   92

WORD LIST

Write _E_ if the answer is NOT listed.

all—A	foremost—C	power—A
alleys—B	founded—D	powerful—D
allied—D	founding—C	
allies—C		ran—A
	horse sense—A	repaint—C
became—D		repair—A
become—A	ideal—C	roll—C
began—C		rolled—B
begin—D	kin—B	run—B
black—A	kind—A	
blacked—C		seven—B
blocked—D	learn—A	small—B
	learned—C	
carriage—A	little—D	threw—A
carried—C		through—D
	machine—D	to rule—B
earned—D	made—D	to run—D
every—C	make—B	trampled—A
everything—D		trundled—D
	passion—C	
finding—B	pasture—A	year—A
first—A	patient—D	yours—B

TRANSCRIPT (continued)

...His ___ for ___ ___ an ___, and the
93   94   95   96

___ of that idea has ___ on ___ the ___.
97   98   99   100

He ___ ___ ___ , ___, and ___ ___
101 102 103 104   105 106

___ of ___ there was. Then he ___ on the
107 108   109

machine that wasn't—a ___ ___.
110 111

In 1896, ___ ___ before the ___ of the
112 113   114

Ford Motor Company, he ___ his ___ ___
115   116 117

two-passenger machine out into one of the ___ of
118

Detroit and ___ it around the ___.
119   120

ANSWERS FOR PRACTICE SET 3

1. A	25. C	49. A	73. C	97. A
2. D	26. B	50. B	74. B	98. B
3. C	27. D	51. E	75. D	99. D
4. E	28. A	52. E	76. C	100. A
5. A	29. E	53. D	77. A	101. C
6. B	30. B	54. C	78. B	102. E
7. D	31. E	55. B	79. D	103. D
8. C	32. D	56. E	80. E	104. A
9. E	33. B	57. C	81. E	105. B
10. E	34. C	58. B	82. A	106. C
11. A	35. A	59. D	83. C	107. A
12. C	36. D	60. E	84. B	108. D
13. D	37. C	61. B	85. D	109. C
14. B	38. B	62. A	86. B	110. E
15. A	39. E	63. E	87. A	111. A
16. C	40. E	64. C	88. B	112. B
17. E	41. D	65. D	89. E	113. A
18. A	42. E	66. A	90. A	114. C
19. E	43. A	67. E	91. C	115. D
20. C	44. E	68. D	92. D	116. A
21. B	45. B	69. B	93. C	117. D
22. D	46. D	70. C	94. B	118. B
23. E	47. C	71. E	95. D	119. A
24. A	48. D	72. A	96. E	120. C

PRACTICE SET 4

The Dictation

Finish reading
each two lines
at the number
of seconds in-
dicated below

The retail salesperson who plays such a vital part in the process of distribution	10
may well be considered one of the most important spark plugs of our economy. (Period)	20
He makes our free-enterprise system work. (Period) He persuades us to exchange	30
our money for the things that make for better and more enjoyable living. (Period)	40
By keeping the cash registers of America ringing, he also keeps our factories	50
humming. (Period) The high-pressure salesperson of yesterday, who misrepresented	1 min.
merchandise, is as obsolete today as the Model T and the patent-medicine man. (Period)	10
In the buyer's market of today, the good salesperson is the one who induces the	20
customer to purchase by showing him how he will benefit. (Period) The retail salesperson	30
should not only make people want what he has to sell, but he should also make them want to	40
but it from him. (Period) What a challenge! (Exclamation Point) What he does in the place of business in which	50
he serves reflects upon the firm, and the firm's reputation reflects upon	2 min.
him. (Period) The successful salesperson is more interested in keeping the customer's	10
good will than in turning a quick sale. (Period) Good will is an intangible	20
asset that is not visible except as it is reflected in the faces of satisfied	30
customers. (Period) However, it is the most valuable asset that any business can possess. (Period)	40
It is indeed more valuable than the building, the merchandise, or the equipment. (Period) Every	50
salesperson holds the good will of the establishment in his hands. (Period)	3 min.

The Transcript

Compare your notes with the transcript. Then select the correct word for each blank space and write the letter of your choice in the space.

WORD LIST

Write E if the answer is NOT listed.

allow—A	improved—C	retail—C
American—A	items—B	role—A
business—B	key—D	salesman—B
		salesperson—A
can—C	life—C	seller—C
cash—D	living—D	such—C
considered—C		system—A
considering—A	make—B	systems—C
convinces—D	may—D	
	money—C	takes—C
demonstrates—A	most—D	the—C
distribution—A	much—A	things—D
		thought of—D
economy—B	our—D	to exchange—A
enjoyable—A		to trade—C
enjoyed—B	part—B	
essential—D	perhaps—A	very—C
	persuades—B	
goods—A	plays—D	way—B
	plug—D	well—B
happen—C	plugs—C	wholesale—A
	procedure—C	work—D
important—B	process—A	worthwhile—D

TRANSCRIPT

The _____ _____ who _____ _____ a _____ _____ in
　　　1　　2　　　　 3　　 4　　 5　　6

the _____ of _____ _____ _____ be _____ one of the
　　　7　　　　8　　 9　　10　　　 11

_____ _____ _____ _____ _____ of our _____. He makes
　12　　13　　14　　15　　　　　　16

_____ _____ _____ _____ _____. He _____ us _____ our
　17　　18　　19　　20　　　　　21　　 22

_____ for the _____ that _____ for _____ and more
　23　　　　　24　　　　25　　　 26

_____ _____....
　27　　28

WORD LIST

Write E if the answer is NOT listed.

allowing—B	industries—C	past—B
America—A	introduces—C	pressure—A
benefitting—B	keeping—C	registers—B
buyer—C	keeps—A	represented—B
buyer's—A		
	machines—C	show—B
cash—D	making—A	showing—C
coin—C	man—B	
consumer—C	market—D	to buy—D
continues—C	marketing—C	to peruse—B
customer—B	medical—D	to purchase—A
	medicinal—B	today—C
factories—D	medicine—C	
	mercantile—B	when—D
going—A	merchandise—A	where—C
good—B	merchant—B	who—C
goods—A	mistaken—C	whom—A
	Model T—B	why—D
high—C		working—B
how—A	now—B	
humming—B		yesterday—D
	obsolete—D	yesteryear—C
induces—A	opposite—C	

TRANSCRIPT (continued)

... By _____ the _____ _____ of _____ _____, he also
　　　 29　　　 30　　31　　　 32　　33

_____ our _____ _____. The _____ - _____ salesper-
　34　　　 35　　36　　　　 37　　 38

son of _____, _____ _____ _____ _____, is as _____ _____ as
　　　　 39　　40　　41　　42　　　　　 43　　44

the _____ and the patent-_____ _____. In the _____
　　　45　　　　　　　　　　　　46　　 47　　　　　 48

_____ of today, the _____ salesperson is the _____
　49　　　　　　　　　50　　　　　　　　　　　　　 51

who _____ the _____ _____ by _____ him _____ he
　　　52　　　　 53　　54　　　 55　　　　56

will _____....
　57

WORD LIST

Write *E* if the answer is NOT listed.

business—D
buying—A

challenge—A
could—C
customer—D
customer's—A

do—D

faith—B
firm—D
from—C

goes—B
good—C

he—B
her—A

interest—B
interested—D

keep—C
keeping—B

make—D
may—C
might—A

office—B
one—C
only—A
over—D

people—D
persons—A
place—A
placed—C

quiet—b

reflected—A
reflects—B
reputation—A
reputed—C
retail—B

sale—A
serve—D
serves—C

sold—C
success—C
successful—A

than—B
them—A
then—D
they—C
to bring—D
to buy—B
to say—B
to sell—A
turning—C

up—C
upon—B

want—D
wanted—C
which—A
will—A
with—B

TRANSCRIPT (continued)

...The ____ salesperson ____ not ____ make
         58   59   60
____ ____what he has ____, but ____ ____ also
61   62   63   64   65
____ ____ want ____ it ____ him. **What a**
66   67   68   69
____! What he____ in the ____ of ____
70   71   72   73
in ____ he ____ ____ ____ the ____, and the
    74   75   76   77   78
firm's ____ reflects ____ ____. The ____
         79   80   81   82
salesperson is more ____ in ____ the ____
                      83   84   85
____ ____ ____ in ____ a ____ ____....
86   87   88   89   90   91

WORD LIST

Write *E* if the answer is NOT listed.

accept—D
am—B
any—A
are—D
assist—D

built—A
business—C
busy—B

can—A
can't—B
could—D

established—B
establishment—A
except—A
exception—B

faced—D
faces—B

hands—A
has—C

helps—A
his—D
holds—B
honor—C
hour—A

indeed—A
indication—C
intangible—D
invisible—C
is—A
it—C
its—B

many—A
merchandise—A
merchant—B
more—B
most—D
much—C

or—C
our—B

possess—B
possessed—C
possession—D

reflect—B
reflected—A
reflects—C

satisfaction—C
satisfying—B

than—D
the—B
then—C

valuable—A
value—D
valued—B
viable—A
visible—B

was—D
will—C
won't—B

TRANSCRIPT (continued)

...Good ____ ____ an ____ ____ that is not
        92   93   94   95
____ ____ as ____ is ____ in the ____ of
96   97   98   99   100
____ customers.
101
    However, it is the ____ ____ ____ that ____
                        102   103   104   105
____ ____ ____. It is ____ ____ valuable
106   107   108   109   110
____ the ____, the ____, ____ the ____.
111   112   113   114   115
Every ____ ____ the good will of the ____ in
        116   117   118
____ ____.
119   120

ANSWERS FOR PRACTICE SET 4

1. C	25. B	49. D	73. D	97. A
2. A	26. E	50. B	74. A	98. C
3. D	27. A	51. E	75. C	99. A
4. C	28. D	52. A	76. B	100. B
5. E	29. C	53. B	77. B	101. E
6. B	30. D	54. A	78. D	102. D
7. A	31. B	55. C	79. A	103. A
8. A	32. A	56. A	80. B	104. E
9. D	33. E	57. E	81. E	105. A
10. B	34. A	58. B	82. A	106. C
11. C	35. D	59. E	83. D	107. A
12. D	36. B	60. A	84. B	108. B
13. B	37. C	61. D	85. A	109. A
14. E	38. A	62. D	86. C	110. B
15. C	39. D	63. A	87. A	111. D
16. B	40. C	64. B	88. B	112. E
17. D	41. E	65. E	89. C	113. A
18. E	42. A	66. D	90. E	114. C
19. A	43. D	67. A	91. A	115. E
20. D	44. C	68. B	92. C	116. E
21. B	45. B	69. C	93. A	117. B
22. A	46. C	70. A	94. D	118. A
23. C	47. B	71. E	95. E	119. D
24. D	48. A	72. A	96. B	120. A

PRACTICE SET 5

The Dictation

We say that Father keeps the house running. (Period) Father says that the house	10
keeps him running. (Period) Probably both statements are true. (Period) Let us look	20
at it in the most favorable light— the light of a lovely summer evening. (Period)	30
Father has come home from the office, has had his dinner, and has arbitrated	40
all the children's quarrels. (Period) He has settled down in his favorite chair	50
on the porch to relax and enjoy the summer evening. (Period) Right away we know	1 min.
that Father is either new to country living or that he is an incurable	10
optimist. (Period) Every beautiful summer evening he sits in that same chair to	20
relax, and every beautiful summer evening something drags him out of the chair. (Period)	30
This evening perhaps the telephone bell rings. (Period) Almost immediately Father hears	40
Mother say, "Of course, he will be delighted." (Period) Then Mother	50
comes out and breaks the news to Father that Mrs. Jones, their neighbor,	2 min.
has offered to give her some plants if Father will get them	10
now. (Period) So, Father climbs into the car and drives over to get the	20
plants and drives back, only to find, naturally, that he is to plant	30
the plants for Mother and that they are very delicate plants	40
that must be planted immediately. (Period) By this time the beautiful	50
summer evening has faded and the mosquitoes have come out. (Period)	3 min.

Reprinted with permission from Gregg Shorthand Simplified for Colleges, Leslie, Zoubeck, and Hosler, 1958, Gregg Publishing Division, McGraw-Hill Book Co., Inc.

The Transcript

Compare your notes with the transcript. Then select the correct word for each blank space and write the letter of your choice in the space.

WORD LIST
Write _E_ if the answer is NOT listed.

arbiter—B
arbitrated—A
are—B
as—C

boat—B
both—A

came—B
children's—C
child's—B
come—D

dined—C

even—C
evening—A
every—D

farther—B
favorable—D
favorite—B
fro—C
from—A

hard—D
he's—B
hid—B
him—C
his—D
home—B
horse—C
house—A
hut—D
if—D
it—A
it's—D

keep—D
keeps—B

light—A
lit—C
lively—A
look—C
lovely—C
luck—B
many—C
most—B
much—A

of—B
office—C
often—A
orbited—C
our—D

pair—C

quakes—C
quarrels—B

racing—B
running—D

said—D
say—C
simmer—D
stated—A
summer—A

true—A
truth—B

us—D

TRANSCRIPT

We ____ that ____ ____ the ____ ____. Father
   1   2   3   4   5

____ that the house keeps ____ running. Probably
 6   7

____ ____ ____ ____.
 8   9   10   11

Let ____ ____ at ____ in the ____ ____ ____
    12   13   14   15   16   17

— the light ____ a ____ ____ ____. Father has
          18   19   20   21

____ ____ ____ the ____, has ____ his ____,
 22   23   24   25   26   27

and has ____ ____ the ____ ____....
       28   29   30   31

- -

WORD LIST
Write _E_ if the answer is NOT listed.

always—C

beautiful—D
beauty—C
bountiful—A

continent—D

done—A
down—D
drag—C
drugs—A

either—A
enjoy—D
ether—C
even—C
evening—A
ever—C
every—D

farther—B
Father—D
favorable—D
favored—B

he—B
him—D

incubate—B
incurable—C
injure—A

knew—C
know—B
known—D

life—B
live—C
living—A

new—B

optometrist—A
our—D
out—B

porch—A
pouch—C

relapse—A
relax—C

saddled—C
same—C
sat—B
sets—C
settled—B
share—B
sits—A
some—D
someone—C
something—B

than—C
that—D
to relapse—D
to relax—B

us—A

we—C
when—D

TRANSCRIPT (continued)

... He has ____ ____ in his ____ chair on the
        32   33   34

____ ____ and ____ the ____ ____. Right
 35   36   37   38   39

____ ____ ____ that ____ is ____ ____ to
 40   41   42   43   44   45

____ ____ or ____ he is an ____ ____. Every
 46   47   48   49   50

____ summer evening ____ ____ in that ____
 51   52   53   54

____ to ____, and ____ ____ summer
 55   56   57   58

evening ____ ____ ____ ____ of
         59   60   61   62

the ____....
   63

WORD LIST

Write E if the answer is NOT listed.

be—C	hers—A	offhand—B
being—D	herself—D	our—A
bell—C		out—C
bowl—A	if—A	
bricks—A	immediate—C	perchance—C
bride—B	immediately—B	perhaps—D
		plans—D
came—C	James—D	plants—B
come—B	Jones—C	purchase—A
comes—A		
	knew—A	ring—D
delighted—B		rings—A
deluded—D	Miss—B	
	mom—B	said—D
even—B	Mrs.—A	says—A
evening—A		sum—C
	neighbor—A	
get—C	new—D	telegraph—D
got—D	news—D	telephone—B
	night—C	their—B
hear—A	now—A	them—B
heard—C		they're—A
hears—D	of—C	those—A
her—C	offered—D	

TRANSCRIPT (continued)

. . . This ____ ____ the ____ ____ ____. Almost
64 65 66 67 68

____ Father ____ ____ ____, "Of course, he will
69 70 71 72

____ ____." Then Mother ____ ____ and ____
73 74 75 76 77

the ____ to Father that ____ ____, ____ ____,
78 79 80 81 82

has ____ ____ ____ ____ ____ ____ Father
83 84 85 86 87 88

will ____ ____ ____ . . . .
89 90 91

- -

WORD LIST

Write E if the answer is NOT listed.

above—B	even—B	our—D
and—A	evening—C	over—C
are—A	ever—C	
	every—C	part—A
back—D		partial—C
bake—B	faded—B	planted—B
barge—D	faith—C	plants—B
bargain—B	Father—E	
beautiful—D	feted—D	solely—D
begin—A	found—A	soon—D
bountiful—C		
	immaterially—C	than—C
came—B	immediately—A	that—D
car—A	into—B	them—B
cart—D	is—E	they—A
climbs—C		time—B
climbed—D	masked—A	to find—B
come—C	most—B	to get—C
	must—C	to have—B
delicate—D		to plant—D
delicious—A	naturally—C	
driven—C	neutral—A	very—B
drives—D		
drove—D	one—A	
dug—A	only—C	

TRANSCRIPT (continued)

So, ____ ____ ____ the ____ and ____ ____
92 93 94 95 96 97

____ the ____ ____ ____ ____, only to
98 99 100 101 102

find, ____, that he ____ ____ the plants for
103 104 105

Mother and ____ ____ ____ ____ ____ plants
106 107 108 109 110

that ____ be ____ ____. By this ____ the
111 112 113 114

____ ____ ____ has ____ and the ____
115 116 117 118 119

have ____ out.
120

ANSWERS FOR PRACTICE SET 5

1. C	25. C	49. C	73. C	97. C
2. E	26. E	50. E	74. B	98. C
3. B	27. E	51. D	75. A	99. B
4. A	28. A	52. B	76. C	100. A
5. D	29. E	53. A	77. E	101. D
6. B	30. C	54. C	78. D	102. D
7. C	31. B	55. E	79. A	103. C
8. A	32. B	56. C	80. C	104. E
9. E	33. D	57. D	81. B	105. D
10. B	34. E	58. D	82. A	106. D
11. A	35. A	59. B	83. D	107. A
12. D	36. B	60. E	84. E	108. A
13. C	37. D	61. D	85. C	109. B
14. A	38. E	62. B	86. E	110. D
15. B	39. A	63. E	87. B	111. C
16. D	40. E	64. A	88. A	112. B
17. A	41. C	65. D	89. C	113. A
18. B	42. B	66. B	90. B	114. B
19. C	43. D	67. C	91. A	115. D
20. A	44. A	68. A	92. E	116. E
21. A	45. C	69. B	93. C	117. C
22. D	46. E	70. D	94. B	118. B
23. B	47. A	71. E	95. A	119. E
24. A	48. D	72. E	96. D	120. C

The Office Machine Operator Special Tests— Simplified Typing Test/Letter Series Test

PART FIVE

The Office Machine Operator Special Tests—Simplified Typing Test/Letter Series Test

CHAPTER 11

Introduction to the Simplified Typing Test A Diagnostic Test

THE SIMPLIFIED TYPING TEST

Special tests are added when Office Machine Operator positions are covered by the examination. If the Office Assistant examination has not included a typing test, then a Simplified Typing Test is given for positions such as Data Transcriber, which may require knowledge of a typewriter-style keyboard. Applicants for Electric Accounting Machine Operator (Tabulating Machine Operator) and Cryptographic Equipment Operator are required to take a reasoning test in the form of Letter Series (see Chapter 13).

If the examination for Office Machine Operator positions is announced separately, verbal abilities and clerical tests are given with the appropriate special tests. All applicants for Office Machine Operator positions are required to pass the Verbal Abilities Test and the Clerical Abilities Test.

The simplified or short typing test is used by agencies at the agencies' discretion. Agencies may use the tests developed by the Office of Personnel Management or a different test.

NATURE OF THE TEST

Persons who have passed the Clerk-Typist examination may be appointed as Cold-Type Composing Machine Operators. Otherwise, applicants for positions requiring knowledge of the typewriter-style keyboard must pass the 10-minute Simplified Typing Test. This test does not include any punctuation, and the interchangeable use of capital or small letters is permitted since the machines that appointees will operate have no shift key.

HOW THE TEST IS ADMINISTERED AND SCORED

The Simplified Typing Test is administered in the same manner as the Typing Test. Each competitor will need a copy of the test and two sheets of typewriter paper. About 25 minutes will be needed for the Simplified Typing Test.

Five minutes will be allowed for reading the instructions on the face of the test. Ten minutes will be allowed for the practice exercise. After the practice typing, competitors put fresh paper in their machines, and turn the page over and begin the test. Ten minutes are allowed for the test proper. As the test is scored by the number of correct lines, no erasures or corrections are allowed.

HOW TO DETERMINE THE TEST SCORE

For the Simplified Typing Test, the minimum passing score for GS–2 is 25 correct lines.

A DIAGNOSTIC TEST

The purpose of this diagnostic exam is to familiarize you with the Simplified Typing Test. This unique exam type requires a great deal of practice. Chapter 12 will give you seven full-length practice sets.

Directions

This is a test of your knowledge of the typewriter keyboard.

Type each line precisely as it is in the exercise.

Double space between lines; *single space* between words; use all *capitals*.

Type *one column down the center* of the sheet.

Leave about a 2½-inch *margin* on the left.

If you notice that you made an error, double space and begin the same line again. *Do not make any erasures or any other kinds of corrections.*

If you finish before time is called, begin typing the exercise again.

If you were copying from a list like the practice exercise at the bottom of this page and you abandoned incorrect lines, you would be credited for having the first three lines of the exercise correctly typed if your paper looked like this —

NESBIT ED ELECTRICIAN TRANSIT BELMONT

FOLEY, DA

FOLEY DAVID SURVV

FOLEY DAVID SURVEYOR BAY COMPANY AVON

LEWIS DAN LINEMAN HYDROPOWER B

LEWIS DAN LINEMAN HYDRO POWER BEDFORD

Now copy the ten lines of the practice exercise below, in one column. If you finish before time is called, begin copying the exercise a second time. You will not be rated on this practice. The purpose of this practice is to let you exercise your fingers and to see that your machine is working properly.

Practice List

NESBIT ED ELECTRICIAN TRANSIT BELMONT

FOLEY DAVID SURVEYOR BAY COMPANY AVON

LEWIS DAN LINEMAN HYDRO POWER BEDFORD

BURKERT KARL MINER PENN COLLIERY GARY

NESBITT GUY WELDER UNITED STEEL AKRON

PRICE IRA DRYCLEANING SERVICE MANAGER

ADAM FRED ASSEMBLER AND BENCH GRINDER

BROWN MAX AUTOMOBILE MECHANIC SKILLED

WEST CORA DEMONSTRATOR OFFICE DEVICES

LOMAN LEO CALCULATING MACHINE REPAIRS

THE TEST

Time allotted—10 minutes

Type as many of these lines as you can in the time allowed. Double space. Type them in one column down the center of your sheet.

If you notice that you have made an error, double space and begin the same line again. Do NOT make any ERASURES or other corrections.

BABB FRIEDA AMESBURY MD BILTMORE BLVD
BACKUS EARL PONTIAC OREG RADCLIF APTS
BERRY ELMER CLAYTONA MINN ROSLYN ARMS
BEAUMONT WM SHERWOOD ILL GUNTHER CORP
BOWMAN LOIS GREENVILLE ALA HILL HOUSE
BUTCHER BOB BARPORT MISS ROSWELL STRT
CAPARELLO A GRANTLAND WIS FOREST LANE
DONAHUE EDW PORTLAND MO WHITELAW AVEN
ESSEX LOUIS HANOVER KANS HUNTERS APTS
FOWLER JOHN LOGANPORT LA ST PIERRE CT
HARTLEY GEO SUNCLIFFE LA CHESTER STRT
ISERMAN JOE HUNTSVILLE WY MARINE CLUB
JACOBS FRED FAIRPORT ILL GRENADA DRIV
KEMPER SAML PERDUE IND BEVERIDGE BLDG
KENNEDY LEO SEWARDS WASH TARBORO PARK
LAWRENSON W GASTONIA CONN SOCONY BLVD
LINDERMAN F LEWISTOWN IND SEWELL AVEN
LONG GERALD GALESBURG KY NICHOLS REST
MARTIN BRAD SHAMROCK TEX FEDERAL BLDG
MORTON CHAS MEMPHIS GA CARSTAIRS VIEW
NAYLOR PAUL MANHATTAN TENN WOODY REST
NATHANSON L CLARENDON VT SEAVIEW PKWY
OBERG CAREY KNOXVILLE VA WINSTON HALL
PARKER HUGH GLENLEY WASH HOOVERS LANE
PINCKERTS M BLYFIELD ALA BURKARD BROS
POTTER ROBT WASHINGTON FLA CITRUS WAY
SKUPCEK JAS PULLMAN ME STOCKERLY BLDG
SNYDER WILL BLUERIDGE MINN OAKEN YARD
TREADWELL R GRISSBY MASS PIRATES PIKE
WALKER CARL KITTANING PA JOHNSON CORP

CONTINUE WITH NEXT COLUMN.

ACME ELECTRIC INC ADAIRSVILLE AERIALS
ARTHURS DRUG CORP EAST WILTON POWDERS
A SIMPSON TOOL CO RICHARDSTON HAMMERS
BRIGHTWOOD AND CO WALLA WALLA BASKETS
BROOKE PAINTS INC SIOUX FALLS SIZINGS
CARLTON AND BLOCK WINTON CITY GASKETS
CROWN TOOL CO INC MITCHELBURG SHOVELS
CRUCIBLE STEEL CO E SANDERTON ROLLERS
DANIEL V GENTZ CO WHITNYVILLE KETTLES
DUNN AND SONS INC BELLINGSHAM BOILERS
ELI WYNN AND BROS YELLOWSTONE CUTTERS
E WYLAND AND SONS NORFORDTOWN HANDLES
EXPERT IRON WORKS CALLENSBURG ENGINES
F A GREGORY STORE STEUBENVINE CHISELS
FARMERS SUPPLY CO GREAT RIVER HALTERS
FREY GAS LIGHT CO FREYCHESTER BURNERS
GRECIAN MARBLE CO FAIRDEALING STATUES
HAMDEN MUSIC MART GREENCASTLE VIOLINS
I MASON TOOL SHOP CORTANNINGS GIMLETS
JOHN WEST AND SON HENSONVILLE SPRINGS
JOHN W WILLIS INC GEORGESBURG BEAKERS
LA BANTA PRODUCTS GRAY ISLAND MATCHES
LEIGH IMPORTS INC LANDISVILLE WOOLENS
L PARKER GLASS CO SHREVESTOWN BOTTLES
MURRAY OPTICAL CO MILLERVILLE GLASSES
NEW YORK BAR CORP BARTHOLOMEW LANCETS
OFFICE SUPPLY INC NUTTALLBURG LEDGERS
PAPER PRODUCTS CO PAXTONVILLE TISSUES
P FRY ELECTRIC CO MONTGOMEREY MAGNETS
REO VARIETY STORE RUTERSVILLE LADDERS
R J HOWARDS MILLS HYATTSVILLE TROWELS
S TODT AND COOPER SPRINGFIELD RIPSAWS
TREIK BROS AND CO LOGANSVILLE REAMERS
UTAH SUPPLY STORE CEDAR WOODS TRIPODS
V G CORNELL SHOPS FREEMANPORT WINCHES

IF YOU FINISH BEFORE TIME IS CALLED, BEGIN
COPYING THE LIST THE SECOND TIME.

CHAPTER 12

Practice, Practice, Practice

This chapter gives you seven full-length practice tests, which should be taken under strict timed conditions. Allow only 10 minutes for each practice set.

Because this method of testing your knowledge of the typewriter keyboard is unique and probably unfamiliar to you, it is essential that you do additional practice. Repeating the practice sets can be helpful.

Remember, this test is scored by the number of *correct* lines; therefore, you must not erase or correct any errors.

PRACTICE SET 1

Type as many of these lines as you can in the time allowed. Double space. Type them in one column down the center of your sheet.

If you notice that you have made an error, double space and begin the same line again. Do NOT make any ERASURES or other corrections.

ANGEL GRACE BRINKLEY AR SURFSIDE WALK
BERRY ALICE BRIGHTON AL TAMARIND LANE
MATTHEWS WM CULLMAN IL ROWLAND CIRCLE
MORELAND ED DAYVILLE CT VENTURA HOUSE
MULLIN MARK CORSSWELL MI VICTORIA AVE
OSTER HELEN CARBONDALE PA MOLINA CORP
PARISH KIRK CARROLLTON GA MANVIEW AVE
POPE MARCIA CEDARVILLE OH MANOR DRIVE
QUINN KELLY CHALMETTE LA COLOARDO WAY
RADER EDWIN BOULDER CO EASTLAKE HOUSE
REAGAN PAUL BUCHANAN MI DURANGO COURT
REID GEORGE MIDDLEBURY VT DOROTHY AVE
RUSSELL JAS TAMASQUA PA MANSFIELD STR
SANDERSON I WOODVILLE MS ISABEL DRIVE
SAVAGE CARL SYRACUSE NY MICHELLE PKWY
SHAPIRO BEA SWEETWATER ND MILLER CORP
SINCLAIR WM SYCAMORE IL RICHVIEW ARMS
SLATER CHAS TOWNSEND MT REDCLIFF LANE
SMALL STEVE TORRINGTON WY LINCOLN AVE
SPENCER JOE ZANESVILLE OH LOMBARD WAY
STOKES GARY WOODBINE IA LILLIAN HOUSE
TAYLOR STAN ONEONTA NY HEATHER CIRCLE
TOMLINSON P YERINGTON NV HUTCHINS CIR
TUCKER ENID OWENSBORO KY HAYWORTH WAY
VALDEZ PAUL MARINETTE WI HIGHLAND AVE
VAZQUEZ LON PROVIDENCE RI HAYFORD APT
WADE NORMAN MEDFIELD MA CLARIDGE LANE
WARREN LYNN DUCHESS UT COGSWELL HOUSE
WOODS DIANE DULUTH MN COHASSETT DRIVE
YOUNG VINCE BRADDOCK PA CENTINELA STR

CONTINUE WITH NEXT COLUMN.

ALARM SUPPLIES CO TAYLORVILLE BURGLAR
AMERICAN TILE INC E ROSSVILLE CERAMIC
B AND D AVIATIONS LOS ANGELES CHARTER
COMER AND FUENTES PUTNAM CITY CANDLES
DEWEY PLUMBING CO SANTA CLARA SHOWERS
FORTSONS WORD PRO MT PROSPECT RESUMES
GANTERS LUMBER CO EAGLE RIVER ROOFING
HAMILTON BROTHERS GREENCASTLE HAMMERS
JOANS UNIFORMS CO SHELBYVILLE CLOTHES
JOYCE AND MARTINI JOHNSONBURG LAWYERS
KIDS R US SERVICE TUNKHANNOCK CLOTHES
MAIN DISTRIBUTING MONROE PARK STATUES
MARINAS BIKE SHOP FOREST HILL BICYCLE
MEYERS AND DURHAM STURGIS BAY ROOFING
NAKAHARA BROTHERS GREAT FALLS ROOFING
PACIFIC BLINDS CO UPPER MILLS AWNINGS
PEDRINO WINDOW CO SANTA MARIA FRAMING
QMC SERVICES CORP MADISONBURG IMPORTS
ROSS AVIATION INC GRAND BANKS AIRLINE
SECURITY GATES CO EAST SEWARD CLOSERS
STONEWALL SHOE CO JOPLIN CITY BOOTERY
SUNRISE GIFT SHOP LENOIR CITY FLOWERS
TAUB AND THORNTON OLIVER HILL LAWYERS
THOMPSONS FABRICS HOLDENVILLE BATTING
TRIANGLE CLEANERS SPRINGFIELD LAUNDRY
VALLEY PORCELAINS LIVINGSTONE BATHTUB
WLM AIR CARGO INC MOUNT OLIVE FREIGHT
XENOS REFINISHING LITTLE ROCK SANDERS
YODERS FISHING CO MONDOVI BAY NETTING
ZIMMERMANS PHOTOS PORT ARTHUR CAMERAS

IF YOU FINISH BEFORE TIME IS CALLED, BEGIN COPYING THE LIST THE SECOND TIME.

PRACTICE SET 2

Type as many of these lines as you can in the time allowed. Double space. Type them in one column down the center of your sheet.

If you notice that you have made an error, double space and begin the same line again. Do NOT make any ERASURES or other corrections.

ABEL HORACE TAYLORVILLE IL JACKMAN ST
ARMSTRONG N TILLAMOOK OR IRONDALE AVE
AUSTIN DOUG WILTON ND PICKERING DRIVE
AYERS FRANK SHELBYVILLE IN JALAPAN WY
BARTON ROBT SHERIDAN OR PEARTREE BLVD
CADMAN THOS IOWA FALLS IA VANOWEN WAY
DIAMOND BEN JEFFERSON GA VERONICA AVE
FLOYD OSCAR GABRIEL TX MONTEZUMA GLEN
GAINES MARY PAYNESVILLE MN HERALD HWY
GRIMES BERT PASADENA CA MOUNTAIN ROAD
HARRISON WM FREDONIA KS LIBERTY HOUSE
HUELSMANN S FORT MEADE FL LOOKOUT AVE
ISHIKAWA LE BUSHNELL IL OAKLAWN COURT
MENDOZA MAX BYESVILLE OH NOVELDA CORP
METKOVICH R COATESVILLE PA WEBSTER ST
MYERS LARRY CODY WY CARMELITA LANE NE
OGONOWSKI A FRANKLIN LA BONSALLO LANE
POTTER FRED SCOTT CITY KS CALGROVE PL
PURCELL JAS PROVIDENCE RI BENFIELD ST
QUICK CRAIG ROSSVILLE GA HUNSAKER WAY
QUINN STEVE ST GEORGE UT BENJAMIN HWY
RADA HAROLD MARSHFIELD MO LIGGETT CTY
RAMIREZ TED DES MOINES IA LEADWELL CT
RASMUSSEN N EAST MEDFORD OK SHARON ST
RAY WILLARD MAYSVILLE KY BERMUDA ROAD
ROYAL SUSAN SAN BENITO CA GUNNISON ST
RUSCH KEVIN OSGOOD IN HALLWOOD LANE S
TAYLOR LEON OVERLAND MO PARK OAK ROAD
WHEATLEY ED ZEELAND MI QUEENSIDE CLUB
WISE ARTHUR SANTA MONICA CA PURDUE ST

CONTINUE WITH NEXT COLUMN.

ADRA SERVICES INC FORESTVILLE MAILING
AVALON MAILING CO BRIDGEVILLE PRINTER
AVION AIR FREIGHT BUNKER HILL EXPRESS
BOBS LOCK AND KEY WEST AUBURN LOCKERS
CHILDRENS BOOK CO EAGLE GROVE RECORDS
CREATIVE HAIR INC MILLERSBURG BARBERS
CROWNS APPLIANCES EATONE PARK FREEZER
DANAN ADVERTISING MT PLEASANT CONCERT
EMPIRE PROPERTIES NEW HOLLAND ESCROWS
FENNELL INSURANCE PORT HERALD LEASING
GROSSMAN AND HALL ITHACA CITY LAWYERS
HERTWOOD ANTIQUES MORAN BLUFF GALLERY
HUGHES TERMITE CO NORTH PEASE CONTROL
HUNTERS BOOKS INC JERSEYVILLE RECORDS
INFO MGMT SYSTEMS BRACEBRIDGE COPYING
JONES PLUMBING CO BEDSIN HILL HEATING
KESON CAMERA SHOP CARLINVILLE LEDGERS
LAWNDALE BLOCK CO KENTON CITY CENTERS
MASTER TATTAN INC AYDEN RIVER BASKETS
NIPPON EXPRESS CO FREDERICTON FREIGHT
ORVAL ENTERPRISES MORNINGSIDE MAGNETS
PARAMOUNT RV CORP POWELL CITY CAMPERS
RAND MUFFLER CORP CENTERSBURG SPRINGS
RICKERTS CABINETS BUENA VISTA HANDLES
ROCKYS SANDWICHES GUNTERVILLE LUNCHES
SECURITY AVIATION CEDAR FALLS ENGINES
SMITH AND STAKINS AMBERG CITY LAWYERS
TRI CITY TITLE CO MOUNDSVILLE ESCROWS
UNIVERSAL FORWARD NORTH OGDEN FREIGHT
V L DECORATING CO ALCOVE CITY FIXTURE
WESTWOODS LEASING BELLA VISTA RENTALS
WIDE AREA PAGINGS ALMAN RIVER MESSAGE

IF YOU FINISH BEFORE TIME IS CALLED, BEGIN
COPYING THE LIST THE SECOND TIME.

PRACTICE SET 3

Type as many of these lines as you can in the time allowed. Double space. Type them in one column down the center of your sheet.

If you notice that you have made an error, double space and begin the same line again. Do NOT make any ERASURES or other corrections.

ADCOCK MAYE AUSTIN TX SUNFLOWER DRIVE

BABB ANDREW INDEPENDENCE MO WILCOX CT

BEYER JAMES KNOXVILLE TN COUNTRY VIEW

CAIN SHARON CALVERTON NY ANNETTE APTS

DAVIS LARRY ALEXANDRIA VA WATSON REST

GRAY EDWINA PHOENIX AZ SOUTHERN DRIVE

JACKSON JAS FAIRBANKS AL DOUGLAS REST

KAUFMAN RON ASHDOWN AR VALENCIA DRIVE

KLEIN LYNNE SHAWNEE OK ROSECRANS APTS

LAMMERS SUE MARYVILLE MO CRESTVIEW CT

LAPIN FRANK PITTSBURGH PA CRESCENT ST

LOGAN HARRY DEARBORN MI HYACINTH CLUB

MELNICK VAL WINNFIELD LA MAYBROOK WAY

NEWMAN ALAN LAWRENCEVILLE GA PALM AVE

PEREZ GLENN NASHVILLE TN SIERRA HOUSE

PEYTONS VAL BELLEVILLE IL ZELZAH LANE

PLINER JEFF ROCHESTER NY ABBOTT DRIVE

RAMAGE LISA GREENSBORO NC GUNDRY VIEW

REEVES DAVE SHENANDOAH IA YUKON DRIVE

ROLFE SALLY JACKSONVILLE FL HALSEY CT

SHIBATA JAS WATERTOWN WI CENTRAL BLDG

SILVERMAN M MANCHESTER NH CHESTER STR

SINGLETON L WATERBURY CT CAMPUS DRIVE

SMITH PETER ELLENVILLE NY CANAL HOUSE

STANEK ROSE PORTLAND ME CAMPBELL APTS

TESDAHL RAY LANCASTER NY ADDISON CORP

THORPE JOHN LUNENBURG MD BLAKELY BLDG

VARNUM MIKE WILMINGTON PA BEVERLY WAY

WEBER ROBIN CARRIZOZO NM VIVIAN HOUSE

WILLIAMS ED COLDWATER KS WILLIAMS STR

CONTINUE WITH NEXT COLUMN.

A TO Z LEGAL SRVS LOS ANGELES LAWYERS

ALS WAVE MATE INC IMPERIALCTY CONSULT

BARRYS BAR SUPPLY GREEN RIVER BURNERS

BATEMAN PEST CORP MIDDLERIDGE TERMITE

CALIFORNIA FINISH HADDONFIELD WINDOWS

CAREER SERVICE CO WILLOWBROOK RESUMES

CHRIS PIZZA STOPS EAGLE RIDGE PARTIES

DIANES AND ROCKYS HAPPY TRAIL LUNCHES

DIRECT A PAGE INC NORTH CLIFF BEEPERS

EVANS BABY SHOPPE KINGS RIDGE CLOTHES

FURMANTI AND SONS MAPLE WOODS LAWYERS

HONEYCUTT ASPHALT PARKWESTERN PATCHES

J OCEAN CLOTHIERS OCEAN RIDGE DRESSES

JAYS POODLE SALON HALLEYVILLE KENNELS

KELL PICTURES INC SIGNAL HILL FRAMING

LINNS CARD SHOPPE MULBERRY PK LEDGERS

LONGS ELECTRONICS GRAND LAKES RECORDS

MARKS WORKCLOTHES TRIDENT CTY CLOTHES

MORRISON ALUMINUM WAGON TRAIL PATCHES

NYLANDERS STUDIOS CULVER CITY PASTELS

PHILS ENTERPRISES BELLINGBURG LAWYERS

QUINN AND SON INC N HOLLYWOOD CONSULT

ROLFE ROLFE ROLFE SPRINGSTEIN CHISELS

ROSE POOL AND SPA GRAHAM CITY HEATERS

ROYS POOL SERVICE GOLDENFIELD FILTERS

S TOOM AND LINDEN LOGANSVILLE REAMERS

SLUMBER BABY SHOP EMERY LAKES CLOTHES

TIMOTHY BERG CORP PARKWESTERN STYLING

UTAH SUPPLIES INC NORTH WILEN KETTLES

VARGAS AND SON CO LOS ANGELES AERIALS

ZIPPERS AND STUFF WESTERN WAY FABRICS

ZOO ANIMALS TO GO LARRYSVILLE ANIMALS

IF YOU FINISH BEFORE TIME IS CALLED, BEGIN COPYING THE LIST THE SECOND TIME.

PRACTICE SET 4

Type as many of these lines as you can in the time allowed. Double space. Type them in one column down the center of your sheet.

If you notice that you have made an error, double space and begin the same line again. Do NOT make any ERASURES or other corrections.

ADLER DAVID CINCINNATI OH SUPERIOR CT

ATKINSON JO ROANOKE VA CAVALIER HOUSE

BAIRD MYRON PONTIAC MI BILTMORE HOUSE

BLACK DIANE SEATTLE WA RICHMOND DRIVE

ESSIE LOWEN ABERDEEN SD SHOEMAKER AVE

FOX ROBERT OGALLALA NE LOWEMONT ARMS

FREEMAN JIM CHEYENNE WY ASHWORTH BLVD

GARNER KENT LOVELAND CO HIGHDALE LANE

GASS DANIEL WATERLOO IA WHITAKER CORP

JOHNSON BOB SACRAMENTO CA WESTERN WAY

KLOOSTER ED MINNEAPOLIS MN CENTURY CT

LINN RANDAL PELLA IA PARAMOUNT COURTS

LITTLE ANDY BUFFALO NY IRONWOOD DRIVE

LONG ARTHUR BROWNSVILLE TX PARADE AVE

MARASCO EVE LOUISVILLE KY JAVELIN WAY

MARIS LOUIS CHICAGO IL FLORENCE HOUSE

MCPHERSON E OMAHA NE MANCHESTER HOUSE

MORTON DANE SAN DIEGO CA CARROLL LANE

MURPHY DEAN BRANCHVILLE SC PALERMO CT

NEAL GERALD HONOLULU HI PROSPECT APTS

ORTEGA RYAN LOGAN UT MORNINGSIDE PKWY

OSTERHOLT A AMARILLO TX GILBERT HOUSE

PARKER LYNN DALLAS TX QUEENSLAND BLVD

PATTERSON J BROOKHAVEN MI SIMMONS STR

RUSTAD JOHN MEMPHIS TN HOLLYWOOD CLUB

SHERLOCK WM DAYTON IA WESTCHESTER AVE

SIDMAN GREG SCRANTON PA HAWTHORNE AVE

VARGAS EARL PORTLAND OR WEBSTER HOUSE

WASSON JEFF INGLEWOOD CA OVERLAND AVE

YOUNG COREY FT DODGE WI GARDENIA BLVD

CONTINUE WITH NEXT COLUMN.

A TO Z SOUND CORP W GREENBELT PAGINGS

AGENCY RENT A CAR GLOVERTOWNE LEASING

AMERICAN PLUMBING MONTMORENCY HEATERS

AMY LAMINATING CO GLENS FALLS PLASTIC

ASHLEY ART CENTER CULVER CITY FRAMING

BURNS TYPESETTING SANTAFE SPG GRAPHIC

C AND L TOWING CO CERISE CITY CARRIER

DIAL ONE PEST INC SOUTH HILLS TERMITE

EAGLE AUDIO VIDEO GREEN HILLS REPAIRS

GORDON INDUSTRIES MARLBOROUGH BEEPERS

HILL PET GROOMING HALLETTBURG KITTENS

JETTONS GALLERIES STUDIO CITY FRAMING

KENTWOOD CLEANERS FORESTVILLE LAUNDRY

KITCHENS AND MORE SAXTON CITY BASKETS

LAWRENCE JEWELERS MORRISVILLE WATCHES

LYNNES AUTOMOTIVE SHREVESPORT REPAIRS

M WILSON GLASS CO HAMLIN CITY BOTTLES

MARIES INDUSTRIES W HOLLYWOOD PILLOWS

MEDICAL ARTS LABS FOREST HILL TESTING

MILLER TELEVISION GRAND HAVEN REPAIRS

MURPHY STUDIO INC SIGNAL HILL PASTELS

NEW WATCH REPAIRS FRIEDLANDER JEWELRY

ORIGINAL PIZZA CO CANOGA PARK PARTIES

PIONEER VIDEO INC LOS ANGELES RENTALS

PROFESSIONAL WORD DAYTON CITY RESUMES

RANDALLS PHARMACY KINGS CREST POWDERS

SPARKLING LAUNDRY GAITHERBURG CLEANER

SUZANNES KITCHENS MAPLE GROVE BASKETS

TIDELINE IMPORTER SIOUX FALLS BOTTLES

VILLAGE DRUGS INC HIDDEN PINE POWDERS

WESTSIDE CAB CORP HEARTSHORNE TAXICAB

YOUNG AUTO REPAIR JACKSONBURG REPAIRS

IF YOU FINISH BEFORE TIME IS CALLED, BEGIN COPYING THE LIST THE SECOND TIME.

PRACTICE SET 5

Type as many of these lines as you can in the time allowed. Double space. Type them in one column down the center of your sheet.

If you notice that you have made an error, double space and begin the same line again. Do NOT make any ERASURES or other corrections.

BOOTH KELLY REEDSPORT OR RINDGE HOUSE

BROWN NORMA PENDLETON OR RAYMOND PKWY

CAMPBELL WM COOPERSTOWN ND SHAVER WAY

CARTER ALAN FARMINGTON UT GOTHIC REST

CLARRIDGE T SEWARD NH SEPULVEDA PLACE

COOK RODNEY CHAMPAIGN IL SEADLER BROS

CURREY FRED DARLINGTON WI TRAVIS PARK

DONALDSON C LORDSBURG NM THOMAS PLACE

GARCIA BILL GOLDFIELD NV TELFAIR YARD

GARDNER ROY MORNINGSIDE IA SWEET LANE

HANDEL SAML POCATELLO ID SERRANO BLVD

HODSON KENT ENGLEWOOD CO TRENTON PKWY

JOSEPH JOHN WATERLOO IA FRANKLIN ARMS

KAPLAN CARL SHELBY NC UNIVERSITY BLVD

KATZ DANIEL HUMBOLDT IA VALINDA DRIVE

LANDON BART OCEANSIDE CA SHADOW PLACE

LAWSON JACK PLACERVILLE CA UNION ROAD

MADISON ANN ROSEVILLE MN ARMY POST RD

MARTINEZ WM RUSSELL KS ALVERSTONE WAY

MOORE AARON APPLETON MN TYBURNE HOUSE

NASH GORDON OKANOGAN WA E VALLEY VIEW

OWEN DONALD LIVINGSTON MT MAYFAIR AVE

PATTON JUDY HURRICANE UT UPLAND PLACE

PETERSON ED MONTAGUE MI TUSCANY HOUSE

POWERS ANNE MOUNT AYR IA DELGANY CLUB

PULIDO ADAM COLUMBIA KY WATKINS DRIVE

RICE DENNIS REPUBLIC WA RELIANCE LANE

ROSE ARTHUR SPRINGFIELD IL HARVEY WAY

SULLIVAN ED MUSKEGON MI TRUXTON DRIVE

THOMAS ERIC MONTPELIER ID SEVILLE WAY
CONTINUE WITH NEXT COLUMN.

ALARM SYSTEMS INC BLUE ISLAND PATROLS

ARMANS VACUUM INC WERNERVILLE VACUUMS

BELLOTTO AUTO INC GRAND RIVER LININGS

BEST AND SONS INC PORTERVILLE SHOVELS

BILLS CAMERA SHOP LOS ANGELES PICTURE

CRES CLINICAL LAB FOREST CITY TESTING

DELIAN MUSIC CORP NORTONSBURG VIOLINS

DIAMONDS PLUMBING MONTEREY PK HEATERS

GOODS SHEET METAL VIKING CITY WELDING

HEALTH HABIT CLUB WEST OAKMAN WORKOUT

JAY OF CALIFORNIA N TARRYTOWN COPYING

MAGIC FIGURE CLUB PARTONVILLE WORKOUT

MCPHERSON AND SON GRANDEVILLE WOOLENS

MURPHY STUDIO INC VISTA FALLS PICTURE

NATIONAL TRAILERS DANTONSPORT RENTALS

NATIONWIDE CREDIT OTTERSVILLE FINANCE

RESTER INDUSTRIES GREENCASTLE PAGINGS

ROYS POOL SERVICE GOLDENFIELD FILTERS

RUSSELLS JEWELERS FRANKLIN PK WATCHES

SELF STORAGE CORP MINNEAPOLIS STORAGE

SMILEY ASSOCIATES GRAND FORKS PUMPERS

SPECIALTY WELDING HANSONVILLE SIZINGS

TUCKWOOD MUSIC CO E PARAMOUNT GUITARS

UNITED LEASING CO GREAT BLUFF LEASING

V A LAMINATING CO GLOVERVILLE PLASTIC

VIDEO FILMEX CORP CEDAR FALLS RENTALS

WESTERN MOVING CO N URBANDALE STORAGE

WESTSIDER LAUNDRY GALLATIN PK CLEANER

WHITMORE CLEANERS GAINESVILLE LAUNDRY

YALE MUSIC STUDIO MILTONVILLE VIOLINS

YOUNG SHAVER SHOP N URBANDALE SHAVERS

YUKON AVE NURSERY WESTCHESTER GARDENS

IF YOU FINISH BEFORE TIME IS CALLED, BEGIN
COPYING THE LIST THE SECOND TIME.

PRACTICE SET 6

Type as many of these lines as you can in the time allowed. Double space. Type them in one column down the center of your sheet.

If you notice that you have made an error, double space and begin the same line again. Do NOT make any ERASURES or other corrections.

ADAMS MARIA KENNEWICK WA NATHENE CORP

ASHE MARTIN WHEATLAND WY NEWCOMB ARMS

BEATTY CHAD LENNOX CA NATHANSON CREST

BRYANT MARY STEVENSVILLE MT MEAD HALL

CARROLL JOE WELLSVILLE UT MAYNARD WAY

GREENE OWEN MIDVILLE NY HUBBARD COURT

HALEY KAREN HAMILTON VA BREMAND HOUSE

HALL THOMAS VILLISCA IA BRANDON HILLS

HARTMAN DON WARREN IN MACDONNELL APTS

JONES FRANK WATERVILLE WA STEWART AVE

JOSEPH JOHN WATERLOO IA FRANKLIN ARMS

KAPLAN JOAN SHELBY AK UNIVERSITY BLVD

LARSEN LYLE SIKESTON MO MADISON COURT

QUINN DAVID MONDOVI WI LONGTON SQUARE

REAVES DALE MORRISON IL HARVARD COURT

RUSSELL GUY MOUNT PLEASANT SC LUND ST

SAKAI ALVIN MADISON FL NORTH ILLINOIS

SCHULTZ RON GARRISON ND JASMINE HOUSE

SIMON JAMES GENEVA NY JEFFERSON COURT

STROCK GARY GILLETTE WY WASHINGTON WY

TAYLOR LYLE DENISON TX SOUTH JENNINGS

TURNER NINA DODGE CITY KS BEVERLY WAY

VANCE BRUCE DUBUQUE IA STANFORD CLUBS

WAKEFIELD S DUCKTOWN TN MARYLAND CORP

WARD EUGENE BOLLINGTON MT EUCLID BLVD

WELCH MARIA BOONTON NJ WELLESLEY LANE

WHITE JAMES BLOOMFIELD NE SEAFIELD ST

WILSON ANDY HARTWELL GA SHERBOURNE CT

WOOD JANICE HARTFORD CT NEARSIDE LANE

WYMAN SUSAN HAMILTON MO NEWBROOK APTS

CONTINUE WITH NEXT COLUMN.

ACE FREIGHT LINES ORANGEVILLE SENDERS

ADEC LABORATORIES E WATERTOWN POWDERS

AIRPORT STATIONER WESTCHESTER PENCILS

ALPHA DATA SYSTEM SPRINGSTEIN RIBBONS

AMERICAN PRODUCTS CHILLICOTHE MATCHES

BAY OFFICE SUPPLY OLMOSE PARK COPYING

BRITE RUGS CO INC CARTERVILLE CARPETS

CARAVAN MOTEL INC GROTON CITY ROOMING

COMPUTERS R US CO MOUNT PEALE RIBBONS

FABRICS AND STUFF MONTE VISTA FABRICS

FLAME CUTTERS INC BLUE ISLAND GRINDER

G AND L ENGINEERS GREAT FALLS HAMMERS

GARDEN SPOT HOTEL GREENEWOODS ROOMING

GOLD STAR NURSERY WESTCHESTER GARDENS

GRAND CHARTER INC W KERRVILLE CRUISES

H FRONER CONCRETE BRIDGEVILLE CEMENTS

HAIR IS US SHOPPE MURRYSVILLE STYLING

HOUSE OF STYLINGS ALBUQUERQUE SHAMPOO

JOHNSON AND ALROD EAST DAYTON LAWYERS

LANDSCAPE ARTISTS N COACHELLA FLOWERS

LEWIS ELECTRIC CO WEST SAMSON WIRINGS

LINDSEYS LIMOSINE N KNOXVILLE DRIVERS

RALFS PHOTOGRAPHY VENTUR CITY PICTURE

SANCTION SECURITY RICHARDTOWN PATROLS

SHERIDAN HARDWARE GREAT RIVER HAMMERS

SQUIRE TUXEDO INC CEDAR WOODS RENTALS

STEVES JANITORIAL BROWNSVILLE CLEANER

SUPREME GARDENING NEWTONVILLE SHOVELS

WESTWOOD BUILDING SANTA CLARA SIZINGS

WORLD TRAVEL CORP OVAR ISLAND CRUISES

YOUNG BROS MOVING FLOWER CITY STORAGE

YALE MUSIC STUDIO MILTONVILLE VIOLINS

IF YOU FINISH BEFORE TIME IS CALLED, BEGIN COPYING THE LIST THE SECOND TIME.

PRACTICE SET 7

Type as many of these lines as you can in the time allowed. Double space. Type them in one column down the center of your sheet.

If you notice that you have made an error, double space and begin the same line again. Do NOT make any ERASURES or other corrections.

ADKINS KATY HAMMONTON NJ HYPERION WAY

BALDWIN PAT LYNDONVILLE VT JACKSON CT

BECKER GENE LUMBERTON MS IMPERIAL AVE

BERG WALTER LOUISVILLE KY CRESTWAY ST

CHAN SANDRA MACKENZIE OR CROCKER ROAD

CLARK ALLEN MIDDLESBORO KY LOMITA WAY

COBB HAROLD NIOBRARA NE LINDBLADE AVE

CURTIS RUTH NORMAN OK MARAVILLA DRIVE

DECKER RICK NOBLETON IN MARIMBA COURT

DOUGLAS DEE OGDENSBURG NY MARKTON CIR

EDWARDS ART OAKDALE LA MULHOLLAND HWY

EVANS ALICE NORWICH CT MOONRIDGE ROAD

FELIX PETER RICE LAKE WI LINDLEY WALK

FONTANA ANN ROGERS CITY MI OAKLAWN DR

GELLER EARL SAN ANTONIO TX NORMAN WAY

GOODE CLARA SANDERSVILLE GA OAKLEY ST

GRAY GEORGE SANDPOINT ID REXFORD CLUB

GRIGGS PAUL SYLVANIA GA RINALDI DRIVE

HARRIS JOHN FULLERTON LA RAYMOND ARMS

HAYES CRAIG GIBSON CITY IL WAVERLY ST

HOLM DONALD FAIRVIEW OK WALGROVE BLVD

HUNTLEY BOB EVANSTON WY YARNELL COURT

JOHNSON JAN ESSEXVILLE MI HUSTON LANE

KING THOMAS ENTERPRISE AL ISABEL PKWY

KNIGHT DALE FAYETTEVILLE NC CLOVIS PK

KAMACHI SAM FALCONER NY CLIFTON VISTA

LOUFF BRIAN DES MOINES IA COLFAX ARMS

MANNING LEE DODGEVILLE WI AVALON BLVD

MATHIS DOUG DOUGLAS TN ATLANTIC DRIVE

MATSUMOTO F CUMBERLAND MD MORGAN ROAD

CONTINUE WITH NEXT COLUMN.

ANDRE BEAUTY MART E INGLEWOOD STYLING

ANNS CATERING INC W BIG SANDY LUNCHES

ASTROS CAR FINISH YELLOWSTONE WAXINGS

BELL HOTEL CO INC W GREYCOURT ROOMING

BROWN CORNELL LTD W KITTANING BEAKERS

COASTAL CLEANINGS WALLA WALLA CARPETS

CONN AND SONS INC E PRINCETON ENGINES

CURRY AND PICKARD GRANBY CITY LAWYERS

EXPOS TRAVEL SRVS PAINESVILLE CRUISES

FLOWERS BY ANDREW E MANHATTAN FLOWERS

JAMES AND BENNETT N SUMMERTON CUTTERS

JOES ITALIAN DELI WARRENSBURG LUNCHES

KENT AND SONS INC LEVERSVILLE SPRINGS

LEIGH FENCING INC MONROEVILLE STATUES

LINCOLN INTERIORS CAMPBELLTON CARPETS

MARK I CUTLER INC MORRISVILLE GASKETS

MAYOR BROS TRAVEL MOUNDSVILLE CRUISES

N E TIME PLUMBING S CLARINDON PLUMBER

OFFICE SUPPLY INC CLEARFIELDS LEDGERS

OPTICAL DISCOUNTS CIRCLE CITY GLASSES

PHILLIPS GLASS CO BISHOPVILLE BOTTLES

QUALITY WORK CORP NORTHBRIDGE BOTTLES

RAINBOW CARPET CO W LEXINGTON CARPETS

RELIABLE IRON INC NORTHBRIDGE ENGINES

RIVIERA FINANCIAL NEW HAMPTON LENDERS

ROBERTS BEAUTY CO LOS ANGELES SHAMPOO

ROYALTY TUX SHOPS SIOUX FALLS RENTALS

SILK SCREEN ASSOC W STOCKHOLM ROLLERS

SUNSET LUMBER INC MOUNDSVILLE SIZINGS

THE MESSENGER INC WALLINGFORD SENDERS

TITAN TOOL CO INC SHELBYVILLE SHOVELS

ZAIN TRADING CORP GRAND FALLS WOOLENS

IF YOU FINISH BEFORE TIME IS CALLED, BEGIN COPYING THE LIST THE SECOND TIME.

CHAPTER 13

Introduction to the Letter Series Test
Diagnostic Test
with Answer Explanations

THE LETTER SERIES TEST

The Letter Series Test is *no longer used* on the Federal Civil Service Examinations. We have not deleted this chapter because some state and local agencies may still use the Letter Series type question on their exams.

NATURE OF THE TEST

The Letter Series Test consists of 30 sets of letters that follow a definite order determined by a rule. The applicant must study each set of letters to discover the rule governing the order and then apply the rule in selecting the next two letters from the suggested answers that will continue the set of letters in the same order.

HOW THE TEST IS ADMINISTERED AND SCORED

For the Letter Series Test, students or applicants are allowed up to 2 minutes for each sample question and a total of 20 minutes for the 30 questions. The sample questions are explained in detail before the test itself is begun. For the first sample question, the following statement is read to students or applicants. "The order in this series of letters is the letter x alternating with letters in alphabetical order starting with c so that if the series where continued for two more letters it would read x c x d x e x f x, and f x are the two letters you would look for. In your sample , the set f x is labeled 'A.' This is the answer for this question."

The other sample questions are based on the following rules. The order in the second sample question is pairs of letters starting with u u and going backward through the alphabet. The order in the third sample question is the letter a alternating with letters in alphabetical order. The order in the fourth sample question is two consecutive letters; the next letter is skipped; then come the next two consecutive letters. The last sample question has two alternating groups of letters: the first group consists of every second letter, a c e g, skipping a letter each time; the second group consists of letters in consecutive order, beginning r s t.

The score for the Letter Series Test is the number of correct answers.

HOW TO DETERMINE THE TEST SCORE

Since the Letter Series Test is no longer used on the Federal Examination, state or local agencies may have their own scoring system. Check with the local agency for the requirements.

THE LETTER SERIES DIAGNOSTIC TEST

The purpose of this diagnostic test is to familiarize you with the Letter Series Test and offer you some insight into the reasoning process.

Chapter 14 will give you five full-length practice sets with explanations.

Now tear out the answer sheet on the next page, and read the samples that follow.

ANSWER SHEET

SIGNATURE: _____
(Please Sign)

EXAMINATION TITLE: _____

PLACE OF EXAMINATION: _____
City   State

TODAY'S DATE: _____

SAMPLE Ⓐ ● Ⓒ Ⓓ Ⓔ

DIRECTIONS FOR MARKING ANSWER SHEET

Use only a **No. 2 (or softer) lead pencil.** Darken completely the circle corresponding to your answer. You **must** keep your mark within the circle. Stray marks may be counted as errors. Erase **completely** all marks except your answer.

SAMPLE NAME GRID

LAST NAME — F.I. — M.I.

1. In the boxes below, **PRINT** your name. Print only as many letters as will fit within the areas for the last name, first initial (F.I.), and middle initial (M.I.) Below each box, darken the circle containing the same letter. SEE SAMPLE NAME GRID

2. In the boxes below, enter your 9-digit Social Security Number. Below each box, darken the circle in each column corresponding to the number you have entered.

SOCIAL SECURITY NUMBER

3. OCCUPATIONAL GROUP NUMBER

LAST NAME — F.I. — M.I.

SECTION 1

PART: Ⓐ Ⓑ Ⓒ Ⓓ Ⓔ Ⓕ Ⓖ Ⓗ Ⓘ Ⓙ

TEST SERIES

TEST NUMBER

Make no marks or entries in the columns to the right until you receive instructions from the administrator.

1 Ⓐ Ⓑ Ⓒ Ⓓ Ⓔ
2 Ⓐ Ⓑ Ⓒ Ⓓ Ⓔ
3 Ⓐ Ⓑ Ⓒ Ⓓ Ⓔ
4 Ⓐ Ⓑ Ⓒ Ⓓ Ⓔ
5 Ⓐ Ⓑ Ⓒ Ⓓ Ⓔ
6 Ⓐ Ⓑ Ⓒ Ⓓ Ⓔ
7 Ⓐ Ⓑ Ⓒ Ⓓ Ⓔ
8 Ⓐ Ⓑ Ⓒ Ⓓ Ⓔ
9 Ⓐ Ⓑ Ⓒ Ⓓ Ⓔ
10 Ⓐ Ⓑ Ⓒ Ⓓ Ⓔ

11 Ⓐ Ⓑ Ⓒ Ⓓ Ⓔ
12 Ⓐ Ⓑ Ⓒ Ⓓ Ⓔ
13 Ⓐ Ⓑ Ⓒ Ⓓ Ⓔ
14 Ⓐ Ⓑ Ⓒ Ⓓ Ⓔ
15 Ⓐ Ⓑ Ⓒ Ⓓ Ⓔ
16 Ⓐ Ⓑ Ⓒ Ⓓ Ⓔ
17 Ⓐ Ⓑ Ⓒ Ⓓ Ⓔ
18 Ⓐ Ⓑ Ⓒ Ⓓ Ⓔ
19 Ⓐ Ⓑ Ⓒ Ⓓ Ⓔ
20 Ⓐ Ⓑ Ⓒ Ⓓ Ⓔ
21 Ⓐ Ⓑ Ⓒ Ⓓ Ⓔ
22 Ⓐ Ⓑ Ⓒ Ⓓ Ⓔ
23 Ⓐ Ⓑ Ⓒ Ⓓ Ⓔ
24 Ⓐ Ⓑ Ⓒ Ⓓ Ⓔ
25 Ⓐ Ⓑ Ⓒ Ⓓ Ⓔ
26 Ⓐ Ⓑ Ⓒ Ⓓ Ⓔ
27 Ⓐ Ⓑ Ⓒ Ⓓ Ⓔ
28 Ⓐ Ⓑ Ⓒ Ⓓ Ⓔ
29 Ⓐ Ⓑ Ⓒ Ⓓ Ⓔ
30 Ⓐ Ⓑ Ⓒ Ⓓ Ⓔ

31 Ⓐ Ⓑ Ⓒ Ⓓ Ⓔ
32 Ⓐ Ⓑ Ⓒ Ⓓ Ⓔ
33 Ⓐ Ⓑ Ⓒ Ⓓ Ⓔ
34 Ⓐ Ⓑ Ⓒ Ⓓ Ⓔ
35 Ⓐ Ⓑ Ⓒ Ⓓ Ⓔ
36 Ⓐ Ⓑ Ⓒ Ⓓ Ⓔ
37 Ⓐ Ⓑ Ⓒ Ⓓ Ⓔ
38 Ⓐ Ⓑ Ⓒ Ⓓ Ⓔ
39 Ⓐ Ⓑ Ⓒ Ⓓ Ⓔ
40 Ⓐ Ⓑ Ⓒ Ⓓ Ⓔ
41 Ⓐ Ⓑ Ⓒ Ⓓ Ⓔ
42 Ⓐ Ⓑ Ⓒ Ⓓ Ⓔ
43 Ⓐ Ⓑ Ⓒ Ⓓ Ⓔ
44 Ⓐ Ⓑ Ⓒ Ⓓ Ⓔ
45 Ⓐ Ⓑ Ⓒ Ⓓ Ⓔ
46 Ⓐ Ⓑ Ⓒ Ⓓ Ⓔ
47 Ⓐ Ⓑ Ⓒ Ⓓ Ⓔ
48 Ⓐ Ⓑ Ⓒ Ⓓ Ⓔ
49 Ⓐ Ⓑ Ⓒ Ⓓ Ⓔ
50 Ⓐ Ⓑ Ⓒ Ⓓ Ⓔ

51 Ⓐ Ⓑ Ⓒ Ⓓ Ⓔ
52 Ⓐ Ⓑ Ⓒ Ⓓ Ⓔ
53 Ⓐ Ⓑ Ⓒ Ⓓ Ⓔ
54 Ⓐ Ⓑ Ⓒ Ⓓ Ⓔ
55 Ⓐ Ⓑ Ⓒ Ⓓ Ⓔ
56 Ⓐ Ⓑ Ⓒ Ⓓ Ⓔ
57 Ⓐ Ⓑ Ⓒ Ⓓ Ⓔ
58 Ⓐ Ⓑ Ⓒ Ⓓ Ⓔ
59 Ⓐ Ⓑ Ⓒ Ⓓ Ⓔ
60 Ⓐ Ⓑ Ⓒ Ⓓ Ⓔ
61 Ⓐ Ⓑ Ⓒ Ⓓ Ⓔ
62 Ⓐ Ⓑ Ⓒ Ⓓ Ⓔ
63 Ⓐ Ⓑ Ⓒ Ⓓ Ⓔ
64 Ⓐ Ⓑ Ⓒ Ⓓ Ⓔ
65 Ⓐ Ⓑ Ⓒ Ⓓ Ⓔ
66 Ⓐ Ⓑ Ⓒ Ⓓ Ⓔ
67 Ⓐ Ⓑ Ⓒ Ⓓ Ⓔ
68 Ⓐ Ⓑ Ⓒ Ⓓ Ⓔ
69 Ⓐ Ⓑ Ⓒ Ⓓ Ⓔ
70 Ⓐ Ⓑ Ⓒ Ⓓ Ⓔ

71 Ⓐ Ⓑ Ⓒ Ⓓ Ⓔ
72 Ⓐ Ⓑ Ⓒ Ⓓ Ⓔ
73 Ⓐ Ⓑ Ⓒ Ⓓ Ⓔ
74 Ⓐ Ⓑ Ⓒ Ⓓ Ⓔ
75 Ⓐ Ⓑ Ⓒ Ⓓ Ⓔ
76 Ⓐ Ⓑ Ⓒ Ⓓ Ⓔ
77 Ⓐ Ⓑ Ⓒ Ⓓ Ⓔ
78 Ⓐ Ⓑ Ⓒ Ⓓ Ⓔ
79 Ⓐ Ⓑ Ⓒ Ⓓ Ⓔ
80 Ⓐ Ⓑ Ⓒ Ⓓ Ⓔ
81 Ⓐ Ⓑ Ⓒ Ⓓ Ⓔ
82 Ⓐ Ⓑ Ⓒ Ⓓ Ⓔ
83 Ⓐ Ⓑ Ⓒ Ⓓ Ⓔ
84 Ⓐ Ⓑ Ⓒ Ⓓ Ⓔ
85 Ⓐ Ⓑ Ⓒ Ⓓ Ⓔ
86 Ⓐ Ⓑ Ⓒ Ⓓ Ⓔ
87 Ⓐ Ⓑ Ⓒ Ⓓ Ⓔ
88 Ⓐ Ⓑ Ⓒ Ⓓ Ⓔ
89 Ⓐ Ⓑ Ⓒ Ⓓ Ⓔ
90 Ⓐ Ⓑ Ⓒ Ⓓ Ⓔ

91 Ⓐ Ⓑ Ⓒ Ⓓ Ⓔ
92 Ⓐ Ⓑ Ⓒ Ⓓ Ⓔ
93 Ⓐ Ⓑ Ⓒ Ⓓ Ⓔ
94 Ⓐ Ⓑ Ⓒ Ⓓ Ⓔ
95 Ⓐ Ⓑ Ⓒ Ⓓ Ⓔ
96 Ⓐ Ⓑ Ⓒ Ⓓ Ⓔ
97 Ⓐ Ⓑ Ⓒ Ⓓ Ⓔ
98 Ⓐ Ⓑ Ⓒ Ⓓ Ⓔ
99 Ⓐ Ⓑ Ⓒ Ⓓ Ⓔ
100 Ⓐ Ⓑ Ⓒ Ⓓ Ⓔ
101 Ⓐ Ⓑ Ⓒ Ⓓ Ⓔ
102 Ⓐ Ⓑ Ⓒ Ⓓ Ⓔ
103 Ⓐ Ⓑ Ⓒ Ⓓ Ⓔ
104 Ⓐ Ⓑ Ⓒ Ⓓ Ⓔ
105 Ⓐ Ⓑ Ⓒ Ⓓ Ⓔ
106 Ⓐ Ⓑ Ⓒ Ⓓ Ⓔ
107 Ⓐ Ⓑ Ⓒ Ⓓ Ⓔ
108 Ⓐ Ⓑ Ⓒ Ⓓ Ⓔ
109 Ⓐ Ⓑ Ⓒ Ⓓ Ⓔ
110 Ⓐ Ⓑ Ⓒ Ⓓ Ⓔ

111 Ⓐ Ⓑ Ⓒ Ⓓ Ⓔ
112 Ⓐ Ⓑ Ⓒ Ⓓ Ⓔ
113 Ⓐ Ⓑ Ⓒ Ⓓ Ⓔ
114 Ⓐ Ⓑ Ⓒ Ⓓ Ⓔ
115 Ⓐ Ⓑ Ⓒ Ⓓ Ⓔ
116 Ⓐ Ⓑ Ⓒ Ⓓ Ⓔ
117 Ⓐ Ⓑ Ⓒ Ⓓ Ⓔ
118 Ⓐ Ⓑ Ⓒ Ⓓ Ⓔ
119 Ⓐ Ⓑ Ⓒ Ⓓ Ⓔ
120 Ⓐ Ⓑ Ⓒ Ⓓ Ⓔ
121 Ⓐ Ⓑ Ⓒ Ⓓ Ⓔ
122 Ⓐ Ⓑ Ⓒ Ⓓ Ⓔ
123 Ⓐ Ⓑ Ⓒ Ⓓ Ⓔ
124 Ⓐ Ⓑ Ⓒ Ⓓ Ⓔ
125 Ⓐ Ⓑ Ⓒ Ⓓ Ⓔ
126 Ⓐ Ⓑ Ⓒ Ⓓ Ⓔ
127 Ⓐ Ⓑ Ⓒ Ⓓ Ⓔ
128 Ⓐ Ⓑ Ⓒ Ⓓ Ⓔ
129 Ⓐ Ⓑ Ⓒ Ⓓ Ⓔ
130 Ⓐ Ⓑ Ⓒ Ⓓ Ⓔ

Directions

In each question in this test, there is at the left a series of letters that follow some definite order, and, at the right, five sets of two letters each.

Look at the letters in each series at the left and find out what order they follow. Now decide what the next two letters in that series would be if the order were continued. Then find that set in one of the five suggested answers at the right and darken completely the correct letter space on your answer sheet.

Sample questions 1, 2, 3, 4, and 5 are given below. Mark the answer to each on your answer sheet in spaces 1 through 5.

1. x c x d x e x .... A) f x   B) f g   C) x f   D) e f   E) x g

The order of this series is the letter *x* alternating with letters in alphabetical order starting with c so that if the series were continued for two more letters, it would read: x c x d x e x f x and *f x* are those two letters you would look for.

In the five sets of letters on the right, in question 1, the set *f x* is labeled A. Therefore, you should mark space A on your answer sheet for sample question 1. Do it now.

2. u u t t s s r .... A) r r   B) r q   C) q r   D) q q   E) r s

The order of this series is pairs of letters starting with *u u* and going *backward* through the alphabet so that if the series were continued for two more letters, it would read: u u t t s s r r q and *r q* are those two letters you would look for.

In the five sets of letters on the right, in question 2, the set *r q* is labeled B. Therefore, you should mark space B on your answer sheet for sample question 2. Do it now.

3. a v a w a x a .... A) z a   B) y z   C) y a   D) a z   E) a y

If you discover the order in this series, you will see that the next two letters should be *y a*. In the five sets of letters on the right, the set *y a* is labeled C. Therefore, you should mark space C on your answer sheet for sample question 3. Do it now.

Now work sample questions 4 and 5 and mark the answers on the answer sheet.

4. a b d e g h j .... A) k l   B) l n   C) j m   D) l m   E) k m

5. a r c s e t g .... A) h i   B) h u   C) u j   D) u i   E) i v

If you worked the sample questions correctly, you should have marked space E for question 4 and space D for question 5.

You will have 20 minutes to answer the test questions. The first question is number 6, so be sure to start with space 6 on your answer sheet.

DO NOT TURN THIS PAGE UNTIL TOLD TO DO SO.

THE TEST

In each series of letters below determine what the order of the letters is and decide what the next two letters should be. From the suggested answers at the right choose the one that gives the next two letters in the series and darken the corresponding space on your answer sheet.

a b c d e f g h i j k l m n o p q r s t u v w x y z

6. m n o m n o m .... A) m n   B) n o   C) n m   D) o n   E) o m

7. e e a e e b e .... A) e e   B) e f   C) c e   D) f e   E) e c

8. f g g f h h f .... A) f f   B) f i   C) i i   D) i f   E) j j

9. p p q r r s t .... A) t t   B) u v   C) u u   D) t u   E) t v

10. l c d l e f l .... A) l g   B) g h   C) l e   D) f g   E) g g

11. g n v h o w i .... A) p j   B) x j   C) i p   D) p x   E) x q

12. r l s m t n u .... A) o v   B) u v   C) v w   D) o w   E) v o

13. s h r i q j p .... A) k o   B) k l   C) o k   D) p k   E) o n

14. a b z c d y e .... A) x g   B) x w   C) f w   D) f x   E) f g

15. e e g i i k m .... A) m n   B) o o   C) o q   D) m o   E) n m

16. j h n l r p v .... A) t x   B) s z   C) t z   D) s y   E) z t

17. q g r i s k t .... A) u l   B) m u   C) l u   D) m n   E) l m

18. e h i f i j g .... A) h i   B) j k   C) i k   D) h j   E) i j

19. t g h u e f v .... A) d c   B) d w   C) d e   D) c d   E) c w

20. h g f k j i n .... A) m l   B) p o   C) l m   D) o p   E) m o

21. r p n l j h f .... A) e c   B) d c   C) e b   D) d b   E) e d

22. e g t h j t k .... A) l t   B) m t   C) l m   D) t l   E) m n

23. b d c e g f h .... A) g i   B) i k   C) j i   D) j l   E) h j

24. e h j m o r t .... A) v y   B) w z   C) v x   D) x z   E) w y

25. f r h t j v l .... A) m n   B) w y   C) x n   D) n w   E) x m

26. m p n q o r p .... A) s q   B) q r   C) t q   D) q s   E) s r

27. g i k h j l i .... A) k l   B) j k   C) j l   D) j m   E) k m

28. a c f h k m p .... A) s v   B) r t   C) r u   D) s u   E) q r

GO ON TO THE NEXT PAGE.

abcdefghijklmnopqrstuvwxyz

29. c d f g j k m .... A) n q   B) p q   C) o p   D) n p   E) o r

30. h g l m l q r .... A) q r   B) q w   C) r w   D) q v   E) r q

31. c d f g j k o .... A) p t   B) p u   C) t x   D) t z   E) s x

32. f d h f j h l .... A) j m   B) i n   C) j n   D) k m   E) i m

33. r n p t p r v .... A) s u   B) r t   C) x z   D) z x   E) t r

34. d f h h e g i i f h j .... A) j g   B) g g   C) g i   D) j i   E) l l

35. y x v t s q o n l j i .... A) h f   B) h g   C) g e   D) f e   E) g f

If you finish before the time is up, you may go back and check your answers.

ANSWER KEY

1. **A**		8. **C**		15. **D**		22. **B**	29. **A**
2. **B**		9. **D**		16. **C**		23. **C**	30. **D**
3. **C**		10. **B**		17. **B**		24. **E**	31. **B**
4. **E**		11. **D**		18. **B**		25. **C**	32. **C**
5. **D**		12. **A**		19. **D**		26. **A**	33. **B**
6. **B**		13. **A**		20. **A**		27. **E**	34. **A**
7. **E**		14. **D**		21. **D**		28. **C**	35. **C**

ANSWER EXPLANATIONS

Explanations for questions 1 through 3 are given on page 307.

4. **(E)** a b d e g h j <u>k m</u>
Two consecutive letters, the next letter is skipped; then two consecutive letters, the next letter is skipped; and so on.

5. **(D)** a r c s e t g <u>u i</u>
Two alternating groups of letters: the first group (*a, c, e, g, i*) skips a letter each time; the second group is letters in consecutive order (*r, s, t, u*).

6. **(B)** m n o m n o m n <u>o</u>
The letters *m n o* repeating.

7. **(E)** e e a e e b e <u>e c</u>
Double *e*, then *a*; double *e*, then *b*; double *e*, then *c*; and so on.

8. **(C)** f g g f h h f <u>i i</u>
f, then double *g*; *f*, then double *h*; *f*, then double *i*; and so on.

9. **(D)** p p q r r s t <u>t u</u>
A pair of the same letter followed by the next consecutive letter once; then a pair of the next consecutive letter followed by the next consecutive letter once; and so on.

10. **(B)** l c d l e f l <u>g h</u>
l followed by two consecutive letters, starting with *c*; then *l* again followed by the next two consecutive letters; repeat sequence.

11. **(D)** g n v h o w i p <u>x</u>
Three alternating groups of letters: each group is in consecutive order—(*g, h, i*); (*n, o, p*); and (*v, w, x*). Note how a part of each group appears every third letter.

12. **(A)** r l s m t n u <u>o v</u>
Two alternating groups of letters: each group is in consecutive order—(*r, s, t, u, v*) and (*l, m, n, o*).

13. **(A)** s h r i q j p k <u>o</u>
Two alternating groups of letters: the first group goes backward consecutively (*s, r, q, p, o*); the other group is in forward consecutive order (*h, i, j, k*).

14. **(D)** a b z c d y e <u>f x</u>
The first two letters of the alphabet, then the last letter; the next two letters after *a b*, followed by the next to last; the next two letters after *c d*, followed by the one before the next to last; and so on.

15. **(D)** e e g i i k m <u>m o</u>
Double letter, then skip a letter, single letter, then skip a letter; repeat.

16. **(C)** j h n l r p v t z
Begin with j: second letter back, then sixth letter forward; second letter back, then sixth letter forward: and so on.

17. **(B)** q g r i s k t m u
Two alternating groups of letters: the first group goes forward consecutively (*q, r, s, t, u*); the second group goes forward skipping a letter each time (*g, i, k, m*).

18. **(B)** e h i f i j g j k
Three alternating groups of letters, each consecutive and interspersed: (e ⓗ i f ⓘ j g ⓙk̄)

19. **(D)** t g h u e f v c d
Two alternating groups of letters: the first group is consecutive and appears every third letter (*t, u, v*); the other group consists of pairs of consecutive letters, each pair coming before the previous pair (*g h, e f, c d*).

20. **(A)** h g f k j i n m l
Three backward consecutive letters, followed by the next three backward consecutive letters: (*h g f, k j i, n m l*).

21. **(D)** r p n l j h f d b
Goes consecutively backward but skips every other letter: (*r*, skips *q*, then *p*, skips *o*, then *n*, skips *m*, then *l*, skips *k*, then *j*, skips *i*, then *h*, etc.).

22. **(B)** e g t h j t k m t
A forward pair skipping the middle letter (*e, g*), then *t*; the next consecutive pair, skipping the middle letter (*h, j*), then *t*; then the next consecutive pair (*k, m*), then *t*.

23. **(C)** b d c e g f h j i
Ahead two, back one, ahead two; ahead two, back one, ahead two; ahead two, back one, and so on.

24. **(E)** e h j m o r t w y
Ahead three, ahead two; repeat.

25. **(C)** f r h t j v l x n
Two alternating groups of letters: each group skips a letter (*f, h, j, l, n*, and *r, t, v, x*).

26. **(A)** m p n q o r p s q
Two alternating groups of letters, each consecutive: (*m, n, o, p, q* and *p, q, r, s*).

27. **(E)** g i k h j l i k m
Three letters, skipping a letter each time (*g, i, k*); then the next consecutive set of three skipping letters (*h, j, l*); followed by the next consecutive set of three skipping letters (*i, k, m*).

28. **(C)** a c f h k m p r u
Two ahead, then three ahead; repeat.

29. **(A)** c d f g j k m n q
A pair of consecutive letters, then skip one letter, the next pair of consecutive letters, then skip two letters; repeat.

30. **(D)** h g l m l q r g v
Back one, ahead five, ahead one; repeat.

31. **(B)** c d f g j k o p u
A pair of consecutive letters then skip one; the next pair of consecutive letters, then skip two; the next pair of consecutive letters, then skip three; and so on.

32. **(C)** f d h f j h l j n
Back two, up four; repeat.

33. **(B)** r n p t p r v r t
Back four, up two, up four; repeat.

34. **(A)** d f h h e g i i f h j j g
Each set of four letters follows the order skip one, skip one, double the last letter (*d, f, h, h*); then repeat this sequence starting with the next consecutive letter after the *first* from the last sequence (*e, g, i, i*); then (*f, h, j, j*); then (*g, i, k, k*); and so on.

35. **(C)** y x v t s q o n l j i g e
Going backward only: a pair of consecutive letters, skip one, then a single letter, skip one; repeat.

CHAPTER 14

Practice, Practice, Practice

(NOTE: Allow 20 minutes for each practice set.)

PRACTICE SET 1

In each series of letters below determine what the order of the letters is and decide what the next two letters should be. From the suggested answers at the right choose the one that gives the next two letters in the series.

a b c d e f g h i j k l m n o p q r s t u v w x y z

1. c d f g i j l .... A) m n   B) m o   C) m p   D) o p   E) o q   _____

2. y x v u s r p .... A) m o   B) q m   C) o n   D) o m   E) n o   _____

3. j k l n o p r .... A) t u   B) s t   C) s u   D) u v   E) s v   _____

4. b c f g j k n .... A) o r   B) o p   C) q r   D) p q   E) p r   _____

5. b b c d d e f .... A) f f   B) g g   C) g h   D) h i   E) f g   _____

6. p p o n n m l .... A) l k   B) k l   C) k j   D) l l   E) k i   _____

7. y y x w w v u .... A) t u   B) u t   C) u v   D) t s   E) s t   _____

8. c b a f e d i .... A) g h   B) h g   C) g f   D) k j   E) f g   _____

9. n o m l j k i .... A) h g   B) h i   C) h f   D) h e   E) f h   _____

10. d e f d e f d .... A) d e   B) f d   C) e d   D) e f   E) f e   _____

11. y x w u t s q .... A) p o   B) o n   C) p n   D) r p   E) o p   _____

12. t t a b u u c .... A) c v   B) d e   C) d v   D) v v   E) v d   _____

13. l l z k k y j .... A) x j   B) j i   C) j x   D) j l   E) v j   _____

14. e f d h i g k .... A) l j   B) j l   C) j m   D) m j   E) l m   _____

15. o n l k i h f .... A) e d   B) e c   C) e b   D) d b   E) d c   _____

16. b r c s d t e .... A) f g   B) u v   C) v f   D) u f   E) u g   _____

17. e w h u k s n .... A) p q   B) p q   C) q q   D) q r   E) r q   _____

18. a a d e g i j .... A) m m   B) m n   C) n m   D) l m   E) m l   _____

19. n o p p q r s .... A) t s   B) s t   C) u t   D) t u   E) u v   ____

20. g h i i j k k .... A) l m   B) m n   C) n o   D) k l   E) k i   ____

21. a b t c d s e .... A) f g   B) f g   C) f r   D) f u   E) g f   ____

22. z a x c v e t .... A) f s   B) f r   C) g s   D) g u   E) g r   ____

23. y l m w n o u .... A) q s   B) p s   C) p q   D) q r   E) p r   ____

24. t s s r r r q .... A) q p   B) p p   C) q q   D) o p   E) o o   ____

25. j j h h f f d .... A) d d   B) d c   C) d b   D) d a   E) d e   ____

26. v u u t t t s .... A) r r   B) s t   C) p r   D) r s   E) s s   ____

27. n s p q r o t .... A) s p   B) m v   C) v m   D) p s   E) u v   ____

28. g h a j k b m .... A) n o   B) n d   C) n c   D) o c   E) c o   ____

29. v c t f r i p .... A) j n   B) l n   C) j m   D) l m   E) j o   ____

30. a c d d e g h h i .... A) k k   B) l l   C) k l   D) k m   E) m m   ____

ANSWER EXPLANATIONS FOR PRACTICE SET 1

1. **(B)** c d f g i j l m o
   Two consecutive letters, then skip a letter; repeat.

2. **(D)** y x v u s r p o m
   Going backward: two consecutive letters, then skip one; repeat.

3. **(B)** j k l n o p r s t
   Three consecutive letters, then skip one; repeat.

4. **(A)** b c f g j k n o r
   Two consecutive letters, then skip two; repeat.

5. **(E)** b b c d d e f f g
   Consecutive letters, but every other one is doubled.

6. **(A)** p p o n n m l l k
   Consecutive letters backward, but every other one is doubled.

7. **(B)** y y x w w v u u t
   Consecutive letters backward, but every other one is doubled.

8. **(B)** c b a f e d i h g
   Continuing sets of three consecutively backward letters.

9. **(C)** n o m l j k i h f
   One forward, two back, one back, two back; repeat. This is a difficult one.

10. **(D)** d e f d e f d e f
    The letters d e f repeating.

11. **(A)** y x w u t s q p o
    Consecutive letters backward, skipping every fourth letter.

12. **(C)** t t a b u u c d v
    Two alternating groups of letters: the first group is repeating pairs of consecutive letters (t t, u u, v v, etc.); the second group is pairs of consecutive letters (a b, c d, e f, etc).

13. **(C)** l l z k k y j j x
    Two alternating groups of letters: the first group is pairs of doubled letters backward consecutively (l l, k k, j j, etc.); the other group is single letters backward consecutively (z, y, x, w, etc.)

14. **(A)** e f d h i g k l j
    One ahead, two back, four ahead; repeat.

15. **(B)** o n l k i h f e c
    Consecutive letters backward, skipping every third letter.

16. **(D)** b r c s d t e u f
    Two alternating groups of letters, each consecutive: b, c, d, e, f and r, s, t, u.

17. **(C)** e w h u k s n q q
    Two alternating groups of letters: the first group goes forward, skipping every two letters (e, h, k, n, q); the other group goes backward, skipping every other letter (w, u, s, q).

18. **(A)** a a d e g i j m m
    Two alternating groups of letters: the first group goes forward, skipping every two letters (a, d, g, j, m); the second group goes forward, skipping every three letters (a, e, i, m).

19. **(B)** n o p p q r s s t
Consecutive letters forward, with every third letter doubled.

20. **(A)** g h i i j k k l m
Consecutive letters forward, but the third letter of a set becomes the first letter of the next set.

21. **(C)** a b t c d s e f r
Two alternating groups of letters. The first group is pairs of consecutive letters (*a b, c d, e f*); the other group is single letters, consecutively backward (*t, s, r*).

22. **(E)** z a x c v e t g r
Two alternating groups of letters: the first group goes backward, skipping every other letter (*z, x, v, t, r*); the second group goes forward, skipping every other letter (*a, c, e, g*).

23. **(C)** y l m w n o u p q
Two alternating groups of letters: the first group is single letters going backward, skipping every other letter (*y, w, u*); the second group is pairs of consecutive letters going forward (*l m, n o, p q*).

24. **(C)** t s s r r r q q q
Consecutive letters going backward, each letter increasing in number by one: one *t*, two *s*'s, three *r*'s, four *q*'s, and so on.

25. **(C)** j j h h f f d d b
Going backward: a pair of the same letters, skip the next letter; repeat (*j j, h h, f f, d d, b b*).

26. **(E)** v u u t t t s s s
Going backward: consecutive letters increasing in number by one (one *v*, two *u*'s, three *t*'s, four *s*'s, and so on).

27. **(B)** n s p q r o t m v
Two alternating groups of letters: the first group goes forward, skipping every other letter (*n, p, r, t, v*); the second group goes backward, skipping every other letter (*s, q, o, m*).

28. **(C)** g h a j k b m n c
Two alternating groups of letters: the first group is consecutive letters in pairs, skipping every third letter (*g h, j k, m n*); the other group is consecutive single letters (*a, b, c,*).

29. **(B)** v c t f r i p l n
Two alternating groups of letters: the first group goes backward, skipping every other letter (*v, t, r, p, n*); the other group goes forward, skipping every two letters (*c, f, i, l*).

30. **(C)** a c d d e g h h k l
Forward as follows: beginning with *a*, skip a letter, then double the next consecutive letter, then go to the next consecutive letter; repeat.

PRACTICE SET 2

In each series of letters below determine what the order of the letters is and decide what the next two letters should be. From the suggested answers at the right choose the one that gives the next two letters in the series.

a b c d e f g h i j k l m n o p q r s t u v w x y z

1. f g i j m n p .... A) r u   B) q t   C) s t   D) r s   E) q s   _____

2. k j o p o t u .... A) t u   B) u t   C) t z   D) u z   E) t y   _____

3. f g i j m n r .... A) s w   B) s x   C) w a   D) w c   E) v q   _____

4. i g k i m k o .... A) l p   B) m p   C) l q   D) m q   E) n p   _____

5. u q s w s u y .... A) w y   B) v x   C) u w   D) a c   E) c a   _____

6. d g e h f i g .... A) j h   B) k h   C) j k   D) k j   E) h k   _____

7. c y x t s o n .... A) j i   B) i j   C) k j   D) l k   E) i h   _____

8. g y h x i w j .... A) k x   B) x k   C) v k   D) v i   E) k v   _____

9. m n n o p p q .... A) r s   B) q r   C) r r   D) s r   E) s s   _____

10. n b p z r x t .... A) v v   B) v x   C) x v   D) w v   E) u w   _____

11. h g r j i r l .... A) r k   B) r n   C) k r   D) m r   E) r m   _____

a b c d e f g h i j k l m n o p q r s t u v w x y z

12.	d c e b f a g	A) h z	B) z h	C) z i	D) i h	E) y h	____
13.	g j i l k n m	A) p o	B) p q	C) q r	D) q p	E) o n	____
14.	d e g j k m p	A) r t	B) q r	C) q t	D) q s	E) r s	____
15.	g r j s m t p	A) u r	B) u s	C) u p	D) u w	E) u u	____
16.	a d e h i l m	A) n q	B) q p	C) p q	D) o p	E) r s	____
17.	j i m l p o	A) n r	B) s w	C) q u	D) s r	E) n m	____
18.	d h e i f j g	A) k h	B) h k	C) h i	D) i j	E) k l	____
19.	n k m j l i	A) g j	B) k h	C) l j	D) f h	E) k l	____
20.	e e b e e c e	A) e e	B) a a	C) e d	D) e f	E) d e	____
21.	z w y v x u w	A) t v	B) s v	C) t s	D) s t	E) v s	____
22.	w e v f u g t	A) s f	B) f s	C) h s	D) h u	E) s h	____
23.	q p p o n n m	A) l k	B) m l	C) k l	D) l l	E) k k	____
24.	a e f j k o p	A) u v	B) t u	C) u t	D) s t	E) r s	____
25.	p b n d l f j	A) h f	B) j h	C) g h	D) i g	E) h h	____
26.	v w l t u l r	A) l p	B) s l	C) q l	D) l q	E) l s	____
27.	z a y b x c w	A) v d	B) d v	C) d u	D) u v	E) e v	____
28.	w t u r s p q	A) n o	B) n m	C) m l	D) m n	E) o p	____
29.	b c w v d e u t f	A) g t	B) t h	C) g s	D) h i	E) h s	____
30.	a e c g e i g k i	A) i k	B) m k	C) o m	D) m o	E) j m	____

ANSWER EXPLANATIONS FOR PRACTICE SET 2

1. **(B)** f g i j m n p q t
   A pair of consecutive letters, then skip one letter, the next pair of consecutive letters, then skip two letters; repeat.

2. **(E)** k j o p o t u t y
   Back one, ahead five, ahead one; repeat.

3. **(B)** f g i j m n r s x
   A pair of consecutive letters, then skip one letter; the next pair of consecutive letters, then skip two; the next pair of consecutive letters, then skip three; and so on.

4. **(D)** i g k i m k o m q
   Back two, up four; repeat.

5. **(C)** u q s w s u y u w
   Back four, up two, up four; repeat.

6. **(A)** d g e h f i g j h
   Alternating consecutive sets: (d e f g h) (g h i j).

7. **(A)** c y x t s o n j i
   Back four, back one; repeat.

8. **(C)** g y h x i w j v k
   Two alternating groups: the first group goes forward consecutively (g, h, i, j, k); the second group goes backward consecutively (y, x, w, v).

9. **(C)** m n n o p p q r r
   A single letter, then the next consecutive letter doubled; the next consecutive single letter, then the next consecutive letter doubled; and so on.

10. **(A)** n b p z r x t v v
Two alternating groups of letters: the first group skips one letter as it goes forward; the other group skips one letter as it goes backward.

11. **(C)** h g r j i r l k r
Consecutive backward pairs, separated by the letter *r*.

12. **(B)** d c e b f a g z h
Two alternating groups of letters: one consecutive forward; the other consecutive backward.

13. **(A)** g j i l k n m p o
Ahead three, back one; repeat.

14. **(D)** d e g j k m p q s
Beginning with *d*, the next consecutive letter, then skip one letter, then skip two letters; repeat.

15. **(B)** g r j s m t p u s
Two alternating groups of letters: the first group goes forward skipping two letters (*g, j, m, p, s*); the second group goes forward consecutively (*r, s, t, u*).

16. **(C)** a d e h i l m p q
Three ahead, then one ahead; repeat.

17. **(D)** j i m l p o s r
Back one, ahead four; repeat.

18. **(A)** d h e i f j g k h
Two alternating groups of letters, each consecutive: (*d, e, f, g, h*) and (*h, i, j, k*).

19. **(B)** n k m j l i k h
Back three, ahead two; repeat.

20. **(C)** e e b e e c e e d
Double *e*, then *b*; double *e*, then *c*; and so on.

21. **(A)** z w y v x u w t v
Working backward starting at *z*, go three back, then two forward; three back, two forward; and so on.

22. **(C)** w e v f u g t h s
Two alternating groups: the first group goes backward consecutively (*w, v, u, t, s*); the second group goes forward consecutively (*e, f, g, h*).

23. **(D)** q p p o n n m l l
Going backward only: a single letter, then the next consecutive letter doubled; the next consecutive letter single, then the next consecutive letter doubled; and so on.

24. **(B)** a e f j k o p t u
Ahead four, ahead one; repeat.

25. **(E)** p b n d l f j h h
Two alternating groups of letters: the first group skips one letter as it goes backward; the other group skips one letter as it goes forward.

26. **(B)** v w l t u l r s l
Consecutive forward pair followed by letter *l*; then go two backward from starting letter *v* to get next consecutive forward pair (*t u*), followed by letter *l*; go two backward from *t* to get next consecutive pair (*r s*), followed by *l*.

27. **(B)** z a y b x c w d v
Two alternating groups of letters: one consecutive backward; the other consecutive forward.

28. **(A)** w t u r s p q n o
Back three, ahead one; repeat.

29. **(C)** b c w v d e u t f g s
Two alternating groups of letters: the first group, consecutive pairs going forward (*b c, d e, f g*); the second group, consecutive pairs going backward (*w v, u t, s r*).

30. **(B)** a e c g e i g k i m k
Ahead four, then back two; repeat.

PRACTICE SET 3

In each series of letters below determine what the order of the letters is and decide what the next two letters should be. From the suggested answers at the right choose the one that gives the next two letters in the series.

a b c d e f g h i j k l m n o p q r s t u v w x y z

1. a f a g a h a .... A) i a   B) i j   C) a i   D) h i   E) a j   _____

2. x x w w v v u .... A) u u   B) u t   C) t u   D) t t   E) u v   _____

3. d y d z d a d .... A) c k   B) b c   C) b d   D) d c   E) d b   _____

4. d e g h j k m .... A) n o   B) o q   C) m p   D) o p   E) n p   _____

5. d u f v h w j .... A) k x   B) k l   C) x l   D) f y   E) x m   _____

6. p q r p q r p .... A) r p   B) r q   C) q p   D) q r   E) p q   _____

7. h h d h h h e h .... A) h h   B) h i   C) f h   D) i h   E) h f   _____

8. i j j i k k i .... A) i i   B) l l   C) i l   D) l i   E) m m   _____

abcdefghijklmnopqrstuvwxyz

9. sstuuvw .... A) wy   B) wx   C) xx   D) xy   E) ww   _____

10. ofgohio .... A) jj   B) ij   C) oh   D) jk   E) oj   _____

11. jqykrzl .... A) at   B) sa   C) ls   D) am   E) sm   _____

12. uovpwqx .... A) yr   B) rz   C) yz   D) xy   E) ry   _____

13. vkultms .... A) rq   B) sn   C) rn   D) no   E) nr   _____

14. decfgbh .... A) az   B) aj   C) ij   D) iz   E) ia   _____

15. hhjllnp .... A) rt   B) pr   C) rr   D) qp   E) pq   _____

16. mkqousy .... A) vc   B) wq   C) vb   D) wc   E) cw   _____

17. tjulvnw .... A) px   B) so   C) ox   D) pq   E) op   _____

18. hklilmj .... A) kl   B) ln   C) mn   D) km   E) lm   _____

19. wjkxhiy .... A) gf   B) gz   C) gh   D) fg   E) fz   _____

20. kjinmlq .... A) po   B) sr   C) op   D) rs   E) pr   _____

21. usqomki .... A) hf   B) gf   C) he   D) ge   E) hg   _____

22. hjwkmwn .... A) ow   B) pw   C) op   D) wo   E) pq   _____

23. egfhjik .... A) jl   B) ln   C) ml   D) mo   E) km   _____

24. hkmpruw .... A) yb   B) zc   C) ya   D) ac   E) zb   _____

25. iukwmyo .... A) pq   B) zb   C) aq   D) qz   E) ap   _____

26. psqtrus .... A) vt   B) tu   C) wt   D) tv   E) pu   _____

27. jlnkmol .... A) no   B) mn   C) mo   D) mp   E) np   _____

28. dfiknps .... A) vy   B) uw   C) ux   D) vx   E) tu   _____

29. gikkhjllikm .... A) mj   B) jj   C) jl   D) ml   E) oo   _____

30. baywvtrqoml .... A) ki   B) kj   C) jh   D) ih   E) ji   _____

ANSWER EXPLANATIONS FOR PRACTICE SET 3

1. **(A)** afagahaia
   The letter $\bar{a}$ alternating with letters in alphabetical order, starting with f.

2. **(B)** xxwwvvuut
   Pairs of letters, starting with x x and going backward through the alphabet.

3. **(C)** dydzdadbd
   The letter d alternating with letters in alphabetical order, starting with y.

4. **(E)** deghjkmnp
   Two consecutive letters, then skip the next letter; the next two consecutive letters, then skip the next letter; and so on.

5. **(C)** d u f v h w j x̲ l̲

Two alternating groups of letters: the first group (*d, f, h, j*) skips a letter each time; the second group consists of letters in consecutive order (*u, v, w, x*).

6. **(D)** p q r p q r p q̲ r̲

The letters *p q r* repeating.

7. **(E)** h h d h h e h h̲ f̲

Double *h*, then *d*; double *h*, then *e*; double *h*, then *f*; and so on.

8. **(B)** i j j i k k i l̲ l̲

i, then double *j*; *i*, then double *k*; *i*, then double *l*; and so on.

9. **(B)** s s t u u v w w̲ x̲

A pair of the same letter, then the next consecutive letter once; a pair of the next consecutive letter, then the next consecutive letter once; and so on.

10. **(D)** o f g o h i o j̲ k̲

o, then, starting with *f*, two consecutive letters; then *o* again, followed by the next two consecutive letters; then *o* again and so on.

11. **(B)** j q y k r z l s̲ a̲

Three alternating groups of letters: each group is in consecutive order (*j, k, l*), (*q, r, s*), (*y, z, a*).

12. **(E)** u o v p w q x r̲ y̲

Two alternating groups of letters: each group is in consecutive order (*u, v, w, x, y*), (*o, p, q, r*).

13. **(E)** v k u l t m s n̲ r̲

Two alternating groups of letters: the first group goes backward consecutively (*v, u, t, s, r*); the other group goes forward consecutively (*k, l, m, n*).

14. **(E)** d e c f g b h i̲ a̲

The fourth and fifth letters of the alphabet, then the third letter; the next two letters (sixth and seventh), then the second; and so on.

15. **(B)** h h j l l n p p̲ r̲

Double letter, then skip one letter, then single letter, then skip one letter; repeat.

16. **(D)** m k q o u s y w̲ c̲

Begin with *m*: second letter back, then sixth letter forward; repeat.

17. **(A)** t j u l v n w p̲ x̲

Two alternating groups of letters: the first group goes forward consecutively (*t, u, v, w, x*); the second group goes forward skipping a letter each time (*j, l, n, p*).

18. **(C)** h k l i l m j m̲ n̲

Three alternating groups of letters, each consecutive: (*h, i, j*), (*k, l, m*), (*l, m, n*).

19. **(D)** w j k x h i j f̲ g̲

Two alternating groups of letters: the first group is consecutive and appears every third letter (*w, x, y*); the other group consists of pairs of consecutive letters, each pair coming before the previous pair (*jk, hi, fg*).

20. **(A)** k j i n m l q p̲ o̲

Three backward consecutive letters, followed by the next three backward consecutive letters: (*k, ji, nml, qpo*).

21. **(D)** u s q o m k i g e̲

Goes consecutively backward but skips every other letter: *u*, skips *t*; then *s*, skips *r*; then *q*, skips *p*, then *o*, skips *n*; then *m*, skips *l*; and so on.

22. **(B)** h j w k m w n p̲ w̲

A forward pair skipping the middle letter (*h, j*), then *w*; the next consecutive pair, still skipping the middle letter (*k, m*), then *w*; the next consecutive pair (*n, p*), then *w*.

23. **(C)** e g f h j i k m̲ l̲

Ahead two, back one, ahead two; ahead two, back one, ahead two; ahead two, back one, and so on.

24. **(E)** h k m p r u w z̲ b̲

Ahead three, ahead two; repeat.

25. **(C)** i u k w m y o a̲ q̲

Two alternating groups of letters, each group skips a letter: *i, k, m, o, q* and *u, w, y, a*.

26. **(A)** p s q t r u s v̲ t̲

Two alternating groups of letters, each consecutive: *p, q, r, s, t* and *s, t, u, v*.

27. **(E)** j l n k m o l n̲ p̲

Three letters, skipping a letter each time (*j, l, n*); then the next consecutive set of three skipping letters (*k, m, o*), followed by the next consecutive set of three skipping letters (*l, n, p*).

28. **(C)** d f i k n p s u̲ x̲

Two ahead, then three ahead; repeat.

29. **(A)** g i k k h j l l i k m m̲ j̲

Each set of four letters follows the order skip one, skip one, double the third letter (*g, i, k, k*); then the sequence is repeated, starting with the next consecutive letter after the *first* from the last sequence (*h, j, l, l*); and so on.

30. **(C)** b a y w v t r q o m l j̲ h̲

Going backward only: a pair of consecutive letters (*b a*), skip one (*z*), then a single letter (*y*), skip one (*x*); a pair of consecutive letters (*wv*), skip one (*y*), then a single letter (*t*), skip one (*s*); and so on.

PRACTICE SET 4

In each series of letters below determine what the order of the letters is and decide what the next two letters should be. From the suggested answers at the right choose the one that gives the next two letters in the series.

abcdefghijklmnopqrstuvwxyz

1. adbecfd .... A) ge   B) he   C) gh   D) hg   E) eh   _____

2. dveuftg .... A) hu   B) uh   C) sh   D) sf   E) hs   _____

3. jkklmmn .... A) po   B) no   C) oo   D) op   E) pp   _____

4. zvuqplk .... A) gf   B) fg   C) hg   D) ih   E) fe   _____

5. kymwouq .... A) su   B) us   C) ts   D) rt   E) ss   _____

6. edogfoi .... A) ok   B) ho   C) jo   D) oj   E) oh   _____

7. azbycxd .... A) ew   B) we   C) wf   D) fe   E) ve   _____

8. zywtsqn .... A) ml   B) mj   C) lj   D) mk   E) lk   _____

9. wltkqjn .... A) il   B) ik   C) in   D) ig   E) ii   _____

10. qsmoike .... A) gc   B) ha   C) ga   D) hb   E) ag   _____

11. jtirhpg .... A) fo   B) nf   C) of   D) nm   E) on   _____

12. vsrurqt .... A) sr   B) qp   C) rp   D) wq   E) rq   _____

13. gtsfvue .... A) wx   B) wd   C) wv   D) xw   E) xd   _____

14. stupqrm .... A) no   B) kl   C) on   D) lk   E) nl   _____

15. ikmoqsu .... A) vx   B) wx   C) vy   D) wy   E) vw   _____

16. vtgsqgp .... A) og   B) ng   C) on   D) go   E) nm   _____

17. ywxvtus .... A) tr   B) rp   C) qr   D) qo   E) sq   _____

18. vsqnlig .... A) eb   B) dc   C) ec   D) ca   E) db   _____

19. uisgqeo .... A) nm   B) db   C) cm   D) nd   E) cn   _____

20. nkmjlik .... A) ji   B) hj   C) gj   D) jn   E) hi   _____

21. trpsqor .... A) po   B) qp   C) pn   D) qo   E) qn   _____

22. zxuspnk .... A) he   B) ig   C) if   D) hf   E) ji   _____

23. xwutqpn .... A) mj   B) kj   C) lk   D) mk   E) li   _____

24. stonoji .... A) ji   B) jd   C) id   D) je   E) ij   _____

abcdefghijklmnopqrstuvwxyz

25. xwutqpl .... A) kg   B) gc   C) kf   D) ga   E) hc   _____

26. uwsuqso .... A) qn   B) rm   C) pn   D) qm   E) rn   _____

27. imkgkie .... A) ig   B) hf   C) ca   D) ac   E) gi   _____

28. vvtrrpn .... A) nm   B) ll   C) lj   D) nl   E) mn   _____

29. bceghjlmoqr .... A) su   B) st   C) tv.   D) uv   E) tu   _____

30. ywuusrppn .... A) jj   B) lj   C) hf   D) mj   E) nl   _____

ANSWER EXPLANATIONS FOR PRACTICE SET 4

1. **(A)** adbecfdge
   Ahead three, back two; repeat.
2. **(C)** dveuftgsh
   Two alternating groups: the first group goes forward consecutively (*d, e, f, g, h*); the second group goes backward consecutively (*v, u, t, s*).
3. **(C)** jkklmmnoo
   A single letter, then the next consecutive letter doubled; then the next consecutive letter single, then the next consecutive letter doubled; and so on.
4. **(A)** zvuqplkgf
   Back four, back one; repeat.
5. **(E)** kymwouqss
   Two alternating groups of letters: the first group skips one letter as it goes forward; the other group skips one letter as it goes backward.
6. **(B)** edogfoiho
   Consecutive backward pairs, separated by the letter *o*.
7. **(B)** azbycxdwe
   Two alternating groups of letters: one consecutive forward, the other consecutive backward.
8. **(D)** zywtsqnmk
   Going backward from *z*: the next consecutive letter, then skip one letter, then skip two letters; repeat.
9. **(B)** wltkqjnik
   Two alternating groups of letters: the first group goes backward skipping two letters (*w, t, q, n, k*); the second group goes backward consecutively (*l, k, j, i*).
10. **(C)** qsmoikega
    Beginning with *q*: second letter forward, then sixth letter backward; repeat.
11. **(B)** jtirhpgnf
    Two alternating groups of letters: the first group goes backward consecutively (*j, i, h, g, f*); the second group goes backward skipping one letter (*t, r, p, n*).

12. **(B)** vsrurqtqp
    Three alternating groups of letters, each consecutively backward (*v, u, t*), (*s, r, q*), (*r, q, p*).
13. **(D)** gtsfvuexw
    Two alternating groups of letters: the first group goes backward consecutively and appears every third letter (*g, f, e*); the other group consists of pairs of consecutive backward letters (*t s, v u, x w*), with two letters skipped between pairs.
14. **(A)** stupqrmno
    Three consecutive letters; then three letters back from *s* to begin the next three consecutive letters (*p q r*); then three back from *p* to start the next three consecutive letters (*m n o*).
15. **(D)** ikmoqsuwy
    Goes forward but skips every other letter (*i*, skips *j*; then *k*, skips *l*; then *m*, skips *n*; etc.).
16. **(B)** vtgsqgpng
    A backward pair, skipping the middle letter (*v, t*), then *g*; followed by the next consecutive backward pair, skipping the middle letter (*s, q*), then *g*; and so on.
17. **(C)** ywxvtusqr
    Back two, ahead one, back two; back two, ahead one, back two; back two, ahead one, and so on.
18. **(E)** vsqnligdb
    Back three, back two; repeat.
19. **(C)** uisgqeocm
    Two alternating groups of letters: each group goes backward and skips a letter: *u, s, q, o, m* and *i, g, e, c*.
20. **(B)** nkmjlikhj
    Two alternating groups of letters, each consecutively backward: *n, m, l, k, j* and *k, j, i, h*.
21. **(C)** trpsqorpn
    Three letters of the alphabet in reverse order, skipping a letter each time (*t, r, p*); then the next consecutive backward set, skipping letters (*s, q, o*); followed by the next consecutive backward set, skipping letters (*r, p, n*).

22. **(C)** z x u s p n k i f
Two back, then three back; repeat.

23. **(A)** x w u t q p n m j
Going backward: pair of consecutive letters, then skip one, the next pair of consecutive letters, then skip two; the next pair of consecutive letters, then skip one, the next pair of consecutive letters, then skip two.

24. **(D)** s t o n o j i j e
Ahead one, back five, back one; repeat.

25. **(C)** x w u t q p l k f
Going backward: pair of consecutive letters, then skip one; the next pair of consecutive letters, then skip two; the next pair of consecutive letters, then skip three; and so on.

26. **(D)** u w s u q s o q m
Ahead two, back four; repeat.

27. **(A)** i m k g k i e i g
Ahead four, back two, back four; repeat.

28. **(D)** v v t r r p n n l
Going backward: double letter, then skip a letter, then a single letter, then skip a letter; repeat.

29. **(C)** b c e g h j l m o q r t v
going forward: a pair of consecutive letters, skip 1, then a single letter, skip 1; repeat.

30. **(B)** y w u u s r p p n l j
Going backward: skip every other letter, doubling the third letter of the set; then repeat.

PRACTICE SET 5

In each series of letters below determine what the order of the letters is and decide what the next two letters should be. From the suggested answers at the right choose the one that gives the next two letters in the series.

a b c d e f g h i j k l m n o p q r s t u v w x y z

1. a b x c d x e	A) f x	B) g x	C) g h	D) j x	E) e x
2. a a b c c d e	A) e e	B) f f	C) e f	D) e g	E) g g
3. z p y p x p w	A) p v	B) v p	C) w p	D) p w	E) o p
4. r s t r s t r	A) t r	B) s t	C) r s	D) r t	E) t u
5. j l n p r t v	A) x z	B) w x	C) y z	D) r t	E) w y
6. j a k b l c m	A) e d	B) n o	C) d n	D) l c	E) n p
7. a d t e h t i	A) i j	B) l t	C) k m	D) m k	E) n p
8. z z a y y b x	A) z x	B) c c	C) c x	D) x x	E) x c
9. i i j k k l m	A) z i	B) m o	C) m n	D) m i	E) n m
10. a d e f g j k	A) l m	B) n o	C) a d	D) m n	E) o p
11. z l w m t n q	A) p o	B) o n	C) l v	D) k r	E) q r
12. f p h n j l l	A) j n	B) l m	C) m p	D) j k	E) l n
13. a g e k i o m	A) s q	B) q s	C) p r	D) n o	E) a g
14. e h g j i l k	A) l m	B) n m	C) m l	D) p o	E) e h
15. b c f g h k l	A) n m	B) p q	C) m p	D) m n	E) p n
16. a y b v c s d	A) r p	B) r q	C) e e	D) p e	E) q e

abcdefghijklmnopqrstuvwxyz

17. abdabea .... A) bc   B) bf   C) ba   D) af   E) aa   _____

18. azbycxd .... A) we   B) ew   C) vu   D) ft   E) ue   _____

19. agdjgmj .... A) pm   B) ro   C) or   D) kd   E) jo   _____

20. gdjgmjp .... A) ms   B) jl   C) jn   D) kp   E) ps   _____

21. fetjitn .... A) tm   B) mt   C) po   D) ot   E) nm   _____

22. cqeogmi .... A) oq   B) ik   C) kk   D) km   E) kn   _____

23. abscdte .... A) hi   B) fg   C) he   D) eu   E) fu   _____

24. yhwiujs .... A) kq   B) rq   C) qp   D) yh   E) tr   _____

25. afbgchd .... A) ef   B) ie   C) ij   D) jk   E) jr   _____

26. dgfihkj .... A) ml   B) mn   C) no   D) nm   E) lk   _____

27. abdghjm .... A) no   B) nq   C) oq   D) np   E) op   _____

28. dogpjqm .... A) ro   B) rp   C) rm   D) rt   E) rr   _____

29. bcefhikln .... A) rs   B) oq   C) pt   D) op   E) ps   _____

30. aycweugsi .... A) mk   B) mn   C) qm   D) qk   E) si   _____

ANSWER EXPLANATIONS FOR PRACTICE SET 5

1. **(A)** abxcdxefx
   Two consecutive letters, then the letter *x*, followed by the next two consecutive letters, then *x*, and so on.

2. **(C)** aabccdeef
   A letter twice, then the next consecutive letter once; the next consecutive letter twice, then the next consecutive letter once; and so on.

3. **(A)** zpypxpwpv
   The letter *p* alternating with consecutive letters going backward.

4. **(B)** rstrstrst
   The letters *r s t* repeating.

5. **(A)** jlnprtvxz
   Consecutive letters skipping every other letter.

6. **(C)** jakblcmdn
   Two alternating groups of consecutive letters: *j k l m n* and *a b c d*.

7. **(B)** adtehtilt
   Beginning with *a*, skip two letters, then the next letter, insert a *t*; the next letter, skip two, then the next letter *h*, insert a *t*; and so on. This is a difficult problem.

8. **(E)** zzayybxxc
   Two alternating groups of letters: the first group doubles each letter and goes backward consecutively; the second group goes forward consecutively.

9. **(C)** iijkklmmn
   Consecutive letters forward; however, every other letter is doubled.

10. **(A)** adefgjklm
    Beginning with *a*, skip two letters, then the next three consecutive letters; then skip two letters, then the next three consecutive letters.

11. **(B)** zlwmtnqon
    Two alternating groups of letters: the first group goes backward skipping two letters (*z, w, t, q, n*); the other group goes forward consecutively (*l, m, n, o*).

12. **(A)** fphnjlljn
    Two alternating groups of letters: one group goes forward skipping every other letter (*f, h, j, l, n*); the other group goes backward skipping every other letter (*p, n, l, j*).

13. **(A)** a g e k i o m s q
Ahead six, back two; repeat.

14. **(B)** e h g j i l k n m
Ahead three, back one; repeat.

15. **(C)** b c f g h k l m p
The pattern is three consecutive letters, then skip the next two, then repeat. Note that the pattern begins one letter in on the first group of three ($b\,c$ instead of $a\,b\,c$).

16. **(D)** a y b v c s d p e
Two alternating groups of letters: the first group is consecutive letters going forward (a, b, c, d, e); the second group skips two letters (y, v, s, p) going backward.

17. **(B)** a b d a b e a b f
Consecutive letters beginning with d (d, e, f), each preceded by $a\,b$: $a\,b\,d$, $a\,b\,e$, $a\,b\,f$.

18. **(A)** a z b y c x d w e
Two alternating groups of letters: the first group goes forward consecutively (a, b, c, d, e); the other group goes backward consecutively (z, y, x, w).

19. **(A)** a g d j g m j p m
Two alternating groups of letters: both groups go forward skipping every two letters (a, d, g, j, m and g, j, m, p).

20. **(A)** g d j g m j p m s
Two alternating groups of letters: both groups go forward, skipping every two letters (g, j, m, p, s and d, g, j, m).

21. **(B)** f e t j i t n m t
Two letters backward, insert t, skip four letters forward; two letters backward, insert t, skip four letters forward; and so on.

22. **(C)** c q e o g m i k k
Two alternating groups of letters: the first group goes forward, skipping every other letter ($c, e,$

g, i, k); the other group goes backward, skipping every other letter (q, o, m, k).

23. **(E)** a b s c d t e f u
Two alternating groups of letters: the first group consists of pairs of consecutive letters ($a\,b, c\,d, e\,f, g\,h$); the other group, beginning with s, goes backward consecutively (s, t, u).

24. **(A)** y h w i u j s k q
Two alternating groups of letters: the first group goes backward, skipping every other letter (y, w, u, s, q); the other group goes forward consecutively (h, i, j, k).

25. **(B)** a f b g c h d i e
Two alternating groups of letters: each group goes forward consecutively (a, b, c, d, e and f, g, h, i).

26. **(A)** d g f i h k j m l
Ahead three, back one; repeat.

27. **(D)** a b d g h j m n p
Beginning with a, the next consecutive letter, then skip one letter, then skip two letters; repeat.

28. **(B)** d o g p j q m r p
Two alternating groups of letters: the first goes forward but skips two letters (d, g, j, m, p); the second group goes forward consecutively (o, p, q, r).

29. **(B)** b c e f h i k l n o q
Going forward: a pair of consecutive letters, then skip one letter; the next consecutive pair, then skip one letter; and so on.

30. **(D)** a y c w e u g s i q k
Two alternating groups of letters: the first group goes forward skipping every other letter (a, c, e, g, i, k); the other group goes backward skipping every other letter (y, w, u, s, q).

Appendix A

Samples of questions for the

Telephone Operator Test
Accounting Clerk Test
Computation Test
Clerical Checking Test

The following four types of tests are *no longer used* on the Federal Civil Service Examinations. We have not deleted them from our appendix because some state and local agencies may still use one or all of these types.

THE TELEPHONE OPERATOR TEST
MEASURES SKILL IN HEARING AND REMEMBERING NUMBERS

Questions like samples 29 through 39 are to test the accuracy with which you hear numbers like telephone numbers and make correct connections for the numbers that you hear. In the test, the examiner will give you a number as the first question, then pause for you to answer the question, then give you a number as the second question, and so on. For almost every number that the examiner gives, you have that number below, together with three wrong numbers. You are to pick out the number you hear and make a check mark at the right of it. If the number is not one of the four listed for the question, check "none of these."

Part of a list such as the examiner would use in reading these sample questions is shown in the column at the right. Have someone dictate these practice numbers to you.

Just as in the actual test do not ask the examiner to repeat any number. If you miss one, try to get the next question. As you will notice, the dictation is slow at first and then becomes faster. In the first sample, the answer has been checked for you.

SAMPLE QUESTIONS

29. A) 1 3 4 4
    B) 3 1 3 4
    C) 3 1 4 4
    D) 4 1 3 3
    E) none of these

30. A) 2 6 8 7
    B) 2 7 6 8
    C) 2 8 6 7
    D) 2 8 7 6
    E) none of these

31. A) 1 0 0 9 3
    B) 1 0 9 0 3
    C) 1 9 0 0 3
    D) 1 9 3 0 0
    E) none of these

32. A) 6 2 3 7 5
    B) 6 7 2 3 5
    C) 6 7 2 5 3
    D) 7 6 2 3 5
    E) none of these

33. A) 1 5 5 9 6
    B) 5 1 1 6 9
    C) 5 1 9 9 6
    D) 5 5 1 9 6
    E) none of these

34. A) 3 2 8 9 7
    B) 3 8 2 9 7
    C) 3 8 9 2 7
    D) 8 3 2 9 7
    E) none of these

35. A) 4 1 3 6 2
    B) 4 1 6 2 3
    C) 4 1 6 3 2
    D) 4 6 1 3 2
    none of these

36. A) 6 6 8 1
    B) 8 1 6 6
    C) 8 8 6 1
    D) 8 0 6 6 1
    E) none of these

37. A) 5 7 6 8 5
    B) 5 7 6 8 9
    C) 5 7 8 6 9
    D) 7 5 6 8 9
    E) none of these

38. A) 4 7 2 8
    B) 4 7 8 2
    C) 4 0 7 2 8
    D) 4 7 2 0 8
    E) none of these

39. A) 3 6 2 8
    B) 3 8 2 8
    C) 3 8 2 6 8
    D) 8 3 6 2 8
    E) none of these

On the Sample Answer Sheet in the column at the right, you are to show the answer you have checked for each question. Do this by darkening completely the oval under the letter that is the same as the letter of the answer you checked. Be accurate because a check mark beside a correct answer in the list of questions will not do you any good unless you darken the same answer space on the answer sheet.

Sample Examiner's List

The rates at which the examiner is to read are shown by the 10-second markings at the right. He or she should read each number as rapidly as he or she would tell an operator what phone number he or she wants, and then he or she should pause before reading the next. For example, in the first 10 seconds he or she should read 3144, pause, read 2687, pause, and be ready to begin 19300. The pauses become shorter as he or she moves down the list of numbers.

3 1 4 4	
2 6 8 7	10 sec.
1 9 3 0 0	
6 7 2 3 5	20 sec.
5 1 1 9 6	
3 8 2 9 7	
4 1 6 3 2	30 sec.
8 6 6 1	
5 7 6 8 9	
4 7 2 8	
8 3 6 2 8	40 sec.

Sample Answer Sheet

29 A B C D E
30 A B C D E
31 A B C D E
32 A B C D E
33 A B C D E
34 A B C D E
35 A B C D E
36 A B C D E
37 A B C D E
38 A B C D E
39 A B C D E

Correct Answers to Sample Questions

29 A B C D E — C
30 A B C D E — A
31 A B C D E — D
32 A B C D E — B
33 A B C D E — E
34 A B C D E — B
35 A B C D E — C
36 A B C D E — E
37 A B C D E — B
38 A B C D E — A
39 A B C D E — D

ACCOUNTING CLERK TEST

Questions 9 and 10 are based on the application of the regulation presented below. All information necessary to answer the questions is given in the regulation and in the paragraph of directions following the regulation.

Regulation (on which sample questions 9 and 10 are based):
Full-time employees shall earn and be credited with sick leave at the rate of 4 hours per pay period of two workweeks duration. Four work hours are equal to ½ workday.

Directions (for sample questions 9 and 10):
The following table gives the sick-leave records of two full-time employees for the current leave year. For each of these employees the workweek consists of five 8-hour days and the leave year consists of 26 pay periods. For each employee, determine the balance of accumulated sick leave to the credit of the employee at the end of the current leave year. At the right side of the table are four suggested answers designated A, B, C, and D, at the top of the columns. If one of the suggested answers is correct, darken the proper space on the Sample Answer Sheet. If the correct answer is not given under A, B, C, or D, darken the space under E on the Sample Answer Sheet.

Questions:

Employee	Accumulated Sick Leave from Preceding Year	Sick Leave Used in Current Year	Balance of Accumulated Sick Leave at End of Current Year				
			A	B	C	D	E
	Days Hours	Days Hours	Days Hours	Days Hours	Days Hours	Days Hours	Days Hours
9. No. 9	8 — 4	2 — 1	6 — 3	19 — 3	23 — 5	32 — 3	None of these
10. No. 10	60 — 0	8 — 7	51 — 3	51 — 7	64 — 3	68 — 7	

11. A voucher contained the following items:

   6 desks   @ $89.20 . . . . . $525.20
   8 chairs   @ $32.50 . . . . .   260.00
                        Total $885.20

   The terms were given on the voucher as 3%, 10 days; net, 30 days. Verify the computations, which may be incorrect, and calculate the correct amount to be paid. If payment is made within the discount period, the amount to be paid is
   A) $761.64   D) $858.64
   B) $771.34   E) none of these
   C) $795.20

Questions 12 and 13 are based on the following portion of a withholding tax table:

If the payroll period with respect to an employee is MONTHLY:

And wages are —		And number of withholding exemptions claimed is				
At least	But less than	0	1	2	3	4
		The amount of income tax to be withheld shall be				
$688	$704	$125.50	$85.20	$45.20	$5.20	0
704	720	128.00	88.00	48.00	8.00	0
720	736	131.20	91.20	51.20	11.20	0

12. K received a monthly wage of $705.60 the first 3 months of the year and $730.00 the remaining 9 months. He claimed 3 exemptions for the first 4 months and 4 for the remaining 8 months. What was the total income tax withheld during the year?
   A) $ 0.00   D) $44.80
   B) $24.00   E) none of these
   C) $35.20

13. L, who has 2 exemptions, receives a monthly wage of $702.00 If no amounts other than income tax were withheld, his monthly take-home pay would be
   A) $616.80   D) $702.00
   B) $656.80   E) none of these
   C) $696.80

COMPUTATION TEST

These sample questions show how the questions are to be recorded. Read the directions for each set of questions and then answer them. Record your answers on the Sample Answer Sheets provided on each page of this booklet. Then compare your answers with those given in the Correct Answers to Sample Questions on the same page. Solve each problem and see which of the suggested answers is correct. Darken the space on the Sample Answer Sheet corresponding to the correct answer. Some questions have four suggested answers, other have five.

Computations

1. Add:
963
257
416
——

Answers
A) 1,516
B) 1,526
C) 1,636
D) 1,726
E) none of these

2. Add:
1,725
881
40
——

Answers
A) 2,556
B) 2,546
C) 2,646
D) 2,456
E) none of these

3. Add:
245
413
——

Answers
A) 658
B) 657
C) 655
D) 656
E) none of these

4. Add:
653
972
148
——

Answers
A) 1,752
B) 6,673
C) 1,773
D) 1,653
E) none of these

5. Add:
75
6
89
—

Answers
A) 168
B) 170
C) 196
D) 171
E) none of these

6. Multiply:
45
5

Answers
A) 200
B) 215
C) 225
D) 235
E) none of these

7. Multiply:
70
9
—

Answers
A) 629
B) 620
C) 639
D) 640
E) none of these

8. Multiply:
952
34
——

Answers
A) 33,378
B) 31,367
C) 30,267
D) 32,368
E) none of these

9. Multiply:
280
62
—

Answers
A) 17,360
B) 17,267
C) 17,362
D) 17,260
E) none of these

10. Multiply:
346.05
83
——

Answers
A) 287.2225
B) 287.2015
C) 287.2215
D) 287.2205
E) none of these

Sample Answer Sheet

	A	B	C	D	E
1	○	○	○	○	○
2	○	○	○	○	○
3	○	○	○	○	○
4	○	○	○	○	○
5	○	○	○	○	○
6	○	○	○	○	○
7	○	○	○	○	○
8	○	○	○	○	○
9	○	○	○	○	○
10	○	○	○	○	○

Correct Answers to Sample Questions

	A	B	C	D	E
1	○	○	●	○	○
2	○	○	●	○	○
3	○	●	○	○	○
4	○	●	○	○	○
5	○	●	○	○	○
6	○	○	●	○	○
7	○	○	○	○	●
8	○	○	●	○	○
9	●	○	○	○	○
10	○	○	●	○	○

11. Subtract:
33
8
___

Answers
A) 25
B) 26
C) 35
D) 36
E) none of these

12. Subtract:
685
74
___

Answers
A) 621
B) 611
C) 521
D) 601
E) none of these

13. Subtract:
1,970
858
___

Answers
A) 1,110
B) 1,112
C) 1,111
D) 1,100
E) none of these

14. Subtract:
2,973
2,284
___

Answers
A) 688
B) 678
C) 679
D) 689
E) none of these

15. Subtract:
790
281
___

Answers
A) 509
B) 500
C) 508
D) 501
E) none of these

16. Divide:
40)1,208

Answers
A) 3
B) 30
C) 33
D) 40
E) none of these

17. Divide:
9)189

Answers
A) 12
B) 20
C) 22
D) 21
E) none of these

18. Divide:
6)126

Answers
A) 20
B) 24
C) 22
D) 26
E) none of these

19. Divide:
85)170,850

Answers
A) 2,110
B) 2,000
C) 2,010
D) 2,001
E) none of these

20. Divide:
.005).000025

Answers
A) .0000025
B) .000025
C) .0025
D) .025
E) none of these

Sample Answer Sheet

	A	B	C	D	E
11	○	○	○	○	○
12	○	○	○	○	○
13	○	○	○	○	○
14	○	○	○	○	○
15	○	○	○	○	○
16	○	○	○	○	○
17	○	○	○	○	○
18	○	○	○	○	○
19	○	○	○	○	○
20	○	○	○	○	○

Correct Answers to Sample Questions

	A	B	C	D	E
11	●	○	○	○	○
12	○	●	○	○	○
13	○	○	●	○	○
14	○	○	○	●	○
15	●	○	○	○	○
16	○	○	○	○	●
17	○	○	○	●	○
18	○	○	○	○	●
19	○	○	●	○	○
20	○	○	○	○	●

THE CLERICAL CHECKING TEST

This type of test has been used in the past, but is presently *no longer used* by the federal government. It is used by some companies and state and local governments.

The test takes 8 minutes total for both parts. It is scored rights minus wrongs. There are 125 proper name pairs and 125 digit span pairs. The digit pairs range from 3 digits to 9 digits.

The name pairs use proper people and corporate names. First name, middle initial, and last names; first initial, middle name, and last names; and first and middle initial and last names are all used in the pairs.

1.   Robert Levenson - Roberta Levenson
2.   E. G. Cummings - E. G. Cummings
3.   Arthur Jerome Ash - Arthur Jerome Asch
4.   William M. Smythe - William N. Smythe
5.   etc.

1.   27349801 - 17134801
2.   493 - 492
3.   58700 - 58709
4.   98001 - 98001
5.   etc.

Mark A if the two names or numbers are exactly alike.
Mark B if the two names or numbers differ in any way.

Appendix B

Getting a Federal Government Job (Flow Chart)
Applying for a Federal Job (Brochure)
OPM's Self-Service System for Employment Information (Brochure)
1999 General Schedule - Hourly Basic Rates & Hourly Overtime
1999 General Schedule - Annual Rates by Grade and Step
Qualification Standards
Group Coverage Qualification Standard for
    Clerical and Administrative Support Positions
Clerical and Administrative Support Positions
Qualification Requirements
Other Testing Locations
Clerical and Administrative Support Exam
Additional Testing Locations in Washington, D.C. area
Typing Proficiency Exam Locations in Washington, D.C. area
Special Pay Rates (Typing)
Official Sample Questions
Occupational Duty Sheet, Secretary
Secretary Positions
Declaration for Federal Employment (Sample Form)
Optional Application for Federal Employment (Sample Form)
Qualifications & Availability Form (Sample Grid Form)
Answer Booklet (Sample Grid Form)

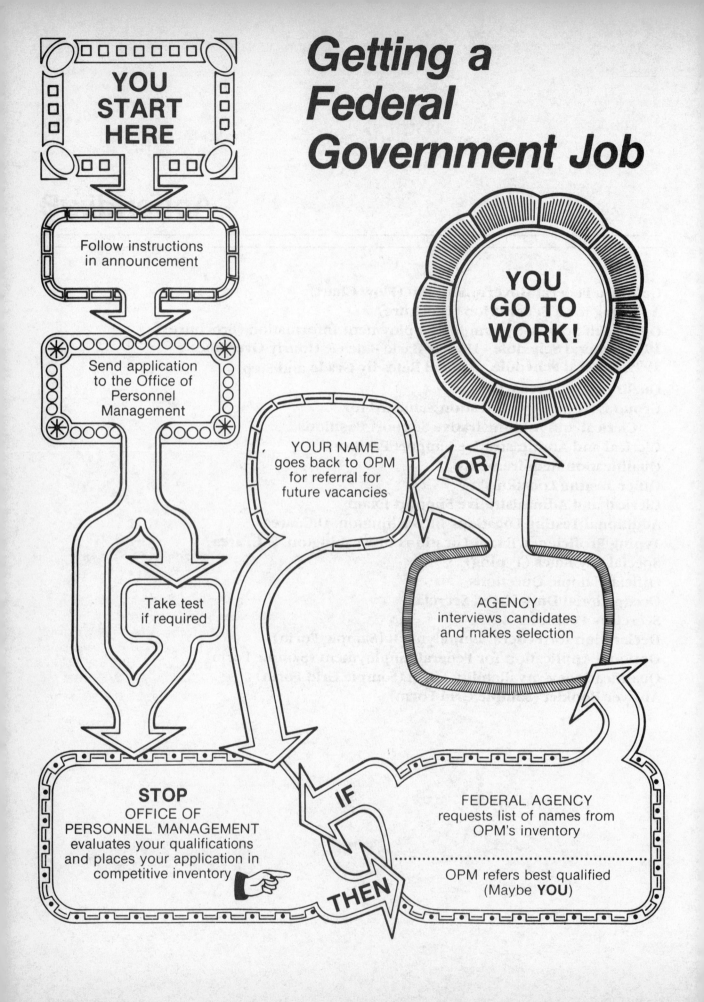

Getting a Federal Government Job

YOU START HERE

Follow instructions in announcement

Send application to the Office of Personnel Management

Take test if required

STOP
OFFICE OF PERSONNEL MANAGEMENT evaluates your qualifications and places your application in competitive inventory

YOUR NAME goes back to OPM for referral for future vacancies

AGENCY interviews candidates and makes selection

FEDERAL AGENCY requests list of names from OPM's inventory

OPM refers best qualified (Maybe YOU)

IF

THEN

OR

YOU GO TO WORK!

Applying for a Federal Job

JOB OPENINGS

For job information 24 hours a day, 7 days a week, call **912-757-3000**, the U.S. Office of Personnel Management (OPM) automated telephone system. Or, with a computer modem dial **912-757-3100** for job information from an OPM electronic bulletin board. You can also reach the board through the Internet (Telnet only) at FJOB.MAIL.OPM.GOV.

APPLICANTS WITH DISABILITIES

You can find out about alternative formats by calling OPM or dialing the electronic bulletin board at the numbers above. Select "Federal Employment Topics" and then "People with Disabilities." If you have a hearing disability, call **TDD 912-744-2299**.

HOW TO APPLY

Review the list of openings, decide which jobs you are interested in, and follow the instructions given. **You may apply for most jobs with a resume, the *Optional Application for Federal Employment*, or any other written format you choose.** For jobs that are unique or filled through automated procedures, you will be given special forms to complete. (You can get an *Optional Application* by calling OPM or dialing our electronic bulletin board at the numbers above.)

WHAT TO INCLUDE

Although the Federal Government does not require a standard application form for most jobs, we do need certain information to evaluate your qualifications and determine if you meet legal requirements for Federal employment. If your resume or application does not provide all the information requested in the job vacancy announcement and in this brochure, you may lose consideration for a job. Help speed the selection process by keeping your resume or application brief and by sending only the requested material. Type or print clearly in dark ink.

**United States
Office of
Personnel
Management**

OF 510
(September 1994)

Here's what your resume or application must contain

(in addition to specific information requested in the job vacancy announcement)

JOB INFORMATION

- ❏ Announcement number, and title and grade(s) of the job you are applying for

PERSONAL INFORMATION

- ❏ Full name, mailing address *(with ZIP Code)* and day and evening phone numbers *(with area code)*
- ❏ Social Security Number
- ❏ Country of citizenship *(Most Federal jobs require United States citizenship.)*
- ❏ Veterans' preference *(See reverse.)*
- ❏ Reinstatement eligibility *(If requested, attach SF 50 proof of your career or career-conditional status.)*
- ❏ Highest Federal civilian grade held *(Also give job series and dates held.)*

EDUCATION

- ❏ High school
  - Name, city, and State *(ZIP Code if known)*
  - Date of diploma or GED
- ❏ Colleges or universities
  - Name, city, and State *(ZIP Code if known)*
  - Majors
  - Type and year of any degrees received
  - *(If no degree, show total credits earned and indicate whether semester or quarter hours.)*
- ❏ Send a copy of your college transcript only if the job vacancy announcement requests it.

WORK EXPERIENCE

- ❏ Give the following information for your paid and nonpaid work experience related to the job you are applying for. *(Do not send job descriptions.)*
  - Job title *(include series and grade if Federal job)*
  - Duties and accomplishments
  - Employer's name and address
  - Supervisor's name and phone number
  - Starting and ending dates *(month and year)*
  - Hours per week
  - Salary
- ❏ Indicate if we may contact your current supervisor.

OTHER QUALIFICATIONS

- ❏ **Job-related** training courses *(title and year)*
- ❏ **Job-related** skills, for example, other languages, computer software/hardware, tools, machinery, typing speed
- ❏ **Job-related** certificates and licenses *(current only)*
- ❏ **Job-related** honors, awards, and special accomplishments, for example, publica– tions, memberships in professional or honor societies, leadership activities, public speaking, and performance awards *(Give dates but do not send documents unless requested.)*

> **THE FEDERAL GOVERNMENT IS**
> **AN EQUAL OPPORTUNITY EMPLOYER**

VETERANS' PREFERENCE IN HIRING

❏ If you served on active duty in the United States Military and were separated under honorable conditions, you may be eligible for veterans' preference. To receive preference if your service began after October 15, 1976, you must have a Campaign Badge, Expeditionary Medal, or a service-connected disability. For further details, call OPM at **912-757-3000**. Select "Federal Employment Topics" and then "Veterans." Or, dial our electronic bulletin board at **912-757-3100**.

❏ Veterans' preference is not a factor for Senior Executive Service jobs or when competition is limited to status candidates (current or former Federal career or career-conditional employees).

❏ To claim 5-point veterans' preference, attach a copy of your DD-214, *Certificate of Release or Discharge from Active Duty*, or other proof of eligibility.

❏ To claim 10-point veterans' preference, attach an SF 15, *Application for 10-Point Veterans' Preference*, plus the proof required by that form.

OTHER IMPORTANT INFORMATION

❏ Before hiring, an agency will ask you to complete a *Declaration for Federal Employment* to determine your suitability for Federal employment and to authorize a background investigation. The agency will also ask you to sign and certify the accuracy of all the information in your application. **If you make a false statement in any part of your application, you may not be hired; you may be fired after you begin work; or you may be fined or jailed.**

❏ If you are a male over age 18 who was born after December 31, 1959, you must have registered with the Selective Service System (or have an exemption) to be eligible for a Federal job.

❏ The law prohibits public officials from appointing, promoting, or recommending their relatives.

❏ Federal annuitants (military and civilian) may have their salaries or annuities reduced. All employees must pay any valid delinquent debts or the agency may garnish their salary.

PRIVACY AND PUBLIC BURDEN STATEMENTS

The Office of Personnel Management and other Federal agencies rate applicants for Federal jobs under the authority of sections 1104, 1302, 3301, 3304, 3320, 3361, 3393, and 3394 of title 5 of the United States Code. We need the information requested in this brochure and in the associated vacancy announcements to evaluate your qualifications. Other laws require us to ask about citizenship, military service, etc.

❏ We request your Social Security Number (SSN) under the authority of Executive Order 9397 in order to keep your records straight; other people may have the same name. As allowed by law or Presidential directive, we use your SSN to seek information about you from employers, schools, banks, and others who know you. Your SSN may also be used in studies and computer matching with other Government files, for example, files on unpaid student loans.

❏ If you do not give us your SSN or any other information requested, we cannot process your application, which is the first step in getting a job. Also, incomplete addresses and ZIP Codes will slow processing.

❏ We may give information from your records to: training facilities; organizations deciding claims for retirement, insurance, unemployment or health benefits; officials in litigation or administrative proceedings where the Government is a party; law enforcement agencies concerning violations of law or regulation; Federal agencies for statistical reports and studies; officials of labor organizations recognized by law in connection with representing employees; Federal agencies or other sources requesting information for Federal agencies in connection with hiring or retaining, security clearances, security or suitability investigations, classifying jobs, contracting, or issuing licenses, grants, or other benefits; public or private organizations including news media that grant or publicize employee recognition and awards; and the Merit Systems Protection Board, the Office of Special Counsel, the Equal Employment Opportunity Commission, the Federal Labor Relations Authority, the National Archives, the Federal Acquisition Institute, and congressional offices in connection with their official functions.

❏ We may also give information from your records to: prospective nonfederal employers concerning tenure of employment, civil service status, length of service, and date and nature of action for separation as shown on personnel action forms of specifically identified individuals; requesting organizations or individuals concerning the home address and other relevant information on those who might have contracted an illness or been exposed to a health hazard; authorized Federal and nonfederal agencies for use in computer matching; spouses or dependent children asking whether an employee has changed from self-and-family to self-only health benefits enrollment; individuals working on a contract, service, grant, cooperative agreement or job for the Federal Government; non-agency members of an agency's performance or other panel; and agency-appointed representatives of employees concerning information issued to an employee about fitness-for-duty or agency-filed disability retirement procedures.

❏ We estimate the public burden for reporting the employment information will vary from 20 to 240 minutes with an average of 40 minutes per response, including time for reviewing instructions, searching existing data sources, gathering data, and completing and reviewing the information. You may send comments regarding the burden estimate or any other aspect of the collection of information, including suggestions for reducing this burden, to the U.S. Office of Personnel Management, Reports and Forms Management Officer, Washington, DC 20415-0001.

Send your application to the agency announcing the vacancy.

Form Approved: OMB 3206-0219   50510-101   NSN 7540-01-351-9177

Step 1 — Use OPM's Self-Service System for Employment Information

The Federal Employment Information Highway will assist you in your job search. The Information Highway provides listings of the latest Federal worldwide job openings, state/local government jobs, private industry jobs and access to application materials. Information on a wide variety of employment-related topics and programs, such as special information for veterans, students, people with disabilities and outplacement information for current Federal employees, is also available. When using the system you can obtain vacancy announcements with complete information about a job and the application process. The system is available to you 24 hours a day, 7 days a week and is updated daily.

Here is how you can access the Federal Employment Information Highway:

Visit our USA JOBS Web Site!

Our address is www.usajobs.opm.gov USA JOBS lets you tailor your job search (e.g., by occupational category, geographic location, pay), view daily updated listings, receive vacancy announcements, access employment information, and much more via your personal computer.

Turn On Your Computer and Dial Up!

Access the Federal Job Opportunities Board (FJOB) from your personal computer by dialing (912) 757-3100. You can also access FJOB by Telnet at fjob.opm.gov or File Transfer Protocol at ftp.fjob.opm.gov.

Visit a Touch Screen Kiosk!

Employment Information (Touch Screen) Computer Kiosks are located in major cities throughout the nation, in OPM offices, career transition centers, and in some Federal office buildings. For a listing of OPM touch screen locations request the "Employment Information Sources" factsheet from any of the system's components.

Use Your Telephone!

Call the Career America Connection (CAC) at (912) 757-3000 or TDD service at (912) 744-2299. You can request full-text vacancy announcements through fax delivery and receive complete information about the job and the application process. For a complete listing of CAC's telephone numbers see the back of this postcard.

...And,

for your convenience, use FedFax, a nationwide "telephone / fax-to-fax" document request system. You may obtain information sheets on Federal employment-related topics and application materials. FedFax will not contain vacancy announcements or job listings. For a complete listing of FedFax telephone numbers see the back of this card.

Step 2 — Find the Right Job!

You can obtain agency vacancy announcements by using the Federal Employment Information Highway. This enables you to determine upfront if this is the job for you. The announcement provides complete application instructions and details about the job, i.e., duties, open period, job location, salary, education/experience requirements, testing requirements, etc. In addition, you can even apply for some jobs over the telephone or from a computer.

Step 3 — See How Easy It Is to Apply!

The Federal Employment Information Highway provides instructions on how to apply for jobs and what application information will be required. For example, you may be requested to apply for a job using your resume or the Optional Application for Federal Employment (OF-612). The vacancy announcements will specify if any additional or special forms are required. Use any of the methods to request *"Applying for a Federal Job"*, a factsheet with complete details on preparing a resume for Federal employment.

Helpful Hints when using the Federal Employment Information Highway...

Be prepared. . . Before searching the Federal Employment Information Highway, think about the type of job that interests you (e.g., professional, clerical, technical, or trades and labor). Develop a clear idea of the career field you want to pursue (e.g., engineer, computer specialist, accountant) and the specific requirements you have (e.g., geographic location, salary range, educational level, work experience). We list over 3,500 jobs daily. A focused job search will help you find the best job that meets your qualifications, personal career goals, and saves you time and effort!

Know your skills. . . Select a Federal job that matches your skills and interests. Thoughtful consideration about the type of skills you can bring to a job is important. When searching the Information Highway, look for jobs that would be a good match. Vacancy announcements are provided with most job listings. Pay close attention to the job duties that are listed. Identifying your skills will help you find the right job match!

Follow through. . . Searching the Federal Employment Information Highway is the first step in finding a job. Our system helps you follow through with complete application instructions. In addition, vacancy announcements will tell you if there are any special hiring criteria (e.g., whether the job is open to the general public, or to current Federal employees, or former Federal employees with reinstatement eligibility, special appointing authorities for veterans, the disabled... etc.); if there are special application procedures/forms that need to be completed; or if there are any tests required for the job. Following through is a key component in completing a job search!

for your recent inquiry about employment with the United States Government. Although the government is streamlining to work better and cost less, we remain interested in talented individuals for critical occupations.

We encourage you to use the Federal Employment Information Highway and the 3-step job search strategy. On this card you will find information on how to use our systems to obtain employment information and locate specific job opportunities that match your experience and education.

ES-20 10/96

United States
Office of
Personnel
Management

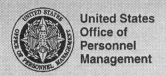

United States
Office of
Personnel
Management

The Federal Government, leading the way as an equal opportunity employer

Search the Federal Employment Information Highway

Here's How

USA JOBS – OPM's Web site:
www.usajobs.opm.gov

Federal Job Opportunities Board (FJOB):
(912) 757-3100

Touch Screen Computer Kiosks:

For a complete listing of touch screen locations request the "Employment Information Sources" factsheet via the employment information system.

FedFax:

Atlanta, GA	(404) 331-5267
Denver, CO	(303) 969-7764
Detroit, MI	(313) 226-2593
San Francisco, CA	(415) 744-7002
Washington, DC	(202) 606-2600

Career America Connection (CAC):

Atlanta, GA	404-331-4315
Chicago, IL	312-353-6192
Dayton, OH	513-225-2720
Denver, CO	303-969-7050
Detroit, MI	313-226-6950
Honolulu, HI	808-541-2791
Huntsville, AL	205-837-0894
Kansas City, MO	816-426-5702
Norfolk, VA	757-441-3355
Philadelphia, PA	215-597-7440
Raleigh, NC	919-790-2822
San Antonio, TX	210-805-2402
San Francisco, CA	415-744-5627
Seattle, WA	206-553-0888
Twin Cities, MN	612-725-3430
Washington, DC	202-606-2700
Nationwide	912-757-3000
TDD Service	912-744-2299

Todays Technology Working for You 24 Hours a Day, 7 Days a Week!
Updated Daily!

U.S. Office of Personnel Management
1999 General Schedule
Excluding Locality Rates of Pay*
Effective January 1999

HOURLY BASIC (B) Rates by Grade and Step

HOURLY OVERTIME (O) Rates by Grade and Step

Grade		1	2	3	4	5	6	7	8	9	10
1	B	6.40	6.62	6.83	7.04	7.25	7.38	7.59	7.80	7.81	8.01
	O	9.60	9.93	10.25	10.56	10.88	11.07	11.39	11.70	11.72	12.02
2	B	7.20	7.37	7.61	7.81	7.90	8.13	8.36	8.59	8.83	9.06
	O	10.80	11.06	11.42	11.72	11.85	12.20	12.54	12.89	13.25	13.59
3	B	7.85	8.12	8.38	8.64	8.90	9.16	9.42	9.69	9.95	10.21
	O	11.78	12.18	12.57	12.96	13.35	13.74	14.13	14.54	14.93	15.32
4	B	8.82	9.11	9.40	9.70	9.99	10.29	10.58	10.87	11.17	11.46
	O	13.23	13.67	14.10	14.55	14.99	15.44	15.87	16.31	16.76	17.19
5	B	9.86	10.19	10.52	10.85	11.18	11.51	11.84	12.17	12.49	12.82
	O	14.79	15.29	15.78	16.28	16.77	17.27	17.76	18.26	18.74	19.23
6	B	11.00	11.36	11.73	12.10	12.46	12.83	13.20	13.56	13.93	14.29
	O	16.50	17.04	17.60	18.15	18.69	19.25	19.80	20.34	20.90	21.44
7	B	12.22	12.63	13.03	13.44	13.85	14.26	14.66	15.07	15.48	15.88
	O	18.33	18.95	19.55	20.16	20.78	21.39	21.99	22.61	23.22	23.82
8	B	13.53	13.98	14.43	14.89	15.34	15.79	16.24	16.69	17.14	17.59
	O	20.30	20.97	21.65	22.34	23.01	23.69	24.36	24.69	24.69	24.69
9	B	14.95	15.45	15.94	16.44	16.94	17.44	17.94	18.44	18.93	19.43
	O	22.43	23.18	23.91	24.66	24.69	24.69	24.69	24.69	24.69	24.69
10	B	16.46	17.01	17.56	18.11	18.66	19.20	19.75	20.30	20.85	21.40
	O	24.69	24.69	24.69	24.69	24.69	24.69	24.69	24.69	24.69	24.69
11	B	18.09	18.69	19.29	19.89	20.50	21.10	21.70	22.30	22.91	23.51
	O	24.69	24.69	24.69	24.69	24.69	24.69	24.69	24.69	24.69	24.69
12	B	21.68	22.40	23.12	23.84	24.57	25.29	26.01	26.73	27.46	28.18
	O	24.69	24.69	24.69	24.69	24.69	24.69	24.69	24.69	24.69	24.69
13	B	25.78	26.63	27.49	28.35	29.21	30.07	30.93	31.79	32.65	33.51
	O	24.69	24.69	24.69	24.69	24.69	24.69	24.69	24.69	24.69	24.69
14	B	30.46	31.47	32.49	33.50	34.52	35.54	36.55	37.57	38.58	39.60
	O	24.69	24.69	24.69	24.69	24.69	24.69	24.69	24.69	24.69	24.69
15	B	35.83	37.02	38.22	39.41	40.60	41.80	42.99	44.19	45.38	46.57
	O	24.69	24.69	24.69	24.69	24.69	24.69	24.69	24.69	24.69	24.69

* INCORPORATING A 3.10% INCREASE

U.S. Office of Personnel Management

1999 General Schedule*
(Not Including Locality Rates of Pay)

Effective January 1999

Grade	Annual Rates for Steps (in dollars)									
	1	*2*	*3*	*4*	*5*	*6*	*7*	*8*	*9*	*10*
1	13,362	13,807	14,252	14,694	15,140	15,401	15,838	16,281	16,299	16,718
2	15,023	15,380	15,878	16,299	16,482	16,967	17,452	17,937	18,422	18,907
3	16,392	16,938	17,484	18,030	18,576	19,122	19,668	20,214	20,760	21,306
4	18,401	19,014	19,627	20,240	20,853	21,466	22,079	22,692	23,305	23,918
5	20,588	21,274	21,960	22,646	23,332	24,018	24,704	25,390	26,076	26,762
6	22,948	23,713	24,478	25,243	26,008	26,773	27,538	28,303	29,068	29,833
7	25,501	26,351	27,201	28,051	28,901	29,751	30,601	31,451	32,301	33,151
8	28,242	29,183	30,124	31,065	32,006	32,947	33,888	34,829	35,770	36,711
9	31,195	32,235	33,275	34,315	35,355	36,395	37,435	38,475	39,515	40,555
10	34,353	35,498	36,643	37,788	38,933	40,078	41,223	42,368	43,513	44,658
11	37,744	39,002	40,260	41,518	42,776	44,034	45,292	46,550	47,808	49,066
12	45,236	46,744	48,252	49,760	51,268	52,776	54,284	55,792	57,300	58,808
13	53,793	55,586	57,379	59,172	60,965	62,758	64,551	66,344	68,137	69,930
14	63,567	65,686	67,805	69,924	72,043	74,162	76,281	78,400	80,519	82,638
15	74,773	77,265	79,757	82,249	84,741	87,233	89,725	92,217	94,709	97,201

* INCORPORATING A 3.10% GENERAL INCREASE

QUALIFICATIONS STANDARDS

All of the jobs listed on the next page are covered by the Verbal Abilities Test and Clerical Abilities Test, except for Sales Store Clerical and Date Transcriber, which are covered by the Clerical Speed Test only.

Also any *seasonal* job at the Internal Revenue Service would probably use the Clerical Speed Test only. (Seasonal jobs are jobs that exist only during the first half of a year when tax returns are being processed.)

The two tests are used at grades GS—2, GS—3, GS—4. No test is required for GS—1, or GS—5, with one exception: the Clerk-Stenographer requires the two tests at the GS—5 level.

The typing and stenographer speeds described on the following pages are the official speeds. The length of education and experience qualifications that are shown here reflect the new standards.

MINIMUM QUALIFICATION REQUIREMENTS FOR ONE-GRADE INTERVAL CLERICAL AND ADMINISTRATIVE SUPPORT POSITIONS (p.1)

This qualification standard covers positions in the General Schedule which involve the performance of one-grade interval clerical and administrative support work. A list of the occupational series covered by this standard is provided below. This standard may also be used for other one-grade interval positions for which the education and experience pattern is determined to be appropriate. While some of the occupational series covered by this standard include both one- and two-grade interval work, the qualification requirements described in this standard apply only to those positions which follow a one-grade interval pattern. For a description of the work in these occupations, refer to the series definitions in the *Handbook of Occupational Groups and Series* and/or to individual position classification standards.

GS-029 Environmental Protection Assistant	GS-561 Budget Clerical and Assistance
GS-072 Fingerprint Identification	GS-592 Tax Examining
GS-086 Security Clerical and Assistance	GS-593 Insurance Accounts
GS-135 Intelligence Air and Clerk	GS-675 Medical Records Technician
GS-203 Personnel Clerical and Assistance	GS-679 Medical Clerk[2]
GS-204 Military Personnel Clerical and Technician	GS-962 Contact Representative
GS-302 Messenger[1]	GS-963 Legal Instruments Examining
GS-303 Miscellaneous Clerk and Assistant	GS-986 Legal Clerical and Assistance
GS-304 Information Receptionist	GS-990 General Claims Examining
GS-305 Mail and File	GS-998 Claims Clerical
GS-309 Correspondence Clerk	GS-1001 General Arts and Information
GS-312 Clerk-Stenographer and Reporter	GS-1046 Language Clerical
GS-318 Secretary	GS-1087 Editorial Assistance
GS-319 Closed Microphone Reporting	GS-1101 General Business and Industry
GS-322 Clerk-Typist	GS-1105 Purchasing
GS-326 Office Automation Clerical and Assistance	GS-1106 Procurement Clerical and Assistance
GS-332 Computer Operation	GS-1107 Property Disposal Clerical and Technician
GS-335 Computer Clerk and Assistant	GS-1152 Production Control
GS-344 Management Clerical and Assistance	GS-1411 Library Technician[2]
GS-350 Equipment Operator	GS-1421 Archives Technician
GS-351 Printing Clerical	GS-1531 Statistical Assistant
GS-356 Data Transcriber	GS-1702 Education and Training Technician
GS-357 Coding	GS-1802 Compliance Inspection and Support
GS-359 Electric Accounting Machine Operation	GS-1897 Customs Aid
GS-361 Equal Opportunity Assistance	GS-2005 Supply Clerical and Technician
GS-382 Telephone Operating	GS-2102 Transportation Clerk and Assistant
GS-390 Telecommunications Processing	GS-2111 Transportation Rate and Tariff Examining
GS-392 General Telecommunications	GS-2131 Freight Rate
GS-394 Communications Clerical	GS-2132 Travel
GS-503 Financial Clerical and Assistance	GS-2133 Passenger Rate
GS-525 Accounting Technician	GS-2134 Shipment Clerical and Assistance
GS-530 Cash Processing	GS-2135 Transportation Loss and Damage Claims Examining
GS-540 Voucher Examining	GS-2151 Dispatching
GS-544 Civilian Pay	
GS-545 Military Pay	

---

[1]Under 5 U.S.C. 3310, appointment to Messenger positions is restricted to persons entitled to veteran preference as long as such persons are available.

[2]These qualification requirements have been approved for use within the Veterans Health Administration of the Department of Veterans Affairs under the provisions of section 7402, title 38, U.S.C.

(TS-234)
July 1992

Group Coverage Qualification Standard for
Clerical and Administrative Support Positions

This qualification standard covers positions in the General Schedule that involve the performance of one-grade interval clerical and administrative support work. It contains common patterns of creditable experience and education to be used in making qualifications determinations. Section IV-B of this Manual contains individual occupational requirements for a few occupations that are to be used in conjunction with this standard. Section V identifies the occupations that have test requirements.

A list of the occupational series covered by this standard is provided on page IV-A-1. This standard may also be used for one-grade interval positions other than those listed if the education and experience pattern is determined to be appropriate.

EXPERIENCE AND EDUCATION REQUIREMENTS

The following table shows the amounts of education and/or experience required to qualify for positions covered by this standard.

GRADE/POSITIONS	EXPERIENCE		OR EDUCATION
	GENERAL	SPECIALIZED	
GS-1 All positions	None	None	None
GS-2 All positions	3 months	None	High school graduation or equivalent
GS-3 Clerk-Steno	6 months	None	High school graduation or equivalent
All other positions			1 year above high school
GS-4 All positions	1 year	None	2 years above high school
GS-5 Clerk-Steno	2 years	None	4 years above high school (except Reporting Stenographer)
All other positions	None	1 year equivalent to at least GS-4	
GS-6 and above All positions	None	1 year equivalent to at least next lower grade level	Generally, not applicable

Equivalent combinations of education and experience are qualifying for all grade levels and positions for which both education and experience are acceptable. Proficiency requirements are described on pages IV-A-5 and IV-A-6.

Some of the occupational series covered by this standard include both one- and two-grade interval work. The qualification requirements described in this standard apply only to those positions that typically follow a one-grade interval pattern. While the levels of experience shown for most positions covered by this standard follow the grade level progression pattern outlined in the table, users of the standard should refer to E.3.(o) in the "General Policies and Instructions" (Section II of this Manual) for guidance on crediting experience for positions with different lines of progression.

General Experience (All positions except Reporting Stenographer, Shorthand Reporter, and Closed Microphone Reporter)—Progressively responsible clerical, office, or other work that indicates ability to acquire the particular knowledge and skills needed to perform the duties of the position to be filled.

Specialized Experience (All positions except Reporting Stenographer, Shorthand Reporter, and Closed Microphone Reporter)—Experience that equipped the applicant with the particular knowledge, skills, and abilities (KSA's) to perform successfully the duties of the position, and that is typically in or related to the position to be filled. To be creditable, specialized experience must have been equivalent to at least the next lower grade level. Applicants who have the 1 year of appropriate specialized experience, as indicated in the table, are not required by this standard to have general experience, education above the high school level, or any additional specialized experience to meet the minimum qualification requirements.

Experience for Reporting Stenographer, Shorthand Reporter, and Closed Microphone Reporter—One year of experience equivalent to at least the next lower grade level using the skills and equipment appropriate to the position to be filled is required for all positions. Following is a description of qualifying experience for these positions.

- Reporting Stenographer, GS-5: Experience as a clerk-stenographer, secretary, reporting stenographer, or in other positions that included application of stenography and typing skills as a significant part of the work.

Group Coverage Qualification Standard for
Clerical and Administrative Support Positions

- Reporting Stenographer, Shorthand Reporter, and Closed Microphone Reporter, GS-6: Experience as a reporting stenographer, hearing reporter, or in other positions in which the primary duty was to make and transcribe manual or machine-written shorthand records of hearings, interviews, or similar proceedings.

- Shorthand Reporter and Closed Microphone Reporter, GS-7 and above: Experience as a court reporter, or hearing reporter, or in other positions in which the primary duty was to make verbatim records of proceedings.

Education: High school graduation or the equivalent is creditable at the GS-2 level for the occupations listed, except Clerk-Stenographer, where it is creditable at the GS-3 entry level.

Successfully completed education above the high school level in any field for which high school graduation or the equivalent is the normal prerequisite is creditable at grades GS-3 through GS-5 for all positions except Reporting Stenographer, GS-5. This education must have been obtained in an accredited business, secretarial or technical school, junior college, college or university. One year of full-time academic study is defined as 30 semester hours, 45 quarter hours, or the equivalent in a college or university, or at least 20 hours of classroom instruction per week for approximately 36 weeks in a business, secretarial, or technical school.

As a general rule, education is not creditable above GS-5 for most positions covered by this standard; however, graduate education may be credited in those few instances where the graduate education is directly related to the work of the position.

Intensive Short-Term Training—Completion of an intensive, specialized course of study of less than 1 year may meet in full the experience requirements for GS-3. Courses of this type normally require completion of up to 40 hours per week of instruction rather than the usual 20 hours per week, and are usually of *at least* 3 months duration. Such courses may have been obtained through a variety of programs such as those offered by business or technical schools, and through military training programs. To be creditable, such a course must have

been designed specifically as career preparation for the work of the position being filled, and must have provided the applicant with the necessary knowledge, skills, and abilities to do the work.

Combining Education and Experience: Equivalent combinations of successfully completed post-high school education and experience may be used to meet total experience requirements at grades GS-5 and below, except for Reporting Stenographer, GS-5.

- For GS-3 and GS-4 level positions, determine the applicant's total qualifying experience as a percentage of the experience required for the grade level; then determine the applicant's education as a percentage of the education required for the grade level; then add the two percentages. The total percentage must equal at least 100 percent to qualify an applicant for that grade level.

- For GS-5 level positions (except Clerk-Stenographer, which does not require specialized experience), only education in excess of the first 60 semester hours (i.e., beyond the second year) is creditable toward meeting the specialized experience requirement. One full academic year of study (30 semester hours) *beyond the second year* is equivalent to 6 months of specialized experience.

The following are examples of how education and experience may be combined. They are examples only, and are not all inclusive:

- The position to be filled is a Payroll Clerk, GS-4. An applicant has 8 months of qualifying experience and 20 semester hours of college. The applicant meets 67 percent of the required experience and 33 percent of the required education. The applicant meets 100 percent of the total requirements and is qualified for the position.

- The position to be filled is a Clerk-Typist, GS-4. The applicant has 4 months of qualifying experience and 1 year of business school. The applicant meets 33 percent of the required experience and 50 percent of the required education. The applicant meets 83 percent of the total requirements and is not qualified for the position.

Group Coverage Qualification Standard for
Clerical and Administrative Support Positions

- The position to be filled is a Clerk-Stenographer, GS-5. An applicant has 1 year of qualifying experience and 90 semester hours of college. The applicant meets 50 percent of the required experience and 75 percent of the required education. The applicant exceeds 100 percent of the total requirements and is qualified for the position.

- The position to be filled is an Editorial Assistant, GS-5. The applicant has 9 months of specialized experience and 75 semester hours of college (15 semester hours beyond the second year and the equivalent of 3 months of specialized experience). The applicant meets 75 percent of the required experience and 25 percent of the required education. The applicant meets 100 percent of the requirement for 1 year of specialized experience and is qualified for the position.

PROFICIENCY REQUIREMENTS

Clerk-Typist, Office Automation Clerk/Assistant, Clerk-Stenographer, Data Transcriber, and Positions with Parenthetical Titles of (Typing), (Office Automation), (Stenography), or (Data Transcription)

In addition to meeting experience or education requirements, applicants for these positions must show possession of the following skills, as appropriate. Applicants may meet these requirements by passing the appropriate performance test, presenting a certificate of proficiency from a school or other organization authorized to issue such certificates by the Office of Personnel Management local office, or by self-certifying their proficiency. Performance test results and certificates of proficiency are acceptable for 3 years. Agencies may verify proficiency skills of self-certified applicants by administering the appropriate performance test.

- Clerk-Typist, GS-2/4; Office Automation Clerk/Assistant (any grade); (Typing) (any grade); and (Office Automation) (any grade):

  40 words per minute typing speed

- Data Transcriber, GS-2/4; and (Data Transcription) (any grade):

  skill in operating an alphanumeric data transcribing machine,

  or 20 words per minute typing speed[1] for GS-2 transcription duties

  or 25 words per minute typing speed[1] for GS-3 and GS-4 transcription duties

- Clerk-Stenographer, GS-3/4:

  40 words per minute typing speed[1] *and*

  80 words per minute dictation speed[2]

- Clerk-Stenographer, GS-5:

  40 words per minute typing speed[1] *and*

  120 words per minute dictation speed[2]

- (Stenography) (any grade):

  40 words per minute typing speed[1] *and either*

  80 words per minute dictation speed[2] for GS-3 and GS-4 stenographic duties

  or 120 words per minute dictation speed[2] for GS-5 stenographic duties

NOTE: The level of proficiency for stenographic and data transcribing duties required by positions with parenthetical titles is based on the grade level of those duties and not necessarily on the overall grade of the position. For example, a position classified as Secretary (Stenography), GS-318-5, may require either 80 or 120 words per minute dictation speed depending upon the level of difficulty of the stenographic duties. A position classified as Payroll Clerk (Data Transcription), GS-544-4, may require either 20 or 25 words per minute typing speed depending upon the level of difficulty of the transcribing duties. Therefore, before filling positions of this type, first determine the grade

---

[1]Words per minute are based on a 5 minute sample with three or fewer errors.

[2]The maximum number of errors allowed in a dictation sample equals 10 percent of the required dictation speed (80 words per minute or 120 words per minute) multiplied by the number of minutes in the sample.

level of the duties that require the additional skill, and then determine the skill level required.

Reporting Stenographer, Shorthand Reporter, and Closed Microphone Reporter

In addition to meeting the experience requirements, applicants for these positions must show possession of the following skills with equipment appropriate to the specific position.

- Reporting Stenographer, GS-5/6: 120 words per minute dictation speed[3]

- Shorthand Reporter and Closed Microphone Reporter, GS-6: 160 words per minute dictation speed[3]

- Shorthand Reporter and Closed Microphone Reporter, GS-7 and above: 175 words per minute dictation speed[3]

Applicants must also be able to produce accurate typewritten transcripts of recorded proceedings.

Applicants for competitive appointment and inservice applicants for initial assignment to these three positions at all grade levels must demonstrate the specific skill and level of proficiency required by the position to be filled. Also, inservice applicants for promotion to positions that have a higher proficiency requirement than the position previously held must demonstrate the higher level of proficiency. Applicants may demonstrate

that proficiency by either passing a dictation test at the required speed or presenting a certificate of proficiency showing speed and accuracy equivalent to those used in the Office of Personnel Management performance tests for these positions. The certificate must show that the candidate demonstrated the required proficiency, i.e., dictation speed and accuracy, to a teacher of stenography, shorthand reporting, or closed microphone reporting, within the past year. Applicants for these positions may not self-certify dictation proficiency.

USING SELECTIVE FACTORS FOR POSITIONS COVERED BY THIS STANDARD

Selective factors must represent knowledge, skills, or abilities that are essential for successful job performance and cannot reasonably be acquired on the job during the period of orientation/training customary for the position being filled. It is unlikely, for example, that a requirement for experience with a particular brand of word processing software could be justified as a selective factor for an Office Automation Clerk position. Since knowledge of that software may be desirable, such knowledge could be appropriately used as a quality ranking factor. On the other hand, proficiency in the correct use of medical terminology may be needed immediately to perform the duties of a Medical Records Technician position to provide continuity in an agency's medical records program. If that is the case, knowledge of medical terminology could be used as a selective factor in filling the position.

---

[3]The maximum number of errors allowed in a dictation sample for these three positions equals 5 percent of the required dictation speed multiplied by the number of minutes in the sample.

United States
Office of
Personnel Management

Office of Washington Examining Services
P.O. Box 52
Washington, D.C. 20415-0001

Clerical and Administrative Support Positions, GS-2/3/4

This announcement supersedes previous editions.

Do Not Apply Under This Announcement for Summer Jobs

Location of Jobs:
Washington, DC; Maryland: Counties of Charles, Montgomery, and Prince Georges; **Virginia:** Cities of Alexandria, Fairfax, Falls Church, Manassas and Manassas Park, and Counties of Arlington, Fairfax, King George, Loudoun, Prince William, and Stafford; and Overseas Atlantic.

Salary
Federal salary rates are adjusted periodically. Current information regarding salaries may be obtained from the Federal Job Information/Testing Center in the Office of Personnel Management, 1900 E Street NW., Room 1416, Washington DC 20415.

A written test is required for the occupations covered under this announcement.

GS-029	Environmental Protection Clerk	
GS-072	Fingerprint Identification Clerk	
GS-086	Security Clerk	
GS-134	Intelligence Clerk	
GS-203	Personnel Clerk	
GS-204	Military Personnel Clerk	
GS-301	Clerk	
GS-302	Messenger*	
GS-303	General Clerk	
GS-304	Information Receptionist	
GS-305	Mail and File Clerk	
GS-309	Correspondence Clerk	
GS-312	Clerk-Stenographer	
GS-318	Secretary	
GS-322	Clerk-Typist	
GS-326	Office Automation Clerk	
GS-332	Computer Operator	
GS-335	Computer Clerk	
GS-344	Management Clerk	
GS-350	Office Equipment Operator	
GS-351	Printing Clerk	
GS-357	Coding Clerk	

GS-359	Electronic Accounting Machine Operator
GS-382	Telephone Operator
GS-390	Telecommunication Processing Clerk
GS-392	Telecommunications Clerk
GS-394	Communications Clerk
GS-503	Financial Clerk
GS-525	Accounting Clerk
GS-530	Cash Processing Clerk
GS-540	Voucher Examining Clerk
GS-544	Civilian Pay Clerk
GS-545	Military Pay Clerk
GS-561	Budget Clerk
GS-592	Tax Examining Clerk
GS-593	Insurance Accounts Clerk
GS-675	Medical Records Clerk
GS-679	Medical Clerk
GS-963	Legal Instruments Examining Clerk
GS-986	Legal Clerk
GS-998	Claims Clerk
GS-1001	Arts & Information Clerk
GS-1046	Language Clerk

GS-1087	Editorial Clerk
GS-1101	General Business & Industry Clerk
GS-1105	Purchasing Clerk
GS-1106	Procurement Clerk
GS-1107	Property Disposal Clerk
GS-1152	Production Control Clerk
GS-1411	Library Clerk
GS-1421	Archives Clerk
GS-1531	Statistical Clerk
GS-1802	Compliance Inspection & Support Clerk
GS-1897	Customs Clerk
GS-2005	Supply Clerk
GS-2102	Transportation Clerk
GS-2111	Transportation Rate & Tariff Examining Clerk
GS-2131	Freight Rate Clerk
GS-2132	Travel Clerk
GS-2133	Passenger Rate Clerk
GS-2134	Shipping Clerk
GS-2135	Transportation Loss & Damage Claim Examining Clerk
GS-2151	Dispatching Clerk

Direct-Hire Authority is restricted to the above listed positions.

---

*Under 5 U.S.C. 3310, appointment to Messenger positions is restricted to persons entitled to veteran preference as long as such positions are available.

WA-8-06   Mar 93

Qualification Requirements

A WRITTEN TEST IS REQUIRED FOR ALL OCCUPATIONS COVERED BY THIS ANNOUNCEMENT

In addition, the following chart reflects the minimum education or experience requirements:

GRADE/POSITIONS	EDUCATION		EXPERIENCE	
GS-2 ALL POSITIONS	HIGH SCHOOL GRADUATION OR EQUIVALENT	OR	3 MONTHS	GENERAL
GS-3 CLERK-STENO	HIGH SCHOOL GRADUATION OR EQUIVALENT	OR	6 MONTHS	GENERAL
GS-3 ALL OTHER POSITIONS	1 YEAR ABOVE HIGH SCHOOL	OR	6 MONTHS	GENERAL
GS-4 ALL POSITIONS	2 YEARS ABOVE HIGH SCHOOL	OR	1 YEAR	GENERAL
GS-5 CLERK-STENO	4 YEARS ABOVE HIGH SCHOOL	OR	2 YEARS	GENERAL

Equivalent combinations of education and experience are qualifying for all grade levels and positions for which both education and experience are acceptable.

For all positions requiring a qualified typist the minimum typing speed is 40 words per minute (wpm) with three errors or less. Clerk-Stenographer, GS-3/4 and any other occupation at the GS-3/4 grade level with parenthetical title of (Stenography) must have a minimum shorthand speed of 80wpm with 24 errors or less. Clerk-Stenographer, GS-5, must have a minimum shorthand speed of 120wpm with 36 errors or less. You may meet these requirements at the time of appointment by indicating these skills on your Application for Federal Employment (SF-171), presenting a Certificate of Proficiency (OPM Form 680) or taking a performance test given by the agency.

FOR ALL POSITIONS

"General experience" is progressively responsible clerical, office OR other work which indicates ability to acquire the particular knowledge and skill needed to perform the duties of the position to be filled. Specialized experience directly related to the position may be substituted for general experience. Unpaid or volunteer work will be credited on the same basis as salaried experience.

EDUCATION

Successfully completed education above the high school level in any field for which high school graduation or the equivalent is a prerequisite may be substituted for the experience required for all positions at grades GS-3 through GS-5. This education must have been obtained in an accredited business, secretarial or technical school, junior college, college or university. One full year of full-time academic study is 30 semester hours, 45 quarter hours, or the equivalent, of college or at least 20 hours of classroom instruction per week for approximately 36 weeks in business, secretarial, or technical school.

Intensive Short-Term Training—Completion of an intensive, specialized course of study of less than one year (for example, specialized computer operator) may meet in full the experience requirements of GS-3. Courses of this type normally require completion of up to 40 hours per week of instruction rather than the usual 20 hours per week and are usually of at least three months duration. Such courses may have been obtained through a variety of programs such as those offered by business or technical schools, or through military training programs. To be creditable, such a course must have been designed specifically as a career preparation for the work of the position being filled and must have provided the applicant with the necessary knowledge, skills, and abilities to do the work.

CERTIFICATES OF PROFICIENCY

If you wish, you may present a Certificate of Proficiency in typing and/or shorthand which meets the speed and accuracy requirements. To be acceptable, the certification must be made on OPM Form 680 or on an official form or letterhead of the testing organization and include the following information:
* The date the test was administered;
* The length of the test in minutes;
* The total number of words typed per minute on at least a 5-minute test, and the total number of errors made; and
* For stenographer, the rate of dictation in words per minute on a 3-minute test, and the total number of errors made.

We accept Certificates of Proficiency from the following sources:
* Public and parochial schools;
* Accredited private high schools;
* Business, commercial, and secretarial schools accredited by such accrediting organizations as the Association of Independent Colleges and Schools or the appropriate State Education Department.

CERTIFICATES OF PROFICIENCY (cont.)

* Junior colleges and colleges which are accredited or whose work is accepted for advance credit by the State University of the State in which they are located;
* Schools approved by the Veterans Administration for the education of veterans and their dependents;
* Public and private social and welfare agencies conducting programs sponsored or approved by the U.S. Office of Education or by an appropriate State Office of Education to provide training or retraining of people with disabilities for vocational rehabilitation purposes;
* Federal, State, or other public or private agencies with programs in supporting of personnel utilization and economic opportunity, such as the Neighborhood Youth Corps, Job Corps, Opportunities Industrialization Centers, and other agencies that provide training under provisions of the Comprehensive Employment and Training Act;
* State Employment Service Offices;
* Military hospitals or agencies and other Federal hospitals or agencies which provide training in connection with occupational therapy or vocational rehabilitation programs in typing and/or shorthand; and
* Federal agencies which provide in-service training in typing or shorthand to civilian or military personnel.

Time Limitations on Certificates of Proficiency

The test on which the Certificate of Proficiency is based must have been taken within one year of the date on which the certificate was issued. The certificate is good for three years from the date of issue.

How to Apply

The first step is to take the written test.

Information About the Test

Written Test - The written test consists of two parts, clerical aptitude and verbal abilities. To pass the written test, applicants must make a minimum score of 33 on the verbal abilities and a minimum combined total score of 80 on both the clerical and verbal parts. A score of 80 converts to a numerical rating of 70.0. In addition to taking the written test, applicants must complete the Occupational Supplement for Clerical Positions (OPM Form 1203-AI). With this form OPM will be able to determine applicants' minimum qualifications based on a review of their education and work experience. Applicants will select the occupational specialities, grade levels and geographic preferences they wish to be considered for by Federal agencies. A final rating will be generated from the written examination and Form 1203-AI, with 5 or 10 points added for veterans entitled to preference. The test process takes approximately two and a half hours. The test is given every Monday through Friday at 8:30 am and every third Friday of the Month at 12:30 pm on a walk-in basis with 130 seats available at the Office of Personnel Management's (OPM), Federal Job Information and Testing Center(FJITC), 1900 E Street, NW., Washington, DC, in Room 1416. Applicants must bring identification with a picture and signature to be admitted to the testing room. **OPM will no longer issue Notice of Results (NOR's) on the same day. Applicants will receive the NOR through the mail within 5 to 10 working days of testing.**

Testing of Applicants With Physical Impairments

The Visually Impaired-If you are blind, you will be required to take the test of verbal abilities but not the clerical aptitude test.

The Hearing Impaired-If you are deaf, you will be required to take the clerical aptitude test, but not the verbal abilities test.

Other-Appropriate modifications in the testing procedure may be authorized, depending on the nature of the disability. For special testing arrangements in the Washington, DC, metropolitan area, applicants with disabilities may call the Office of Personnel Management on (202) 606-1030 or dial TDD number (202) 606-0591.

Minimum Age Requirements

You must meet the age requirement. The usual minimum is 18, but high school graduates may apply at 16. If you are 16 or 17 and are out of school but not a high school graduate you may be hired only if (1) you have successfully completed a formal training program preparing you for work (for example, training provided under the comprehensive Employment and Training Act or in similar government or private programs), or (2) you have been out of school for at least three months, not counting the summer vacation, and school authorities write a letter on their official stationery agreeing with your preference for work instead of additional schooling. Appropriate forms will be given to you by the agency that wants to hire you.

How to Get a job

Simplified hiring procedures make it easier for persons seeking Clerical and Administrative Support positions to be given immediate employment consideration in the Washington, DC, metropolitan area. When seeking employment, you should submit an application for Federal Employment (SF-171) and a copy of your NOR directly to agencies where you wish to work. Effective July 1, 1993, NOR's dated on or after March 15, 1993 will be the only notices accepted by Federal agencies in the Washington, DC, metropolitan area. Applicants with old notices will not have to retest. In order to receive a new NOR applicants must call (202) 606-2700 or visit OPM's FJITC, 1900 E Street NW., Room 1416, Washington, DC 20044 to request the OPM Form 1203-AI. Upon completion and return to OPM's FJITC, P. O. Box 52, Washington DC 20415 applicants will be sent acceptable notices. Agencies will only accept the new notice beginning June 1, 1993. NORs' 0300X issued by OPM Service Centers may be used by Federal agencies to direct hire applicants in the Washington DC, metropolitan area regardless of the issue date.

Job Information

The Office of Personnel Management furnishes information about Federal employment opportunities, qualification requirements, and application procedures without charge. Residents of the Washington, DC, metropolitan area may call the Federal Job Information/Testing Center on (202) 606-2700 for information. Residents of other areas should check the local telephone directory under "United States Government" for the address and telephone number of the nearest Federal Job Information/Testing Center.

"Civil Service Schools"

The Office of Personnel Management has no connection with any so-called "civil service" school or private employment agency. No "civil service" school or employment agency can guarantee that you will be found qualified for a particular position.

Equal Employment Opportunity

All qualified applicants will receive consideration for appointment without regard to race, religion, color, national origin, sex, political affiliations, disability, or any other nonmerit factor.

CLERICAL AND ADMINISTRATIVE SUPPORT EXAM
GRADES GS-2, -3, AND -4

(LOCATION: U.S. OFFICE OF PERSONNEL MANAGEMENT, 1900 E STREET, NW., ROOM 1416, WASHINGTON, DC 20415

REQUIREMENTS/ENTRANCE TO THE EXAM ROOM:

This exam is open to **United States CITIZENS only**. A picture identification is required to enter the building and the examining room; **there will be no exceptions**.

TESTING PROCEDURES!! The Clerical exam will be conducted on a **by appointment only** basis. Weekly sessions will be conducted every Wednesday. Admittance into the exam room will begin ½ hour before the scheduled exam. Applicants wishing to reserve a seat for the exam should call (202) 606-2701, Monday through Friday between 9:00 a.m. and 4:00 p.m., for scheduling.

Applicant(s) with special needs (e.g., hearing-impaired, dyslexia, motor-skill impairment, etc.) should notify this office at (202) 606-2701 or TDD (202) 606-0591.

ABOUT THE EXAM

A *Qualifications and Availability Form* (Form C) is used to collect basic qualification information and is completed in the exam room. Completing the Form C and examination takes approximately 2½ hours.

The written test consists of two parts, clerical aptitude and verbal abilities. Questions are multiple-choice covering vocabulary, grammar, spelling, word relations, and general math. This is a timed examination with no permitted breaks.

JOB QUALIFICATIONS

The Clerical Exam only covers clerical and administrative support occupations at the GS-2, -3, or -4 grade levels. Annual salary is between $17,865 to $20,228 for the Washington, DC, metropolitan area.

For grade GS-2, you are required to have a high school diploma (or equivalent) or three months of experience. For grades GS-3 and GS-4, additional education and/or experience are required.

Some positions may have special requirements in addition to passing this exam. For example, clerk-typist, office automation clerk, and computer-related positions require typing or other skills.

RECEIVING YOUR TEST RESULTS

Results are based on your test and the information you provide on the Form C. You should receive a Notice of Results (NOR) approximately two to four weeks. A total of 33 on the verbal and a combined "total score" of 80 is needed to be considered passing. The notice does <u>not</u> have an expiration date and may be accepted by agencies indefinitely.

Once you have received a passing notice of results, you may apply directly to Federal agencies that are accepting applications for Clerical job opportunities. Vacancies are listed on OPM USAJOBS Network of Systems; i.e., USAJOBS by Touch touchscreen computers at the OPM building at 1900 E Street; the USAJOBS by Phone at (202) 606-2700; the web site http://www.usajobs.opm.gov; and the USAJOBS electronic bulletin board at (912) 757-3100. These will be actual vacancies and you will need to apply separately for each position.

For all positions requiring a qualified typist, you must be able to type a minimum speed of 40 words per minute with three fewer errors. Agencies will tell you whether a Certificate Proficiency or typing performance test is required.

FOR FURTHER INFORMATION . . .

A listing of OTHER LOCATIONS WHERE YOU MAY TAKE THE CLERICAL AND ADMINISTRATIVE SUPPORT EXAM and the PROFICIENCY EXAM (if required) is on the reverse side.

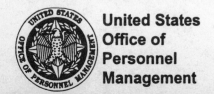

**United States
Office of
Personnel
Management**

OTHER LOCATIONS WHERE YOU MAY TAKE THE CLERICAL AND ADMINISTRATIVE SUPPORT EXAM

The following is a list of agencies that administer the written test for Clerical and Administrative Support Positions in the Washington, DC, metropolitan area. Applicants are encouraged to call the locations where they wish to be tested to obtain specific agency testing instructions. Photo identification is needed for all locations.

COMMERCE, DEPARTMENT OF
Bureau of the Census
Silver Hill Executive Plaza
3701 St. Barnabus Road
Suitland, MD 20233
Test is given every Friday at 8:30 a.m.
Must call each Monday to register
Limited to 25 people per test
By appointment only.
(301) 457-3587

HEALTH AND HUMAN SERVICES
DIVISION OF CAREER RESOURCES
National Institutes of Health
9000 Rockville Pike
Building 31, Room B3C02B
Bethesda, MD 20892
Walk-in test on
Tuesday at 9:00 a.m.
Arrive 7:45 - 8:15 a.m.
Limited to 14 people per test.
(301) 496-2403

GEOLOGICAL SURVEY
12201 Sunrise Valley Drive
Room 1A315, MS-601
Reston, VA 22092
Test is given once a month.
30 people per test.
By appointment only.
(703) 648-6131

NATIONAL ARCHIVES AT COLLEGE PARK
8601 Adelphi Road
College Park, MD 20740-6001
Walk-in test on the first Wednesday
each month at 8:30 a.m.
Limited to 20 people per test
(301) 713-6760

Contact the agency directly for additional information.
PLEASE NOTE: Those agencies identified "By appointment only" must be contacted directly as early as possible.

LOCATIONS WHERE YOU MAY TAKE THE TYPING PROFICIENCY EXAM

<u>DC Employment Services</u>: Picture I.D. required at all sites. Some locations require a referral.

1000 U Street, NW.
Monday-Friday, 9:00 a.m.
(202) 673-6995

1217 Goodhope Road, SE.
Monday-Friday, 9:00 a.m. *
(202) 645-4040

4120 Kansas Avenue, NW.
Monday-Friday, 9:00 a.m. *
(202) 576-7450

25 K Street, NE.
Monday-Friday, 9:00 a.m.
(202) 724-2316

4049 South Capitol Street, SW.
Tuesday-Thursday, 9:00 a.m.
(202) 645-4000

* Sign in before 8:45 a.m.

<u>Library of Congress</u>:   101 Independence Avenue, SE., Madison Building, Room LM-107, (202) 707-4315
Monday-Friday, 9:00 a.m. to 3:00 p.m. Test given once an hour on the half hour.

SPECIAL PAY RATES (TYPING) - (EFFECTIVE JANUARY 1998)

	1	2	3	4	5	6	7	8	9	10
GS-2	$17,865	$18,335	$18,805	$19,275	$19,745	$20,215	$20,685	$21,155	$21,625	$22,095
3	19,079	19,609	20,139	20,669	21,199	21,729	22,259	22,789	23,319	23,849
4	20,228	20,823	21,418	22,013	22,608	23,203	23,798	24,393	24,988	25,583
5	21,967	22,633	23,299	23,965	24,631	25,297	25,963	26,629	27,295	27,961
6	23,742	24,484	25,226	25,968	26,710	27,452	28,194	28,936	29,678	30,420
7	25,558	26,382	27,206	28,030	28,854	29,678	30,502	31,326	32,150	32,974

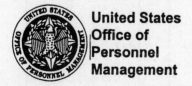

**United States
Office of
Personnel
Management**

Pg. 2 of 2
DC-2
02-26-98

SAMPLE QUESTIONS

The following sample questions show types of questions found in the written test you will take. They also show how your answers to the questions are to be recorded on a separate answer sheet. The questions on the test may be harder or easier than those shown here, but a sample of each *kind* of question on the test is given.

Read these directions, then look at the sample questions and try to answer them. Each question has several suggested answers lettered A, B, C, etc. Decide which one is the best answer to the question. Then, in the Sample Answer Sheet box, find the answer space that is numbered the same as the number of the question, and darken completely the oval that is lettered the same as the letter of your answer. Then compare your answers with those given in the Correct Answers to Sample Questions box. For some questions an explanation of the correct answer is given immediately following the sample question.

Vocabulary. For each question like 1 through 3, choose the one of the four suggested answers that means most nearly the same as the word in *italics*.

1. *Option* means most nearly
   A) use   C) value
   B) choice   D) blame

2. *Innate* means most nearly
   A) eternal   C) native
   B) well-developed D) prospective

3. To *confine* means most nearly to
   A) restrict   C) eliminate
   B) hide   D) punish

Grammar. In questions 4, 5, and 6, decide which sentence is preferable with respect to grammar and usage suitable for a formal letter or report.

4. A) If properly addressed, the letter will reach my mother and I.
   B) The letter had been addressed to myself and my mother.
   C) I believe the letter was addressed to either my mother or I.
   D) My mother's name, as well as mine, was on the letter.

The answer to question 4 is D. The answer is not A because the word *me* (reach . . . me) should have been used, not the word *I*. The answer is not B. The expression, to myself, is sometimes used in spoken English, but it is not acceptable in a formal letter or report. The answer is not C, because the word *I* has been used incorrectly, just as it was in A.

5. A) Most all these statements have been supported by persons who are reliable and can be depended upon.
   B) The persons which have guaranteed these statements are reliable.
   C) Reliable persons guarantee the facts with regards to the truth of these statements.
   D) These statements can be depended on, for their truth has been guaranteed by reliable persons.

6. A) Brown's & Company employees have recently received increases in salary.
   B) Brown & Company recently increased the salaries of all its employees.
   C) Recently Brown & Company has increased their employees' salaries.
   D) Brown & Company have recently increased the salaries of all its employees.

Spelling. In questions 7 through 9, find the correct spelling of the word among the choices lettered A, B, or C and darken the proper answer space. If no suggested spelling is correct, darken space D.

7. A) athalete   C) athlete
   B) athelete   D) none of these

In question 7 an extra letter has been added to both A and B. The fourth letter in A makes that spelling of *athlete* wrong. The fourth letter in B makes that spelling of *athlete* wrong. Spelling C is correct.

8. A) predesessor   C) predecesser
   B) predecesar   D) none of these

All three spellings of the word are wrong. The correct answer, therefore, is D because none of the printed spellings of *predecessor* is right.

9. A) occassion   C) ocassion
   B) occasion   D) none of these

Sample Answer Sheet

1 A B C D E ⊘○○○○
2 A B C D E ○○○○○
3 A B C D E ○○○○○
4 A B C D E ○○○○○
5 A B C D E ○○○○○
6 A B C D E ○○○○○
7 A B C D E ○○○○○
8 A B C D E ○○○○○
9 A B C D E ○○○○○

Correct Answers to Sample Questions

1 A B C D E ○⬤○○○
2 A B C D E ○⬤○○○
3 A B C D E ⬤○○○○
4 A B C D E ○○○⬤○
5 A B C D E ○○○⬤○
6 A B C D E ○⬤○○○
7 A B C D E ○○⬤○○
8 A B C D E ○○○⬤○
9 A B C D E ○⬤○○○

Sample questions 16 through 20 require name and number comparisons. In each line across the page there are three names or numbers that are very similar. Compare the three names or numbers and decide which ones are exactly alike. On the Sample Answer Sheet, mark the answer—

A if ALL THREE names or numbers are exactly ALIKE
B if only the FIRST and SECOND names or numbers are exactly ALIKE
C if only the FIRST and THIRD names or numbers are exactly ALIKE
D if only the SECOND and THIRD names or numbers are exactly ALIKE
E if ALL THREE names or numbers are DIFFERENT

16. Davis Hazen	David Hozen	David Hazen
17. Lois Appel	Lois Appel	Lois Apfel
18. June Allan	Jane Allan	Jane Allan
19. 10235	10235	10235
20. 32614	32164	32614

In the next group of sample questions, there is a name in a box at the left, and four other names in alphabetical order at the right. Find the correct space for the boxed name so that it will be in alphabetical order with the others, and mark the letter of that space as your answer.

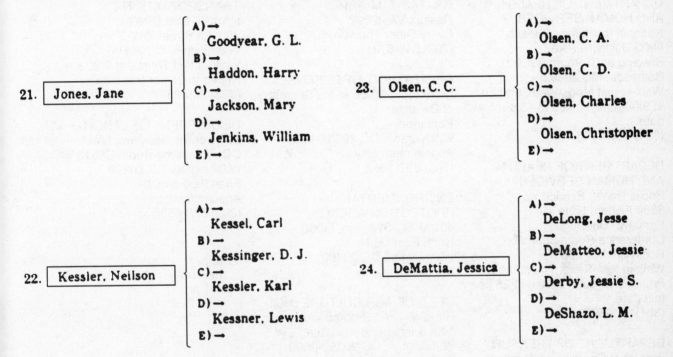

21. Jones, Jane
A) →
   Goodyear, G. L.
B) →
   Haddon, Harry
C) →
   Jackson, Mary
D) →
   Jenkins, William
E) →

23. Olsen, C. C.
A) →
   Olsen, C. A.
B) →
   Olsen, C. D.
C) →
   Olsen, Charles
D) →
   Olsen, Christopher
E) →

22. Kessler, Neilson
A) →
   Kessel, Carl
B) →
   Kessinger, D. J.
C) →
   Kessler, Karl
D) →
   Kessner, Lewis
E) →

24. DeMattia, Jessica
A) →
   DeLong, Jesse
B) →
   DeMatteo, Jessie
C) →
   Derby, Jessie S.
D) →
   DeShazo, L. M.
E) →

Sample Answer Sheet

16 A B C D E
17 A B C D E
18 A B C D E
19 A B C D E
20 A B C D E

21 A B C D E
22 A B C D E
23 A B C D E
24 A B C D E

Correct Answers to Sample Questions

16 A B C D ●
17 A B C D E
18 A B C D E
19 A B C D E
20 A B C D E

21 A B C D ●
22 A B C D E
23 A B C D E
24 A B C D E

3

Other Testing Locations

DEPARTMENT OF COMMERCE
Patent & Trademark Office
2011 Crystal Drive, Suite 700
Crystal Park One
Arlington, VA 22202
Walk-in test Tues. at 7:30 a.m.
limited to 15 people per test date
(703) 305-8231

AGRICULTURAL RESEARCH SERVICE
Personnel Division
6303 Ivy Lane, Room 106
Greenbelt, MD 20770-1435
Appointment only
(301) 344-3961

DEPARTMENT OF HEALTH AND HUMAN SERVICES
National Institutes of Health
9000 Rockville Pike
Building 31C, Room B3C02
Bethesda, MD 20892
Walk-in test Mon., Wed., and Fri., at 9:00 a.m.; limited to 16 per test date.
(301) 496-2403

DEPARTMENT OF HEALTH AND HUMAN SERVICES
Public Health Service
5600 Fishers Lane
Parklawn Building
Conference Room 3rd Floor
Rockville, MD 20857
Walk-in test Tues., Thurs., and Fri., at 9:00 a.m.; limited to 25 per test date.
(301) 443-6900

DEPARTMENT OF TREASURY
Bureau of Engraving & Printing
14th & C Street, SW.
Washington, DC 20228
Walk-in test 1st & 3rd Wed. of the month at 8:30 a.m.; limited to 14 per test date.
(202) 874-2094

DEFENSE LOGISTICS AGENCY
DASC-KSE Cameron Station
Alexandria, VA 22304-6130
Appointment only
(703)274-7087/88

DEPARTMENT OF VETERANS AFFAIRS (Central Office)
Room 175
810 Vermont Ave., NW.
Washington, DC 20420
Thurs. at 8:30 a.m. by Appointment only
(202) 233-2459

GEOLOGICAL SURVEY
12201 Sunrise Valley Dr.
Rm. 1A315, MS-215
Reston, VA 22092
Every Other Thursday
(703) 648-6131

DEPARTMENT OF DEFENSE
(Pentagon) Office of the Secretary of Defense
Pentagon,
Washington, DC 20301-1155
Appointment only
(703) 697-1062

ENVIRONMENTAL PROTECTION AGENCY
401 M St., SW., Rm. G050
North East Mall
Washington, DC 20460
Appointment only

DEPT. OF AGRICULTURE (HQ)
Rm. SM-7, Ag Promenade
14th & Independence Ave., SW.
Washington, DC 20250-9600
Walk-in test Tues., at 8 a.m. & 11 a.m.; limited to 18 per test date
(202) 720-5625

DEPARTMENT OF COMMERCE
Bureau of the Census
Personnel Division, Rm. G256
Suitland, MD 20233
Walk-in test Wed., & Fri., at 9:00 a.m.; limited to 25 per test date
(301) 763-6064

BOLLING AFB
Main Entrance
Build., P20   Room 240
Washington, DC 20332-5000
Appointment only
(202) 767-5449

DEPARTMENT OF TRANSPORTATION
NASSIF BUILDING
400 7th Street, SW.
Washington, DC 20590
Walk-in test Thurs., at 9:30 a.m.; limited to 24 per test date
(202) 366-9397

DEPARTMENT OF LABOR
200 Constitution Ave., NW.
DOL Academy-Room C5515
Washington, DC 20210
Fri at 9:00 a.m. by Appointment only
(202) 523-6525

OFFICE OF PERSONNEL MANAGEMENT
Office of Washington Area Examining Operations

OCCUPATIONAL DUTY SHEET

Secretary
GS-318

DUTIES OF THE POSITION:
Secretaries are responsible for the performance of a variety of tasks, including telephone and receptionist duties; scheduling appointments and conferences; receiving mail and preparing replies; reviewing outgoing mail; maintaining records and files; making travel arrangements; assembling and disassembling information; transmitting staff instructions; and performing stenographic or typing services when required.

QUALIFICATIONS REQUIREMENTS:
Applicants for these positions must have had progressively responsible experience of the length shown in the table below and of the nature described in the paragraphs following.

GRADE	TOTAL EXPERIENCE
GS-3	6 months at the next lower grade level or equivalent experience
GS-4 or 5	1 year at the next lower grade level or equivalent experience
GS-6	6 months at the next lower grade level or equivalent experience
GS-7 through GS-9	6 months at the next lower grade level or equivalent experience

OR

1 year at the second lower grade level

QUALIFYING EXPERIENCE FOR GS-3:
Candidates must have a general background in the performance of routine clerical duties which demonstrate *all* of the following:

- basic knowledge of office routines and functions sufficient to refer visitors and telephone calls and to route correspondence by name or function area;

AND

- knowledge of clerical practices and procedures sufficient to file material and obtain requested information from the file;

AND

- knowledge of spelling, punctuation, and syntax sufficient to identify and correct grammatical errors.

QUALIFYING EXPERIENCE FOR GS-4:
Candidates must have a background in the performance of a variety of clerical duties which demonstrates *all* of the following:

- working knowledge of many different office procedures such as those needed to request a variety of office equipment, supplies, publication material, and maintenance services, when each of these requires a different procedure;

AND

- ability to understand an organization and its functions sufficient to establish file systems for classifying, retrieving, and disposing of materials; refer telephone calls and visitors; distribute and control mail; maintain leave records; and provide general and nontechnical information.

QUALIFYING EXPERIENCE FOR GS-5 AND ABOVE:
Candidates must have a background in the performance of a variety of clerical duties which demonstrates *all* of the following:

- ability to organize effectively the flow of clerical processes in an office;

AND

- ability to organize and design a filing system;

AND

- ability to make arrangements for such things as travel, conferences, meetings;

AND

- ability to locate and assemble information for various reports, briefings, and conferences;

AND

- ability to compose nontechnical correspondence.

SUBSTITUTION OF EDUCATION FOR EXPERIENCE:

Except for any requirement for passing performance tests to demonstrate skill in shorthand and/or typing (when required), the following will apply:

GRADE	EDUCATION
GS-3	1 academic year of full-time business school
	OR
	1 academic year of education above the high school level
GS-4	2 academic years of full-time business school
	OR
	2 academic years of education above the high school level
GS-5	4 academic years of education in an accredited college or university

There is no substitution of education for experience above the GS-5 level. Thirty semester hours or 45 quarter hours or equivalent is considered one year of academic study.

BASIS OF RATING:

Applicants will be rated on achievements, training and information contained in their Supplemental Qualifications Statement (EWA-505) Resume and cover letter.

FORMS TO FILE:

Resume and cover letter
OPM 1203-X (Form B, Employment Availability Statement)
SSW-560 (Supplemental Instructions for Completing OPM Form 1203-X)
EWA-505 (Supplemental Qualifications Statement for Secretarial Positions)
SSW-32 (Supplemental Qualifications Statement)—self-certification of proficiency.

SECRETARY POSITIONS

GS-318-5 AND 6

Duties of the Positions

Secretaries at these levels perform duties such as: receives all visitors and telephone calls to the office and determines appropriate action; keeps the supervisor's calendar and schedules appointments; responds to requests for information concerning office functions; maintains files, reads incoming correspondence, and directs to appropriate staff person; reviews documents prepared for signature; makes travel arrangements; drafts routine responses and types.

AGENCIES HAVE BEEN GRANTED DIRECT HIRE AUTHORITY FOR THESE POSITIONS.

Applicants may apply directly to federal agencies for employment consideration by submitting a Standard Form 171.

THERE IS NO WRITTEN TEST REQUIREMENT AND THE OFFICE OF PERSONNEL MANAGEMENT DOES NOT ISSUE A NOTICE OF RESULTS OR MAINTAIN A REGISTER FOR THESE POSITIONS.

Qualification Requirements

GRADE	SPECIALIZED EXPERIENCE
5	1 year
6	1 year

TO BE CREDITABLE, SPECIALIZED EXPERIENCE MUST HAVE BEEN AT LEAST EQUIVALENT TO THE NEXT LOWER GRADE LEVEL IN THE FEDERAL SERVICE.

SPECIALIZED EXPERIENCE is experience that demonstrates possession of particular knowledge, skills, and abilities necessary to successfully perform secretarial duties.

Proficiency Requirements

For positions requiring typing skills, applicants must demonstrate an acceptable level of proficiency. Minimum speed for typing positions is 40 words per minute. Applicants may meet the requirement by passing the appropriate performance test, presenting a certificate of proficiency, or self-certifying their proficiency. Applicants who self-certify their proficiency may be required to pass a performance test.

Optional Form 306
September 1994
U.S. Office of Personnel Management

Declaration for Federal Employment

Form Approved:
O.M.B. No. 3206-0182
NSN 7540-01-368-7775
50306-101

GENERAL INFORMATION

1 FULL NAME
►

2 SOCIAL SECURITY NUMBER
►

3 PLACE OF BIRTH (Include City and State or Country)
►

4 DATE OF BIRTH (MM/DD/YY)
►

5 OTHER NAMES EVER USED (For example, maiden name, nickname, etc.)
►
►

6 PHONE NUMBERS (Include Area Codes)
DAY ►
NIGHT ►

MILITARY SERVICE

7 Have you served in the United States Military Service? *If your only active duty was training in the Reserves or National Guard, answer "NO".*

	Yes	No

If you answered "YES", list the branch, dates (MM/DD/YY), and type of discharge for all active duty military service.

BRANCH	FROM	TO	TYPE OF DISCHARGE

BACKGROUND INFORMATION

For all questions, provide all additional requested information under item 15 or on attached sheets. The circumstances of each event you list will be considered. However, in most cases you can still be considered for Federal jobs.

For questions 8, 9, and 10, your answers should include convictions resulting from a plea of nolo contendere *(no contest),* but omit (1) traffic fines of $300 or less, (2) any violation of law committed before your 16th birthday, (3) any violation of law committed before your 18th birthday if finally decided in juvenile court or under a Youth Offender law, (4) any conviction set aside under the Federal Youth Corrections Act or similar State law, and (5) any conviction whose record was expunged under Federal or State law.

		Yes	No
8	During the last 10 years, have you been convicted, been imprisoned, been on probation, or been on parole? (Includes felonies, firearms or explosives violations, misdemeanors, and all other offenses.) *If "Yes", use item 15 to provide the date, explanation of the violation, place of occurrence, and the name and address of the police department or court involved.*		
9	Have you been convicted by a military court-martial in the past 10 years? (If no military service, answer "NO".) *If "Yes", use item 15 to provide the date, explanation of the violation, place of occurrence, and the name and address of the military authority or court involved.*		
10	Are you now under charges for any violation of law? *If "Yes", use item 15 to provide the date, explanation of the violation, place of occurrence, and the name and address of the police department or court involved.*		
11	During the last 5 years, were you fired from any job for any reason, did you quit after being told that you would be fired, did you leave any job by mutual agreement because of specific problems, or were you debarred from Federal employment by the Office of Personnel Management? *If "Yes", use item 15 to provide the date, an explanation of the problem and reason for leaving, and the employer's name and address.*		
12	Are you delinquent on any Federal debt? (Includes delinquencies arising from Federal taxes, loans, overpayment of benefits, and other debts to the U.S. Government, plus defaults of Federally guaranteed or insured loans such as student and home mortgage loans.) *If "Yes", use item 15 to provide the type, length, and amount of the delinquency or default, and steps that you are taking to correct the error or repay the debt:*		

ADDITIONAL QUESTIONS

		Yes	No
13	Do any of your relatives work for the agency or organization to which you are submitting this form? (Includes father, mother, husband, wife, son, daughter, brother, sister, uncle, aunt, first cousin, nephew, niece, father-in-law, mother-in-law, son-in-law, daughter-in-law, brother-in-law, sister-in-law, stepfather, stepmother, stepson, stepdaughter, stepbrother, stepsister, half brother, and half sister.) *If "Yes", use item 15 to provide the name, relationship, and the Department, Agency, or Branch of the Armed Forces for which your relative works.*		
14	Do you receive, or have you ever applied for, retirement pay, pension, or other pay based on military, Federal civilian, or District of Columbia Government service?		

CONTINUATION SPACE / AGENCY OPTIONAL QUESTIONS

15 Provide details requested in items 8 through 13 and 17c in the continuation space below or on attached sheets. Be sure to identify attached sheets with your name, Social Security Number, and item number, and to include ZIP Codes in all addresses. If any questions are printed below, please answer as instructed (these questions are specific to your position, and your agency is authorized to ask them).

CERTIFICATIONS / ADDITIONAL QUESTION

APPLICANT: If you are applying for a position and have not yet been selected. Carefully review your answers on this form and any attached sheets. When this form and all attached materials are accurate, complete item 16/16a.

APPOINTEE: If you are being appointed. Carefully review your answers on this form and any attached sheets, including any other application materials that your agency has attached to this form. If any information requires correction to be accurate as of the date you are signing, make changes on this form or the attachments and/or provide updated information on additional sheets, initialing and dating all changes and additions. When this form and all attached materials are accurate, complete item 16/16b and answer item 17.

16 **I certify** that, to the best of my knowledge and belief, all of the information on and attached to this Declaration for Federal Employment, including any attached application materials, is true, correct, complete, and made in good faith. **I understand** that a false or fraudulent answer to any question on any part of this declaration or its attachments may be grounds for not hiring me, or for firing me after I begin work, and may be punishable by fine or imprisonment. **I understand** that any information I give may be investigated for purposes of determining eligibility for Federal employment as allowed by law or Presidential order. **I consent** to the release of information about my ability and fitness for Federal employment by *employers, schools, law enforcement agencies,* and *other individuals and organizations* to *investigators, personnel specialists,* and *other authorized employees of the Federal Government.* **I understand** that for financial or lending institutions, medical institutions, hospitals, health care professionals, and some other sources of information, a separate specific release may be needed, and I may be contacted for such a release at a later date.

16a Applicant's Signature ▶
(Sign in ink)   Date ▶

16b Appointee's Signature ▶
(Sign in ink)   Date ▶   APPOINTING OFFICER: Enter Date of Appointment or Conversion ▶

17 **Appointee Only** *(Respond only if you have been employed by the Federal Government before):* Your elections of life insurance during previous Federal employment may affect your eligibility for life insurance during your new appointment. These questions are asked to help your personnel office make a correct determination.

	Date (MM/DD/YY)		
		Yes	No	Don't Know

17a When did you leave your last Federal job? . . . .

17b When you worked for the Federal Government the last time, did you waive Basic Life Insurance or any type of optional life insurance? · · · · · · · · · · ·

17c If you answered "Yes" to item 17b, did you later cancel the waiver(s)? *If your answer to item 17c is "No," use item 15 to identify the type(s) of insurance for which waivers were not cancelled.* · · · · · · · · · · ·

Optional Form 306 (Back)   September 1994

Optional Form 306
U.S. Office of Personnel
Management

Declaration for Federal Employment

Form Approved:
O.M.B. No. 3206-0182
NSN 7540-01-368-7775
50306-101

INSTRUCTIONS

The information collected on this form is used to determine your acceptability for Federal employment and your enrollment status in the Government's Life Insurance program. You may be asked to complete this form at any time during the hiring process. Follow instructions that the agency provides. If you are selected, you will be asked to update your responses on this form and on other materials submitted during the application process and then to recertify that your answers are true before you are appointed.

Your Social Security Number is needed to keep our records accurate, because people may have the same name and birthdate. Executive Order 9397 also asks Federal agencies to use this number to help identify individuals in agency records. Giving us your SSN or any other information is voluntary. However,

if you do not give us your SSN or any other information requested, we cannot process your application. Incomplete addresses and ZIP Codes may also slow processing.

You must answer all questions truthfully and completely. A false statement on any part of this declaration or attached forms or sheets may be grounds for not hiring you, or for firing you after you begin work. Also, you may be punished by fine or imprisonment (U.S. Code, title 18, section 1001).

Either type your responses to this form or print clearly in dark ink. If you need additional space, attach letter-size sheets (8.5" X 11"), including your name, Social Security Number, and item number on each sheet. It is recommended that you keep a photocopy of your completed form for your records.

OPTIONAL APPLICATION FOR FEDERAL EMPLOYMENT - OF 612

You may apply for most jobs with a resume, this form, or other written format. If your resume or application does not provide all the information requested on this form and in the job vacancy announcement, you may lose consideration for a job.

1 Job title in announcement		**2** Grade(s) applying for	**3** Announcement number

4 Last name	First and middle names	**5** Social Security Number

6 Mailing address	**7** Phone numbers (include area code)
	Daytime ( )
City State ZIP Code	Evening ( )

WORK EXPERIENCE

8 Describe your paid and nonpaid work experience related to the job for which you are applying. Do **not** attach job descriptions.

1) Job title (if Federal, include series and grade)

From (MM/YY)	To (MM/YY)	Salary $	per	Hours per week

Employer's name and address	Supervisor's name and phone number ( )

Describe your duties and accomplishments

2) Job title (if Federal, include series and grade)

From (MM/YY)	To (MM/YY)	Salary $	per	Hours per week

Employer's name and address	Supervisor's name and phone number ( )

Describe your duties and accomplishments

GENERAL INFORMATION

You may apply for most Federal jobs with a resume, the attached *Optional Application for Federal Employment* or other written format. If your resume or application does not provide all the information requested on this form and in the job vacancy announcement, you may lose consideration for a job. Type or print clearly in dark ink. Help speed the selection process by keeping your application brief and sending only the requested information. If essential to attach additional pages, include your name and Social Security Number on each page.

- For information on Federal employment, including job lists, alternative formats for persons with disabilities, and veterans' preference, call the U.S. Office of Personnel Management at **912-757-3000**, TDD **912-744-2299**, by computer modem **912-757-3100**, or via the Internet (Telnet only) at FJOB.MAIL.OPM.GOV.
- If you served on active duty in the United States Military and were separated under honorable conditions, you may be eligible for veterans' preference. To receive preference if your service began after October 15, 1976, you must have a Campaign Badge, Expeditionary Medal, or a service-connected disability. Veterans' preference is not a factor for Senior Executive Service jobs or when competition is limited to status candidates (current or former career or career-conditional Federal employees).
- Most Federal jobs require United States citizenship and also that males over age 18 born after December 31, 1959, have registered with the Selective Service System or have an exemption.
- The law prohibits public officials from appointing, promoting, or recommending their relatives.
- Federal annuitants (military and civilian) may have their salaries or annuities reduced. All employees must pay any valid delinquent debts or the agency may garnish their salary.
- Send your application to the office announcing the vacancy. If you have questions, contact that office.

THE FEDERAL GOVERNMENT IS AN EQUAL OPPORTUNITY EMPLOYER

9 May we contact your current supervisor?

YES [   ]   NO [   ] ▶ If we need to contact your current supervisor before making an offer, we will contact you first.

EDUCATION

10 Mark highest level completed. **Some HS** [   ] **HS/GED** [   ] **Associate** [   ] **Bachelor** [   ] **Master** [   ] **Doctoral** [   ]

11 Last high school (HS) or GED school. Give the school's name, city, State, ZIP Code (if known), and year diploma or GED received.

12 Colleges and universities attended. Do **not** attach a copy of your transcript unless requested.

Name		Total Credits Earned		Major(s)	Degree - Year
		Semester	Quarter		(if any) Received
1) City	State ZIP Code				
2)					
3)					

OTHER QUALIFICATIONS

13 **Job-related** training courses (give title and year). **Job-related** skills (other languages, computer software/hardware, tools, machinery, typing speed, etc.). **Job-related** certificates and licenses (current only). **Job-related** honors, awards, and special accomplishments (publications, memberships in professional/honor societies, leadership activities, public speaking, and performance awards). Give dates, but do **not** send documents unless requested.

GENERAL

14 Are you a U.S. citizen?   YES [   ]   NO [   ] ▶ Give the country of your citizenship. _____

15 Do you claim veterans' preference? **NO** [   ] **YES** [   ] ▶ Mark your claim of 5 or 10 points below.

5 points [   ] ▶ Attach your DD 214 or other proof.   **10 points** [   ] ▶ Attach an *Application for 10-Point Veterans' Preference* (SF 15) and proof required.

16 Were you ever a Federal civilian employee?

NO [   ] **YES** [   ] ▶ For highest civilian grade give: Series   Grade   From (MM/YY)   To (MM/YY)

17 Are you eligible for reinstatement based on career or career-conditional Federal status?

NO [   ] **YES** [   ] ▶ If requested, attach SF 50 proof.

APPLICANT CERTIFICATION

18 **I certify** that, to the best of my knowledge and belief, all of the information on and attached to this application is true, correct, complete and made in good faith. **I understand** that false or fraudulent information on or attached to this application may be grounds for not hiring me or for firing me after I begin work, and may be punishable by fine or imprisonment. **I understand** that any information I give may be investigated.

SIGNATURE   **DATE SIGNED**

SAMPLE QUALIFICATIONS & AVAILABILITY FORM

The following 4 pages show a sample QUALIFICATIONS & AVAILABILITY FORM (Form C), and although the question booklet is not included, you can at least see what the form looks like.

U.S. OFFICE OF PERSONNEL MANAGEMENT
QUALIFICATIONS & AVAILABILITY FORM

FORM APPROVED
OMB No. 3206-0040

FORM C

PRINT YOUR RESPONSE IN THE BOXES AND BLACKEN IN THE APPROPRIATE OVALS.

USE A NO. 2 PENCIL

DO NOT FOLD, STAPLE, TEAR OR PAPER CLIP THIS FORM.
DO NOT SUBMIT PHOTOCOPIES OF THIS FORM.
We can process this form only if you:
- Use a number 2 lead pencil.
- Completely blacken each oval you choose.
- Completely erase any mistakes or stray marks.

1 YOUR NAME: _____

2 JOB APPLYING FOR: _____

3 ANNOUNCEMENT NUMBER: _____

EXAMPLES

0 1 2 - 3 4

	YES	NO
	●	Ⓝ
	Ⓨ	●
	Ⓨ	●
	●	Ⓝ

CORRECT MARK

INCORRECT MARKS

FOLLOW THE DIRECTIONS ON THE
"FORM C INSTRUCTION SHEET"

4 OCCUPATION (OCC)

5 CASE NO. (CNO)

6 LOWEST GRADE (LAG)

7 EMPLOYMENT AVAILABILITY

ARE YOU AVAILABLE FOR:

	YES	NO
A) full-time employment -40 hours per week?	Ⓨ	Ⓝ (FTE)
B) part-time employment of		(PTE)
-16 or fewer hrs/week?	Ⓨ	Ⓝ
-17 to 24 hrs/week?	Ⓨ	Ⓝ
-25 to 32 hrs/week?	Ⓨ	Ⓝ
C) temporary employment lasting		(TMP)
-less than 1 month?	Ⓨ	Ⓝ
-1 to 4 months?	Ⓨ	Ⓝ
-5 to 12 months?	Ⓨ	Ⓝ

	YES	NO
D) jobs requiring travel away from home for		(TRV)
-1 to 5 nights/month?	Ⓨ	Ⓝ
-6 to 10 nights/month?	Ⓨ	Ⓝ
-11 plus nights/month?	Ⓨ	Ⓝ
E) other employment questions (see directions)		(OEM)
Question 1?	Ⓨ	Ⓝ
Question 2?	Ⓨ	Ⓝ
Question 3?	Ⓨ	Ⓝ
Question 4?	Ⓨ	Ⓝ

8 (OSP) OCCUPATIONAL SPECIALTIES

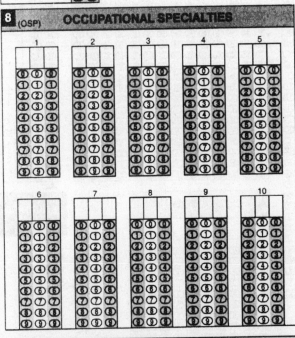

9 (GFP) GEOGRAPHIC AVAILABILITY

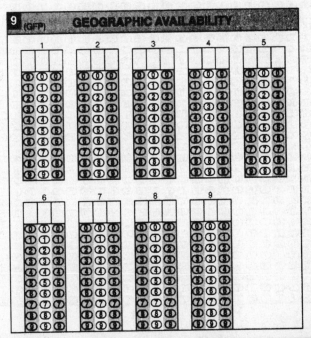

4591742

OPM FORM 1203-A/W
(7-92)

10 FIRST NAME (FNM)   MI (MIN)   LAST NAME (LNM)

11 SOCIAL SECURITY NUMBER (SSN)

12 TELEPHONE NUMBER (TEL)   AREA CODE   CONTACT TIME (TCT)

○ Day

○ Night

○ Either

13 STREET, ADDRESS (HOUSE NUMBER AND STREET AND APT. NO., WHERE YOU WANT TO RECEIVE MAIL.) (ADR)

LEAVE BLANK COLUMN BETWEEN NUMBER, STREET, NAME, ETC.

14 CITY (CTY)

15 STATE CODE (STE)

IF OUTSIDE THE U.S.A. BLACKEN "0V" AND PRINT COUNTRY HERE →

USE STANDARD STATE CODES

16 ZIP CODE + 4 (ZIP)   OPTIONAL

17 (OCQ) — OCCUPATIONAL QUESTIONS

1 Ⓐ Ⓑ Ⓒ Ⓓ Ⓔ Ⓕ Ⓖ Ⓗ Ⓘ	41 Ⓐ Ⓑ Ⓒ Ⓓ Ⓔ Ⓕ Ⓖ Ⓗ Ⓘ	81 Ⓐ Ⓑ Ⓒ Ⓓ Ⓔ Ⓕ Ⓖ Ⓗ Ⓘ	121 Ⓐ Ⓑ Ⓒ Ⓓ Ⓔ Ⓕ Ⓖ Ⓗ Ⓘ
2	42	82	122
3	43	83	123
4	44	84	124
5	45	85	125
6	46	86	126
7	47	87	127
8	48	88	128
9	49	89	129
10	50	90	130
11	51	91	131
12	52	92	132
13	53	93	133
14	54	94	134
15	55	95	135
16	56	96	136
17	57	97	137
18	58	98	138
19	59	99	139
20	60	100	140
21	61	101	141
22	62	102	142
23	63	103	143
24	64	104	144
25	65	105	145
26	66	106	146
27	67	107	147
28	68	108	148
29	69	109	149
30	70	110	150
31	71	111	151
32	72	112	152
33	73	113	153
34	74	114	154
35	75	115	155
36	76	116	156
37	77	117	157
38	78	118	158
39	79	119	159
40	80	120	160

(Each question row provides bubbles Ⓐ Ⓑ Ⓒ Ⓓ Ⓔ Ⓕ Ⓖ Ⓗ Ⓘ)

18 (JBF) — JOB PREFERENCE

01 ○	06 ○	11 ○	16 ○	21 ○	26 ○	31 ○	36 ○	41 ○	46 ○	51 ○	56 ○	61 ○	66 ○
02 ○	07 ○	12 ○	17 ○	22 ○	27 ○	32 ○	37 ○	42 ○	47 ○	52 ○	57 ○	62 ○	67 ○
03 ○	08 ○	13 ○	18 ○	23 ○	28 ○	33 ○	38 ○	43 ○	48 ○	53 ○	58 ○	63 ○	68 ○
04 ○	09 ○	14 ○	19 ○	24 ○	29 ○	34 ○	39 ○	44 ○	49 ○	54 ○	59 ○	64 ○	69 ○
05 ○	10 ○	15 ○	20 ○	25 ○	30 ○	35 ○	40 ○	45 ○	50 ○	55 ○	60 ○	65 ○	70 ○

19 LANGUAGES (LNG)

Three columns of bubbles 0–9.

20 DATE BLOCK (SDF)

M M | D D | Y Y columns of bubbles 0–9.

21 OTHER INFORMATION (MSC)

Columns of bubbles 0–9.

22 SPECIAL KNOWLEDGE (SPK)

Columns of bubbles 0–9.

Page 3

23 VETERAN PREFERENCE CLAIM
(VET)

○ No preference claimed

○ 5 points preference claimed

10 POINT PREFERENCE- You must enclose a completed Standard Form 15.

○ 10 points preference claimed (award of a Purple Heart or noncompensable service-connected disability)

○ 10 points compensable disability preference claimed (disability rating of less than 30%)

○ 10 points other (wife, widow, husband, widower, mother preference claimed)

○ 10 points compensable disability preference claimed (disability rating of 30% or more)

24 BACKGROUND INFORMATION
(SB1)

	YES	NO
1. Are you a citizen of the United States?	Ⓨ	Ⓝ
2. During the last 10 years, were you fired from any job for any reason or did you quit after being told that you would be fired?	Ⓨ	Ⓝ
3. Are you now or have you ever been: (Answer the following questions.)		
a) convicted of or forfeited collateral for any felony?	Ⓨ	Ⓝ
b) convicted of or forfeited collateral for any firearms or explosive violation?	Ⓨ	Ⓝ
c) convicted, forfeited collateral, imprisoned, on probation, or on parole, during the last 10 years?	Ⓨ	Ⓝ
d) convicted by a court martial?	Ⓨ	Ⓝ
4. Are you currently under charges for any violation of law?	Ⓨ	Ⓝ

25 DATES OF ACTIVE DUTY - MILITARY SERVICE

(ASD) FROM   (ETS) TO

MM DD YY   MM DD YY

26 SIGNATURE/DATE

I certify that the information on this form is true and correct to the best of my knowledge. **NOTE:** A false statement on any part of your application may be grounds for not hiring you, or for firing you after you begin work. Also, you may be punished by fine or imprisonment (U.S. Code, title 18, section 1001).

_____
Signature

_____
Date signed

PRIVACY ACT

The Office of Personnel Management is authorized to rate applicants for Federal jobs under sections 1302, 3301, and 3304 of title 5 of the U.S. Code. Section 1104 of title 5 allows the Office of Personnel Management to authorize other Federal agencies to rate applicants for Federal jobs. We need the information you put on this form to see how well your education and work skills qualify you for a Federal job. We also need information on matters such as citizenship and military service to see whether you are affected by laws we must follow in deciding who may be employed by the Federal Government.

We must have your Social Security Number (SSN) to identify your records because other people may have the same name and birthdate. The Office of Personnel Management may also use your SSN to make requests for information about you from employers, schools, banks, and others who know you, but only as allowed by law or Presidential directive. The information we collect by using your SSN will be used for employment purposes and also for studies and statistics that will not identify you.

Information we have about you may also be given to Federal, State and local agencies for checking on law violations or for other lawful purposes. We may send your name and address to State and local Government agencies, Congressional and other public offices, and public international organizations, if they request names of people to consider for employment. We may also notify your school placement office if you are selected for a Federal job.

Giving us your SSN or any of the other information is voluntary. However, we cannot process your application, which is the first step toward getting a job, if you do not give us the information we request.

PUBLIC REPORTING BURDEN

The public reporting burden of information is estimated to vary from 20 minutes to 45 minutes to complete this form including time for reviewing instructions, gathering the data needed, and completing and reviewing entries. The average time to complete this form is 30 minutes. Send comments regarding the burden estimate or any other aspect of this collection of information, including suggestions for reducing this burden to: US Office of Personnel Management, Office of Information Management, 1900 E Street, NW, CHP 500, Washington, DC 20415; and to the Office of Information and Regulatory Affairs, Office of Management and Budget, Paperwork Reduction Project 3206-0040, Washington, DC 20503.

OFFICE USE ONLY – DO NOT MARK BELOW

○ NV   ○ OK

○ TP   ○ Hold

○ XPP

○ CP

○ XPO

○ CPS

4591742

SAMPLE ANSWER BOOKLET

The following pages include a typical sample ANSWER BOOKLET to help you become familiar with the booklet.

UNITED STATES OF AMERICA

OFFICE OF PERSONNEL MANAGEMENT

ANSWER BOOKLET

SIGNATURE _____ DATE _____
                        PLEASE SIGN

PLACE OF EXAMINATION _____
                              CITY   STATE

EXAMINATION TITLE _____

DIRECTIONS FOR COMPLETING APPLICANT INFORMATION

SAMPLE NAME GRID

1	FIRST NAME	MI	LAST NAME
	J A N E	B	D O E

On Page 2, you will complete information about yourself. Enter the appropriate letter or number in the box and completely blacken the corresponding circle below the box. See Sample Name Grid to the right.

CORRECT MARK   INCORRECT MARKS

DIRECTIONS FOR MARKING RESPONSES TO TEST QUESTIONS

Use only a **No. 2 pencil**. Darken completely the oval corresponding to your answer. You **must** keep your mark within the oval. Stray marks may be counted as errors. Erase **completely** all marks except your answer.

SAMPLE   Ⓐ ● Ⓒ Ⓓ Ⓔ

OPM Form 1603 (2-91)

0700195

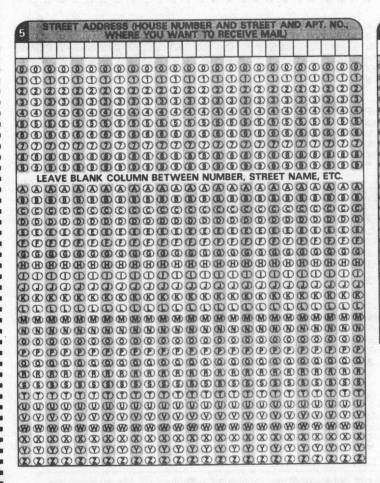

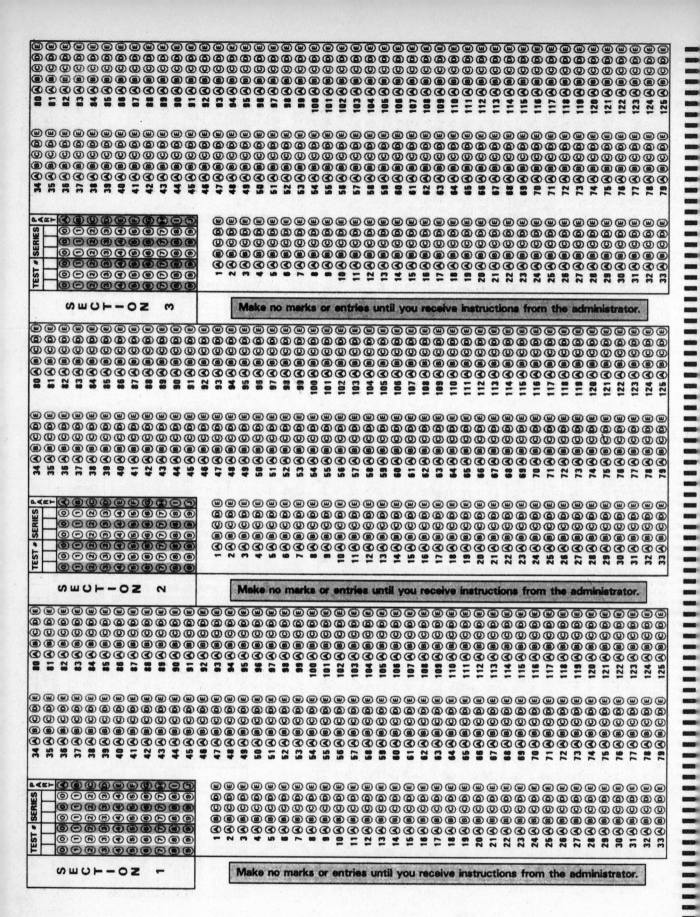

Make no marks or entries until you receive instructions from the administrator.

Make no marks or entries until you receive instructions from the administrator.

Make no marks or entries until you receive instructions from the administrator.

PAGE 3

366   Appendix B

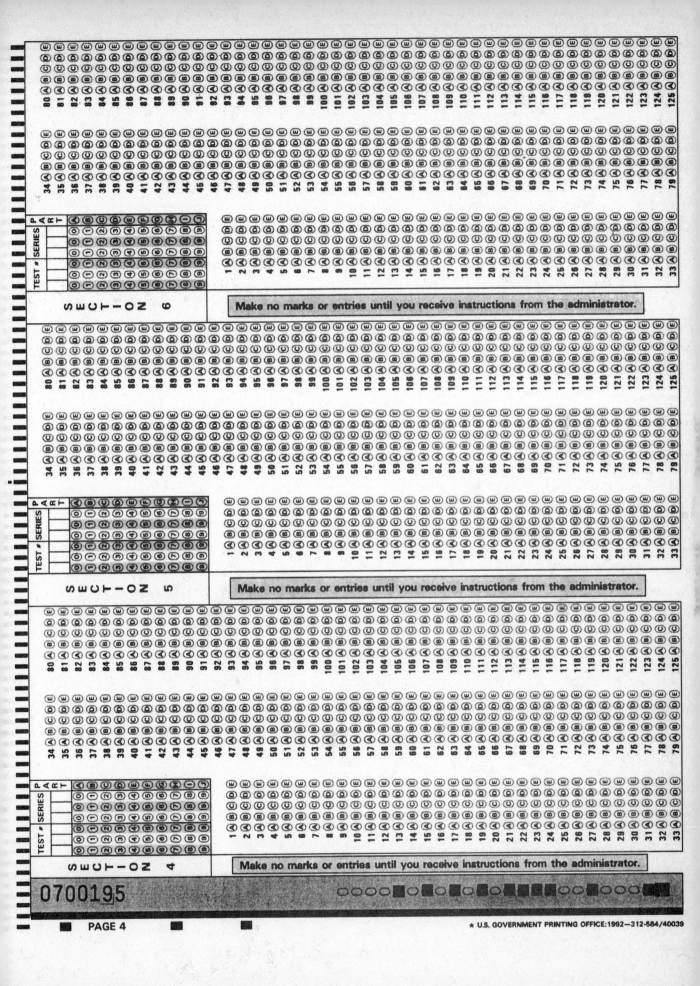

NOTES

NOTES

NOTES

NOTES